# THE SHAKESPEARE GAME

# THE SHAKESPEARE GAME

## The Mystery of the Great Phoenix

## Ilya Gililov

Translated from Russian by
Gennady Bashkov & Galina Kozlova
with the help of Evelina Melenevskaia

Algora Publishing
New York

ISBN: 0-87586-181-4 (softcover)

ISBN: 0-87586-182-2 (hardcover)

English Editor: Andrea L. Secara

Library of Congress Cataloging-in-Publication Data:

Gililov, I. (Ilia)
 [Igra ob Uiliame Shekspire, ili, Taina velikogo feniksa. English]
 The Shakespeare game, or, The mystery of the great phoenix / by Ilya M. Gililov.
    p. cm.
Includes bibliographical references and index.
Originally published as: Igra ob Uiliame Shekspire, ili, Taina velikogo feniksa. Moskva : Artist,
Rezhisser, Teatr, 1997.
  ISBN 0-87586-182-2 (alk. paper) — ISBN 0-87586-181-4 (pbk. : alk. paper)
  1.  Shakespeare, William, 1564-1616—Authorship. 2.  Rutland, Roger Manners, Lord, 1576-1612—
Authorship. I. Title: Shakespeare game. II. Title: Mystery of the great phoenix. III. Title.

PR2947.R8G555 2003
822.3'3—dc21

                        2003001921

*A writer hiding behind a curtain.*
Engraving from a book by H. Peacham, 1612.
The Latin inscription on the banner reads, "The creations of man's genius will live on in the hearts of mankind; let the rest die."

# TABLE OF CONTENTS

# LIST OF ILLUSTRATIONS

(1) As a witness testifying in Belott's suit. 1612. — (2) On the deed for the purchase of the house. 1613. — (3) On the mortgage paper for the same house. 1613. — (4) On the first page of his will. — (5) On the second page of the will. — (6) On the third page of the will.

## A NOTE ON THE ENGLISH EDITION

*The Shakespeare Game* was translated from Russian into English according to the text of the second Russian edition, published by the publishing house "International Relations," Moscow, 2001. (The first edition, printed in 1997 and 1998, was published by "Artist.Rezhisser.Teatr.")

During the process of translation, the author took the opportunity to make some editorial enhancements and to add a few important facts.

The quotation of original English sources from the $16^{th}$-$17^{th}$ centuries is known to be problematical. The original spelling is given whenever possible, that is, when the meaning of the words quoted is clear. In other cases, the modern spelling is used. The older form of a letter (*v* for *u*, and *i* for *j*) has generally been changed. Titles of books are italicized, and when first cited are given in the original spelling (e.g., *Loves Martyr*); after that, they are modernized (e.g., *Love's Martyr*). When original sources are cited, proper names are given in the old spelling; subsequently, in the author's words, it seems reasonable to use the modern spelling (e.g., the original Salisburie or Willobie are now spelled "Salusbury" and "Willoughby").

Algora Publishing wishes to acknowledge Evelina Melenevskaia for her contribution and effort in finalizing this translation.

# PREFACE:   THE UNKNOWN SHAKESPEARE

Ilya Gililov's book *The Shakespeare Game, or The Mystery of the Great Phoenix* was originally published in Russia and quickly went through several printings, becoming an intellectual bestseller. It has been covered by some hundred reviews, interviews and comments in the press, on the radio and TV. For an academic book, it turns out to have elicited a lively response from many different circles of readers.

For a long time, we here in Russia knew very little about the great controversy surrounding Shakespeare. Since the 1930s, any doubts about the authenticity of the Stratfordian tradition were branded "ideologically harmful," which, in the context of a totalitarian establishment, amounted to banning the public expression of such doubts and impeding access to objective information about the discussion of a most important and wonderful problem of world culture beyond the Iron Curtain. Several generations of Soviet intellectuals were brought up under the conditions of this absurd ideological taboo, the consequences of which are still felt even now.

In December of 1987, in the early days of *perestroika*, a Soviet-British colloquium on Shakespeare took place in Moscow at the Art Studies Institute. My attention was drawn to a man who was talking about some unknown (at the time) poetry collection from Shakespearean times. But really, would anyone believe that something new about Shakespeare would be discovered in Moscow?

The man, however, knew that the rare book contained the solution to the great mystery. I made his acquaintance some five years later: It turned out that Ilya Gililov was a secretary of the Shakespeare Committee with the Russian Academy of Sciences, compiler of an academic periodical *Shakespeare Readings*, and author of several works on specific problems in Shakespeare studies. When I learned about some of his discoveries, I was deeply and sincerely impressed.

There are few riddles in world history that are as provoking and essentially important for all of human culture. The mystery of Shakespeare is akin to the riddle of Atlantis. Shakespeare is a vast, miraculous country that patiently waits to have its secret treasures, buried in the depths of the unknown, brought to the surface. Right now, thanks to this book, the mystery land of "Shakespeare" is beginning to take shape.

Humanity cannot live without myths. But there is a time to create myths and a time to learn the truth about them. Everyone who takes the trouble to read Gililov's book carefully, without prejudice, will harbor no more doubts that humanity has been made a partner in an enormous hoax.

Since the beginning of the debate many a surmise has been put forward and many a guess has been hazarded as to who is hiding under the mask of Shakespeare — and why. Now, we have not just one more interesting but insufficiently substantiated version, but the very solution of the great Mystery, supported by authentic interconnected facts. One should not assert (and Gililov does not claim) that all the intricate details of the Shakespeare mystery have now been understood, that there are no more blank spots; but the main thrust is clear. The circle of major figures behind the pretence has been identified, and their line of thought has been defined.

I read *The Shakespeare Game* as a captivating detective story, following the author in his meticulous investigation, disentangling the knots of a momentous mystification in history which cannot be explained by mundane everyday motives. Each sentence is substantiated with documents and historical and literary facts.

The beginning of the book seems to be a digression from the major problem of Shakespeare's authorship, which for many is all encompassing. Here the author examines the contents of the poetic collection *Love's Martyr* (where Shakespeare's most enigmatic poetic requiem, "The Phoenix and Turtle," first appeared) and the circumstances under which it was published. It turns out, by the way, that in the past four centuries nobody in England, or in America, had taken the trouble to hold the pages of the three extant copies of that peculiar book up to the light, to make drawings of the watermarks and compare them! This was done only by researchers who came from faraway Moscow and established that, despite different dates and typographic emblems on the title pages, the watermarks, including the unique ones, are the same on every copy. Together with certain other facts newly discovered, this helped to establish the book's authentic date of publication and to identify, at last, the heroes' prototypes — an unusual platonic couple, whose nearly simultaneous death was secretly mourned by the most celebrated poets of England. The Requiem, heard centuries later, made it possible to unveil the mystery.

Then, the author examines just as meticulously certain curious books issued in Shakespearean times under the name of one Thomas Coryate of Odcombe, who was proclaimed during his lifetime "The Prince of Poets, Greatest Traveler and Writer of the World," who surpassed Homer, Ulysses, Columbus and Magellan all together. Readers can learn about his exceptional "deeds" from modern British and American encyclopedias and biographical directories. They tell us that this court jester and drunkard not only covered all of Europe by foot in record time (and wrote a huge book about it), but also reached India the same way — maybe the only one to do so in the history of mankind! Poetic "panegyrics" in his honor, written in a dozen languages (including some imaginary ones) were issued (by the same publisher who first produced Shakespeare's sonnets) as a separate book and signed by the names of some fifty poets. This was another brazen mystification, a spoof (and again, discovered only now).

Gradually, step by step, these traces (and many others) keep leading us to the same circle of wonderful people bound together by unusual relationships, by a spiritual unity, perceiving Life as Theater, who played games meant to go on for centuries.

Many of the facts and discoveries which readers shall first learn from this book are quite important on their own, aside from the "Shakespeare question," the problem of Shakespeare's identity. They have been accepted even outside of that context by a number of English and American literature professors who do not entertain any doubt as to the Stratfordian tradition. It would be interesting to hear the opinions of these scholars and their colleagues after *The Shakespeare Game* appears in English.

The author's greatest achievement certainly lies in probing the Shakespeare phenomenon as a Game of unprecedented scale — this concept radically changes the whole picture of the epoch which is customarily called Shakespearean. This new picture is shocking in its authenticity.

Perhaps, in time, the saga of the lofty love of the Turtle and the Phoenix will become as current as the myths of Romeo and Juliet, Othello and Desdemona, Tristan and Iseult. Today, they show their faces to the readers of this book — creators of the great spiritual wonder that has come down to us under the name of the Great Bard William Shakespeare.

Alexandr Lipkov, PhD
Moscow

# FOREWORD AND ACKNOWLEDGEMENTS

This book is the result of a long investigation of literary and historical facts pertaining to the Shakespeare phenomenon. Once I began studying Shakespeare's works and his biographies, I found quite soon (like many others before me) that I could not possibly match them together. The information provided by the biographies drastically contradicts the various images of the Great Bard in his dramas and poems. I cannot imagine the person who is described in those biographies writing "Hamlet," "Lear," "Julius Caesar," or the sonnets. The authentic biographical facts that have been repeated over and over again speak about a person who was separated from Shakespeare's works by a deep abyss, both intellectual and spiritual. We do not even have any objective evidence that the person who is considered the greatest writer in all of mankind could read or write, and there are good reasons to doubt it — for, how could he allow his wife and children to remain illiterate? The Shakespeare era was not that long ago; the missing artifacts cannot be blamed on the intervening millennia. Nothing in the history of world literature compares to this incredible situation.

At first, when almost nothing was known about Shakespeare's life (and his works were studied rather superficially), there was little ground to doubt his identity; the problems only appeared when the Stratford archives were examined, and in-depth research on his works was begun. The more that was learned, the more doubts and questions arose. A number of renowned writers and historians came to the conclusion that the moniker "Shakespeare" was the penname of an authentic author who wished to remain unknown. Since the middle of the 19$^{th}$ century, a heated and rather convoluted controversy about Shakespeare began that thousands of minds all over the world actively joined.

A thorough investigation of the Shakespeare authorship question convinced me that the solution might be found only through new research. The first object of this investigation, for me, was the most mysterious of Shakespeare's works: the poem "The Phoenix and the Turtle," and Robert Chester's poetic collection, *Love's*

*Martyr*, where the poem first appeared. My research revealed the true date of publication of the poem, and the identity of its heroes and prototypes; these results were confirmed empirically when unique watermarks were found in the copies kept in Washington, DC, and in London. The mysterious work turned out to be (as the outstanding American philosopher R. W. Emerson had supposed) a long sought key to Shakespeare's mystery.

I also examined some other unusual and baffling books and portraits that heretofore had remained unidentified. Working with the inestimable rarities in the Folger Shakespeare Library in Washington, DC, and the British Library in London, I turned up many valuable details.

Shakespeare's biographers were in a bind when it came to explaining the fact that the Great Bard's death had passed virtually unnoticed, and nobody in England mourned it according to the custom prevailing at the time. Reading this book, the reader will learn that that was not so — that the best English poets secretly took farewell of their great fellows, mourning their demise in a striking Requiem.

Certainly, not everyone is concerned to reveal the meaning of what is truly the most mysterious Shakespeare work — the Game of William Shakespeare. Many people find it difficult to give up the customary image that we were all taught during school — the image of a common provincial apprentice without any education who suddenly and miraculously turned into a sophisticated erudite, a brilliant poet and a playwright of genius. As happens not infrequently, the irrevocable progress of science (including historical) towards the truth may be greeted only as an encroachment on time-honored traditions and values, and even as something harmful to world culture. As a matter of fact, it actually enriches it with marvelous and tragic truth.

The book is not intended only for specialists in Shakespeare studies, though newly established facts that have been confirmed empirically could be of special interest to them. It is also an invitation to take part in an academic discussion. First of all, I shall dwell on the date when Chester's book was issued, and the identity of its heroes, then the history of the Prince of Poet, Thomas Coryate from Odcombe, and also Ben Jonson's and John Donne's connection with the Rutlands. I hope that this invitation will be heard and accepted by English and American scholars who have at their disposal the original publications, manuscripts, portraits and so on.

I am happy to acknowledge those who, after my first publications, have lent me active assistance in moving ahead with this complex enquiry: M. D. Litvinova, L. A. Pichkhadze, I. S. Shoulzhenko, A. I. Lipkov, S. A. Makourenkova, Lynn Visson, Boris Rabbot, Joseph Rabbot, I. N. Kravchenko, and A. V. Daniushevskaya. E. D. Melenevskaia has provided invaluable assistance in preparing the English-language edition. I am grateful to the Soros Foundation, and the Folger Shakespeare Library in Washington, DC for providing me with a grant for work in that treasury of knowledge in 1992, and to the Moscow Alba Alliance Bank that made possible my travel to Great Britain, to work in the wonderful libraries and museums there, in 1995.

April 2003
I. G.

# CHAPTER 1. ROBERT CHESTER'S MYSTERIOUS BIRDS

*A poetic requiem. For whom? The legend of that wonderful bird, the Phoenix — Only three copies of the book extant, and every one different — "Love's Martyr": The story of the life and death of the Turtle and the Phoenix — The Turtle Cantoes and Shakespeare's sonnets — Mourned by a whole chorus of poets — John Marston sees a wonder of perfection — Ben Jonson knew them well — Behind the shroud of mystery — Awakening: first guesses and hypotheses — "Enjoy the music of the verses." — Take another look at those dates! — A strange "misprint" in the British Museum — The most famous publisher — Dead Salusbury helps to open the curtain — There was no other couple like that in England —A platonic marriage — Hamlet's fellow student*

## A POETIC REQUIEM — FOR WHOM?

Each year more than one hundred books and articles about Shakespeare's sonnets appear throughout the world in different languages. By comparison, Shakespeare's other poetic works may seem to be neglected, not only by scholars but by the reading public, as well. The same is true of a small poem that for about two centuries has been printed under the title of "The Phoenix and the Turtle" (meaning "turtledove" — which, by the way, was always erroneously translated into Russian as "The Phoenix and She-Turtle," that is, *golubka* rather than *golub*).

Academic discussion of what without exaggeration could be called Shakespeare's most mysterious poem has gone on for 120 years, though it never attained such a wide scale and notorious character as the famous and vociferous chorus about his sonnets, about the Fair Friend and Dark Lady, about the love and sufferings of the Great Bard. In Russian Shakespeare studies, discussion of this poem was not made public at all, for a long time.

I should note that the complex and controversial problems of dating and identifying the prototypes for a number of Shakespeare's works have been examined rather seldom by our scholars, for all the resources necessary for such investigation — original editions and manuscripts — were accessible only to British and American historians of English literature. Nowadays, however, the opportunity to conduct such research has been greatly expanded: now libraries in Russia, in addition to a great number of foreign specialists' works, also possess valuable reprints of many sources including the so called *Variorums*; there are also microfilms of the original issues. And, recently, the doors of American and British research centers and libraries with their inestimable collections were opened up to our researchers.

The poem that we shall consider now is usually placed after Shakespeare's other poetic works and is often put at the very end of his full collections. Studying Shakespeare's heritage, I long ago began to pay special attention to this strange piece of art, time and again coming back to it, trying to penetrate its meaning. I spent several years intensively researching the poem and the book of collected poems named *Love's Martyr*, where it appeared for the first time. I also studied works by the other authors whose poems are included in the collection, and the biographies of Shakespeare's contemporaries, and I read through the works of several generations of scholars; and then, after strictly selecting the facts on the basis of authentic historic and literary evidence, my first ideas and hypotheses evolved into a trustworthy version that later on acquired both theoretical and empirical confirmation.

So, here we have the most mysterious Shakespeare poem. Not every line can be adequately rendered into modern English; various English and American scholars have treated some images differently. But it is extremely important to get a clear and accurate understanding of the sense of each sentence. The spelling has been modernized, as in every modern Shakespeare edition, but it should be noted that in the original, the words Phoenix, Turtle, Reason, Swan, Crow and Eagle are capitalized.

680314 10/25(4R23)

## The Phoenix and the Turtle

*Let the bird of loudest lay*
*On the sole Arabian tree,*
*Herald sad and trumpet be,*
*To whose sound chaste wings obey.*

*But thou shrieking harbinger,*
*Foul precurrer of the fiend,*
*Augur of the fever's end,*
*To this troop come thou not near.*

*From this session interdict*
*Every fowl of tyrant wing*
*Save the eagle, feather'd king,*
*Keep the obsequy so strict.*

*Let the priest in surplice white*
*That defunctive music can,*
*Be the death-divining swan,*
*Lest the requiem lack his right.*

*And thou, treble-dated crow,*
*That thy sable gender mak'st*
*With the breath thou giv'st and tak'st,*
*'Mongst our mourners shalt thou go.*

*Here the anthem doth commence:*
*Love and constancy is dead;*
*Phoenix and the turtle fled*
*In a mutual flame from hence.*

*So they lov'd, as love in twain*
*Had the essence but in one;*
*Two distincts, division none;*
*Number there in love was slain.*

*Hearts remote, yet not asunder;*
*Distance, and no space was seen*
*'Twixt the turtle and his queen:*
*But in them it were a wonder.*

So between them love did shine,
That the turtle saw his right
Flaming in the phoenix' sight;
Either was the other's mine.

Property was thus appall'd,
That the self was not the same;
Single nature's double name
Neither two nor one was call'd.

Reason, in itself confounded,
Saw division grow together;
To themselves yet either neither;
Simple were so well compounded,

That it cried, "How true a twain
Seemeth this concordant one!
Love hath reason, reason none
If what parts can so remain."

Whereupon it made this threne
To the phoenix and the dove,
Co-supremes and stars of love,
As chorus to their tragic scene.

## Threnos

Beauty, truth and rarity,
Grace in all simplicity,
Here enclosed in cinders lie.

Death is now the phoenix' nest;
And the turtle's loyal breast
To eternity doth rest.

Leaving no posterity:
'Twas not their infirmity,
It was married chastity.

Truth may seem, but cannot be;
Beauty brag, but 'tis not she;
Truth and beauty buried be.

> *To this urn let those repair*
> *That are either true or fair;*
> *For these dead birds, sigh a prayer.*

Having read the poem, we can see that it mourns the departure from life of a wonderful couple that is called by the allegorical names of Turtle and Phoenix. During their life, they were tied by a purely spiritual marriage, but they were so close that it would be hard to say where one began and the other ended. Though they each had their own heart, one cannot imagine them separate; that is, they exist both as two beings and as one and the same simultaneously — this is unheard of, a great wonder.

The Requiem is performed in memory of them both, though we learn that they did not die at the same time, but one after the other. First departs the Turtle; he burns away before the eyes of his friend, and then she follows him, disappearing in the same flame. The amazed spectators see how two beings finally become one, bearing a double name. Here the poet creates extremely enigmatic images; he several times emphasizes the wonder and confusion of those who had not been privy to the secret.

Everything in the poem makes one ponder its heroes, their unusual relations, the uncommon funeral services. First the poet makes an address to a wonderful vociferous bird that from a sole Arabian tree is to announce to the "chaste wings" the sad news. Then some enemy forces are vaguely mentioned (birds of prey — "tyrant wings") and "harbinger of death" that should not approach the righteous persons who were gathered for the sad ceremony. But an ominous crow that lives three human lives, however, is permitted to take part in it. The swan, a priest in a white surplice — is invited to perform the funeral paean. The solemn background, and the careful choice and disposition of verbs, from the very first lines, underscore the special significance and deeply mournful character of the proceedings.

The poem begins in the imperative voice: "Let the bird of loudest lay. . . "; one comes across this voice in the text several times. The poet not only depicts the proceedings, he seems to be conducting the funeral ceremony that slowly develops and shows each participant his role and place. Along with the words we can hear the sound of an organ, the melody of the requiem that flows behind the lines.

In conclusion, the character who is called Reason performs a threne (dirge) for both of the deceased, which the poet compares to the "chorus to their tragic scene." The threnos is different in form from the main part of the poem — in the first edition, these five three-line stanzas were placed on a separate page with a distinct heading.

The Turtle and the Phoenix are mourned as the rarest creatures that have ever adorned this world; with their demise, the real beauty and truth have disappeared. The third stanza of the "Threnos" emphatically shows the unusual relations between the Turtle and the Phoenix during their life. Let's look again at this very important strophe:

*Leaving no posterity:*
*'Twas not their infirmity,*
*It was married chastity.*

So the relations of the couple that became one were at the same time platonic, and this adds another mysterious feature to the portrait. Mysterious, but taken together with the others, it shows that it is not some mythical birds the poet mourns, but a real man and woman who lived on this earth among their contemporaries and who possessed uncommon virtues; he deeply worships them.

The fact that behind the allegorical "birds'" names stand real personalities is clear enough from the poem itself, and the works of other participants in *Love's Martyr* leave no doubt about it. I would like to emphasize that especially, for there have been attempts to discard the sense of the poem which could not be interpreted in a simple way and it is often treated as a purely allegorical piece of art dedicated to the traditional topic of the Phoenix bird, or as just an example of so-called "Renaissance Neo-Platonism." Such a simplified approach, though, is not uncommon in Shakespeare studies, when vague literary and historical facts are discarded at the outset. As we shall see later, such an approach is not accidental.

A requiem . . . a threne . . . For whom? Whose death inspired the poet to create such a poem? Who are these two, a wonderful couple, "stars of love," that adorned this earth and left it nearly at the same time, without issue, but with a double name?

It is common knowledge that the want of fundamental information about the Bard's life makes it a difficult and sometimes an intractable task to decipher his lyrical works; this is a case in point. Even now, four centuries later, biographers have little to say about the events and circumstances that prompted the writing of one or another piece of Shakespeare's poetry. We do not know what in his lyrics is an expression of real personal feeling and what is the fruit of his creative imagination determined by the literary custom of the time. This adds to the difficulties when trying to identify Shakespeare's lyric heroes with his real contemporaries.

World Shakespeare studies have accumulated vast and edifying experience in interpreting the Great Bard's sonnets and in searching for their prototypes, first of all the Dark Lady and Fair Friend. There is an immense literature about this famous segment of his works, consisting of 154 verses; the list grows each year. In some cases there are several score of mutually exclusive versions. Though such poets as Goethe and Wordsworth asserted that in Shakespeare's sonnets there is no single letter that had not been deeply felt by the poet, that the sonnets are the clue to the heart of Shakespeare, today surveying the pyramid of all that has been written about them we still consider that the study is far from complete. The most intricate literary problem with all its imponderables still remains open, and may remain so until scholars acquire more knowledge not only about Shakespeare's creative milieu and social life, but about Shakespeare himself, as well.

What should one say then about "The Phoenix and the Turtle" — a piece of poetry far more knotty to comprehend than the sonnets — when it contains enigmatic hints in nearly every line? What could we hope to learn about its heroes hidden under allegorical names, what could we establish about William Shakespeare himself, when the study of his sonnets for more than two centuries has been so discouraging? One may add that some scholars long ago voiced their doubts as to Shakespeare's authorship of the poem. Late in the 19th century, the eminent Shakespeare biographer Sidney Lee, speaking of the enigmatic character of this piece, said: "Happily, Shakespeare wrote nothing of like character."[1]

There is no doubt that the fate of the poem would have been like that of the sonnets, which enable us to hear the heartbeat of the poet but do not reveal his face, if it were not part of a poetry collection which is definitely odd and unusual in many respects. It, too, is dedicated to the very mysterious Turtle and Phoenix.

Before we start our travels through the maze that this strange volume presents (where only strict methodology and a quest for truth may serve as Ariadne's thread) one should recollect the mythical Phoenix as it appeared in the English literature of the Shakespearean era.

## THE LEGEND OF THE WONDERFUL BIRD, THE PHOENIX

According to an ancient legend reflected in classical literature, the wonderful bird the Phoenix lived all alone in the fairytale Arabia; her nest was situated in a solitary tree. The bird lived to the age of five hundred years, after which she prepared her own funeral pyre in which she burned to ashes. Then from the cinders miraculously appeared a new Phoenix, which was again the only one in the world. The beautiful legend could symbolize immortality and the uninterrupted renewal of the wonder of Being . . .

In English literature, the image of the Phoenix appeared as far back as the Middle Ages (8th–9th centuries), first as an allegory for Christ, who died and was resurrected according to God's providence. In Elizabethan times the image appears frequently, but without religious connotations. It came to England along with other contributions from the Italian and French Renaissance and bears traces of Petrarch's and Ronsard's treatment of the legendary image. Petrarch, speaking of his Laura's beauty and celestial charm, several times compares her to the Phoenix; Ronsard does the same in his "Sonnets à Hélène." English poets of the 16th and 17th centuries most often used the term Phoenix as a synonym to the word "wonder," in order to indicate the unique and extraordinary virtues of prominent personalities. Many a time Queen Elizabeth was called Phoenix, a choice compliment to the monarch who so long and "happily" ruled

---

1. Lee S. *A Life of Shakespeare.* L., p.184

the country, who overcame so many foes and managed to escape so many dangers. Some others of the epoch were also called Phoenix. For instance, the great poet Philip Sidney, idolized by Elizabethans — mostly in elegies for his tragic and untimely death. In Matthew Roydon's Elegy in the poetic anthology, *The Phoenix' Nest* (1593),[2] the Dove, the Nightingale, the Swan, the Phoenix and the Eagle mourn Astrophel; this poetic allegory has much in common with the Shakespeare poem. Earlier in 1591, in the elegy published in the collection *Brittons Bowre of Delights*,[3] poet Nicholas Breton rebukes death, saying that by taking away Philip Sidney it killed the Phoenix; but several lines further down, among the "birds" mourning the irrevocable loss, we see the Phoenix again; as with Roydon, this is a new Phoenix arisen from the ashes of its predecessor. The epithet was not infrequently used to underscore the succession and heritage of rare qualities and great talent.

In each separate case, the context in which one comes across the image of the Phoenix must be carefully analyzed in order to determine which elements of the ancient legend and later traditions the author used, to what extent those elements were transformed, and what new traits were added. The analysis must combine a literary and a historical approach, for only the combination allows us to determine the possibility and probability of identification of given events and/or personalities. Pursuing only one side of the analysis may lead to the type of mistake so frequently met in this kind of work — hasty and unfounded identification or, conversely, the reduction of a work's artistic imagery to a hollow traditional form or to some abstraction devoid of relevance to the time.

Shakespeare mentions the name "Phoenix" in eight plays: in the first and third parts of "Henry VI," in "As You Like It," "The Comedy of Errors," "Timon of Athens," "Henry VIII," "Cymbeline," "Tempest" — and, besides, in Sonnet 19 and in "Lover's Complaint." In "Henry VI," the Phoenix is an expected avenger who rises from the ashes of the perished; in other plays it is synonymous with traits such as exceptional character, magnificence and grandeur. In "The Tempest," Sebastian, moved by the sounds of music coming from the heavens and other wonders on the desert island, exclaims that now he is ready to believe in unicorns and in the Phoenix, living in Arabia and reigning at this hour on its throne — the one tree (let us keep this association in mind — the Phoenix and the unicorn — we shall come to it later on). In Sonnet 19, "devouring Time burns the long-lived phoenix in her blood."

In the poem about the Turtle and the Phoenix there are some features of the ancient myth: the sole Arabian tree, the flame devouring both birds. But all in all, the Phoenix here does not conform to the framework of traditional perceptions. This can be seen in the fact that the Phoenix here appears as a female creature, and in its relations with another "bird," the Turtle (which is absent in the legend but present in Roydon's elegy on the death of Philip Sidney). The legendary Phoenix is a genderless

---

2. *The Phoenix Nest*, 1593. Ed. by H.E.Rollins. Cambridge (MA). 1931, reiss.1969
3. *Brittons Bowre of Delight*, 1591. Ed. by H.E.Rollins. Cambridge (MA), 1933.

creature and has no friend whatsoever, male or female. Thus the love of Shakespeare's Turtle and the Phoenix, though platonic, is not rooted in the legend any more than the other characters in the poem (the members of the funeral ceremony) are; and the same is true of the whole of its mournful requiem leitmotif.

The image of the turtle and she-dove — "an inseparable couple" — may be found in Philip Sidney's "The Countess of Pembroke's Arcadia." In Shakespeare's works, doves are met quite frequently — in twelve plays, in the first poem, "Venus and Adonis," and in the "*Passionate Pilgrim*." They are incarnations of modesty, chastity, and pure service to Aphrodite — fidelity. But in "Hamlet" the term has a more intimate ring, when the mad Ophelia interrupts her *ante mortem* song with an unexpected exclamation: "Fare you well, my dove!"

## ONLY THREE COPIES OF THE BOOK EXTANT, AND EACH ONE DIFFERENT

In the second half of the 16<sup>th</sup> century, it became fashionable in England to publish various literary collections, books of songs and airs. The poetic collection *The Phoenix' Nest*, containing poems by various authors and several elegies on the death of Philip Sidney, started a series of invaluable publications connected with the poetic circle around Mary Sidney (upon marriage, the Countess of Pembroke), the sister and pupil of the prematurely departed poet. In 1600, "Englands Helicon" and the "Englands Parnassus" appeared; followed in 1602 by "A Poetical Rhapsody."[4] Somewhat earlier "Politeuphia, or Wits Commonwealth," "Palladis Tamia: Wits Treasure," "Wits Theatre of the Little World," and "Belvedere or the Garden of the Muses" were issued. Many details about the publication of these collections (including the real names of their compilers and participants) are still unknown. The opening address of the "Englands Helicon" is rather mysterious; it hails a John Bodenham as the chief initiator and compiler of these excellent publications that had such a profound impact on the history of English literature. Now, Bodenham was a member of the Grocers' Guild and, as far as anyone knows, never had anything to do with printing or literary affairs . . . and there are many such challenges for those who study these books.

Nonetheless, *Love's Martyr*, the poetic collection by Robert Chester, is rightly considered the most mysterious of the books of those times. The collection is noteworthy first and foremost because of the fact that Shakespeare's poem about the Turtle and the Phoenix first appeared in it. This is the only occasion when Shakespeare voluntarily participated in a collective literary work (although on that score there are some other, extremely doubtful, opinions), and alongside such famous

---

4. *Englands Helicon*, 1600, 1614. Ed. by H. Macdonald. L., 1949; *Englands Parnassus* 1600. Ed. by Ch. Crawford, Oxford, 1917; *A Poetical Rhapsody* 1601-1621, Ed. by H.E. Rollins. Cambridge (Mass), 1931-1932. Vol.1, 2.

writers as Ben Jonson, George Chapman and John Marston, at that! It is clear that if they could determine the reason for such collaboration and learn more about the circumstances of its publication, Shakespeare's researchers would have a precious opportunity to fill in some of the most vexing gaps in his biography.

Nevertheless, it was more than two and a half centuries before any profound study of the Chester book was made — in this field of knowledge, time flows slowly. The book was first reissued only in 1878, in small numbers, and was annotated by Alexander Grossart for the New Shakspere Society."[5] As of today this edition is still the only one, and it is a rarity. Needless to say, the collection has never been translated into Russian; of all the poems incorporated there, only Shakespeare's is translated, and as we have seen, with a gross error at that.

There are only a few extant copies of the original Chester volume. One is kept at the John Huntington Library (San Marino, CA), the second in the Folger Shakespeare Library (Washington, DC), and the third one in the British Library in London. The title pages of these copies are each quite different. The Huntington copy lacks a date. Some scholars used to think it was cut off by the bookbinder, but meticulous examination shows that it was absent from the very beginning, probably having been cut off on purpose at the printing house. A special inscription by a former owner attests to that. The Folger copy shows the date 1601. And lastly, the title page of the British Library copy (the "London" copy) has quite a different title for the collection and shows a different date — 1611. Recently, a fourth copy was discovered at the National Library of Wales; it has no opening pages at all. The title page and some pages at the end are also missing. Nobody has ever seen any other copies of the book. One more strange circumstance: there is no authentic mention of the book in the literature or letters of that time, despite the fact that a number of highly distinguished poets contributed to it. Contrary to existing rules, the book was not entered into the Register of the Stationers' Company.

The format of the book is in quarto. The title pages of the Huntington and Folger copies bear the legend:

> Loves Martyr: or, Rosalin's Complaint. Allegorically shadowing the truth of Love, in the constant fate of the Phoenix and Turtle. A poeme enterlaced with much varietie and raritie; now first translated out of the venerable Italian Torquato Caeliano, by Robert Chester. With the true legend of famous King Arthur, the last of the nine Worthies, being the first essay of a new British Poet: collected out of diverse Authenticall Records. To these are added some new compositions, of several moderne writers whose names are subscribed to their severall workes, upon the first Subject: viz. the Phoenix and Turtle. Mar: "Mutare dominum non potest liber notus.[6]" London. Imprinted for E.B. 1601.[7]

---

5. Grossart A.B. *Robert Chester's Loves Martyr or Rosalin's Complaint*. L., 1878

# LOVES MARTYR,

## OR,

## ROSALINS COMPLAINT

*Allegorically shadowing the truth of Loue*
in the constant Fate of the Phœnix
*and Turtle.*

A Poeme enterlaced with much varietie and raritie;
*now first translated out of the venerable Italian* Torquato
Cæliano, *by* ROBERT CHESTER.

With the true legend of famous King *Arthur*, the last of the nine
Worthies, being the first *Essay* of a new *Brytish* Poet: collected
out of diuerse Authenticall Records.

*To these are added some new compositions, of seuerall moderne Writers
whose names are subscribed to their seuerall workes, vpon the
first Subiect: viz. the Phœnix and*
Turtle.

*Mar:* —— *Mutare dominum non potest liber notus.*

## LONDON

Imprinted ~~by~~

**1601**

# LOVES MARTYR:

## OR,

## ROSALINS COMPLAINT.

*Allegorically shadowing the truth of Loue,*
in the constant Fate of the Phœnix
*and Turtle.*

A Poeme enterlaced with much varietie and raritie;
*now first translated out of the venerable Italian* Torquato
Cæliano, *by* ROBERT CHESTER.

With the true legend of famous King *Arthur*, the last of the nine
Worthies, being the first *Essay* of a new *British* Poet: collected
out of diuerse Authenticall Records.

*To these are added some new compositions, of seuerall moderne Writers*
*whose names are subscribed to their seuerall workes, vpon the*
*first Subiect: viz. the* Phœnix *and*
Turtle.

*Mar:* —— *Mutare dominum non potest liber notus.*

## LONDON

Imprinted for E. B.

The title page of the Huntington copy. The date is missing.

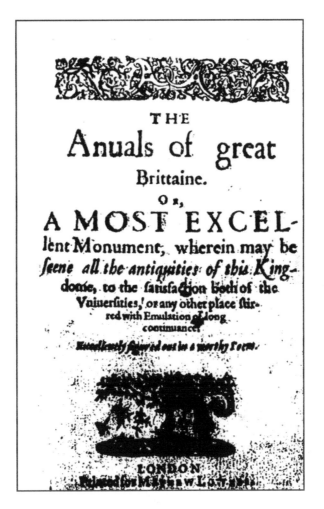

THE

Anuals of great

Brittaine.

Or,

A MOST EXCEL-
lent Monument, wherein may be
seene all the antiquities of this Kingdome, to the satisfaction both of the
Vniuersities, or any other place stirred with Emulation of long
continuance.

Excellently figured out in a worthy Forme.

LONDON
Printed for Mathew Lownes.

The title page of the London copy. Quite different:
strange title, different date and publisher, and the emblem of
another printer.

Let us note that E.B. means publisher Edward Blount; that Robert Chester bears a name that has not been heard before or after in English poetry; and that no Italian writer or poet Torquato Caeliano has ever existed at all.

The heading on the title page of the London copy is quite different:

> **The Anuals of the great Brittaine**. Or a most excellent Monument, wherein may be seene all the antiquities of this Kingdome to the satisfaction both of the Universities, or any other place stirred with Emulation of long continuance. Excellently figured out in a worthy poem. London. Printed for Mathew Lownes. 1611.[8]

We shall come back to the title later on, but now let us focus on the first, key, word which is rather odd: "Anuals," printed in large letters. Insofar as there is no such word in the English language, one has to assume that we have a misprint of one letter (the compositor allegedly turned the second letter "n" upside down). This "misprint" is often corrected by replacing the strange word by the seemingly more suitable "Annals." Let us also note the changes to the name of the publisher and the date. For, despite such difference in the title pages, all three copies were printed, as researchers have noted, with one and the same set of type (as well as the fourth one, Welsh, that has no title page).

## LOVE'S MARTYR — THE STORY OF THE LIFE AND DEATH OF THE TURTLE AND THE PHOENIX

Robert Chester's poem (for we know that the Italian Torquato Caeliano is a fiction, and no one has ever found any trace of an Italian original in this indisputably British work) is placed first in the book and comprises an overwhelming portion of it — 168 pages out of 195. The poem is prefaced with three author's introductions on unnumbered pages. The first, in prose, is an address to Sir John Salusbury (in the 19th century it was established that he was a gentleman from the county of Denbighshire).

---

6. "A noted book cannot change its master"(Martial). Probably this sentence contains an even more intriguing hint. If we consider that Muta is the name of a nymph whom Jupiter punished for her chattering by making by her mute, this line may be understood to mean that the book should not make public the name of its "master" (author, or main hero).

7. *Loves Martyr or Rosalins Complaint*. Allegorically shadowing the truth of Love in the constant Fate of the Phoenix and the Turtle. A Poem enterlaced with much variete and raritie; now first translated out of the venerable Italian Torquato Caeliano, by Robert Chester . . . Mar.: Mutare dominum not potest liber notus. London. Imprinted for E.B. 1601 (Spelling as in original)

8. *The Anuals of Great Britain*. Or a most excellent Monument, wherein may be seene all the antiquities of this Kingdome, to the satisfaction both of the Universities, or any other place stirred with Emulation of long continuance. Excellently figured out in a worthy Poem. London. Printed for Mathew Lownes. 1611.

To the honorable, and (for me before all other) honored Knight, Sir John Salisburie one of the Esquires of the bodie to the Queenes most excellent Majestie, Robert Chester wisheth increase of vertue and honour.

Posse & nolle, nobile.

HONORABLE SIR, having according to the directions of some of my best-minded friends, finished my long expected labour; knowing this ripe iudging world to be full of envie, every one (as sound reason requireth) thinking his owne child be fairest although an Aethopean, I am emboldened to put my infant wit to the eye of the world under your protection knowing that if Absurditie like a theefe have crept into any part of these Poems, your well-graced name will over-shadow these defaults, and the knowne Character of your vertues, cause the common back-biting enemies of good spirits to be silent.

Further on, Chester repeats and develops the idea:

To the World I put my Child to nurse, at the expence of your favour, whose glorie will stop the mouthes of the vulgar, and I hope cause the learned to rocke it asleepe (for your sake) in the bosome of good will. Thus wishing you all the blessings of heaven and earth; I end.

Yours in all service,

Ro. Chester

The next address, a poetic one, is to the Phoenix herself:

*Phoenix of beautie, beauteous Bird of any*
*To thee I do entitle all my labour,*
*More precious in mine eye by far than many,*
*That feedst all earthly senses with thy favour:*
*Accept my home-writ praises of thy love,*
*And kind acceptance of thy Turtle-dove.*
*Some deepe-read scholler fam'd for Poetrie,*
*Whose wit-enchanting verse deserved fame,*
*Should sing of thy perfections passing beauty,*
*And elevate thy famous worthy name:*
*Yet I the least, and meanest in degree,*
*Endeavoured have to please in praising thee.*

Chester's third and final address is "To the kind Reader," whom he warns that the story awaiting him will not tell of "bloody warres, nor of the sacke of Troy, of Pryams murdered sonnes, nor Didoes fall . . . of Caesars victories, nor Pompeys thrall, of Lucrece rape . . . of none of these, of sweete Conceit I sing." Then Chester concludes:

> *Then, (gentle Reader) over-reade my Muse,*
> *That armes herselfe to flie a lowly flight,*
> *My untun'd stringed verse do thou excuse,*
> *That may perhaps accepted, yeeld delight:*
> *I cannot clime in praises to the skie,*
> *Least falling, I be drown'd with infamie.*

The Chester poem itself comprises a mixture of material of varying degrees of perfection: from highly poetic lines, in which one can feel the hand of a master, to raw allegories with colorful and voluble deviations, rhymed with compilations that have no apparent connection with the major theme but are necessary to the author for some as yet obscure reason.

In the poem one can discern three principal parts: "Dame Nature Before the Gods," "The Dialogue of Dame Nature and the Phoenix," "The Dialogue of the Dove and the Phoenix"; there is also a "Conclusion."

The first third of the poem has a subheading: "Rosalins Complaint, metaphorically applied to Dame Nature at a Parliament held (in the high Star-chamber) by the Gods, for the preservation and increase of Earths beauteous Phoenix." Rosalin's name in the poem's text is presented only in this subheading and in the running title, and nowhere else. We know the witty maiden Rosalin by Shakespeare's play "Love's Labour's Lost," and the similar name Rosalind belongs to one of the heroines of "As You Like It." Both these characters and Chester's Phoenix have much in common, and readers will comprehend the reason for it later on.

> *"A solemne day of meeting mongst the Gods,*
> *And royal parliament there was ordained;*
> *The heavenly Sinod was at open ods,*
> *And many harts with earthly wrongs were painted;*
> *Some came to crave excuse, some to complaine*
> *Of heavie burdend griefes they did sustaine.*

The weeping Dame Nature speaks before the "Parliament of Gods." She is pale; the handkerchief with which she wipes her cheeks is soaked through (an interesting detail to note while describing the scene on Olympus!). Dame Nature kneels before Jupiter, seated on a golden throne, and speaks of the wonderful woman Phoenix, whom she has brought up and introduced to the world. Now Phoenix is in danger of being left without issue, and then her dynasty would cease to exist. A description of the Phoenix's appearance takes up to five pages: her face and hands are beautiful, her neck and head are adorned with "locks of hair taken by Nature from Apollo himself." Her forehead hides deep thoughts and excellent conceptions.

> *Her lippes — two rubie Gates from whence doth springe*
> *Sweet honied dew by an intangled kisse,*
> *From forth these glories doth the Night-bird sing,*
> *A Nightingale that no right notes will misse;*
> *True learned Eloquence and Poetrie,*
> *Do come between these dores of excellencie.*

The applicant shows the Gods a portrait of the beautiful Phoenix. They are delighted and ask Jupiter to help Dame Nature and her protégé.

The stern potentate of the world yields to their petition. He orders Dame Nature to take Apollo's chariot and deliver the Phoenix to the "Isle of Paphos," a veritable paradise on Earth; there is a high and steep mountain over a beautiful valley.

> *There shalt thou find true Honours lovely Squire*
> *That for this Phoenix keepes Prometheus fire.*
> *.. … … … … …*
> *His name is Liberall honor, and his hart*
> *Aymes at true faithfull service and desart.*

Jupiter gives to Dame Nature some precious balsam to bring to the man:

> *Give him this Ointment to anoint his head,*
> *This precious Balme to lay unto his feet,*
> *These shall direct him to this Phoenix bed,*
> *Where on a high hill he this Bird shall meet:*
> *And from their Ashes by my doome shall rise*
> *Another Phoenix her to equalize.*

The Gods hail Jupiter's decision, and Venus composes for the Phoenix a prayer for the salvation of silver Dove's soul, who is suffering for his sins. It is ironic that the heathen goddess Venus, addressing Jupiter, calls him Jehovah; she also mentions Christ's name. Judging by many texts in the book, Chester was well aware of the difference between the pagan religions of the Greeks and Romans and Christianity. Such confusion is evidently intentional, the more so as the prayer is supplied with a special address by the author "To those of light beleefe," wherein he recommends trying to understand his intent, though it is not easy.

So Dame Nature meets the Phoenix, whose beauty matches "true eloquence and poetry." Here and further on the heroine is constantly associated by Chester with poetry and its godly patron Apollo. The Phoenix complains that her life is full of suffering; she is not the Phoenix of yesteryear. She is apprehensive of Envy harassing her and hampering her to come with her feelings, she is afraid that the time of love for her is over:

> *.. .. .. .. .. ....I am defaced*
> *Upon the Arabian mountaines I must die,*
> *And never with a poore young Turtle graced;*
> *Such operation in me is not placed...*

Dame Nature convinces the Phoenix that all is not lost, that love and motherhood are still possible for her, despite weariness of life and "dead blood." Nature promises to find and severely punish Envy and to perform even greater deeds. The Phoenix speaks of another predicament, about the "dark dimme Taper that I must adore"; her beauty and virtue are prisoners of "false love." Nature tells her that Jupiter has charged her with taking the Phoenix to the blessed island of Paphos, and the Phoenix expresses hope that that could revive her, for the Turtle's nest is there.

Apollo's chariot takes them to the sky and they fly over the planet, over countries and cities, valleys, rivers, high mountains. Now they are over Britain and Nature points out the cities and what they are famous for. Here are the famous university cities of Oxford and Cambridge; here is Leicester, the Thames, Windsor... Special attention is paid to Scotland, Edinburgh with its noteworthy sights. In the meantime Nature tells the Phoenix about nine celebrated women whose images are carved in stone in the Edinburgh Maidens Castle. When the Windsor castle appears that, the belief goes, was erected by the legendary King Arthur, the poem is interrupted with the title: "Here followeth the Birth, Life and Death of the honourable Arthur, King of Brittaine." This rhymed "story" takes up 44 pages, though it does not seem to have the least connection with the poem's topic. Then Chester announces: "and now, to where we left," and Dame Nature goes on explaining to the Phoenix that now they are flying over London. At last they reach their destination.

Here, Chester deemed it necessary to insert one more huge digression — a whole catalogue of flowers, herbs, trees, fishes, gems, animals, snakes, worms and birds — that takes up 43 pages. It has been established that Chester used (retold in rhyme) the books on flora and fauna known at the time. All those digressions take up more than a half of Chester's poem. It is definitely done on purpose: having nothing to do with either Turtle or the Phoenix, these digressions may more likely repel than attract an "outside" reader. It seems that is exactly the reason . . .  Other not so cyclopic digressions, short historical fragments, lyric verses and songs are scattered all over Chester's poem, and right after it (but before the works of the other poets) we come across a collection of verses written by another, much more skilled hand, and presented as "Cantoes Alphabet-wise to faire Phoenix maide by the Paphian Dove." We shall speak later about those magnificent verses, many of them extremely close to Shakespeare's sonnets and true masterpieces.

One may notice that the images of the Turtle and the Phoenix did not acquire their final traits with Chester at once. At first Nature describes the heroine as a "Marvellous Phoenix of Exceptional Beauty" and right after that as a "milk-white

Dove." The Turtle calls his beloved either Phoenix, or Rose, Sun, Dove, or "my Queen." It seems that Chester, while creating (or revising, which is more probable) the poem, "accommodated" the images of the heroes to traditional ones, but did it rather carelessly. But perhaps these and other "inconsistencies" are not accidental.

In the last (third) part of the poem the allegory takes an unexpected turn. Dame Nature and the Phoenix arrive at Paphos Island, which is like paradise, "a sacred nook," where evil forces, "crocodiles and hissing snakes" do not dare to appear. However, instead of the beloved who was supposed to give the Phoenix a new *esprit*, to help her ensure the lineage, the two ladies meet an ailing creature, a grieving soul, "the perfect picture of heart-pining woes." This is "True Honors lovely Squire," the same Turtle, to whom the Phoenix came by order of Jupiter himself. From their words one may conclude that the meeting is not their first. The Phoenix observes that his condition is worse than before, and the Turtle craves pardon for a "presumptious foule offence," the timing and sense of which are not quite clear. It is also unclear what the Turtle has to do with the "false love" and "burning taper" to which the Phoenix had vowed herself. It seems that the ill Turtle "at Paphos island" is the very "dim taper" himself, though Chester's images, as we have noted already, are not really clear.

Having accomplished her mission, Dame Nature departs Paphos, leaving the Turtle and the Phoenix to be alone. The Turtle kneels down and asks the Phoenix to believe his fidelity and devotion. He speaks about his wretched condition, and, indeed, the Phoenix notes that

> *His features fade away, and make him looke*
> *As if his name were writ in death's pale booke.*

The Turtle is desperate:

> *I am not living, though I seeme to go,*
> *Already buried in the grave of woe.*

The Phoenix tries to console him, and reaches to wipe his tears, but he declines: "he is not clean," he is not worthy to be touched by her fair hand. Still, she insists on staying with him:

> *Why I have left Arabia for thy sake,*
> *Because those fires have no working substance,*
> *And for to find thee out did I undertake:*
> *Where on the montaine top we may advance*
> *Our fiery alter; let me tell thee this*
> *Solamen miseris socios habuisse doloris.*[9]

---

9. One who is miserable is comforted by having a companion in distress.

*Come poore lamenting soule, come sit by me,*
*We are all one, thy sorrow shall be mine,*
*Fall thou a teare, and thou shalt plainly see,*
*Mine eyes shall answer teare for teare of thine*
*Sigh thou, I'll sigh, and if thou give a grone,*
*I shall be dead in answering of thy mone.*

*… … … … … … … … … …I will beare*
*Half of the burdenous yoke thou dost sustaine,*
*Two bodies may with greater ease outweare*
*A troublesome labor, then I'll brooke some paine …*
*… … … … … … … … … … … …*
*Thou shalt not be no more the Turtle-Dove,*
*Thou shalt no more go weeping all alone,*
*For thou shalt be my selfe, my perfect Love,*
*Thy griefe is mine, thy sorrow is my mone …*

They speak of their mutual service to the god Apollo — patron of poetry and other arts. They decide to erect a burning altar, a sacrificial fire, dedicated to their godly benefactor.

But first the Phoenix asks the Turtle some not so easy questions: "What is the difference betwixt false love and true Sincerity?" And:

*"What may we wonder at? O where is learning?*
*Where is all difference twixt the good and bad?*
*Where is Apelles[10] Art? Where is true cunning?*
*Nay where is all the vertue may be had?"*

It is a pity, but the Turtle has time to answer only the first question; then they go out to gather twigs and sticks for the sacred fire. Burning, in the poem, initially symbolizes service to Apollo, but then[11] death, which both heroes wish for. The sacrificial fire dedicated to Apollo is to consume them, so that, in the Phoenix's words,

*… in a manner sacrificingly,*
*Burn both our bodies to revive one name.*

The Turtle says:

---

10. A noted painter of ancient Greece.
11. Quite unexpectedly!

> *Why now my heart is light, this very doome*
> *Hath banisht sorrow from my pensive breast;*
> *And in my bosome there is left no room,*
> *To set blacke melancholy, or let him rest …*

They address Apollo with a plea to accept this voluntary sacrifice, to send a spark from which would arise the fire destined to consume them. Then the Phoenix notices that somebody is watching them, but the Turtle assures her: this is the Pelican, their friend:

> *Let her alone to view our Tragedie,*
> *And then report our love that she did see.*

Tragedy! The Turtle is about to step first into the burning fire when the Phoenix stops him:

> *Stay Turtle stay, for I will first prepare;*
> *Of my bones must the princely Phoenix rise*
> *And if it be possibly thy blood well spare,*
> *For none but for my sake, dost thou despise*
> *  This frailty of thy life, o live thou still,*
> *  And teach the base deceitful world Love's will.*

She urges him to stay alive in order to "keep on teaching and enlighten this coarse and lying world," but the Turtle insists on his right to die:

> *Do not deny me Phoenix, I must be*
> *A partner in this happy Tragedy.*

And then they appeal to the sacred flame, lit by Apollo:

> *Phoenix:*
> > *Oh, holy, sacred and pure perfect fire*
> > … … … … … … … … … … … … … … …
> > *Accept into your ever hallowed flame*
> > *Two bodies, from the which may spring one name.*

> *Turtle:*
> > *O sweet perfumed flame, made of those trees,*
> > *Under the which the Muses nine have song*
> > *The praise of virtuous maids in misteries,*
> > *To whom the faire-fac'd Nymphs did often throng,*

> *Accept my body as a Sacrifice*
> *Into your flame, of whom one name may rise."*

This repeated image — some mysterious name that will remain after both heroes, emerging, like the Phoenix from their ashes — evidently carries considerable significance. We come across it further on, in verses by other contributors to the collection. In the poem with which we began and which is signed in Shakespeare's name, the image is made more precise: "Single Nature's double name." With Marston it acquires other more meaningful attributes missing in the legend about the wonderful bird.

The Turtle nevertheless steps first into the fire and burns up in it. The Chester poem concludes with the story told by the Phoenix of how staunchly, even with a smile, her friend accepted his last ordeal:

> *O willfulnesse, see how with smiling cheare*
> *My poore deare hart hath long himself to thrall,*
> *Looke what a mirthfull countenance he doth beare*
> *Spreading his wings abroad, and joyes withal:*
> *Learne thou corrupted world, learne, heare, and see,*
> *Friendships unspotted true sincerity.*

Then she hurries after him:

> *I come, sweet Turtle, and with my bright wings,*
> *I will embrace thy burnt bones as they lye,*
> *I hope of these another Creature springs,*
> *That shall possesse both our authority:*
> *I stay too long, o take me to your glory,*
> *And thus I end the Turtle Doves true story.*

Let us take note of the "Creature" that would own everything created by both heroes — it is, without doubt, the same enigmatic image, "the Name, rising from their ashes," but there is also some precision: it speaks of "authority," that is, creative heritage. A corner of the shroud of mystery is lifted. . . And what is this? The Phoenix's dead (or dying) friend smiled. We can make no mistake; for right beside "mirthfull" we see the word "joyes." He was laughing, even on the verge of eternity.

Under the last line of the Phoenix's monologue it is written: "Finis. R.C. (Robert Chester)." Still, after that on three pages there are two more poems,[12] which are not divided into strophes; the lines are rhymed in pairs. The first is entitled "The Pelican" and contains its testimony about the Turtle's death and that of the Phoenix:

---

12. They also bear Chester's signature and evidently were added later.

> *What wondrous hart-grieving spectacle*
> *Hast thou beheld the world's true miracle?*

The Pelican speaks of the courage with which the Turtle met death, then relates how the Phoenix ("Nature's deare adopted child") valiantly followed her friend, and both burned in Apollo's fire.

> *O, if the rarest creatures of the earth,*
> *Because but one at once did ere take breath*
> *Within the world, should with a second he,*
> *A perfect forme of love and amitie*
> *Burne both together, what should there arise*
> *And be presented to our mortal eyes,*
> *Out of the fire, but not a more perfect creature?*
> *Because that two in one is put by Nature...*

The "Creature" that emerges from the Turtle and the Phoenix's ashes received from them all the gifts of noble minds seeking good, love, beauty. The Phoenix's input cannot be separated from what the Turtle gave to the "Creature" — those two became one, thanks to Nature. As for Nature, it's clear that we have Dame Nature here again, Dame Nature who brought her foster daughter to this sacred island of Apollo. It is much more difficult to recognize the most wonderful and most perfect "Creature," which Chester has hinted at several times before. To this Creature he turns his exalted gaze in his last verse, entitled "Conclusion," which begins with the author apologizing that his talent is not great enough to speak about such momentous events, about such a rare subject. But it so happens

> *That had no better skill, but let it passe,*
> *For burdnous logs are set upon an Asse...*

After this, Chester informs us that another royal Phoenix did arise from the flames, and that this magnificent creature would long astound the world. Chester expresses his hope that "gentle minds" will approve his efforts and again concludes with: "Finis. R. Ch."

## THE TURTLE'S CANTOES AND SHAKESPEARE'S SONNETS

Then the reader comes across a large collection of poems which take up 34 pages and are presented as "Cantoes made by the Paphian Dove to faire Phoenix."[13] Such a subtitle, the character of the poetic works and the fact that Chester has introduced them as someone else's writings only cited by him, prevent us from seeing the poems as a mere sequel to Chester's opus. The "Dove's Cantoes," with their bright poetic imagery and virtuoso versification, surpass not only the work of Chester, whose name is otherwise unknown in the history of literature, but also that of collection participants including Chapman, Jonson, and Marston. It is a cascade of master acrostics that are surprisingly close to Shakespeare's sonnets in their topics and figurative style.

The first group of acrostics is called "alphabetical"; it consists of 24 verses on seven pages. They are seven-line verses with the rhyme scheme "ab abb cc," in which the first word of each line begins with the same letter. The verses are given in alphabetical order from "A" to "Z." The second, much more voluminous, section of acrostics was created according to a different principle: the first words of each line, read from top to bottom, form a sentence, which is the first, key line of the verse or even several lines of the verse. Here, depending on the number of words in the key sentence, we come across a gamut of strophes — from six line verses to fourteen lines (when it is a sonnet), and rhyme schemes.

The "Dove's Cantoes" are difficult, exquisite acrostics that have long attracted the astonished (sometimes puzzled) attention of specialists in English poetry. They display a baffling multitude of metaphors, individual words and even whole sentences that seem to come straight from the poems and sonnets of William Shakespeare. As in his sonnets, the topic of tender love, which is at the same time friendship, is predominant here, and along with creativity determines the meaning of the poet's life. The highest happiness is to love and know that you are loved.

The beautiful Phoenix is "a glorious comet," "her ever growing beautie like the Rose." The poet's love for her is full of endless fidelity, sincerity and purity. But it is not passion that unites them: their union is based on spiritual kinship, on joy "of mutual service to Apollo," whose fire they selflessly uphold, believing in their high destiny.

"Myself and mine are always thine" — this sentence is formed by the first words of one acrostic. The incomparable Phoenix — the poet's Muse, instills in him "the spirit of the ancient Homer." Their creative union is indivisible: "My lines are thine," "Grant me to play my sonnet on thy Harp," "Pray thou for me and I will make a song, pend [penned — *ed.*] in thine honor, none shall equalize" . . .

But cloudless joy and happiness are not in store for our Turtle. Many of his lines are full of bitterness and pain; by an unjust fate he is doomed to suffering. As we are given to understand by another acrostic he has suffered some misfortune; he is seriously ill. He repeatedly asks her pardon for his condition, and calls for sympathy and help:

---

13. *Cantoes Alphabet -wise to faire Phoenix made by the Paphian Dove. Cantoes Verbally written.*

*Yf thou have pity, pity my complaining,*
*Yt is a badge of Vertue in thy sexe.*

*Pittie is writ in gold upon thy hart,*
*Me promising to cure a curelesse smart.*

*Cure of my wound is past all Phisickes skill*
*Thou maist be gracious, at thy very looke*
*My wounds will close, that would my bodie kill,*
*Smart will be easie that could no plasters brooke…*

*Death haunts me at the heeles, yet is afraid,*
*To touch my bosome, knowing thou lov'st me.*

The repeated return to this theme, the very nature of these lines that are almost medical in terminology (illness, pains, medicine, plaster), leave little doubt that we are dealing not so much with spiritual and romantic sufferings, languor and lamentations, where poetic tradition and fashion may play a significant role, but also with physical sufferings that color the relations of this uncommon couple with tragic, even sacrificial notes.

The Turtle renders to the Phoenix his knowledge, his art. Along with the theme of pure, platonic love, compassion, fidelity, adoration of Apollo and the Muses, the motif of mystery and secret is always present. There is some understanding between the Turtle and the Phoenix, not only about the exalted purity of their relations and shared service to arts, but also about the mystery that should envelop them — though it is hard for the reader to perceive why such noble relations and occupations should be kept secret.

*Me may you count your unknowne Turtle-Dove.*

*Ah, be my Phoenix, I will be thy Dove*
*And thou and I in secrecie will love.*

*Blasé not my love, thou Herald of the day…*

*Other sweet motions now I will conceale*
*Grace these rude lines that my hearts thoughts reveale.*

Even the first person to research the Chester collection, Alexander Grossart, was much puzzled by the presence of such a great number of Shakespeare's thoughts, images, metaphors, and delicate euphuistic turns, and by the similarity of the poetic form of the "Dove's Cantoes" and Shakespeare's poems and sonnets. Some more recent

| | |
|---|---|
| *Not* | Not all the world could profer me difgrace, |
| *being* | Being maintained faireft faire by thee, |
| *hard,* | Hard-fortune fhall thy feruant nere outface, |
| *no* | No ftormes of Difcord fhould difcomfort me : |
| *plague* | Plague all the world with frownes my *Turtle-Doue,* |
| *fo* | So that thou fmile on me and be my loue. |
| | |
| *great* | Great Miftris, matchleffe in thy foueraigntie, |
| *in* | In lue and recompence of my affection, |
| *loue* | Loue me againe, this do I beg of thee, |
| *being* | Being bound by *Cupids* kind direction : |
| *long* | Long haue I fu'd for grace, yet ftil I find, |
| *deferd.* | Deferd I am by her that's moft vnkind. |

*And if my loue fhall be releeu'd by thee,*
*My heart is thine, and fo account of me.*

| | |
|---|---|
| *And* | And yet a ftedfaft hope maintaines my hart, |
| *if* | If anie fauour fauourably proceede |
| *my* | My deare from thee, the curer of my fmart, |
| *loue* | Loue that eafeth minds oppreft with neede, |
| *fhal be* | Shall be the true Phifition of my griefe, |
| *releeu'd* | Releeu'd alone by thee that yeeld'ft reliefe. |
| | |
| *by* | By all the holy rites that Loue adoreth, |
| *thee,* | Thee haue I lou'd aboue the loue of any, |
| *My* | My heart in truth thee alwayes fauoureth, |
| *heart* | Heart freed from any one, then freed from many : |
| *is* | Is it not bafe to change ? yea fo they fay, |
| *thine* | Thine owne confeffion loue denies delay. |
| | |
| *and* | And by the high imperiall feate of *Ioue,* |
| *fo* | So am I forc'd by *Cupid* for to fweare, |
| *account* | Account I muft of thee my *Turtle-doue,* |

Of

Some pages from the Chester collection, *The Turtle-Dove Cantoes* (A. Grossart's reissue). One of the most virtuoso acrostics, surprisingly similar to Shakespeare's sonnets.

*of*
*me.*

Of thee that Times long memorie fhall outweare:
Me by thy ftedfaft truth and faith denying,
To promife any hope on thee relying.

*My paffions are a hell and death to me,*
*Vnleffe you feele remorce and pitie me.*

*My*
*paffions*
*are*
*a*
*hell*
*and*

My fweeteft thoughts fweet loue to thee I fend,
Paffions deeply ingrafted, vnremouable
Are my affections, and I muft commend
A ftedfaft truft in thee moft admirable :
  Hell round enwraps my bodie by difdaine,
  And then a heauen if thou loue againe.

*death*
*to*
*me,*
*vnleffe*
*you*
*feele*

Death haunts me at the heeles, yet is afraid,
To touch my bofome, knowing thou lou'ft me,
Me fometimes terrifying by him betraid,
Vnleffe fweete helpfull fuccour come from thee:
  You well I know, the honor of mine eie,
  Feele fome remorcefull helpe in miferie.

*remorce*
*and*
*pittie*
*me.*

Remorce fits on thy brow triumphantly,
And fmiles vpon my face with gentle cheere ;
Pittie, loues gracious mother dwels in thee,
Me fauouring, abandoning bafe ieare,
  Death is amazed, viewing of thy beautie,
  Thinking thy felfe perfect eternitie.

*My pureft loue doth none but thee adore,*
*My heartie thoughts are thine, I loue no more.*

*My,*
*pureft*
*loue*

My comfortable fweete approued Miftris,
Pureft of all the pure that nature framed,
Loue in the height of all our happineffe,

scholars, trying to explain the phenomenon, have noted that this goes beyond any possible coincidence; they are compelled to assume that Shakespeare for some unknown reason not only gave his poem to the collection, but also may have taken part in editing Chester's poetic material and maybe even rewrote some of it. But, what is Shakespeare's connection with the enigmatic Turtle?

In his book *The Mutual Flame* (1955),[14] the eminent English poetry specialist G.W. Knight conducted a meticulous analysis of the "Dove's Cantoes." Paying special attention to the "Shakespeare places" in these "Cantoes," he notes on 20 pages of his book: "Very close to Shakespeare," "There is a quality here in the use of abstraction and personification that I would call deeply Shakespearean" and, finally, — "This is pure Shakespeare!"

The well-known metaphor, "this fell sergeant death is strict in his arrest" ("Hamlet," V. 2), was repeated in Sonnet 74 ("that fell arrest without all bail"); we also come across it ("death — arrest") in the Turtle Cantoes. The "map of sorrow" and "great map of beauty" in the Cantoes recalls "thus in his cheek the map of days outworn" in Sonnet 68 and "thou map of honour" in "Richard II," V. I). The euphuistic "Shame is ashamed to see thee obstinate" we find not only in the Turtle Cantoes but also in "Romeo and Juliet": "Upon her brow shame is ashamed to sit" (II, 5); and in the same place, "thoughts — Love's heralds." A charming expression, "Thy sweet self," adorns not only the 19th alphabetic acrostic of the Turtle, but also Shakespeare's Sonnets 114 and 126. The list of coincidences, which are unique, never encountered anywhere else in the poetry of the time, goes on and on; they cannot be accidental and cannot be treated as borrowed — these words are too closely woven into the poetic fabric of the acrostics.

And it's not just the neologisms, metaphors, and euphuistic turns that call to mind Shakespeare. Dangers and sins, which are mentioned in Sonnets 69, 70, 94, and 95, also trouble the Turtle. The Fair Friend becomes a target of slander and indecent rumors, and Shakespeare suffers deeply on her account. The same vituperative assaults on the part of certain malevolent people against the cherished Phoenix also anger the Turtle, who threatens to "pull out these weeds." Many other problems and concerns are common to the sonnets' author and the Chester Turtle.

Thus, Knight came to the conclusion that the poetic material, so reminiscent of Shakespeare's poems and sonnets and of such high artistic quality, is quite worthy of the Great Bard's pen, and one cannot exclude the possibility that Shakespeare really "had a finger in it." In any case, the "Dove's Cantoes" could not possibly have been written by Robert Chester: the level of his poetic texts in the collection and also those in his home manuscripts (we shall touch upon them later) is incomparably lower. I am ready to agree, myself, with Knight's conclusion — though I deem it incomplete. Chester could not have created anything like that; but it could have been written by the Turtle himself, that is, by the person hidden under that allegoric name.

---

14. Knight, G.W. *The Mutual Flame.* L., Methuen, 1955, p.161-178.

Knight could not help but notice a strange confusion of pronouns in some of the acrostics: the Phoenix is sometimes referred to as "she," sometimes as "he"; the same is also true of the Turtle. Some epithets describing the Phoenix seem to be more becoming to a man, and, conversely, the Turtle sometimes acquires some of the traits of his beloved lady friend, that is, becomes a She-Turtle! Knight notes that the gender confusions are so frequent and are so organically introduced into the text that they seem intentional, as if they served some important function. But, what? Knight's erudite ruminations about Renaissance poetry where love was often presented as a great potentate, a self-dominant essence, an active beginning, even if it were a woman, in this case cannot provide even a remotely plausible answer. But many difficulties are eliminated if one understands that some of the acrostics of the second group are in essence dialogues between the Turtle and the Phoenix and are the fruit of their common creativity (that is, their prototypes').

The English scholar concludes his analysis of the Turtle acrostics by admitting: "As for the acrostics, they leave the mind dizzy. . . . It seems that here we come to a limit beyond which any analysis becomes fruitless. But that may perhaps involve rather more than is usually supposed."

That is correct, as we shall see later — and *much* more, indeed!

## MOURNED BY A CHORUS OF POETS

Having turned the last page of the "Dove's Cantoes," the reader can see a second title page (half-title), opening the part of the collection where other contributors' poetic works are placed. The half-title goes as follows:

> Hereafter follow diverse Poetical Essays on the former Subject, viz The Turtle and the Phoenix. Done by the best and chiefest of our moderne writers with their names subscribed to their particular workes: never before extant. And (now first) consecrated by them generally to the love and merite of the true-noble Knight, Sir John Salisburie. Dignum laude virum Musa vetat mori.[15]

Beneath, there is the typographic emblem of the publisher Richard Field, who in 1593 issued the first Shakespeare poem, "Venus and Adonis," and the date MDCI (1601).

The title page of Chester's collection carried a notice promising that it contained new works by several contemporary authors, each signed with their names; the inscription on the second title page is more precise, and repeats the promise to publish

---

15. The man worthy of praise/ The Muse will not let die. Horace, Odes, IV, 8, 28.

their names. However, the first four poems of this section are signed by pennames. Under two, there is the Latin inscription, "Vatum Chorus" (A Chorus of Poets).

First comes an "Invocatio ad Apollinem and Pierides"; the Chorus of Poets asks the godly patrons of the arts to grant their minds such force and ability that they may pay a worthy tribute to the *noble friend*:

> *To your high influence we commend*
> *Our following Labours, and sustend*
> *Our mutual palmes, prepar's to gratulate*
> *An honorable friend: then propagate*
> *With your illustrate faculties*
> *Our mental powers: Instruct us how to rise*
> *In weighty Numbers, well pursu'd,*
> *And varied from the Multitude:*
> *Be lavish once, and plenteously profuse*
> *Your holy waters, to our thirstie Muse,*
> *That we may give a Round to him*
> *In a Castalian boule, crown'd to the brim.*

The second verse by the Chorus of Poets develops the idea further, emphasizing that the godly patronage was granted to them so that they could pay a creditable tribute to the most unusual and lofty heroes — the Turtle and the Phoenix. However, the title of the second verse says: "To the worthily honor'd Knight Sir John Salisburie."[16] On this basis, some researchers have assumed that the image of the Turtle is an allegory of John Salusbury. However, one can detect no sign of that gentleman in any of these works, nor of any of his relatives (in contrast to the virtuous Turtle and the Phoenix, the Salusbury couple produced no fewer than ten children). John Salusbury has no direct connection to the contents of the book or the tragic fate of the enigmatic couple. That is why some scholars assume that the name of Salusbury serves here as a sort of "smokescreen" masking the truth about the Turtle and the Phoenix, as testified in the key sentence on the title page. We must recall that at the beginning of the book Chester expressed the hope that Salusbury's *name* would protect it from the curiosity and the evil tongues of the mob; with the quotation from Horatio the poets show that, invoking his name, the Muse bestows Sir John with great honor and brings to him immortality.

The Chorus of Poets presents to the "noblest of minds" their hymns, born from a flowing source of poetic inspiration, the Muses' spring.

---

16. He was knighted in June of 1601. Hence, the verse was not written earlier than this date. The correct spelling of the family name of the owners of Lleveny, as accepted by Grossart, Matchett, Knight, Stanley Wells and many other scholars, is Salusbury.

L Et the bird of lowdeſt lay,
   On the ſole *Arabian* tree,
Herauld ſad and trumpet be :
To whoſe ſound chaſte wings obay.

But thou ſhriking harbinger,
Foule precurrer of the fiend,
Augour of the feuers end,
To this troupe come thou not neere.

From this Seſſion interdict
Euery foule of tyrant wing,
Saue the Eagle feath'red King,
Keepe the obſequie ſo ſtrict.

Let the Prieſt in Surples white,
That defunctiue Muſicke can,
Be the death-deuining Swan,
Leſt the *Requiem* lacke his right.

And thou treble dated Crow,
That thy ſable gender mak'ſt.
With the breath thou giu'ſt and tak'ſt,
Mongſt our mourners ſhalt thou go.

Here the Antheme doth commence,
Loue and Conſtancie is dead,
*Phœnix* and the *Turtle* fled,
In a mutuall flame from hence.

So they loued as loue in twaine,
Had the eſſence but in one,

Two

The first two pages of the Shakespeare poem
about the Turtle and Phoenix. There is no heading.

Two diſtinᶜts, Diuiſion none,
Number there in loue was ſlaine.

Hearts remote, yet not aſunder;
Diſtance and no ſpace was ſeene,
Twixt this *Turtle* and his Queene;
But in them it were a wonder.

So betweene them Loue did ſhine,
That the *Turtle* ſaw his right,
Flaming in the *Phœnix* ſight;
Either was the others mine.

Propertie was thus appalled,
That the ſelfe was not the ſame:
Single Natures double name,
Neither two nor one was called.

Reaſon in itſelfe confounded,
Saw Diuiſion grow together,
To themſelues yet either neither,
Simple were ſo well compounded.

That it cried, how true a twaine,
Seemeth this concordant one,
Loue hath Reaſon, Reaſon none,
If what parts, can ſo remaine.

Whereupon it made this *Threne*,
To the *Phœnix* and the *Doue*,
Co-ſupremes and ſtarres of Loue,
As *Chorus* to their Tragique Scene.

> *Pure juice that flow'd from the Pierian springs,*
> *Not filch'd, not borrow'd, but exhaust*
> *By the flame-hair'd Apollo's hand:*
> *And at his well observ'd command,*
> *For you infus'd in our retentive braine,*
> *Is now distil'd thence, through our quilles againe.*

At first, it seems that they are addressing Salusbury, but then it becomes clear that their thoughts are directed towards Chester's heroes — either one or both of them:

> *Value our verse, as you approve the worth;*
> *And thinke of what they are create,*
> *No Mercenarie hope did bring them forth,*
> *They tread not in that servile Gate;*
> *But a true Zeale, borne in our Spirites,*
> *Responsible to your high Merites,*
> *And an Invention, freer from the Times,*
> *These were the Parents to our severall Rimes,*
> *Werein Kind, Lerned, Envious, all may view,*
> *That we have writ worthy our selves and you.*

The signature under each of these verses is indeed significant — "Vatum Chorus." Not only did the best of England's poets deem it necessary to attach their works dedicated to mysterious heroes hidden under bird-mask pennames to a weak poem by the nearly unknown Chester, but they preceded their works with paeans performed by a whole poetic chorus! The telling signature, the solemn tone of the address to Apollo, the pronoun "we" and the fact that these addresses open up the second part of the collection once again speak for the fact that behind allegorical images of the Turtle and the Phoenix are hidden people of uncommon, outstanding virtues, a platonic couple whose death deeply moved the poets who knew of their secret "service to Apollo." The world had lost its finest ornament, one that had profoundly influenced the entire environment and made it purer. A chorus sings about it — not an ordinary choir of choristers, but the Chorus of Poets — who mourn and glorify their noble friends consumed by Apollo's flame.

The two short verses (six and eight lines), placed on one page are signed by a penname "Ignoto." Under this name hides an active contributor to the collection "England's Helicon." The opening verse, entitled "The First," presents a figurative description of the unique Phoenix.

> *The silver Vault of Heaven, hath but one Eie,*
> *And that is the Sunne: the foule-maskt Ladie, Night*

> *(Which blots the Cloudes, the white Booke of the Skie),*
> *But one sicke Phoebe, fever-shaking Light:*
> *The heart, one string: so, thus in single turnes,*
> *The world one Phoenix, till another burnes.*

The second verse, "Burning," is a direct continuation of the first. It speaks of the Phoenix again, and the name Turtle is not mentioned here, either.

> *Suppose here burnes this wonder of a breath*
> *In righteous flames, and holy-heated fires:*
> *(Like Musike which doth rapt it selfe to death,*
> *Sweet'ning the inward roome of man's Desires);*
> *So she wast's both her wings in piteous strife,*
> *The flame that eates her, feeds the others life:*
> *Her rare-dead ashes, fill a rare-live urne:*
> *One Phoenix borne, another Phoenix burne.*

A "rare-live urne"? — this is obviously the very "Creature" of which Chester spoke.

The Ignoto's verses are followed by the Shakespeare poem that drew scholarly interest to the Chester collection and that is known to the world as "The Phoenix and the Turtle." This is the title that was so misleadingly translated into Russian (as "The Phoenix and the She-Turtle") — but there is more to it than that. The most peculiar thing is that it is the only poem in the collection, the only work in the whole book, to be printed without any title! The title to which we are now accustomed was appended to the poem only in 1807, two centuries later. It was in 1807 that the editors of an American publisher (in Boston) of Shakespeare's works decided to provide a title for the heretofore-untitled poem. This invention took root and since then the title 'The Phoenix and the Turtle," which by the way fully corresponds to the contents of the poem, though it is not exhaustive, has become an integral part of it. But there is no such title in the Chester book!

The poem takes up three pages. The first part, 13 four-line verses, is given on two pages (170-171) without a title or signature. It ends with a notice that Reason created (or performed) a threne on the Turtle and Phoenix, "as Chorus to their Tragique Scene."

The lament itself, five three-line strophes, is placed on the next page, 172. It bears the title "Threnos," and, after the last line, the signature "William Shake-speare." Besides the heading, and the name of William Shakespeare, spelled the same way as on the title page of the only edition of the sonnets published during his lifetime (that is, with a hyphen[17]), this page also carries a special polygraphic decoration — it is adorned at the top and at the bottom by a border. Thus, the two parts of the poem look

### *Threnos.*

BEautie, Truth, and Raritie,
Grace in all ſimplicitie,
Here encloſde, in cinders lie.

Death is now the *Phœnix* neſt,
And the *Turtles* loyall breſt,
To eternitie doth reſt.

Leauing no poſteritie,
Twas not their infirmitie,
It was married Chaſtitie.

Truth may ſeeme, but cannot be,
Beautie bragge, but tis not ſhe,
Truth and Beautie buried be.

To this vrne let thoſe repaire,
That are either true or faire,
For theſe dead Birds, ſigh a prayer.

*William Shake-ſpeare.*

The Threnos from the poem about the Turtle and Phoenix. Signed Shake-speare.

like quite independent works, different in the poetic form of the strophes; and the second part has both the title and signature, whereas the first one has neither.

Researchers have tried to understand the reason for and meaning of the strange placement and polygraphic arrangement of the poem — if it is a single poem, indeed. The assumption that these are two different works would entail the following: that the poem on the first two pages was written by an author who shrank from signing his poem even with a penname (like, for example, the Ignoto) and supplying it with a heading. That hypothesis seems to contradict the fact that the second part is a lamentation, the creation of which is announced in the first part. All the authors of the collection are represented by two or four verses, and usually the second continues and develops the ideas and images of the previous one. The same principle with some qualifications could be traced here (if only we discard the indication that the "Threnos" was created or performed by someone called Reason, and ignore the difference in the poetic language). But in any case, the absence of a heading either before the entire poem or before its first part, sets this poem apart from the others and presents a problem that cannot be casually dismissed.

The Boston "invention" removes the question for the reading public, but not for scholars. Perhaps the text of the first part took up two full pages and left no room to the compositor (or type-setter) to set a title? In similar cases — Chapman's or Marston's poems — he did not omit the headings, though he had to move two last lines of Marston's verse to the following page, where Chapman's verse is placed, and to use a smaller font for Chapman's title and signature and crowd the renowned poet in every regard. Here, the compositor could have easily made room for a heading (if the author had provided one) by moving the final strophe of the first part to the next page, by removing at least one of the border decorations there (for instance, the top one); such borders were generally used to fill up the blank space. But this was not done. Why?

Some other questions remain. Do these poetic lines, so distinctly different from authentic Shakespeare works, really belong to him? At any rate, the "Dove's Cantoes" are much closer to the Sonnets, "Lucrece," "Venus and Adonis" than this poem is, so that we find ourselves in the company of the silent sphinxes of Chester's book. Some have noticed the likeness of the "Threnos" (its poetical form, and language) to the poetic texts of two plays by John Fletcher, and have presumed that he was the author. As to the poem's contents, it clearly indicates that both heroes of the poem, the Turtle and the Phoenix, are dead. And it especially notes that they left no issue and that the reason for that is not their impotence but the vow of chastity by which their marriage was conditioned. How much does this agree with what the other poets say about the unusual "birds"?

---

17. It was not customary at the time to spell proper names with a hyphen, but as one can see, for Shakespeare an exception was made.

## JOHN MARSTON SEES THE WONDER OF PERFECTION

The satirical poet and playwright John Marston was 26 years old in 1601 and until then, he had not published any poetic works under his own name. We come across four of his verses in the Chester collection. The first one is placed on the page opposite the Shakespeare "Threnos" and bears the title: "A narration and description of a most wondrous creature, arising out of the Phoenix and Turtle Doves ashes." Such a heading puzzles some English and American researchers: it seems to contradict the words from Shakespeare's "Threnos" — "leaving no posteritie." Let us, however, take another look:

> *O Twas a moving Epicidium!*
> *Can Fire? can Time? can blackest Fate consume*
> *So rare creation? No; tis thwart to sence,*
> *Corruption quakes to touch such excellence,*
> *Nature exclaimes for Justice, Justice Fate*
> *Ought into nought can never remigrate.*
> *Then looke; for see what glorious issue (brighter*
> *Then clearest fire, and beyond faith farre whiter*
> *Then Dians tier) now springs from younder flame?*
> *Let me stand numb'd with wonder, never came*
> *So strong amaizment on astonish'd eie*
> *As this, this measurelesse pure Raritie.*
> *Lo now; th'xtracture of devinest Essence*
> *The Soule of heavens labour'd Quintessence,*
> *(Peans to Phoebus) from dear Lovers death,*
> *Takes sweete creation and all blessing breath.*
> *What strangenes is't that from the Turtles ashes*
> *Assumes such forme? (whose splendor clearer flashes*
> *Then mounted Delius) tell me genuine Muse.*
> *Now yeeld your aides, you spirites that infuse*
> *A sacred rapture, light my weaker eie:*
> *Raise my invention on swift Phantasie,*
> *That whilst of this fame Metaphisicall*
> *God, Man, nor Woman, but elix'd of all*
> *My labouring thoughts, with strained ardor sing,*
> *My Muse may mount with an uncommon wing.*

Marston asks his godly patrons in poetry to help him see and sing (the praises of) this astonishing creation, who, according to the poet, is "metaphysical, for it is not a

## A narration and description of a
moſt exact wondrous creature, ariſing
*out of the Phœnix and Turtle*
*Doues aſhes.*

O Twas a mouing *Epicidium!*
Can Fire? can Time? can blackeſt Fate conſume
So rare creation? No; tis thwart to fence,
Corruption quakes to touch ſuch excellence,
Nature exclaimes for Iuſtice, Iuſtice Fate,
Ought into nought can neuer remigrate.
Then looke; for ſee what glorious iſſue (brighter
Then cleareſt fire, and beyond faith farre whiter
Then *Dians* tier) now ſprings from yonder flame?
  Let me ſtand numb'd with wonder, neuer came
So ſtrong amazement on aſtoniſh'd eie
As this, this meaſureleſſe pure Raritie.
  Lo now; th' xtracture of deuineſt *Eſſence,*
The Soule of heauens labour'd *Quinteſſence,*
(*Peans* to *Phœbus*) from deare Louers death,
Takes ſweete creation and all bleſſing breath.
  What ſtrangeneſſe is't that from the *Turtles* aſhes
Aſſumes ſuch forme? (whoſe ſplendor clearer flaſhes,
Then mounted *Delius*) tell me genuine Muſe.
  Now yeeld your aides, you ſpirites that infuſe
A ſacred rapture, light my weaker eie:
Raiſe my inuention on ſwift Phantaſie,
That whilſt of this fame *Metaphiſicall*
God, Man, nor Woman, but elix'd of all
My labouring thoughts, with ſtrained ardor ſing,
My Muſe may mount with an vncommon wing.
A 2

John Marston talks about the unusual Perfection
left behind by the Turtle and Phoenix

God, not a man nor woman, but elix'd of all"! And the poet feels that his Muse "mounts an uncommon wing."

In the second poem, entitled "The Description of this Perfection," Marston calls this creature, this wonder, "limitless Ens" — thus in scholastic philosophy was designated the highest abstract form of Being. It would be "impertinent" to give a clear definition of such a creation: it is transcendental, though palpable, and the poet's Muse attempts only to glorify it. But even for that, the poet lacks adequate words, adequate means. This Perfection is higher than anything imaginable; in speaking about it, one cannot exaggerate; no lofty praise, no dithyrambs whatsoever could be excessive.

> *No speech is Hyperbollical*
> *To this perfection blessed.*
> *Thus close my Rimes, this all that can be sayd,*
> *This wonder never can be flattered.*

It is interesting to note that in speaking about this wonderful Perfection, Marston uses verbs in the past tense.

In the third, eighteen-line poem entitled "To Perfection. A sonnet," Marston underlines the contrast between the spoilt world and the unstained purity of Perfection. Squalor, unshapeliness, all physical and mental deficiencies that other creatures possess may be explained, in the poet's opinion, by the fact that nature had long been selecting all possible merits from everywhere, so that it could adorn its new Perfection, this incomparable rarity.

In his last, fourth poem, "Perfectioni Hymnus," Marston exclaims:

> *What should I call this Creature*
> *Which now is growne into maturitie?*

This line also puzzles some scholars. Earlier, Marston spoke of the appearance of the new Creation, excellent and perfect in every respect, either in the present or in the past tense. Now, he directly asserts that it has reached maturity, that is, it did not emerge just now; although one page before, the poet saw this perfect being born from the Turtle's ashes. One can only feel compassion for the conscientious scholars: such a manner of expression could positively drive one into an impasse. Seeking a way out, they started looking for a couple whose female issue might have come of age by 1601. They ignored Marston's warning that it was not a human issue, and explained that away as the whimsy of Platonism. But to no avail. . .

In the last verse the poet carries further the idea of the unattainable height of this wonderful Perfection, the impossibility of finding adequate words for its description. Even such epithets and similes as "Heaven's Mirror," "Deepe Contemplation's wonder," even the word chosen by the poet, "Perfection," is too feeble; one should add to each of them the superlative case: "the best," "the highest." This Perfection teaches virtue itself; it serves as an example to everything that is mundane; it is in itself the Highest Absolute Existence. Sometimes Marston uses such hyperboles that one cannot but call them astonishing. And the poet, in anticipation of his readers' embarrassment (including ours), had warned that in glorifying this Wonder one could not fall into exaggeration.

The Creation is neither a man, nor woman, nor god (though it exists in reality and even reached maturity), but the Turtle himself is an allegory of a certain personality whose death is mourned by Marston. It is no accident that the Creature emerging (or discovered?) from the ashes of the Turtle and the Phoenix is so perfect, for the dead Turtle had also been such.

What is then this mysterious Creation, extract of human and godly essence, influencing the whole world? Shakespeare's "Threnos," asserting that the Turtle and the Phoenix did not leave any posterity because their marriage was platonic, does not contradict Marston's poems about Perfection (though one may assume that, at cursory reading). The poets complement one another and help us to understand their meaning better. In light of the information provided by the Chorus of Poets, the Ignoto, Shakespeare and especially Marston, and the repeated invocation of Apollo and the Muses (whom the heroes of the book had secretly served) — it becomes clear that it deals with the creative activity of the Turtle and the Phoenix. The name of Homer serves the same purpose, as do Marston's important words about poetry (paeans to Phoebus), that survived after the heroes left this life — that is the Perfection that they bequeathed to the world. By the time of their death, their creative heritage was significant — thus are explained Marston's words about the "maturity" of the Creation and the fact that sometimes he refers to it in the past tense. This heritage, as it were, had excelled everything created, or even conceivable, before! Sometimes Marston refers to the magnificent Creation as an Idea; still, it is not an abstract but a materialized Idea. The poet knows well the man, his lady, and their creative heritage that blossomed after their demise.

Even in the poetry of the time, when excessive rapture and extravagant eulogizing were common, one can hardly find anything equal to these four verses of Marston. The more so that one does not feel in them either exaggerated exaltation or servility. The poet is perfectly sincere in his adoration of the wonder, whose contemporary and witness he happened to be. I repeat, one can hardly find anything like that. But . . . reading Ben Jonson's famous ode in the Great Folio, the first posthumous collection of Shakespeare's plays,[18] under the heading of "To the Memory of my Beloved, the Author Mr. William Shakespeare: and What He Has Left Us," we come across lines that almost literally repeat Marston's definition of the Perfection — the Creature that arose from the Turtle and the Phoenix's ashes. "Shakespeare . . . I

---

18. This edition is commonly called the "Great Folio" or "the "First Folio," and so I shall refer to it henceforth.

confess thy writings to be such, as neither man, nor muse, can praise too much. 'Tis true, and all men's suffrage." Can it be a coincidence?

George Chapman is the only contributor to the Chester book who provided just one poem, "Peristeros, or Male Turtle." In this heading the poet formed a male version of the Greek word "peristera," which had been used before only in the feminine gender. Chapman helps us to better understand Chester's allegory. The poet depicts the Turtle in the past tense (while speaking of himself in the present), when the former, as it turns out, was inclined to extremes. Despite the title, the highest eulogy is directed to a woman, who in this book bears the name of "Phoenix." The Turtle's and the Phoenix's hearts were tightly united; she was for him the world of joy. The poet emphasizes his loyalty to the Turtle and his deep fidelity to the Phoenix.

> *And Time nor Change (that all things else devoures,*
> *But truth eterniz'd in a constant heart)*
> *Can change me more from her, then her from merit,*
> *That is my forme, and gives my being, spirit.*

Chapman speaks perfectly clearly about his close personal ties with the heroes of the book and leaves no doubt that he means specific people, his very own friends. Chapman's verse shows that the allegorical images, repeated addresses to classical mythology, and language permeated with philosophical terminology, was clearly intended for a narrow circle of the initiated, concealing not only an intricate game in abstraction, but certain specific people and a certain none too simple life, connected with the very art of poetry. The difficulty lies not in absence of any authentic reality hidden behind those symbolic figures, but in the fact that even today we still do not have a readily accessible key to them.

## BEN JONSON KNEW THEM WELL

Ben Jonson, like Marston, is represented in the book by four pieces.[19] The first one is "Praeludium." The poet who is about to sing his heroes' praise first tries to find a worthy patron on Mount Olympus. Hercules? Phoebus? Bacchus? Athena, Cupid? Wily Hermes? No!

> *… … … … … … …No, we bring*
> *Our owne true Fire; now our Thought takes wing,*
> *And now an Epode to deep Ears we sing.*

---

19. Beside Chester's book, these verses can be found in collections of B. Jonson's poetic works. Rf. Jonson, B. *The Complete Poems.* Ed. by G.Parfitt. Penguin 1975, p.106, 107, 278, 341.

So, Jonson makes his address to those who understand about whom and about what he is going to speak. Then follows "Epos" — a poem that occupies four pages and is surpassed in volume only by the works of Chester himself. In the center of the poem is a Turtle, which is referred to in the present tense. There is no indication or hint as to his death or the death of the Phoenix. The poem extols chastity, cleanness, and the renunciation of passionate fleshly love, which are characteristic of the hero.

Though our actions are controlled by reason, sometimes reason is overwhelmed by passion. "The thing they call Love, is blind Desire." True love is pure, selfless, perfect; it is like a gold chain coming from the heavens in order to unite the noblest minds into a godly union of those equal in spirit. It does not need base tricks to attain such a high aim. There are people who are chaste because their time for passion is past; others fear for their reputation — their chastity is compelled. Authentic purity is based on love of virtue and not on fear or calculation.

> But we propose a person like our Dove,
> Crac'd with a Phoenix love;
> A beauty of that cleare and sparkling light,
> Would make a day of night,
> And turne the blackest sorrows to bright joys…
>
> Oh, who is he, that (in this peace) enjoys
> The elixir of all joys?
> A form more fresh, than are the Eden bowers
> And lasting, as her flowers…

Who is he, who can suppress his desire, who can renounce such happiness, who would refrain from possessing the one who loves him?

> … … …. But soft: I hear
> Some vicious fool draw near,
> That cries, we dream, and swears, there is no such thing
> As this chaste love we sing…
> … … … … … … … … … … …..
> No, vice, we let thee know
> Though thy wild thoughts with sparrows' wings do fly
> Turtles can chastely die ….

The concluding lines of the poem are heavy with meaning, but can be understood in different ways. Speaking of the Phoenix, the poet writes:

Iudgement (adornd with Learning)
Doth shine in her discerning,
Cleare as a naked vestall
Closde in an orbe of Christall.

Her breath for sweete exceeding
The *Phœnix* place of breeding,
But mixt with sound, transcending
All *Nature* of commending

Alas : then whither wade I,
In thought to praise this *Ladie*,
When seeking her renowning,
My selfe am so neare drowning ?

Retire, and say ; Her *Graces*
Are deeper then their Faces :
Yet shee's nor nice to shew them,
Nor takes she pride to know them.

*Ben : Iohnson.*


FINIS.

The last page of the Chester book — the ending of
the 'Ode Enthusiastic' by Ben Jonson. Speaking of the
Phoenix, he calls her "Lady" and regrets that he may not
openly tell the truth about her.

> *What savage, brute affection,*
> *Would not be fearful to offend a dame*
> *Of this excelling frame?*
> *Much more a noble, and right generous mind*
> *(To virtuous moods inclined)*
> *That knows the weight of guilt: he will refrain*
> *From thoughts of such a strain.*
> *And to his sense object this sentence ever,*
> Man may securely sin, but safely never.

It looks as though Jonson is hinting here at some intimate circumstances connected with the Turtle. Whatever it may be, the poem also confirms the spiritual character of the relationship between the Turtle and the Phoenix that excludes physical intimate relations.

As one can see, Jonson accorded great importance to these two poems. In 1616, he published the "Works" — the collection of his poetic and dramatic compositions which in academic circles is known under the name of "Folio 1616." For this book Jonson carefully selected the verses himself, he grouped them, edited them, and watched over the typographic process. He did not publish everything he had written by that time. But the "Praeludium" and "Epos" from the Chester book he did include, and placed them in the most important, "program" part of the book — the poetic cycle "Forest," next to the address to a noble lady who had died several years before. To this lady we shall return later on.

The third Jonson poem in Chester's book consists only of two four-line stanzas and is called "The Phoenix Analysed." In the first line, he states: now, nobody can doubt that the magnificent creature the Phoenix turned out to be a woman. The second strophe says that no one should wonder that she only appears to be the Turtle's wife.

> *Now, after all, let no man*
> *Receive it for a Fable,*
> *If a Bird so amiable,*
> *Do turn into a Woman.*
>
> *Or (by our Turtle's Augur)*
> *That Nature's fairest Creature,*
> *Prove of his Mistress' Feature,*
> *But a bare Type and Figure.*

Once again, and quite definitely, Jonson indicates the chaste nature of their relations. It is quite apparent that the authors of Chester's book thought the uncommon, "pure" marriage of their heroes an extremely important feature of their relationship, something that sets them apart from others and requires certain explanations.

In the last poem, the "Ode Enthusiastic," which concludes the whole collection, Jonson speaks about the Phoenix as a real person, calls her a "Lady" and highly praises her intellectual qualities.

### Ode Enthusiastic

> Splendour! O more than mortal,
> For other forms come short all
> Of her illustrate brightness,
> As far as sin's from lightness.
>
> Her wit as quick, and sprightful
> As fire; and more delightful
> Than the stol'n sports of lovers,
> When night their meeting covers.
>
> Judgement (adorned with Learning)
> Doth shine in her discerning,
> Clear as a naked vestall
> Closed in an orb of Chrystall.
>
> Her breath for sweete exceeding
> The Phoenix place of breeding,
> **But mixed with sound, transcending**
> **All nature of commending.**[20]
>
> Alas: then whither wade I,
> In thought to praise this ladie;
> When seeking her renowning,
> Myself am so near drowning?
>
> Retire, and say; her Graces
> Are deeper than their Faces:
> Yet shee's nor nice to shew them,
> Nor takes she pride to know them.

---

20. Emphasis mine (Author).

This last line by Jonson is the last line in the book. Now let me repeat myself: not only in the "Praeludium" but also in other verses, Jonson refers to the Turtle and the Phoenix in the present tense. He does not mention their death. His poems conclude the book and could not possibly leave such an important and tragic event without due attention. Why then did Ben Jonson kept silent on the subject of his heroes' departure?

## BEHIND THE SHROUD OF MYSTERY

Such is the content of the poetic collection *Love's Martyr*. (Now, having met its heroes, we can assume that the title most probably refers to the Phoenix who voluntary followed her late consort). The poets, contributors to the book, as they had promised, talked in allegorical form about the wonderful couple, whom they knew well and whose demise they (all but Jonson) mourn. One might come to the conclusion that the couple died shortly before the book appeared. Chester's poem is concluded by the Phoenix's story about the demise of her friend; she is about to follow the Turtle. Ignoto (an unknown) makes an address to the Phoenix, who is still alive. In Chester's final verses (the "Pelican" and "Conclusion") we are told that the Phoenix also took her life. Shakespeare and Marston grieve the dead couple: the latter venerates some perfect creation they left behind. Jonson's poems, as one may judge, were written while both heroes were still alive.

All the poets observe the most general agreement about the nature of the allegory and call the man Turtle and the woman Phoenix, paying little attention to the classical legend and addressing their heroes as real persons who existed in life. They shrink from calling them by name and do not give such details as could divulge their real identities to an uninitiated reader. Each poet treats the images of the Turtle and the Phoenix somewhat differently; the details, however, are not of great importance. Some pay more attention to the Turtle, others to the Phoenix; in some cases one may trace the acquaintance and even friendship of the poet with his heroes. There are natural discrepancies in some details of these stories by several witnesses about the same people and events; the differences are caused by the writers' various degrees of knowledge and acquaintance, and their dissimilar intellectual and spiritual interests. It is also caused by their respective poetical vision and manners.

In the main, their evidence coincides, for the poets' vision is aimed in the same direction; they are speaking about the same people. The authors do not contradict but add to each other's evidence a certain detail or trait that is important to them, some peculiarities of their personal relations with the prototypes of the heroes. Such a cross section of this authoritative and multifaceted evidence reveals from the darkness first a vague and then a clearer silhouette of two unusual personalities, contemporaries and friends of the greatest poets in England, who paid tribute to them with their works but abstained from calling them by name.

Chester's poem and the "additional" verses of the renowned English poets convincingly testify that under the allegorical name-masks are hidden not characters from ancient legends, or abstractions, but quite real people, exceptional in their virtues and by the influence they exerted on their milieu. Though they were consorts, their relations remained chaste — it was confirmed more than once by the poets; common spiritual interests tied them by service to Apollo and the Muses, i.e. by creativity. The reader has an opportunity to get acquainted with a portion of the heritage — the collection of the "Turtle Dove's Cantoes," marked with an imprint of sophisticated poetic mastery and wonderfully close to Shakespeare's poems and sonnets.

They definitely occupied a high position (speaking of them, such epithets as "royal," "godly," "most noble," "glorious," "perfect" are often used), but for some reason the life of this couple and their poetic occupation are kept in deep secret, shrouded in mystery, inaccessible to the uninitiated. The secrecy, as one can see from multiple poets' hints and aposiopesis, from the intent declared on the title page to shroud the truth, covered even the demise of the enigmatic couple. But we still learn that they died nearly at the same time — first he, then she. From the flame of Apollo's service, from their ashes arose a name, one name, possessing everything unattainable and perfect that they had created during their lifetime.

The mystery of the Turtle and the Phoenix covers their memory, their heritage, the Chester book itself, making the latter an intractable riddle for several generations of researchers.

Who, then, are these two, this unusual couple that left behind only one name? What united them with England's best poets and, first of all, with Shakespeare? Why was the publication of the book laden with so much mystery; why are there so many riddles? What is the relationship between the 1601 edition and the London copy dated 1611 and named with so very strange a title?

Such are the major questions confronting the researchers of the Chester collection. It is clear that the first question is crucial: only by finding the prototypes of the Turtle and the Phoenix, individuals who really existed in Shakespeare's Elizabethan and Jacobean England, can we understand everything else.

## AWAKENING — FIRST CONJECTURES AND HYPOTHESES

As far as is known, nobody remembered and studied Chester's collection in the 17th century. In 1616, Ben Jonson issued his "Works," where he placed a somewhat amended "Praeludium" and "Epos," and in 1640 John Benson published Shakespeare's poetic works, including there the poem about the Turtle and the Phoenix from Chester's book — without any title or reference to the source. He placed it just before the elegies on Shakespeare's death. In 1710, the poem appeared in a new collection of

Shakespeare's poetry published by Gildon, and then in other editions. In 1780, one of the first researchers of Shakespeare, Edmund Malone, in his edition for some reason issued the poem as the 20th verse from the *Passionate Pilgrim*;[21] it was likewise published several times during the 18th and 19th centuries. There were no serious commentaries on the poem, nor even attempts to fathom its meaning. In 1865, J.O. Halliwell published some short notes on Chester's book[22] — that was essentially its first presentation to the reading public. Halliwell especially pointed out that this is the only case wherein Shakespeare took part in a collective book by his contemporaries, and he came to the conclusion that Chester must have been an intimate friend of the Great Bard (though Halliwell knew nothing about the man). He treated the book as one of the rarest and most valuable in English literature.

He also mentioned the location of both known copies of *Love's Martyr*. The first was acquired at auction during the sale of George Daniel's library. There is no date on the title page but the former owner, Daniel, in 1838 made an inscription testifying that the date had not been cut off by the bookbinder — it was absent from the very beginning. Consequently, this is the copy that is now in California. The other one (which is now in Washington, DC), was purchased in the 19th century by a renowned book lover named Miller. Halliwell also made it known that the book was reissued in 1611 under the title "The Anuals of great Brittaine or . . . ," and took pains to correct the "misprint" in the key word of the title.

So, only in the 19th century was the strange book noticed and given some interest. Most probably the collection would have shared the fate of other books of the Shakespearean epoch, lost in neglect, were it not for the name of the Great Bard under one of the works published there. Researchers' attempts to probe the meaning of the poem "Phoenix and the Turtle" inevitably lead to Chester's book. R.W. Emerson, the outstanding American philosopher and writer, regarded the poem highly and deemed it to be a mourning elegy on the death of a certain poet and his poetic lady friend. In 1875, he proposed to introduce a special academic prize for study of the poem and of Chester's collection — though he himself did not have the chance to read it (all the copies were still in England).

Soon after that, in 1878, the Chester book was at last reissued in a small quantity and annotated by a well-known editor of the time, Alexander B. Grosart. The scholar has great merits in the study and publishing of rare books, though nowadays some errors and unsubstantiated assertions can be found in his work. For instance, the double pagination he invented for the Chester book: the original book has no pagination at the introduction, and there are some mistakes in the pagination of the main text. In "correcting" it, Grosart printed at the top of each page (excluding the introduction) an ordinal number, and at the bottom the number of the page from the

---

21. It is known that Malone owned one of the very rare copies of the *Passionate Pilgrim*, dated 1612.

22. Halliwell, J.O. *Some Account of Robert Chester's Loves Martyr or Rosalin's Complaint, a very rare volume published in the the year of 1601, including a remarkable poem by Shakespeare.* L., 1865

very beginning. Thus he offers the reader two paginations, neither of which coincides with the original; this causes confusion and hampers investigation.

Also troublesome is a decorative emblem (a tragic mask — which is rather significant in itself) that Grosart placed at the second title page, without any explanation, instead of the usual emblem used by the printer Field on all three original copies of the book. The Grosart reissue is still the only one, though it is high time we had a new edition reflecting the results of more than a century of academic work and all the hypotheses that have been put forward in the meantime.

Grosart prefaced his reprint with a special verse addressed to the president and members of the New Shakspere Society, offering for their enlightened attention the pages of an enigmatic book that had been extracted by him from "hidden nooks." Grosart identified the personality of Robert Chester (1566-1640), a gentleman from Royston in Hertfortshire County, who was knighted by James I in 1603. Grosart also found traces of Sir John Salusbury, owner of the Lleweny estate in Denbighshire county and head of a large family, who was not too successful in his career. Grosart did not establish the exact date of Salusbury's death, nor did he find his will, but he noticed the name in a small poetic collection by one Robert Parry (1597), without the designation Sir. He was either one of the authors or a patron of the book. The volume has the strange title "Sinetes." There is only one copy left and it is now waiting to be investigated in the context of the most urgent literary problems of the epoch.

In analyzing the Robert Chester book, Grosart did not find in the texts any connection with John Salusbury, to whose name the authors of the collection appeal for protection from the curiosity and suspicion of the ignorant mob. Grosart definitely established that Chester's poem in no way is a translation, and that the "Italian poet Torquato Caeliano" is a pure fiction. Grosart accepted the date of "1601" on the title page without question, although he could not have failed to notice some grounds for doubt; instead, he took it as a convenient confirmation of his conjectures, and he relied on it in forming a hypothesis that he himself called "a golden clue" to probing the meaning of the book and the purport of its poetic contents. Grosart decided that behind the allegoric names of the Phoenix and the Turtle were hidden Queen Elizabeth I herself, and her favorite, the Earl of Essex. Such a hypothesis is based on the assumption that poets and court flatterers often called their queen a phoenix; this practice was usual not only during her lifetime. In the last scene of Shakespeare's "Henry VIII," written a decade after the queen's death, Cranmer — while forecasting the future splendor of the newborn Elizabeth — speaks of her as a wonderful Phoenix:

> … … … … … … … … … … … *but as when*
> *The bird of wonder dies, the maiden Phoenix*
> *Her ashes new create another heir,*
> *As great in admiration as herself,*
> *So shall she leave her blessedness to one,—*
> *When heaven shall call her from this cloud of darkness —*

*Who from the sacred ashes of her honour*
*Shall star-like rise, as great in fame as she was…*

In Grosart's opinion the unmatched veneration of the Chester heroine, the epithets "royal," "heavenly," "majestie," showed not only high but exceptional, i.e. royal position. Given the jealous nature of the queen, nobody would dare during her lifetime to make public compliments of such a nature to any other lady in England (note that "during her lifetime").

Having thus identified the Phoenix with Queen Elizabeth, the scholar started to look for a suitable personality for the Turtle. And who could he be, but the magnificent and ill-fated Robert Devereux, the 2$^{nd}$ Earl of Essex (1566-1601), considered by many historians not only a favorite but also a paramour of the elderly monarch? The merciless execution of the Earl of Essex after his clumsy, nearly farcical mutiny in the very year of 1601, was the most tragic event of the year. During his lifetime many poets sang Essex, and William Shakespeare also expressed his sympathy for him in the "Henry V."

This seemed the only possible solution to the enigma and Grosart did not hesitate to use this "golden clue" to explain all the texts from *Love's Martyr*. Sometimes he stretched it much too far. The hypothesis relies on certain unfounded assumptions and in many ways contradicts the contents of the collection. In fact, Chester's Phoenix is presented before the Turtle as an obedient pupil to whom he passes his knowledge of the world and of people. Nobody would depict the relations of the very mature Queen with her young subject in such a way, even under the most allegorical of names. Dame Nature also sometimes treats the Phoenix without due respect, and that would have been impermissible for any author if the Queen was intended. For instance, "Fie peevish Bird, what art thou frantic mad, wilt thou confound thy selfe with foolish griefe?" At other times, the poets speak of the Phoenix's fresh blossoming beauty — in respect to the aging Queen (even if she tried to seem young and was prone to flattery), that could have been taken as mockery. The militant, courageous, sometimes even tempestuous Essex could hardly be taken for the sickly hero who could walk only with difficulty. Essex was beheaded by order of the Queen (or at least with her consent); that, too, conflicts rather strongly with the touching idyllic relations of the Turtle and the Phoenix. And lastly, the Turtle dies before the eyes of the Phoenix, after which she follows him, and Shakespeare describes the funerals of them both. Queen Elizabeth died in fact only in 1603! It is quite inconceivable that the poets could describe her death and funeral two years beforehand, mourning her as dead while she was their live and ruling Queen. This point is the most vulnerable to criticism, though some Grosart adherents attempted to explain it by suggesting that Shakespeare and other poets sensed the Queen's approaching demise and even two years before could present it as a *fait accomplis*!

As to the Creation (Creature) that arose from the ashes of the Turtle and the Phoenix, the Grosart allies had to assume that the elderly monarch and the young count might have had some secret posterity and that Chester and his fellows (having somehow found out about it) and thus symbolized the pure love of these exalted lovers as tragically terminated. One may note that there is no credible evidence that Elizabeth ever had any descendants or, more generally, about the nature of her relations with those courtiers whom some contemporaries and, later on, fiction writers believed to be her favorites and paramours. How far she went in her relations with her favorites is a mystery that she took to her grave.

And Essex in this relation is even more improbable than others; Leicester for instance. For Elizabeth was not only 34 years his senior but was also his grandmother's (Catherine Carey's) cousin. H. Dickson, a biographer of Francis Bacon, says that even the inference that the 65-year-old Elizabeth could be a paramour of her cousin's grandson is a monstrous thing that could only be conceived in the feverish mind of a monk. As can be seen from the correspondence, the Queen had always thought of Essex as a wild youngster capable of heroic foolishness. But she also saw in him the progeny of the Boleyns, whose blood was also in her veins. For that, she forgave him his pranks, for a time, until he encroached on sacred ground: her throne and crown. In Elizabeth's letters to him, there is not a line that she could not have written to her own grandson (if only she'd had one).

As to their "pure love" and its fruit, well, the image of the head of Essex, bloodied and deformed by the executioner's axe, would have been a more suitable symbol for their love than Marston's Perfection. Practically all the authors of the Chester book and the publisher himself were known to have sympathy for Essex, and they never expressed their sorrow when the Queen died in 1603. They could not forgive her the execution of their idol. One can hardly imagine them describing her with such vivid colors right after his death. What was the sense of publishing, at the time, a book that has all the hallmarks of the strictest conspiracy? Weren't other outstanding personalities of the epoch also called Phoenix — most often, the great poet Philip Sidney?

In general, Grosart's hypothesis spurred considerable inquiry, critical and even satirical reaction on the part of many scholars. But it also launched an academic discussion and attempts to probe the meaning of the strange phenomenon that was in some curious way linked to the Great Bard. All credit is due to Alexander Grosart in this respect.

Carlton Brown went further in researching John Salusbury (1566-1612), his life and his milieu, and in 1913 Brown published a work[23] that played an important role in furthering studies of the Chester book. Brown studied manuscripts in English and Welsh in the Oxford library — manuscripts that contained poems signed by Salusbury and Chester, and other documents related to them — copies of letters, household notes and even medical prescriptions. Brown established many telling facts about the proprietor of Lleweny estate.

---

23. *Poems by Sir John Salisbury and Robert Chester.* Ed. by C. Brown. L., 1913.1914

John Salusbury studied at Oxford but it is not known whether he completed his course. In 1586, his elder brother was executed for taking part in the conspiracy to liberate Mary Stuart; three months after that, John Salusbury married Ursula Stanley, the illegitimate daughter born to the Earl of Derby and the foster sister of William Stanley, the sixth Earl of Derby (one of the "Shakespeare pretenders"). By 1600, the parish registers featured ten children with the Salusbury couple. Under the patronage of his father-in-law, he received a position at the court and tried to find a way to some lucrative position in his own county, but strained relations with the neighbors disrupted his plans and projects. As far as one can judge, Salusbury was a loyal subject to the Queen and did not side with Essex (Brown even thinks him an opponent, for after the failure of Essex's mutiny he called the Earl a traitor); in June of the same year, 1601, he was made a knight. After James Stuart's ascension to the throne, Salusbury left London for Denbighshire and took part in the local ceremony swearing allegiance to the new ruler. He expected to be invited to resume his former service with the court, but that never happened, and he remained forever at his estate. Some documents show that during the last years of his life he suffered financial difficulties. Salusbury died in 1612, leaving behind his wife, four surviving lawful descendants and a son born out of wedlock.

Brown noticed some strange circumstances in connection with Salusbury's demise. The exact date of his death is registered with the notary Roberts as July 24, 1612; the notary also noted that *the body was interred the same night*. However, in the parish register there is no mention of any nighttime funeral (as is usually done in such cases), but there is a normal entry about the funeral on July 25. Why? And why so much haste to inter the body of the proprietor of the Lleweny estate?

Brown examined some manuscripts, a kind of family album, and found some comments in verse addressed to Salusbury and his family, signed by his neighbors and friends. There are acrostics signed by Salusbury and Chester; their first letters form the name of Blanche Winn, a relative of the proprietor, but there are many more verses where the name of Salusbury is linked with another lady, Dorothy Halsall, who was his wife's sister. Clearly, Dorothy was the object of blatant propositions on the part of Salusbury. Some of the documents are dated and are attributed to the period from 1586 to 1608. Among the verses of this "personal" character he found a poem by Ben Jonson (written in his own hand), and a poem by Daniel. Among the documents were copies of Essex's letter to Lord Thomas Egerton, and letters to the poet Philip Sidney from his father and sister. Essex's letter to Egerton (1598) was made public and was disseminated in copies. It dealt with his argument with the Queen, when she publicly slapped him in the face for being mulish. The letter was full of noble wrath and hurt feelings, as one may judge by the following sentences: "I owe to Her Majesty the duty of an Earl and Lord Marshal of England. I have been content to do her Majesty the service of a clerk, but can never serve her as a villein or slave." Explanations may be found for the letter being in Salusbury's archive (it was copied by Essex' friends and foes alike); but it is much harder to see how the personal letters to Philip Sidney from his father and sister (Countess of Pembroke, poet and translator) found their way there. Brown did not even try; he just noted that Mary's husband, the Earl of Pembroke, tried to help Salusbury when he was seeking a position in Denbighshire.

Following Grosart, Brown studied Robert Parry's volume of poems, "Sinetes," (Brown calls it enigmatic, but does not voice the natural assumption that the word could be formed from the English word "sins") with a dedication to John Salusbury. In the acrostics of the first section, the author's name is linked to two female names — a Frances Willoughby and an Elizabeth Wolfreston. In the second part of the book these three names are met in an acrostic alongside the names of John Salusbury and Dorothy Halsall, and after that the latter couple is met several times in other verses. Brown wrote that more remarkable and puzzling verses could be found only in the minds of the most fanatic Baconians (he meant those seekers of a secret code allegedly used by Francis Bacon.). Brown decided that most of verses that Robert Parry attributed to a certain Patron were actually written by John Salusbury. He disregarded thirty magnificent sonnets that closely resemble the "Dove's Cantoes" and, consequently, Shakespeare's sonnets, for he was too much preoccupied with the idea that the Turtle in the Chester book was none other than the proprietor of the Lleweny estate in Denbighshire.

The role of the fair Phoenix, however, Brown assigned not to Dorothy Halsall (as one could have expected) but to the lawful consort of John Salusbury, Ursula, who bore him ten children and after his death lived to a rather old age. On the basis of the opening episodes of Chester's poem, Brown decided that it was dedicated to their marriage in 1586; he had to close his eyes to the title of the book, which was not at all appropriate for such an occasion ("Love's Martyr") and to the poem's tragic ending. As to the new Phoenix — a Creature arising from the ashes — Brown calculated that in 1601 the elder daughter Jane turned 14; here is your new Phoenix, here is the Perfection that could not be described in words! There is no place in his hypothesis for the other nine children of John and Ursula, or at least for the four surviving ones.

Brown did not agree with Grosart's identification of Robert Chester as a gentleman from Royston and proposed another person, a proposition that, in our opinion, is even less convincing. But the major flaw in Brown's hypothesis lies elsewhere. In order to substantiate his identification of the Turtle and the Phoenix with the Salusbury couple and their many children, he had to interpret Chester's poem very loosely. As to the "additional" verses by Shakespeare, Marston, Chapman, Jonson and several anonymous contributors, they cannot be accounted for, no matter how much the symbolism is stretched, and Brown had to admit that it is impossible to find any correspondence (in his opinion, of course) between Shakespeare's poem and Chester's allegory. The only explanation that he could submit was this: "Obviously, Shakespeare was not a good acquaintance of Salusbury."

How can one correlate a wedding poem with a story of death and funerals? A Requiem with a gift on the occasion of a wedding or a daughter's coming of age? The numerous progeny of the Salusbury couple also fails to concord with the poets' repeated testimony to the purely spiritual nature of the union of the Turtle with the Phoenix, and their lack of descendants. One cannot but notice the efforts Brown exerted with Chester's texts in order to link the deep mourning feelings to the marriage and further routine events in the life of a provincial gentleman with a large family. Now, in the London example dated 1611, the former title page and the pages with the address to John Salusbury, and the name of Chester himself, are missing. Such unscrupulous treatment of Salusbury, who was still alive in 1611, indicates that he was hardly a central figure in this project.

Carlton Brown's research into the manuscripts from Lleweny is of great value, for it allows the figure of John Salusbury, his milieu, their interests and concerns to be correctly presented. One cannot possibly ignore the fact that aside from several poets and publishers, Salusbury is the only contemporary who was called by name in the book, albeit ambiguously. The creators of the book needed him, for some reason or other; some of them, including Chester, knew Salusbury and his environment well enough, and they knew of the poetic exercises of his friends and admirers. That is about all that one can definitely say — even after Brown's investigation — about Salusbury in connection with the publication of the still mysterious *Love's Martyr*. Brown's conjectures about the book's meaning and his hasty identification of the enigmatic Turtle and the Phoenix with the Salusbury couple contradict historical and literary facts (including those discovered by Brown himself) and are totally unconvincing.

However, in the minds of some modern historians of English literature, Brown's publication of the Oxford manuscripts, which contain many heretofore-unknown texts and names, lends a certain credibility to his theory despite its obvious incoherence. It is still mentioned, with some straining, in many theses, notes and articles.


### "ENJOY THE MUSIC OF THE VERSES . . . "


Since Brown's ruminations were never convincingly confirmed, the search for the Turtle and the Phoenix went on, and not only around John Salusbury. In 1937, an entirely new idea was suggested by B. Newdigate, who found, in a manuscript preserved at the Bodleian Library in Oxford, a copy of Ben Jonson's "Ode Enthusiastic," inscribed "To L.C:of: B," i.e., "To Lucy, Countess of Bedford."

The Countess of Bedford, née Harington (1581-1627), a sister of the poet John Harington, is known to historians and literature scholars as a very well-educated lady who was close to King James' court. She was a friend and patron of many renowned poets such as Jonson, Donne, Chapman, Drayton, and Daniel. "The Bright Lucy," as she was called by the poets, was a frequent participant in theatrical entertainments at the Court. On the basis of these hand-written initials on Jonson's verse, "Phoenix

Analyzed" (wherein the poet says directly that the Phoenix is a real woman), Newdigate identifies Chester's heroine with the Countess of Bedford, and her husband Edward with the Turtle.

However, relations between the couple (who were married in December of 1594) were not chaste at all; they had children, and were both alive after 1601 and 1611 — the dates on the title pages of *Love's Martyr* — and so cannot possibly be equated with the Chester story about the Turtle and the Phoenix. Newdigate did not really try to do that, hoping that future research in this direction would make the picture clear. Newdigate's hypothesis remains unproven, but the inscription he found is very important: it testifies that the "Bright Lucy" had something to do with the issuing of Chester's volume (and with its heroes). At the very least, the Countess of Bedford and Ben Jonson, who sent her (or who wrote in her album) his "Ode," knew who was the woman in question and were well acquainted with her. Still, who was she?

Attempts have been made to find a solution by combining various details from these hypotheses. Thus, T. Harrison, while in agreement with Grosart in identifying the Phoenix with Queen Elizabeth, followed Brown in the case of the Turtle and considered the allegorical image to be that of John Salusbury. Historical sources, letters, and diaries of their contemporaries show no evidence of any relationship between Salusbury and the Queen. He outlived her by nearly ten years, while Chester's Turtle dies before the Phoenix's eyes. Poor Virgin Queen, historians have tried to find her one lover or another at every opportunity. . . This kind of interpretation is easy to poke holes in — their artificiality and internal conflicts are not denied by the authors themselves.

Twenty five years later, a detailed and objective review of works on the Shakespeare poem and Chester's book appeared: *A new Variorum Edition of Shakespeare*, issued and annotated by H.E. Rollins in 1938.[24] R.A. Underwood analyzed the last few decades of research in a 1974 academic series devoted to the Elizabethan-Jacobean period of English literature and issued by Salzburg University, Austria.[25]

A thorough investigation of the Shakespeare poem, Chester's collection and all previous attempts to explain them was produced by the American scholar W. Matchett (1965).[26] He treats with great skepticism Brown's idea of assigning the Salusbury family these roles in the high tragedy. Matchett conceded that Grosart's idea is not satisfactory on a number of critically important points, but still he tried to accommodate the surmise that the book is dedicated to the memory of the executed Essex — perhaps they had begun creating the book during his lifetime, and only later on, for conspiracy's sake, inserted Salusbury's name instead of his. The scholar posits that initially the publisher, E. Blount, who was known for his sympathy to Essex (in

---

24. *A New Variorum Edition of Shakespeare.* Ed. by H.E. Rollins. Philadelphia, 1938. Vol.1. The poems, p. 583.

25. *The Phoenix and the Turtle. A Survey of Scholarship* by R.A. Underwood. Salzburg, 1974

26. Matchett, W. *The Phoenix and the Turtle. Shakespeare's Poem and Chester's Love's Martyr.* L. Mouton, 1965.

fact, Matchett thinks he played the leading role in producing the book), and his friends were seeking by this means to reconcile the stubborn Earl with the Queen. But after his execution they decided to go on with the enterprise and removed or masked some of the most apparent allusions. Only in such a convoluted way does Matchett find it possible to explain the mind-boggling camouflage used by the authors and publishers and their contemporaries' total lack of response when the book came out. He did not quite manage to give a satisfactory explanation for the fact that the poets mourned the Queen's death while she was alive, and many other details. But given Matchett's research, no Shakespeare scholar should have any doubt that Chester's book is steeped with some important secret.

As the fruitless quest for prototypes whose biographies more or less coincided with Chester's and his fellows' went on, some literary scholars were induced to consider Shakespeare's poem (and the whole book along with it) as an elaborate poetic exercise with philosophic abstractions, where the Turtle, for instance, is an incarnation of Fidelity, the Phoenix — Love, and the Creature appearing after them — a metaphysical harmony of a Platonic love. Those authors dwell on Renaissance neo-Platonism, but that can hardly explain why the greatest English writers decided one fine day to glorify an ideal metaphysical Love, with the help of prominent London publishers, without registering it. These verses dedicated to an innocent topic were put together in a strange collection, with false dedications, dubious title pages and many hints as to some highly significant but allegorically masked persons and events that are unknown to us. The poets, as can be seen from their works, were well aware of the "abstractions" and knew whose funeral they were describing, whose death they so deeply mourned. One should say that not all Shakespeare scholars share such "metaphysical" persuasions, but hardly anyone has studied the real circumstances under which Chester's book was published.

Such far fetched interpretations and unconvincing use of "pure Neo-Platonic" approaches makes their authors to concede that there were some real personalities whose unusual relations and nearly simultaneous death served as an occasion for the joint address of the poets to glorification and mourning of an ideal love and fidelity. These works give scattered details of the major ideas by Grosart, Brown, Newdigate in various combinations which are concluded by an appeal not to search for slipping away, urgent for the times past sense of the Shakespeare's poem, but seek to assess its poetic merits and specially analyze the so-called "motives of the Renaissance Neo-Platonism."[27]

A renowned Shakespeare scholar of the early 20th century, Sir Edmund Chambers, did not make a special study of the Chester book but adhering to Brown's conjecture spoke of it as "an awkward collection of poetical verses honouring the love of Sir John Salusbury and his wife, Ursula, represented by the Phoenix (Love) and the

---

27. Strictly speaking, nobody has ever been able to come up with anything resembling a complete and clear "neoplatonic" or any other metaphysical interpretation of Chester's book.

Turtle (Constancy) and the fruit of their union, their daughter, Jane. Shakespeare, Jonson, Chapman, and Marston develop the theme of the Phoenix in their verses. Shakespeare's poem does not show evidence of any deep study of Chester's poem by the Bard, as it mourned the childless death of the Turtle and the Phoenix."[28] This was written in 1930 and since then several generations of scholars have formed their ideas about Chester's book under the influence of this short and not very original note by the patriarch of British Shakespeare studies.

It is no wonder that four decades later the readers of *The Oxford Anthology of the Literature of Renaissance England* (1973) were treated to information about the Chester book like this:

> To this muddled poem of Robert Chester's, Ben Jonson, Shakespeare, and others, for unknown reasons, consented to add their shorter pieces. Chester was celebrating his patron Sir John Salisbury (sic! — I.G.) as the Turtle-dove (Constancy) and his wife as the Phoenix (Love), and the daughter of that union. The other contributors, including Shakespeare, treat his new-made myth with great freedom. Shakespeare appears to have found in it an occasion to combine the image of the phoenix with a bird-funeral of the kind known in folklore; one analogue to his poem is 'Cock Robin.' But in doing so he also wrote his most obscure and metaphysical poem. Shakespeare's birds left no posterity, the Phoenix also did not rise at the time from the ashes. There may have been some actual events that could have explained it — Essex' execution, that accelerated the Phoenix's death — Queen Elizabeth, but there is no satisfactory testimony to it. The best course is to read the poem for its own sake — in rhythm, movement of thought, and lexical inventiveness a great work, and itself a Phoenix.[29]

The American professor D. M. Zesmer, in his *Guide to Shakespeare* (1976),[30] advises that the Phoenix in Shakespeare's poem is a symbol of beauty, the Turtle — honesty and constancy in love. Making a cursory mention of attempts to identify the heroes of the poem and of the whole book, he does not exclude the possibility that the poets wrote their verses with Queen Elizabeth and the Earl of Essex in mind, or under the impression of such events as John Salusbury's marriage or the death of the Countess of Bedford's first son. Zesmer notes that "more and more scholars are inclined to concentrate their attention on the philosophical aspect of the poem and on the themes of Renaissance Neo-Platonism," on the possibility that it is poetry as such that is the subject here. Moreover, the scholar supposes that Shakespeare, in this case, like John Donne in the "Canonization" (which we shall come to later on), is not as serious as many academics would like to believe. "The poem remains an artful pattern of a delightful lyric."

28. Chambers, E.K. *William Shakespeare. A Study of Facts and Problems.* Oxford, Clarendon press, 1930

29. *Oxford Anthology: The Literature of Renaissance England.* Ed. by J.Hollander, F. Kermode. Oxford University Press, 1973, p. 424.

30. Zesmer, D. M. *Guide to Shakespeare.* N.Y. 1976, p.88

And here is a more recent commentary by the eminent English Shakespeare scholar Stanley Wells, in the *Oxford Edition of Shakespeare Works* (1994): "Chester's poem appears to have been composed as a compliment to Sir John and Lady Salusbury, his patron. We know of no link between Shakespeare and the Salusbury family; possibly his poem was not written specifically for the volume in which it appeared . . . An incantatory elegy, it may well have irrecoverable allegorical significance." [31]

Such pronouncements by English and American university professors show almost overt attempts to shirk the alarming difficulties and enigmas of the Chester book and to ascribe them to nebulous Neo-platonism and the idealism of the Renaissance. They call on scholars and readers to enjoy the musicality of Shakespeare's (and not only his) poems without troubling their minds over what was their real meaning at the time, and to ignore the problem of identifying the heroes and events. Such an approach has become more than common — for some contemporary compilers and editors of reference books, anthologies, academic journals and reviews on Shakespeare it appears to be the only one possible.

In 1992, while I was in the United States, I saw that Western Shakespeare scholars have made very little progress in recent decades in studying Chester's book. After Matchett, there have been no substantive works on the collection, it has not been re-published, and it is unheard of to attempt any critical reassessment of the old hypotheses that fly in the face of the facts. Shakespeare's Requiem is still being treated — I even heard there was something like a "consensus" on the matter — as something that got into the "marriage" collection by mistake (even some specialists on Shakespeare's poetry do not know that Chester's poem also ends with death of the Turtle and the Phoenix and not in a wedding ceremony).

Still, as a result of more than a century of research and debate, we now know much more about the Chester book, the epoch and the people, and about many aspects of the culture of the time, than did those who first extracted the strange book from "dusty oblivion." The ideas that have come up in the course of this effort are only steps along the difficult path that brings science to the perception of complex truth: as such, they deserve objective consideration. But even objective reasoning requires that we acknowledge that all these hypotheses — both of historical and metaphysical nature — in their main features contradict the contents of the book so completely that they can in no way serve as clues to its true meaning. They only point in certain directions, which have proved to be futile. The main question still remains to be answered satisfactorily: whose death were Shakespeare and his fellows mourning?

This gives rise to some pessimism about the chance of finding a solution of this so much puzzling problem. In 1904, A. Fairchild compared the position of those who had tried to probe the meaning of the poetic works of the collection and the real situations that served as a pretext for their creation, with great sufferings of pilgrims who were

---

31. *William Shakespeare. The Complete Works.* General Editors Stanley Wells and Gary Taylor. Clarendon Press, 1994, pp.777-778.

tried in the desert by false visions and hopes. In 1938, the outstanding American editor and critic H.E. Rollins, commenting in *The New Variorum*, stated that the solution to the riddle of the poem and the entire Chester volume had not been found, and he voiced serious doubts that an answer would ever be found that could satisfy every scholar.

## TAKE ANOTHER LOOK AT THOSE DATES!

So, after some hundred years of research and debate, the Shakespearean establishment came to an impasse that could not be glossed over by any polite agreement about an "interim consensus." The situation is not, however, hopeless.

The book contains so much convincing evidence of the fact that England's most outstanding poets were expressing themselves in response to the death of two people who were known to them and who were bound together in such extraordinary ways that a modern researcher cannot and should not accept a conclusion that it is impossible to establish their identities, no matter how difficult the task would appear to be. Acknowledging that all the theories hazarded thus far are unsatisfactory should not provoke pessimism (within the scope of the problem); instead, we may take it only as a sign that so far we have been searching in the wrong places, wherever anyone has succeeded in finding some interesting detail which, however, has turned out to be secondary to the main question. Scholars can take this as a motivation to start the search afresh, and to approach their predecessors' findings with a new and critical eye.

As a matter of fact, the major starting point for every theory promoted heretofore was the dating of the book to the year 1601. That led its first researcher to think of the most tragic event of the year — the mutiny of the Queen's favorite, Essex, and his execution — the more so since the name "Phoenix" (with some strained interpretations) could be attributed to the Queen herself. This date seemingly did not prevent anyone from linking the contents of the book with the aforementioned (in the preface) John Salusbury, with the family affairs and amorous inclinations of this gentleman who had so many children. The search for another prominent couple whose relations resembled those of the Turtle and the Phoenix and whose death occurred in this year (or even close to it) was fruitless. The year of sixteen hundred and one has led to a dead end.

But on what premises, after all, do we accept that dating? In all my research I have found that the traditional dating accepted in Shakespeare studies is based *only* on the title page of one of the three extant copies and on the half-title which is the same in all of them (it is printed there in Roman numerals: MDCI). *There is no other confirmation of this dating!* The Huntington copy has no date on the title page; the London copy has quite a different title page with another title and another date — 1611. In the past four centuries no one has found anything to corroborate the date printed on the title page;

rather, in the course of that research, a number of facts were revealed that raise doubts as to its authenticity and even refute it altogether.

Let us return to fact that the book was not entered into the Stationers' Company[32] Register. According to established procedure, the members of the Company had the right to publish only those books that had been approved by persons who were appointed by the Queen: several members of the Privy Council, top church dignitaries and the chancellors of both universities. These high officials often delegated to their subordinates the right to look through manuscripts and give permission for publication. The permission was noted on the manuscript (in some cases, it was printed on the title page), after which the printer entered it into the register and, having paid only sixpence, could begin printing. Sometimes books that were already printed were registered, but there are also some that are not mentioned in the Stationers' Register.

The registration fee was small; it would not prompt anyone to violate the rule (for which the guilty were punished). Printers and publishers avoided registration only if for some reason they wanted to conceal the fact of publication of a certain book or the date of its issue. In such cases the printer either did not show the date on the title page or printed a false date (thus causing headaches for latter-day scholars). There may have been other reasons for evading registration, but they would have to have been pretty sound, for an entry in the Stationers' Register established a publisher's exclusive rights and protected his financial interests. In our case, the printers and publishers are of great importance: Blount, Field and Lownes were distinguished members of the Guild, and many times were elected its managers (Masters and Wardens); they would not risk their reputations on a mere whim.

The title pages of our collection bear the real names of respected publishers and printers and their emblems; the texts contain the names of famous poets. This speaks for the fact that the book was intentionally not registered. The registration fixed the date of issue— and the date could be a clue to the book's meaning. The reason was to conceal the actual date of issue, which was soon after a significant event — the death of an eminent married (but platonic!) couple. As to obtaining permission — that would not have been hard; the influential friends of the deceased could have secured that — the more so as the book did not tread on any political or religious sensibilities.

Obviously, the lack of registration (both in 1601 and 1611) in itself is not a definite proof that the date on the title page is false, but it certainly does not confirm it as true. There is no confirmation at all! So far as renowned poets, publishers and printers took part in creation of the book, the lack of registration gives good reason (and even obliges scholars) to question the traditional but unsubstantiated dating. One may only wonder why this question has not been raised earlier.[33]

There are other significant reasons to doubt the premise that the book really appeared in 1601. It is known that during this very period the so-called war of theaters

---

32. In Russian publications, it is often called the Guild.

A Renaissance print shop

was in full swing, when Ben Jonson was fighting John Marston and Thomas Dekker. Later, Jonson told the poet Drummond[34] that the quarrel went as far as fist fighting: he had disarmed Marston of his pistol and given him a severe beating. Many researches of Chester's collection (including Matchett) are at a loss: how could one reconcile this longstanding animosity, taking into consideration Ben Jonson's wild nature, which sometimes went as far as mutual vituperative public clashes, insults and even street brawls, with the fact of both poets collaborating on a book in 1601? Jonson's and Marston's contribution to the collection is the greatest; each had four verses in it. Matchett was even obliged to assume that those mutual fierce attacks (including the well-known plays published in 1601, "What You Will" by Marston and "Poetaster" by Jonson) were launched in order to mask their participation in the secret collection (which was connected, in his opinion, with Essex's fate). Clearly, any suggestion that these rival poets could have been collaborating in 1601 is farfetched. It is much more logical to think that the collaboration (and, consequently, the publication of Chester's book) took place much later — in any case, not before the poets reconciled in 1602-1603.

In 1601, Marston was a young and impudent satirical poet (theatrical entrepreneur Philip Henslow called him "a new one") who did not publish anything under his own name,[35] and one could hardly attribute to him the name printed on the second title page among other participants as "the best and chiefest of our modern writers." Ben Jonson became well-known only several years after the notorious "war of theaters" was over; one may also note that Marston's verses in the Chester collection are different from his earlier works in their earnest and philosophical nature.

Even the first reviewer of the book, Grosart, was puzzled to note the subservient allusion to James Stuart contained in Chester's poem (in the Dialogue of Dame Nature with the Phoenix). But in 1601, Mary Stuart's son was only the ruler of Scotland; he was not King of England or even the formally proclaimed the successor to Elizabeth.

---

33. It is not so difficult to understand why scholars took such a negligent attitude. Registrations are not found for many English books issued in the 16th and 17th centuries (some estimates put the figure as high as 30 per cent), so that many scholars gave little thought to specific omissions — never mind trying to ascertain the circumstances and reasons for them. However, such an approach is flawed. Publishers with solid reputations, who were in the first ranks of the Guild, were mindful of their positions and did not violate the registration rule without any special necessity.

Having verified all of Blount's publications for the years of 1598-1623, I have calculated that during that period he issued (or participated in) 62 books, and failed to register only three of them (including one book that had been published in Scotland, and another that he was only selling). M. Lownes in 1600-1607 and 1611 published 44 books altogether, and only two of them were not registered (one with invectives against the Pope, and the other contained a dangerous letter to Walter Raleigh, who was at the time in prison). Thus, both Blount and Lownes registered nearly all their publications (including reissues, cession of rights etc.); Chester's book, which they both declined to register, is a unique case; thus the reason for its dating needs a special inquiry. I hope that English and American scholars by now would agree to that.

34. "Jonson's Conversations with Drummond," l. 150. In Jonson, B. *The Complete Poems*, p. 465.

35. His penname at the time, interestingly, was William Kinsider.

The Chester book does not seem to have anything to do with Scotland, so Grosart, not seeing any sign of a later insertion (the idea that the whole book may have been published later did not even cross his mind) was compelled to assume that Elizabeth's subjects several years before her death treated Scotland's monarch as their future king and were not averse to voicing such sentiments in public. Such an assumption contradicts historical facts. Until the last day of Elizabeth's life, nobody in England dared openly to call the Scottish King James successor to the English crown; only several high-ranking courtiers, foreseeing what was to come, could afford some allusions to the succession in their secret correspondence with Edinburgh. One would have paid dearly for printing such treasonous compliments. In a secret report on Christopher Marlowe, the author also indicates his connection with the Scottish court. Later on, scholars studying Chester's book did not even try to explain this strange "slip of the tongue" by Robert Chester; but it clearly shows that he wrote his poem (or at least a part of it) during James'[36] incumbency, that is, *not earlier than 1603*.

Grosart also mentions (without dwelling on it in particular) a small volume, of which a single copy existed, "Four Birds From Noah's Ark" by Thomas Dekker. The book contains prayers attributed by the author to the Turtle, Eagle, Pelican and Phoenix; each character is featured in a separate chapter with its own second title page. The author pays special attention in his addresses to the Turtle and the Phoenix. The birds and their prototypes here are clearly the same as with Chester, and the author's attitude toward them is of greatest veneration, but the overtones of mourning characteristic of the Chester book are entirely absent in Dekker's. Those prototypes were still alive in 1609, when the book about "the four birds" is dated. This is one more fact speaking for a later dating of Chester's book.

The title page of the Folger and Huntington copies has an inscription alleging that the book had been translated from the Italian and even giving the name of the imaginary author, Torquato Caeliano. This is *an outright mystification*, for literary scholars have not been able to turn up any trace of such an Italian poem or poet. All the works in the collection are of British origin (and thank God, all researchers agree on that). Such a mystification, however, is fully consistent with the warning the author placed on the same title page, just two lines above: that the truth about the Turtle and the Phoenix would be allegorically veiled. The appearance of a mythical Italian is one element of such veiling. Of the same nature are the allegoric names, and the deliberately long digressions intended to confound and deter uninitiated readers ("the mob"). Judging by all appearances, the editors did not want to advertise their fantastical child; this was destined only for "deep ears," i.e. for those who knew the secret of the Turtle and the Phoenix. Taking care to avoid giving "the mob" a clue to the allegory, the editors understood that the publication date could give away the

---

36. The reminiscence of King James serves as the image of stern Jupiter sitting on the throne in the "High Star Chamber," listening to Rosalyn's complaint and sending to the ill Turtle a miracle potion in order "to direct him to Phoenix's bed."

entire game, and as we have seen they took pains to conceal it. Fortunately for us, they could not hide the traces altogether (or, perhaps, did not want to).

## A Strange "Misprint" in the British Library's Copy

An important and convincing proof that the Chester book appeared not in 1601 but much later is found in the copy kept in the British Museum (now the British Library), which is dated 1611. It has usually been called a reissue or a second edition of the book. But a number of rather strange circumstances speak against such a simple approach.

The London copy, dated "1611" on the title page, was printed with the same set of type as the Folger and Huntington ones dated 1601. This is an uncontested fact, for all the text is identical, including misprints and certain peculiar features and defects of the set. However, the title page with the heading "Love's Martyr . . . " together with Chester's foreword (without page numbering) is absent and instead we see another title page with quite another, rather flowery, heading that does not match the contents of the book: "Anuals of Great Brittaine or a most excellent monument . . . " As mentioned above, "Anuals," the first word, printed in large letters, is nowadays quite often "corrected" to "Annals," without raising any questions. But in its actual form (not distorted some four centuries later) this word resembles a word new coined from the Latin "anus." Then the heading may acquire an indecent Rabelaisian overtone and take on the appearance of a hint at homosexuality. The final ambiguous part of the heading also contributes to such an interpretation.

The possibility that an unintended misprint appeared in the key word of the title page, and that neither the owner of the print shop nor anyone else noticed it, is approximately nil. One may wonder why not only the former title of the book disappeared from this page (does "Love's Martyr" lack market appeal?), but also any mention of its principal heroes, the Turtle and the Phoenix, and even the name of the author, Robert Chester. There is no longer any notice that the book contains pieces by some "modern writers," and out with the first pages went Chester's dedication to the name of John Salusbury. Instead of publisher Edward Blount the name of his colleague Mathew Lownes appears, with the emblem of the printer Edward Allde. The second title page, with the same date of "1601" and Field's emblem, remained intact, in the same place. So who, after all, printed the book — Field or Allde?

There are few books in this world that would puzzle researchers so much as the London copy of Chester's collection. And in the last four centuries few people chose to fret over such riddles: it was much easier to record the book as a "second edition" and leave it at that.

What happened to the London copy of Chester's volume, that it nearly lost its right to be called so? (While in the Folger copy Chester's name appears eight times, in the London one it is mentioned only three times, at the very end of the poem — once in full and twice as initials — where they were difficult to eliminate). How is it that copies of the same book, printed with one and the same set of type, on the same paper, were issued ten years apart? This should have been clarified by entries in the Stationers' Register, but we already know that Blount and Lownes both forswore to register the book, in 1601 and again in 1611.

Proponents of Grosart's hypothesis can only surmise, as did Matchett, that Blount printed too many copies and did not have time to sell them all at the time. For some reason (maybe he was afraid he would be harassed for producing a book touching upon the queen's relations with Essex), Blount hid the rest of the copies (or unstitched pages) and ten years later handed them over to Lownes. The latter, for reasons of his own (for instance, thinking the title of the book obsolete or not commercial enough), tore off the title page and several others — that bore no page numbers. Then he inserted a new specially printed page with a curious and bizarre "misprint" in the title and in such an "amended" form sent the book out for sale. During this operation the name of John Salusbury and also the name of the author, Robert Chester, were discarded, though both of them were still alive at the time. Why did Lownes eliminate the mention of works by other poets? During the ten years that had elapsed, those poets had indeed become "the best and chiefest" in England, and their names could only attract the attention of readers (if Lownes was indeed anxious for "commercial success").

The motives that guided Blount and then Lownes may appear illogical. If, in the period between 1601 and 1611, there really was any risk associated with the book, the simplest and most natural thing to do was to destroy the unsold copies or the pages left behind. However, they chose to hide the (allegedly extant) remains for ten long years, despite the many serious changes that took place in the country during the period. Even if we assume (with some difficulty) that some person of rank saw the book as an impertinent hint at Queen Elizabeth and the Earl of Essex (though it would not have been much easier at the time than it is today to find such hints), what could it matter after the queen's death, that is, after 1603? Even in 1601, neither Blount, Field, nor any of the authors was in trouble, as would have been expected in such a case; for example, in 1605, both Jonson and Chapman were sent to prison for certain politically ticklish sentences in the play "Eastward Ho!"

King James's gracious attitude to the Earl of Essex' surviving comrades in arms is well known; he was also quite unconcerned about the memory of the late Queen Elizabeth. In any case, after 1603 Blount (who was very active and influential at this very period) could easily have sold the remaining copies — if he had any. Still, he allegedly kept the book hidden for many years (or maybe he forgot about it altogether), and after that he purportedly handed over the "remainders" to another publisher, who destroyed the publication data, inserted the emblem of another printer, and put the book on sale again. And, as before, although the book contains nothing forbidden (does it?), and it contains works by renowned poets, Lownes failed to register it. Why? What stopped them now?

Proponents of Brown's hypothesis usually call the London copy "the second edition" of the collection. But explaining the ten-year difference by which its title page varies from the Folger's, they certainly cannot invoke the Essex affair and the risks associated with it for the publisher. Instead, they assume there were some kind of purely commercial considerations. First is the misguided idea that Blount was unable to sell all the copies printed at the time. It is known that he handed over his bookshop, "Bishop's Head," to Lownes in approximately 1609. This gives rise to the assumption that he also handed over the remaining copies of the unsold books, including *Love's Martyr* (allegedly kept in the shop for eight years). Then we hear the familiar assertion: the book was not in demand, so Lownes had to tear off the title pages two years later, and so on.

As we can see, the usual assertion that in 1611 the remaining copies were sold off, with a new title page, entails many essential inconsistencies. And, what is most fundamental: *there is no evidence* that Chester's book was ever available for sale at all, and especially that Blount had "extra copies" to pass on to Lownes many years later.

Still worse is the assumption that the old composition frames were kept intact for ten years. This assumption was finally discarded after it was established that the London copy was published on the same batch of paper as the Folger, and this batch of paper is unique. To the analytically acquired evidence that Chester's book was a mystification, several significant empirically proven facts have been added. Here is how it happened.

At first I had access to Chester's book only on microfilm and via Grosart's reissue, so I could not compare the paper on which the original copies were printed. In Western academic literature, there was no information about the paper and watermarks; as it turned out, in 400 years, nobody had taken the trouble to hold the pages up to the light and compare them. But the watermarks bear information that is essential in establishing the date of publication. That is why, after publication of the first article about the Chester collection, I started asking my friends and colleagues on their way to England and the US to lend a hand in the next stage of the investigation. In December of 1988, at last, Marina Litvinova, an eminent translator, a lecturer at Moscow's Foreign Languages Institute and a Shakespeare enthusiast who was in Washington, DC, managed to get a pass to the Folger Shakespeare Library and asked to have a look at the copy of *Love's Martyr*. She was the first person in four centuries to hold the darkened pages up to the light; and she clearly saw there the contours of old marks, among them a weird-looking unicorn with crooked hind legs. The library consultants rallied around, checking reference books on watermarks and confirming that, while one might occasionally come across a mythological unicorn on ancient paper, this was the first time that this kind of unicorn was discovered;[37] the

---

37. In the very heart of Washington!

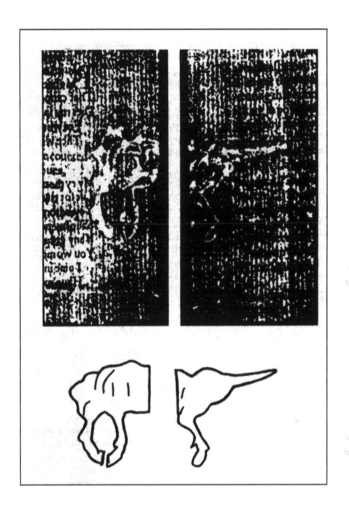

The unique watermark we discovered in the Chester book
— the unicorn with crooked hind legs. Bottom — my tracing of
the outline of the watermark.

watermark is unique! To the list of the Chester book's strange features was added one more, and quite an essential one, at that.

Now it was necessary to verify the watermarks on the London copy. Having received from the Folger Library facsimile images of the watermarks, I sent them to the British Library (which by then was separate from the British Museum) and asked them to compare them with the marks in the London copy. The reply was slow in coming, and I plagued everyone I knew (and some whom I did not know) who might be going to London . . . At last, in July of 1989, historian Igor Kravchenko got hold of the coveted book, held the pages up to the light and made sketches of the watermarks. In Moscow, we compared the sketches with the Folger prints and found that they are identical. Soon after that, an expert opinion from the British Library also arrived. Altogether there are six types of watermarks (including the unusual unicorn) in the book, in each copy; pages with such marks make up about two thirds of the volume. The rest of the text is printed on paper without definite watermarks, but with the paper factory's water net. Everything coincided. Thus it was discovered that the Folger copy with the "1601" date and the London copy with the "1611" date were printed with the same type and with identical watermarks (including some that are unique!). Later on, in Washington, with Laetitia Yeandle, Curator of Early Books and Manuscripts in the Folger Library, I asked the Huntington Library in California and the National Library of Wales to check their copies. We received confirmation that the watermarks are all identical. The circle was complete.

As to the curious title page of the London copy, I got a chance to study it in the British Library myself in 1995. Like the other copies, one third of its pages have no particular watermarks but only the paper factory's water net. I measured the distance between the lines forming the water net on the title page and found that they accurately match the parameters of the water net on several other pages at the end of the book.

## THE MOST FAMOUS PUBLISHER

Now it is time to focus on the publisher of the Chester collection, who took such pains to keep the uninitiated reader from divining what, or whom, the book is about. The name of this publisher is forever enshrined in the history of world culture, for Edward Blount is the very person who, on November 8, 1623, presented the Master and Wardens of the Stationers' Register with *Master William Shakespeare's Comedies, Histories and Tragedies* — the Great First Folio, for the first time featuring 20 of 37 plays that now comprise the canon of Shakespeare the playwright. This came about seven years after Shakespeare's death; without it, posterity likely would never have known "The Tempest," "Macbeth," "Julius Caesar," "Twelfth Night," "Cymbeline," "Coriolanus," "The Winter's Tale" and other plays. Earlier, in 1608, Blount had registered the Shakespeare plays "Pericles" (published by his friend Gosson) and "Antony and Cleopatra" (published only in the First Folio), and his fellow and confidant Thomas Thorpe registered and published Shakespeare's sonnets in 1609 — he had obtained them from a "Mr. W. H.," who remains enigmatic to this day.

Blount is known not only as a publisher, but also as a translator from Spanish and Italian; he probably was the author of several books issued by him. Besides the priceless First Folio, several other Blount editions played an important role in the history of English literature. In 1596 he registered and in 1598 issued an English–Italian dictionary, "The World of Words," by John Florio. Also in 1598, he released a posthumous edition of Christopher Marlowe's "Hero and Leander"; in the dedication to Sir Thomas Walsingham, Blount speaks of himself as an intimate friend of the killed poet. In 1600, Thomas Thorpe published Lucan's poem, translated by Marlowe, with a warm dedication to his (Thorpe's) "true and honest friend Edward Blount." The same year Blount put out a strange book by an unknown author, "Hospital for Incurable Fools." (Some people believe that he himself was its author). Later on, he issued the first translations of Montaigne's "Essais" and "Don Quixote" by Cervantes, and a collection of plays by Lyly with Blount's own preface, where he gives high praise not only to Lyly's plays but also his novel "Euphues." He also registered Jonson's "Sejanus" for the first time, and there ceded his rights for that book to Thomas Thorpe — one of many verifiable facts showing that he knew the laws of the publishing business very well. Blount always registered his editions and observed the standing rules. Only a very serious motive could have induced him to skip registration.

Blount registered in 1610 and released in 1611 a most peculiar book by the traveler Thomas Coryate, who is known to Shakespeare's biographers for his connection with the London tavern "The Mermaid," which was frequented not only by poets and playwrights including Ben Jonson and Francis Beaumont but, it has been presumed, by the very Great Bard. The huge book, queerly entitled *Coryate's Crudities*, contains the story of the author's travels across Europe, but its first hundred pages are filled with poetic eulogies to the author's honor. Under these Rabelaisian "panegyrics," in a dozen of languages (including such fantastic ones as "Bermudan," "Macaronic" and "Antipodean"), are placed the names of 56 English poets of the time, that is, quite a majority of them, including the best. We will take a closer look at this book and its patrons in due course.

All of Blount's editions are significant, though literary scholars have yet to evaluate some of them. He did not engage in trifling matters, even if they were lucrative (Rabelaisian jokes are anything but trifling). In some cases he claimed not to know the name of the author. A number of Blount's publications are dedicated to influential and highly-placed persons such as the Earls of Southampton, Pembroke, and Montgomery, and later on to the all-powerful Buckingham. There is much evidence that Blount was connected to these nobles via Philip Sidney's sister Mary, Countess of Pembroke; he published certain books, including the Shakespeare First Folio dedicated to the Earls of Pembroke and Montgomery, sons of Mary Sidney-

Pembroke, with their patronage and financial help. For such purposes he evidently received quite significant financing.

Such a confidant must not only have known the publishing and printing business well, he was obliged in case of necessity to maintain the confidentiality of any facts his clients and patrons did not wish to make public. In his dedication to the Earl of Southampton, in one of the books, he states this straight out: "I make your Honorable Lordship the first and most competent Censor, wishing that before you begin to read farther, you could but read my silence." Edward Blount and his assistants could keep silence very well; Chester's collection is another eloquent testament to that — an impregnable literary and polygraphic sphinx for nearly four centuries.

## DEAD SALUSBURY HELPS TO OPEN THE CURTAIN

The multilayered mystification in the texts and the printing details of the collection, coupled with Newdigate's discovery of the "Ode Enthusiastic" by Jonson with the inscription addressed to Lucy Bedford, added to the extremely limited number of copies printed, are evidence Robert Chester's poetic volume was not an ordinary commercial undertaking for Blount, but a delicate and critical matter for someone among the highly placed principals behind him. Blount's actions and those of other participants in the publication were aimed first and foremost at protecting the secret from the "mob" (multitude), i.e., from the uninitiated. Those who knew the background were offered ambiguous hints in the texts, cunning dating on the title pages, and sordid Rabelaisian jests in the heading, as so many examples of the delicate art of mystification.

There is absolutely no justification for talking about the putative "surplus remains" of an edition that was never registered and never mentioned in contemporary documents. This was a very limited edition, meant for a few people who knew the secret of the Turtle and the Phoenix. In order to believe that the title pages bear authentic dates of publication — 1601 and 1611 — we would have to close our eyes to facts that contradict this dating, and to the many other strands of mystification, and invent instead some version of the circumstances that would be very hard to substantiate indeed.

The idea that a part of the edition was kept in the bookshop for years, and then "rejuvenated" by a whole decade, is a pure invention. Adherents of Grosart's and Brown's hypotheses use this invention to try to make the dates printed on the title pages credible. These attempts utterly fail to explain the strange fact that a weird new title page was inserted into the London copy, with a Rabelaisian "misprint," without the author's name. Not only are the publisher's dates dubious, there is nothing to substantiate them; and analysis of the physical evidence, both within the book and outside, shows that these dates are a deliberate mystification.

There remains only one convincing explanation: the London copy was not kept for ten years in the bookshop at the gates of St. Paul's Cathedral or in Field or Allde's printing shop. Whatever was the reason (that is a separate question) for publishing it, the unique title page of the London copy is contemporary with the remaining pages, into which it was inserted. This is corroborated by the fact that the water net on the title page is matched on some other pages of the book. Thus, *the London copy is in no way a second edition of the Chester collection.* All the copies of the book, despite the different dates on the title pages, were printed with one and the same set of type, on unique paper, in other words, at the same time.

In those days, it was not so rare to print a book with a false date of publication. The example best known to us is the case publishers Thomas Pavier's and William Jaggard's edition of Shakespeare and apocryphal Shakespeare plays (those whose authorship evokes skepticism). For many years scholars were puzzled by these editions. The dates and names of printers and their emblems raised questions. Only in the 20th century A.W. Pollard focused on the fact that all those quartos were printed on paper with the same watermark, though the dates on the title pages varied from one to nineteen years (1600; 1608 — "King Lear"; 1618; 1619). But one batch of paper could not be kept in a printing shop for such a long time; thus, regardless of the dates indicated, the books were printed at approximately the same time. Clearly, on a book intended for sale, no one would put a date some 10-20 years ahead; therefore, one of the later dates must be closer to the true one. Having analyzed the concrete evidence and everything else that was known about the edition, Pollard, W. W. Greg and other scholars came to the conclusion that Pavier's dates are deliberately misleading, and attributed all the editions to 1619.[38] That dating has gradually been accepted by everybody, but the reasons for the mystification remain unclear to our English and American colleagues, for Jaggard and Pavier had the legal right to publish many of those plays.

This and certain other examples speak for the fact that some publishers and printers of the time were adept at artificially "aging" printed books, though the motives in each may have been different. These motives should be thoroughly inspected, for they do not always have anything to do with commerce.

If all the copies of Chester's book appeared simultaneously, then which date is closer to the event — 1601 or 1611? If one assumes that it happened in 1601, it means that the publisher or the printer dated some portion of the edition ten years ahead, which is quite improbable. And then we have Jonson's animosity toward the young Marston that was in full flare in the year of 1601; the mature style of Marston's works in the collection; Dekker's book "Four Birds from Noah's Ark;" and the subservient allusion to James Stuart, who was not yet enthroned.

---

38. Pollard, A.W. *Shakespeare's fight with the pirates.* L. 1920, pp. IX-XII; Anikst, A.A. *First Editions of Shakespeare's plays* (in Russian). Moscow. 1974. pp. 89-90.

So the year of 1601 can be discarded. That leaves us with 1611; the London copy is the evidence that *Love's Martyr* appeared *no earlier* than that date. I think English and American scholars might have come to such a conclusion long ago, if it were not for Grosart's first hypothesis, based on the year of 1601, the year of Essex's execution. The usual dating of Shakespeare's poem, repeated in hundreds and thousands of editions of the Bard's works, was not questioned by those who went on to construct further hypotheses, who connected with it their notions and assumptions. It may seem odd, but despite all the reasons for doubt, this problem of dating was never seriously investigated. This might become less surprising if the reader takes a closer look at the history of English and American Shakespeare studies and the great weight given to the authority of established opinions.

We have established that the collection — all the extant copies — could not have appeared before 1611. Now we shall try to date it more precisely, for that is indeed possible. A line from Horatio, following the dedicative mention of the "truly noble knight Sir John Salisburie," promises that the Muse would keep alive the memory of the man, so worthy of praise. Any mention of death (mori) in such a context means that such an address to the name of Salusbury is a posthumous feature. It is interesting to note that in a magnificent old Russian edition of Shakespeare (1904), edited by S.A. Vengerov, the commentary to "The Phoenix and the Turtle" notes that the verse was dedicated to "the memory of John Salusbury." We do not know if the author was aware of the date of Salusbury's death, or whether he was familiar with Grosart's work issued in London in 1878, but he hit the bull's eye.

Matchett, who wrote about the Chester book less than four decades ago, knew for certain that the owner of Lleweny estate was still alive both in 1601 and 1611. That is why he thinks that Horatio's words refer not to the living (and not very significant) Salusbury, but to a "recently executed hero," i.e., Essex. One cannot but agree with Matchett: Horatio's line could hardly be addressed to a person who was still alive. But one cannot ignore the fact that Horatio's words directly follow the name of Salusbury and a contemporary, uninitiated reader could connect it only with him. For such a reader Horatio's line was clearly a posthumous epitaph referring to Salusbury and it would look natural only after his death; the editor (or whoever was behind him) certainly took that into account. This meshes very well with the fact that in the London copy Chester's prosaic address to Salusbury was ruthlessly discarded. This negligence would have been an insult, if Salusbury were still alive, and it would appear strange and unmotivated, for the second title page remained the same. But when Salusbury was dead, and only then, the posthumous epitaph would have looked quite natural for an uninitiated reader looking through the book. For those few who really knew who was meant, it was an additional brushstroke to savor in the picture of intricate mystification. Quite a masterful stroke, for it brings us one step closer to a more accurate dating of the book. As we now know, John Salusbury died in the summer of 1612, *ergo* that very year is the earliest probable date that this enigmatic collection could have appeared. The address of renowned poets and publishers to the name of a person whose memory outlived him for a short time speaks in favor of the hypothesis that it was published soon after his demise. Those promoting this mystification took advantage of the coincidence of these sad occasions — the death of the Turtle and the Phoenix and the death of Salusbury — for their own purposes. All the more so, since Chester had known Salusbury well during his lifetime, and was familiar with his verses and with the ambiguous dedication to him in one part of Robert Parry's volume.

On the basis of all available evidence in each of the extant copies of Chester's book, taking into account the historical and literary facts of the epoch, I have established the date of the collection as 1612-1613.[39]

That date corresponds very well with the above-mentioned fact that Ben Jonson, in all of his four verses in the Chester book, depicts the Turtle and the Phoenix as alive; he never mentions their death, which became the rationale for publishing the book. Matchett and other scholars have tried in vain to find some convincing explanation for that. In reality, this fact is one more confirmation that the date of 1612-1613 is correct. At just that time, Jonson was traveling in France with the young son of Sir Walter Raleigh (who was locked in the Tower of London). Jonson was actually playing a new role, that of a tutor. So it was that when the volume was being put together, Jonson was absent from England, and so they used his earlier poems about the couple, masked behind the names of Turtle and Phoenix, written while they were still alive. Researchers have noted that Jonson's name appears in the book twice as a signature, and both times it is spelled with the letter "h" (Johnson). But it is known that he detested that spelling, considering it too commonplace, and when an edition was made under his guidance (for instance, the folio of 1616) or when he was aware of the publication, the printers took into account the author's preference and printed his name without the "h." In this case, there was no one to correct the compositor.

Another confirmation that Jonson's verses appeared in Chester's collection without his knowledge can be found by comparing the text of his "Praeludium" in the Chester book with an earlier one, in manuscript form, and with a later one (in the folio of 1616) that was evidently prepared by Jonson himself. In 1616, he rejected most of the changes made during his absence and the singular restored pronouns "I," "mine" (as had been in the manuscript).

Only by assuming that Chester's and Blount's book was published in 1612-1613, when Jonson was away from England, one can make relatively easily explain the features of Jonson's contribution to the collection that puzzle experts. The new date also corresponds well with many other facts that are of concern; the number of such "coincidences" grows steadily as one goes on exploring them.

---

39. Some facts (that cry out for further investigation) suggest that in 1605-1606 most of Chester's poem (without the additional verses by Chester himself and by some other poets, that is, without any indication of the death of the Turtle and Phoenix) was known to his friends in manuscript form.

After the discovery of the watermarks, in the Folger Library, in the books printed by Field and Allde in the first decades of the 17th century, I learned of another link. In 1612-1613 those two printers participated in one more mystification — they published the pro-catholic compositions of one Roger Widdrington (the penname of the catholic preacher Thomas Preston). Here, Field is named as Theophilus Pratt and Allde as Theophilus Fabri, and the printing locations are accordingly given as Cosmopolis and Albionopolis. Both editions[40] share the same preface, and the same decorative features (partially used in the Chester book!) This explains why the London copy, which is completely identical to the Folger as to the type and paper used, bears Allde's emblem (Field's emblem is featured on all the second title pages, Allde's is on the title page of the London copy) and is an additional and quite point of evidence in favor of dating the book to 1612-1613.

Now, 1612 . . . that was just the time certain prose, poetic and dramatic works started to appear in England, the real meaning of which scholars have found controversial. From Shakespeare's biographies everybody knows that he ceased all creative work in 1612-1613 — the Great Bard, as we are told, wrote not another line more until he died in 1616. Is there any connection between the appearance of the Chester collection and the cessation of Shakespeare's creative activity, or is it a mere coincidence, a pure accident?

## No Other Couple Like Them In All England

English scholars have combed through the history archives in vain for traces of a childless couple of noble origin whose unusual relationship, other circumstances of life and especially their almost simultaneous death in about 1600-1601 would at least approximately correspond to what the authors of the Chester collection said about our Phoenix and Turtle. No such couple was found, and that dashed all hopes of convincingly identifying the prototypes of Chester's heroes and thus decoding Shakespeare's most enigmatic work.

But now, looking at 1612, I can name such a strange married couple, who left this world, like John Salusbury, in the summer of that year and in the same sequence as Chester's Turtle and Phoenix. They were Roger Manners, the 5th Earl of Rutland, and his wife Elizabeth, the only daughter of the great poet Philip Sidney, who was deified by his contemporaries and was called the Phoenix (and his home and family —the "Phoenix's Nest").

For three centuries the names of Philip Sidney's daughter and her husband were lost in the oblivion they longed for; English historians knew very little about them. At

---

40. These books, according to *The Short Titles Catalogue of Books,...* (STC) by Pollard-Redgrave (1948), bear the numbers 25596, 25597, 25602).

best, scholars were aware that Rutland was a member of the Essex mutiny. And only at the beginning of the 20th century, scholars came across a number of heretofore unknown or forgotten facts that testify to their unusual relations and also to their close ties with the famous writers of the epoch, including Jonson, Beaumont, Fletcher and the very William Shakespeare.

According to their contemporaries' testimony, the Rutlands' marriage was fictitious: not only did they lack offspring, but during the entire twelve years of their married life they maintained chaste relations — Jonson and Beaumont speak about it. They died one after the other, first he, then she; it happened in the summer of 1612. Roger passed away in Cambridge on June 26 after a long and grave illness; he was 35. The count's embalmed body was taken in a closed casket to his family castle of Belvoir and that very night he was interred in the family crypt. Contrary to custom, no one was allowed to see the face of the deceased. The solemn funeral ceremony was held only two days later, without the dead man!

For a long time historians did not know anything about the circumstances of the death of Elizabeth, Countess of Rutland; even the year[41] of her demise was questioned. Only quite recently, from a surviving letter from one of her contemporaries, it was learned that she took poison and died in London a week after her husband's funeral. It was also at night, without any publicity, that she was buried in St. Paul's Cathedral in the crypt of her father, Philip Sidney, whose magnificent funeral paid for by the Crown had been a national event some quarter of a century before. She lived less than 27 years and took her life of her own accord, following her husband — like the Phoenix, who went very soon after the Turtle burned away at Apollo's altar.

The death and funerals of the Earl and Countess of Rutland were peculiar in many ways, but so was their life together — quite unusual and enveloped in secrecy. It is not only the chaste relations that matter to us, though such an unusual circumstance certainly helps identify them with the Chester heroes. They never let their occupation be known, difficult as it was to keep it hidden. The fact that Elizabeth was the only daughter, the only child of Philip Sidney — idol of a whole generation of English poets — made her a very notable figure. It is enough to mention that Fulke Greville, who was a poet but also one of the most influential officials of the day, said: "I was a servant to Queen Elizabeth, Counsellor to King James, and a friend to Sir Philip Sidney," thus placing the latter on an even par with the monarchs. Elizabeth, besides being the daughter of the great poet, was the stepdaughter of the Earl of Essex (several years after Philip's demise, his widow became Essex' wife). In spite of all this, the name of Elizabeth Sidney, Countess of Rutland, is seldom mentioned in surviving manuscripts and printed literature of the time, especially compared to other ladies of her milieu — for instance, her cousin and friend Lucy Bedford.

---

41. Even such a dependable source as the (British) *Dictionary of National Biography* gives the date of her death wrongly, as 1615.

However, it hadn't always been that way. Even the fact of her birth was commemorated by poets and her godmother was Queen Elizabeth, who attended her christening. Only after she threw in her lot with Rutland did her name disappear from view. But perhaps she did not inherit from her brilliant father, or from her aunt, the Countess of Pembroke (who brought her up), their deep intellectual bent and literary talents? Perhaps she was so ordinary that even Philip Sidney's and her stepfather Essex' names could not draw the attention of poets and writers?

Not quite. Seven years after her death Ben Jonson, who visited her many times, said: "The Countess of Rutland was nothing inferior to her father Sir Philip Sidney, in poesy."[42] That is an extremely important declaration — such praise at that time was the highest possible; Jonson knew well her poetic talent, and rated it the highest. His estimation could not have been motivated by the desire to flatter; Jonson made this comment while visiting a provincial poet, Drummond, in his house in 1619, and he did not know that the inquisitive host would put to paper all that he had heard from his metropolitan guest. Elizabeth and her husband had been buried long ago, so Jonson had no reason to lie, much less to invent details of that nature. Besides, what was said to Drummond is confirmed by both of Jonson's poetic epistles to Elizabeth Sidney-Rutland, that were first published in his folio of 1616, i.e., four years after her death. In epigram #79, Jonson exclaims: if only Philip Sidney were alive, he could have seen his art reborn and surpassed by his daughter! Modern Jonson scholars are struck by his veneration of her talent, for not a single poetic line signed by Philip Sidney's daughter has come down to us so far.

The other letter in verse was written and sent to her in 1600, but it too was only published in the 1616 folio. Jonson placed it in the small (15 verses) cycle, "Forest," which by his own reckoning is one of the most important pieces of his poetic legacy. Most of those verses are connected in some degree with the Sidney family. Jonson put into this "Sidney" cycle two of his poems from the enigmatic Chester book — "Praeludium" (somewhat modified and without the title) and "Epos" (renamed as "Epode"[43]) — dedicated to the Turtle and the Phoenix! And here we come to a startling and not yet adequately studied detail: "Praeludium" comes under number X, "Epode" was number XI, and under number XII Jonson placed his "Epistle to Elizabeth, Countess of Rutland." We have already noted that Jonson meticulously selected and grouped the works for this edition, which was so important to him; he must have had some purpose in arranging them in this order. That being the case, the epistle to Elizabeth in such close connection with mysterious addresses to Chester's Turtle and Phoenix is another proof confirming our identification of their prototypes, and the more so as it is traced to an earlier manuscript copy. This cannot have happened by chance — for Jonson, these three poems were always inseparable.

---

42. "Jonson's Conversations with Drummond," 1.205-206. In Jonson B. *The Complete Poems*, p. 466.
43. An epos is a heroic song or epic poem; an epode is a lyric poem where a long verse is interlaced with a short one.

In the "Epistle to Elizabeth, Countess of Rutland," Jonson again asserts that Elizabeth inherited from her father, "the godlike Sidney," his love for the Muses, and his art. But out of 150 poems published in the 1616 folio, the "Epistle" is the only one whose text Jonson unexpectedly cut in mid-sentence. The sentence is interrupted as soon as he passes from Elizabeth's father to her "brave friend" (her husband), who also (like the "godlike Sidney") loved the art of poetry, who loved "high and noble matter, such as flies from brains entranced, and billed with ecstasies (rapturous thoughts)." In the text of the folio Jonson made a strange remark: "the rest is lost." The remark is more than strange, for the poet was editing the collection himself and could have restored or replaced the "lost" ending. But he pointedly did not do it. The full text of the verse was found in the 20$^{th}$ century in a manuscript copy; it contained the allegedly "lost" ending — only seven lines, which speak of an "ominous vow" and gratitude to Rutland. Jonson scholars these days have different ways of accounting for this excision (it is unprecedented in all of Jonson's editions throughout his whole life). For instance, they surmise that Rutland was impotent, that he could not fulfill his duties as a husband — although it is not clear why, even if it were true, that would matter four years after the death of both consorts. What is clear is that, for some reason, even after Rutland's death one could not speak about him openly (just as one could not reveal the true names of the Turtle and the Phoenix), and Jonson found a way to attract his contemporaries' and posterity's attention to the matter.

In the third epistle, addressed "To the Honored Countess of _____," (the 50$^{th}$ poem of the "Underwood" cycle, published after Jonson's death), which some renowned Jonson scholars also think was intended for Elizabeth Rutland, her name and title are replaced with dotted lines. Here the poet speaks about her position as a "widowed wife," about books that replace absent friends and certain other high virtues that are safely concealed from the uninitiated. It was like in the "Ode Enthusiastic" describing the Phoenix. Let's take another look at the fourth stanza of the "Ode":

> Her breath for sweet exceeding
> The Phoenix place of breeding,
> But mixed with sound, transcending
> All Nature of commending.

Here "her breath" is a poetic voice, a poetry, supported as well by the word "sound" in the third line. But which marvel voice ("sound") was mixed with the Phoenix? We shall come to that later.

Jonson's pastoral play "The Sad Shepherd" is evidence that Belvoir Castle was the center of a closed poetic circle — Jonson called them "the poets of Belvoir Vale"; and all the participants in Chester's collection belonged to it. The great poet's daughter, a woman of outstanding talent and tragic fate, Elizabeth Sidney occupied a special place in this poetic community. They saw her as a successor to Philip Sidney's service, a new the Phoenix arisen from his ashes — here too are the roots of Chester's allegory. Ben Jonson venerated her beyond all bounds, and further on we shall see that she remained for him the High Muse, nearly always hidden behind the curtain. He often recalled her later, after her death, not only in talks with Drummond but also (usually without revealing her name) in a number of his most outstanding poetic works, and then we recognize her by the incomparable admiration and never ceasing pain in the poet's voice.


## A PLATONIC MARRIAGE


The [British] Dictionary of National Biography (L., 1893, vol. 36) has several columns of text written by the historian Archbald[44] and dedicated to Roger Manners, the 5th Earl of Rutland. Shakespeare's contemporary, the Earl of Rutland (1576-1612) was one of the best-educated men of the time; he held Master of Arts degrees from Cambridge and Oxford universities, and studied at Padua University in Italy and at Gray's Inn in London. His upbringing and education were supervised by Francis Bacon — a great orator, philosopher and friend of the Muses, a man of complex character and not a simple fate.

In his youth, Rutland was a close friend and comrade in arms of the Earl of Southampton, to whom Shakespeare dedicated his first works — the poems "Venus and Adonis" (1593) and "The Rape of Lucrece" (1594). There is an extant letter from a contemporary in which it is said that Rutland and Southampton spent all their time in the theater, to the detriment of their obligations at the court (1599). Together with Essex they took part in military action at sea and in Ireland. In 1601, Rutland was in the first ranks of the Essex mutiny, for which his father-in-law lost his life and Southampton his freedom; Rutland was condemned to pay a ruinous fine and was sent to the provinces under the watchful eye of his relative. James Stuart, upon his ascension to the throne, rehabilitated him and soon sent him on an honorable mission to the Danish King; after his return, Rutland seldom showed up at court. A long and exhausting illness often rendered him bedridden and at last took his life, while he was still a young man. From the surviving correspondence among his acquaintances, one can see that he suffered from a severe disease of the legs, and that during the last years of his life he complained of devastating head aches. As Robert Chester (as has been established recently) was Rutland's distant relative, he must have known about his illness. Now we can understand why the Chester Turtle's "features fade away, and make him looke / As if his name were writ in death's pale booke," and why sending to him Dame Nature and the Phoenix, Jupiter (King James) gives them "this Ointment to anoint his head / This precious Balme to lay unto his feet" for the Turtle. The

---

44. *Dictionary of National Biography.* L., 1893, vol.36.

concordance is astonishingly full, even down to such minute details — and the details have nothing to do with the ancient legend of the Phoenix.[45]

One may add that Chester's description of the place that is the abode of the ailing Turtle coincides very closely with the topography of the Rutlands' estate at Belvoir[46] — a unique touristic site in England. The ancient castle of the Rutlands is located on a high hill (probably of artificial origin) from which a breathtaking view opens out across the surrounding countryside, adorned with two branches of the Devon River and further on to the forested valley for several miles across. Carlton Brown, in his day, specially noted that Chester's heroes several times describe this magnificent dale with the river, this "high hill," which is different from other geographic descriptions in Chester's poem, suggesting that it must actually correspond to some locality that is well known to the author and which he recollects in detail. Brown was sorry that he could not associate Chester's unknown locality with Sir John Salusbury's estate; Grosart and Matchett tried in vain to find it in Ireland along the routes of Essex' travels there in 1599-1600. And one more important "coincidence." The mythical unicorn that we discovered on the paper of Chester's book is also present in the Rutlands' coat of arms — there are even two of them.

The Rutlands' marriage was not always cloudless; from about 1605-1610 they were to a certain extent estranged, and lived apart for most of the time. Elizabeth's friends and relatives, particularly her aunt, the magnificent Mary Sidney Pembroke, were worried by her ambiguous situation as a "widowed wife." They were afraid that Philip Sidney's daughter would be left without descendants and the Phoenixes would cease to exist. Thus, they tried to make peace between the Rutlands, and to make their marriage a normal one. Let us recollect how Chester's Dame Nature (a mask for Mary Sidney Pembroke) begs Jupiter to take some action and how she later goes to the ailing Turtle in order to, in the not so delicate but quite explicit words of Chester, "direct him to this Phoenix' bed." Thus, we have plenty of evidence as to the circumstances of the Phoenix's and Dame Nature's arrival at the Turtle's place — his ailing condition, their balm and ointment for his sick head and sore feet, his request to the Phoenix to forgive the wrongs inflicted earlier — showing that Chester started writing his poem exactly at that period (about 1605) of their complicated and no doubt mutually painful relations, when their friends and relatives hoped for a miracle and tried to make it come true as soon as possible.

But the miracle did not work. Rutland pined away, and several years later he and his platonic wife quit life, at nearly the same time. With the help of Blount and his

---

45. Certainly one may not treat Chester's rhymed story with its many and long digressions as a report from the field. But it is also not just a pure poetic imagination, for the author repeats several times that his "homemade" poem contains an allegorically-shaded truth about its heroes. Fragments of the truth, nearly naturalistic in their presentation, shine through now and then (not always by accident) from the coarsely cut veil of Chester's allegory. The same is true for the verses of other poets, whose poetic properties are far higher than Chester's. Such fragments and allusions are invaluable for a researcher.

46. Belvoir — a nice view (in French).

distinguished patrons, Chester secretly issued his book, supplementing it with the story of the tragic outcome and poems by several other poets mourning the Turtle and the Phoenix. These verses, including the staggering Requiem with the name of Shakespeare, were preceded by the special half-title.

The death of the Earl of Rutland, and what is even more astonishing, the sacrificial death right after of his wife, the daughter of the celebrated Elizabethan Phoenix Philip Sidney, contrary to custom were not *openly* mourned by their friends, the poets, or anyone else in England. How can this be? The poets were silent, though they had to have been shocked by the martyr death of their beloved Muse and the mysterious funerals of their patrons.[47]

All this is further indication that the atmosphere of secrecy, of deep mystery, surrounding Chester's Turtle and the Phoenix, surrounded their Belvoir prototypes as well, so that their friends, and above all the poets, respected it and observed it even after they had passed away. Still, several of them, those who were closest to the Belvoir couple, decided to break the taboo and paid their tribute in Chester's volume, having masked its meaning with an allegory so involved that it could be understood only by a few people. The riddle of Chester's book is the riddle of the Belvoir couple, the Rutlands; it is also closely linked with Shakespeare's mystery. Its solution, after a long and difficult quest, casts a light down through the dark of centuries onto two wonderful people, probably the most wonderful that have ever walked this earth.


## HAMLET'S SCHOOLFELLOW


Not long before the First World War, going through the archives of Padua, where Rutland had studied, the Belgian historian Selesten Demblon discovered the names of two young men from Denmark: Rosencrantz and Guildenstern.

Rosencrantz and Guildenstern! Every one who knows and loves "Hamlet" holds a special place in his memory for these names. Many of those who have written about this Shakespearean tragedy have focused on this inseparable pair of false friends to the Danish prince. They are commonplace personalities, servile and thoughtless executors of the monarch's will. They always appear together; one can hardly imagine them being apart; it is quite impossible to discern any difference between them. It is no wonder that in spite of their faceless appearance, their triviality, and lack of any individual characteristics, they still are discernable among the major dramatis personae of the tragedy. One can see and feel them quite vividly; they stick in the memory. Even Goethe was impressed by the penetrating insight of the great

---

47. The silent conspiracy was broken only by Francis Beaumont, but his elegy on the death of Elizabeth Rutland, filled with deep sorrow, was only published anonymously, ten years later (1622), when Beaumont was no longer alive.

playwright who created the pair who show on the stage what could not have been presented by one person, for they symbolize society itself. The English Shakespeare scholar H. Granville-Barker tersely described their essence: "they are not just a nonentity, but a nonentity split in two."

Those inseparable twins passed through the perennial tragedy, through the minds of millions of people speaking all the languages of the world, both readers and spectators of Shakespeare. Then some three centuries after their first appearance on stage, they again emerged in a most mysterious way. Thus, still as a pair, the shadows of Rosencrantz and Guildenstern rose from dusty shelves of the Padua archives and appeared before us with their unspoken testimony. Their own insignificance, the fact that they came from another country, makes the testimony the more significant; their names do not belong to kings, famous soldiers or English nobles, whose names were current on the lips of their British contemporaries. The author could hardly have read their names from Danish books or chronicles. The chance of this being a haphazard coincidence can practically be excluded; that would be quite a stretch even for one person, not two.

No, Rosencrantz and Guildenstern were not dreamt up by the author of "Hamlet." Two young Danish noblemen studied in the same town with the young Englishman, the Earl of Rutland, in that Italian city so far away from England and Denmark, and several years later they lent their names to two inseparable courtiers in the tragedy created by the great Englishman William Shakespeare.[48] The Paduan specters of Rosencrantz and Guildenstern indicate that this very Roger Manners, Earl of Rutland, had something to do with William Shakespeare and his "Hamlet." And also pointing us in this direction is the fact that certain important details about Denmark appear in the tragedy only in the second quarto — that is, after Rutland's return from Denmark in 1603.

Even if Rutland and his wife were just informants passing ideas on to Shakespeare, that should be sufficient to inspire literature historians to take a closer look at them, especially as there are so few authentic facts by which we can gain insights into the creative milieu of the great playwright and his poetic laboratory. However, the Paduan details and other highly relevant facts connecting Shakespeare to the poetic environment of the Rutlands — the Sidneys — and the Pembrokes — have not been adequately reflected in Shakespeare biographies. Let us take, for instance, a short documented biography by the respected American Shakespeare scholar S. Shoenbaum, which was translated into Russian in 1985. Here all the most important discoveries in the world of Shakespeare studies are enumerated, everything that to some degree could be linked with the life and work of the Great Bard. But in this thoroughly academic book, where nothing was too prosaic, not even mortgages

---

48. Shakespeare directly called Hamlet and Horatio alumni of Wittenberg University, and the prince called Rosencrantz and Guildenstern his schoolfellows. It has been established now that the Rosencrantz and Guildenstern who studied at Padua were indeed graduates of Wittenberg University. It is clear that Shakespeare knew that; there can hardly be any coincidence here.

and invoices, Shakespeare's legal claims on his neighbors for small sums of money and the persecution of debtors and their ill-fated guarantors, you will not find anything concerning Rutland, much less his fellows Rosencrantz and Guildenstern, who passed from an ancient Italian city to the pages of the great tragedy, and acquired there one more fellow — Hamlet, Prince of Denmark.

Sometimes Rutland's name appears in Shakespeare biographies, but only in the context of his friendship with the Earl of Southampton; sometimes even in serious academic works he is confused with other Mannerses, his brother and distant grandfather.[49] Nonetheless, Shakespeare knew the way to Belvoir. This point is made by the inclusion of his name in Chester's collection, and also by a unique record in the household book of the Belvoir steward from whom Shakespeare received several score shillings in gold coins after Roger Rutland's death.

As to the negligence modern Shakespeare biographers have shown to Hamlet's schoolfellow and his consort in life, this can most often be attributed to ignorance about important facts and sources and also a lack of interest in investigating them. Certainly, they are further thwarted by the thick shroud of mystification (resembling to some extent the Masonic mysteries), created around the Turtle and the Phoenix by themselves and their poetic friends. The "poets of Belvoir vale" kept the secret well. They kept the unusual funerals secret, and they masked or omitted countless details in Chester's book and Jonson's pastoral "The Sad Shepherd"; then we have Jonson's poem cut short in mid-sentence, in his surviving letters and the letters of John Donne.

However, it is not only this veil of secrecy that hampers research and impedes the revelation of important evidence that would confirm the existence of this poetic circle (which included the most outstanding poets and playwrights of the epoch, together with Shakespeare). There are other reasons as well. Here we can name tradition and the long-standing authority of previous research, and the influence of the anthology and compilation approach to events whose roots are too deep for a cursory glance. Many researchers are tired of the names that still circulate in vituperative debates on "the Shakespeare Authorship Question." For Roger Manners, the 5th Earl of Rutland, is one of the so called pretenders, that is, one of the persons who lived in the Shakespeare epoch and in the 19th and 20th centuries were named as probable author of the Shakespeare plays, poems and sonnets.

The argument between adherents of "heretical" hypotheses and those who stand for traditional approaches has gone on for a century and a half. However, readers in Russia for many years received meager information about the Great Debate on Shakespeare — a debate that has no precedent in the history of world culture — and what little they did see was glimpsed through a unilateral interpretation, colored by

---

49. Such mistakes may be found in even the most solid of works, such as: Fripp, E.J. *Shakespeare: Man and Artist.* L., 1938, vol.1, p.9; vol.2, p.230; Bald, R.C. *John Donne, A life.* N.Y., Oxford, 1970, p. 203-205; the aforementioned in Matchett's book, p. 173 (see footnote 46 at p. 492); Park, Honan: *"Shakespeare. A Life,"* OUP, 1998, pp.179, 469; O'Connor, Garry. *William Shakespeare,* NY, Applause Books, 2000, pp.191, 374.

simplified ideological considerations. It is high time that our readers learned the real reasons why the Great Debate came about and its none too simple history.

# Chapter 2. A Long-Standing Controversy About Stratford-on-Avon

*"Shakespeare without end." — Who invented "the Shakespeare authorship problem"— and why? The traces of genius — William Shakspere of Stratford, his family and occupation. — The last will of the Lord of Language? The riddle of the signatures. — A close friend of the Earl of Southampton. — A crow in someone else's feathers. — Cambridge and Oxford knew the Shakespeare. — The smug pork-butcher or a melancholic tailor? — The portrait that Ben Jonson did not advise looking at. — The Great Bard acquires a biography. — The Anniversary. — Chests of manuscripts. — The first doubts. Baconian heresy. — Formation of scholarly history. Rutland appears — coincidences, coincidences . . . — Ideological taboo. — The discussion becomes more involved. New candidates, new evolution of the elusive image. — In academic circles, the facts keep piling up. — The hour has struck for the Turtle and the Phoenix.*

## "Shakespeare Without End"

World culture is inconceivable without Shakespeare. His art, his genius, his profound probing into human nature, made this Englishman who lived during the times of Ivan the Terrible and Boris Godunov a full fledged contemporary of all the succeeding epochs and generations. Shakespeare's art seems necessary and immediate to our era, with its tragic cataclysms, rises and falls.

Today, millions of people see his heroes on stage, in movies, on TV and video, and they listen to audio recordings and read his books in all the languages of the world. More than 4000 books and articles are printed every year, directly relating to the Great Bard.[1]

Shakespeare study was established long ago not only as a part of literary and theatrical criticism, but as special branch of knowledge, an international one, with its own traditions and its own history in each country. For example, speaking of Russian Shakespeare studies, one may name at the top of the list N. Karamzin, A. Bestouzhev, V. Kuhelbecker and especially the great Pushkin, who called Shakespeare "our father" and wrote: "Read Shakespeare — this is my permanent refrain." By the middle of the 19th century, all of Shakespeare's works had been translated into Russian. Shakespeare and the Russian culture (mostly literature, theater, and cinema) is a theme of utmost interest reflected in hundreds of books and articles.[2]

Truly, as Goethe foretold, "Shakespeare is without end." That being the case, one might imagine that scholars long since unearthed every important fact about him and his works, leaving only theoretical, critical points to be further discussed — the quality of translations and new editions, problems at various levels in Shakespeare's creative heritage, new findings of biographical interest, the artistic quality of new stagings, directors' and actors' interpretations. Not quite. Serious problems in Shakespeare studies are still unresolved: What are we to make of variations in the texts of editions issued during his life and later on, the conflicting or missing dates on many of his works, the authorship of the so-called apocryphal plays that at various times have been assigned to Shakespeare but not included in the canon, etc.? Many of the heroes of Shakespeare's sonnets have yet to be identified. And many a problem remains in connection with the works of Shakespeare's contemporaries.

Last but hardly least, there is still the famous (some would say "odious") "Shakespeare authorship problem" that erupts from time to time, the Great Controversy about the Great Bard's identity. In the 1920s, this debate was raging in Russia also, but then it (like many other questions) was "closed," and objective information about its progress in the West was reduced to minimum. Lately, the controversy has again flared up in England and the USA; but in Moscow, a long-standing taboo dominated the study and public discussion of this and related issues.

How could such a controversy emerge, and still be raging at this late date? Very few people doubt the traditional identification of Dante, Cervantes, Philip Sidney, Ben Jonson, John Milton and other great or just outstanding writers, dramatists, and poets of the Renaissance. As to the greatest genius of mankind, William Shakespeare, serious doubts have been voiced many times, mostly by people who have the greatest esteem for the Shakespeare works. Views about Shakespeare sometimes come into or

---

1. The yearly bibliographical issue of the Shakespeare Quarterly, produced by the Folger Shakespeare Library in Washington, DC lists for the year of 1988 4.846 headings of books, articles and reviews in all the languages of the world, for 1992 — 5.597.

2. Rf. Shakespeare. Bibliography of Russian translations and critical literature in Russian. 1748-1962. Composed by I.M. Levidova. Moscow. 1964. Shakespeare. Bibliographical index of Russian translations and critical literature in Russian. 1963-1975. By I.M. Levidova. M. 1978. Shakespeare. Bibliographical index of Russian translations and critical literature in Russian. 1976-1987. By Yu. G. Friedstein. M. Library for Foreign Literature. 1989.

go out of fashion; that's not a very academic approach. Like everything in human relations, emotions play a significant role.

Traditionalists suggest, among other reasons, that the "heretics" are simply not familiar enough with the facts of Shakespeare's life, that they are simply looking to stirrup a historic scandal, that they are prejudiced snobs who cannot admit that a common actor without higher education could have written such masterpieces. Here is an example, from Russian literary scholar Yu. F. Shvedov, in his monograph "Shakespeare's creativeness":

> The dearth of authentic information about the life of the great poet gave a pretext to some reactionary literary researchers of the 19th and 20th century to try and deny Shakespeare as the real author of his works. The major argument of those vituperative invectives consists in the snobbish idea that a craftsman's son, educated at the Stratford grammar school, who served as an actor in the theater, could not have created such magnificent pieces of art. Anti-Shakespearean proponents ruminated that under the pen name of Shakespeare hid some aristo-cratic contemporary who was averse to providing the theater with his works and presented them on the stage under the guise of one of the actors. The falsehood of such doctored ideas, whose authors shuffle the facts at will and do not pay any attention to the testimony of people who personally knew Shakespeare and highly valued his works, does not require any special proof.[3]

The book was published in 1959, reprinted in 1977. Compared to the arguments of the 1930s and 1940s, it has fewer ideological rubber stamps and ominous tags applied to opponents; but it still serves to discourage anyone from going down that path.

The other side, i.e. "the heretics," often cite the "blindness" of the first biographers and investigators, who accepted naïve lore and legends about Shakespeare, and who did not understand the great spirit of his works. English politician and writer John Bright (1811-1889) gave a direct and laconic pronouncement on the topic: "Any man who believes that William Shakespeare (i.e. Shakspere, I. G.) of Stratford wrote 'Hamlet' or 'Lear' is a fool." Considering how many diverse opinions have been presented, Bright may have oversimplified to some extent. But the traditionalists, both literary and theater people, have also called their opponents dreamers, lunatics, oddballs, and traitors to the treasury of cultural heritage of the English nation and of all mankind.

More than ideology and ego is involved. Even in academic circles, the discussion carries a certain polemic charge. In order to preserve objectivity while proceeding with the matter, I shall use more neutral terms while naming the parties: "Stratfordians" for those who do not doubt that the Shakespeare works were written by a member of the London actors' troupe, William Shakspere, who was born in 1564 in the city of

---

3. Shvedov Yu.F. *William Shakespeare, Research.* Moscow. 1977. p.276-277.

Stratford-on-Avon, died the same place in 1616 and was buried there; and "non-Stratfordians" for those who do not agree with this opinion. The terminology is conventional enough (it's nothing new), but it is quite convenient and neutral.

## WHO INVENTED "THE SHAKESPEARE AUTHORSHIP PROBLEM" — AND WHY? THE TRACES OF GENIUS

Why do we even have a "Shakespeare authorship problem"? Is it because so little is known about the life of the Great Bard? No; that was true only for the first hundred years after his death. Thanks to meticulous investigation by many generations of scholars, we know much more about him than about other writers and actors of his time. The difficulty is not in the quantity of authentic documents confirming his biography, but in their nature, their shocking incompatibility with what we are told by the Shakespeare works themselves. From 37 plays, two large poems, a cycle of sonnets, and several other verses, many tell-tale signs are bound to emerge. The more we have learned about Shakespeare's biography, and the more we have studied his works, the more obvious this incompatibility became.

The pre-revolutionary Russian author of several works on the history of English literature N. I. Storozhenko, who never doubted the authenticity of the traditional identification of William Shakespeare, noted even so that: "Literature history has not known more incongruity between what we know about the author and what was written by him." R. W. Emerson wrote, even earlier, that he couldn't reconcile Shakespeare's biographies with his creative activity. No modern biographer of Shakespeare can sidestep this controversy, no matter how one may choose to explain it.

While reading Shakespeare's dramatic and poetic pieces, we learn quite a lot about the author: first and foremost, a general impression of deep spiritual values and sense of humanity, standing far above boiling passions of people. His heroes speak not only about their daily concerns and desires, about their friends and foes, but they often dwell on the meaning of life and death, on good and evil, on love, on history. Those thoughts, often tangential to the play's action, let us follow the flight of Shakespeare's ideas, surprisingly insightful and intricate, penetrating into the most complex features of human existence. And like nature, his art again and again creates life on the theater stage encompassing the whole world.

Shakespeare's works testify to the immense artistic mastery of the author but also to the incomparable richness of his language. His vocabulary counts about 20,000 words, that is, two to three times more than his most educated and talented literary contemporaries and even writers of the following generations (John Milton and Francis Bacon used 8,000 words, William Thackeray — 5,000; French writers like Victor Hugo and Hippolyte Taine, who lived two centuries later, used about 9,000 words). Our contemporary Englishmen with university education use not more than 4,000 words; a semi-literate provincial person in Elizabethan England made use of 1,000, or even half as many. Such a great disparity speaks for itself — there is no parallel in literary history. According to the Oxford Dictionary, Shakespeare introduced into the English language about 3,200 new words — more than Bacon, Jonson, and Chapman taken together.

Shakespeare's works testify that he used French, Latin, and Italian, could read Greek and probably several other languages. In "Henry V," the 4$^{th}$ scene of Act III is *completely written in French*, as is the conversation with the prisoner of war in the 4$^{th}$ scene of Act IV. All in all, this play contains about 100 lines in good French. Single words and sentences of Italian and Latin can be found in his many pieces. The plot of "Hamlet" was taken from "Histoires Tragiques," by the Frenchman Belleforest, which was translated into English only a century later; the plots and many other details of "Othello" and "The Merchant of Venice" were borrowed from collections of Italian stories by Giraldi Cinthio and Giovanni Fiorentino that also appeared in English only in the 18$^{th}$ century. Shakespeare knew works by Montaigne, Rabelais, Ronsard, Ariosto, Boccaccio, Bandello. "The Two Gentlemen of Verona" took its plot from a Spanish pastoral novel by Montemayor that had not been printed in English before the play appeared.[4]

The evidence suggests that the author received a classical education based on the Greek and Latin tradition. He was fully conversant on Greek and Roman mythology, literature, and history; he used excerpts from Homer, Plautus, Ovid, Livy, Seneca, Plutarch, and Appian — not only in translation but also in the original. Take a look at his poems, and the Roman cycle of plays, "Timon of Athens." Mythological and historical characters from the classical period are used in 260 instances.

He was also exceedingly well-read in English. In his historical plays he used "Chronicles" by Hollinshed and works by Hall, Grafton, Fabyan, and Stow. He knew the novels about King Arthur, works by Chaucer, and Gower, he was familiar with literature about travel and exploration and the compositions of contemporary poets and playwrights, and he knew the Holy Scriptures. Scholars in the last 150 years have found that Shakespeare was well read in English history, law, rhetoric, music, botany, medicine (of the period), military and even naval affairs (for example, the commands given by the boatswain in "The Tempest" are appropriate for a sailing ship in distress). In Shakespeare's works they counted 124 citations connected with law, 172 with seafaring, and 192 that testify to some knowledge (and experience) of martial affairs; the word "music" and its derivatives are used 170 times. Botanists have noted that Shakespeare's characters mention the names of 63 herbs, flowers, plants and trees. In his day, such erudition could be obtained only at a university, from private tutors, and from people who had been engaged personally in military campaigns. There were no

---

4. The sources used by Shakespeare are listed in the eight-volume book, *Narrative and dramatic sources of Shakespeare*. Ed. by G. Bullough. N.Y. Columbia Univ. Press, 1957-1973.

Such was Shakespeare at work in his study, as conceptualized by the 19th century artist John Fad, with books everywhere...

public libraries in England in the late 16th century. There is every sign that Shakespeare was comfortable with court etiquette, noble titles, family trees, and the language of courtiers and monarchs. Most of the action in his plays takes place in this milieu. In his works there are 196 depictions of the games, diversions, and entertainment of the nobility, including those that were most expensive and of limited following: falcon hunting, hunting with hounds, tennis; one could not acquire such knowledge by hearsay.

Shakespeare's knowledge of the cities and towns in northern Italy is amazing; some biographers assume that he visited there. Many of his plays take place in Venice, Padua, Verona, and Mantua. Lucentio, in "The Taming of the Shrew," appears in Padua with the following words:

> Tranio, since for great desire I had
> To see fair Padua, nursery of arts,
> I am arrived for fruitful Lombardy,
> The pleasant garden of great Italy ...

Lucentio, who was born in Pisa and brought up in Florence, knows what is taught at Padua University. Even his servant Tranio says:

> Mi perdonate, gentle master mine,
> I am in all affected as yourself;
> Glad that you thus continue your resolve
> To suck the sweets of sweet philosophy.
> Only, good master, while we do admire
> This virtue and this moral discipline
> Let's be no stoics nor no stocks, I pray,
> Or so devote to Aristotle's checks,
> As Ovid be an outcast quite abjured:
> Balk logic with acquaintance that you have,
> And practice rhetoric in your common talk;
> Music and poesy use to quicken you;
> The mathematics and the metaphysics,
> Fall to them, as you find your stomach serves you ... (I, I).

Only a person who knows university subjects and how the students take them could write this.

Shakespeare knows the main sites of Venice and some minor side streets and buildings as well, and local words; he also knows Mantua and its surroundings. Many Shakespeare scholars have noted that in his Italian plays (as distinct from Jonson's *Volpone*, which also takes place in Venice) the incomparable spirit of Italian life is vividly felt, the bright colors and the sun of the promised land of the Renaissance, suggesting that its atmosphere had been imbibed and savored in person by the son of foggy Albion. The heroes of the gallant play "Love's Labour's Lost" are contemporaries of Shakespeare: the French King Henry IV (called Ferdinand, in the play); his first wife Margaret Valois and his closest attendants bear their own names: Lords Biron, Longaville and Dumaine; this is refined air, inaccessible to commoners. The sophisticated philosophical discourse and the witty repartee of noblemen who have at their mercy the fate of the country and of the charming young ladies seeking to win their hearts, are interwoven with intricate locutions and allusions, and liberally sprinkled with foreign phrases and words.

Shakespeare's works display a highly diversified and thorough education, nearly encyclopedic knowledge and an immense vocabulary. And certainly the reader (and often the spectator) is struck by the philosophic depth of his perception of this world and man's place in it, is amazed at the momentous dramatic and poetic mastery that allows Shakespeare to probe the most sacred corners of man's heart and show them to us on the theater stage, from generation to generation. One more thing: he makes a clear distinction between Good and Evil, and wants us to do the same. His hand depicts without prejudice (albeit not indifferently) living images of flesh and blood, not some metaphysical abstractions; but Shakespeare leaves no doubt as to whose side he is on, which heroes have a place in his heart: Cordelia or Goneril, Edgar or Edmond, King Claudius or Prince Hamlet, the usurer Shylock or his victims. And how about Iago?

## WILLIAM SHAKSPERE FROM STRATFORD, HIS FAMILY AND OCCUPATION

What do we actually know today about William Shakespeare, from other sources, from authentic documents and the testimony of his contemporaries? His first biographers started collecting information about him just 50-100 years after his death; then, gradually, in the course of three centuries, original documents were found that built up a voluminous asset of hard facts so that modern biographies of Shakespeare differ substantially from those written in the 18th and early 19th centuries.

As biographers tell us, William Shakespeare was born and raised in the small town of Stratford-(up)on-Avon, Warwickshire. Its population was under 2,000. The parish register and other official papers list his name (including on the occasions of his baptism and burial) and the names of his father, mother, wife, and children as "Shakspere" or "Shaxper." The pen name used by the Great Bard was "Shakespeare" or "Shake-speare"; that is how it was printed on the title pages of his works, during his lifetime and in his posthumous editions. The spelling "Shakspere" can still be seen in five out of the six known personal signatures he has left us.[5] That is why non-Stratfordians call the Stratford-born man that, while calling the Author of great works, whoever he might be, Shakespeare (one shaking a spear). Some Stratfordians take the name "William Shakespeare" as a pen name of Shakspere of Stratford. For our discussion, I am going to call the Stratford man Shakspere in order to avoid possible confusion. But I should like to point out that such a distinction in itself does not predetermine the results of a complicated investigation as to who authored the Shakespeare works. No academic examination is possible at all without clear-cut definitions and a delineation of notions and terms. Such definitions may be symbolic and sometimes are even expressed in figures and signs, but one should not confuse them without saying so, at least until the examination is over.

The most important rule in such a discussion is that different phenomena and objects cannot be designated by the same name, sign, or symbol — especially when the focus of the discussion is on just such debatable phenomena, whose identity is questionable. The importance of such a condition becomes clear when we look back over a century and a half of debates, abounding in examples of mutual misunderstanding.

Unfortunately, in Shakespeare's biographies published in Russian, including those translated from English, the authors and translators have usually followed the pattern of unscholarly "unification," often misrepresenting incontestable historic realities in order to simplify a very complicated problem. For instance, the April 26, 1564 record in the Stratford parish register on the baptism of a child reads: "Gulielmus filius Iohannes Shakspere," but the translator writes the name as Shakespeare, thus altering the most important component. The same thing happens with the record made 52 years later in the same Register, about the funeral of "Mr. Will Shakspere, gent." If anyone transcribing the baptismal and funeral records of Marie-Henri Beyle had switched his family name to Stendhal, there would have been protests, though nobody had any doubt whatsoever that "Stendhal" was the pen name of Henri Beyle and none other. Still, the substitution of the real name of the Stratford-born William Shakspere for the pen name Shakespeare is common practice in every language, even when reproducing authentic documents.

But let us come back to the April 26, 1564 entry. As a rule, baptisms took place three days after birth, so it has been thought that William Shakspere came to this world on April 23, 1564. His father's name, John Shakspere, can be found in the city records since 1552, when he was fined for leaving refuse in the street. He evidently had come to town several years before from the village of Snitterfield, where he was a farmer, like his parents. In Stratford he started a gloves-making business, but also had some trade in wool, probably timber, and barley, and he was also a money lender. When his business flourished, the townsfolk elected him constable, then alderman, a member of the town corporation, and during 1568 he was bailiff — the town leader.

---

5. That is why in many English and American publications of the late 19th and early 20th centuries it is spelled "Shakspere." The quite orthodox British academic society established in 1873 was called the New Shakspere Society. Those responsible for it specifically explained that to their mind the Great Bard knew what he was doing when he signed his name as Shakspere.

Then he suffered financial difficulties and the town wardens excluded John Shakspere from their list, as he was skipping the meetings of the city council. He was illiterate, and instead of his signature he would mark documents either with a cross or the image of a compass — which was the gloves maker's tool. In 1557 he married Mary Arden; they had eight children, five of whom survived.

We have nothing definite about William Shakspere's elementary education. There was one school in town, a city-sponsored grammar school, but the lists of pupils have not survived. Since his biographers cannot conceive that perhaps he never set foot in any school at all, it has been commonly assumed that he attended this school for a number of years. We have nothing else to go by. According to a legend that was put to paper late in the 17th century, John Shakspere, finding himself in financial difficulties, took his son out of school at an early age so that he could help him in his business. Looking ahead we shall note that William Shakspere, neither in his youth nor later on, attended any university or any other institution of learning. (This is not a supposition, but an established fact, for the lists of students are extant). It is not easy for Stratfordians to explain where he could have acquired such fundamental knowledge in history, law, classical and modern languages and literature — for in Stratford at the time there were no books other than the Bible, and there were no public libraries in the whole country. Even the assumption that he attended elementary school, for some time, does not change the picture very much — it was a one-room schoolhouse, and one teacher had to cope with all the children.

We do not know for certain how Shakspere spent his time during his early years. Rumor has it that he was attracted to the arts. When, as his father's apprentice, he was assigned to cut the throat of a calf, he was wont to pronounce solemn speeches. The modern Shakespeare biographer S. Schoenbaum calls this legend naïve and even ridiculous,[6] but it would appear natural if the Bard's early fans (in the second part of the 17th century) first attempted to learn from the folks of Stratford something about the background of their long-deceased countryman, who was becoming more and more famous.

In November of 1582, William Shakspere received the Church's permission to marry Anne Hathaway, of the village of Shottery, near Stratford; and he inherited some property. The bride was eight years senior to her eighteen-year-old husband; some six months after the marriage they baptized their first daughter, Susanna. In February of 1585, Anne bore twins — a daughter, Judith, and a son, Hamnet. 1586 to 1594 (some biographers say 1592, but they are relying on undocumented evidence) are counted as so-called lost years. No documents, no notes of any kind have been found for that period — yet traditional biographers say that was the very period during which an uneducated apprentice from a small provincial town moulted into a highly sophisticated and erudite poet and a genius dramatist.

---

6. A glove maker would not have been engaged in cattle slaughtering.

Many attempts have been made to fill in those lost years, that vexing vacuum, with legends and lore. How did he wind up in London? They say that he was very fond of the local hard ale and even took a wager with his neighbors from Bedford. (Late in the 18$^{th}$ and early in the 19$^{th}$ centuries, local "guides" would show tourists a wild apple tree, under which he supposedly fell asleep, unable to walk home, after one such bout.) For a long time Shakespeare's biographies included a tale that the young Stratfordian mixed with bad company, was poaching in Sir Thomas Lucy's park, was found guilty of deer slaughtering, was whipped, and fled to London. Now it has been established that Sir Thomas Lucy had no parks in the vicinity; so all this intriguing story comes unraveled, though some biographers think "there is still something in it." Some have suggested that Shakespeare (i.e. Shakspere), already the head of a family, worked as an assistant to a local lawyer, served as a soldier in the Netherlands, or even was a schoolteacher. No confirmation of these events has ever been found; neither for the rumor that he got his start in London by looking after noblemen's horses left at the theater during the performance. Probably he went to London with one of the actors' troupes that had visited his town around 1586-1587. At the time, many such troupes roamed England; they were under the patronage of one lord or other (otherwise they would be considered tramps), their cast often changed, they broke up or merged, and chose new patrons. Some think that the young Stratfordian could have joined the troupe "The Queen's Men" that played an important role in the theater of the time (it was dissolved soon after 1588, when the leading actor, Richard Tarlton, died). But he may have started with the troupe "The Earl of Pembroke's Servants" as well.

What Shakspere was doing during his first years in London, and with whom, we do not know; but in 1594, he became a member of a newly established troupe, "The Lord Chamberlain's Servants," and probably he was a shareholder.

Now is a good time to note that the name of William Shakespeare (the spear-shaker) first appeared in 1593, under the author's dedication to the Earl of Southampton in the mythological poem "Venus and Adonis," which the writer called "the first heir of my invention." Under the same name and dedicated to the same person, another poem, "The Rape of Lucrece," was published the following year. We shall speak about these poems and dedications later on, when we consider certain literary details pertaining to Shakespeare.

Shakspere left his family in Stratford when he moved to London. However, he often visited his home town, where he conducted some business, purchased houses and land, practiced money-lending and prosecuted debtors.

In 1596, a certain William Wayte, the stepson of Judge Gardiner, sued William Shakspere, Francis Langley and two women on the grounds that he had been threatened with murder. Nothing is known about the women, but Francis Langley was the owner of the "Swan" theater and had been in a feud with Gardiner. Thus we learn that Shakspere had dealings with the owner of the "Swan," and supported him in his affairs.

In August of 1596, "Hamnet, filius (the son of) William Shakspere," died in Stratford, according to the parish register.

In October of 1596, Shakspere's father John received permission to have a family coat of arms drawn up (the son could not seek the privilege while his father was alive; but William certainly worked to obtain it with the help of his London acquaintances). The extant sketch of the coat of arms, made by a clerk at the college of heralds, contains the motto: "Non sanz droict" (Not without right). But, curiously, another version on the same page has a comma, which radically alters the motto's meaning: "Non, sanz droict" (No, without right).[7]

Documents show that in May of 1597, Shakspere bought the second largest house in Stratford, the so called New Place, for 60 pounds sterling; that probably was not the whole sum.

In November of 1597, tax collectors in the London borough of Bishopsgate listed Shakspere among those who had failed to pay the property tax (probably he left the rented flat without paying).

On January 24, A. Sturley of Stratford sent to his fellow citizen Richard Quiney, residing in London, a letter (which has survived) containing Quiney's father's offer to Shakspere for a deal on tithe lands. In October of 1598, Quiney, who was in London on behalf of the Stratford corporation, wrote a letter to Shakspere asking to borrow 30 pounds sterling, with two persons vouchsafing for him. The letter was not sent; probably they discussed it in person, for the same day Quiney wrote to Stratford that Shakspere had promised to provide the requested sum. On November 4, Sturley expressed satisfaction "that our countryman Mr. Wm. Shak. would procure us money . . . I pray let not go that occasion if it may sort to any indifferent conditions."

In February of 1598, due to a bad harvest, the authorities restricted the quantity of grain and malt that could be stored at each house for making beer. When the townsfolk of Stratford were checked, Shakspere turned out to have 10 quarts (80 bushels, or about 3,000 liters) of malt, which was quite a sizable amount.

In October of 1598, Shakspere was again among those who did not pay the tax, and his arrears were not cleared in 1600.

In 1599, William Shakspere, as a shareholder, took part in the construction of the Globe Theater. His share was ten per cent.

1600. In his will, Thomas Whittington, who once was a shepherd with Shakspere's wife's father, asks his executors to take her debt of 40 shillings and donate it to the poor of the city. Presumably she had borrowed the money when her husband was away and then failed to return it in due course.

In September, 1601, his father, John Shakspere, died.

---

7. Ben Jonson in his play "Every man Out of His Humor" scorned Shakspere under the name of Sogligardo, who bought himself a coat of arms with an image of a headless Boar. His pal suggests a motto to go with it: "Not Without Mustard."

In May of 1602, Shakspere purchased a parcel of land near Stratford from the moneylenders Combes. Both Combes, the uncle and the nephew, signed the deed, but Shakspere's signature is absent.

During 1602-1603 he bought and rented some premises in Stratford near New Place.

May of 1603. Soon after the new monarch, James I, ascended to the throne, the actors' troupe "The Chamberlain's Servants" became the "King's Men." The troupe received the king's patent giving them the right "to freely use their skill in presenting comedies, tragedies, chronicles, interludes, moralities, pastorals, dramas etc." Listed among the eight members of the troupe was "Wilm Shakespeare."[8] He was also among the actors of the troupe who, in March of the next year, each received four yards of red worsted cloth in order to make livery for the occasion of the new monarch's gala entry into the capital.

June 1604. Shakspere sued his neighbor, the druggist Philip Rogers, for debt. In the spring, Shakspere had sold him 20 bushels of malt, and on June 25 lent him two shillings. Altogether Roger's debt comprised a bit more than two pounds sterling, of which the druggist managed to give back six shillings. He still owed 35 shillings and 10 pence. Via his attorney, Shakspere demanded payment of 35 shillings 10 pence plus 10 shillings for expenses and loss. The outcome of the suit is not known, for such minor cases were handled by the bailiff.

June 1605. Shakspere bought from a Ralf Hubaud the right to levy half of the "ten per cent tax on grain, hay and thatch" (the church tithe) from those who rented former monastery lands in three nearby villages and also half of the small tithe from the whole of Stratford's parish. He paid a very large sum of 440 pounds sterling for the right. Levying taxes from farmers in the vicinity was certainly not an easy job, but, as modern Shakespeareans have calculated, was a rather lucrative business.

In June 1607, the elder daughter, Susanna, married Doctor Hall. His brother Edmund died.

1608. The granddaughter was baptized; his mother, Mary Shaxpere, died.

In August of 1608, Shakspere became a shareholder in the Blackfriars Theater, along with six other members of the troupe.

Between August of 1608 and June 1609, Shakspere sues another of his fellow townsmen, John Addenbrooke, for the debt of 6 pounds sterling, plus 1 pound sterling and 5 shillings for expenses and losses. Addenbrooke was detained, but he had no money and was bailed out by blacksmith Thomas Hornby. Addenbrooke apparently fled from Stratford, and Shakspere went on to sue the hapless blacksmith. The court proceedings were dragged out for a long time; the jury held several sessions, a number of decisions were taken, and the suitor stubbornly demanded payment of the debt plus losses and expenses. Schoenbaum notes: "His persistence may strike moderns as

---

8. Perhaps the clerk, who wrote the patent, had encountered the name on the title pages of some poems and plays that were already published.

heartless, but the course Shakespeare followed was normal in an age without credit cards, overdrafts and collection agencies."[9] (Actually, it is not clear that things have changed much.)

1611. Along with two others in the tithe-collecting business, he was engaged in court proceedings having to do with arrears in the tithe payments by other tax-farmers.

In May of 1612, he testified as a witness at the London court in Stephen Belott's suit against his father-in-law Chr. Mountjoy, a beauty-parlor owner and wig maker, for failure to pay the entire promised dowry. Shakspere had lodged with the barber from 1603 to 1607 and was present during the marriage negotiations while Belott was courting Mountjoy's daughter, but he could not recollect what and how much had been promised by the father to the bridegroom.

January of 1613. Stratford money-lender John Combe bequeathed to Shakspere 5 pounds sterling.

On March 10, Shakspere purchased in Blackfriars, London, a house for 140 pounds sterling and the next day, March 11, mortgaged it for 60 pounds to the former owner for a period of 18 months.

On March 31, 1613, Shakspere and his friend and partner Richard Burbadge received from the steward of Francis Manners, the Earl of Rutland (brother and heir to the late Roger, who had died the previous summer), at Belvoir Castle, 44 shillings in gold, each: "To Mr. Shakspeare about my Lord's impreso" and to Burbadge "for painting and making it." Some biographers assume that an *impresa (imprese)* is meant, a painted cardboard shield for a knights' tournament. (In March of 1616, Burbadge received another, similar, payment). Soon after that, Shakspere ceded his share in the actors' troupe to someone else, settled all his financial interests in London (no details are available) and moved back to Stratford for good.

1614. Shakspere's name is mentioned several times in documents having to do with the Combes family's attempts to illegally enclose some public land. Shakspere reached an agreement with his friends, the Combes, so that his interests would not be infringed; other members of the Stratford Corporation offered a resolute rebuff to the invaders and protected their pastures from enclosure.

May of 1615. Shakspere's name is listed with other owners of real estate in Blackfriars who applied to court in connection with some documents pertaining to certain premises and real estate lots.

February of 1616. His younger daughter Judith was married. She, like other members of the Shakspere family, was illiterate (she made a sign instead of her signature; that is documented).

On March 25, 1616, notary Francis Collins drew up (certainly based on Shakspere's words) a will, an amended version of one that had been made two months earlier — for "William Shackspeare, gent." We will look at that shortly.

---

9. Schoenbaum S. *William Shakespeare. A compact documentary Life.* NY. 1977.

On April 23, 1616, William Shakspere died in his native Stratford-on-Avon, at the age of 52, on his birthday. Two days later an entry in the parish register announced the burial of "Will Shakspere, gent." Not a single comment was made on this death in Stratford, London or anywhere else.

In 1622, in the Stratford church where William Shakspere was buried, a small wall monument was erected. Who ordered this monument and paid for it is unknown.

Now the reader is familiar with the list of authentic, documented facts about William Shakspere of Stratford. (There are also some insignificant facts relating to the household, which I have not included, and some others that mention his relatives and acquaintances.) Still, as it is, the list is rather impressive; we do not know half as much about many other Elizabethans. It has taken an army of researchers to piece this together over the years; no biographer can ignore these incontestable facts.

A reader may ask: "Where are the documented, authentic facts about Shakespeare's literary activity (i.e., William Shakspere from Stratford), about his relationships with other poets, writers, dramatists, publishers? Where are letters and diaries written either by him or his contemporaries, from which one could see that they had dealings with the great poet and dramatist who was born and died in Stratford, who was a member of a renowned actors' troupe, and was its shareholder?" The answer gives little comfort. There is no such documented evidence and there never has been any. As to certain controversial and peculiar details, mostly posthumous, on which the traditional Stratfordian cult and all other deductions are based, we shall touch upon them later, for they do merit some mention.

For the time being, let us go back to the uncontested, documented and proven facts listed above. If we did not already know whose biography they sketch, is there any chance that we could imagine they had anything to do with a great poet and playwright, an erudite master of language, the author of high tragedies and extravagantly sophisticated sonnets, the creator of "Hamlet," "Lear," "Macbeth," "Othello," "The Tempest," and "Timon of Athens"?

No, we could not.

Having carefully considered these facts, one most probably would assume that they were taken from the life of some mediocre entrepreneur, a shareholder in the London theater troupe, a tenacious businessman who by hook or by crook made himself a fortune. The man purchased buildings and land, bought the privilege of levying the tax on local farmers for their grain, hay and straw; he lent money (not without interest, but on certain conditions, which are described by his compatriot A. Sturley) and mercilessly prosecuted debtors and their guarantors, his own neighbors of modest means. We have seen several cases of such prosecution, but it is clear that most often the debtors paid their creditor on time, and so more cases did not reach the court. One may conclude that William Shakspere had a rather extensive "money-lending practice." The illiterate family, including his parents and his children, adds one more stroke to the portrait of the Stratford man who bought half the church tithe.

(This was characteristic of his social milieu: some 50% of merchants and craftsmen and 90% of their wives in England could not sign their names.) And lastly, William Shakspere's notorious will, found only in the middle of the 18^th century, confirms the picture painted by all the above-mentioned documents.

## THE LAST WILL OF THE LORD OF LANGUAGE? THE RIDDLE OF THE SIGNATURES

"T [estamentum] W [illel]mj Shackspeare [sic!]
. . . In the name of god Amen I William Shackspeare of Stratford upon Avon in the countie of Warr gent in perfect health & memorie god be praysed doe make & Ordayne this my last will & testament in manner & forme followeing. That is to saye first I Comend my Soule into the handes of god my Creator, hoping & assuredlie believing through thonelie merittes of Jesus Christe my Saviour to be made partaker of lyfe everlastinge, And my bodye to the Earth wherof yt ys made."

In a three-page document, the notary Frances Collins wrote down the following, the last will of a man concerned about the disposal of property left after his demise. (The will was found in 1747). Meticulously, taking account of interest to be paid, and the order of inheritance of the future generations, he allocated the money. The instruction on how his daughter Judith is to receive her share takes up a whole page.

"Item I Gyve & bequeath unto my daughter Judyth One Hundred & fyftie pounds of lawfull English money to be paied unto her in manner & forme followeing; That ys to saye, One hundred Poundes in discharge of her marriage porcion within one yeare after my deceas, with consideration after the rate of twoe shillings in the pound for soe long tyme as the same shalbe vnpaied unto her after my deceas, & the ffyftie poundes Residewe therof upon her Surrendring of, or giving of such sufficient securitie as the overseers of this my will shal like of to Surrender or graunte. All her estate & Right that shall discend or come unto her after my deceas or that shee nowe hath of in or to one Copiehold tenemente with thappurtenaunces lyeing & being in Stratford upon Avon aforesaied in the saied countie of Warr, being parcel or holden of the mannour of Rowington, unto my daughter Susanna Hall & her heires for ever. Item I Gyve & bequeath unto my saied daughter Judith One Hundred & ffyftie Poundes more if shee or Anie issue of her bodie be Lyvinge att thend of three Yeares next ensueing the date of this my will, during which tyme my executors to paie her consideration from my deceas according to the Rate aforesaied. And if she dye within the saied terme without issue of her bodye then my will ys & I doe gyve & bequeath One Hundred poundes therof of my Neece Elizabeth Hall & the ffiftie Poundes to sett fourth by my executors during the life of my Sister Johane Harte & the vse & profit thereof Cominge shalbe payed to my saied Sister Jone, & after her deceas the said L li [50 pounds] shall Remaine Amongst the children of my saied Sister Equallie to be devided Amongst them. But if my saied daughter Judith be lyving att thend of the saied three Years or anie yssue of her bodye, then my will ys & soe I devise & bequeath the saied Hundred & ffyftie pounds to be sett out by my executours & overseers for the best benrfit of her & her issue & the stock not to be paied unto her soe long as she shalbe marryed & covert Baron (by my executours & overseers) but my will ys that she shal have the consideration yearelie paied unto her during her life & after her deceas the saied stock and consideration yearelie paied to her children if she have Anie & if not to her executours or assignes she lyving the saied terme after my deceas. Provided that yf such husbond as she shall att thend of the saied three Yeares be marryed unto or attaine after doe sufficiente Assure unto her & thissue of her bodie landes Awnswereable to the porcion by this my will given unto her & to be adjudged soe by my executors & overseers then my will ys that the said CL li [150 pounds] shalbe paied to such husbond as shall make such assurance to his owne vse."

Then a list of household items is given, including tableware, small sums of money allocated to friends (among whom are his fellows from "The King's Men" Heminge, Condell and Burbadge, in order to buy them memorial rings).

"Item I gyve & bequeath unto my saied sister Jone XX li [20 pounds] & all my wearing Apparell to be paied & delivered within one yeare after my deceas. And I doe will devise unto her the house with thappurtennaunces in Stratford wherin she dwelleth for her natural life under the earlie Rent of 12 pence. Item I gyve & bequeath unto (her) the saied Elizabeth Hall All my plate (except my brod silver & gilt bole) that I now have att the date of this my will."

Most of his real estate and other property is bequeathed to daughter Susanna Hall, "for & during the terme of her natural life, & after her deceas to the first sonne of her bodie lawfullie yssueing & to heires Males of the bodie of the saied first Sonne lawfullie yssueing, & for defalt of such issue to the Second Sonne lawfullie yssueinge, & for daefalt of such heires to the third Sonne of the bodie of the saied Susanna lawfullie yssueing and the heirs Males of the bodie of the saied third sonne lawfullie yssueing. . . . " and so on till the seventh lawful male son and his descendants! Then he bequeathed to his wife "the second best bed with furniture," and "to my saied daughter Judith my broad silver gilt bole."

So much has been written about the oddities in this will — mostly about such queer details as "the second best bed" bequeathed to his wife or the name of a nephew that he forgot.

But what is most striking is the spiritual and intellectual poverty of the testator. From the grave, he still tries to control every penny of his wealth, down to the seventh lawful heir to his daughter and the descendants of those lawful heirs. He gives his daughter Judith only the interest from the capital, and the capital itself he orders to be placed for the greater profit of her progeny (unknown to him). He bids that her future husband should provide her with land in the same share that he left her etc. The coarse and restricted outlook is typical for a crass wheeler-dealer ambitious to rack up houses, barns and vacant land, interest and rent, all those shillings and "thappurtenaunces" avariciously acquired over the years; even death cannot tear him away from his riches.

No books are mentioned. Yet it is clear from the works of William Shakespeare, poet and dramatist, that there must have been a large collection of books in his house. Books, or at least most of them, were very costly in those days. And, if the man was really a writer, some of his own published works should have been in the house. No, William Shakspere from Stratford, having distributed all his property including cutlery and other trifles, never even mentioned the word "book" in his will. Neither is there any mention of manuscripts, which could have been sold for a good price. (London publishers at the time were after any line written or allegedly written by Shakespeare. Take, for example, the story of how his sonnets or "The Passionate Pilgrim" were published). And not a word is said about pictures or portraits.

All this certainly left such a puzzle for later biographers that some of them (and especially those writing biographical fiction) resort to tales of a mysterious trunk filled with papers that was allegedly taken from the house of the dying playwright by his literary or theater friends. There is nothing, of course, to substantiate such stories. Conjecture on the topic emerged as early as at the beginning of the 18th century when a John Roberts, who called himself "an itinerant actor," spread rumors about "two big trunks full of unsorted papers and manuscripts of the great man, that were in possession of some ignorant baker from Warwick (who had married a woman of Shakespeare's kin). The trunks were broken and their contents were negligently thrown away like some garbage from an attic . . . all of it was consumed during the fire."[10] However, none of Shakspere's descendants lived in Warwick at the end of the 17th century (the great fire connected with this story took place in 1694). Some seventy years later, after the death of the last descendant of William Shakspere, his granddaughter Elizabeth Barnard, rumors began to circulate about an "old legend" that she allegedly had taken away from Stratford many of her grandfather's papers.

At the end of the 18th century, another version of the legend appeared: one Williams, who bought the house from the Clopton family, allegedly found several baskets of papers which bore Shakespeare's name. (The Cloptons had bought the Stratford house, New Place, from Shakspere's heirs.). Of course, it was also said that the unwitting Mr. Williams burned all the papers.

Sometimes Shakespeare biographies suggest that "the library" may have been handed over to Shakspere's son-in-law John Hall even before the will was drawn up, which would account for why nothing is mentioned about it. There is no evidence to substantiate that notion or any of the other attempts that have been made to plausibly explain the absence of books in the house of a man who is credited with such

10. i.e. p.305-306.

accomplishments. No less strange is the fact that every member of Shakspere's family was illiterate. This agrees with the view of the non-Stratfordians — the will illustrates a house inhabited by illiterate people who had no books whatsoever.

William Shakspere's testament conforms to the authenticated biographical facts that have been collected over the centuries and allows us to get a sense of a man and his milieu, to hear his voice, to understand his way of life and his concerns. It is rather a simple world — no books, no sparks of intelligence; his greatest interests were money, litigation over it, and the acquisition of "properties." There is nothing enigmatic or shameful in that — many of his contemporaries lived such a life and shared the same concerns; but what does it have to do with great works of literature?

This is not just a boilerplate document enumerating how property is to be distributed. Whether the attorney wrote in his own words or he wrote it as dictated by the testator, the character and mindset of the latter are clearly reflected in the document. Comparing it to the wills of other writers of that era (for instance, John Donne or John Davies), in which the distribution of property also takes up a good deal of space, we can see how different was his sphere of reference, how different was his outlook on life. Even the will of his fellow actor Heminge (1630) is much more decent, in the style of presentation and in the substance as well: Heminge speaks about his books and specially mentions five pounds in order to purchase textbooks for his grandson.

Even the honest Stratford curate Joseph Greene, who found "the testament of the Great Bard" in the middle of the next century (1747), was shocked with his great discovery. He wrote to a friend: "The Legacies and Bequests therein are undoubtedly as he intended, but the manner of introducing them, appears to me so dull and irregular, so absolutely void of ye least particle of that Spirit which animated our great Poet; that it must lessen his Character as a Writer, to imagine ye least sentence of it his production." One can only agree with this worthy man, who surely had seen his share of wills.

It is often stated that Shakespeare was gravely ill when he was composing the will, and that his condition left an imprint on the document as a whole. It is not known what disease William Shakspere suffered from, but if one assumes that his intellectual capacities were already suffering the effects of a fatal illness, how could it be that this lengthy and detailed paper, prepared over the course of several months, contains not a thought, not a single phrase that calls to mind the Lord of Language (if he were the Great Bard)? Did the illness completely transform his personality, turning him into quite another person, erasing all links with his past? There is no sign that his mental abilities or his memory were significantly impaired, for he makes a very detailed list and enumerates his "properties" and "thappurtenaunces" down to the pounds, pence and interest on them. No, it is not likely that his personality was deformed by illness (either in January 1616, when it was composed, and at the end of March, when it was substantially amended); he was in good control of his thoughts, and those thoughts were focused on the same thing as always, as shown by impartial documents throughout his life — to increase and maintain his properties and capital.

Giving his opinion on this irreconcilable dichotomy between the authentic biographical data of William Shakspere of Stratford and what Shakespeare's works tell us about their author (especially after Greene found the will), the historian and editor of the best pre-revolutionary Russian-language Shakespeare collection Professor S. A. Vengerov said:

> Everyone who values Shakespeare for his brilliant ability to reproduce the feelings of his characters, like nobody else in world literature, is stunned by his deals, acquiring real estate not only for his personal use but taking the mortgaged and pawned property of others and his money-lending in general. . . How can one entertain the notion that while working on "Hamlet," while so eloquently expressing the world's grief and disillusionment, Shakespeare was meticulously and diligently pursuing the acquisition of more property? How can one combine in one's own imagination the pathetic grandeur of "Othello," "Measure for Measure," "Macbeth," and "Lear" with such base and vainglorious affairs as the purchasing of city tax licenses (the church tithe)? Obviously, we must not confound the image of the man Shakespeare, the businessman Shakespeare, and Shakespeare the artist. Obviously, Shakespeare the artist lived in an enchanted world of his own, lofty and unattainable, where he could not be reached by voices from the ground, where his artistic vision was free from the conditions of time and space."[11]

Those who consider the great William Shakespeare and Shakspere the Stratford purchaser of the church tithe to be one and the same person are assuming an inconsistency of personality that has never been seen in the history of culture. Vengerov doesn't touch on the subject of the illiterate family (maybe he did not have much information on Shakspere's daughters, at the time) and although he gently mentions "the money-lending," he doesn't say that such deals not infrequently ended up in litigation and sometimes with the debtor or his hapless neighbor being sent to jail. The obviously usurious nature of William Shakspere's financial affairs mars even the portrait of a sophisticated and calculating entrepreneur drawn by some Victorian biographers who asserted that Shakespeare was obliged to engage in less poetic business only in order to support his family and have ample opportunity to pursue his creative pursuits . . . the man who did not wish to have his works published and accept the lawful and well-earned revenues was not averse to dealing in usury and suing his struggling neighbors!

Shakspere's money lending, his illiterate family, his purchase of the church tithe and the dreadful will are such astonishing discoveries that many biographers just do not dare to face up to them. Attempts have been made to question whether it was

---

11. Vengerov S.A. "William Shakespeare. A sketch." In: *The Complete collection of Shakespeare's works.* Vol. 5. St. Petersbourg. Ed. by Brokgauz and Ephron, 1904. pp. 460,464 (in Russian).

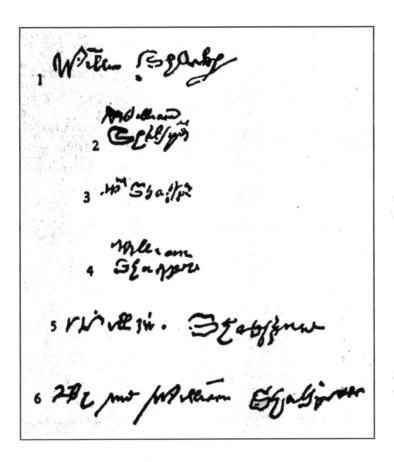

Six signatures by Shakespeare:
1. As a witness testifying in Belott's suit. 1612.
2. On the deed for the purchase of the house. 1613.
3. On the mortgage paper for the same house. 1613.
4. On the first page of his will.
5. On the second page of the will.
6. On the third page of the will.

usury, since there is no mention of the interest the debtor was to pay for the money borrowed. But the sum mentioned in the promissory note was not the amount that had been lent but the amount the debtor was to pay back, inclusive of interest. It appears that Shakspere, out of his good heart, lent money (or malt) to his neighbors and acquaintances, and when they were unable to settle their debt in time, he was obliged to sue them in court and even put them in jail. Sometimes such deals, which ended in serious trouble for the debtors, were presented as practically philanthropic actions for the sake of art. Literary and art critic Anikst tried to explain away the cruel prosecution of John Addenbrooke and his hapless supporter the blacksmith Thomas Hornby by pointing out that in those years (1608-1609) the troupe of the "King's Men" was in the process of acquiring a new theater house, so that perhaps Shakspere needed money for that.[12]

No matter how one explains these facts, they cannot be reconciled with the identity of the playwright who gave us "The Merchant of Venice" and "Timon of Athens," wherein he flagellates usurers with wrath and disdain.

Are we to believe that the great writer — unlike most of his contemporary poets and playwrights — left no manuscripts, not even a scrap of paper, written in his own hand? Centuries of hunting have turned up only six signatures for the Stratfordian in the archives, and three of them are in his will. These six signatures — the only words presumed to have been written by the Great Bard — have been discussed many times, and handwriting analysis has been done, but there is no consensus. The reader can take a look for himself at the facsimile rendition of these signatures. They were found on the following documents:

1. On his testimony in Belott's suit to his father in law, the lady's wigmaker Mr. Mountjoy, on May 11, 1612, (found in 1910).
2. On the purchase document for the acquisition of the house in Blackfriars on March 10, 1613.
3. On the mortgage bill for the same house on March 11, 1613.
4. On the first page of his will, 1616.
5. On the second page of his will, 1616.
6. On the third page of his will, 1616.

It is clear to the naked eye that the signatures differ markedly; they exhibit different spellings, and none of them matches fully the name of the Great Bard — Shakespeare. There are some strange abbreviations: Wilm Shaksp, William Shakspe, Wm Shaksper, though such abbreviations were not customary when signing documents. The signatures under the will are also spelt differently: on each page — William Shakspere, Willim Shakspere, and William Shakspeare. Only the last one is relatively close to the literary name that was rather widely known by that time

12. Anikst A.A. *Shakespeare.* Moscow, 1964, p. 274. (In Russian.)

(although it lacks the letter *e* after the *k*). Why would he sign his name differently every time, even in the same document? Why did not he use the "noble" name Shakespeare that was current in literature and associated with the spear in the coat of arms granted to his family?

Furthermore, the name of the signatory is written in a shaky, rough handwriting. All the experts agree, one way or another, that the penmanship displayed in "Shakespeare's autographs" is exceedingly strange for a person who is supposed to have written thousands and thousands of pages during his lifetime. This is the writing of a man who is simply not used to handling a pen.

Some unconvincing explanations have been proposed. H. Gibson points out that it was not easy to signa document with a goose quill, using the thick ink in use at the time. But other writers and poets managed to do it. The renowned scholar, text expert and bibliographer W. W. Gregg went as far as to verify that by examining the manuscripts and signatures of 70 prose writers and playwrights and 42 poets for the period of 1550-1650.

Most of Shakespeare's biographers are inclined to blame the poor writing on illness. George Bernard Shaw assumed, in his day, that Shakespeare suffered from spasms in the hands. Perhaps he suffered from this ailment throughout the latter years of his life (though he was actively practicing his usual commercial business)?

Most non-Strafordians see these signatures as unsurprising, coming from Shakspere of Stratford. He was illiterate and at best could scrawl his name on documents. Some non-Stratfordians (for instance, F. Shipoulinsky) have focused especially on the dot, which is seen best under the signature from his testimony in the Belott vs Mountjoy case. They think it is the real "signature" of Shakspere: that is how an illiterate person "put his hand" to a document; then a scribe would add the (sometimes abbreviated) spelling of his name.

For my part, I think that the last page of the will deserves the most attention. For, here we have nearly a phrase: "by me William Shakspeare." Everyone who has examined this signature can see (and readers of this book can, too) that the first three words are written in a normal, clear handwriting, but the last one — the family name — is in nearly the same ragged letters as on the second page of the will. Why would there be such a difference in one line of text, if it was written at the same time by the same person? Stratfordians again invoke illness: the poor man pulled himself together for a brief moment, and he managed to jot down the first words. By then he was exhausted and could barely scrawl the last word. That seems far-fetched; it is quite apparent that the line at the end of the will was not written by one person. The first three words could have been written by Collins or his clerk; but they knew that Shakspere could manage his family name, more or less, so they had him do it. On the previous page he had attempted to render his first name, in the same contorted letters, and they may have decided to handle it otherwise on the last page.

In any case, these are the only writing samples we have from William Shakspere, the only evidence that he ever held a quill in his hand, and they still have biographers guessing. Some Stratfordians, however, have no doubt about these signatures and even think it possible to go on to identify the provenance of Elizabethan manuscripts on this basis. For instance, the manuscript of the play "Thomas More," which was barred from publication by a censor and kept in the archives for two and a half centuries (it was found only in 1844), is written in six different handwritings; some scholars think three pages are written in "Shakespeare's hand." On what grounds? The handwriting is allegedly similar to that of "Shakespeare's signatures" (all six of them?). For these scholars, on those three pages of "Thomas More" the orthography shows an even clearer "resemblance" to the spellings in the Great Bard's works. Well, one can understand the ardent desire of Shakespeare's fans to find at least one manuscript by the great playwright, but stretching scholarly methods so implausibly is no way to arrive at a convincing identification.

The six William Shakspere autographs are very important pieces of concrete evidence. They correlate well with other facts pertaining to the Stratfordian; they amend and confirm them, and they help us to understand the real nature of the shrewd shareholder in the London actors' troupe.

## A CLOSE FRIEND OF THE EARL OF SOUTHAMPTON

Having gradually dug up these authentic documents from the life of William Shakspere of Stratford, we find that it is not at all clear what this might have to do with literature, creative work, and poetry. So far, there is nothing to suggest that the man was a writer, playwright, or poet; moreover, some facts even seem to rule out such a possibility (his lack of education, illiterate family, crude will, lack of books and manuscripts, and strange autographs). Maybe there is something in the appearance of Shakespeare's works, in his contemporaries' response to them, in their letters and diaries, that contains some authentic indication as to the identity of the Great Bard?

Let's fill in some background on the literary and theater life of the age. As we already know, Shakespeare's name first appeared in print in 1593, when printer Richard Field registered and published in quarto a select poem on the theme taken from "Metamorphoses," by Ovid, about the romantic difficulties of the goddess Venus, who had fallen passionately in love with a chaste young man, Adonis. The poem was entitled "Venus and Adonis"; the book was very neat, with almost no misprints or other printing flaws, on excellent paper. The name of the author was not featured on the title page, but there was a Latin epigraph, also from Ovid: "Vilia miretur vulgus; milhi flavus Apollo / Pocula Castalia plena ministret aqua" (Let base conceited wits admire vile things; fair Phoebus lead me to the Muses springs). The author's name appears only in the dedication of the book to the Earl of Southampton:

To the right honourable Henry Wriothesley,
Earl of Southampton, and baron of Titchfield.

Right Honorable,
 I know not how I shall offend in dedicating my unpolished lines to your
Lordship, nor how the world will censure me for choosing so strong a prop to
support so weak a burden: only, if your honour seem but pleased, I account myself
highly praised, and vow to take advantage of all idle hours, till I have honour'd you
with some graver labour. But if the first heir of my invention prove deform'd, I shall
be sorry it had so noble a godfather; and never after ear so barren a land, for fear it
yield me still so bad a harvest. I leave it to your honourable survey, and your honour
to your heart's content; which I wish may always answer your own wish, and the
world's hopeful expectation.
 Your Honour's in all duty,
 William Shakespeare.

The poem at once attracted attention both by its erotic theme, with picturesque
images of fleshly temptations (though formally it asserted the preeminence of sublime
platonic love) and by the high poetic mastery of the author; it was reprinted several
times in the ensuing years. But modern Shakespeareans are most of all drawn to the
book because it is the first in which the name of the Shake-speare appeared. First, it
appears that William Shakspere, who had not been heard of after his disappearance
from Stratford, turned up in London, where he found a patron in the person of one of
the most influential representatives of the English aristocracy — the Earl of
Southampton. Second, nearly every biographer is impressed with the peculiar form of
the dedication: one does not feel the enormous social distance between the author and
the person he addresses. The tone of the dedication is deferential, even elaborately
courteous, but the author speaks to the powerful lord without giving up his dignity;
his courtesy and civility never verge on the servility or fawning so typical of the
addresses of his contemporary writers to their high patrons.
 The next spring, the same Field published the second Shakespeare poem, "The
Rape of Lucrece," wherein the poet relates how the voluptuous and wild King
Tarquinius raped the proud and virtuous Roman lady, who could not live with the
disgrace and took her own life. The new poem demonstrates, even more than the first,
that the author was perfectly conversant with both Latin and English sources: Ovid,
Livy, Chaucer etc. It was also reprinted several times, though not so often as "Venus
and Adonis." Again, the author's name appeared only in the dedication, addressed to
the same person, the Earl of Southampton:

 The love I dedicate to your Lordship is without end; whereof this pamphlet,
 without beginning, is but a superfluous moiety. The warrant I have of your honourable
 disposition, not the worth of my untutor'd lines, makes it assured of acceptance. What I
 have done is yours; what I have to do is yours; being part in all I have, devoted yours.

Were my worth greater, my duty would show greater, meantime, as it is, it is bound to your Lordship, to whom I wish long life, still lengthened with all happiness.
>    Your Lordship's in all duty,
>    William Shakespeare.

Here again, the dedication shows no self-abasement or servility; it expresses personal warmth for the earl — but now he feels freer to express his feelings: love, respect, even friendship. Modesty is conveyed in delicate and carefully chosen genteel turns of phrase that do not infringe the poet's self-respect. All this looks like someone younger (but equal) addressing his senior, rather than a person of humble station addressing someone incomparably higher on the social ladder — which was rigidly defined at the time.[13]

All the theories Shakespeareans like to promote about the close (and extraordinary, for those days) friendship between the actor/playwright William Shakespeare (i.e., Shakspere from Stratford) and the noble Earl of Southampton are based on these two consecutive dedications alone. On this basis the biographers then conclude that the former provincial glove-maker's apprentice joined a "circle of young and exceptionally well-educated aristocrats," from whom he could acquire knowledge of the refined culture of the Renaissance that had made its way to England from the continent; for, signs of such knowledge are clearly visible throughout the Bard's work. Much has been written about the long sought "circle," about the phenomenon of "the Bard's first entry into culture"; many scholars have sought to find evidence of that circle and Shakespeare's relationship to it, and of course they began their research with that eminent figure known as Southampton.

Henry Wriothesley, the 3<sup>rd</sup> Earl of Southampton (1573-1624), was born while his father, a staunch catholic, was in jail. The boy inherited the title of Earl at the age of eight, after his elder brother and then his father died. Like other sons of English peers who lost their fathers at an early age, he was brought up and educated under the strict surveillance of Lord Treasurer William Cecil (Lord Burghley), subsequently presented by Shakespeare in the image of Polonius in "Hamlet." He studied for four years at Cambridge, in St. John's College, and in 1589 he became a Master of Arts. As a 13-year-old boy, he had delighted his tutor with an unexpectedly mature Latin composition on the theme, "All men are spurred to the pursuit of virtue by the hope of reward." At the age of seventeen he was presented at the court, was noticed by the queen and made friends with the nobleman who was most influential and on closest terms with the queen — the Earl of Essex (who had been also under the tutelage of Lord Burghley). Southampton was true to Essex through all the vicissitudes of his life, to the very end.

Southampton patronized scholars and poets. His teacher in Italian was John Florio, the author of the English–Italian dictionary "A World of Words," which was

---

13. Some Shakespeareans (particularly A.L Rowse) have noted that the dedications were written in the language that was current among the most venerable lords.

dedicated to Southampton and his young friend (three years his junior), the Earl of Rutland — also raised by Lord Burghley. This friendship lasted until Essex's demise, but they were closest in the 1590s, according to extant letters. The young earls were fond of learning and poetry and were so devoted to the theater that it amazed even Elizabethans.

Many poets dedicated their works to Southampton, although none of the other dedications was written as though they were near equals. These two dedications to Southampton are also unique in that Shakespeare never again dedicated his works to any one.

Thus it is possible to discern who was in that circle of exceptional young aristocrats: Essex, Southampton and Rutland. Now, we only have to find some evidence of Shakespeare there, and the tenor of the two dedications seems to promise success. Many Shakespeare researchers still hope to discover Shakespeare at the earl's palace, conversing with his high-ranking host and his enlightened guests, the friends and servants of nearly all nine Muses. I shall quote some passages from the works of our Shakespeare scholars.

In M. M. Morozov's book *Shakespeare* (1947):

> We have every reason to assume that Shakespeare at the beginning of his creative path had access to the palace of the Earl of Southampton, to whom he dedicated two of his poems, "Venus and Adonis" and "Lucrece." He probably visited other aristocratic homes. Many young men among the high English aristocracy frequented theaters (Queen Elizabeth even reprimanded two young nobles who spent all their time at the theater and neglected their duties at the court.)[14] These nobles certainly invited actors to come to their houses and those came as humble visitors there. While visiting, Shakespeare could observe the life of aristocracy, listen to the music, and admire the pictures — in a word, he could imbibe the Renaissance culture that had come there from Italy.[15]

In a biographical sketch by Smirnov (1957), we read:

> About the same time (1592) Shakespeare established close relations with a circle of young aristocrats, theater goers, namely with the Earl of Southampton . . .[16]

In Anikst's book *Shakespeare* (1964), we read:

---

14. Certainly, the earls of Southampton and Rutland are meant, though there is no evidence that the Queen herself reprimanded the two lords for their excessive love for the theater.

15. Morozov M.M. *Shakespeare*. Moscow, 1947, pp. 232-233. (In Russian.)

16. Smirnov A.A. "A Biography Sketch." In: *Shakespeare. Complete Works.* Vol.1 Moscow, 1957. p. 32 (in Russian).

As we know, Shakespeare was protected from Greene's sneers by the young Earl of Southampton. Shakespeare visited him in his palace and took part in the literary diversions of the circle gathered there. They also were fond of poetry . . .[17]

The tentative tone becomes more and more assertive and takes on a note of certainty.

The two dedications are invaluable; maybe there is some other written evidence of Shakespeare's close relations with Southampton, with his milieu? No. There is not a single mention in the earl's letters or documents, or those of people who were close to him, of the actor and playwright William Shakespeare (or Shakspere) of Stratford, though such a low-born person, whose company we are told eminent aristocrats found interesting, could not but attract attention.

G. P. V. Akrigg, author of the book *Shakespeare and the Earl of Southampton*,[18] for many years studied in archives, libraries, and private collections all the documents, letters and diaries we know of that have at least something to do with the Earl of Southampton. Akrigg provided a detailed biography of the earl, the notorious story of his participation in Essex's mutiny that nearly cost him his head, and related other prominent and even trivial events of his life. Akrigg went into detail about Southampton's close friendship with the other two earls, Essex and Rutland, late in the 16th century: how they traveled together, and participated in the Ireland campaign, about their family ties and shared literary and theater interests. The story is substantiated with thorough documentary material.

As to the Earl of Southampton's relations with the actor, poet and playwright William Shakespeare (Shakspere) of Stratford, the scholar did not find anything new to mention in his rather voluminous book; he could find no trace of the man, though he had been looking for him everywhere. Thus, he had to restrict himself to a quotation of the above-mentioned dedications to "Venus and Adonis" and "Lucrece," which inspired Shakespeare scholars to take an interest in the Earl of Southampton in the first place, and to conjectures about the earl's probable links with some of Shakespeare's plays and sonnets.

There has been plenty of conjecture and a great deal of fiction generated along those lines. Writers and screenwriters have had a field day depicting the actor (so recently just a vagabond) Shakespeare wining and dining at the same table as his noble young friends, sleeping in the earl's bed and speaking to his host almost with condescension. Authors of fiction have the right to interpret historical topics and personalities as they see fit, but readers and spectators also have the right to know how preposterous such notions are. The relationship between Southampton and Shakespeare remains enigmatic, to this day. Shakespeare scholars have not yet found Shakespeare near Southampton, though his absence seems hard to believe.

---

17. Anikst A.A. *Shakespeare*. Moscow, 1964, p.91 (In Russian.)
18. Akrigg G. *Shakespeare and the Earl of Southampton*. L. 1968.

## A Crow In Someone Else's Feathers

As mentioned, in his book Anikst put forth the premise that the Earl of Southampton protected Shakespeare from Greene's assaults. The episode pertaining to the name of writer Robert Greene can be found in all of Shakespeare's biographies and, though it remains unclear and even ambiguous, it is very important for, in many biographies, it is connected with the beginning of Shakespeare's creative activity. What is the story about?

In August of 1592, that is, about one year before William Shakespeare's name appeared in print, a pamphlet was published in London by Robert Greene, one of the first professional writers and dramatists in England. Because Greene had died shortly before, the book was prepared for publishing by another writer and playwright, Henry Chettle (at least, that is what Chettle tells us).

Robert Greene was one of the so-called "university wits" — offspring of the middle class, who had come from the provinces and been educated at Cambridge and Oxford. After moving to London, they began earning their living by writing pamphlets for book publishers and plays for actors' troupes. Upon graduating, Greene managed to travel abroad where, as he wrote later, he witnessed "such atrocities that one is averse to mention." Still, he not only witnessed but took part in them himself. After his return he led a wild life, then repented, earned a Master of Arts degree and started a family. Then he lost his way again, took up with bad company, squandered his wife's dowry, abandoned her and their child, and took to drinking. He made some money here and there by writing love and adventure novels and pamphlets decrying whatever was the evil of the day — mostly about thieves and tramps. He also composed plays and managed to sell the same piece to several troupes. After a major bout of drinking, Greene fell ill and became bedridden. Dying in utter misery, he asked the family of the cobbler that had given him bed and board in London to place a laurel wreath on his head in the coffin. They complied.

It was then that his composition on repentance was published: "Greene's Groats-worth of witte, bought with a million of Repentance. Describing the follie of youth, the falshood of make-shifte flatterers, the miserie of the negligent, and mischiefes of deceiving Courtezans. Written before his death and published at his dyeing request." In this piece Greene deeply repents his choice of a life of vice, that he kept company with tramps, wrote plays for public theaters, and left his family. Greene advises readers how to save their souls, and then addresses his "fellow scholars about this city"— without naming names, but from certain hints one may understand that he means Christopher Marlowe and (probably) Thomas Nashe and George Peele. Greene asks them to change their minds, not to believe "those puppets (I mean) that spake from our mouth, those antics garnished in our colours." Then follows a passage that is quoted in all Shakespeare's biographies, discussed endlessly, and still retains its nearly impenetrable mystery.

Yes, trust them not: for there is an upstart Crow, beautified with our feathers, that with his *Tygers hart wrapt in a Players hyde*, supposes he is as well able to bombast out a blanke verse as the best of you: and being an absolute *Johannes fac totum*, is in his own conceit the onely Shake-scene in a countrey. O that I might intreat your rare wits to be imploied in more profitable courses: and let those Apes imitate your past excellence, and never more acquaint them with your admired inventions. I know the best husband of you will never prove an Usurer . . .

The overwhelming majority of Shakespeareans consider this invective to be aimed at Shakespeare. Whom else, they argue, could Greene be calling a "shake-scene"? Besides, "tiger's heart wrapt in a player's hyde" is a quotation from the 3$^{rd}$ part of "Henry VI," with only one word changed: "tiger's heart wrapt in a woman's hyde." Both puns seem to be aimed at Shakespeare.

However, this was 1592. How could Greene write that Shakespeare imagined himself to be the only shake-scene, at a time when not a single Shakespeare line had been published? There is no solid evidence that any of Shakespeare's plays had been staged by the time. How about "Titus Andronicus"? That was presented by the Earl of Sussex's troupe only on January 24, 1594, in the Rose Theater, and the theater entrepreneur Philip Henslowe marked it in his famous diary as "a new one." That corresponds with the fact that it was entered into the Stationers' Register on February 6, 1594. "A Comedy of Errors"? There is no information to suggest that it was staged before December 28, 1594.

There remains only "Henry VI," especially as Greene seems to quote a line from it. Henslowe's diary notes that Lord Strange's troupe played "Harey the VI" (Henslowe's spelling) fourteen times from March to June of 1592, but what play and whose was it? No information is available about any relationship between Shakespeare and this troupe, either. Neither the lists of players nor the letters of actor Alleyn feature the name at all. Maybe the actors presented the play that was printed in 1594 under the title "The First part of the Contention betwixt the two famous Houses of York and Lancaster . . . ," or its sequel, entitled "The true Tragedie of Richard, Duke of York . . . " In contents they correspond to the 2$^{nd}$ and 3$^{rd}$ parts of Shakespeare's "Henry VI," published only in 1623; still, the texts differ greatly. The question of authorship for the predecessors of those two plays has a longstanding history in Shakespeare discussions and we shall touch upon it later; but at the time, there was no basis whatsoever for calling Shakespeare a "shake-scene of the English theater."

What did Greene mean when he spoke of a "crow, beautified with our feathers"? Greene had used the image of that bird with a gift for imitation (but not for creativity), borrowed from such classical writers as Aesop, Martial, and Macrobius, on an earlier occasion. Addressing Alleyn, Greene wrote, in his "Francesco's Fortunes": "Why, Roscius, art thou proud with Esop's crow, being pranked with the glory of other's feathers? Of thyself thou canst say nothing . . . " Many researchers assume that in his posthumous "Groats-worth of witte," Greene used the image of an "upstart crow" in the sense of an actor (i.e. "a clown painted with our colours") trying to vie with the "university wits" in composing pompous blank verse, trying to horn in on their business!

However, Horace offers another image (which was also certainly familiar to Greene) of a crow who was stealing someone else's glory but was caught at it. Another Elizabethan, Richard Brathwaite, features sly crows who steal "selected flowers from others' wits." Thus, starting with E. Malone, a number of scholars have understood Greene's invective to mean that the dying dramatist was accusing Shakespeare of plagiarism. This hypothesis is usually bolstered by an assumption that the young Shakespeare lifted passages from someone else's plays on historical themes, modifying the texts here and there, and that Robert Greene could have been the real author of some of these appropriated plays. During the 19$^{th}$ century many people shared that opinion, but nowadays Shakespeare scholars are much more careful in how they treat the Great Bard's reputation, and such a simplified approach to the famous Greene image is thought to be obsolete.

Finally, it may be that Greene meant to say that the "odious crow" is only decorated with someone else's feathers, that this "clown" is not, in reality, a writer or a dramatist at all, but is a decoy. Did Greene actually know this "Crow"? We cannot rule out the possibility that the charge was based on hearsay — or even that the allegation was introduced into the book by Chettle, who published the book.

Greene uses a tone of censure and vilification when he speaks about the "crow." The expression "Johannes (John) Factotum" denotes a meddler, errand-boy, a servant entrusted with confidential errands, sometimes a pimp. This has been inaccurately rendered in Russian as analogous to "Jack of all trades," but that term fails to suggest the odious nature of the man's business and the scorn expressed by the writer.

That's not all. Several months later, at the very end of 1592, Henry Chettle published his work "Kind-Heart's Dream," and in the foreword to it he refuted accusations that it was he who had added the invectives against the three writers to Greene's book. Chettle said that one or two of them found Greene's composition insulting, "and because on the dead they cannot be avenged, they willfully forge in their conceits a living author" (i.e. Chettle). Chettle then explains that the manuscript was practically illegible and he had had to transcribe it, but did not add a single word, "not mine nor Master Nashe's, as some unjustly have affirmed"; he even had to delete some of strongest expressions. "Everybody knows full well that working in the publishing business I have always prevented fierce assaults on scholars."

According to Chettle, he hadn't even known the people who considered themselves insulted (he apparently met them soon enough). About one of them (most probably Marlowe), Chettle commented that he would have been no worse off for the lack of such an acquaintance. Marlowe was well known for his hot temper. He takes a different attitude toward the second person (Shakespeare, some think). Chettle regrets that he had not made all the necessary corrections to Greene's book before sending it to press (meaning what — removing the attacks against the "crow" — "John Factotum"?); he apologizes for Greene's mistake: "I am as sorry as if the original fault had been my fault." Further explanations suggest that the offended party turned out to be beyond criticism: "myself have seen his demeanor no less civil than he is excellent in the quality he professes; besides, divers of worship have reported, his uprightness of dealing, which argues his honesty, and his facetious grace in writing, that approves his art." One can sense the care with which the author chooses each word; one can sense the fear in his involved and elaborate excuses. It seems that those most worthy people, the "divers of worship" (or their agents) have had a talk with him.

What could Chettle be afraid of — the consequences of insulting a few writers? In the literary circles of those days, no one minced words. They were only careful not to invoke God and the powers that be. Marlowe was actually dangerous — touchy, explosive, and quick to take retribution. Chettle makes no excuses on his account and treats him with contempt. But when it comes to the unknown man from provinces, a mere actor, a person of humble origin (if that is who it was), Chettle begs pardon and prostrates himself, all in very roundabout ways, while avoiding saying anything concrete about him, let alone calling him by name. By the way, Nashe, who later on made public excuses, names Marlowe directly: "I have never insulted Marlowe, Greene, Chettle or any other of my friends, who treated me as a pal." He never mentions Shakespeare's name. Still, it is not out of the question that Chettle was the real author of the Greene pamphlet; some researchers who have done a computer analysis of the vocabulary reached that conclusion.

The reverberations of the story were heard in 1594 in a queer collection entitled "Greene's Funerals." Someone signing his name as "R. B. Gent" (probably the poet Richard Barnfield), playing with Greene's name, made a pun:

> Greene is the pleasing object of an eye:
> Greene pleased the eyes of all that looked upon him,
> Greene is the ground of every painter's dye,
> Greene gave the ground to all that wrote upon him.
> Nay more, the men that so eclipsed his fame,
> Purloined his plumes: can they deny the same?

It seems likely that the "upstart crow" is here accused of plagiarizing the "university wits." Many Shakespeareans take that to be the meaning of "Greene's Funerals," though some think that R. B. was aiming not at Shakespeare but at Gabriel Harvey, who mocked Greene soon after his death: "Thank other for thy borrowed and filched plumes of some little Italianated bravery."

Shakespeare's fans are outraged by these sometimes quite blatant hints at plagiarism, at the notion that the Bard used some of his predecessors' works. One renowned Shakespeare scholar (J. C. Smart) wrote sixty years ago: "This passage from

Greene has had such a devastating effect on Shakespearean study, that we cannot but wish it had never been written or discovered."[19] That is a very candid complaint; adherents of Shakespeare's cult might say the same about many other traces of the Great Bard or William Shakspere. The case of Greene and Chettle is the first link and a very important one in the chain of strange and ambiguous literary facts of the Elizabethan–Jacobean era that are directly or indirectly related to "the Shakespeare mystery." (Its significance is unique, because all the biographers rely on it as establishing the beginning of Shakespeare's creative activity, his first plays). Here and in a few other instances, his contemporaries seem to want to say something about Shakespeare, and we expect to learn a little about his works and also about him. But then the language becomes nebulous; the authors limit themselves to vague, often ambiguous hints. One feels their fear of overstepping some taboo issued by those "divers of worship" who so quickly put the hapless Henry Chettle in his place for inadvertently straying onto forbidden ground.

Those eminent persons quite often got up to strange and curious endeavors (and games). They were very fond of theater; we have seen that the highest nobility either maintained or patronized actors' troupes. They could also improvise shows in day-to-day life, using live "material" that fell into their hands.

The play "The Taming of the Shrew" is a good example. Like nearly all of Shakespeare's plays, this one has its own complicated history and unresolved problems. It was first published in the posthumous Folio of 1623, but an anonymous play with the same theme had appeared in bookshops in 1594 with a title that differed from the one later incorporated into the Shakespeare canon only by the article.[20] All the features of the plot are similar; nearly all the *dramatis personae* with all their peculiarities are also the same. But in the canon edition of Shakespeare the names are changed into Italian (except Katharina) and the setting is changed from Athens to Padua. The whole text was rewritten and only six lines coincide *in toto*. Here, one recollects Greene's hints at plagiarism; we shall turn our attention to certain explanations later. For now, we can consider a strange character who attracted the attention of non-Stratfordians long ago: the tinker called Sly. This character has no direct link to the main plot, but the anonymous author of the first play (and Shakespeare, later on) found it necessary to retain him. He appears in the introduction.

An eminent lord, riding home from the hunt, comes across the drunken tinker Sly[21] sleeping near an alehouse, and decides to play a joke on him. He orders his servants to take the drunk to his house, wash him up, dress him in noblemen's clothes and put him into the lord's bed. When he wakes up, they are to treat him as a

---

19. rf. Schoenbaum. Op.cit. p. 157

20. The old play was "The Taming of a Shrew," Shakespeare's is "The Taming of the Shrew."

21. The name of this Sly is Christopher. The well-known comedic actor of the time was called William.

nobleman and assure him that he was such a person. Then, actors (who apparently happen to be at hand) are ordered to present him (and other spectators) with an amusing comedy — specifically, a story about how to tame a shrewish woman. When the play is over the servants take the sleeping tinker back to his spot near the alehouse and leave him just as they'd found him. When Sly comes to, he tells the alehouse servant about a wonderful dream — from which he now knows how to tame a shrewish woman.

In the old play, Sly twice begins to converse with the lord during the performance, but falls back to sleep. In the text from Shakespeare's canon, the story of Sly is abridged and only the beginning remains intact. The end is discarded (maybe out of negligence), and nearly all his comments on the play are omitted, so that that plot line petered out entirely. The joke of the overbearing lord may seem to today's audiences artificial and even awkward, like the Duke's caprice in Cervantes' *Don Quixote*, when he makes Sancho Panza governor of the Isle of Baratoria. No wonder directors always skip this introduction when staging the play. But the character takes on an enigmatic aura when we learn that the environs of Stratford are mentioned twice in connection with Sly: Wincot (the setting for introductory scene, where Sly owes the alehouse wench 14 pence), and Burton-heath (Barton-on-the-Heath): "Am not I Christopher Sly, old Sly's son of Burton-heath . . . " Of all Shakespeare's plays, the Stratford region is mentioned only here, in connection with Sly, and in "Henry IV," in connection with Falstaff. Even the name of the bar maid, Marian Hacket, whom Sly mentions in his speech, is not fictitious; it has been established that the Hackets lived in Wincot at the time.

All these "coincidences" have led some non-Stratfordians to conclude that the role of the tinker Christopher Sly ("by birth a pedlar, by education a card-maker, by transmutation a bear-herd") is not to be overlooked by any means. They think that this story sheds some light (perhaps as an exaggeration) on how the former glove-maker's apprentice became known to "eminent persons," who for some reason decided he might be a suitable playing piece for a game on a scale that would become apparent only later on.


## CAMBRIDGE AND OXFORD KNEW THE SPEAR-SHAKER


Shakespeare's name came to the attention of his contemporaries soon after his two poems were published. All the comments came from university circles: apparently, those poems and later on the plays were carefully read and highly appreciated both at Cambridge and Oxford.

The first time Shakespeare's name was mentioned, even in an enigmatic way (how often Shakespeare's biographers have to use that epithet!), is in the poem published in 1594 under the title of "Willobie, His Avisa, or the True Picture of a

Modest Maid and of a chaste and Constant Wife." One Hadrian Dorrell tells us, in the foreword, that the poem had been found among the papers of his university buddy Henry Willobie (Willoughby), who went abroad. The poem made such an impression on him that he decided to publish it without the author's knowledge. Henry Willoughby's name is on the list of Oxford students for 1591-1595, but Hadrian Dorrell was never found there — this is a pen name.

The poem dwells upon a certain Avisa, who successfully rebuffs numerous suitors, including Willobie. The latter is consoled and counseled by his close friend W. S. (either Shakespeare or Southampton, it is believed), who had recently recovered from a broken heart. The poem offers many intriguing hints that those concerned know the real name of the author, "who could tell much more about his heroes, if only he wished." The situation with the heroes resembles those presented in Shakespeare's sonnets (which were not yet published at the time), and in the laudatory verses that preface the poem, Shakespeare is directly mentioned for the first time, as well as his "Lucrece," which was produced that same year (1594).

> *Yet Tarquin plucked his glistering grape,*
> *And Shake-speare paints Lucrece's rape.*

The name was spelt with a hyphen, also for the first time; proper names were not usually spelled like that, but it emphasizes its etymological sense.

Cambridge fellow William Covell used the same spelling in his book *Polymanteia* (1595), which was published at Cambridge. Enumerating the writers and poets who were graduates of the University (Spenser, Marlowe, Daniel, Drayton), Covell includes here also "the sweetest Shake-speare." So we learn that Covell considered Shakespeare a university writer, his fellow student.

The same year Thomas Edwards also counted Shakespeare among the best contemporary poets, together with Spenser, Marlowe, and Daniel. Poet John Weever addresses one verse in his book of epigrams to Shakespeare:

> *Honey-tongued Shakespeare, when I saw thine issue*
> *I swore Apollo got them, and none other...* [22]

Weever extols more than Shakespeare's poems; he also mentions "Romeo and Juliet" and "Richard III." Weever, too, is a Cambridge graduate; he earned his bachelors degree in 1598. His book is dated 1599 (but it was not registered).

In 1598, poet Richard Barnfield, whose name came up while we were speaking about stolen "plumes" and Robert Greene, gave Shakespeare's poems the highest rating:

---

22. Weever J. *Epigrams in the oldest cut and newest Fashion.* 1599. Repr.1911 by R.B. McKerrow, p. 75 — Ad Gulielmum Shakespeare.

*And Shakespeare thou, whose honey-flowing Vein*
*(Pleasing the World), thy Praises doth obtain.*
*Whose Venus, and whose Lucrece (sweet and chaste)*
*Thy Name in fame's immortal Book have placed.*
*Live ever you, at least in Fame live ever:*
*Well may the Body die, but Fame dies never.*[23]

In the satirical play "Return from Parnassus," written by a Cambridge graduate and staged at the university in 1599, Shakespeare's name is mentioned several times and there are both direct and indirect quotations from his works. A character by the name of Gullio goes on at length about Shakespeare; he demands that they read to him verses only in the spirit of "sweet Master Shakespeare" and announces: "Let this duncified world esteem of Spenser and Chaucer, I'll worship sweet Mr. Shakespeare and to honour him will lay his 'Venus and Adonis' under my pillow." We shall consider this play and its heroes further on, but for now, let us note that in certain Cambridge circles, Shakespeare was then the "talk of the town."

This is also corroborated by a book by another Cambridge graduate and Master of Arts at both universities, Francis Meres. His thick tome (700 pages) published in 1598 under the title *Palladis Tamia: Wits Treasury Being the Second part of Wits Commonwealth*[24] is one in a series[25] connected with the name of an enigmatic John Bodenham. Meres' book is full of dull, maybe purposely dull, scholastic-like ruminations on various subjects. Then all of a sudden sixteen pages are filled with a "Comparative Discourse of our English poets, with the Greek, Latin and Italian poets." In the lists of English poets, writers and dramatists, compiled by Meres, Shakespeare is mentioned several times. First, Meres appraises him as a poet: "As the soule of Euphorbus was thought to live in Pythagoras, so the sweet, witty soule of Ovid lives in mellifluous and honey-tongued Shakespeare, witness his Venus and Adonis, his Lucrece, his sugared Sonnets among his private friends." "The Muses would speak Shakespeare's fine filed phrase, if they would speak English." Meres adds that Shakespeare is one of the poets by whom "the English tongue is mighty enriched." Shakespeare also is one of "the most passionate among us to bewail and mourn the perplexities of love."

Most important, Meres not only credits Shakespeare as a preeminent playwright but also lists his dramatic works: "As Plautus and Seneca are accounted the best for comedy and tragedy among the Latins, so Shakespeare among the English is the most

---

23. Barnfield R. *Remembrance of Some English Poets.* L., 1598.

24. Meres F.; Palladis Tamia. *Wits Treasure Being the Second part of Wits Commonwealth.* L., 1598.

25. To this series (1597-1600) belong the editions mentioned in the first chapter: "Wits Treasure," "Wits Theater of the Little World," "Belvedere or the Garden of the Muses," "Englands Helicon."

excellent in both kinds for the stage. For comedy, witness his 'Gentlemen of Verona,' his 'Errors,' his 'Love's Labour's Lost,' his 'Midsummer Night's Dream,' and his 'Merchant-of Venice,' his 'Love's Labour's Won,' for tragedy his 'Richard II,' 'Richard III,' 'Henry IV,' 'King John,' 'Titus Andronicus' and his 'Romeo and Juliet'" (spelling modernized).

Thus, Meres names twelve plays, only six of them published by that time, and only three with Shakespeare's name on the title page. Some of the pieces cited by Meres were published a quarter of a century later, and the "sweet sonnets" eleven years later. Meres was apparently exceedingly well-informed about Shakespeare's works, though the sources of his knowledge remain undiscovered. Of course, Shakespeareans have been driven to distraction by Meres' reference to a play known as Labour's Won." What Meres meant, we can only guess; perhaps this is the play we know under a different title; perhaps it is lost forever.

Soon after this book was published, Francis Meres left London for good and became a parish priest in the county of Rutland, but his high regard for Shakespeare and his famous list of Shakespeare's plays have found their way into all Shakespeare biographies, where they are given a place of honor.

In 1599, the publisher and printer W. Jaggard issued a small poetic collection under the title of *The Passionate Pilgrim*. He featured Shakespeare's name on the title page, but of the twenty verses in the collection, only five are definitely considered to be by Shakespeare. Some are thought to be Barnfield's, Marlowe's, and Raleigh's; the authorship of half of the collection is still disputed. Maybe Jaggard picked up an album that fell into his hands, or some orphaned verses, and assumed they were Shakespeare's. The third edition of the collection came out in 1612, and Jaggard included in it two sonnets by Thomas Heywood, an ambitious and prolific author. Heywood did not let such literary piracy pass unnoticed. His book, *An Apology for Actors*, was being printed at the time, and he inserted into it a special epistle citing the obvious harm done to him by the fact that two of his verses had been printed under another name — "which may put the world in opinion I might steal them from him; and he to do himself right, hath since published them in his own name." Then Heywood wrote: "But as I must acknowledge my lines not worthy [of] his patronage, under whom he hath published them, so the author I know much offended with Mr. Jaggard (that altogether unknown to him) presumed to make so bold with his name."

One may note that although he is speaking of the author (W. Shakespeare) who is mentioned on the title page of Jaggard's collection, and *he alone* could be meant, Heywood somehow does not call him by name but uses only the neutral word "author." Heywood, himself not an unknown in the literary circles of the day, writes about Shakespeare with great reverence, even with obsequiousness. He doesn't say that his verses were published under the name of another author, he uses the word "patronage." Everything about this short paragraph seems odd. It is surprising enough that in 1612 Shakespeare should be "not at all acquainted" with Jaggard, who had twice published the collection with his name on it (the first time thirteen years before). The

127

expression "presumed to make so bold with his name" is also unusual, for it seems to indicate that the author (that is, Shakespeare) occupied a high social position. At the time, Jaggard was a well-known editor and publisher (several years later he would be entrusted with publishing the first collection of Shakespeare's plays — the Great Folio). His social status was certainly not less than that of a member of an actors' troupe like William Shakspere from Stratford. We shall note also that, from this point onward, Shakespeare's name (which had been a major selling point) disappeared from the title page of some part of edition of *The Passionate Pilgrim*, though it would have been more logical to delete the two Heywood sonnets from the book. Such was the publisher's hasty and radical response to Heywood's rather temperate and polite "Epistle." It seems likely that he, like Chettle, was favored with a little talking to from certain people who possessed a great deal of influence.

In 1609 Thomas Thorpe, a friend and a confidant of Edward Blount, whom we already know, published the first edition of Shakespeare's sonnets, containing 154 poems. In the title, *Shake-speares Sonnets*, the name was hyphenated. The book was duly registered, but there are indications that it was issued without the author's consent and without his participation. In distinction to the meticulously printed first editions of Shakespeare poems, *Sonnets* is riddled with misprints. Judging by Meres' words and by *The Passionate Pilgrim*, at least some of the sonnets had been written in the 1590s and were known to the poet's close friends, but for some reason Shakespeare chose not to publish them. It is not known whether the sequence in which they were arranged in this famous edition corresponds to the author's intention, for some thirty years later they were arranged differently and were grouped by topic, three to five verses each.

How Thomas Thorpe came by the sonnets, we do not know (perhaps Blount could have shed some light on that). In any event, the publisher deemed it necessary (the publisher, not the author) to include a separate page bearing this enigmatic dedication:

TO. THE. ONLIE. BEGETTER. OF.
THESE. INSVING. SONNETS.
MR. W. H. ALL. HAPPINESSE.
AND. THAT. ETERNITIE.
PROMISED.
BY.
OVR. EVER-LIVING. POET.
WISHETH.
THE. WELL-WISHING.
ADVENTURER. IN.
SETTING.
FORTH.
T. T.

# SHAKE-SPEARES

# SONNETS.

### Neuer before Imprinted.

AT LONDON

By *G. Eld* for *T. T.* and are
to be folde by *Iohn Wright,* dwelling
at Chrift Church gate.
**1609.**

The title page of "Shake-speares Sonnets", issued by T.Thorpe in 1609

Shakespeare's sonnets have been studied from many angles as scholars hunt for any clue as to when they were written, in the context of which historic events, and any other information that might help in identifying the sonnets' heroes, the Fair Friend and the Dark Lady, and how they were related to the poet.

But the mysterious dedication and the riddle of W. H. — "the only begetter" to whom those sonnets (or the book of sonnets) owe their appearance — was of special interest. The enigmatic stranger seems to be the "Fair Friend" to whom Shakespeare promised immortality in his verses (Sonnets 55, 61, 65). Some scholars disagree: They think the publisher meant that person (probably one of Shakespeare's noble sponsors) who had been keeping the sonnets, or who found himself in possession of them by some other means and provided them to Thorpe for publication. I do not see any contradiction here — both views may be correct. Let us say that Thorpe received the sonnets from the very person to whom Shakespeare, in the sonnets, promised immortality. Who is he? Solving the riddle, identifying W. H., would give us the key to the meaning of many sonnets and consequently to the elusive Bard, himself.

Shakespeare had many contemporaries whose initials were W. H. The most noted among them are William Herbert, Earl of Pembroke; Henry Wriothesley, Earl of Southampton; and William Harvey. Each of them has adherents among Shakespeare researchers. Pembroke makes the best case — his initials fit without any permutations, he was known in publishing circles, and the Great Folio dedication was later addressed to him. Eminent scholars such as Edmund Chambers and Dover Wilson favor Pembroke; but some doubt that Thorpe could have addressed such a high nobleman with a title as mundane as "Mr." I find this argument a little weak: this was an address to a person under a pen name, an abbreviation used so that the identity would not be unequivocal to any but those who were closely involved; and this would be an additional means of masking or obscuring it.

Other facts also speak in favor of Pembroke; we will consider them in due course. There were several funny things about how the book was published. Why would Shakespeare not wish to publish his sonnets, as other poets had done? Poesy was deemed a noble enough occupation, even among the most distinguished aristocrats; King James allowed his verses to be published under his own august name. Besides, by withholding his poetic (and other) works from publication, Shakespeare deprived himself of a certain income — while Shakspere never missed the slightest chance, noble or otherwise, to chalk up a bit of profit. One guess was that "Mrs. Shakspere may have prevented it, out of jealousy"; but the woman was illiterate and as far as we know she never left Stratford. Shakespeare could not have been afraid that someone would recognize his poetic heroes, for generations of scholars have been able to turn up very few clues, and the sonnets contain no criminal allusions, no grounds for unwanted revelations, etc. Who was the adventurer mentioned in the dedication? Thorpe, himself? And what is the meaning of all this mystery around what is, essentially, the simple and harmless matter of publishing a little volume of lyrical verses?

In 1610, a poet and tutor to the crown prince, John Davies, from Hereford, included an interesting epigram in his book *Scourge of Folly*: "To our English Terence Mr. William Shake-speare."[26] Many a Shakespearean has puzzled over it. And for good reason:

*Some say, (good Will) — which I, in sport, do sing*
*Hadst thou not played some kingly parts in sport,*
*Thou hadst been a companion for a king,*
*And been a king among the meaner sort.*
*Some others rail; but rail as they think fit,*
*Thou hast no railing but a reigning wit,*
*And honesty thou sow'st, which they do reap*
*So to increase their stock which they do keep.*

How are we to understand — "And been a king among the meaner sort . . . "? How could Shakespeare be "a companion for a king"? Some biographers tentatively suggest that Davies might have meant Shakespeare playing the part of a king in a play; but we have no notion what parts Shakespeare played on stage, or whether he played at all. There is no definite information about that. But these are not all of the epigram's riddles.

The very title is intriguing: "To our English Terence Mr. Will Shakespeare." It would not seem extraordinary if Shakespeare were likened to a great Roman comic writer (although, by that date, "Hamlet" and "King Lear" had been staged and published, not to mention the six plays named by Meres in 1598). The point is not that Davies compared Shakespeare to a master of comedy rather than, say, Seneca; the point is that Davies chose one master of comedy in particular.

Publius Terence (2^nd century BC), nicknamed Afer, arrived in Rome as a slave and was a servant of senator Terence Lucan, who provided him with an education and then set him free and allowed to take his own family name. After Terence's comedies appeared in circulation, his literary adversaries began spreading rumors that he was a fake and that the real authors of the comedies were the influential patricians Scipio and Gaius Laelius, his patrons. Terence did not refute the rumors, and so they came down to posterity. During the Renaissance, this story (taken from such authors as Cicero and Quintilian) was well known; Elizabethan historians wrote about it. Whether or not Terence actually wrote the plays issued under his name in ancient Rome, the superb Latin researcher John Davies and many of his readers knew of the rumors; and in choosing Terence for comparison with Shakespeare (and not Plautus, as Meres did), Davies was consciously referring to these links. A small hint, but broad

---

26. In the Oxford Complete Shakespeare (1988), edited by Stanley Wells and Gary Taylor, the Bard's name is printed here without a hyphen, astonishingly enough.

enough for the initiated — and most modern non-Stratfordians understand it this way.

In 1616, among his other works, Ben Jonson published a highly interesting epigram "On Poet-Ape," which many Western scholars (including Stratfordians) consider aimed at Shakespeare (i.e. Shakspere).

> *Poor poet-ape, that would be thought our chief,*
> *Whose works are e'en the frippery of wit,*
> *From brocade is become so bold a thief,*
> *As we, the robbed, leave rage, and pity it.*

Those Stratfordians who agree that the epigram refers to Shakespeare think that Jonson (like Greene, earlier) was accusing him of plagiarism. But this vituperative attack can be read another way: Jonson's "ape' (Greene's "crow," "John factotum") — is not a writer at all, not a plagiarist, but only a straw man, a stalking horse, who is "decorated with someone else's feathers" (that is, is credited with the authorship of someone else's works) in order to trick people into believing that he is a major poet. The extraordinary Game is under way. This epigram appeared in 1616, after Shakspere's death — but it was probably written several years earlier.

In 1790, theater entrepreneur Philip Henslowe's diary for 1591–1609 was found. That is an extremely important period for Shakespeare biographers. In Henslowe's notes (together with calculations and receipts) are named practically every contemporary dramatist whom Henslowe paid for his plays. Only one name is never mentioned during all those years — years when the majority of Shakespeare's plays were written — the name of William Shakespeare. The diary does contain the names of some Shakespeare plays, and Henslowe had a direct hand in their staging; but Henslowe, who knew everybody in theatrical London and had dealings with all of them, never mentioned Shakespeare! He did not know such a person. No plausible explanation for that has been presented until now.

Since many of Shakespeare's contemporaries esteemed him as the leading poet and playwright of the day, we might expect to find comments from them not only on his works, but about him as the famous author, about his personality, his lifestyle, his friends and acquaintances — that is, at least the kind of tidbits we have about other poets and dramatists of the era whose works were considerably less renowned. No. Nothing was said about this one particular author, as a man who lived somewhere, was of a certain age, had a certain appearance, habits, friends. None of his contemporaries ever mentioned him during his lifetime, not in print and not in the numerous surviving letters and diaries of people who surely would have known him. There are no personal impressions or second-hand information, no hearsay or rumors about the writer.

Still, like the exception that proves the rule, there is an entry in the diary of attorney John Manningham, which is now featured in all Shakespeare biographies.

Manningham recounts a vulgar story from theater life. Richard Burbadge, who was playing the part of Richard III, caught the fancy of a woman who invited him to visit her at home, and they agreed that he would present himself as the king. Having overheard this exchange, Shakespeare allegedly went there earlier, and was received and entertained well. When the hostess was told that King Richard was waiting at the door, Shakespeare gave orders to tell him that William the Conqueror had preempted him. In order to make sure not to miss the innuendo, Manningham made a note to remind himself: "Shakespeare's name is William."

Manningham, as evident from his diary, was a well-educated person. He knew classical, Italian, and contemporary English drama. Thus, in his notes on the performance that took place at the Middle Temple on February, 2, 1602 he wrote: "At our feast we had a play called 'Twelfth Night; or, What You Will,' much like the 'Comedy of Errors' or 'Menachmi' in Plautus, but most like and near to that in Italian called 'Inganni.' A good practice in it to make the steward believe that the lady of the house, a widow, was in love with him, by counterfeiting a letter as from his lady, in general terms, telling him what she liked best in him, and prescribing his gesture in smiling, his apparel, etc., and then when he came to practice making him believe they took him to be mad."

An inveterate theater-goer, Manningham heard plenty of backstage gossip. But he does not seem to give any direct or indirect hint that this story has to do with a renowned dramatist and poet, the author of several plays including the "Twelfth Night" that he had so enjoyed. This single diary entry is the only evidence from a contemporary that shows us Shakspere as a member of the Lord Chamberlain actors' troupe together with Richard Burbadge (facts which are not contested by anyone). As to the identity of William Shakespeare, there is not a word.

We already know that William Shakespeare, unlike most of his literary contemporaries, left behind no manuscripts whatsoever, not a single line written in his own hand (and we have already seen what Shakspere's signatures look like). No document (legal or other) has been found that clearly relates to the poet and playwright William Shakespeare.

In Shakespeare's era, the art of portraiture was flourishing. We have surviving oils, miniatures, engravings, and drawings of many eminent persons in various periods of their life — images of poets, dramatists and actors. Only the greatest writer left no authentic portrait made during his lifetime, and there is no indication that any ever existed, though such talented and prolific portrait painters as Nicholas Hilliard, Isaac Oliver, Robert Peake, William Segar, Paul van Somer and their disciples were active at the time. Only several years after the Bard's death two images were created (or constructed) that biographers had to accept as "confirmed" — but they do not resemble each other. More about that, later. All the other so-called "Shakespeare portraits" that are featured in various publications are either images of unknown figures from those times, or later forgeries[27] (I do not mean illustrations in later editions, when an artist is free to use his imagination to the fullest extent).

The Ashburn "Shakespeare" portrait. A fraud.

The Janssen "Shakespeare" portrait. A fraud.

The Flower "Shakespeare" portrait. A fraud.

The Chandos "Shakespeare" portrait. Actually a portrait of an unknown man.

It is almost enough to make one think that all traces of the great man and his works had been intentionally and carefully eliminated, and that for some unclear reasons he withheld during his life all evidence of his personal links with literary work. He succeeded in keeping such evidence obscured by deep shadows that none of his contemporaries could penetrate. Documented testimony about William Shakspere of Stratford, discovered later, has nothing to do with Shakespeare's (or any other's) creative activity and even precludes the possibility of such a link, as we have seen.

This bizarre circumstance — the total lack of any authentic traces of him as more than a commoner and acquisitive deal-maker — as a writer and a poet (outside of his works) — is now known as the "Shakespeare mystery" both by non-Stratfordians and Stratfordians alike. The utter incompatibility of the Stratfordian documents and Shakespeare's works takes this mystery far deeper, and no inquiring mind can be put off by easy answers. No authority in this world can "close the Shakespeare authorship question" until this mystery is solved in a convincing way.

## A SELF-SATISFIED PORK-BUTCHER OR A MELANCHOLY TAILOR?

Against the will of the biographers, the facts, both literary and historical, which comprise the traditional biographies of Shakespeare seem to coalesce around two opposite (or at least non-coinciding) poles so that two different biographies are formed or, to be more precise, the biographies of two different people.

The first group of facts builds a creative biography of the Great Bard, William Shakespeare, consisting exclusively of the dates when his works appeared, the years when his plays were staged, how they were received, analyses of their incomparable artistic value and how they reveal the exalted soul of the author and his versatile erudition. But they do not contain any real information about his daily life and his social relations.

The other group of findings consists of authentic documents about the life, family and occupation of the man who was born in the town of Stratford-on-Avon, William Shakspere — a shareholder in the London actors' troupe, with no education to speak of, who busied himself acquiring and multiplying his properties and capital. This collection of documented facts comprises a biography that includes no evidence that the man had, or could have had, anything to do with creative activity, with literature.

---

27. In recent decades, X-ray examination has established that many of the supposed "Shakespeare portraits" kept in well-known collections and purchased for large sums of money are counterfeits made during later periods (18$^{th}$ and 19$^{th}$ centuries). These include the famous Ashburn, Janssen and Flower portraits, copies of which have adorned Shakespeare's biographies and works in all languages of the world.

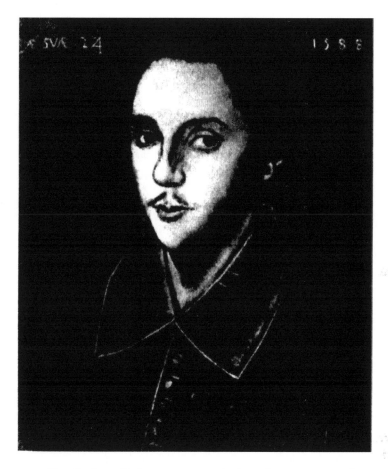

The Grafton "Shakespeare" portrait. In reality, a portrait of an unknown man.

Each of those facts, collected piecemeal by generations of scholars, may be easy to match up with one of these biographies, but there are very few that could be correlated to both biographies at the same time. In spite of a tradition three centuries long, as R. W. Emerson noted, these two life stories do not fit into one whole compatible picture. Non-Stratfordians contend that we are dealing with two absolutely different people, who may not even have had anything in common.

Thus the scarce facts that do appear to cross over between the two biographies are of special interest for scholars. For Stratfordians, these details prove that the shrewd businessman with his occupations so distant from lofty matters did not slip into the story of the Great Bard due to some error made by posterity. These few and nebulous allusions and rather contorted scenarios are truly precious, for they provide some basis (beyond mere respect for the traditional approach) for strengthening their belief in the Stratfordian cult, the conviction that William Shakspere from Stratford was the greatest poet and playwright in this world.

Stratfordian biographers understandably do not like to focus much on things like the tinker Sly and John Davies' clear hint at "our English Terence." That leaves only Greene's and Chettle's attacks on some "crow" clothed in their plumes, and an aside in the Cambridge play "Return from Parnassus."

We'll go into this more later, but as a preview let me say that one of the characters in that play, Kempe, is an actor, a dancer,[28] and a clown in Lord Chamberlain's troupe. He is presented as an unscrupulous and ignorant person: he mistakes the title of a famous Latin book (*Metamorphoses*) for the name of a writer. In the course of the play Kempe says that "our fellow" Shakespeare is far above the university wits. "They smell too much of the writer Ovid and that writer Metamorphosis, and talk too much of Proserpina and Jupiter." Then he mentions Jonson, who presented Horace on stage, and gave a pill to the poets, "but our fellow Shakespeare hath given him a purge that made him bewray his credit." Many non-Stratfordians do not take the words seriously, for an unknown writer placed them in the mouth of an uneducated comic character, and the play was performed by students. The words should be understood, we are told, as "our fellow at the university." However, while some students may have understood that as a hint that Shakespeare was "their own, university" writer, some other students and readers (like today's Stratfordians) take them to mean quite the opposite — that actor Kempe was talking about his fellow actor. Thus, the ambiguous comment was a hint for those who were in the know. Anyhow, the comic character's words testify that William Shakspere, from the troupe of Lord Chamberlain, had something to do with the Great Bard — and someone at Cambridge knew it.

The Stratfordian tradition is based on just two major points which, in the opinion of the true believers, prove that William Shakspere from Stratford and the

---

28. Kempe was known for winning a bet by dancing all the way from London to Norwich.

Trinity Church in Stratford-upon-Avon

Great Bard William Shakespeare are the same person, and both points emerged some six or seven years after the Stratfordian died.

We already know that the only place where any note was taken of William Shakspere's death was in the parish burial registry: "April 25, 1616, Will Shakspere, gent." The demise of the "honey-tongued Shakespeare," whose works had been famous during his lifetime and were repeatedly published, was ignored by poets, diarists and letter-writers alike. There are many elegies, even collections, mourning the deaths of Philip Sidney, Spenser, Drayton, Donne, Jonson and other poets and playwrights, members of the royal family, other eminent persons and their relatives, but the most prominent person of the Elizabethan cohort, William Shakespeare, was left unmourned. Looking to explain such gross negligence, biographers are compelled to assume that Shakespeare (who for unknown reasons retired to Stratford in 1612), was simply forgotten by his London friends and fellows, and that in Stratford, where books and the arts were of little importance, his countrymen knew him only as a prosperous and shrewd man. However, not one of his biographers has failed to invoke the legend that, not long before his death, Shakespeare (Shakspere) received in his house both Ben Jonson and Michael Drayton. On the occasion of that meeting the friends drank liberally, as a result of which Shakespeare developed a fever and died several weeks later. If one believes this legend (that was only written down some fifty years later), his London friends did not forget him; they simply failed to react to his demise! Yet Ben Jonson wrote verses full of pathos on the deaths of his many contemporaries, and when he died in 1637, a special collection dedicated to his memory appeared a year later.[29]

When Michael Drayton died, in 1631, his casket was carried by students from Gray's Inn, Middle Temple, Lincoln Inn and Inner Temple along with other eminent citizens to Westminster Abbey. They walked two by two, leading a procession of mourners that trailed a long way back through the streets of the city. Drayton was not, by the way, of noble origin, nor was he wealthy.

For non-Stratfordians, it is natural that Shakspere's death was passed over in silence. The man was neither a poet nor a dramatist, and so his demise went unremarked. Still, if someone else was the Great Bard, then he too passed away at some time or other and, apparently, that event was also met by silence.

We do not know who buried Shakspere's body in 1616 (by a strange coincidence, he died on April 23, the day of his birth). But in 1622, in the Holy Trinity Church where he was buried, a small wall monument was erected, at the same time that a full collection of Shakespeare's plays, the Great Folio, was scheduled to appear (although, in the end, it was published only a year later). These two essential facts are at the crossroads of biographies of William Shakspere from Stratford and the Great Bard William Shakespeare. They form the essential foundation upon which to build a

---

29. Elegies for the death of Ben Jonson take up 74 pages, appended to a large-format academic edition of his works.

combined biography of the Bard as tradition depicts him and the Stratfordian cult connected to his story.

The monument in Stratford's Holy Trinity Church is a place of pilgrimage for Shakespeare fans the world over. Above the grave there is a stone plaque engraved with a rhymed inscription (according to lore, composed by Shakespeare himself):

> *Good friend for Jesus sake forbeare,*
> *To dig the dust encloased heare:*
> *Bleste be Ye man yt spares thes stones,*
> *And curst be he yt moves my bones.*

The inscription does nothing to evoke the spiritual depth for which the Lord of Language was known; but it is quite consistent with the man we discern in William Shakspere's last will. Some think that the inscription was addressed to church guardians, who used to clear space for new interments by vacating the old graves and taking the bones to a common crypt adjacent to the church. In 1694, Reverend William Hall noted the inscription and thus explained it in a letter to his friend, an expert in Anglo-Saxon literature, A. Thwaites: "The poet being willing to preserve his bones unmoved, lays a curse upon him that moves them, and having to do with clerks and sextons, for the most part a very ignorant sort of people, he descends to the meanest of their capacities; and disrobes himself of that art, which none of his contemporaries wore in greater perfection."[30] Whether the spell was crafted by Shakespeare himself or by someone else, we do not know, but it has played its role; as for the gravestone, according to some sources, it began to look worn and in the 18th century was replaced.

Somewhat distant from the gravestone, about five feet up in the northern wall of the altar, there is a niche holding two small Corinthian columns. Between them is a bust of a man with a quill in hand and a sheet of paper lying on a flat pillow with tassels at the corners. Above the columns is a cornice with two small cherubs: the left figure holds a spade, symbolizing toil; the right one holds a skull and a torch turned upside down, symbolizing eternal peace. Between the cherubs a bas-relief of the coat of arms obtained by William Shakspere's patrons for his father around 1599. At the top is another skull, which is somehow missing the lower jawbone. Naturally, everyone who has written about the monument has concentrated on the head of the bust, and few Shakespeareans are satisfied with it. A plump, expressionless, even a dull face, with a large bald brow, short neck, and a curved moustache upward pointed. John Dover Wilson went as far as to call the Stratford bust "an effigy of a sausage maker." When Wilson wrote about the Stratford bust and Droeshout's engraving (which we shall come to later), he severely asserted: "These effigies stand between us and the true Shakespeare, and are so obviously false images of the greatest poet of all time that the

---

30. Quotation from Schoenbaum, S. Op. cit. p. 307.

The wall monument to Shakespeare in the Stratford church. Present-day view.

world turns from them in disgust and thinks it is turning from Shakespeare himself."[31] (Still, Wilson never went over to the non-Stratfordians).

However, two lines under the bust, in Latin, glorify the man who "was like Nestor in mind, genius — like Socrates, in art — like Marones; earth covers him, people bewail him, Olympus receives him" (JUDICIO PYLIUM, GENIO SOCRATEM, ARTE MARONEM: TERRA TEGIT, POPULUS MAERET, OLIMPUS HABET). Then follow six lines in English verse addressed, not without an odd bit of irony, to "a passerby":

STAY PASSENGER, WHY GOEST THOU BY SO FAST?
READ IF THOU CANST WHOM ENVIOUS DEATH HAS PLAST,
WITH IN THIS MONUMENT SHAKSPEARE[32]: WITH WHOME,
QUICK NATURE DIDE: WHOSE NAME DOTH DECK YS TOMBE,
FAR MORE THEN COST: SIEH (sith) ALL, YT HE HATH WRITT,
LEAVES LIVING ART, BUT PAGE, TO SERVE HIS WITT.

Then, in the right corner, in Latin: "Died in 1616 AD in the 53rd year of his life, Apr. 23."

The inscription and the indication of the date of William Shakspere's death, and his age, may serve as testimony that he was great writer — otherwise what have Socrates, Maron (Vergil), and art to do with him?

It has been established, however, that before the middle of the 18th century the monument, and especially the bust, looked otherwise. This is made evident by a sumptuous book published in 1656: "Antiquities of Warwickshire Illustrated . . . " in which the author, Sir William Dugdale,[33] presents several years of research on, and sketches of, noteworthy places of the county. The monument in the Stratford church is illustrated in the current work by an engraving made by Wenceslaus Hollar according to Dugdale's drawing, and it can hardly be reconciled with what one sees in Stratford today. The capitals of the columns are decorated with leopards' heads (I, for myself, cannot call to mind any other tombstone of a peaceful European burger of the period featuring the image of such an exotic beast of prey). Two cherubs sit on the cornice with their legs dangling. The one on the right holds an hourglass instead of a torch. The face, in Dugdale's drawing, is lean, the cheeks are wrinkled, the beard is unkempt, and moustache is drooping. The modern Shakespeare biographer Schoenbaum noted, in reference to the original version of the bust: "The complacent pork butcher has metamorphosed into a melancholy tailor"[34] (as a matter of fact, the metamorphosis turned out to be the other way around). One more thing: it appears that earlier there

---

31. Wilson J.D. *The essential Shakespeare.* Cambridge, 1932, p. 5-6.
32. The name William is not given.
33. Later he became the head of the Heralds' College.
34. Schoenbaum S. Op.cit. p. 311.

was neither quill, nor paper — tools of a writers art, and instead of a smart pillow was pictured a big shapeless sack (wool? gold?) that the man clutches to his stomach, elbows apart. Schoenbaum asks himself, does this sack symbolize wealth? . . . Some Stratfordians, puzzled by the incongruities, assume that Dugdale may have made his sketches from memory and could have distorted some of the details. But could he have forgotten the obligatory paraphernalia of a writer, the quill and paper? Could he have invented leopards' heads and a big sack?

Besides, the Dugdale book was reprinted in 1730, and two decades before that, in 1709, Nicholas Rowe in his Shakespeare biography (the first Shakespeare biography, it preceded the first 18th-century collection of Shakespeare's works) had placed an image of the Stratford monument that is almost the same as that shown by Dugdale — but this was an original picture, not a copy of Dugdale's image.[35] That means that the monument, even one hundred years after its installation, looked quite different from the current one: with a different face, and without the quill and paper. For a long time nothing was known about the circumstances of the *monument's creation*, and only in the 19th century something new became clear.

The monument in the Stratford church (in its initial aspect) was made by the sculptor (stonecutter) Garrat Janssen, with the help of his elder brother Nicholas,[36] who had not so long before created the tomb for Roger Manners, the 5th Earl of Rutland — the very person whose death was covertly mourned in 1612 by the poets who participated in the Chester collection. Anyhow, the more artful hand of Nicholas Janssen is felt in some of the details of the outer decoration of the Stratford monument, similar to analogous details on the Rutland tomb. A prominent Shakespeare scholar, Sidney Lee, only noted that correspondence at the end of the 19th century. In the surviving letter from Nicholas Janssen (1617) to Francis Rutland, the brother and successor of the late Roger, the sculptor explains his conception, writing that the symbolic figures of the cherubs would be an allegory of Labour and Rest (afterwards, similar figures in a smaller size appeared on the cornice of the Stratford wall monument).

Who paid for the Stratford monument is unknown; in any case, Shakspere did not allocate any funds for that in his will (unlike his friend Combe, who left 60 pounds for his posthumous life in stone — a sizable sum; Shakespeare's must have cost no less). In spite of that, biographers usually assert, with more or less confidence, that the monument was ordered and paid for by the late Shakspere family (the question is, though, who could have composed the complicated inscription in two languages. His son-in-law? He was the only literate member of the family).

---

35. The engraving in Rowe's edition reproduces the first two lines in Latin on the memorial plate under the bust.

36. The *Great Soviet Encyclopedia* (1957, v. 47), in the article about Shakespeare, erroneously says that the monument was made by the sculptors "Garret and Johnson."

The Stratford bust of Shakespeare according to W. Dugdale's engraving. 1656. There is neither a pen nor paper, but there are leopards' heads at the top of the pillars

John Dover Wilson, expanding on his view that the Stratford bust is one of the greatest impediments in comprehending Shakespeare, says: "It is the old story, only too familiar to friends and relatives of most men wealthy or famous enough to fall a prey to the second-rate portrait-painters. The job was given to an Anglo-Flemish mason of London, one Garrat Janssen, who knew what belonged to a monument and executed the task in a workman-like and (as monuments go) highly creditable fashion. The proportions are admirable, and the architectural design, with its pillars and canopy, its mantled shield, and its twin cherubs, is even beautiful. But one thing was clearly quite beyond the workman's scope — the human face, the face that happened to be Shakespeare's. And if Mistress Shakespeare and the poet's daughters disliked the portrait, what could they do? In cases of this kind, the family of the victim is helpless . . . There was the monument . . . no doubt paid for . . . perhaps by friends as well as relatives . . . a fine monument . . . all but the face."[37]

These lines cannot but cause wonder. Wilson should have known that Dugdale's and Rowe's engravings show a different face, and not only the pillow with tassels (which Wilson was so fond of) but even the quill and paper were absent. Still, Wilson, like some other Stratfordians, was capable of dismissing facts that were not convenient for the traditionalist view. Here, he puts the story something like this: the Stratford bust in 1622 looked exactly the way it does today. . . Moreover, he asserts that the sculptor made Shakespeare's image from the mask taken either while the Bard was alive or right after his death. (Wilson probably meant the mask found in an antiques shop in the German city of Mainz in 1869 at the time when the greatest "harvest" of Shakespearean relics took place.) The mask, of unknown provenance, does bear some resemblance to the plump face of the Stratford bust (as it is now). It was much talked about by Stratfordians and was used as evidence to support their view at the end of the 19th and beginning of the 20th centuries. As no information is available about any death mask that might have been taken from Shakespeare, it is certain that the Mainz mask (if it is not a fake) was made somewhere and someplace from a person who had nothing to do with Shakespeare or England. That much was clear to any sound-minded person from the very beginning, but still there were people who wanted to confirm the authenticity of the Stratford monument and to dissipate the more serious doubts in this respect. The notorious mask is seldom mentioned nowadays, like certain other relics of the kind that surface from time to time to bolster arguments in the Shakespeare debate. Still, some scholars will not tolerate any doubts as to what the monument looked like from the very start, though they cannot offer any plausible explanations for why the monument's appearance today has so little in common with the illustrations in Dugdale's and Rowe's books.

So, when did the Stratford monument acquire its present-day canonical aspect? Some documents suggest that it happened in 1748-1749. The monument was deteriorating, by then, while Shakespeare's name was at the zenith of its glory. Local

---

37. Wilson J.D. Op. cit. p. 6.

The Stratford bust of Shakespeare according to N. Rowe. 1709. No pen nor paper, but leopards' heads are present, here, too!

authorities made an agreement with a theater entrepreneur, John Hall, and the latter with some assistants "repaired and beautified" the important historical relic. Shakspere lost his leopards and the large sack of goods, but acquired a quill, paper and a more pious face. The "restorers'" intentions were most noble, and the installation in general came to look much more like a memorial to a poet. Nowadays, such a re-make would be called a travesty, but the notion of artistic restoration was seen differently in those days. Several decades later the bust was painted white, on the initiative of Malone (who was strongly criticized for it). In 1861, an unknown artist painted the bust again, and Shakespeare's cheeks were tinted with a healthy glow. All those renovations did not change anything in principle, for with the invention of photography the 1748-1749 version became definitive. Still, drawings in old books keep reminding us of what the creation of the Janssen brothers and their unknown sponsors looked like in 1622, and it provokes doubts and conjectures.[38]

Judging by Dugdale's and Rowe's engravings, the "restorers," thank God, refrained from editing the inscription under the bust. But what does it mean? Why does it say that the envious death placed Shakespeare "with in this Monument"? This strange legend may be understood in many different ways. Some ardent non-Stratfordians took it literally, in the sense that within the monument or in the wall behind it, Shakespeare's manuscripts were hidden. A prominent non-Stratfordian, Charlton Ogburn, mounted a campaign starting in 1962 to urge the authorities to conduct an investigation of the monument in the Holy Trinity Church (by X-ray, ultrasonic waves or any other safe means), to look for any possible cavities in the bust foundation and the wall behind it. Naturally, he did not receive any favorable response to that. Still, this proposal did not go unnoticed; in September of 1973, someone got into the Holy Trinity Church at night, shifted the heavy bust aside and tried to open the base. They do not seem to have found any secret compartments, much less any manuscripts. The wall itself remains "unexplored"; but at least we can feel secure that the peculiar phrase under the bust is not likely to be meant literally as a hint that the manuscripts are there. Rather, in saying that death placed Shakespeare "with in this Monument" (or behind it), someone was implying (to be understood in full measure only by the initiated) that this image and monument are meant to hide Shake-speare, to serve as his posthumous mask and shelter.

The relics of the Stratford Holy Trinity Church and many other artifacts and events bear testimony that, in spite of their seeming incongruity and incompatibility, there was some bewildering connection between the great writer William Shakespeare and the Stratford-born theater troupe shareholder and church tithe holder William Shakspere. The wall monument with the mystifying epitaph for the

---

38. Looking at the face on Dugdale's drawing, we can imagine approximately what Will Shakspere looked like in reality, for if the bust was not at all like the person, it would have greatly astonished his relatives and countrymen. Non-Stratfordians think that those simple-hearted people would be even more amazed if they saw writing paraphernalia in his hands — as shown in the monument nowadays.

great writer is separated only by a few paces from the stone slab over the ashes of William Shakspere, inscribed with a coarse command not to disturb his bones. Only a few paces. . .

## A PORTRAIT BEN JONSON RECOMMENDED NOT LOOKING AT

The second most important fact, also posthumous, that lies at the crossroads of Shakespeare's two biographies is the Great Folio. Though English poets, writers and publishers evinced no visible response to the demise of the Great Bard, a magnificent volume appeared in 1623: *Mr. William Shakespeare Comedies, Chronicles and Tragedies.* The book is usually called the First, or, because of its significance for all of world culture, the Great Folio.

On November 8, 1623, a famous entry was made in the Stationers' Register: "Master Blount and Isaac Jaggard. Entered for their Copie under the hands of Master Doctor Worrall and Master Cole warden, master William Shakespeare Comedyes Histories, and Tragedyes soe manie of the said Copies as are not formerly entered to other men . . . VII shillings." Then are listed 16 plays (indeed, more than 16 of the plays in the collection had never been registered until then). Altogether in the book 36 plays[39] were printed, 20 of which appeared for the first time, including "Macbeth," "The Tempest," "Twelfth Night," "The Taming of the Shrew," "Henry VI," "Julius Caesar," "Coriolanus," "Antony and Cleopatra," "Cymbeline," "Measure for Measure," "Two Gentlemen of Verona" etc. Where had the texts been kept all those years since the author's death? The addresses to the edition's patrons and to the reader are signed in the names of two members of the actors' troupe, "The King's Men," John Heminge and Henry Condell; this gave rise to the theory that all these texts, including those that had not been staged, had been held by the troupe's shareholders for safekeeping. There is no other confirmation for that supposition, but it is equally hard to imagine that they had been kept in an actor's trunk for so many years. As to Heminge and Condell's participation in the publication (some scholars have gone so far as to call them editors), it should be stated that neither before nor after did these two actors have anything to do with publishing or editing. Heminge, for instance, handled the troupe's financial matters, then, after quitting the company, went into the grocery trade.

Never before had all the plays of one dramatist had been collected in one volume, and it was a tome of impressive dimensions — 998 pages, in a large format, printed in two columns. The press run was huge indeed for the time — about a thousand. Preparation for the edition had begun in 1620. There was a great deal of preliminary

---

39. Of the 37 pieces that now comprise Shakespeare's dramatic canon, the First Folio lacked only "Pericles," which was published in 1609.

work to be done in connection with acquiring the copyrights for plays published earlier and registered by other publishers. The printing was begun by William Jaggard (whom we know in connection with *The Passionate Pilgrim*) but the heart and soul of the enterprise was undoubtedly Edward Blount. Later on, J. Smethwick and A. Aspley joined them. Early in November of 1623, William Jaggard died, so the book was registered with the company by his son and heir, Isaac, together with Blount.

Thomas Pavier and William Jaggard had made an earlier attempt to publish a collection of ten Shakespeare plays; we touched on that in the first chapter. At the time, someone hindered the publication (some scholars assume there was a complaint from the actors). Whatever was behind it, the volumes printed by Pavier and Jaggard were released after all, but separately, and half of them bore false (earlier) dates. Some hard facts about this mysterious publishing event were illuminated in the 20th century as a result of technical examinations of the watermarks and other particulars of printing, printers' emblems, etc.; but the reasons that led the editors, who had legal rights for at least some of those plays, to fake the dates still remain among the many riddles connected with the name and works of Shakespeare. Most often these editors' actions are explained by alleging that they were producing pirated editions. As for Shakespeare, strictly speaking, nearly all his works found their way to publishers by some roundabout way (one guess is that Shakespeare gave them to the troupe as a share of his holdings, and later on lost interest in them; but this pretext can only be seen as forced). Besides, if Jaggard was a "pirate," then why, after the story with *The Passionate Pilgrim* and ten plays with Pavier, would he have been entrusted with the production of the enormous collection of Shakespeare plays? And by whom was he entrusted, by the way — by the actors who supposedly complained to the Earl of Pembroke a year earlier (although, what legal grounds could they have had)?

It is evident that the so-called "piracy" and the alleged actors' complaints had nothing to do with it. In the foreword to the 1609 edition of "Troilus and Cressida," certain "Grand Possessors" (of plays) are directly mentioned, upon whom the publishing of Shakespeare's works depended, and who, incidentally, are highly valued, together with Shakespeare's mind "so sharp that nobody's brains would be sharp enough to make it dull." The author of this address, who did not give his name, speaks of the "Grand Possessors" with the highest esteem, but about the theater and its public with haughty fastidiousness: "play never stalled with the stage, never clapper-clawed with palms of the vulgar ... not being sullied with smoky breath of the multitude ... " It is clear that the "Grand Possessors" are by no means lowly actors. Some very influential, highly placed persons are meant; this is a circle accessible only to the initiated. It seems that Pavier and Jaggard made an attempt to publish a collection of Shakespeare's plays without the consent and patronage of the "Grand Possessors," and found themselves barred. Only after a certain mission was assigned to Edward Blount, a person who had earned the confidence of Mary Sidney Pembroke,[40] could they begin to prepare an expert edition of the complete collection of plays. Blount took on as his partner a skilled and experienced printer, Jaggard, who had considerable resources in the printing industry.

The dedication in the First Folio gives us the names of two "Grand Possessors"; they were the sons of Mary Sidney Pembroke: William, Earl of Pembroke, Lord Chamberlain; and Philip, Earl of Montgomery. As was noted in the dedication, they "were benevolent to the Author when he had been alive, and to his trifles" that they esteemed highly, so the huge book was dedicated to them. Three times Shakespeare's dramas were called "trifles."

Though the dedication was signed "Heminge and Condell", nearly every scholar who has analyzed the addresses has concluded that they were written by none other than Ben Jonson. It is extremely interesting to note that, right during the work on the Great Folio (late 1621 — July of 1623) Lord Chamberlain, Earl of Pembroke suddenly appointed Jonson the Master of Revels (including theater performances). Later on, in July 1623, when a relative of Pembroke, Sir Henry Herbert, took over the position, he found out that the old registers of performances had been burned.

Many of the texts comprising the Great Folio were considerably changed, in comparison with editions published during the author's life. "The Merry Wives of Windsor" had more than 1000 new lines, and a part of the text was reedited; the 2$^{nd}$ part of "Henry VI" had 1139 new lines and about 2000 lines reedited; "Richard III" 193 and 2000 respectively; "King Lear" had 1100 new lines; "Hamlet" gained 83 lines and lost 230, etc. Who so radically edited the texts, and when, if the author had departed this life several years before?

A separate page carries the names of "major actors, who took part in all those plays" and the list begins with Shakespeare (the name is spelled exactly like the name of the author on the title page, but there is no mention that it is the same person).[41] Richard Burbadge stands second; third is John Heminge; Henry Condell is eighth; altogether 26 actors are named who were members of the troupe at different times.

At long last, we come to the very first memorial verses dedicated to Shakespeare. Written by Ben Jonson, two "university wits" (Hugh Holland and Leonard Digges), and the anonymous I. M,[42] they mourn the great poet and dramatist, offer him the highest praise, and predict that his works and his name will endure forever. Hugh Holland wrote:

> *Dried is that vein, dried is the Thespian spring,*
> *Turn'd all to tears, and Phoebus clouds his rays;*
> *That corps, that coffin, now bestrick those bays,*

---

40. Blount began his publishing activity as an apprentice to W. Ponsonby (died 1603), who was often called "the court publisher of the Countess of Pembroke."

41. The case is unique. There is no other book of plays from this period, wherein the author's name is included in the list of actors.

42. There are grounds to think it was John Marston, but most often other candidates are cited.

> *Which crown'd him poet first, then poets' King.*
>
> ......................................................
>
> *For, though his line of life went soon about,*
> *The life yet of his lines shall never out.*

The anonymous I. M.:

> *We wonder'd, Shakespeare, that you went'st so soon*
> *From the world's stage to the grave's tiring-room ...*

These lines have inspired many a spat. Shakespeare died at the age of 52; it was a mature age at the time. Can one attribute the words "so early" to such a man? Non-Stratfordians quote a list of renowned figures from the 16th and 17th centuries who died at the age of 30 or 40. Some Stratfordians counter with a list of people who lived 70 or 80 years. Certainly, the death of a genius is always untimely.

Leonard Digges also sees Shakespeare's immortality in his creations:

> *Shakespeare, at length thy pious fellows give*
> *The world thy works; thy works by which outlive*
> *Thy tomb thy name must; when that stone is rent*
> *And time dissolves thy Stratford monument,* [43]
> *Here we alive shall view thee still ...*

These are very important lines. First, they confirm the fact that in 1623 the monument in the Stratford church already existed. Second, they indisputably assert a link between Shakespeare and Shakspere, but what link? Speaking about time, that would "dissolve" the Stratford "monument," the author deliberately expresses his idea ambiguously. For it could be understood in the sense that a monument erected by man's hands eventually would be demolished by implacable time, while the spiritual monument — Shakespeare's great works — will go on to everlasting life. That is how most Stratfordians interpret this figure of speech. Non-Stratfordians understand it differently: Digges is speaking about a future when the veil, the mask hiding the face of the great man, will have evaporated and the world will be presented with the astonishing truth about him and his work. Here, like in Jonson's poem and, a decade later, in Milton's verse — Shakespeare's works seem to be detached from the monument on which his name is inscribed. At that, the forecast that time would "dissolve" the newly made monument reveals a strange lack of deference to the installation in the church wall, which seemingly was erected in order to mark the

---

43. In some copies of the Great Folio, "monument" is spelled as "Moniment," which in the Scottish dialect means "laughing stock."

grave among many others. Maybe something similar lies behind the suspicious "misprint" (?) in the key word "Moniment."

Neither Holland nor Digges ever mentioned Shakespeare's name during his lifetime, though they esteemed him so highly that they called him not just a "famous stage poet" (Holland), but "poets' King"! They had nothing to say on the occasion of his death. Neither did Ben Jonson, who was much closer to him and treasured him. He never openly said a word about him during Shakespeare's lifetime nor for several years after his death.

In 1619, Jonson undertook to walk to Scotland; at some point, he visited the poet William Drummond and was his guest for several days. In friendly conversations (over a glass of wine, for which Drummond especially noted Jonson had a great predilection) Jonson openly gave his opinion about prominent writers, poets and playwrights, and recollected many an interesting anecdote from his relations with them and, needless to say, he knew nearly every one of his literary contemporaries. Every time after his guest went to bed, Drummond diligently jotted down all these stories. His notes, not without some mishaps, survived, giving us an opportunity to see "live" many prominent Elizabethans and Jacobeans and at the same time greatly enriching our notions about the wild disposition and evil tongue of Ben himself. In his "Conversations with William Drummond," he relates his passionate quarrel with Marston, and describes Philip Sidney's appearance (though Jonson could hardly have seen him alive), and many other things about Donne, Drayton, Daniel, Chapman, Beaumont and certainly most of all about himself. But one may hunt there in vain for any authentic recollections about William Shakespeare, whom Ben Jonson knew well and respected far above his contemporaries and even the great dramatists of the classic theater. That much was clear from the poem he wrote several years later for the Great Folio. In 1619, Jonson mentioned only that Shakespeare was short on art, and observed that in one of his plays ("A Winter's Tale") he staged a shipwreck in Bohemia, which has no sea whatsoever. That's all.

Just three or four years after that, Jonson wrote for the Great Folio a poem that became his most celebrated poetic work, one that would forever place his name together with the Great Bard's: "To the Memory of My Beloved, the Author Mr. William Shakespeare: And What He Hath Left Us." In this brilliant poem impregnated with sincere pathos, there is the highest heartfelt evaluation of Shakespeare's art and a prophetic forecast of the place he was destined to take in the culture of all humanity. Jonson calls Shakespeare the "soul of the age, / The applause, delight, the wonder of our stage." Shakespeare is the pride and glory of England:

> *Triumph, my Britain! Thou hast one to show,*
> *To whom all scenes of Europe homage owe.*
> *He was not of an age, but for all time …*

In conclusion Jonson exclaims:

*Sweet Swan of Avon, what a sight it were*
*To see thee in our waters yet appear,*
*And make those flights upon the banks of Thames,*
*That so did take Eliza and our James!*
*But stay, I see thee in the hemisphere*
*Advanced and made a constellation there:*
*Shine forth, thou star of poets ...*

Now, Shakspere lived in London pretty much full time; and one can hardly imagine the stern ruler of Britain or her successor eagerly waiting for a member of an actors' troupe to arrive in the capital.

One more enigmatic line at the beginning of the poem merits particularly close attention: "Thou art a monument without a tomb . . . " The Stratford memorial had been just erected and Digges mentioned it in his verse. Now, it appears that this monument does not exist for Jonson at all — the only real monument to Shake-speare would be his name and his works, as they were his only incarnation during his lifetime.

One of the most remarkable features of the book is the portrait on the title page, which was presented as an image of William Shakespeare. It was created by a young engraver of Flemish origin, Martin Droeshout (born in 1601). The portrait bears no resemblance to the image of Shakespeare made not so long before, the Stratfordian bust in the Holy Trinity Church (in its initial or its present day appearance).

The face is like a mask, with a huge brow with a strange bulbous protuberance, as if he were ill with dropsy ("horrible hydrocephalus development," noted one scholar); the wide chin is elongated. The upper lip carries a thin moustache and a small beard is under the lower lip; both the chin and the upper lip seem to be in need of a shave. His ear protrudes and his hair seems to be plastered down. The oval of the face starts right at the ear lobe, and behind it there is another sharp line that goes beyond the ear at the top and down under the chin. The light is given from different sides, so one cannot take the line for the natural outline of a shadow. It looks as though this line was drawn on purpose and, as some non-Stratfordians think, it designates the edge of a mask, for those with the eyes to see it. The large head seems to be detached from the body by a flat pleated collar resembling a pole-axe blade.

The clothing of the "figure" (as Ben Jonson called it) produces no less weird an impression. The improbably tight tunic, richly decorated with embroidery and buttons, does not at all recall the attire of a person of humble station. Stranger yet, one half of the tunic is shown correctly, while the other is presented from behind, so that both sleeves appear to be left (this was noted only early in the 20th century, by experts from the London professional review "The Gentleman's Tailor" (April, 1911). Could any artist, even one that was inexperienced, have made such a blunder?[44] No, it can only have been done intentionally, at the behest of the sly sponsors of the Great Folio . . . and it gives us another hint: there was more than one person behind the portrait.

Shakespeare. M. Droeshout's engraving in the First Folio. 1623.

Did Droeshout simply dream up the pole axe-blade ruff and the tight, ornate tunic? Portraits of common people of the 16th and 17th centuries do not look like this, let alone the unique "reversed" tunic. But tunics of similar cut were normal for the most eminent aristocrats of the period, the Earls of Southampton and Dorset, for example, as may be seen in several portraits. In the Earl of Dorset's portrait by I. Oliver (1616), the tunic and the ruff as well show a certain resemblance to Droeshout's "perception." Quite possibly Droeshout had seen Oliver's picture[45] and "borrowed" from it while designing Shakespeare's portrait on order for the "Grand Possessors of the Plays."

Stratfordian biographers find it difficult to account for strangeness of Droeshout's engraving, and most often they take the easy route, ascribing it to Droeshout's young age (in 1623 he was only 22 years old), lack of experience, and modest artistic capabilities. Thus, Schoenbaum writes: "Martin was . . . hardly experienced in his craft. How he obtained the commission we do not know — perhaps his fee was as modest as his gifts."[46] But Droeshout's artistic biography tells another story. Only two years later he made a portrait of the Duke of Buckingham, in a highly professional engraving giving a realistic depiction of all the particulars of his attire, as we can verify by the unquestionable similarity of Buckingham's face with his other portraits. The very fact that Droeshout received this commission from the leading nobleman of the land (or from someone of his milieu) speaks of his high repute as an engraver and portrait painter. One of the Great Folio's patrons, with whom Buckingham was certainly acquainted, as we shall see later, may have recommended him to the Duke.[47]

The same indefatigable Ben Jonson took on the task of presenting and explaining to the public the portrait of the Shake-speare. Besides an excellent poem and the text of the addresses on behalf of two members of the actors' troupe, Ben also wrote one more, special, verse "To the Reader" which was printed on the page opposite to Droeshout's engraving. This is a poetic masterpiece of wit and ambiguity.

> *This figure that thou here seest put,*
> *It was for gentle Shakespeare cut;*

---

44. John Brophey, author of the book, *The Gentleman from Stratford*, hazards the assumption that the reverse feature of the coat was invented by the artist as a way of symbolically representing a duplicitous trait of the Bard's soul, "in which two natures seem to be constantly in argument."

45. The collar in the Dorset picture is decorated with embroidery. The beard and moustache also resemble Shakespeare's, but in the earl's picture they are denser and look more natural, as does the face as a whole.

46. Schoenbaum S. Op. cit.p. 315.

47. Martin Droeshout is known for another, even more famous, work: a highly professional engraving showing John Donne laid out in his death clothes (1632). The work is remarkably similar to the sculpture by Nicholas Stone in St. Paul's Cathedral. Thus, we know that Droeshout was quite able to execute accurate, realistic engraved portraits of the highest quality; the peculiarities in Shakespeare's image indicate that he was not depicting a real person but a "mask."

*Wherein the graver had a strife*
*With nature, to undo the life:*
*O, could he but have drawn his wit*
*As well in brass, as he hath hit*
*His face; the print would then surpass*
*All, that was ever writ in brass,*
*But, since he cannot, reader, look*
*Not on the picture, but his book.*

Some non-Stratfordians point out that the words "has hit his face" (captured the features) are very close to "has hid his face" (disguised the features), and surmise that Jonson intended the second version for the initiated. Such a turn of phrase corresponds nicely to the "figure," which "was for gentle Shakespeare cut" and the "strife with nature" which he had to endure in order to "surpass all." Otherwise, why should the artist surpass nature, in creating the face of the "figure"? Non-Stratfordians suggest that Jonson praises Droeshout for managing to devise such an excellent mask, disguising the authentic author, the Great Bard; but as one cannot represent a person's mind in an image, then readers have to study his works instead. Incidentally, Jonson's poetic heritage includes an interesting verse,[48] intended for an artist whom Jonson "instructed" on how to depict something that cannot be seen. Creating an imaginary portrait, an artist emulates nature itself and strives to surpass life itself.

Thus non-Stratfordians, pointing out multiple questions and ambiguities in the Droeshout portrait and Jonson's verse accompanying it, conclude that the portrait was designed on order and deliberately presents not a certain person, but a lifeless mask. For us, the uninitiated, the problematical engraving and ambiguous address are pulling our collective leg; before our eyes, as Jonson says in his second verse, the invisible Shakespeare "is brandishing his lance."

Stratfordian authors usually avoid "probing" into the ambiguities of Jonson's address to the reader; they gloss over it, noting that Jonson allegedly was critical of Droeshout's work. Others, on the contrary, maintain that Jonson liked the engraving, and probably found some likeness with the late Bard; otherwise, why place it in the folio.

In his biography of Shakespeare, Schoenbaum touches upon the poem, cautiously noting: "Jonson was able to bring himself to supply a few perfunctory lines of commendation, printed on the adjoining leaf. No doubt only an over-subtle reader will detect a latent irony in Jonson's conclusion . . . but the advice is sound enough."[49]

Yes, indeed, the last words from Jonson resound quite definitely. But one could take them to mean something else entirely, taking into account the purport of the whole poem and the specific features of the Droeshout "figure." It is hardly normal

---

48. Eupheme, 4
49. Schoenbaum S. Op. cit. p. 317.

Richard Sackville, Earl of Dorset. Portrait by I. Oliver. The Earl's garment resembles the one shown in M. Droeshout's engraving.

practice to place a special verse next to the author's portrait, in which the reader is advised not to look at the picture.

Droeshout's "figure' was reprinted without any change in the Second Folio that appeared a decade later, in 1632. And eight years after that, in 1640 — that is, after Ben Jonson's death — the editor, John Benson (the name is a curious coincidence) issued a collection of Shakespeare's poetic works (minus two large poems); it incorporated a number of verses dedicated to his memory and an engraving with his image signed with the initials of some other engraver. The picture is not widely known; it is seldom presented even in special literature. The facial features are not so distinct as in the Great Folio (the format is in octavo, a quarter of the folio size), but the influence of the Droeshout engraving is evident, mostly in the presentation of the face, hair and collar. There are some new traits: the face is turned not to the right but to the left, there is a mantle on the right shoulder, the left hand (gloved) is holding an olive branch with fruit, and there is a semblance of a halo around the head.

Under the engraving there is a short verse, which ironically reminds us of Jonson's address to the reader in the Great Folio:

> This Shadow is renowned Shakespeare? Soule of the age
> The applause? delight? the wonder of the stage...

Jonson's "figure" has become a "shadow," and the three interrogation marks are rather intriguing. The address and other poets' verses contained in the book are full of deep veneration for the Bard; then, what could be the meaning of this?

The Droeshout engraving is the only one formally confirmed by contemporaries, one way or another, but Shakespeare's biographers find it suspicious and they are put off by its strange features. They prefer others, which have not been verified as true representations of Shakespeare (or Shakspere); at least the unknown men portrayed in them do resemble people who lived in those times. I have already mentioned the portraits that, after a privileged life on museum walls or in the pages of luxurious Shakespeare editions, turned out to be false. Some of the better-known examples are the so-called Chandos and Grafton portraits. The Grafton picture bears an inscription saying that the person presented on it was 24 years old in 1588, the same as Shakspere. That was enough to allow the well-known Shakespearean John Dover Wilson to support it as a picture of the young Shakespeare. At least Wilson hedged, writing: "Yet there is no real evidence, and I don't ask the reader to believe in it or even to wish to believe in it. All I suggest is that he may find it useful in trying to frame his own image of Shakespeare. It will at any rate help him to forget the Stratford bust."

Clearly, the scholar is unhappy with the lack of a confirmed image. Like some other Stratfordian authorities, he is not satisfied either with the Stratford bust (he does not even mention its first version) or the Droeshout engraving, for they do not conform to his notions about Shakespeare. He would prefer to see some of the other portraits as authentic, despite the absence of any good reason to do so. Wilson really

This Shadowe is renowned Shakespear's Soule of th'age
The applause delight the wonder of the Stage.
Nature her selfe, was proud of his designes
And joy'd to weare the dressing of his lines,
The learned will Confess, his works are such,
As neither man, nor Muse, can prayse to much.
For ever live thy fame, the world to tell,
Thy like, no age, shall ever paralell.
W. M. sculpsit.

Shakespeare. The engraving in John Benson's edition of Shakespeare's poems and sonnets. 1640. What do the three interrogation marks mean?

tried. He took measurements, calculated the proportions of the face in the Grafton portrait, and found that they matched the proportions in the Stratford bust (in its present shape!) and the Droeshout engraving. Thus, despite the disparity of the three images, which is obvious to the casual observer, he asserted that "the proportions of the face features coincide."

There are also Stratfordians who do not criticize the Droeshout engraving and who even try to enliven the "figure" by reproducing enlarged images of its separate parts. For instance, only the face, without the hair, collar and the notorious cloak — which, in Anikst's words, give "the image of Shakespeare an awkward and wooden aspect." Never mind the many stylized representations of the portrait by modern illustrators.

Those who enjoy "transfiguring" artifacts into counterfeits have also tried their hands on the Droeshout engraving. It was assumed long ago that, while preparing his engraving, Droeshout had in mind some portrait made of Shakespeare during his lifetime. Then, in the second half of the 19$^{th}$ century, just such an "original" portrait actually appeared. A Mrs. Flower acquired it and donated it to the Shakespeare Memorial, and the memorial officer Edgar Flower presented experts with a picturesque portrait (oil on a wooden board), which greatly resembled the Droeshout engraving. It had an inscription in the top left corner: "Wilm Shakespeare." Competent experts from the British Museum and the National Arts Gallery pronounced the picture authentic, painted during Shakespeare's lifetime. Of course, it was a sensation — at last, Shakespeare's portrait was found, and with his name on it. Now all those vexing questions about Droeshout's creation could be put to rest! The picture with the relevant explanation was placed in the National Arts Gallery, and the famous Shakespeare researcher Sidney Lee placed a reproduction of it in the frontispiece of his major work, *Shakespeare's Life* (1898). For a long time afterward, it decorated various editions of Shakespeare and works on him in many languages. However, some doubts as to its authenticity still lingered; and in 1966 it was examined by X-ray. Under the picture was an image of the Madonna with child, probably by some mediocre 16$^{th}$-century Italian painter. It is hard to imagine that any painter during Shakespeare's lifetime would paint Shakespeare's (or Shakspere's) portrait on a used Italian panel; it would have been easier and cheaper to start with a new canvass or board. Some other features of the "portrait" led specialists to conclude that it was made much later than the Droeshout engraving, most probably in the next century; that is, it was purposely doctored. The Droeshout engraving was taken as the inspiration for fraud, and the old wooden board, dark with age, added greater authenticity. Still, proponents of the Flower portrait hope that pigment analysis or some other miracle will restore the reputation of the "most valuable and authentic image of the Great Bard that ever existed."

Thus, the Stratford monument and the Great Folio, the two most important pieces of tangible evidence that the baffling Bard left to us posthumously and wherein the creative biography of William Shakespeare crosses paths with the documented biography of William Shakspere, bear testament that despite the evident incompatibility of those two persons, they are somehow intriguingly connected. It is no accident that the Stratford cult emerged. Years after Shakspere's death, when very few people remembered him, certain influential persons took special care in order that posterity should take him for the Great Bard (who also had departed this life by then). As we know, they achieved their aim. For a long time.

## THE GREAT BARD ACQUIRES A BIOGRAPHY

Traditional notions about the identity of the author of "Hamlet," "The Tempest," "King Lear" and the sonnets first came under question as the facts were being dug up. In this day and age, biographies are supposed to be based on an academic approach to reality (or, at least, the appearance of such); and by academic we mean, first of all, based on facts. Shakespeare biographies are loaded with facts — documented facts about the life and occupation of William Shakspere from Stratford and his family, descriptions of various historic events of Elizabethan times in England, its culture, and the European Renaissance in general, facts from the life of outstanding figures — writers, poets, actors, state officials; and, in parallel, with analysis (in various degrees) of Shakespeare's dramatic and poetic craftsmanship. Since researchers long ago matched up the accepted dates when the plays were created with the life events of Shakspere (who is always and without any qualifications simply called Shakespeare) — all this abundance of facts makes it possible to concoct a seemingly coherent description of the life of the Great Bard. On the other hand, an analysis of the facts pertaining to William Shakspere and the content of Shakespeare's texts show them to be utterly incompatible, impossibly mismatched — in other words, they belong to the biographies of two quite different men. Thus the first doubts crept in as to the identification of the Great Bard, doubts that were then substantiated as more and more facts came to light.

In the first decades after Shakespeare's death, nobody in the whole of England tried to document his biography or even to record any observations about his life. We know how highly his educated contemporaries valued his dramatic skill and his poetry; however, they did not tell us any concrete details about the author. One might think that these people, who were educated in Greek and Roman cultural traditions, had never heard of biography as a genre, had never read Plutarch and Svetonius, and were not interested in the outstanding figures of their own time. The life and death of William Shakespeare are enveloped in the strange silence of his contemporaries; there is only the name, without flesh and blood.

If that was where the matter ended, then Shakespeare's identity crisis, the notorious "Shakespeare question," might never have taken on such enormous proportions, would not have preoccupied so many minds in so many countries, would have dissipated calmly like so many other ephemeral controversies. When only the author's works have survived and nothing definite is known about him, then literary studies are the only basis for research. There are no particular discussions now about the identity of Homer, after all . . .

But in 1623, the Shakespeare Great Folio was issued with hints and allusions to Stratford and the recently erected small monument in the local church; and in 1632, the edition was reissued. The seed was sown, and a framework for future researchers and biographers was established; but the time for harvest was not yet ripe. The great playwright's glory was growing. Thousands of people read his works, but still nothing was known about him. Nobody went to Stratford to look into his background. In 1634, Lieutenant Hammond, who made a chance visit to Stratford, noted in his diary that in the local church there was a "neat monument of that famous English poet Mr. Shakespeare"; there was also a monument to his friend Combe, for whom, as Hammond was told, Shakespeare once composed a humorous epitaph.

Milton, who was young at the time, wrote a verse dedicated to Shakespeare that was published in 1632 in the Second Folio; in it, he tried to explain somehow the absence of at least a modest description of the life of the great poet:

> *What need my Shakespeare for his honored bones*
> *The labour of an age in piled stones,*
> *Or that his hallowed relics should be hid*
> *Under a stary-pointing pyramid?*
> *Dear son of memory, great heir of fame,*
> *What need'st thou such dull witness of thy name?*
> *Thou in our wonder and astonishment*
> *Has built thyself a lasting monument . . .*

Here Milton repeats and develops further the image of a "monument without a tomb" taken from Ben Jonson. Here again the highest regard is shown to Shakespeare's works, and here again we see that the eternal glory that awaits his great creations is completely in contrast with, is distinct from, the place where his earthly remains were buried — although that, too, should be hallowed. These lines are supposed to have been written by Milton in 1630, when the Stratford monument had been in its place in the Trinity Church for about eight years. He participated in the republication of the Great Folio (though it is not clear who could have recommended the young poet to the editors); and so, of course, he had read the poems by Jonson and Digges prefacing it and should have known about the Stratford monument. However, he completely ignores its existence, which cannot but add to our wonder.

Still, time went on, and the seeds sown by the creators of the Great Folio and the Stratford "monument" came to bear fruit. Those seeking information about the great writer Shakespeare cast their gaze toward Stratford, and little by little information began to be exchanged. Rumors about the famous poet and playwright Shakespeare reached Stratford; and from Stratford, a few facts and anecdotes were received about Shakspere, the former member of an actors' troupe. All the participants of this slowly unfolding drama thought they were dealing with one and the same person, and gradually the information came to be combined for the "mutual enrichment" of the two biographies.[50] Still, as we now know, the two biographies did not merge into a single one, for they are irrevocably incompatible — which becomes evident only when enough information is gathered together and it becomes clear that the differences are critical.

Thomas Fuller (1608-1661) may be called the first Shakespeare biographer; in his book *Worthies of England* (published posthumously in 1662), in the part entitled "Warwickshire," after Jonson, Digges and Milton he gives Shakespeare's works a very high rating, and tells us in passing that Shakespeare was born and was buried in Stratford-on-Avon. Fuller evidently did not know the date of Shakespeare's death, for in the book printed from his manuscript it is given as: "Died in 16 . . . ." Had he visited Stratford, it would not have been hard for him to learn the year of Shakspere's death.

In Fuller's short notes (presumed to have been written in 1640s) — just a few dozen lines — one can sense his awareness of F. Meres' critique and Ben Jonson's comment about Shakespeare's poor command of Latin and Greek. Fuller remarks that Shakespeare was poorly educated and compares him with a gem which, like Cornwall diamonds, owed everything to nature but not to external polishing. Then Fuller writes (without mentioning where he had heard it) that Shakespeare and Jonson frequently found themselves in verbal sparring, with the more educated Jonson coming across like a heavily armed but awkward Spanish galleon whereas Shakespeare — like a lighter but more agile English navy ship — had the advantage, owing to his wit and inventiveness. The purely biographic data that Fuller was able to obtain and bring to the reader thus are minimal: Shakespeare was born and died in Stratford-on-Avon, and he was a poorly-educated man. Still, for Fuller to describe the great poet and playwright as poorly educated shows that Fuller was had only a cursory acquaintance with Shakespearean works; for later on more attentive experts found uncontested and multiple traces of unique education and deep culture of their author.

In any case, an English priest wrote those lines based on someone else's word, some thirty years after Shakspere's death and twenty years after the Great Folio was published, and they served as a basis for many other biographers. Those several lines were what, for the first time quite definitely (as opposed to the hints given by the monument and the Great Folio) connected the works of the Shake-spear with the Stratford relics or, to be more precise, with a single relic, for other than the tomb in the Holy Trinity Church, all the authentic artifacts related to William Shakspere, still unknown to the public, were tucked away in attics or book shelves.

---

50. The more so that in the 1630s and 1640s, some of the sponsors of the Great Folio and the Stratford monument were still alive, and they could have had a hand in directing that process.

It may be remarked that Fuller, in his notes about Ben Jonson (which are also rather brief, albeit not half as brief as those concerning Shakespeare) tells us something about Jonson's family, his childhood, education and the date of his death (not quite accurately: 1638 instead of 1637). In spite of the cursory nature of Fuller's notes about Jonson, by modern standards, considering they are based on information received second- or even third-hand, he gives us an image of this poet that is much more vivid than Shakespeare's, thanks to the more complete biographical facts.

As far as we know, the first attempt to study the biographical facts of Shakespeare (i.e. Shakspere) was made in Stratford at about the same time that Fuller's book came out. Vicar Ward was assigned a parish in Stratford in 1662. At the time, there were probably several people in the city who remembered Shakspere or had heard about him. Not far from Stratford lived Shakspere's granddaughter, Lady Barnard, who died only in 1670 at the age of 61. Still, Ward learned very little during his 19 years of service in Stratford, as may be judged by his diary. He wrote: "I have heard that Mr. Shakespear (sic) was a natural wit, without any art at all; he frequented the plays all his younger time; but in his elder days lived at Stratford and supplied the stage with two plays every year, and for that had allowance so large, that he spent at the rate of a thousand pounds a year, as I have heard." Ward also found out that Shakspere had two daughters, and he knew where Lady Barnard lived (in her second marriage), but it is not clear whether he ever met her. Ward was told that Shakspere died of a "fever" that began after his liberal drinking bout with Drayton and Ben Jonson.

Many Shakespeareans nowadays are skeptical of these notes, for they present an unacceptable image of the great man. One may agree that Ward could hardly question the information he was given by his parishioners, but some of it does coincide with other evidence that we now have (but that Ward did not) about William Shakspere, his occupations, and his will. The traces of the real William Shakspere are easily distinguished in Ward's notes from naïve fantasies and ruminations about any connection between the Stratfordian and creative activity and huge profits reaped from it. Indeed, the memory of one of the most famous men of the city, whose memorial survived in the local church, may have been preserved among parishioners for several decades, especially since his daughter Judith died the same year that Ward appeared in Stratford (1662). The Stratford man had lived for a long time in London, was in touch with theaters, and provided well for his family. The Harts — descendants of Shakspere's sister Joan — still lived in the house in Henley Street. It was not hard even after forty or fifty years to find out who the members of Shakspere's family had been and to ascertain that all of them, and Shakspere himself, were uneducated. Shakspere's neighbors could hardly say what he had been doing in London, and none of his countrymen had ever called him a dramatist or a poet during his lifetime.

But when rumors reached the city that the late Stratfordian was not only in touch with the London theaters but had been also a famous composer of plays, when visiting dignitaries became interested in his life and even the parish priest began to make inquiries, then some "particulars" about his life began to appear, colored by the locals in accordance with their notions of such matters as theater, drama and poetry. Thus some mixture of truth and invention emerged, some "legends," which several decades later became an important source for Shakespeare biographers. Today's researchers are more skeptical about these "legends," for it is difficult to get at any underlying truth. In Ward's case, it is easier because traces of real life were still maintained in the memory of his countrymen.

Vicar Ward was a diligent person. He made a note in his diary "to peruse Shakespear's plays and be versed in them" so as not to be "ignorant in that matter." It may mean that he had not read them before (or not carefully), but he also mentions the names of Jonson and Drayton, so the priest was an educated man and knew contemporary literature. Having made such a reminder in his diary, Ward clearly anticipated further talks with his parishioners; and he intended to go on with his investigation, for he certainly could not be totally unaware of the importance of such an activity.

However, Shakespeare's name is found only in one of Ward's sixteen surviving diaries, at the very beginning of his sojourn in Stratford. He never wrote about Shakespeare again. Is it possible that he did not learn anything new about him, or lost interest in the man? Did he, perhaps, learn something that would discourage an honest priest, and put his soul in turmoil? Or, perhaps, parts of his diary dealing with Shakespeare were lost or disappeared? Another mystery! And still, practically at first hand, Ward confirmed Shakspere's lack of education, which coincides with what we know today. Also, the merry drinking bout with Shakspere's London friends, which caused his illness and death, deserves special attention for there must be some seed of truth in it. There must have been many witnesses to such an affair; there must have been a lot of talk when it ended in the death of the host.

But Ward's diary was found many years later; and the same goes for John Aubrey's (1627-1697) book on famous people in England. The book was not finished during his lifetime, but was published much later. Aubrey wrote what he had heard about Shakespeare from various people, including some hearsay from the actor William Biston, who is supposed to have learned about Shakespeare from his father, a player in the troupe of Lord Chamberlain in 1598. Probably Aubrey visited Stratford in 1681. He wrote down a lot of stories about Shakespeare, many of which were recognized later as fake. For instance, it was he who wrote that Shakespeare was a butcher's son and recited tragic monologues while helping his father to slaughter cattle. He also wrote that Shakespeare was once a schoolteacher; and that a not very well-known poet and dramatist, William Davenant, told him that while going through Oxford, Shakespeare would often stay at his father's inn and flirt with his mother. Davenant hinted that Shakespeare was his natural father, and this invention is evidence that Shakespeare's name already carried some weight in England.

John Dryden's "An Essay of dramatic poesy" appeared in 1668, and in it the "god-like, divine Shakespear" was placed above all contemporary and ancient poets alike.

Those who accused him of scant scholarship, wrote Dryden, by this very fact praised him most, for he learned from nature and did not need books. The premise that Shakespeare lacked education, originating in Stratford and matching Ben Jonson's vague words about his limited knowledge of Latin and Greek, now was "theoretically substantiated" and went along with the creative heritage of the genius.

New editions of the Folio came out in 1663, 1664 and 1685, the last two with additional seven plays that are now considered apocryphal and are not included in the canon. Shakespeare was more and more widely read, but no coherent biography was ever created in the 17th century.

The first such biography appeared only in 1709. Its author, the poet and dramatist Nicholas Rowe, positioned it as a foreword to his six-volume edition of Shakespeare's plays; the book included an engraving featuring the Stratford monument, nearly the same as it appeared in Dugdale's book — a lean-faced elderly man with a drooping moustache, without pen or paper, with a shapeless sack clinging to his stomach. Also included was an engraving from the Chandos portrait, which was very popular throughout the 18th century. This biography stated for the first time that Shakespeare was born in 1564, that his father was a trader in wool who could not give the boy better education than he had himself. Rowe also tells us of Shakespeare's marriage to Anne Hathaway, and for the first time mentions the story about his poaching in Sir Thomas Lucy's park (later repeated in most Shakespeare biographies). He gives Shakespeare's age when he died, and quotes a part of the inscription on the Stratford tomb. Then Rowe repeats the words of William Davenant (the man who not spare his own mother in his ambition to claim to be a son of Shakespeare[51]). There is also an assertion that Shakespeare received one thousand pounds sterling as a gift from Lord Southampton, which is a pure fantasy.

The Rowe biography, together with rumors and legends, contains some factual data about William Shakspere, but Rowe never went to Stratford himself and got all his information about it from Thomas Betterton (1635-1710). Betterton made a pilgrimage to Stratford and certainly saw the wall monument in the Trinity church. There are some errors in the information provided: for instance, instead of two daughters and a son, Rowe said that Shakspere had three daughters, the elder being Judith and not Susanna. Rowe does not give the spelling of Shakspere's name as it is given in the Stratford documents and always calls him Shakespeare; probably, he did not know about the difference in the names, or, like many other biographers after him, he did not see any significance in it. But the major feature of this biography was the confounding, in all good faith, of the facts and rumors about both Shakspere and Shakespeare, presenting a unified, if not, perhaps, an entirely coherent, story. The

---

51. The rumor was passed on from one biography to another, and two and a half centuries later reached the Russian writer Yu. Dombrovsky, who together with other legends accorded it a prominent place in his book *The Dark Lady*.

Stratford monument and the Great Folio (reprinted several times during the previous century) served as links, as did later legends and inventions.

Rowe also did some editing: he divided into scenes and acts Shakespeare's plays; they had been printed in the Folio without such a subdivision. He provided each play with the full list of *dramatis personae* and, judging by the text, gave the location of the action. But he is most interesting to us as a Shakespeare biographer, the one who completed the first, most important period in the construction of a biography of the Great Bard. We can see how people began creating it, some 50-70 years after Shakspere's death, on the basis of the hints in the Great Folio and the inscription on the Stratford tomb, on hearsay, legends and unverified data, reflecting and adorning the scarce authentic facts about the life of a shrewd shareholder in an actors' troupe and purchaser of the church tithe.

One can hardly trace the origin of many of the rumors and anecdotes that gradually were incorporated into Shakespeare's biographies, but it is clear they emerged together with the burgeoning fame and glory of the works and the name of Shakespeare. As to the naïve credulity of the first biographers, which is much discussed today by non-Stratfordians, one should not forget that history became a science only later, and the most surprising of the authentic documents about William Shakspere, such as the notorious will, evidence of usury, court papers etc., were found only in the middle of the 18th century, and their significance only began to sink in later.

After Rowe, Shakespeare's plays were published in the same century by Alexander Pope (1725), Lewis Theobald (1733), Thomas Hanmer (1744), William Warburton (1747), Samuel Johnson (1765), Edward Cappel (1768) George Steevens (1773, 1778, 1785, 1793), and Edmund Malone (1790). Altogether, from 1709 to 1799, no fewer than sixty editions of Shakespeare's plays were published in England. He was pronounced a classic writer, indeed, the premier among classics. Meticulous academic work on Shakespeare's texts began in the 18th century, and much new data was obtained. Shakespeare's poetry did not fare so well: even the prominent scholar George Steevens, who made a major contribution to the study and publication of Shakespeare's plays, flatly refused to include Shakespeare's poems in his editions, declaring that even the most severe parliamentary act would not make Englishmen read them!

As to the description of Shakespeare's life, the sketch by Rowe remained the major source of information about him, nearly until the very end of the 18th century (nothing was known yet about Ward's diary and Aubrey's book). Prominent Shakespeareans in their century, Alexander Pope, L. Theobald, and S. Johnson were still musing on Dryden's notion of Shakespeare's greatness as a Poet, through whom Nature herself was speaking so that there was no need of book knowledge to reproduce Her creativity. Compared to the meticulous work on Shakespeare's texts, the literary criticism, and many reprints, much less effort was exerted in systematic study and examination of new biographical data about the Stratfordian. Meanwhile,

Stratfordian "relics" and "legends" multiplied, and strengthened the gradually evolving cult.

## THE ANNIVERSARY

A notable event contributing to the consolidation of the Stratfordian cult was the so-called "Shakespeare Anniversary." As a matter of fact, the two-hundred-year anniversary of Shakespeare (i.e. Shakspere) fell in April 1764, but they managed to celebrate it only some five odd years later, in September 1769. The affair was headed by the famous actor David Garrick, who revered Shakespeare: he even built a chapel on his estate, where he placed a bust of Shakespeare made by the French sculptor Roubiliac.

On the bank of the Avon River in Stratford, a wooden amphitheater (rotunda) was erected, with a stage big enough for a hundred participants in the show; the dance floor accommodated one thousand dancers. On September 5, 1769, a 30-gun salvo and chiming church bells toll announced the start of the jubilee. To the sound of clarinets, flutes and guitars, a chorus of motley clad actors began singing: "Let beauty with the sun arise to Shakespeare tribute pay!" The Town Hall held a lunch for the public, during which the choir sang: "The Will of all Wills was a Warwickshire Will" and even: "The thief of all thieves was a Warwickshire thief." By this, they meant the notorious episode of "Shakespeare's poaching" in Sir Lucy's park. The bust of the Great Bard in the Holy Trinity Church was drifted over with flowers; the choir of the Drury Lane Theater performed the oratory "Judith." Then the Bard's fans, decorated in rainbow-colored ribbons (symbolizing universal character of Shakespeare's genius), accompanied by musicians, went to the house on Henley Street "where Shakespeare was born" and sang the song composed by Garrick, celebrating the city that gave the world the incomparable genius: "Here Nature nurs'd her darling boy . . . " At night there was singing, dancing, fireworks.

The next day began with a march of Shakespeare's heroes, following a triumphant chariot drawn by satyrs. Melpomena, Thalia and the Graces rode in the chariot. A heavy rain forced the hosts to modify the day's agenda, and all the participants had to seek shelter in the "Rotunda" (which could not accommodate so many people). The organizers had to skip the planned "Coronation." The gala "Ode to Shakespeare," also written by Garrick, was performed instead, and when the singer got to the "quietly flowing waters of the Avon," the doors of the theater were wide open and the singer's voice was accompanied by torrents of rain falling from the sky. Garrick gave a gala speech, ending with the words that were the motto of the jubilee: "We shall not look upon his like again." Then the famous actor put on the gloves that, as he was assured, had been worn by Shakespeare himself when he appeared on the theater stage. Despite the driving rain, this night also ended with a masquerade ball. On the last day, the crowd had thinned. The major event of the day was horse racing, and the winner received a valuable prize — a cup with Shakespeare's coat of arms. The final ball ensued, and then the jubilee was over.

Though the rain visibly marred the celebration, the "jubilee" entered history as the first national event in honor of the Great Bard and the city, which now became inseparable from the name. Though the leading British Shakespeareans of the time did not take part in the event and the press came up with many scornful articles deriding the primitive idolatry and lack of taste, these fastidious opinions did not hamper the subsequent development of the Stratford cult and its character.

The production of "relics" visibly increased during the jubilee and after it. Garrick and his brother George both obtained "gloves from Shakespeare." In the house that was considered Anne Hathaway's, George managed to acquire, just think! Shakespeare's inkwell! Somebody found a Shakespeare armchair, and some parts of it, a shoe horn, a signet ring with his stamp, a bench on which the Bard was fond of sitting, and a big beer mug which he had used while partaking of his favorite ale. And a tablecloth, given to the Bard as a gift "by his friend and fan — Queen Elizabeth I," was also found.

Only the house purchased by Shakspere in 1597 (the so-called New Place), where his family dwelled, where he spent the last years of his life and died, suffered from all this success. The house, bought in 1702 by descendants of the former owners, the Cloptons, was extensively rebuilt. It was acquired in 1753 by Francis Gastrell, a retired priest from another town, a coarse and willful man. Fans of the Great Bard, who frequented the city, were after Shakespeare relics and got on the nerves of the retired priest. First, he hired a woodcutter and ordered him to make firewood out of the mulberry tree venerated by pilgrims and reputed to have been planted by the Bard himself. The watchmaker Thomas Sharpe found even the firewood valuable, and he bought it; thus for a good forty years fans were able to purchase souvenirs (for a hefty price) made out of "Shakespeare's tree." By 1759, Gastrell had had enough of such visitors and, deciding to leave Stratford, he ordered the building demolished, for which act he was justly censored and would be cursed until Doomsday.

Together with relics grew the number of "legends" and folk stories, according to which Shakespeare was a crack wit always ready with a joke suitable for lords, fellow actors or Stratford neighbors . . .

Edmund Malone, an attorney, writer and theater expert, launched a systematic and scrupulous analysis of all the information gathered about Shakespeare by the end of the 18th century. First, he helped Steevens in the preparation of the 1778 edition for which he wrote an extensive commentary after that, he worked on his own. His ten-volume edition of Shakespeare's works, with a review of efforts made by many scholars in the 18th century, issued in 1790, became a solid basis for future research. In a sense, his efforts constituted the beginning of Shakespeare scholarship beyond the examination of texts. Malone's and his followers' research started to lift the curtain that obscured the identity of the Great Bard and inspired many people to give more thought to the Stratford documents.

Early in the 19<sup>th</sup> century a new type of edition appeared, which heralded new progress in Shakespeare studies: the variorum. Such an edition comprises all the different versions of the texts, enumerates the different readings with scholarly explanations and explications, and with complete and exhaustive commentary. The first Shakespeare variorum was issued in 1803 by Isaac Reed; in 1813 it was reissued. The third variorum was started by Malone, and after his untimely demise the edition was completed by James Boswell the Younger (the 21<sup>st</sup> volume was published in 1821). It included Shakespeare's poems. Among the introductory material (that took up three volumes) there was also a new Shakespeare biography. Malone was first to try to create a substantiated chronology of Shakespeare's works. The new biography was much more complete than Rowe's sketch; it contained more facts, it clarified some details, and introduced corrections. But what an irony — not one of the newly obtained Stratford documents, obtained through such great efforts, not one factual entry or signature had anything to do with the creative activity of Shakespeare, no connection with it whatsoever. On the contrary, many of the facts seemed to directly contradict the possibility of such a link.

## CHESTS OF MANUSCRIPTS

Time went on, but in spite of all efforts, manuscripts, letters, and papers documenting any literary activity or literary connections on the part of Shakspere (or even showing that he could read and write) stubbornly eluded every hunter. This phenomenon could hardly be overlooked by certain clever and enterprising people. And thus, the late 18<sup>th</sup> century witnessed the appearance of interesting new legends and relics from the "Shakespearean tree," and the long sought "old papers" as well.

John Jordan, a wheelwright from Stratford-on-Avon, should head the list of those who actively worked to provide Shakespeare biographers with the missing evidence. Failing to find success in his principal occupation, he earned money by guiding visitors interested in Shakespeare around Stratford and its environs. Neither did he shy away from making an occasional rhyme or two, which, to his way of thinking, put him on a closer footing with his great fellow countryman. He came into the history of Shakespeare studies as a composer of "stories" and a fabricator. Now and then, he was lucky enough to deceive even Edmund Malone. Some things he invented himself, some he borrowed from the anecdotes already in circulation.

Among Jordan's creations, the so-called spiritual testament of Shakespeare's father became most widely known. In 1784, Jordan approached the "Gentleman's Magazine" in London to publish the transcript he had made from a document which he claimed had been found a quarter of a century before, during repairs to the roof in the house on Henley Street — that same house that is commonly believed to be the birth-place of Shakspere, where the descendants of his sister, Joan Hart, were living at the time in question. Wedged between the rafters and the tiling, the discovery comprised six sheets of paper aced together. It was the Catholic profession of faith, each chapter beginning with the written name of John Shakspere. In the copy forwarded by Jordan, the first leaf was missing. Jordan informed them that the original document had "fine and readable handwriting." The magazine preferred not to print Jordan's copy, but rumors about the discovery came to the ears of scholars, and they managed to have the original forwarded from Stratford-on-Avon to Malone. At first, Malone believed that the document was genuine and decided to publish it (fragmentarily) in his *Historical Account of the English Stage*, which in 1790 was being prepared for publication. When it was already going to press, the scholar made an attempt to clarify the circumstances under which the find was made. A small notebook was sent to him, with the full text of the "Spiritual Testament" written in Jordan's hand. Where did the missing first leaf suddenly appear from? Jordan's answers to Malone's questions were evasive and inconsistent. Competent antiquarians thought the document was a forgery, but Malone nevertheless published the full text, including the unexpectedly supplied beginning. Later on, he too came to the conclusion that the "testament" had nothing to do with John Shakspere.

After the death of Edmund Malone, the document was not found and the question of its authenticity remained open for a long time. The picture, however, became clearer, at a surprisingly late date. In the 20th century it was learned that the text of "The Spiritual Last Will and Testament" had been drawn up by Carlo Borromeo, Archbishop of Milan, in the late 1570s, during the terrible plague epidemic. Instilled with fervent faith, the "Last Will" was adopted by the Catholic Church in its campaign against the Protestants in Europe. A group of British Jesuit missionaries stayed for some time in 1580 at the archbishop's home in Milan on their way from Rome, setting out for a very dangerous mission — to propagate Catholicism in England. Leaving Borromeo's home, they took the English translation of his "last will"; there are some indications that thousands of copies of this document were sent to them later on. The missionaries roamed all over England, served secret masses, and inscribed the newly Catholicized persons' names onto texts of the "last will." Secrecy was ensured, since those who provided refuge for Catholic missionaries did so at the risk of being sentenced to death. Most likely, Jordan obtained one of these "last wills," then transcribed, it inserting John Shakspere's name; later on, he destroyed all traces of his "find."

Cardinal Borromeo "last will" was popular, and not only among British Catholics. There is also a Spanish translation that was printed in Mexico in 1661 (and found only recently). This fact is provided in Schoenbaum's work *William Shakespeare. A compact documentary life*. After Jordan's "find," many scholars came to suspect John Shakspere of secret Catholicism (some of them still do, thinking it a reasonable explanation for Shakespeare (the Great Bard)'s apparently tolerant attitude toward the Catholic faith, which was then being persecuted in England). And that is how a legend is born. Based on Schoenbaum's reference to the Spanish version of the "last will," a Russian literary critic recently concluded that "Shakespeare's father" was no ordinary Catholic but a "prominent Catholic publicist" who allowed his work to be translated into Spanish.

As to Jordan, his memory often let him down. Thus, after a quarrel with the owners of the house on Henley Street, he came up with the claim that the Bard had been born in quite another house — apparently forgetting that he had presented the "Spiritual Testament of John Shakspere" as having been "discovered under the roof of the house on Henley Street where his (John's — *I.G.*) son William was born."

In the summer of 1793, Jordan met two inquisitive tourists from London. These were Samuel Ireland and his son, the 18-year-old William-Henry. Samuel Ireland was known for his engravings picturing England's landscapes and old houses. He was the first to portray the lodge where young Shakespeare was believed to have been locked up for a night after being caught in poaching. Ireland Sr. was distinguished for his boundless enthusiasm for Shakespeare. His family used to learn and recite his plays when gathering at dinner, the main roles being naturally performed by the head of the family. Another passion of his was collecting books and antiquarian items; he would acquire them as the occasion offered (and then profitably resell them); some truly rare books and documents came into his possession. He could show a guest a copy of Shakespeare's First Folio, several pictures by old artists, clothes and trinkets once belonging to King Henry VIII, Charles I, and James II, not to mention Philip Sidney, Oliver Cromwell, et al. His cherished dream, however, was to obtain a rarity directly associated with the Great Bard; he used to say that he would give up half of his treasures in exchange for a scrap of paper signed by the genius.

Ireland Jr., being of too recent issue to merit his father's full attention, grew up as an obedient but dreamy young man. From his favorite book, the epistolary novel *Love and Madness*, he learnt that the poet Thomas Chatterton used to present his poems as ancient works allegedly found in some mysterious long-forgotten chests, and this idea impressed the youth greatly. Ireland Sr. prepared his son for a career in law, and to give him a start got him a position as a clerk in a transportation office. The work was not much of a burden and the young man had enough time for other occupations, more suited to his character and cast of mind.

In Stratford-on-Avon the Irelands, accompanied by Jordan, went to visit a shop whose owner made good money selling souvenirs made out of the notorious "Shakespeare mulberry tree"; the visitors bought a goblet and some trifles. They also made a tour to the neighboring Shottery to visit the "House of Anne Hathaway," where the engraver purchased the old oak armchair, "in which Shakespeare liked to sit when courting his future wife." An old bed, obviously used by generations of farmers, also caught the artist's fancy, but the aged owner's wife would not part with it for the world. Samuel Ireland painted this thatched farmer's house, and the engraving was soon published. Thus the reading public saw for the first time the "House of Anne

Hathaway," one of the major sights in today's Stratford. Of course, Ireland inquired of all and sundry whether anyone knew of any manuscripts or papers relating to the Great Bard. The Londoner was told that a very long time before, during a fire, all the papers had been taken from the former Shakespeare house and moved to the Clopton house, located a mile from Stratford. The Irelands rushed over, but the owner, farmer Williams, said they were late: just two weeks before, he had decided to clear the room of a few crates filled with old papers; on several, he saw the name Shakespeare. The papers took up a lot of room, so he burned them! Ireland's distress was inconsolable. Actually, one authoritative Stratford antiquarian would later note in his diary that Williams recounted to him what a good trick he had played on the metropolitan manuscript chasers . . .

So the Irelands, father and son, bade farewell to John Jordan and went back to London, having enriched the family collection of memorabilia with "Shakespeare's chair" and a mulberry goblet. But the young clerk was already nurturing in his head the plan to obtain far more significant things. He started with a collection of prayers dedicated to Queen Elizabeth, bound in parchment bearing the royal blazon; William-Henry purchased the book from an antiquarian he knew well. With some expert assistance William-Henry prepared special ink, wrote a dedicatory epistle to the queen on a leaf of old paper, and glued it into the prayer book next to the cover; as it dried, the ink acquired a somewhat rusty tint and did not look suspicious. Thus enriched, the rarity was presented to his father, who accepted it favorably.

Looking through a book by Malone taken from his father's bookshelf, William-Henry then focused on Shakespeare's (that is, Shakspere's) facsimile signatures, and trained himself in their reproduction; he also tried to gain some knowledge as to how personal letters and legal deeds were written and drawn up in the times of Shakespeare. Thus, a piece of old parchment appeared to bear the agreement of July 14, 1610, between William Shakespeare from Stratford-on-Avon, gentleman, now a resident of London, and John Heminge, Michael Fraser as well as the latter's wife, Elizabeth. Applying spelling that he deemed similar to that in use in Shakespeare's day, William-Henry put the signatures of the participants to the deed (using in turn his right and left hands). With a red-hot blade, he cut the wax seal from a minor document of the King James I era, fortuitously purchased in advance, and then used the fresh wax, ash and cinder to "certify" the result of his work with the old seal. This document he also presented to his father, who again heartily thanked him for such a valuable gift.

To answer the natural question on the document's origin, William-Henry invented a story about a young gentleman whose family had kept many unsorted papers, a century and half old. The said gentleman gave the deed (and then other papers) to the younger Ireland, but on the strict condition that his (the gentleman's) name and address must remain anonymous under any circumstances. It is unknown whether Ireland-père believed this cock-and-bull story, but he never expressed any doubt, either at first or later on, when the "finds" poured down one after another. He

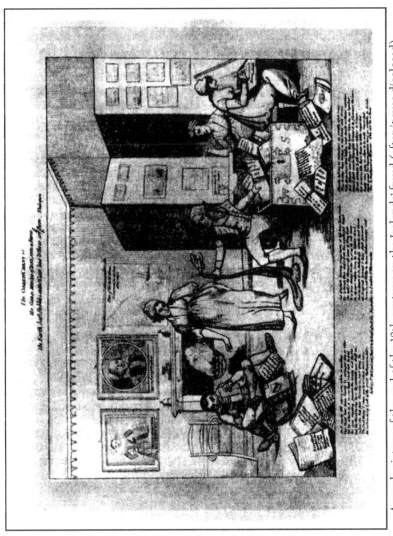

A mock picture of the end of the 18th century on the Irelands' fraud (after it was disclosed).

showed the "deed" in the Great Bard's handwriting to the officers of the Heralds' College, and the heralds officially authenticated it. In addition, an authority on ancient seals found that Ireland's seal featured the image of a quintain, which was erected for the knightly jousts with spears; this fact could already be associated with the name of the Great Bard (the Shake-speare), which quite surprised and encouraged young Ireland in his budding career as an expert on Shakespeare's signatures and manuscripts.

The house on Norfolk Street, where the engraver's family resided, began to receive regular visits from antiquarians and literary critics full of hopes that they might finally learn something definite about the Great Bard. Shakespeare, they argued, lived in the very heart of England; he could not but have been in contact with the most outstanding of his contemporaries, and each of them left some evidence in writing — some more, some less; it was unthinkable that the greatest luminary of the era could remain a strange and mysterious exception! Surely the manuscripts, letters and papers were simply hidden somewhere and waiting for the proper moment to appear before the people of England. Even the cautious Malone expressed the hope that the priceless, long-sought documents would now reveal much about Shakespeare, his relationship with other men of letters and his patrons, about how his masterpieces were created. Malone appealed to the mysterious owner of the precious papers (referred to by Ireland Jr.) to allow the experts, including of course himself, to take part in their study.

Such attention from the educated public, such anxious expectations obliged the young "discoverer of manuscripts" not to stop at half measures. The next document dated 1589 was to demonstrate the noble-mindedness of Shakespeare and his scrupulous dealings. Shakespeare undertook to pay John Heminge 5 pounds and 5 shillings "for his efforts and the services he rendered to me in the 'Globe' theater and when visiting me in Stratford." To this was attached Heminge's receipt, which William-Henry inscribed with his left hand. Today we would be surprised to see a document from 1589 referring to the Globe Theater, which was erected ten years later. But the public did not know that, and therefore neither did William-Henry — otherwise, he could just as easily have used some other, more appropriate date. But the obvious absurdities in spelling were there for anyone who wanted to see them.

The tale of the huge sum that the Earl of Southampton supposedly gave to Shakespeare, and the ardent desire to learn more details regarding this rich gift expressed by an esteemed friend of the Irelands (he was proud to have been lucky enough to purchase the cross-piece of the chair Shakespeare used to sit in) spurred William-Henry to make public a gratifying letter from the Great Bard and the warm response from the Earl of Southampton. Apart from the friendly relationship between the earl and Shakespeare, the letters demonstrated the noble mind of the latter, for he agreed to accept only the half of the proposed lavish donation! Anticipating the likely questions as to how the letter sent to Lord Southampton could have been left with Shakespeare, William-Henry marked it ("in the Bard's hand") as a copy. The "discoverer" used his other — left — hand to improvise Southampton's handwriting and signature. He was not aware that other letters existed, actually written by this lord.

The young clerk's imagination was never at rest. He informed his father that the country house of the same mysterious gentleman held treasures beyond their dreams: a signet ring in gold, with a precious stone and featuring the carved image of the quintain, two uncut copies of Shakespeare's First Folio and a life portrait of the Bard on stage — wearing a black gown and a pair of fine long gloves ... This time, the father pressed his son, wishing to see the treasures as quickly as possible. The first thing presented to his attention was a rough sketch in ink, apparently influenced by Martin Droeshout's engraved portrait from the First Folio; the older Ireland ridiculed the picture. Next came a Shakespeare letter to Richard Cowley, the comedian, in which the Bard offered to his partner's attention a "whymsycalle conceyte." To produce this "whymsycalle conceyte," William-Henry used a sheet of old paper with color drawings, which he had bought at a second-hand bookshop. One side of the sheet portrayed an elderly Dutchman, the other, a young cavalier dressed in the costume of the era of King James I. It was child's play to modify the young knight's face to make it more closely resemble the one on Droeshout's portrait; Shakespeare's initials appeared in the background, with the names of several plays and some semblance of the dramatist's coat of arms. Shakespeare connoisseurs ascertained at once that this was a portrait of the Bard in the role of Bassanio from "The Merchant of Venice." As to the Dutchman, he had acquired a set of scales and a knife, so that he was readily identified him as none other than the bloodthirsty Shylock. Experts also detected faint "traces" of a signature by a famous artist of the early 17$^{th}$ century. Many Shakespeare lovers were happy with the letter that confirmed the adherence of the playwright to the Anglican Church. Public agitation increased, and general expectations were soon satisfied.

Next, an agreement came to light between Shakespeare and the players Condell and Lowin as to the distribution of profits, and Shakespeare's receipt of a neat amount of 50 pounds for playing before the Earl of Leicester in his house. However, the latter document dated back to 1590, and it occurred to Ireland Sr. that the earl was no longer among the living at that time. The son was panic-stricken and wanted to burn the ill-fated receipt, but the father supposed that this might be some two-century-old error, and therefore they decided to merely cut the date from the document. This episode gives rise to some doubts whether the elder Ireland could have been so desperately innocent as to blindly give credit to the fairytales and none too masterly handiwork of his enterprising offspring.

And the public did not fail to notice Shakespeare's annotations in the margins of several old but not especially valuable books (purchased from a secondhand bookshop); this confirmed the existence of the Bard's own library. Soon, the catalogue of the library — personally drawn up by Shakespeare — surfaced, and since it included an entry pertaining to two books from 1613, it suggested that the catalogue was prepared toward the end of Shakespeare's life, probably in Stratford where the books would have been brought from London. Some people were surprised that no letters to Shakespeare from the members of the royal family had yet been found, and naturally those interested were soon able to behold with their own eyes a personal letter from Queen Elizabeth, in which she addressed "goode Master William Shakespeare atte the *Globe* bye Thames," with gratitude for his "prettye Verses," and reminded him that he should bring the best players to the royal palace "to give pleasure to me and Lord Leicester who will be with us." Some scholars of the time assumed that such a warm, almost friendly correspondence with the queen belied the absurd rumors that Shakespeare had begun his stage career by looking after the spectators' horses and performing other base jobs of that sort, and demonstrated that from the very start he was recognized and treated kindly by the high and mighty of this world. Not knowing the year when the Globe Theater was built, the scholars failed to notice another chronological blunder (as great as eleven years!) — again relating to the Earl of Leicester and the Globe. Actually, there was no time for reflection and in-depth analysis: they now had to digest the still more striking discovery — a love letter from Shakespeare with a lock of his own hair enclosed! The Bard's vows of love, his request to "kiss my poore lock" could not leave his admirers indifferent. The letter also comprised a poem of about two dozens lines. Needless to say, it demonstrated no outstanding artistic merit, but let's give credit where it's due — the young clerk had some courage, if he dared to challenge the Great Bard himself! Hairs from the precious lock were set in gold and became part of memorable rings to adorn the fingers of the Bard's most fervent admirers.

Meanwhile, the elder Ireland was working on an edition of his album of engravings entitled "Picturesque Views on the Upper, or Warwickshire Avon," in which he was going to give a detailed account of Shakespeare's manuscripts found by his son. Before publishing, he decided to have the text of this report looked through by the mysterious source of the discoveries — the young gentleman known to his son. The parties began a correspondence; the funniest aspect of which is that, in composing the letters to his father on behalf of the anonymous benefactor, William-Henry did not even take the trouble to disguise his handwriting! Mister X drew Samuel Ireland's special attention to the extraordinary intellectual and moral qualities of his son, his obvious literary gift, a play composed by him (a soliloquy from the play was attached) not inferior to any of Shakespeare's in its style and profundity. "Your son is brother in Genius to Shakespeare and is the only man that ever walked with him hand in hand." Indeed, there is no denying that Ireland Jr. possessed some wits and a creative gift. However, his reach clearly exceeded his grasp, though the success of such an enterprise could have turned the head of a more cautious and mature person.

The danger of exposure sometimes seemed imminent, and oddly enough, not from the literary erudite, not from the connoisseurs of history and ancient manuscripts. Once a visitor accidentally dropped a document, and the wax seal by which it was "certified" broke into two pieces; once a housemaid spotted him writing a letter from Queen Elizabeth; and again, Heminge's true signature was found and it looked very different from Ireland's "hook." Yet he somehow managed to get out of all such dilemmas.

For the time being, nobody publicly accused William-Henry of forgery, and his work went on, fabricating Shakespearean rarities, completing the elder Ireland's collection. A version of "King Lear" appeared, "cleared of black spaces and additions foisted in by the players," as well as the several pages of "the most true author's variants" of "Hamlet." Moreover, the outlines of a new, hitherto unheard of historical tragedy by Shakespeare emerged, a "play of Vortigern and Rowena." Having no such actually in hand, he showed his father a few pages written in his own hand, explaining that "Mister X" would not part with the original till he had transcribed the whole . . .

Finally, in February of 1795, Samuel Ireland deemed his collection quite complete and decided to open it to the public. This seems to have been a fatal mistake. If, instead of this ambitious idea, they had simply announced that the priceless manuscripts had disappeared, been lost, stolen, or burned, today's Shakespeare studies would have been built on a different foundation.

At first, everything went smoothly. More people than expected were anxious to acquaint themselves with the curiosities. The renowned authority on literature history and a friend of Malone, James Boswell Sr., not content with mere words of approbation and delight, fell to his knees, kissed one of the items and thanked God for making it possible for him to see these treasures. The Secretary of the Heralds' College, Francis Webb, was no less enchanted: "These papers bear not only the Signature of his hand, but the Stamp of his Soul, and the traits of his Genius — his Mind is as manifest, as his hand . . . The Papers exhibit him full of Friendship, Benevolence, Pity, Gratitude and Love . . . Here we see the Man, as well as the Poet."

Some visitors, however, shook their heads in doubt. Historian Joseph Ritson attentively examined everything, put some questions to William-Henry, and retired without saying a word. Then he wrote to a friend, "Shakespeare's papers, so much spoken of, — is a set of forgeries aimed at public deception." However, for some reason he did not express his opinion in public, and most people still believed the Irelands; the list of subscribers for the future edition of Ireland's "manuscripts" continued to grow, and included the names of some quite honorable persons.

Then the thought occurred to someone that in case Shakespeare had any lawful heirs, they might insist that the treasure trove be transferred to their ownership. This worried William-Henry, but shortly a new document was turned up, written personally, in William Shakespeare's hand, in October of 1604! By this deed, Shakespeare left the manuscripts of his plays to William-Henry Ireland, explaining the reason for such a gift. It just so happens that a party of drinking companions capsized the boat in which he was crossing the Thames, and Shakespeare found himself in danger of drowning. The valiant William-Henry Ireland had dragged him to the bank and fished him out, at risk to his own life. The deed of gift even enclosed a sketch, depicting the house in Blackfriars "where Mister Ireland lives." Also enclosed was a leaf of parchment depicting Shakespeare's and Ireland's coats of arms, chained together, with gratifying verses from the Great Bard placed under the picture.

It should be noted that by a whim of history there actually was a man named William Ireland who lived at the same time with Shakespeare and Shakspere. In December of 1604, he rented Londoner Henry Walker's building (gatehouse), the same house that William Shakspere would buy from Walker in March of 1613. The deed of purchase for the building, with the name of the tenant Ireland mentioned, as well as the mortgage on the building, were found late in the 18th century; both documents became widely known because they comprised two out of six discovered signatures of Shakspere. One can imagine the joy of our clerk when he saw almost his own name in the facsimile copy of a *true* Shakespeare document!

To "fine-tune" the name of William Ireland as William-Henry Ireland was no big deal. He told his father that "Mister X" was also in possession of papers that testified to the fact that their family originated from that very Ireland who lived in the times of Shakespeare. Coming like a bolt from the blue sky, the news made his father's head spin. In the meantime, some influential friends suggested that the Heralds' College would not object, should Samuel Ireland wish to unite his coat of arms with Shakespeare's.

But what dwarfed all the rest of William-Henry's fabrications was "The Act of February 23, 1611" — a sort of provisional will. In contrast to Shakspere's true will, discovered in 1747, the work of William-Henry Ireland was intended to dispel any doubt that Shakspere cared less about the fate of his literary heritage than, say, the second best bed. John Heminge was appointed to unlock the big oak chest at the Globe Theater, and take out the manuscripts of several plays, including "Titus Andronicus," "The Two Gentlemen of Verona," and "Henry VIII," and duly give them to Burbadge and other two players, and to take for himself five plays, including the "never printed play, Henry VII." The will prescribed that the love letters the Bard had written to his wife in bygone days should be returned to her — she was also to receive his small portrait, a few rings, and a pretty amount of 180 pounds — which of course explained why she was not remembered in the will of 1616.

His daughter (name not stated — obviously, the younger Ireland was in a hurry, or forgot that Shakspere had two daughters) was bequeathed a smaller sum but to her was allocated her father's "favourite ring presented by the Earl of Southampton." Heminge was entrusted with the most delicate and moving mission, relating to a certain unnamed child. He was instructed to hand over to the child, upon its reaching the age of 15 years, a considerable amount of money, as well as to take out from the precious chest and deliver to the same child 18 unpublished plays, and 8 plays more, including "King Vortigern." In accordance with this legal instrument, all the above plays (and any more that the playwright might create, by divine mercy of the Lord), as well as the income from their publication and performance, were to be transferred to the full ownership of this mysterious child, his progeny! The outlines of a striking conjunction began to show — the clerk William-Henry Ireland, living late in the 18th century on Norfolk Street in London, was about to be revealed as the direct offspring, and hence an heir, of the Great Bard!

Everything seemed to take its course. A luxurious edition was published, reproducing the "Miscellaneous Papers and Legal Instruments under the Hand and Seal of William Shakespeare: including the Tragedy of King Lear, and a Small Fragment of Hamlet: from the Original MSS. In the Possession of Samuel Ireland, of Norfolk Street." Shakespeare's hitherto unknown tragedy "King Vortigern" was about to have its premiere on stage . . . However, the publication of the "Miscellaneous Papers" finally gave Malone the chance to interfere. Malone did not want to examine Ireland's collection at his home, and Ireland had missed a meeting someplace else. Now that they were published, Malone had copies of the "papers," "letters" and "manuscripts" in his own hands, and his study of them immediately confirmed his worst fears. Unlike Ritson, Malone preferred not to keep his opinion to himself. He declared that all Ireland's papers were clumsy forgeries. His book *An Inquiry into the Authenticity of Certain Miscellaneous Papers and Legal Instruments . . . Attributed to Shakspeare, Queen Elizabeth, and Henry, Earl of Southampton* appeared at the end of March, 1796. The contents, spelling, and circumstances by which the sensational papers had appeared undeniably pointed to a gross falsification, and for Malone, with all his knowledge, it was easy to prove. Point by point, he revealed all the traces of the forgery: the counterfeiter's ignorance of the date of Leicester's death, as well as of the date (approximate, at least) of the construction of the Globe Theater; the "signatures" of Queen Elizabeth, Lord Southampton, and actor Heminge, that bore no resemblance to the genuine ones; the ridiculous spelling (an amateurish imitation of "old English"), etc. The conclusion that this was gross forgery was indisputable, and Malone expressed his regret for the damage this story caused to the Great Bard's good name and reputation the world over.

Malone's statement demolished Ireland's "rarities." The shock was considerable — how could everyone have fallen for the lures of this ill-educated youth? The scholars who had believed Ireland now tried to justify themselves by noting that the paper, parchment and seals were genuine.

Ireland Sr. struggled to defend his treasures, but the game was up. "King Vortigern" closed in disgrace after its one and only performance. Malicious parodies and burlesque references to the contents of Ireland's chest appeared in the press. Ireland Sr. did not long survive the calamity, but died in 1800. Ireland Jr., the central figure in this charade, took it more in stride. He wrote "A Full and Explanatory Account of the Shakespearean Forgery," and even published his "Confessions" in 1805. Quite openly and apparently repentant, occasionally showing off and admiring his own inventiveness, he narrated the story of his sensational fabrication. He claimed that his father had never suspected, to the very end — and it cannot be ruled out that this Philistine fell victim to his own excessive confidence and ardent but blind love for the Great Bard of Stratford-on-Avon. Ireland Jr. never amounted to much, but consoled himself with the fact that his name would be forever linked to that of Shakespeare — even if in such an unflattering way.

This 18th-century scandal is often regarded as an amusing anecdote or a regrettable incident created by an imaginative youth whose mind had been softened by historical novels, and his ambitious and stupid father. But none of this could have happened if there were not already a conspicuous (though still indistinct) gap between the extraordinarily passionate Stratfordian cult and the absolute absence of any documentary evidence to support it. That evidence is still missing today.

Of course, it is hard to imagine a scenario like this succeeding nowadays, when we have the technical means to see through forgeries. However, attempts to somehow fill the gap dividing Shakspere from Shakespeare are ongoing, and some of the conjectures are almost as fantastic as Ireland's inventions. Quite recently, a certain Western Shakespeare scholar repeated an old and long forgotten tale that in his younger years Shakspere allegedly had been a school teacher; another scholar surmises that in the course of the "Lost Years" he served as a secretary to Francis Bacon himself! The authors of such fantasies naturally fail to advance any factual arguments, but the theories are occasionally discussed in public nevertheless, which leaves an impression with some people that there "might be something in it." The same thing happens with the new "portraits of Shakespeare" that crop up from time to time.

The first and largest falsification of "Shakespeare's" papers exposed the weakest point in the Stratfordian legend — the lack of any authentic evidence to document not only William Shakspere's writing activities or relationship with prominent figures of his age, but even of his, at best, elementary literacy.

The Irelands' downfall had almost no effect upon the Stratford relics as, fortunately, no "Shakespeare manuscripts" were on display in Stratford-on-Avon, and the town's other "exhibits" seemed relatively harmless. In his book of essays published in 1820, Washington Irving wrote that during his visit to Stratford he saw pieces of the gun that Shakespeare had used to kill a deer in Sir Thomas Lucy's Charlecote Park, as well as the rapier he had used in playing the part of Hamlet (!), and so on. And a few miles outside of Stratford, the American was shown "the very same" crab apple tree under which the young Shakespeare once fell asleep on the way home after a beer-drinking contest with his neighbors in Bedford.

In the 19th century, Stratford-on-Avon gradually began to turn into a revered site. The "Shakespearean Trust" was established and, bit by bit, purchased all the buildings that were related to Shakspere and his family, renovated them, and opened them up to visitors. There still are no books, writing materials or other evidence of the former tenants' intellectual occupations, but the guests (whose numbers increase every year) have the pleasure of viewing a rich collection of old beds, blankets, pillows, cast-iron pots, crocks, plates and other simple implements illustrating England's everyday life in the 16th-17th centuries.

## THE FIRST DOUBTS; BACONIAN HERESY

Early in the 19th century, the Great Bard's status continued its steady rise as the depth of his creativity was more fully appreciated. Coleridge and Carlyle considered him not only a great English dramatist but a prophet and genius, a godlike figure embodying the spiritual power of the English nation. Against this backdrop, Stratfordian "stories" and the archival documents looked strange. His portrayal by biographers as a provincial, half-educated lad who suddenly moulted into a great writer, thinker and man of vast erudition came to perplex people. "He was a titan, in a vacuum, without any links to his time, his place or his contemporaries,"[52] noted Shakespeare scholar G. Harrison, as late as the 20th century. He speaks about past times, but the Stratfordians are still eager to fill the vacuum.

Reservations about the accuracy of the generally accepted identity of Shakespeare were expressed as far back as the late 18th century by Herbert Lawrence and James Wilmot, although their works were not widely known then.

Samuel Taylor Coleridge (1772-1834), for whom Shakespeare was more than a demigod, was the first to state his doubts openly and publicly. However, it was not the Stratfordian's authorship that he questioned — that seemed beyond doubt, based on the Stratford monument and other relics of the already functioning cult. Coleridge questioned the credibility and completeness of the facts provided by the biographers of his day, though these were the result of bona fide and laborious attempts to reconcile such incompatible materials as the Shakespearean works and the Stratford documents, legends and tales. Coleridge can be credited with being first to draw public attention to this discrepancy and to attack the "few pedants, who . . . talk of Shakespeare as a sort of a beautiful *lusus naturae*, a delightful monster, . . . the wild and irregular genius."

But the will and other Stratfordian documents were not fabricated by Shakespeare's simple-minded biographers. They (like Coleridge himself) simply took it as a given that the man buried in Holy Trinity Church of Stratford, to whom the above documents related, was really the Great Bard William Shakespeare. By confounding the facts from two completely separate biographies, they drove themselves into a dead end — of which, unlike Coleridge, they were not aware.

There was plenty of evidence from the life of the man from Stratford-on-Avon, and for the most part it was quite authentic, but it was so completely incompatible with the Shakespearean creations that it could mean only one thing: William Shakspere was neither a poet nor a playwright; someone else must have been writing under the name of William Shakespeare — the Shake-spear.

In *The Romance of Yachting*, (1848) Joseph Hart was the first to formulate this idea clearly and plainly. Since then, the dispute about Shakespeare's authorship — "the

---

52. Harrison G.B. *Introducing Shakespeare*. N.Y., 1941. Preface.

Shakespeare question" — has never let up. All that has changed is that the number of proposed solutions has increased, the opponents' names have changed, their store of arguments and counter-arguments has widened, and the degree of readers' interest in the discussions has varied.

The first critics noted obvious blunders in the traditional Shakespeare biographies written by "respectable" authors of maturity and authority, the complete dissonance between their image of the Bard and the works he supposedly produced, the lack of any authentic evidence of writing activity on the part of the Stratfordian, as well as the miserly will that is fundamentally impossible to associate with this Titan of thought and word. The first non-Stratfordians did not, at that time, have many facts to work with to support and refine their arguments; these began to come to light later. Some of their hypotheses were not well founded, and some of their conclusions were too hastily drawn, as they underestimated both the complexity of this unprecedented problem and the vision of those who once stood at the legend's source.

And of course, those who confront traditional myths and dogmas always have an uphill battle. On the other hand, in this case their initial adversary was not too strong, either, once the discussion went beyond the limits of textual subtleties, obscure passages and alternative interpretations. The ingenious tales and anecdotes that abounded in Shakespeare's biographies of those days were of evidently recent origin and quite open to rational criticism.

These old biographies are now considered to be thoroughly obsolete, of interest only to someone researching the history of Shakespeare studies. But their principal postulates nevertheless did pass on into 20th-century Shakespeare studies, and strangely coexisted there with the latest discoveries and results of research made by generations of textual critics, historians of literature and theater and other scholars who have provided a broad picture of the political and cultural life of England in the late 16th-early 17th centuries.

In the 19th century, many people were openly expressing doubt that William Shakspere of Stratford-on-Avon, as he is characterized in Shakespeare biographies and historical documents, could have written the plays, poems and sonnets and that he was really the Great Bard. Charles Dickens, Mark Twain, Ralph Waldo Emerson, Bismarck, Disraeli, Palmerston, Walt Whitman and John Whittier — writers, historians, philosophers and statesmen — joined the list of questioners. Whittier admitted: "Whether Bacon wrote the wonderful plays or not, I am quite sure the man Shakspere neither did nor could." As early as 1847, Dickens wrote: "It is a fine mystery; and I tremble every day lest something should turn up."[53] At the beginning of this chapter I already quoted the less delicate words of John Bright, characterizing those who believe that William Shakspere of Stratford wrote "Hamlet" or "Lear."

---

53. Dickens Ch. Letter to W. Sandys. 13.6.1847. — *The letters of Charles Dickens, edited by his sister-in-law and his eldest Daughter*. Leipzig, B. Tauchnits, 1880, vol. 1, p. 190.

However, the doubts and perplexities alone could not quench the thirst for truth of those many people who were worried and harassed by the exciting proximity of the "Shakespeare mystery." If William Shakspere of Stratford was not and could not be the Great Bard, then who was? And why did he hide behind such a strange disguise? What is the meaning of all this?

For many years, James Wilmot (1726-1808) collected materials relating to William Shakspere in Stratford and the environs. Unfortunately, shortly before his death Wilmot ordered that his archive be incinerated. It is possible that among those papers burned and lost forever there may have been original and valuable documents.

In 1856, Delia S. Bacon published the results of her study in an article, and the next year released her book, *The Philosophy of the Plays of Shakespeare Unfolded.*[54] In the plays she saw many features of a confrontation with Queen Elizabeth's regime, as well as efforts to give the ideals of high culture and political freedom a stronger foothold. Though the authorship problem was not her greatest concern, she did declare that it would be impossible to grasp the plays' meaning if we were "condemned to refer the origin of those works to the illiterate man who kept the theater, compelled to regard them as merely the result of an extraordinary talent for pecuniary speculation ..." She argued that the plays attributed to him had really been jointly written by a coterie of the most prominent minds of the epoch: that the authorship belonged mainly to the great philosopher, orator and statesman Francis Bacon[55] (1561-1626) and to the poet, writer and naval commander Sir Walter Raleigh (1552-1618), with the participation of other poets and playwrights as well.

To support her thesis, Delia Bacon cited the enormous erudition of the outstanding philosopher, and the affinity of many of his ideas to Shakespeare's worldview; and some ambiguous allusions of Shakespeare's contemporaries seemed to indicate likewise. She believed that the authorship was a closely kept secret because it amounted to a political conspiracy. Moreover, she came to believe that the documents that could solve the mystery were in the church in Stratford, under the tombstone (bearing that inscription imploring us not to disturb the ashes). She became obsessed with the idea, and once attempted to shift the stone in order to open the grave. Unable to persuade other people of her convictions, exhausted by the decades-long investigation of such an intricate problem, she fell ill and died at a mental clinic in 1859. In the bitter controversy of the next years (and more recent years, too), even her mental disease and death were quite often used as arguments against Delia Bacon's hypothesis — à la guerre comme à la guerre.

Though the researcher failed to find the direct evidence to back up her case, her surmise came as a revelation to all those who had already felt strong doubts. Even Ralph Waldo Emerson and some literature historians supported her premise. That

---

54. Bacon D.S. *The Philosophy of the plays of Shakespeare.* N.Y., 1856. Reiss. N.Y., 1970.

55. Delia Bacon is a namesake of the great philosopher; she had no family relationship to Francis Bacon.

same year, author and dramatist W.G. Smith sent a letter to the English Shakespeare Society and published his book entitled *Bacon and Shakespeare: an inquiry touching players, playhouses and play-writers in the days of Elizabeth,* in which he claimed that it was Bacon himself who wrote under the pen name/mask of "William Shakespeare." The number of works on the authorship problem and Shakespeare's identity increased dramatically, amounting to hundreds by the end of the 19$^{th}$ century. At times, the Baconian theory was almost in vogue in intellectual circles. The debates went on for many years at various levels and inspired a heretofore-unequalled interest in the body of work and identity of Shakespeare, contributing to a wider range of historical and literary studies of Elizabethan England. This led in turn to the discovery of many hitherto unknown facts, the discovery of documents in archives and private collections, and the republication of numerous rare books from the days of Shakespeare (including Chester's collection, *Love's Martyr*). The sum of knowledge about Shakespeare's England became remarkably large. It comprised, of course, much that was new about Shakspere of Stratford as well, and rather than contradict the prevailing view of him, they served to supplement what was already known; his image became more definite and more strikingly irreconcilable with that of the Great Bard.

The scholarly-based study of Shakespeare's texts finally demonstrated how blind and naive were the generations of biographers who all shared the idea of the Bard as a man of innate wit but limited and self-taught knowledge. It was proved beyond doubt that the works in question had been written by a person (if it was *one* person) of very great education, who possessed a tremendous vocabulary — a truth that still continues to be downplayed or sophistically disputed by those who see in it (rightly) a serious threat to the system of traditional conceptions. Being of the same level of education and culture as Francis Bacon, the Great Bard owned and actively used a vocabulary more than twice his.

Incidentally, there is a common opinion that Bacon wrote in a dry, scholastic, lifeless style. Let us, however, read how he portrays his dependent position in a message to Queen Elizabeth: "I am now like a falcon in rage, see the chance to serve but cannot fly, being tied to the fist of another man." Such could be the words of one of Shakespeare's characters! Bacon's works abound in such examples of figurative richness and artistic allegory. Ben Jonson is known to have praised Bacon very highly for his eloquence. The philosophical writings of Francis Bacon are outstanding for their lucidity and depth, as well as for original and aphoristic presentation of material. It is worth mentioning, for instance, his widely known aphorism that pertains well to the subject of this study: "Truth is rightly named the daughter of Time, not of Authority." He knew the immense potentials of the word and skillfully used it; depending on the nature of his works and letters he was a master in using abstract concepts and all kinds of imagery. The idea that Bacon's style was imperfect apparently originated with David Hume, who characterized it as clumsy and blundering. Interestingly, Hume used the same words to characterize the style of Shakespeare!

All the foregoing does not mean that there is no difference between the style of Bacon's philosophical writings and Shakespeare's artistic manner, but it should be borne in mind that we have here to compare the elements of different disciplines; as to fiction or literature, we know only a few poems by Bacon.

Bacon was one man who might apparently be the author or co-author of some of Shakespeare's works. Supporting this surmise, in 1867 the so-called Northumberland manuscript was found — 22 pages plus cover. The cover featured a list the manuscript's contents — the names of Bacon's works (a masque, several orations and essays) and Shakespeare's plays ("Richard II" and "Richard III"), the names of "William Shakespeare" and "Francis Bacon" both together and separately, several times, a line from "Lucrece," the funnily Latinized word from "Love's Labour's Lost" (honorificabilitudino), all written by hand of, supposedly, one of Bacon's relatives and one or two other people. The interpretations of the "Northumberland Manuscript" are controversial, but it apparently testifies to some relationship between Bacon and Shakespeare, though he was never mentioned by Bacon in his works and numerous letters . . . Why?

Nevertheless, there were obviously not enough facts to credibly assert that Francis Bacon was really William Shakespeare. Then the most ardent of Bacon's proponents started to look for the confirmation of their hypothesis directly in the texts of Bacon's and Shakespeare's works, making use of keys and ciphers especially invented for that purpose. Perhaps the first "decoders" took as a starting point Jonson's vague hints that the Shakespeare works contained allusions to the true author. But the hints were understood in too straightforward a way, and were followed in ways that were too arcane and arbitrary: special "deciphering systems" were invented, and attempts were even made to "read" Bacon's coded messages on the basis of changes in the fonts in his works (including postmortem changes).

It should be noted that Francis Bacon took an interest in many things, including ciphers, and wrote a special essay on the latter.[56] Therefore, the possibility that some encoded messages might exist in his (or Shakespeare's) writings should not be ruled out at all. However, the arbitrary pseudo-mathematical operations (isolated, at that, from the historic and literary context) failed to lead to any conclusive reading of Bacon's anticipated secret messages. At the same time, the seeming simplicity of such calculations resulted in a great number of imitators who often went to extremes. It is quite understandable that those who cared deeply about Shakespeare's heritage took great umbrage toward Bacon's "decipherers." In the eyes of many literary notables of the time, the technique used by this category of Baconians not only discredited its most fervent inventors, it also undermined any critical research of the traditional ideas about Shakespeare's identity in general and made a mockery of the attempts to make sense of the insuperable contradictions in Shakespeare's biographies.

---

56. Bacon F. *On the Dignity and Purpose of Sciences*. Book 6. Compositions vol. 1. M. 1977, p.215 (in Russian).

Francis Bacon

In those days, the controversy was focused on two alternatives: either Shakspere of Stratford, or Francis Bacon. Anyone who denied the Stratfordian's authorship (or even doubted it) was almost automatically treated as a Baconian. Closing the door on other possibilities clearly hindered further studies. It was unfortunate that the discussion was so limited; there were enough questions to justify a thorough research and study of the documented facts and a closer evaluation of many aspects of the social, cultural and political life of the period in question. Hopes for finding a quick and easy solution of the most difficult problem in literary history appeared to be ephemeral.

Baconians became the object of severe criticism, especially those who pinned all their hopes on the "deciphering." Unscholarly methods, excessive haste, and a willingness to bend the rules in order to attain the goal are often the downfall of those who prefer to resort to them, and not only when it comes to studies on Shakespeare authorship. One of the harshest rebukes came from the Russian scholar N.I. Storozhenko, whose article "Shakespeare — Bacon's Question"[57] was published by Brokgauz and Ephron in their excellent edition of Shakespeare's collected works (1904). It is worth noting that while justly criticizing the research methods of some Baconians, Storozhenko goes as far as to discard, along with their unfounded guesses, the whole question of Shakespeare's authorship — although he had implicitly acknowledged the problem before. Defending, as he thought, the Great Bard against his adversaries, Storozhenko pulled no punches in attacking the late Delia Bacon and her followers. Arguments similar to his would continue to surface, as we shall see, later on when the controversy would shift from the notorious "decipherers" to the results of historical research and literary criticism, the scrupulous analysis of the extensive factual material and new finds. Doubters would also be blamed for neglecting the artistic side of Shakespeare's heritage, as well as for being impious and disrespectful towards the name of the great genius, etc.

Thus, Delia Bacon and her adherents were unable to prove that it was that great philosopher hid behind the literary disguise of "William Shakespeare." The Baconians did come up with many points of evidence indicating that Francis Bacon had some connection with "the Shakespeare mystery," but they failed to address several serious objections to their hypothesis. First of all, the Great Folio was published in 1623, when Bacon was alive and well (he died on April 6, 1626, having caught a chill while experimenting with the effect of cold on the decay of meat), whereas everything in the Great Folio indicates that the edition was published as a postmortem collection — especially the poems by Jonson, Digges and an anonymous author, and the dedication to the brothers Herbert. Secondly, Shakespeare's plays show signs of sympathy for the Earl of Essex, whereas Francis Bacon, as the royal prosecutor at the trial of the unfortunate favorite, played an important role in ordering Essex to be sent to the

---

57. Storozhenko N.I. "Shakespeare — the Baconian problem." In the book *Shakespeare. Complete Works.* Vol. 5. by Brokgauz and Ephron. P. 497-515. (In Russian.)

scaffold. Moreover, after Essex was beheaded, Bacon served as an official literary mouthpiece, writing a special "Declaration" about Essex' "treasons," blackening the memory of the executed man.

There were also other, minor objections. For instance, in "The Two Gentlemen of Verona," the main character puts out to sea to travel from Verona to Milan. Could such an educated man as Bacon fail to know that the cities were not both located on the water? But the Baconians ascertained that Milan in those days was connected with the Adriatic Sea by a channel, and other cities of Northern Italy were inter-connected by channels, too; so this was not, in fact, an error. Besides, in the other act of the play the characters go from Milan to Verona through the forest, which actually existed at the time; and detour to Mantua is mentioned, which shows that the play's author knew the topography as well as the geography of Northern Italy, in detail. In "A Winter's Tale" Bohemia appears to be a maritime state — an error which was impossible to associate with Bacon. However, 13th-century Bohemia stretched to the coast of the Adriatic — so, in this case as in some others, the Stratfordians' counter-arguments (that Shakspere could afford to make such mistakes, whereas the highly educated Bacon might not) are unfounded as well— which in itself is not, of course, proof of Bacon's authorship, either.

The non-Stratfordians' first thrusts caught the traditional Shakespeareans of guard. Used to fondly retelling the "life story of Shakespeare, of Stratford" as it was shaped in the 18th century, thoroughly engrossed in the problems of textual studies, scholars found it difficult and uncomfortable to have to debate with people who, rather than simply doubt this or that fact or "legend," would actually maintain — imagine that! — "that Shakespeare was not Shakespeare"! Sheltering under the reliable cover of the Stratfordian cult and tradition, scholars rarely entered into serious arguments on the principal issue — whether Shakspere was Shakespeare. The heretics had a weak and indefensible factual base for their thesis (that is, Bacon's authorship), and that became the main target of their critique. In discrediting their adversaries' views, the Stratfordians were very much assisted by the decipherers' own failings.

The Baconians are sometimes believed to have suffered a complete defeat. This is not quite so. Adherents of the Baconian hypothesis are still active today, and although they have failed to prove that Francis Bacon was the author (particularly, the only one) of Shakespeare's plays, poems and sonnets, their discoveries and studies have made it hard to deny that Bacon had some involvement, and apparently quite a serious one, in the "Shakespeare mystery." However, the nature of this involvement is still obscure. The (unfinished) story of the first non-Stratfordian hypothesis is illuminating in many respects: it illustrates the strong force of inertia preserving traditions and customs, even those of shady origin, and reminds us that only academic methods should be used to debate them. No matter what.

FORMATION OF THE SCHOLARLY HISTORY. RUTLAND APPEARS — COINCIDENCES, COINCIDENCES . . .

The Baconians' criticism helped break academic Shakespeare scholarship free from the most dubious and odious tales and legends, from the image of an illiterate provincial apprentice who all at once converted into the Titan of intelligence and art. The Bard's erudition and high level of culture were now partially acknowledged, though it was still unexplained, and it was even more difficult to explain where and when could Shakspere have acquired such vast knowledge, and how did such a metamorphosis take place? Though the controversy had quite a specific focus, it stimulated both sides to engage in very broad research and analysis of documents in archives and private collections, and to study the biographies of many of Shakespeare's contemporaries — statesmen and notables of literature and stage. The scholarly approach to historical studies was beginning to extend its influence to the problems of literature, too. The vast quantity of new facts coming to light in the field of Shakespeare studies could neither be forced to fit into the Procrustean bed of pre-scholarly "stories" nor into the precocious schemes of the "decipherers." In the process of examining the hard, cold facts around Stratford and the exalted creations of the Great Bard, the disjuncture between them gradually became more obvious and hard to step over.

After visiting Stratford-on-Avon, the famous writer Henry James, weary of struggling to fathom the Shakespeare mystery and finding neither the Baconian conjecture nor the Stratfordian gospel persuasive, wrote: "I am sort of haunted by the conviction that the divine William is the biggest and most successful fraud ever practiced on a patient world..."[58]

In the 19th century, scholars continued their minute examination of Shakespeare's texts, comparing the texts of the quartos published during his lifetime with the posthumous folios. The nine-volume Cambridge edition of Shakespeare's works, published in the 1860s, was considered to be the most authoritative version and it comprised all the principal alternatives. In 1871, H.H. Furness started the US publication of the New Variorum — with a separate volume dedicated to each of Shakespeare's works. Later, other scholars (including H. E. Rollins) also participated in this colossal edition. Many efforts were made to study and reprint the works of Shakespeare's contemporaries, as well as to publish the complete collection of Ben Jonson's works, with commentary — that was published only in the 20th-century. The first volumes of the profound British Dictionary of National Biography appeared, holding the biographies of many of Shakespeare's contemporaries. The vacuum was being filled by real persons of the Elizabethan age, with documentation of their actual artistic and domestic concerns; but the central figure of the "Shakespearean" epoch

---

58. Edel L. *The Life of Henry James.* Vol. 2. Penguin, 1977, p. 475

stubbornly lived on only in his works, as if separated from all his contemporaries by a magic screen of silence and Stratfordian artifacts.

While we are on the topic of Shakespeare's 19th-century editions and the work that was done on his texts, we should also mention, at least in passing, that curious page in the history of Shakespeare studies that was written by the energetic John Payne Collier (1789-1883). Widely reputed as a connoisseur of old English literature, Collier published quite a number of books, including works by Shakespeare, Philip Sidney, Edmund Spenser, Christopher Marlowe, Munday and Henry Chettle. However, it turned out later that he regularly used period documents that he personally fabricated or forged. Tampering with the handwriting and the ink, he made his "manuscripts" look old, and then fabricated whatever "letters" he needed at the moment, citing Shakespeare's name, or entering the name onto genuine documents from the 16th-17th centuries. The most scandalous and most infamous episode had to do with his machinations with a copy of the Second Folio of 1632. He inscribed a great number of "emendations" into the book and announced that he had discovered the genuine proofreading copy of the same date as the book. He then proceeded to enter the "emendations" into the texts of Shakespeare's plays published in his editions (1842-1853), and ensured their extensive publicity. Newspaper and magazines commentators greeted the "great findings of the most learned expert of Shakespeare" with enthusiasm.

Quite a lot of time passed before Collier's forgeries were disclosed (and even then, he was exposed only through his own carelessness). Nevertheless, many of his "facts" and "emendations" had taken root and spread all over the world (particularly via translations), and for quite a long while were taken in all good faith. This is another episode illustrating the irresistible attractive force of the great "black hole" (or "blank spot") at the core of our view of culture under Elizabeth and James; this void demands to be filled, and filled it will be, by people who have "discovered Shakespeare's portraits" or other astounding artifacts and by a certain genre of "literary expert" as well.

During the 19th century, biographies of Shakespeare began to abound in facts (and pseudo-facts), a marked improvement over the previous attempts. They include data about the performances and editions of Shakespeare's plays, their literary and theatrical reviews, contemporary opinions, and above all, of course — the documents, the stories about William Shakspere, his financial and real estate (buildings, barns, etc.) transactions, his relatives close and distant, what had become of the real estate he had purchased in Stratford, etc. London theaters, players' companies and individual players were described in detail. It was not easy to tie together all these voluminous and diverse materials, but the inertial force of tradition helped.

James Halliwell-Phillips stands out as one of the 19th-century scholars who contributed most to the final formation of Shakespeare's biography. A prolific writer, he devoted particular attention to researching and painstakingly reproducing and evaluating documentary artifacts. He proved that some of the legends were unfounded, and he elucidated a number of quite important facts. He was the first to take special note of Chester's collection and treated the unique book very seriously. Unfortunately, Halliwell-Phillips' scholarly investigations went hand in hand with an eccentric habit of stealing books and rare manuscripts from university libraries, or tearing out whatever pages he needed from them.

Many Shakespeare experts (F.J. Furnivall, F.G. Fleay, Edward Dowden and others), who united in 1874 in the New Shakspere Society, also worked on Shakespeare's biography. The Society's founder, Furnivall, was especially irked that British specialists, preoccupied with the problems of textual studies, had still not come up with an overall picture of the Great Bard. ("It is a disgrace . . . to England, that even now, 258 years after Shakspere's death, the study of him has been so narrow, and his criticism, however good, so devoted to the mere text and its illustration, and to studies of single plays, that no book by an Englishman exists which deals in any worthy manner with Shakspere as a whole.") He urged his compatriots to fill that gaping need, using the advances in scholarly methods with which the luminous 19th century was so blessed.

A new generation of Shakespeare biographies is exemplified by the 1898 book *A Life of William Shakespeare*[59] by historian and literary critic Sidney Lee (who initiated and edited the British Dictionary of National Biography). The book went on to see many reprintings and amended editions. It is a serious work by a highly competent expert on the period in question, summarizing the evidence revealed in the latter half of the 19th century. Interestingly, Lee himself never expressed his doubts as to the verity of the Stratfordian biographic tradition or sympathy for the Baconian approach. But his book, or to be more precise, his account of the facts, by itself generated further doubts. As a historian, he naturally tried to link and rationally correlate the results of the study of Shakespeare's cultural legacy with the Stratford papers, but, contrary to his intentions, this effort did more to reveal the disparity and incompatibility of those elements. It was no wonder that the next generation of Shakespeare scholars were less than enthusiastic about the book. As the reader has probably established, the biographical aspect is terribly convoluted in Shakespeare studies, which is rather the fault of Shakespeare than of the biographers.

The next important study appeared in 1930, and was penned by the eminent Shakespeare scholar Sir Edmund Chambers (1866-1953). The book was quite different from what is commonly regarded as a biography, that is, a coherent and consistent life story — it was, rather, a monumental collection of all the documents and facts relating to Shakespeare, as emphasized by its careful title — *William Shakespeare. A Study of Facts and Problems.*[60] Unlike Lee, Chambers does not attempt to piece together a vivid image of the Great Bard on the basis of the available evidence — literary sources, on the one hand, and Stratfordian documents, "stories" and relics, on the other. His sterile

59. Lee S. *A Life of William Shakespeare.* L., 1898
60. Chambers, E.K. *William Shakespeare. A Study of Facts and Problems:* Oxford, 1930.

approach to the presentation of facts enabled him to bypass the eye of the storm. Though Chambers created this, his life's work, over decades that were wracked by strong polemics on this very issue, he refused to engage in debates with the non-Stratfordians and sought to avoid mentioning their hypotheses and interpretations of the facts. And Chambers is not the only one who chose to go forward by ignoring his fundamental opponents.

As the massive quest for documents swept across England, many vital papers were found at the estates and castles owned by the scions of aristocratic families, who were often unaware of the great value of their ancestors' letters, diaries and even ordinary household records. Throughout the centuries, the bulk of these documents had remained unsorted and unread; fires and negligent storage destroyed innumerable priceless manuscripts. To carry out a systematic and purposeful search, a special Historical Manuscripts Commission was established, and the activities also involved several societies.

The name of Shakespeare was seldom mentioned in these old manuscripts, notes and letters (in fact, even Shakspere's name showed up more often, in the Stratfordian documents), so that every instance when it was mentioned required a thorough examination. The fact that the first poems by Shakespeare were dedicated to the Earl of Southampton, and the posthumous First Folio, to the Earls of Pembroke and Montgomery — mentioning the support they had rendered to Shakespeare — undoubtedly testified to a close relationship between the Bard and this aristocratic milieu. The same idea was expressed in the words of the chorus in "Henry V" that drew a sudden parallel between the victorious return of the King, having crushed the once hostile France, and the Earl of Essex' expected return from Ireland in 1599 ("as in good time he may"). The author wishes to see Ireland's "rebellion broached on his sword," and foresees the crowds of triumphant Londoners coming out to greet the victor. Since such a reference was entirely optional, even awkward, in the context of a historical play, the comparison (which also appears to be unique for Shakespeare) is particularly revealing of the Bard's personal sympathies. It would seem that the search for traces of Shakespeare in this aristocratic environment would be productive, even if some of these traces were already lost in the 19th century.

According to Sidney Lee, historian W. Cory wrote in his diary in 1865 that in the course of his visit to Wilton House, Wiltshire, the former home of poetess Mary Sidney Pembroke, the hosts showed (or wanted to show) him a hitherto unpublished 1603 letter from the Countess of Pembroke to her son. In this letter she asks her son to persuade King James to come to Wilton and watch the performance of the play "As You Like It." She wrote in the postscript: "We have the man Shakespeare with us."[61] It is hard to imagine that the Countess of Pembroke would hope to pique the interest of the sovereign with the prospect of meeting a member of a players' company. Moreover,

---

61. The meaning of this phrase, especially "the man Shakespeare," — may be interpreted (and translated) ambiguously.

there is no evidence of anyone ever seeing Shakspere at the Pembrokes' (or at the Southamptons'), frequented as they were by writers and poets. Clearly, the message means a certain person who was no stranger to this elevated circle; he was an acquaintance of the king himself, and he was Shakespeare! The letter contains references to Sir Walter Raleigh, then in disfavor, for whom the Countess wanted to plead with the King — who actually was in Wales in the autumn of 1603; all these details give the letter credibility. Unfortunately, this invaluable piece of evidence was apparently lost; Chambers, at any rate, states that its whereabouts are unknown. Neither the letter nor any facsimile of it was ever made public — its owners, perhaps, used to show the message to their occasional guests, until it went astray. It is lucky indeed that Cory transcribed the note's contents into his diary, thus saving it from full oblivion. The indication in the letter that "As You Like It" was performed at Wilton House is commonly regarded as true (although the play's text was published only later, in the First Folio).

Lee also informs us that in 1897 the then Earl of Pembroke purchased from a London trader an old portrait of his ancestor William Herbert, 3$^{rd}$ Earl of Pembroke. It was to him that his mother had sent the above-mentioned note suggesting that he should invite the King to Wilton House, where among the guests was "the man Shakespeare." On the reverse side of the canvas a sheet of paper was pasted with a few lines from Shakespeare's Sonnet 81:

> *Your monument shall be my gentle verse,*
> *Which eyes not yet created shall o'er-read,*
> *And tongues to be your being shall rehearse*
> *When all the breathers of this world are dead;*
>
> *You still shall live — such virtue hath my pen —*
> *Where breath most breathes, even in the mouths of men.*

It was inscribed, "Shakespeare — to the Earl of Pembroke, 1603." The seller asserted that the note was genuine and contemporary to the date of the portrait. The next year, the purchaser consulted group of experts, who certified the portrait as authentic, but declined to say the same about the note, finding the handwriting and ink too recent. It would be natural to suppose that either the experts or Sidney Lee, relating the episode, had difficulty in conceiving that the ignoble William Shakspere of Stratford could present a noble aristocrat with his portrait, from equal to equal, especially with such an accompanying note; the sonnet's lines promised immortality to the earl only in union with Shakespeare's poetry, while the laconic signature bore no trace of the humility that would be fitting in a player and drama maker. This was a period that was particularly fertile in forgeries related to the name of the Great Bard; the note was never facsimiled, and nothing is known about where it might be now —

apparently lost, as well. How interesting it would be to apply modern technical expertise to these documents now. . .

It is commonly known that the fire of 1627 at Wilton, six years after the death of the mistress of the house, destroyed a great number of documents, books and manuscripts. In addition to the fire at the Globe Theater in 1613, Ben Jonson's study and library burned down in 1623, and finally, with the Great London Fire of 1666, the volume of irretrievably lost evidence is obviously quite appalling.

In the late 19th century the Historical Manuscripts Commission examined the papers that had survived at the Belvoir Castle, Leicestershire. For the past four centuries the castle had been the residence of the earls of Rutland, from the family of Manners. Many important documents and records were found; of particular significance were the papers dating back to the Elizabethan-Jacobean age. And then, the following record was found among the steward's bookkeeping papers: "31 March (1613) to Mr. Shakspeare[62] in gold about my Lord's impreso 44 S; to Richard Burbadge for painting and making it 44 S, in all — 3 lb.16 s." [63] Richard Burbadge was a leading tragic player and shareholder of the "King's Men" company; the fact that he and Shakspere performed such work, unrelated to the stage and, moreover, so far from London, is strange enough. But in addition, Shakspere was by that time quite well off.

Like any find relating to Shakespeare and Shakspere, this notation attracted public attention, and was reproduced in the Commission's report and commented on in Sidney Lee's 1906 article. It is assumed that the players actually made a shield emblem in connection with the forthcoming knightly tournament, in which the owner of Belvoir, Francis Manners, Earl of Rutland, was going to take part. Francis had become the 6th Earl of Rutland eight months before, upon the death of his older brother Roger, the 5th Earl of Rutland. According to Lee, it was Roger Manners who obtained the coat of arms for Shakespeare (that is, Shakspere of Stratford) from the Heralds' College.

The first to link the name of Roger Manners with the Shakespeare authorship question was a New York lawyer, Glisson Ziegler, who published an article in 1893, tackling the mysterious figure who was always present where the Great Bard might appear and at the same time always trying to stay in the shadows. Family ties and friendly relations with the earls of Essex and Southampton; active participation in the ill-fated Essex rebellion — resulting in severe punishment; study at Cambridge, Oxford and Padua University in Italy; the vague hints from Ben Jonson, who knew him well; death in 1612, precisely coinciding with the end of Shakespeare's activities — all these and other facts that were known by the end of the 19th century gave Zeigler

---

62. The steward, Screven, writes "Shakspeare" — neatly in between "Shakespeare" and "Shakspere."

63. In reference to Shakspere, he uses the preposition "about" ("about my Lord's impreso"), but when stating the job Burbadge was paid for, he applies a more definite preposition "for" ("for painting and making it"). There is a difference in the meaning, and it is still unclear what actual work was Shakspere paid for.

reasons to conclude that it was Roger Manners, the 5th Earl of Rutland, who was precisely that man hiding behind the pen name of "William Shakespeare." The hypothesis did not go unnoticed — it was actively picked up in America and Germany by L. Bostelman, P. Alvor and C. Bleibtreu.

Belgian historian Celestin Demblon studied Roger Manners' biography particularly intensely in an effort to substantiate and develop the Rutland hypothesis. Demblon personally ties the beginning of his studies to Sidney Lee's highlighting of the Belvoir steward's records. Prior to that, searching for traces of Shakespeare, Demblon had explored the lives of the Earl of Southampton, Sir Walter Raleigh, poet Richard Barnfield and other contemporaries of Shakespeare's activities. This research extended and deepened his knowledge of the history and literature of the age in question. One of Demblon's significant contributions was to study the archives of Padua University in Italy, where he found the name of the Earl of Rutland and the names of two Danish students — Rosencrantz and Guildenstern. Demblon also investigated the circumstances of the Earl of Rutland's honorable mission to Denmark in 1603, and its reflection in the second edition (second quarto) of "Hamlet" that appeared in 1604-1605. Published in France on the eve of World War I, Demblon's works[64] marked a turning point in the development of Shakespeare studies. In his further studies Demblon expected to find conclusive documentary evidence of Rutland's authorship, but at that time he had yet to discover such materials so that he could successfully complete his tremendous work. Demblon's arguments and the facts he revealed testified to the indisputable involvement of Rutland in the "Shakespeare mystery" and in the creation of Shakespeare's works, but the nature and degree of his involvement could be questioned. Besides, there were many challenges (mainly related to the dating of the first of Shakespeare's plays), which still had to be soundly addressed. More and more research was required, and that takes time.

After Demblon, the Rutland hypothesis was further developed in the works of C. Schneider (Germany), C. Sykes (UK) and Russian professor P. Porohovchikov, who emigrated to the US during the Civil War in Russia. Studying a manuscript copy of the song from "Twelfth Night," found in Belvoir in the late 19th century, Porohovchikov ascertained that it was genuine and written in Rutland's hand.

In the 1920s, the Rutlandian theory was rather widely accepted in Russia (contrary to the Baconian theory, which seems not to have taken hold there). In 1924 F. Shipoulinsky produced the book *Shakespeare — Rutland's Mask. The Three-century-long Conspirational Mystery of History*.[65] Shipoulinsky expounded the history of "The Shakespeare question" and used Demblon's study to elucidate the principal points of the Rutland hypothesis, which he ardently supported and advocated. This fascinating book has an added curiosity due to the timing of its publication — it suffers from an

---

64. Demblon, C. *Lord Rutland est Shakespeare*. P., 1912. *L'Auteur d'Hamlet et sa Monde*. P., 1913.

65. Shipoulinsky F. *Shakespeare — Rutland's Mask. The Three-century-long Conspirational Mystery of History*. Moscow, 1924 (In Russian).

overlay of revolutionary ideology, treating the Earl of Rutland as a revolutionary fighting against autocracy.

Shipoulinsky did not mince words in characterizing Shakspere of Stratford and the authors of Stratfordian biographies: "To identify an illiterate butcher, trader, and usurer with the author of 'Hamlet' and 'The Tempest,' one must not simply be blind, but must also be not able to understand and feel Shakespeare."

The eminent literary critic (and Marxist) V. Friche backed up the Rutlandian theory, arguing that "as opposed to the traditional, orthodox standpoint, it enables us to more satisfactorily interpret the origin and spirit of Shakespeare's creations . . . there is no such yawning contradiction in it . . ." In his small volume on Shakespeare Friche provides no new facts, unlike Shipoulinsky, but he notes the profusion of elements in the works of the Great Bard indicating an aristocratic worldview.

A.V. Lounacharsky, whose authority on cultural issues was still high in the 1920s, believed that the Rutland hypothesis was the most likely solution of the problem of William Shakespeare's identity. In his article "Shakespeare and His Age," he emphasized the profusion of coincidences between Rutland's biographical data with "the life of the plays' author as we might picture it . . . This coincidence is surprisingly great. . . . So many coincidences cannot be explained otherwise but by the fact that the Earl of Rutland was the author . . . it is almost indisputable." In response to some of his opponents, who were already beginning to express their "discontent" with the aristocratic origin of Roger Manners, the People's Commissar of education wrote: "We would perhaps be more pleased if this world-greatest writer descended not from the nobility, but from the lower classes . . . However, we have to admit that Shakespeare and Rutland are apparently one and the same person."[66]

In his analysis of "Julius Caesar" and "Coriolanus," Lounacharsky pointed out that the plays featured traces of the author's sympathy for the views of the pro-Essex feudal-aristocratic Fronde. Today, these assertions still seem valid, for irrespective of the sequence in which the "Roman" tragedies were created, they definitely reflect the problems of the Essex rebellion, appraisals (or later re-evaluations) of its leader and his environment, the tone of the debates and the aspirations of those involved in this ill-considered endeavor.

Later on, under ideological fire and ousted from the Kremlin Areopagus (though managing to die a timely, natural death), Lounacharsky refused to support the Rutland hypothesis in public, but left his article "Shakespeare and his Age" in later editions almost unmodified.

---

66. Lounacharsky, A.V. *About Theater and Dramaturgy*. Vol.2 M. 1958. pp.425-426. (In Russian.)

## AN IDEOLOGICAL TABOO

In the 1930s, Soviet Shakespeare scholarship reassessed its attitude to the non-Stratfordian theories. This was caused by both weakening of Lounacharsky's position in the Kremlin, and the appearance in the West of new hypotheses on the anti-Stratfordian side (that is, the Derbian and Oxfordian views), as well as fresh trends in British Shakespeare studies (the F.G. Fleay and J.M. Robertson school) that used the analysis of texts as a basis to deny the personal authorship of Shakespeare and to consign to him a role as literary corrector of texts that had been written by others. It appeared that there was a long way to go before the West could come to a final and commonly accepted solution regarding Shakespeare's identity and authorship. Hence, there was no need and certainly no urgency to "officially" revise (what other kind of revision could there be, in the ideological atmosphere of those days?) traditional beliefs in Moscow, which, despite being dubious, had at least been blessed by time. Looking back, today, we might note that it is generally undesirable to have *any* "official" views on such specific problems.

In a biographical article on Shakespeare published in the Great Soviet Encyclopedia, in 1932, literary critic I. A. Aksionov wrote about the non-Stratfordian camp: "All these hypotheses are nothing but a captivating and ingenious read, part of the 'historic riddles' literature. They do not and cannot provide any solution to the problem of the texts' authorship."

Aksionov personally held with the Fleay-Robertson school, then popular in the West, and in his book *Shakespeare* (1937 posthumous edition) thus formulated his views on the role of Shakespeare in the creation of the plays bearing his name: "Above all, his work was connected with theater. He did not write much on his own behalf . . . Shakespeare's drama is not a work of one person. It is composite. It is based . . . on old texts. Shakespeare and his collaborators worked on it more and more, up to 1608, after which Shakespeare's participation in the work on the text itself weakens."[67]

The scholars of this school stated that Shakespeare's texts were not written by one person, though many of them bear the traces of revision. However, they did not touch upon the issue of Shakespeare's identity, and moreover did not encroach upon the Stratford cult.

The "Shakespeare question" was still under discussion in early 1930s, but in a very limited way already. The then prolific literary critic P. Kogan mentioned that "mysterious author, whose name science has still failed to precisely ascertain, in spite of all the tremendous efforts of scholars." Referring to the pro-Rutland arguments as "sound," Kogan nevertheless declines to say anything definite in its favor. However, he writes (not forgetting Marxist terminology): "Whoever is the author of Shakespeare's works originated from the British aristocratic milieu, and, what is more, from that

---

67. Aksionov, I.A. *Shakespeare.* M. 1937. pp.251,267. (In Russian.)

group of noblemen who went through their own troubles in the course of the complex historical process resulting in the rise of the bourgeoisie and the decline of the feudal gentry."[68]

Taking advantage of Lounacharsky's weakened position, conservatively-minded Soviet scholars soon silenced their adversaries (including Lounacharsky), using not only factual arguments but the usual procedures of ideological interdiction as well. The basic theses underlying the Soviet Shakespeare establishment's rejection of all unconventional — non-Stratfordian — hypotheses were set forth by professor A.A. Smirnov in his foreword to M. Zhizhmor's undistinguished play "Shakespeare. (Rutland's Mask)" (1932). The name of this play reflected its contents, but Smirnov's foreword dismissed any criticism of traditional ideas about Shakespeare's identity (the play had been apparently written several years before it was published).

Smirnov accused the non-Stratfordians (he called them anti-Shakespearists) of adhering to "the simplified positions of the old biographical method in the history of literature" — that is, of taking a non-Marxist approach — and therefore, he argued, their surmises were based on flawed methodology and were unscholarly. Smirnov went on to assert that "in itself, the factual basis of the anti-Shakespeare versions is weak because it exposes the authors' poor knowledge of the literary conditions in those times . . . As regards the manuscripts and scanty biography, the fate of Shakespeare differs not a bit from that of most other playwrights of the age when tragedies written for the stage were treated as works of a very low genre." Smirnov's assertion is incorrect, for innumerable dramatists and poets of the epoch left a trace in the form of either manuscripts, or letters and diaries of the contemporaries, which proves that they were actually regarded as the authors.

And William Shakspere's biography is far from meager: in the number of facts it surpasses most biographies of his coevals. What is missing, however, is any information indicating that this man (Shakspere, not Shakespeare!), who left no piece of paper with any words written in his hand, and no evidence of having possessed at least elementary literacy — was or even could have been an author, poet or playwright. Instead, the existing facts argue against such an assumption.

Smirnov asserted (thus surpassing even the most conservative British scholars) that there was nothing to prove the player (Shakspere)'s illiteracy, and that the multifaceted erudition of the author (Shakespeare) was exaggerated. "All his learning... is covered by a score of popular books of the semi-educational and semi-entertaining sort that was quite widespread at the time."

And this was written after the results of many studies were already published and well known, proving Shakespeare's unprecedented breadth of knowledge and the use of a great variety of authoritative sources, including books in many languages.

However, besides arguing on the basis of facts, which could be disputed, Smirnov also enunciates the hard-line thesis of the "ideological virulence" of all anti-

---

68. Kogan P.S. *William Shakespeare.* M. 1931, pp.71, 78 (In Russian.)

Stratfordian hypotheses: "Summing up all these 'theories,' we must strongly emphasize the points that not only make them unacceptable for us, but 'ideologically adverse' as well." There were two points. First, their "being founded upon the basis of a non-scientific psychological-biographical method, in the manner of Brandes, who aspired to explain the entire contents of the author's works (right down to the individual characters) by the purely personal circumstances of his life, his intimate emotions and impressions. . . . The second feature is the aristocratic tendency that is dominant in anti-Shakespeare literature (not incidentally, all the strong candidates for Shakespeare are persons with noble titles)."

Smirnov further concludes: "We suppose that these two factors are enough to admit that the penetration of 'Rutland's hypothesis' into our academic literature was a regrettable mistake. And generally speaking, this long and complex dispute about Shakespeare's authorship is interesting merely as an anecdote, and has nothing in common with the scientifically-based study of Shakespeare's creative activities. What is important for us is not the author's name and his personal daily life, but the class subject of the 34 plays, which contemporaries and progeny attributed, probably with good reason, to William Shakespeare."[69]

Smirnov's 1932 arguments set the framework within which the next generations of Soviet scholars would operate. The verdict of ideological unacceptability, applied to all anti-Stratfordian doubts and hypotheses, sounded quite ominous under Soviet conditions in the 1930s, and it was properly understood. Today, however, we may note that the "factual basis" of his arguments is extremely poor. Incidentally, George Brandes never expressed any personal doubts as to the authenticity of the Stratfordian tradition. Since Smirnov was interested neither in the author's name nor in his "personal daily life," but solely in the "class subject," in his eyes the whole dispute over "the Shakespeare question" was just a collection of anecdotes.

Naturally, the problems in Shakespeare scholarship are not limited to the issue of Shakespeare as a person; but to neglect this question and blindly adhere to the traditional approach would be incompatible with any true study of the Great Bard's work. What is needed is a comprehensive biography of Shakespeare, constructed on the basis of responsible scholarship, that would convincingly explain the various dichotomies and resolve the profound contradiction underlying the traditional ideas. And if the investigations eventually ascertain that the Great Bard was of aristocratic descent and education (as so much evidence suggests), then recognizing this fact will be no more reactionary than acknowledging the aristocratic origins of Byron, Pushkin, and Lermontov. Indeed, it was their noble birth and independent status that enabled them to immerse themselves in the treasures of world culture from childhood and to develop their in-born abilities to the highest level. Yet this sort of ideological concern was permitted to derail scholarly investigation for decades.

---

69. Smirnov A.A. *Preface* to Zhizhmor's play "Shakespeare (Rutland's Mask)." M., 1932. pp.6,7,8-9. (In Russian.)

In fact, ideological obstructions still crop up, and certainly not only in Russia. But research and debate based on facts do not "dishonor Shakespeare" or hamper the development of Shakespeare's heritage; on the contrary, they enhance our appreciation and encourage further study. Today, sixty years after Smirnov's "excommunication" of the non-Stratfordians it is still worth repeating.

In the 1930s, the taboo was effective in curtailing the debate; articles on "the Shakespeare question" disappeared from Soviet literature and the problem was not studied, even in the universities. Nonconformists could be sure they would never see their opuses published. Since then, until quite recently, the approach to Shakespeare was dominated by the study of drama, literary criticism and theory. And though some interesting and valuable works appeared in this domain and a series of talented innovations were presented on stage and screen, there was an apparent loss of taste for specific historical-biographical studies — they were regarded as something of a prerogative of Western Shakespeare researchers.

However, new generations grew up and, reading Shakespeare, they too were perplexed. Information drifted in from the West, where the controversy was still alive. It became necessary to remind the general public, from time to time, of the correct way to view these things. In early 1960s, on the eve of Shakespeare's 400-year anniversary, the press began to reiterate the thesis that it was ideologically unacceptable "for us" to question the Stratfordian view; any who questioned it were branded as aristocratically-snobbish "anti-Shakespearists," uncultured muckrakers who were not interested in the aesthetic aspect of the Shakespearean heritage. "Anti-Shakespearists" were also accused of treating Shakespeare as only a writer, whereas, they asserted, he was above all a man of the stage.

The last argument comes up often enough to merit our attention. Certainly, neither the dramatic nor poetic heritage of Shakespeare should be ignored (although the fact that he was not only a playwright, but also a refined poet, "the Bard," is more often neglected). The argument that Shakespeare was primarily a man of the theater is supposed to support the notion that only an actor who had theater in his bones could have written Shakespeare's plays, — which is rather naive. Of course, the man (if it was the same one) who wrote the plays also knew and deeply loved the theater. But to conclude that only a professional actor could know theater so well is absolutely indefensible, especially considering the simplicity of the public (and home) theaters in those days. And in any case, how many of the world's greatest playwrights, with their excellent knowledge of the theater (much more technically sophisticated, at that), were professional actors?

Implausible as it is, this argument is often repeated, and clearly that is no accident. For the public, Shakespeare lives on, and will always live on, on stage and on the screen. The people who most often reflect upon his plays and the images of his heroes are primarily theater people — producers, actors, theater and film critics. And to them, one assumes, this argument may seem flattering. But it is not only unfounded, we should remember that nobody knows what roles William Shakspere played, if any, on stage. He was in the cast of the players' company and was one of its main shareholders — these are the only definite and proven facts relating to his role in theater and to him as a "professional actor." Of course, it is quite likely that he participated with other members of the company in crowd scenes, or even played some episodic roles, but like his friends Heminge and Condell, his function was not artistic but economic — it was not easy for a actors' company to survive in those days.

Stratfordian adherents assert that Shakspere's main responsibility in the company was to create new plays and adapt old ones. Non-Stratfordians reject this assertion, since a semiliterate man could not have written plays or poems. However, some of them surmise that in certain cases plays did appear in the company through him, and he thus served as an intermediary between the true author (or someone of his milieu) and the company, and that that was precisely how he became rich so quickly. The fact that he was in some way connected with the Rutlands and Pembrokes also lends credibility to this view.

Ideological taboos dominated Russian Shakespeare Studies for some sixty years and could not but hinder the development of this scholarship. Though violators of the taboo were not summoned for interrogation, their opuses would never be published. Even relatively recently, to turn the most stubborn "heretics" to the right path, zealots were still trying to enlist the support of the Communist Party organs to protect the purity of Soviet Shakespeare scholarship.

The end of censorship opened the door to new information and the Great Dispute now rages in Moscow almost as energetically as it does in the West.


THE DISCUSSION BECOMES MORE INVOLVED. NEW CANDIDATES, NEW EVOLU-
TIONS OF THE ELUSIVE IMAGE


In the meantime, the debate had not stagnated in the West. In 1918, with the Rutland hypothesis not yet in full swing, the French scholar A. Lefranc released a book arguing that "William Shakespeare" concealed William Stanley, the 6$^{th}$ Earl of Derby (1561-1642); such suppositions had been voiced before.

William Stanley's elder brother, Ferdinando (Lord Strange), ran a players' company where William Shakspere is often believed to have started his career. Ferdinando is known to have written poems and was celebrated in verse by Edmund Spenser under the name of Amint. After Ferdinando's sudden death in 1594, William Stanley succeeded as the Earl of Derby. Married to the daughter of the Earl of Oxford; he was among the people close to the Earl of Essex. However, he did not participate in the Essex rebellion and escaped punishment. In 1583, Derby visited the Court of the King of Navarre where, later on, the action of "Love's Labour's Lost" would take place among *dramatis personae* comprising the French nobles well known to the Earl of Derby. The play was printed under Shakespeare's name in 1598, but certain features bear witness that the edition was a revised version of an earlier text. One character in "Love's Labour's Lost" — Holofernes — may be a caricature of Richard Lloyd, Derby's irksome tutor and author of a long and tedious poem about the "Nine Worthies."

A 1599 letter from a Spanish agent indicates that the Earl of Derby was "busy writing comedies for public theaters." His initials "W. S." (William Stanley) coincide with those on some of Shakespeare's works. The pro-Derbian camp believes that Queen Elizabeth's well-known conversation with the archivist William Lambard, in which the queen referred to the author of "Richard II" ("The one who is ready to forget God shall also forget his benefactors") — also refers to William Stanley and confirms that the tragedy "Richard II" was authored by him. The performance staged by the craftsmen in "Midsummer Night's Dream" recalls the folk shows organized in the town of Chester, patronized by the earls of Derby.

The Derbian hypothesis, comprising several interesting surmises and exploring important and hitherto neglected facts and circumstances, is nonetheless short on concrete evidence. As in the case with Bacon, the pro-Derby lobby has trouble explaining the appearance of the Great Folio — which is obviously posthumous — in 1623, when Derby was still alive and well. That the Earl of Derby is somehow implicated in "The Shakespeare authorship mystery" is very likely, but there is more work to be done before we can say more. He also had something to do with the publication of Robert Chester's collection. Ursula, the wife of John Salusbury, to whose memory the collection was nominally dedicated, was the half-sister of William Stanley, Earl of Derby (she was born from an extramarital liaison of his father); he visited the family quite often and was well informed about how and what they were doing. He might have known about Chester's collection.

In 1920, having thoroughly verified the results of his many years study, the British scholar Thomas Looney finally published his book on the problem of Shakespeare's authorship.[70] In his analysis of "The Merchant of Venice," Looney came to the strong conviction that the play could have been authored only by a person who knew Italy from his personal impressions, not from other people's stories and books; that meant that William Shakespeare must have visited Italy. The study of other Shakespeare works made him increasingly doubtful about the authenticity of the Stratford Gospel.

In search of the true author, Looney painstakingly studied the literature of Elizabethan England. The poetry of Edward de Vere, Earl of Oxford, who more than once published poems under his own name, attracted Looney's attention by its similarity to "Venus and Adonis." Sidney Lee's article about the Earl of Oxford, written for the Dictionary of National Biography, gave a fairly complete image of the man; by then, Looney had developed a fairly clear conception of what the author of Shakespeare's works would have to be like, and the two were very similar.

---

70. Looney, J. T. *Shakespeare Identified in Edward de Vere, 17-th Earl of Oxford.* N.Y., 1984; first American edition by Frederick A. Stokes Company, New York: 1920.

William Stanley, Earl of Derby

Thus Thomas Looney came to identify William Shakespeare with Edward de Vere, the 17<sup>th</sup> Earl of Oxford (1550-1604). Oxford was close to the royal court; he was the son-in-law of the all-powerful Lord Burghley, whose features are associated by Shakespeare researchers with the character of Polonius. This explained Shakespeare's intimacy with the world of court secrets and intrigue, with the world of power. Oxford's coat of arms was crowned with the image of a lion shaking a broken spear. In 1578, Gabriel Harvey made a speech at Cambridge University, giving the Earl's literary achievements the highest praise, but he appealed to him to put aside his pen for a while and to direct his talent and courage to the defense of England. Harvey used the Latin phrase: "Vultus tela vibrat" ("Thy countenance shakes a spear"). Shake-speare?

Looney also quoted the evidence by Francis Meres (1598) that the Earl of Oxford was acquainted with the best English authors of comedies; many writers dedicated their books to him. John Lyly and Anthony Munday were his secretaries; he patronized several companies of players. Thus, his active participation in the literary and theatrical life of Elizabethan England is beyond doubt.

Like the founders of other non-Stratfordian approaches, in his book Looney first sharply criticized traditional biographies of Shakespeare, emphasizing their discrepancies and contradictions. After an intensive study of the whole of Shakespeare's creative heritage, Looney outlined the "general features" and "special characteristics" of the true author, the real Shakespeare, as can be deduced from his works. Generally, he describes the writer, whoever it may be, as —

- A mature man of recognized genius, and mysterious
- Evidently eccentric
- A man apart, and unconventional
- Apparent inadequacy
- A man of pronounced and known literary tastes
- A lyric poet of recognized talent
- Of superior education and an associate of educated people
- Enthusiast for drama

Looney indicates more specific traits ("special characteristics") that would almost surely characterize the writer of the Shakespeare oeuvre:

- A man of feudal connections
- A member of the higher aristocracy
- Connected with Lancastrian sympathies
- An enthusiast for Italy
- A music lover
- A follower of sports, including hunting and falconry
- Improvident in money matters
- Doubtful and somewhat conflicted in his attitude toward women
- Probably somewhat pro-Catholic, but with a touch of skepticism

In Looney's opinion, the Earl of Oxford met all these general qualifications. Today, we may agree with the results of his analysis of Shakespeare's personality as

Edward de Vere, Earl of Oxford

revealed in his works (although the list is hardly exhaustive), but the Earl of Oxford is not the only one of Shakespeare's contemporaries who fit the bill. An even closer match is found in the Earl of Rutland, especially when it comes to a penchant for mystery or secrecy, and misgivings as far as women. As we see, Oxford now and then published works under his own name and did not hide his patronage of writers and players' companies. Rutland, on the other hand, took great pains to conceal such activities and during the last decade of his life he even did not allow other authors and poets to mention his name (as proven by Ben Jonson's emphatic abbreviation of his poem XII in the "Forest" collection). The bizarre secret funerals of the Earl of Rutland and his wife underscore the point.

As to women, Oxford had a family, legitimate children, mistresses, and illegitimate children — he seems to have been quite comfortable with women. Rutland's marriage was strange, by any standard, and till the very end his relationship with his wife remained platonic — this is implicitly confirmed by Ben Jonson and Francis Beaumont, and, as we know now, by Chester's book. Rutland's odd married life and Beaumont's direct hint at his inability or unwillingness to perform his conjugal duties (for whatever reasons) are far more consistent with Shakespeare's "doubtful and somewhat conflicting" characterizations of women than the Earl of Oxford's family life and love affairs. I am not sure that Looney studied the life of Rutland and his partner in life.

It would be probably correct to single out as a separate "general feature" Shakespeare's unprecedentedly vast vocabulary, which supports the supposition that "other pens" participated in his works, as well; tests on that would certainly be useful in this investigation.

Looney also published a small volume of Oxford's poems and verses, which, by the way, also comprised works by famous writers and poets such as Walter Raleigh, Fulke Greville and Richard Barnfield, as well as by some unknown authors.

In 1922, B.R. Ward founded a special Shakespeare's society in England, with the mission "to oppose the Stratfordian orthodoxy by applying the principles of historical criticism to the problem of Shakespeare's authorship." In 1928 his son, B.M. Ward, published a detailed biography of the Earl of Oxford; he conceded that in some cases there may have been cooperation between the earls of Oxford and Derby.

The Oxfordian hypothesis is widespread in Britain and US. Most non-Stratfordian theorists in these countries hold that view today, so that anyone who does not share the traditional idea of the Great Bard's identity is almost automatically labeled as Oxfordian. The American writer Charleton Ogburn was leading Oxford proponent. His life's work was published in 1984: *The Mysterious William Shakespeare. The Myth and Reality*,[71] — a true Oxfordian encyclopedia. In the late 1980s, Oxfordians staged a series of mock trials to hear the case of Oxford's "claims" for the authorship of Shakespeare's plays. Held in Washington, D.C. and London, the trials attracted wide

---

71. Ogburn Ch. *The Mysterious William Shakespeare. The Myth and Reality.* N.Y., 1984.

public attention to the "Shakespeare question," although in the end the majority of the judges (including members of the Supreme Courts of both countries) did not find the arguments in defense of Oxford's authorship convincing.

A weakness in the Oxfordian thesis is the lack of direct proof (manuscripts, for instance — but, of course, the Stratfordians cannot produce any, either), and in particular the very early date of Oxford's death — 1604, whereas many of Shakespeare's plays were apparently created later. Pro-Oxfordians have to accept that the plays that appeared after this date were created before 1604, but published later. However, the plays contain allusions to events of 1605-1610, so that theory does not hold water. Attempts have been made to identify the plays staged by various companies of players in the 1576-1590s with Shakespearean works ("Timon of Athens," "Titus Andronicus," "Cymbeline") to draw their dates nearer to the years of Oxford's life.

The Oxford authorship theory also fails to provide a cogent explanation of such important facts as the dedication of the 1623 Great Folio to the earls of Pembroke and Montgomery and the active involvement of Ben Jonson in the release of this edition. In recent years, a new controversy among Oxfordians arose over the question of whether the Earl of Oxford was once not only a favorite but also a lover of Queen Elizabeth, and that Southampton was the secret offspring of their liaison. In the absence of documented evidence, the authors of such speculations have been unable to prove them, so that in the end their conjecture contributed more to the cause of the Stratfordians than to any real solution to the "Shakespeare problem."

As a matter of fact, historians have no real evidence that Oxford (in contrast to Rutland) had any close relationship with Southampton. Nor of his relations with Shakspere — there is absolutely no trace of that man around the Earl of Oxford (in contrast to Rutland). That is a very important point. Present day followers of Looney claim as evidence a 1569 copy of the Bible in the Folger Library, where the texts used in Shakespeare's plays are marked (by Oxford himself, as they believe). That Oxford and his milieu had some connection to the earliest period of Shakespeare's play-writing activities is quite possible, but such ties should be proved by facts.

The introductory part of the Oxfordian hypothesis — the critique of the Stratfordian biographical canon on the basis of all the accumulated facts about William Shakspere from Stratford — is sounder than its adherents' arguments in favor of Oxford's authorship. Nevertheless, the study of Oxford's biography, like that of the other "contenders" for authorship, as well as their involvement in literature and theater, doubtlessly advances our knowledge of the Shakespearean age.

In addition to the names of Bacon, Rutland, Derby, and Oxford, theorists have also submitted as "pretenders" the Earl of Essex, Sir Walter Raleigh, Sir Robert Cecil and other renowned state figures and literary men of Elizabethan-Jacobian England, including even the sovereigns, Queen Elizabeth I and King James I.

In the 1950s, a popular hypothesis was making the rounds suggesting that the pen name "Shake-speare" was a disguise for the prominent playwright Christopher

Christropher Marlowe

Marlowe, as his later works had much in common in both style and language with Shakespeare's chronicles. The cessation of Marlowe's literary work and his assassination in 1593 coincided with the start of Shakespeare's creative activities. Recent revelations about the circumstances of Marlowe's assassination suggest many odd and dubious things. It appears that the young poet and dramatist, known for his rebellious character and liberal ideas, was also performing secret missions for Sir Francis Walsingham, Elizabeth's intelligence chief.

The American scholar Calvin Hoffman questioned whether Christopher Marlowe was really killed in May 30, 1593. In his book *The Man Who Was Shakespeare* (1955),[72] Hoffman asserted that it was not Marlowe but an unknown man who was killed at a lodging house in Deptford, and that after the would-be assassination the playwright himself allegedly went into hiding at Walsingham's estate, and sent his works to be published under the pen name of "William Shakespeare," through Sir Francis Walsingham (or his cousin). In 1956, Hoffman attempted to excavate the Walsinghams' vault, where he hoped (for reasons that are unclear to me) to find Marlowe's manuscripts. To be sure, nothing of the sort was found.

Other Marlowe proponents surmise that after 1593 he lived under an assumed name and was part of the milieu of Countess Mary Sidney Pembroke and King James himself.

Proceeding from the circumstances of Marlowe's assassination, which were strange indeed, from the fact that the date of the murder was close to the time when the name of William Shakespeare emerged in literature, as well as from all the commonalities between Shakespeare's first chronicle plays and Marlowe's last plays, Hoffman extrapolates too widely and constructs a theory that is unsupported by facts. A great number of scholars of different eras have advanced the opinion (which I share) that the first historic tragedies by Shakespeare, in particular the three parts of "Henry VI," were to some extent reworked variants of material left after Christopher Marlowe, Robert Greene, George Peele or somebody else from the circle of "University Wits." As far as the rest — the sham assassination of Christopher Marlowe, his "posthumous" life and literary work under the name of William Shakespeare, etc. — these intriguing notions are shots in the dark.

In addition to the non-Stratfordian theories favoring one or another individual candidate, some scholars have been convinced that group authorship was the answer. As early as in the 19th century Delia Bacon attributed the authorship to Sir Walter Raleigh and Edmund Spenser, as well as Francis Bacon. In 1925, C. Muscat named as possible co-authors Francis Bacon, the Earl of Oxford, and the Earl and Countess of Rutland. G. Slater (1931)[73] maintained that the evidence favored partial authorship by Christopher Marlowe ("Henry VI"), Francis Bacon ("Richard II" and "Richard III"), the Earl of Derby ("Love's Labour's Lost," "Midsummer Night's Dream"), the Earl of

72. Hoffman C. *The Man who was Shakespere.* L., 1955
73. Slater G. *Seven Shakespeares.* Oxford, 1931.

Oxford ("Hamlet"), Mary, Countess of Pembroke ("As You Like It"), Sir Walter Raleigh, and the Earl of Rutland. Sharing the view of Thomas Looney, Slater believed Oxford to have been the brightest star in this constellation. However, considerably more research will have to be done to support these suppositions.

Advocates of the group authorship theories base their arguments in part on the unparalleled vocabulary used by Shakespeare — such an extensive vocabulary could not be mastered by one person, however brilliant and educated he might be. Besides, in some plays another hand is clearly felt; even most Stratfordian theorists acknowledge that — they who disagree only on the number of such works and the nature of Shakespeare's partnership with other authors in each separate case. J. M. Robertson and his school (his Russian counterpart would be I. A. Aksionov) went quite far in acknowledging the possibility of such collaboration. In any event, various forms of collaboration in creative activity not at all uncommon, the most famous example being the play "Sir Thomas More," which "bears the hand" of a whole group of prominent dramatists!

Some non-Stratfordians, rather than proposing a candidate for authorship, restrict themselves to criticism of Stratford biographies and the documentary evidence about William Shakspere. Like George Greenwood, writing in the early 20th century, they emphasize that Shakspere could not have had a hand in any literary activity and that the construction of the myth about his being the Great Bard was apparently deliberate; but they decline to speculate as to who was, in fact, behind that strange mask, assuming that far more research will be required before any conclusive answer is found. A bibliography of the works of non-Stratfordian researchers and of their opponents would fill a book in itself.[74]

Since the 1920s, the plurality of non-Stratfordian theories has had a peculiar effect on the nature of discussions on the subject. Henceforth united (despite differences of views on certain particular issues), the "official" biographical version based on the almost four-centuries-old tradition, school textbooks and the flourishing veneration of the Stratford relics, now faced a non-Stratfordian opposition that consisted of isolated and rival schools, each defending its own candidate for the role of Shakespeare. This alignment naturally somewhat lessens the pressure on the traditionalists, but as the reader will have understood by now, in their criticism of the traditional approach the arguments of all the non-Stratfordians are basically the same. They also agree on the principal conclusion: Shakspere was not and could not have been the Great Bard. Of all the "Shakespeare candidates," Shakspere is the only one whose elementary literacy is not only unproven but is, in fact, seriously in doubt.

Certainly, along with the meticulous and insightful studies that have been produced over the course of time, the field has seen its share of facile, sensationalist and even tongue-in-cheek writings promoting whimsical notions and fantasies, which makes this intensely complicated problem even more impenetrable to the lay person.

---

74. Galland J.S. *Digesta anti-shakespeareana*. Ann Arbor. 1970

The authors of such works seem not to be concerned about the significance of the whole matter for the culture of humankind.

Looking for reasons why Shakespeare always seems to be just out of view (meaning perhaps that Shakspere was not among the contemporary men of letters, and there is no visible link between him and Shakespeare's works), some authors suggest alcoholism! Quite recently, some British authors have alleged that Shakespeare (i.e. Shakspere of Stratford) was a spy or a secret agent. All these things rather apply to some sort of literary divertissement.[75]

Today, even professional Shakespeare scholars find it difficult to orient themselves in the wilderness of details and divergent paths in the dispute. The problem of Shakespeare's identity and the controversy around him has become an academic discipline in itself. In this context, efforts to brush off the problem seem highly inappropriate and bound to fail.

## IN ACADEMIC CIRCLES — THE FACTS KEEP PILING UP

In the first quarter of the 20th century, many new Stratfordian theories came out. As mentioned above, the Cambridge school, J.M. Robertson and his disciples, concluded that most Shakespeare plays were either the reworked texts of his predecessors (Robert Greene, Christopher Marlowe, George Peele, Thomas Kyd), or were written in collaboration with such authors as George Chapman, Philip Massinger and John Fletcher, the role of Shakespeare himself often being limited to some final literary proof-reading. While avoiding stepping on any Stratfordian toes, these scholars at least provided some kind of rational explanation of the apparent involvement of "other quills," and of the huge vocabulary, as well.

Robertson's approach to Shakespeare's texts as products of collaborative work led to attempts to split up the texts and attribute this or that scene or even a soliloquy to a certain literary contemporary of Shakespeare on the basis of stylistic and lexical differences. Authorities in British Shakespeare studies objected. In May of 1924, a special session of the British Academy heard the report of Edmund Chambers, in which he criticized Robertson's views but recognized the validity of his assertions that some parts of "Timon of Athens," "Troilus and Cressida," "Pericles" and "Henry

---

75. Opinions were advanced in public that one might as well invent whatever stories one likes on Shakespeare's identity, "for in any case it is impossible to either prove or deny them after the elapse of four centuries." This is a highly erroneous judgment that proves a poor knowledge of both the background of the "Shakespeare question" and the considerable potential of modern historic methods. Besides, four centuries are not so great a time span — 17th century England was no primeval desert. However, everything is open to parody and a good laugh, and the challenge of the Shakespeare mystery cannot be discounted on these grounds. Especially so as a Rabelaisian-type of mockery is an essential ingredient of the Shakespearean legend.

VIII" seemed non-Shakespearean in nature. Robertson's views were attacked as a "Bolshevist nationalization of Shakespeare." Robertson does not have many followers today, but most scholars now admit, with some reservations and in very limited cases, that they cannot rule out the possibility of Shakespeare's having collaborated with other authors. Thus, Robertson's approach should not be rejected in its entirety; rather, we must consider the lack of reliable methods available in those days for comparative text analysis. Now that we have computers, we have the prospect of reaching more solid conclusions in each individual case (such as, for instance, the use of Marlowe's texts in Shakespearean historical plays, which has been documented by new analytical data).

Another group of Cambridge scholars is called the "bibliographical school." A. W. Pollard, R. B. McKerrow, W. W. Greg and their followers studied the texts in close connection with the circumstances of how and when they appeared. These scholars engaged in a deep and systematic study of how printing and publishing were conducted in Shakespeare's times, and they developed academic methods by which to reconstruct the original texts. On the basis of these techniques they were able to resolve several difficult textual problems and to provide an analysis of such literary monuments as Shakespeare's First Folio and the quartos, and the early works of Ben Jonson, Francis Beaumont, John Fletcher and other prominent Elizabethan writers. No other era, and certainly no other writer, would require such specialized and complicated methods to study the actual publishing context of literary works as that of Shakespeare — the background of almost every text of each of his works is a challenge, as proved by "The Phoenix and the Turtle." These difficulties are so ubiquitous as to suggest that they are not incidental but are organically tied to the "Shakespeare authorship question," although scholars of the respectable "bibliographic school" preferred not to address that awkward notion directly. This school gave us many reference tools essential for further work, including such fundamental editions as "A Short Title Catalogue of books, printed in England, Scotland and Ireland, and of English books, printed abroad 1475-1640" (A.W. Pollard and G.R. Redgrave); "Dictionary of Printers and Booksellers in England, Scotland and Ireland 1557-1640" (R. B. McKerrow); "Printers and Publishers Devises in England and Scotland 1485-1640" (R. B. McKerrow); "The Shakespeare First Folio" (W. W. Greg). *A Short Title Catalogue* (STC), published by Pollard and Redgrave in 1926, was re-issued with addenda in 1948, 1976 and 1986. The final volume of the STC, in which the old books are grouped by publisher and printer, was compiled by K. Pantzer in 1986 and released in 1991; the STC-assigned numbers for each old edition are now standard in academic libraries.

British scholarship of the second quarter of the 20$^{th}$ century was deeply influenced by the ideas advanced by John Dover Wilson, also a supporter of the "bibliographic school." The reader has already come across this scholar's name in relation to his comments on the bust in the Stratford church and the Grafton portrait. In his works, especially the slender "The Essential Shakespeare" (1932) and the collection of Shakespeare's plays released under his editorship (New Shakespeare), Wilson showed a new approach not only to specific problems of text studies, but also to some of the Stratfordian biographers' traditional ideas. An ardent Stratfordian himself, Wilson nevertheless strongly objects to the image of a wheeler-dealer with a golden touch that emerges from the pages of the biography written by Sidney Lee. Wilson excoriates the Stratford bust, considering it to be one of the main reasons why the great poet came to be seen as resembling a loathsome "self-satisfied pork butcher." According to Wilson, not only Sidney Lee's book but even the engraved portrait by Martin Droeshout turns out to have been created under the influence of that ill-fated work by an unqualified artisan-sculptor; these two pictures stand between us and the true Shakespeare, evoking the disgust of all who understand the Great Bard in the depths of their hearts. Hence, Wilson's aversion to Sidney Lee's work, which was reprinted so many times and was long considered a classic: "In a word, the Life that Lee gave us, was not the Life of William Shakespeare the man and the poet, but the life that 'William Shakespeare,' the bust in Stratford Church, might have lived had he ever existed in flesh and blood."

And then, in his campaign to save the true poetic Shakespeare, Wilson raises the "colors of the crusade" against Janssen, Droeshout and the Victorian biographers of the Bard. Wilson took great exception to the widespread assertion (then as now) alleging that Shakespeare is "absent" in his works, and demanded that biographers and researchers constantly look for the "living Shakespeare." "The essential Shakespeare will be altogether misconceived if we think of him as one who stood apart from the life of his time. On the contrary we may look for him . . . at the very heart of that life . . . Not his 'tragic story,' of which we know nothing, but the life at the courts of Elizabeth and James, the persons and doings of the great men of the land, the political and social events of the hour — these form the real background of his plays."[76] At the same time, Wilson justly reminds us that Shakespeare was not a reporter, but a poet.

As for Shakespeare's relationship with the events of his time, Wilson emphasized how the outstanding personality of the Earl of Essex and his tragic fate affected the poet. In "Henry V" and particularly in "Hamlet," Wilson sensed Shakespeare's anxiety about Essex, his adoration and inescapable anguish. "Hamlet's mystery is the mystery of Essex, the mystery of his heart," — wrote Wilson.

Wilson's quest to force his way through what he calls the "Victorian images" of the great writer to the "living" Shakespeare, as well as his strong repugnance for the Stratford bust, certainly catch our attention. But it should be borne in mind that the "bust,"[77] which in Wilson's eyes represents that dark image, so irreconcilable with Shakespeare's creative activities and so much in the way of people's search to find a

---

76. Wilson J.D. *The Essential Shakespeare*, Cambridge, 1932,p.5-6

77. Like many others, Wilson pays no attention to the fact that when it originally appeared the bust in the church of Stratford looked even less poetic than now, featuring no agreeable-looking ink-pad, quill and paper, but a shapeless bag clasped to the belly instead.

true image of the Bard, is just one element in a whole package of mutually reinforcing Stratfordian facts that work together to shape the outlines of one and the same person — William Shakspere of Stratford.

Wilson, however, seems rather to tear the Stratford bust out of context — away from Shakspere's illiterate parents, wife and even children, his money-lending business and the notorious will. Wilson practically ignores these facts, although they are well documented and irrefutable. He has too deep a sense of the Shakespeare as an artist and poet to be able to embrace or even try to explain these awful papers. But he cannot refuse to acknowledge them, as he did with the bust on the wall, for unlike the sculptor's work, these documents are part and parcel of the life of the man whose ashes lie in the Holy Trinity Church of Stratford.

Focusing all his antipathy and sarcasm on the "bust" and the associated Victorian wingless middle-class concept of Shakespeare, Wilson neglects a crucial circumstance. These ideas did not come out of nowhere, and they were certainly not inspired by the "bust" alone. Wilson's charges against the "Victorian" Shakespeare scholars, first of all against Lee's book, are unjust, for a biographer is not entitled either to ignore or gloss over the facts, whether he likes them or not. Using a historical method based on an analysis of the whole range of evidence and sources does not hamper or conflict with our insight into the creative heritage of an artist — when we are examining the biography of the same person. The life story of a prominent writer or poet comprises all the details of his origin, upbringing, education, family and environment, his deeds and conduct, in relation to the events in his country and the world he witnessed. And this social and personal life aspect of a life story intertwines with the creative biography, that is, the background of his works, the story of the poetic world born of his genius. Rather than being mutually exclusive, these two aspects of an academic biography supplement and enrich each other, although their relationship might often be not simple and implicit. All of this applies in those cases where both aspects relate to one and the same person.

But matters stand otherwise with Shakespeare. Whether intentionally or not, Wilson actually defends the biography of the poet William Shakespeare against the biography of Shakspere of Stratford, and attempts to filter out of the former those elements of the latter that have found their way in, at the same time trying to retain the basic premises of the Stratfordian tradition — in vain.

The "Victorian" image of a shrewd and successful trader who treated his work in the theater and literature mainly as means to secure his material independence did not emerge as a result of Lee's and the other Stratfordian biographers' lack of imagination; such a "moderate" view of the great playwright was a deliberate compromise in the attempt to square, as far as possible, the two conflicting biographies of Shakespeare and to unite all the literary and historically-documented facts in a single consistent portrait, even if not a highly "poetical" one.

While assaulting his Victorian tutors and defending his piously revered Bard against the inimical Stratford "bust,"[78] Wilson undermines the basis for the "peaceful coexistence" of both Shakespeare's and Shakspere's biographies, and in exposing the gap between them goes to the limit that threatens the Stratfordian canon and cult.

Wilson's bold attempts to visualize the "living" Shakespeare (i.e. Shakspere) of Stratford invoked the resistance of authoritative British and American Shakespeareans, who labeled his approach as "romantic" and called his critical judgments on some issues "inspired." Indeed, Wilson's peculiar treatment of the historic facts, while not devoid of some innovative elements (as illustrated by the way he interprets the course of events preceding the appearance of the Stratford bust, or by the preference he shows for the Grafton portrait with the image of an unknown young man) is quite vulnerable to criticism.

All that being said, many of the Shakespearean biographies and biographical studies of recent decades show the influence of, or at least a familiar with, Dover Wilson's ideas (he died in 1970). This is reflected in frequent deviations from the matter-of-fact "protocol-like" approach of Edmund Chambers and his followers to a more free and easy way of telling things, along with some guesses here and there, particularly when it comes to the miraculous spontaneous transformation of the uneducated glover's apprentice into the great poetic dramatist and highly-learned person.

In 1938, Edgar Fripp completed his two-volume edition *Shakespeare. Man and Artist*,[79] with a summary of the facts already established plus some hitherto unpublished details relating to Shakespeare's biography. Leslie Hotson, an assiduous researcher who delved deep into the archive materials and portrait painting of the Shakespearean age, also produced worthwhile books. Though some of his identifications are not sufficiently substantiated, his studies contribute to filling in the "blank spots" around Shakspere and Shakespeare, and to the elucidation of what it was that allowed the Great Bard's literary contemporaries to liken him to the resourceful and elusive Mercury and the shape-changing Proteus of ancient mythology.

We have already mentioned the latest major biographic works, Schoenbaum's books *Shakespeare's Lives*[80] (1970) and *Shakespeare. A Compact Documentary Life* (1977). The former is a substantial work describing the long evolution of Shakespeare biographies (in Stratfordian interpretation, of course). Schoenbaum tackles the non-Stratfordian theories quite superficially, and has a rather fuzzy idea of why they appeared, but treats them (each and all) with pronounced hostility. Judging from *Shakespeare's Lives*, the author does not know much about the Rutland hypothesis. Schoenbaum provides fairly detailed life stories of the Shakespearean biographers themselves, and it should

---

78. Wilson even blamed the Stratfordian "bust" and the "bust-influenced" biography by S. Lee as the chief precursors of the "campaign against the man from Stratford," that is, the rise of the non-Strafordian hypotheses! Similar concepts on the origin of "Shakespeare question" are quite common.

79. Fripp E.I. *Shakespeare. Man and Artist*. L., 1938

80. Schoenbaum S. *Shakespeare's Lives*. N.Y. 1970

be noted that they come across in living color in a way that eludes the Great Bard in his traditional biographies. Significantly, Schoenbaum concluded his solid work with the melancholic statement that although each generation of scholars has applied its own approaches and techniques in this quite thankless endeavor and we have gradually learned so much about Shakespeare, for some reason no one yet has been able to provide a convincing life story of the Great Bard, and we have no choice but to hope for the future.

Schoenbaum's *A Compact Documentary Life* is intended for a wider audience, and is a coherent and chronological recitation of the documented facts of William Shakspere's life. The author also relates some stories and evaluates their possible authenticity. The book provides a detailed description of the theatrical life and players' companies in Elizabethan London, touching upon the subject of Shakespeare's literary activities only from time to time, since its link with Shakspere has never been established (although, of course, that link is by no means questioned by the biographer). As a result, the biographical study features a great number of facts and in this respect is unequaled by the life story of any other poet or playwright of the epoch, but it produces a strange impression even on those who have been brought up in the Stratfordian spirit: what does it have to do with the author of "Hamlet" and "King Lear"? It proves once again the point that, devoid of conjectures, the Stratfordian biography of Shakespeare (i.e. Shakspere) turns into the life story of a mediocre, aggressively enterprising person of average capacity. And the more scholars learn about him, the more factually well-founded the biographies of Shakespeare become, the more apparent is this effect. Anikst wrote in the foreword to the Russian translation of this book: "I am afraid, Schoenbaum's book may further the cause of skeptics and those who do not believe in the authorship of Shakespeare [that is, — Shakspere — I.G.]. The author always deals with documentation that is generally not related to the creative activities of Shakespeare."

Intensive studies of the culture and people of Shakespeare's England carried out over the last two centuries have created a vast wealth of information that far exceeds the knowledge base of century and a half ago, when the Great Dispute on Shakespeare was first emerging. It will be appropriate to mention here the most remarkable Russian-language editions of Shakespeare's complete works. The first of the kind was released by N. Ketcher (1841-1850 and 1858-1879); this was almost a word-for-word translation. A complete edition of poetically translated works was published in 1865 by N. A. Nekrasov and N. V. Gerbel', and went on to be reprinted several times. Shakespeare's plays, translated by A. L. Sokolovsky, came out between 1894 and 1898. In 1902-1904, a finely designed edition of Shakespeare's works, annotated by Russian literary scholars, was issued under the editorship of S. A. Vengerov. The most authoritative of the complete collections released during the Soviet era was the eight-volume edition by Smirnov and Anikst (1957-1960), featuring the best translations of the preceding decades, including those by M. Lozinsky, A. Radlova, and B. Pasternak.

The traditional ideas of the Great Bard's identity were most comprehensively presented in Anikst's *Shakespeare*, published in Russian in 1964. Anikst (1910-1988) was a major contributor to the study and popularization of Shakespeare's heritage, albeit in a Stratfordian vein. Apart from a brief period when the Rutland hypothesis came into vogue in Russia, Russian and Soviet Shakespeare scholars have generally relied upon their British and American colleagues to shed more light on the biographical conundrum. Today, technological advances have made it easier to disseminate both original and auxiliary literature, offering scholars everywhere the chance to conduct original and independent studies. These opportunities, however, have yet to be used to full advantage.

## THE HOUR HAS STRUCK FOR THE TURTLE AND THE PHOENIX

As the blank spots in the imaginary map of 16th-17th century England's political, social and cultural life are filled in, it becomes more and more difficult to plausibly explain the lack of any trace or clue that would associate the man of Stratford with the literary life of the times. As an author, poet and playwright, he is still missing, from the Pembrokes' and the Earl of Southampton's entourages, and among the students of Cambridge or London Inns of Court — that is, from those very circles to which the works of Shakespeare directly point. Neither he is found near Ben Jonson, John Donne, Michael Drayton, Samuel Daniel, George Chapman, John Marston, Francis Beaumont, John Fletcher or the other writers and dramatists whose life and environment have gradually become more transparent. As if separated from all his literary contemporaries by a mysterious curtain, the Great Bard's figure still seems to dwell in sort of fourth dimension. The more documents we have on the life, occupations and interests of William Shakspere, the clearer it is that the man never was and never could be involved in literary activities of any kind.

The "Shakespeare mystery" still exists. The elements of the two biographies resist being put together in one life story — the artificial combination of incompatible materials is obvious. Modern authors of Shakespeare biographies aspire to overcome this inconsistency by saturating their books with generalizations about life in that era, and with stories about other people of renown and about theaters and players' companies, and by striving to synchronize the historical events with the canonical (though often controversial) dates when Shakespeare's works appeared. All this is accompanied by information on the "business" occupations of William Shakspere. As the example of Schoenbaum illustrates, the use (and appropriate presentation) of such supplementary material in Stratfordian biographies may shade but in no way eliminate the striking incongruity between William Shakspere and the role of the Great Bard ascribed to him.

But not everybody reads academic biographies of Shakespeare, and most people start to form their ideas of history, literature and great writers fairly early in their education, on the basis of information provided by schoolbooks, lecturers, historical fiction, and even from tourist brochures on the Stratfordian relics or personal visits to Stratford-on-Avon.

At times, the quasi-biographical literature about Shakespeare presents intriguing notions that capture the public's fancy. R. Sisson's book *Young Shakespeare* shows young William studying at grammar school, then being forced to quit due to his family's financial difficulties. He begins writing poems; becomes a page to Fulke Greville; the latter introduces him to Sir Philip Sidney, as well as to poet Henry Goodiere and his page Michael Drayton; he competes with them in composing verses dedicated to fair ladies, and amazes them by his art, etc. The book fails to mention that these naive tales were invented by the author, so that many readers take them seriously. Similar problems arise with the much talked-about move *Shakespeare in Love*, or the best-selling novel by Anthony Burgess.

Present day Western academic (university) Shakespeare studies emphasize two opposing trends. On the one hand, modern methods of historical research continue to be applied, adding to the accumulation of facts that make Stratfordian theorists more and more uncomfortable (for not one of the latest discoveries has supported their thesis). On the other, there is an obvious resistance to the steadfast, though not always visible, erosion of the Stratfordian tradition and Stratfordian worship, which are part and parcel of the official Shakespeare scholarship.

Over the last 150 years the non-Stratfordians have been able to draw the world's attention to the irreducible contradictions in the traditional view of the Great Bard's identity, as well as to question and make them the subject of scholarly debates. This is a big step in the right direction. In their further research, the non-Stratfordians bump up against the most difficult question: "If not Shakspere, then who?" and offer many (too many) alternative answers. The plurality of hypotheses is normal when facing intricate problems; and let's not forget that the Great Bard's footprints seem to come from more than one pair of feet. However, the isolated non-Stratfordian schools, each supporting their own candidate(s), could not, of course, depose their adversaries, backed up as they are by the four-centuries old commonly accepted tradition and cult of the Stratford relics. The Stratfordists, for now, still occupy the dominating position in Shakespeare scholarship. Educated in the traditional notions of Shakespeare, the scholars still maintain their ground while defending, as they believe, the Great Bard against the profane attacks of his critics and abusers. The key arguments of the "heretics" as a rule are simply ignored, but even minor factual inaccuracies, not to mention groundless assertions, are used to generally discredit any criticism of traditional Stratfordian fundamentals, right up to the rejection of the Shakespeare authorship question as a historical problem. However, this longstanding controversy arose neither by chance nor as a result of some scheme designed by sensation seekers or haughty British lords — the question is a problem of fundamental importance for

A jester effigy erected in recent times in Stratford-upon-Avon.

the history of world culture. And British-American Shakespeare scholarship, tied to the Stratfordian cult, is unable to close itself off from this challenge. The Shakespeare authorship question crops up anew with every generation.

Reading the works of eminent British and US scholars who have devoted their lives to the study of Shakespeare and his contemporaries, one is forced to ask: Do they really not notice the inexplicable absence of the least bit of evidence from these contemporaries to indicate that their great compatriot was a real flesh-and-blood person? Is it conceivable that they fail to note the apparent oddities of Droeshout's portrait and the Stratford "monument," the painful impression the Stratfordian papers leave, and a great variety of other facts that revile everyone who honors literary (and especially Shakespeare) heritage? Do these theorists really believe that all the arguments advanced by several generations of critics are just silly conjectures and aristocratic plots? Is it possible that in the face of such a huge mass of established facts, they have never doubted the truthfulness of the traditional biographic canon? Indeed, who but they ought to know perfectly well when and how it originated?

No, to my mind, they are not all that naive. It is not only the ideas they've absorbed since childhood, it is their official status (their priest-like commentaries on the Stratfordian-Shakespearean icon) that puts these scholars in a difficult position whenever they begin to have any doubts about the central figure to their cult. Since there are actually no reliable barriers to restrict the free circulation of ideas in the humanities to a closed circle of specialists, such scholars generally try not to go beyond the bounds and restrictions imposed by the Stratfordian symbol of faith. This, naturally, has a dramatic impact on their own works and studies. As to the non-Stratfordian hypotheses, their outright rejection on the part of the official Shakespeare priesthood is, in a sense, even beneficial: in a Darwinian sense, the test of time and of non-recognition promotes the selection of prospective ideas and helps to weed out some of the baseless conjectures that are so prevalent nowadays.

The 150-year-old controversy over the "Shakespeare authorship question," like so many other characteristics of the Great Bard and his works, has been unprecedented. It would be a mistake to refer to the debate in the past tense — it is still in the first phase of its decisive development. Today we can speak of two disciplines competing with each other but focusing on the same, unique object — the Great Bard William Shakespeare. Two Shakespearologies. And the final result of this illuminating confrontation of ideas and approaches is unquestionable — the truth about the wonderful mystery bequeathed to humanity will finally become its precious possession, to be cherished by all.

Even if the great writer and his assistants and followers took special care to conceal his true face from their coevals and the generations to come, even if he wished to live only through his creations and to turn them into his sole monument — the only way to learn that is to identify him and understand his intentions. Such as quest by no means disrespects the great man or dishonors his memory. Such investigations cannot be to the detriment of anyone's or anything's image — either the prestige of England, or that of the world literature and theater, or the charming town of Stratford-on-Avon. No matter how the dispute around Shakespeare develops, the authority of the great writer shall always remain unshakable, for it is based on his unequaled creations rather than on the documents of the Stratford parish or the judicial records showing actions taken against insolvent neighbors.

This is not a quest to "denounce" Shakespeare but to arrive at a deeper comprehension of the entire Shakespeare phenomenon. A multiplicity of facts indicate that we are facing a Great Game, the ingenious dramatist's most brilliant creation, with Time itself as the stage, and generations of mere mortals playing the roles of not only the audience but also the players. And those who in all good faith assiduously guard the sealed entrances to the inner sanctum of this Theater of Time, not realizing what is behind the doors, also perform their destined role.

Unraveling the mystery of this Great Game about William Shakespeare would not be a loss, as feared by those "guardians of the doorstep," but an unfathomable enrichment. As to William Shakspere, when, as the First Folio predicted, "time dissolves the Stratford monument," that is, when it becomes clear that Shakspere was not the Great Bard but merely performed the role of his mask, his "impreso," throughout the ages, the world will revere the old relics in a new way, rather than discard them. For Shakspere, as one of the leading players of the Great Game, will take a well-deserved place in its history — for mankind's amazement and edification!

Of course, there will come a day when the details of the dispute will recede into the background — indeed, everyone maintained his personal notion, his personal image of the Shake-spear, and everyone was an active participant in the theater designed by him. But it is too early to speak about that today. At present, what matters most is not the debate itself, but rather the actual exploration of the facts that might be keys to disclosing the mystery of the Great Bard, keys to the door to the sanctuary of his Theater. And Robert Chester's Love's Martyr is one of most important keys.

Humanity will by all means discover the truth about the Great Game, as long as we have the strength and wisdom to force our way through all the obstacles and labyrinths piled up not only by the merciless Time, but also by the brilliant design of those who are still so near to us — we feel the pulsation of their high thought. Invisible and unrecognized, they seem to mock at our attempts to piece together the remnants of Ariadne's thread scattered here, there and everywhere.

But the hour has struck for the Turtle and the Phoenix.

# Chapter 3. The Chaste Lords of Sherwood Forest

*The trail leads to Belvoir — A child of state — Oh, Padua, Padua … The portrait decoded — Phoenix, daughter of Phoenix: Rosalind. Jaques-the-melancholic craves to play a fool — Cambridge games on the Muses' home turf — A favorite on the scaffold. Downfall — The ship is bound for Elsinore: Two "Hamlet" quartos — The poets of Belvoir Vale — The Countess of Pembroke, Mistress of poetic Arcadia in foggy Albion — The transfiguration of Captain Lanyer's wife.*

## The Trail Leads to Belvoir

Now, let us return to the Rutlands, the platonic couple whose unusual relationship and activities as well as the strange circumstances of their almost simultaneous departure precisely coincide with what Robert Chester and the other poets who wrote the *Love's Martyr* collection said about the Turtle and the Phoenix.

Even if Roger Manners, the 5th Earl of Rutland, were not under serious suspicion of hiding behind the penname-mask of "Shake-speare," the facts uncovered in the last century would be enough to focus one's rapt attention on this strange individual who was always appearing just where the Great Bard and quite often William Shakspere from Stratford might be turn up; it is high time we set out to learn everything possible about Rutland and his poet-wife who were, as gradually becomes apparent, a true center of literary life in the England of those days.

Authentic documents found at Belvoir and other locations were made public in studies by G. Zeigler, K. Bleibtreu, C. Demblon, P. Porohovchikov,[1] and C.

Sykes[2] and have finally shed light on this mysterious couple who until a few decades ago were almost fully obscured by the veil created by themselves and their faithful friends. At present, although most Western non-Stratfordians tend to concentrate more on such figures as the Earl of Oxford and on Marlowe, the foundation of the Rutland hypothesis is undeniable. In fact, my research has yielded new facts related to Elizabeth Sidney and her role in the literary process, and also to an immense Rabelaisian farce created around the "Greatest Traveler and Prince of Poets," Thomas Coryate. The significance of these, for our understanding of the mysterious events in the literature of England during the reigns of Elizabeth and James, including the "Shakespearean Mystery," is evident not only from Chester's collection but also from other books which I will discuss later.

Much work still needs to be done to clarify the images of these unique personalities, to understand their intentions, to perceive the high tragedy of their service to art, their life and death. However, the main point is evident — the first stage on the path toward the solution of the mystery of the Great Bard is to fathom the secret of the Rutlands, the enigma of the Turtle and the Phoenix.

Roger Manners was born on October 6, 1576, in the castle of Belvoir,[3] Leicestershire, located at the end of the small Belvoir Vale, not far from the famous Sherwood Forest where the legendary Robin Hood performed his feats in bygone days.

Like many other English aristocratic families, the Manners descended from the Norman knights who had settled in England after William the Conqueror's victory over the Anglo-Saxons. During the War of the Roses (to which the trilogy "Henry VI" was dedicated), one of Roger's ancestors fought on the king's side, while another fought for the Earl of Warwick. Roger's great grandfather, Thomas Manners, was a favorite of King Henry VIII and in 1525 was awarded the title of the Earl of Rutland (the previous bearer of the title, the young son of Richard, Duke of York, had been killed in 1460 at the battle of Wakefield). The grandson of Thomas Manners, Edward, the 3rd Earl of Rutland, was a highly educated person (Master of Arts from both Cambridge and Oxford universities) and an expert in law, as testified by the renowned historian William Camden. Edward enjoyed the confidence of Queen Elizabeth, who once visited Belvoir while on a tour around the country. Surprisingly, though he was believed to be a perfectly loyal subject of the queen, Edward appears in the Jesuits' list of aristocrats upon whom the Spanish king could rely in case of an incursion into England (a letter containing such information, from Parsons, a Jesuit, was found in the

---

1. Porohovchikov P. *Shakespeare unmasked.* L., 1955.

2. Sykes C.M. *Alias William Shakespeare?* L., 1947.

3. This is assumed by most historians. However, A. Daniushevskaya argues that he was most likely born at the other estate, Kirk Daton, where his parents were living at the time and where he was baptized.

Roger Manners, Earl of Rutland (from Demblon's book)

Belvoir Castle. From a 19th-century drawing.

Spanish archives in the 19th century). Perhaps, in some way or another, he had evinced sympathy for Catholicism, which was banned.

After Edward died in 1587, the title passed on to his younger brother John. The next year the latter passed away and 11-year-old Roger Manners became the 5th Earl of Rutland. Historians note that in addition to love of knowledge and the arts, many members of the Manners family were also known for their eccentricity.

We have already mentioned the magnificent Belvoir Castle, standing on a high hill, described in Robert Chester's poem. However, the castle deserves a more detailed treatment. I have visited the place and can say that I have never seen anything more beautiful in Britain than Belvoir. From a small village at the foot of the hill, stone steps lead up to the castle. The route to the fortress is planted with rows of cedars and rhododendrons, and in the olden days the entrance was protected by cannons mounted on the bulwark. In front of the castle walls there is an esplanade where one may take a promenade and enjoy a poetic view of the environs. In fair weather the visibility extends to thirty miles, and one can make out the roofs of Nottingham and the belfries of Lincoln Cathedral in the distance. The esplanade is located over a vertical cliff in which a doorway was cut, leading to the vast cellar of the castle. The building had been improved and decorated by all Roger's predecessors; the Belvoir picture gallery counted hundreds of canvases, including French, Italian and Flemish masterpieces.

An unusually rich and constantly expanding library was at the disposal of hosts and guests alike. The steward, in his household notes, recorded the sizable and frequent expenses for the purchase of books.[4] In September of 1585, 20 shillings were paid to buy the Paris edition (in French) of Belleforest's work *Histoires Tragiques*, which is known to have been a source for "Hamlet." The library also held both Hall's and Holinshed's *Chronicles*, important sources for Shakespeare's historical plays, as well as other books Shakespeare used. Book purchasing increased noticeably while Roger was in charge of Belvoir. I must say in advance that, a few decades after his death, in 1643-1645, Belvoir became the scene of severe battles between the followers of the king and the parliament army, and in the early 19th century the building was greatly damaged by fire, so that many valuable canvases and documents were destroyed. Later on, the castle was rebuilt.

The closest friend of Roger's father John Manners was Henry Herbert, the 2nd Earl of Pembroke and husband of Mary Sidney. Until the end of his life, Roger Manners would keep up a friendship with Pembroke's two sons, William and Philip, especially with the former. The postmortem edition of Shakespeare's plays would be dedicated to them, underscoring the attention they showed to Shakespeare during his life.

---

4. See: Rutland's Papers. Historical MS Commission, vol. 1-4. L., 1888-1894. Among the hand-written materials from Belvoir there are letters, household and other record. They were also used in this work.

Upon his death, John Manners left behind a wife and eight children: four sons (Roger, Francis, George, Oliver), and four daughters (Bridget, Elizabeth, Ann and Frances). Curiously enough, William Shakspere from Stratford also had three brothers and four sisters. Also interesting is the fact that, of the four brothers, two — Roger and George — belonged to the Anglican Church, whereas Francis and Oliver were Catholics. This would seem to indicate that the children were brought up in a climate of religious tolerance, including lenience or maybe even sympathy towards Catholicism. Researchers noticed long ago that there are no signs of hostility toward Catholics in the works of Shakespeare, while the Franciscan monk in "Romeo and Juliet" is beyond doubt a positive character who selflessly and disinterestedly helps the lovers.

The monument on the grave of John Manners, the 4th Earl of Rutland, inside the church of Bottesford, was erected by Garrat Janssen Sr. (father of Nicholas and Garrat Jr., who would later put up the monuments to Roger Manners and William Shakspere). It is such an outstanding masterpiece of monumental art that it is used to illustrate the article on sculpture in the famous *Chamber's Encyclopaedia*. It is really a theatrical scene in stone. Around the tombstone — reclining statues of the father and mother — their children are shown paying genuflectory obeisance, hands folded in prayer. The concept for such a monument to his father and mother was probably discussed between the sculptor and the new earl; or, perhaps Roger was its sole author.

After Roger's demise in 1612, the title passed to his brother Francis, who became the 6th Earl of Rutland. It was he who several months later ordered that a payment be made to Shakspere and Burbadge, and some Shakespeareans assume that after a decade had passed he also paid the Janssens for the wall monument to Shakspere at the church in Stratford, as well as for Roger's, in Bottesford. According to a family legend, Francis made a strange farewell speech on his deathbed (in the words of historian Archbold, the oration was in the spirit of "the Manners' eccentricities"). In due course, Francis's daughter Catherine married the Duke of Buckingham, who is so widely known today from historical novels.

Roger's sister Bridget rejected two marriage proposals in succession, in 1593, from noble young friends of Roger's — the Earl of Southampton and the Earl of Bedford (Edward Russell), because she believed both were "dreamers." In due course Russell consoled himself by marrying Lucy Harington, and after a few years the Earl of Southampton married Elizabeth Vernon, a relative of the Earl of Essex.

Another of Rutland's sisters, Frances, married William Willoughby, a kinsman of the Oxford student Henry Willoughby who was mentioned above in relation to the mysterious poem of 1594, entitled "Willobie[5] his Avisa, or a True Picture of the modest Maid and a Chaste and Constant wife."

---

5. Right spelling — Willoughby.

There is a rather involved story about this poem. Aware of Willobie's difficulties in love, his friend (called W. S.) set out to provoke and stir up his hopes, for he wanted to see whether "some other actor would be able to play the role better than it was played by himself, and to see whether this love comedy would have a happier end for the new actor than for the old one." Disguised under the name of "Hadrian Dorell," one of Willobie's fellow students allegedly found the poem in his papers and decided to publish it. Two years later, the poem "Penelope's Complaint" appeared, signed by a certain Peter Colse, mentioning an "unknown author" who had published the "poem of Willobie." Afterwards, "Willobie and his Avisa" was reprinted with some additions, one of which was signed by "Hadrian Dorell" and dated the "30th of June, 1596, city of Oxford." The other addition, signed by Thomas Willobie, "The Victory of English Chastity," announces that the rivalry between Penelope and Avisa has come to an end in favor of the latter, and that the rivalry has been arbitrated by certain Rogero (i.e. Roger; the name of Henry Willobie is also Italianized — Enrico). Hadrian Dorell (Demblon assumes that this is an anagram) teases Peter Colse (apparently an alias as well), who could not fail to know the author, "whose true name is open on every page."

As to the name of "Avisa," its origin is interpreted by Hadrian Dorell in different editions of the poem in various ways. In one case it is "explained" that the name derives from the first letters of Latin words meaning: loving wife, unblemished, always love worthy; however, later on Hadrian says that the name "Avisa" is made up of the Greek negation "a" and the Latin "visa" (visible), but also may derive from Latin "avis" (bird), and thus means a bird that is invisible or has never been seen.

It is obvious that all these editions and counter-editions are a joke, a masquerade intelligible only to insiders. But the abbreviation "W. S." (matching both William Shakespeare and the Earl of Southampton[6]), the anagram "Hadrian Dorell" and the name of Rogero-Roger help to target our sights on one circle, encompassing authors and the milieu of the aristocratic university youth — the Rutlands, the Southamptons, the Bedfords. This literary game may also concern the unsuccessful proposals to Bridget Manners by her unfortunate admirers. And the name Frances Willoughby is found in the acrostics of the strange poetic book *Sinnets*, by Robert Parry, linked to the circle of Chester and Salusbury and thus possibly related to the Chester collection as well.

Since the verses of praise introducing "Avisa" contain the first time the name of Shake-speare (hyphenated) was ever mentioned in literature, few biographies of Shakespeare fail to mention the poem, one way or another. Lesley Hotson, a well-known Shakespeare researcher, even discovered that the wife of Henry Willoughby's elder brother had a sister whose husband was a certain Thomas Russel, who, like Shakspere, hailed from Stratford. Hotson took that as proof that the poem originated from somewhere "in the circle of personal acquaintances and literary interests of William Shakespeare" (meaning Shakspere). Which specific "circle" that would be,

---

6. Wriothesley Southampton.

Shakespeare scholars generally prefer not to specify, for they have learned to be circumspect when making such claims.

Shakespeare scholars have neglected "Rogero," who judges the rivalry of Avisa and Penelope. Given that Roger Manners, Earl of Rutland, was Willoughby's kinsman, that omission is striking and, I think, must be eliminated. And so, for now, let us leave aside the young earl's brothers and sisters and take another look at Roger himself.


## A CHILD OF STATE


Like other fatherless young offspring of noble families, Roger Manners was under the wardship of Queen Elizabeth's chief minister, Sir William Cecil, Lord Burghley, and was considered to be "a child of the state."[7] Earlier, the earls of Oxford, Essex, Southampton and Bedford had experienced the same strict guardianship. Burdened with state affairs, Lord Burghley assigned the daily education of the young Earl of Rutland to his relative, Francis Bacon, a philosopher, lawyer, and writer; such a tutor could of course teach the capable young ward many things. And it happens that Shakespeare was well acquainted with Bacon's thought.

In 1587, Roger was sent to Cambridge and entered the Queen's College, where his principal mentor was John Jegon, later to become Bishop of Norwich. Two years later, Jegon began teaching at the College of Corpus Christi and transferred Roger there as well. Rutland maintained the relationship with his buddies from both colleges, even while studying at Cambridge and later on as well. He had a personal study at Cambridge, where he stayed when visiting his alma mater and working there. It was also at Cambridge that he died, in 1612, having provided in his will funds for the assistance of Cambridge scholars.

In 1589, Lord Burghley called Roger to London in order to be presented to the Queen, who received him affably (according to a letter to his mother, which still exists today), said that she had known his father to be an honest man, and had heard many good things about his mother. At that point in time, Rutland became very close with another of Burghley's wards — the young Earl of Southampton. Later on, they were both patronized by the royal favorite, the brilliant Essex, and they became his faithful admirers and adherents. Thus, under the wing of Sir William Cecil, Lord Burghley, was born the friendship of three earls which later on would be severely tested when the Earl of Essex dramatically and theatrically challenged the power of the Cecil family and Queen Elizabeth herself.

---

7. The first line of Shakespearean Sonnet 124 strikes many readers as odd: "If my dear love were but the child of state." Where did Shakespeare take this image, this expression — "child of state" — which is hardly on every poet's tongue?

An extant letter sent by Roger's trusted servant to his mother in 1591 announces that "Southampton has informed [us] that he is going to visit my lord." The same year, in June, Roger stayed at Southampton's home for a few days.

Two years later, "Venus and Adonis" appeared, exquisitely and warmly dedicated to the Earl of Southampton, and signed by William Shakespeare. This was the first printed work by Shakespeare, and the first time the name appeared in literature. The next year, the poem "The Rape of Lucrece" came out, with a new dedication to Southampton. We discussed earlier the familiar style in which both dedications were written, unconstrained by subservience and obsequiousness; as many Shakespeare scholars agree (to varying degrees), the dedications do not convey an impression of any great difference in social status. (How could an ordinary actor from a provincial town have addressed a titled aristocrat, close to the royal court, in such a tone?) Only a person who was equal to Southampton and on friendly terms with him could write so. And sorting through all of Southampton's friends at that period of time, whose closeness to him is proven by extant documents, it would appear that the dedications addressed in 1593 to the 20-year-old Earl of Southampton were most likely written by the 17-year-old Earl of Rutland; equal in status (and also "a child of the state"), he spoke under a penname to his older and admired friend.

The friendship between Rutland and Southampton must have revealed the clear differences in their personalities. While the latter, along with his great intellectual interests, never missed an opportunity to enjoy the short-lived pleasures of life, Rutland was already more inclined to spiritual solitude, to in-depth studies of the sciences and arts, and tended to stand aside from the empty life of high society — although its doors were open to him by virtue of his blue blood. Rutland's contact with British and continental scholars over the years is documented in their correspondence, which has partially survived, as well as by his infrequent appearances at court. It is also possible that Roger was physically inferior to his older friend — he was often ill, especially after his voyage to Europe.

Studies at the college were rather intensive — the students took Latin, ancient Greek, ancient Hebrew, theology, law, medicine, philosophy, logic, and rhetoric. The syllabus also included reading and staging classical Latin plays. The students especially liked to stage plays. Many teachers and senior students composed plays themselves, and some of them were presented on solemn occasions at the colleges' assembly halls. Thus we have Polonius recalling, in "Hamlet," that he once played Caesar during a play that was given while he was at university. The plays by mentors and students were generally presented just once, and were not published. The name of the author, as one of "their own," was usually not a secret, though there were some exceptions. Thus, early in 1595, when the Master of Arts degrees were being awarded, an anonymous play entitled "Laelia" was staged. The plot was borrowed from the French recast of an Italian comedy. Analyzing the text of this splendid play, researchers have found that it has much in common with some of Shakespeare's

Roger Manners as a child. The sculpture on the tomb of his father, the 4th Earl of Rutland (about 1591).

William Cecil, Lord Burghley

Henry Wriothesley,
Earl of Southampton

comedies, especially "Twelfth Night," and have surmised that Shakespeare read "Laelia" and borrowed certain elements from it.

Porohovchikov believes that "Laelia" and some other anonymous plays staged at Cambridge in the mid-1590s were written by Rutland during his graduation course. Anyhow, young Roger Manners, Earl of Rutland, was among the graduates of the university who received the Masters degree in February of 1595 and saw "Laelia" performed (or, perhaps, played a role in it), while the guests of honor included the Earl of Essex himself.

The letters Jegon wrote to Roger's mother attest to Rutland's extraordinary progress in his studies. However, the years at Cambridge were not entirely serene. Roger's uncle and father had left his mother heavily in debt, and she was not always able to send the necessary support to Cambridge on time. Though Jegon was pleased with him, one of the young earl's relatives (his grand-uncle, also Roger Manners) informed his mother that he had heard that the youth was not always scrupulous in choosing his acquaintances, which might adversely affect his conduct and manners.

The seven years as a student left a clear imprint. Scholars find the influence of Cambridge in many Shakespeare works, not only in the knowledge of the classics, law, and rhetoric, but also a special Cambridge slang — expressions and jargon which were in vogue only among local students; we hear them even from the lips of King Lear.

The first rapturous reviews and assessments of Shakespeare as a poet and playwright also came from the university, mostly Cambridge, milieu. That first reaction was voiced by Rutland's fellows: his teacher William Covell (who in 1595 included Shake-Speare in a list of writers that were Cambridge alumni), and student John Weever (1598), as well as Cambridge students Richard Barnfield and Francis Meres (1598).

Those were the years when his personality was in the making, when he acquired his knowledge of and his first experiences with poetry and the stage. The impression of youthful exaltation felt in the dedication to "Venus and Adonis" becomes even stronger when reading the poem itself abounding in erotic motives; the eroticism here is also youthful and literary. In his dedication to Southampton, Shakespeare referred to his poem "Venus and Adonis" (based on the classical, mythological plot) as "The first heir of my invention." By this, the Great Bard dates the beginning of his creative development, and the date is 1593. Certain scholars, in order to somehow make these words fit with their theory that some of Shakespeare's plays had been created earlier, began to claim that the expression "the first heir of my invention" was intended to apply only to poetic works: in those days, they said, dramas were considered lesser creations, so that Shakespeare allegedly did not take them into consideration. However, such an interpretation, no matter which experts support it, is quite far-fetched: Shakespeare never said anything of the kind either in the above dedication or anywhere else.

There are certainly more complex problems relating to the first (or, what is considered to be the first) Shakespearean plays and when they appeared; they will be discussed later on.

Upon graduation from university, young men from noble families traditionally set out on a journey across the Continent, and the Earl of Rutland was no exception. In December 1594, Lord Burghley notified the dowager Countess of Rutland that the Queen would allow her son to go abroad. The royal minister wrote in the same letter that his conversation with the young earl had left him with the impression that the young man was not well informed as to the state of affairs at his estates, and advised his mother to fill this void in his knowledge (indeed, the family's financial state left much to be desired).

His mother died in the spring of 1595. Throughout the summer and early autumn, Rutland stayed at Belvoir, delving into family matters and trying to put things straight. And by habit, he spent quite a lot of time in his library and at the writing table; Shakespeare's plays "Midsummer Night's Dream" and "King John" were written in about that year.

In October 1595, he started his travels. The first destination was the Dutch port of Flushing (Vlissingen), leased to the British in exchange for English assistance in the war with Spain. The governor of Flushing was Sir Robert Sidney, brother of the great poet Philip Sidney and a poet himself (like almost every member of that extraordinary family). In his letter to England, Robert Sidney judged Rutland's intellect very highly.

Together with all the other necessaries, the young traveler's luggage contained special "Letters of Advice" written for him by the versatile Francis Bacon, on the instruction of the Earl of Essex who, by then, had already showed the warmest concern for Rutland. This interesting document survived, in manuscript form, and was even printed in 1613. In addition, the watchful mentor Jegon had expressly warned the forerunner of Childe Harold about the frivolous nature of the Frenchmen and the various dangers lurking in wait for a traveler in their country. All those careful instructions were not disregarded; our young traveler possessed a good memory. In "Hamlet," their simple essence comes forth from the mouth of the royal minister Polonius, counseling his son Laertes before his departure to France. Bacon's biographers noted long ago the similarity between Polonius' orations, flavored with the author's irony, and the "Letters of Advice"; historians have also noticed that many features of the Shakespearean Polonius satirically recall the exacting Lord Treasurer Burghley (who certainly was personally known to his charge Roger Manners, Earl of Rutland, and equally certainly was not known to William Shakspere from Stratford, except by hearsay).

Leaving Holland, Rutland went to Germany. An extant letter shows that in early February of 1596 he was in Heidelberg, enjoying a visit to its famed university. He surely took the opportunity to see the notorious Great Tun of Heidelberg, and fifteen years later it is pictured and described in "Coryate's Crudities." However, his major goal was Italy, and the University of Padua. Keeping Anthony Bacon (brother of

Francis) informed about the Englishmen then traveling in Italy, Doctor Hawkins, who was staying in Venice, reported on February 24 that Rutland had not yet crossed the Alps. Through his trusted people Anthony followed events on the Continent and kept the Earl of Essex well posted on developments there; the latter was thus able to report to the Queen on foreign affairs without being dependent on Lord Burghley and his son.

Soon, having crossed Brenner Pass, Rutland found himself in Italy, and the first city he came to in the valley at the foot of the mountains was Verona, with its remarkable Roman amphitheater. A splendid engraving with the image of this ancient construction subsequently illuminated Coryate's book; and, of course, Verona is the city where the action takes place in "Two Gentlemen of Verona" and "Romeo and Juliet."

## OH, PADUA, PADUA . . . THE PORTRAIT DECODED

On March 28, 1596, Rutland was entered in the student list of the University of Padua, linked as it is with names like Galileo and Giordano Bruno. In 1574, Philip Sidney had also visited Padua; it was a true Mecca for any well-educated Englishman of the time. The university was especially famous for its professors of medicine, law and Latin — "Paduan Latin" was renowned throughout Europe in those days (a hero of the play "Return from Parnassas" even mentions it).

The sobriquet "the Paduan student" clung to Rutland long after his stay there; and two students from Denmark, Rosencrantz and Guildenstern, as Demblon established, both were in Padua. Padua is mentioned in Shakespeare's plays, starting with "The Taming of the Shrew."

We already know that that play, part of the Shakespearean canon, first appeared in the Great Folio, in 1623, and that it was preceded in 1594 by another play that shared all three plot lines (the introduction with the drunkard Sly, the taming of Katharina and the marriage of her sister) and whose title differed from the Shakespearean one only in the article. However, though the development is similar in both plays, the text of the Shakespearean comedy is completely different — it was entirely rewritten. Moreover, Shakespeare named all the characters (except Katharina) in Italian and transferred the action from a hypothetical Athens to the real Padua. Scholars have come up with many attempts to explain the relationship between these plays, so alike and at the same time so different. Some hypothesize that the earlier play was written by a different author; others are inclined to think that it was the first version of Shakespeare's comedy. But of greatest interest for us is the fact that the stage rendition of Katharina's taming became Italian, or, to be more precise, "Paduan," immediately after Rutland had visited that town.

We have already noted Lucentio's comments about realizing his dream, "To see fair Padua, nursery of arts," and the detailed enumeration his servant Tranio provides regarding the principal subjects studied at the university there. Interestingly, the witty Benedick of "Much Ado About Nothing" — an associate of the Prince of Aragon (his prototype is Essex) — suddenly turns out to be from Padua, while "The Two Gentlemen of Verona" features a curious slip of the pen: Speed greets Lance upon his arrival in Padua (not Milan). Padua, Padua...

Apparently, Rutland's studies at the University of Padua did not last long: at the end of May, Dr. Hawkins informed Anthony Bacon that the earl had been seriously ill (with a fever) but was now on the mend. However, the fever recurred, and the situation seemed so grave that Dr. Hawkins made a special trip from Venice in July to bear witness to Rutland's will. Nonetheless, the earl recovered, and rather than drawing up a testament Hawkins produced the Italian translation of an ode praising the English fleet, which Rutland had given to him — Hawkins evidently used such works to undermine the Spanish influence and to raise British prestige in the Republic of Venice.

Another letter from Hawkins makes it clear that Rutland was planning to visit Rome. But from all appearances, he did not make it to the "eternal city"; possibly due to the arraignment of Papal authorities, and the persecution and even arrests of a few Protestant Englishmen in Rome just at that time. Instead, he took the opportunity to steep himself in the essence of Venice, and the city left a lasting impression on him. The real atmosphere of Venice's turbulent life, bright colors, and the mingling religions and races at the markets and piazzas of that merchant republic, sights so unusual in the eyes of an Englishman, vividly manifest themselves in "The Merchant of Venice" and the Venetian scenes of "Othello." Shakespeare not only shows us the major sights of this "pearl of the Adriatic" (as described by many a traveler), he appears to know a dark alley named Sagittary and the Italian word "traghetto" — the Venetian ferry . . . Contemporary Rome, however, does not figure in Shakespeare's works at all.

At the end of September, 1596, Rutland left Venice, heading for France via Padua and Milan. While in Milan, a visitor could contemplate Correggio's famous creation "Jupiter and Io." By the way, a copy of this fresco adorns the ceiling of a drawing room at Belvoir; and the Lord seems to talk about it to the awakening Sly in the introduction to "The Taming of the Shrew." A knowledge of Milan is also apparent in "The Two Gentlemen of Verona," where the characters make an appointment to meet "at Saint Gregory's wall." Milan did feature a Hospital and Church of St. Gregory, with a stone wall around them. Shakespeare is also aware that there were two roads leading from Milan to Verona via Mantua, and that the one starting from the northern city gates passed through a forest known to harbor outlaws (who seize Valentine).

Rutland's further route ran through Switzerland, including Geneva and Zurich. Staying in Zurich, he developed a friendship with Gaspar Waser, a polyglot philologist. Based on common interests, the relationship continued over the years and the men kept up a correspondence, part of which was later found in Waser's papers. After a visit to England with a letter of introduction from Waser, a correspondent informed him of the cordial welcome accorded to him by the Earl of Rutland. A parodic "letter" from the same Zurich professor also appeared in 1611 in the Thomas Coryate book; and it is a known fact that Waser corresponded with Rutland.

Passing through Marseilles and Lyons, Rutland moved on to Paris. According to a report by one of Essex's agents, he arrived there by mid-February of 1597. Though the king — Henry IV of Navarre — was personally not present in Paris at that time, court life was pretty lively. In Shakespeare's exquisite comedy "Love's Labour's Lost," which was written (or, more likely, revised) at about that period, the action takes place at the court of the "King of Navarre" and, besides the sovereign himself and his first wife (Margaret of Valois), the characters include the noblemen of the royal retinue. Despite their genuine French names — Dukes Longaville and Dumaine (Dumain), Marshal Berowne (Biron) — scholars decided long since, based on the many allusions, that they should be seen as stand-ins for such English lords as Essex, Southampton and Rutland. Of special interest, of course, is the character Berowne (who has much in common with Benedick in "Much Ado About Nothing"); quite often his words reflect the color of the author's thought. A. A. Smirnov wrote: "As a mouthpiece of Shakespeare's ideas in this comedy Berowne serves as the most clever, lively and attractive of the characters." Among other things, Berowne happens to write sonnets.

Also colorful is the comic figure of the school teacher, the pedantic Holofernes, and many scholars believe he was used to satirically portray John Florio, an Italian by birth who lived in England and taught Italian to Southampton, Rutland, and Lucy Bedford, and who was also close to Mary Sidney Pembroke. He appeared in London (where he might have been seen by any actor of the "Theater" or the "Globe") only several years later. In 1598, Blount published John (Giovanni) Florio's Italian-English dictionary, "A Worlde of Wordes," which the author dedicated to Southampton, Rutland and Lucy Bedford. In his introduction, Florio mentions "a sonnet by a friend of mine, who prefers to be a true poet rather than to use that name"; out of the fairly constricted circle of his friends and patrons, whom could the Italian have meant? In 1603, he dedicated his major translation of Michel de Montaigne's "*Essais*" to six noble ladies, including Lucy Bedford and Elizabeth Sidney Rutland. In the 4th Act of "Love's Labour's Lost," Holofernes recites (or sings) an Italian distich from Florio's dictionary.[8] For all that, there are some hints that the hero of the first variant of the play, which did not come down to us, probably looked and was named differently (after some other prototype).

And it turns out that another character from "Love's Labour's Lost" — Don Adriano de Armado — was also known to Rutland. The preposterous Spaniard is surely a grotesque portrait of Antonio Perez, an unfortunate contender for the Portuguese crown who made too much of his fabulous plans to achieve his goals through an anti-Spanish coalition with the active participation of England. From the same above-mentioned letter sent in February to the Earl of Essex by his agent, we

---

8. "Venegia, Venegia, /Chi non te vede, non te pregia."

("Venice, Venice/ Who sees thee not, values thee not.")

learn that Rutland received messages for Essex from Perez and took measures to deliver them to the addressee.[9] Thus, after meeting Rutland, Don Antonio found himself in the Shakespearean comedy.

In mid-July of 1597, from Paris, Rutland wrote to a relative that he was going to return to England to take part in the expedition planned by the Earl of Essex — this was the naval advance on the Azores. At first, Essex planned to strike the main Spanish forces concentrated on the Ferrol Inlet, on the Atlantic Ocean; unfortunately, setting sail from Plymouth, the English fleet was caught in a terrible storm and ten days later had to struggle back to port, with great difficulty and loss of life. A second attempt was made in August, but again storms kept the English at bay. Essex then decided to sail towards the Azores to intercept Spanish ships making their homeward journey laden with treasures from the West Indies. Without waiting for Essex's ships to arrive, Sir Walter Raleigh took Horta, capital of Fayal (a key island), by storm, which infuriated the Earl, who then decided to try to capture another Spanish stronghold, San Miguel. Meanwhile, the anticipated convoy of treasure ships managed to take shelter at the strongly fortified bay of Terceira, thus leaving the English naval commanders with nothing. Moreover, taking advantage of the fact that the English fleet was busy around the Azores, the Spanish King Philip II sent a new armada with a great army on board to attack England, putting into motion his far-reaching design to capture that hateful bulwark of Protestantism. Again, storms interfered, and the remains of that armada barely limped back to the home shore.

In the winter of 1597-98, Philip II made a final attempt to launch his fleet against England, but the English met the Spanish naval force near Calais and inflicted serious damage and casualties in action.

The naval expedition to the Azores won no great laurels its participants (whose prominent members included Rutland and the Earl of Southampton, the poet John Donne and many of Essex's other followers as well), but the terrible storm left a lasting impression on them. And an attentive reader of the "Tempest" feels that the author had firsthand experience of how the crew acts aboard a sailing ship in distress on the high seas.

Three months after making it home from this naval adventure, on February 2, 1598, Rutland enrolled in Gray's Inn — one of the four London-based Inns of Court. In addition to studying law and practicing the interpretation and application of laws, the students at Gray's Inn, Lincoln's Inn, Middle Temple and Inner Temple had a reputation for putting on spectacular entertainments, which coincidentally helped establish closer bonds among them. The students were actively interested in theater and literature; Christmas festivities included theatrical shows, mock legal proceedings and ceremonies, masques, pageants and street processions — all of which might extend over several weeks. To manage the festivities, each corporation elected a Prince (in the Inner Temple, even an Emperor); they exchanged "embassies," etc. At least two

---

9. See: Sykes C.M. Op. cit., p. 166.

of Shakespeare's comedies were staged during such festivals; and Shakespeare's "Henry IV" reveals an insider's knowledge of some of the customs and rites from Gray's Inn.

While studying at Gray's Inn, Rutland found the time to pass examinations at Oxford and on July 10, 1598, he added an Oxford Masters degree to that of Cambridge.

Having returned from the Azores campaign, in 1598-1599 the earls of Essex, Southampton and Rutland were each absorbed in their own anxieties and troubles. Essex, who was appointed to the post of Lord Marshal of England in December 1597, engaged in a sharp rivalry with Burghley and his supporters in the Privy Council, and devoted his leisure time to pursuing the ladies of the court. Britain's Lord Deputy in Ireland died, and the problem of his successor became the focus of various disputes and intrigues; meanwhile, the Irish rebels led by Tyrone struck some heavy blows on English positions.

During one of the disputes at the Council over the appointment of a new Lord Deputy to Ireland, Essex, in a temper, deliberately turned his back upon the Queen. Elizabeth promptly slapped his face; the Earl lost his head, and gripped his sword. Other lords held him back. He rushed out of the hall, jumped on his horse and galloped off to his estate. A cataclysmic reaction from the Queen was universally anticipated, but did not ensue. The affair appeared to blow over, although Elizabeth of course did not forget this unthinkably impertinent escapade.

Loyal old Burghley, the Queen's trusty supporter, died; but he left an adequate successor — his son, the shrewd hunchback Sir Robert Cecil, who in turn gradually made himself indispensable to Elizabeth. However, the chivalrous Earl of Essex was still highly popular with the common people. He was elected to the honorary post of the Chancellor of Cambridge University, vacant after Burghley's demise; books were dedicated to him, and he had many supporters who were ready to follow him anywhere. In the fever of another bitter dispute at the Privy Council, Essex proposed his candidacy for Lord Deputy in Ireland and, after her usual hesitations, the Queen suddenly gave her approval in January 1599. Assigned to a dangerous and unpromising post, Essex was overwhelmed by doubts and foreboding — but the die had been cast. To outward appearances, his relationship with the Queen was undamaged: at the ball at the Danish Embassy on the eve of Epiphany, Her Majesty wished to dance with the earl.

These were not easy times for Southampton, either. His relations with Elizabeth Vernon, one of Essex's relatives, went too far, and while serving as an envoy in Paris in August of 1598 he received the news that she was pregnant. He went back at once and secretly married her. As in earlier cases (Essex's and Raleigh's marriages, for instance), the Queen was furious — or gave that impression. In view of such willfulness, she threw the newly weds into prison. They were eventually released, but the Earl of Southampton's career at the court of Elizabeth I was considered finished.

Rutland stayed either in London, or Oxford, or at his home at Belvoir Castle. In addition to his legal studies and examinations, he devoted his time to music. In the household records, his steward noted the purchase of a viola-da-gamba, a six-stringed violoncello (like the one that is mentioned in "Twelfth Night"). In February 1598, Rutland was invited to supper at the home of the Earl of Essex, according to a report to Robert Sidney by his steward and regular informer, Rowland Whyte. Also present at the reception were the Countess of Essex, the mother of Rutland's future wife; Lady Rich, sister of the Earl of Essex; and Lucy, Countess of Bedford. It seems unlikely that Essex's young stepdaughter, Elizabeth Sidney, would not have been among the guests as well.

In 1598-1599, the Earl of Rutland and Elizabeth Sidney were often seen together, probably at someone's purposeful instigation. The meetings gradually turned into a kind of good-natured war as they matched wits and sparred with words, exchanging puns and sharp remarks. This is reminiscent of the continuous word play between Benedick, the Paduan writer of sonnets, and Beatrice in "Much Ado About Nothing" — the comedy which appeared at just that period in time. We should also mention Don Pedro's equivocal hint about Benedick, asking whether Cupid has not spent all his quiver on him in Venice — though the city seems to have no relation to the play's action and characters, and is never referred to again — whereas Rutland, recently returned from Europe, had visited Venice for certain.

Elizabeth Sidney's education and social introductions were carefully overseen by her mother and stepfather, and by her father's relatives as well, primarily her aunt, the poet and patroness of arts Mary Sidney, Countess of Pembroke. Many noble suitors aspired to the hand of the daughter of the "godlike Sidney" (including the powerful Secretary of State, Sir Robert Cecil). However, both Essex and Mary Sidney seemed to think that wealth, gentility and influence alone were not enough to earn that honor — Elizabeth's choice ought to be a man who was ready to serve Apollo and the Muses. And so it was not by chance that they (and Elizabeth herself) chose the "Paduan student," who "preferred to be a true poet rather than use this name," the Earl of Rutland. However, the latter, like Benedick and Berowne, was in no haste to bind himself with hymeneal bonds; that happened only late in 1599, as dark clouds were gathering on the horizon for Essex and his trusty friends.

Authentic portraits of Rutland, and of his wife, are few. However, a very interesting miniature painted by Isaac Oliver in the late 1590s aroused the curiosity of art experts and historians years ago. It portrays a young man sitting with his back against a tree. His seat is a sort of natural elevation formed by the tree roots and lumpy soil. The young man's clothes and his knightly sword with cleverly wrought grip and hilt bespeak his gentility. In the background, a long Italianate roofed gallery[10] runs the width of the picture and a park with lawns and walkways form a complex pattern which may have some meaning of its own. Still farther in the distance, the upper story of a baroque house with small towers can be seen.

---

10. Such covered street galleries were an emblematic feature of Padua.

A portrait long deemed to be of Philip Sidney. In fact, it is the image
of the young Rutland against the background of an Italian street gallery.

For a long time the miniature was assumed to be a portrait of Philip Sidney, made after his travels to the Continent (1574-1575); then it was understood from certain features that it was painted far later (never mind that in 1575 artist Isaac Oliver was only ten years old). But if it is not Philip Sidney, then who is it?

The drawing illuminating the title page of Richard Burton's *Anatomy of Melancholy* (1621) has also attracted scholars' attention. The picture features Democritus sitting on a stone under a tree, in a posture similar to that of the young lord in Oliver's miniature; also similar is the pattern formed by the lawns and walks. The drawing in Burton's book apparently was especially intended to remind the well-informed reader of the person portrayed by Oliver. The similarity is not incidental, any more than is the similarity of Burton's philosophical and artistic ideas and those of Shakespeare — including the many textual coincidences and polemics.

As it turns out, Ben Jonson knew this miniature by Oliver — he refers to it in his poem sent to Drummond (1619), recalling the "subtle feet . . ./As hath the youngest he/ That sits in shadow of Apollo's tree"[11]; which further tells us that this young aristocrat, familiar to Jonson, had something to do with poetry.

Having studied the mysterious "portrait of an unknown young man" — as it is known after this long-running controversy — I also noted the drawing in Burton's book, the verse from Ben Jonson, and the Padua-style roofed street gallery. After the experts had revised the dating of the miniature to the late 1590s, all the above factors, taken as a whole, pointed in one and the same direction: the portrait depicts the young Earl of Rutland in the course of, or immediately after, his stay in Padua, Italy. And in 1596, Oliver was in Italy himself. On the reverse of the portrait of Lord Talbot, a kinsman of Rutland, the painter wrote: "Done 13 May's 1596. In Venezia. Isaac Olivero Francese." So, Oliver was in Venice and Padua *at the same time as Rutland*, and surely would have met him there. Oliver's brush also bequeathed to us portraits of other people close to Rutland: The Earl of Dorset and Lucy Bedford. Later on, the artist won royal patronage and painted the portraits of Queen Anne and the Prince of Wales, but his career seems to have started with the Earl of Rutland.

Recently some Western researches have become intrigued by a certain resemblance between this young lord's face and Shakespeare's representation in Droeshout's engraving; however, they have yet to find any explanation for this phenomenon.

Today, the miniature is the property of the Queen of England and is kept at Windsor Castle. Owing to the courtesy of Mrs. Vanessa Remington, curator of the Royal Picture Collection, M. D. Litvinova and I received the kind permission in April, 1995 to study the mysterious (like everything related to the owner of Belvoir) portrait. It is set into a solid brass frame, the reverse side of which bears an engraved inscription

11. The tree is quite possibly the very one that was planted by the parents of Philip Sidney on the day of his birth (November 30, 1554) at Penshurst Estate. Jonson mentioned it in the second verse of the "Forest" cycle: The tree of Apollo, tree of the great Sidney.

Robert Devereux, Earl of Essex

(apparently made by the 19<sup>th</sup> century): "Sir Philip Sidney." According to Mrs. Remington, the miniature was painted on a parchment glued onto a playing card.

Here is Roger Manners, Earl of Rutland, sitting in the shade of Apollo's tree. Behind him we see Italy, Padua. He is back in England, at his Belvoir Castle, in Cambridge, among the "university wits" and their artful amusements, with the friends of the brilliant Earl of Essex, on stage at the Theater of Life where the lively comedy of Youth is still being played. But there is no smile on his lips; his eyes are pensive and melancholic. And ahead, the road will be hard.


## PHOENIX, DAUGHTER OF PHOENIX: ROSALIND

## JAQUES-THE-MELANCHOLIC CRAVES TO PLAY A FOOL


At the end of March, 1599, Essex set sail for Ireland, leading a great force with the aim of suppressing the rebellion and doing away with the Earl of Tyrone. Loyal to Essex, the earls of Southampton and Rutland followed him. Essex assigned Southampton to the post of Commander of Cavalry, but the queen was angered and cancelled the appointment. At first, the queen allowed Rutland to go to Ireland, then changed her mind and withdrew her permission; Rutland crossed the Irish Sea in April nevertheless and joined his idol, who made him a Colonel of Infantry. However, in June the queen recalled Rutland, flatly ordering him to return. Still, he was able to take part in the capture of Cahir Fortress (which seems to have been Essex's sole successful operation throughout the campaign), and was knighted by Essex.

Upon Rutland's return to England, many courtiers expected him to be punished, perhaps even imprisoned, but the queen was graciously disposed and, learning that he was ill, deigned to send her doctor to him. He also underwent medical treatment (for ailing feet) at Bath, the hot mineral springs which had been popular since Roman times. Several years later, his future wife, Elizabeth Sidney, also took treatment there. Would it be surprising that the Great Bard poetized the Bath springs in his Sonnets 153 and 154? Shall we chalk that up to another one of the countless "coincidences"?

Meanwhile, Essex's progress in Ireland was far from good. The queen demanded decisive measures, while the Lord Deputy (who was Governor-General of Ireland, too) wasted time in minor clashes and stayed in Dublin writing eloquent but unconvincing letters to the queen. His faithful friends and followers in London worried for their patron and prayed God to send him good luck and victory. In "Henry V," written during just that period of expectations and hopes, the Chorus relates the victorious return of that King from France and describes the crowds of Londoners who rapturously greet him. Suddenly, and not quite appropriately for a historical play, the Chorus adds:

*As, by a lower but loving likelihood,*
*Were now the general of our gracious empress,*
*As in good time he may, from Ireland coming,*
*Bringing rebellion broached on his sword*
*How many would the peaceful city quit,*
*To welcome him!*

These lines clearly convey not only hope but also anxiety for Essex, the anxiety of a close and loyal friend (although William Shakspere from Stratford was never said to have been seen anywhere near Essex). Moreover, knowing the queen's jealousy over the fame of others, the playwright uses the Chorus as his mouthpiece to purposefully and tactfully concede that far more people came to greet the King:

*. . . Much more, and much more cause,*
*Did they this Harry (Act V. Prologue)*

The play also presents an Irish officer and some other details pertaining to the "Green Island."

But the hopes of the author of "Henry V" and other Essex supporters did not come true. Mired in Irish bogs and unable to gain a decisive victory, the earl started negotiations with Tyrone and concluded an unfavorable truce. Essex thus virtually admitted defeat. Abruptly, he decided to desert his army and the province entrusted to him, and to sail to England — with no definite plan of action. He embarked on September 24, accompanied by a group of officers, and four days later his force entered London.

It was morning. Assisted by her ladies-in-waiting, the aging queen was deep in the complicated ritual of dressing when the earl, wearing dirty jackboots and field cloak, burst into her bedchamber. At first, of course, she was startled, but as it became clear that she was in no danger and the earl began to pour out his confused explanations, the queen sent him off to put himself in order (besides, she too had to finish her toilette). The meeting continued later in the day, but in the presence of the assembled Privy Council, which listened to Essex's report. The earl was ordered to stay at home. A day later, he was transferred to the house of Egerton, Lord Keeper of the State Seal — this already meant arrest. He fell ill and was nearly dying; his letters to the queen were left unread. In November, the inference on Essex's offences was made public; no one was admitted to visit him, not even his wife; but the queen delayed the final decision on his fate.

At the start of 1600 the queen appointed Lord Mountjoy as Lord Deputy in Ireland — a man who once had been close to Essex but later changed his mind. The situation in Ireland was improving, and in a while Lord Mountjoy finally suppressed Tyrone's uprising.

Queen Elizabeth I

Essex was allowed to return to his own home, but he was still under strict surveillance. Finally, in June he appeared before the Privy Council, where he was made to kneel before the lords and only then permitted to take a seat. The disobedient earl was reminded of all his sins. Among those who brought accusations was Francis Bacon, whose advancement in the government had been continuously pressed by Essex, not so long before, and who had enjoyed the earl's financial support, but who began to cool toward him, seeing that the behavior of the former queen's favorite was dangerously unpredictable. Upon instruction from Elizabeth, Bacon recalled one of the earl's seemingly negligible misdemeanors: he had accepted the dedication of John Hayward's "History of Henry IV," narrating the troublesome deposition of the legitimate King Richard II. The unfortunate author had long ago been sent to prison so that others would be discouraged from touching upon such delicate issues and moreover from accompanying them with suspicious dedications. Essex had to stoop to repent of all his sins, and to beg pardon. He was sent home and ordered to await the decision of the queen. And only at the end of August, almost a year after his ill-considered prank, the Earl of Essex was granted freedom.

However, the lesson was ineffective. Debarred from court and from power, seriously pressed for money, Essex was seized by a rebellious spirit that threatened to boil over in rage; his friends feared what might be the eventual result. As before, he continued to bombard the queen with letters of complaint, while at the same time huddling with his friends and drawing up and revising one scheme after another to regain the queen's confidence and counteract Robert Cecil, Walter Raleigh and his other foes.

All the time after their idol's return to England, Essex's faithful shadows Southampton and Rutland worried about his fate, and their anxieties went beyond politics alone. On October 13, 1599 (that is, when Essex had already come back and was under arrest), the all-knowing Rowland Whyte wrote to his patron, Robert Sidney: "My Lord Southampton and Lord Rutland come not to court; they pass away the time in London merely in going to plays every day."[12] This highlights both the close friendship between Rutland and Southampton (if any additional proof of that were needed) and their special interest in the theater.[13] However, while studying this document of paramount importance, Shakespeare's Stratfordian biographers focus only upon the name of Southampton (since it was to him that "Shakespeare heartily dedicated his first poems") and generally they know little about Rutland.

---

12. See: Akrigg G. Op. cit., p. 96.

13. It is worth noting that in the summer of 1599, the Lord Chamberlain's Men quickly erected a new theater building, the largest in London; it was given the pretentious name, *The Globe*. By autumn, the theater was already staging plays, including the September presentation of Shakespeare's tragedy "Julius Caesar" (witnessed on September 21, according to the diary of the Swiss traveler Thomas Platter). The timing coincides exactly, and it is clear where and how Rutland and Southampton were spending their time. It is reasonable to surmise that they also spent some money to facilitate the prompt building of the Globe, along with the necessary patronage of the actors-shareholders.

This was also the time when a great change took place in the Earl of Rutland's life — he became Elizabeth Sidney's husband. According to Whyte's letters, the wedding took place sometime between September 1 and October 16, 1599.[14] There are no records available on any festivities marking the occasion of the wedding of such an eminent couple. Perhaps that was the result of Essex's arrest and the pall this cast over his family, to whom Rutland was now (right after Southampton) related as well.

Philip Sidney's daughter was born in 1585 (we have contradictory information about the exact day and month) and was given the name Elizabeth by her royal godmother, the queen. In 1590, four years after Philip Sidney died from wounds received on the battlefield, his young widow (only 22 years old) married the Earl of Essex. The upbringing of Philip Sidney's daughter and Essex's stepdaughter was closely attended by her aunt, Mary Sidney, Countess of Pembroke. In 1595, Gervase Markham (who later wrote "The English Arcadia") dedicated his "Poem of Poems" to the ten-year-old girl. Elizabeth grew up in a climate of veneration of her great father, in the cult of art and poesy, and was herself a gifted poet as we already know from Jonson and Beaumont. As the Countess of Rutland, Elizabeth gradually slipped into the same shadow that always concealed the private life of her husband; like him, she left not a single poetic or dramatic line signed by her name.

Though Rutland was recognized as the worthiest candidate to qualify for the hand of Philip Sidney's daughter, he himself hesitated for a long time. And even after the marriage had been contracted, it never went beyond platonic relations. The exact dates of various Shakespearean sonnets published as late as 1609 are unknown; however, the poet addresses the first group of sonnets to a friend whom he tries to convince, over and over again, of the need to procreate. There are scholars who do not rule out the possibility that the poet was addressing these (and some other sonnets) to himself. Another view insists that the poet was addressing Pembroke. At any rate, their contents precisely match the situation of the Earl of Rutland before his marriage (and later, when the deficiency of the marriage was no longer a secret to those around).

The anthology of lyrical and pastoral poetry entitled "Englands Helicon," of 1600, comprises the poem entitled "The Countess of Pembroke's Pastorall." The pastoral's author, signed as "Shepherd Tonie," might be Anthony Munday, who was closely related with the milieu of the Countess of Pembroke. However, the title also leaves room for conjecture that the Countess herself might have written or edited it. The poem relates the story of a newly wed "shepherd and shepherdess," that is, poet and poetess, in the terms of pastoral poesy current at the time.

> *His looks did gentle blood expresse,*
> *her beauty was no foode for clownes*
> ............................................

---

14. Other sources provide an earlier date.

Philip Sidney

*They shewed themselves in open sight,*
*poor lovers, Lord how they were mazde?*

But "hope now begins to further love."

*And to confirme a mutual band*
*of love, that at no time should ceasse:*
*They likewise joined hand in hand,*
*The Shepherd and the Shepherdess.*

What couple from Mary Sidney Pembroke's circle could be so described in 1599? The care and anxiety expressed for this newly-married couple, an alliance of poetic souls, makes it sound as though the story is about Roger and Elizabeth, about the union of the Phoenix and the Turtle which thirteen years later would result in unity in death and immortality.

In the October 1599 letter, Whyte says that Belvoir awaits the coming of William Herbert — the son of Mary Sidney Pembroke, the future 3$^{rd}$ Earl of Pembroke. He would become a close and loyal friend of the Rutlands, and a patron of Jonson and many other poets and playwrights.

In June 1600, Rutland went to the Netherlands and fought there against the Spaniards. In a month, the action ceased; he expected to go to France, but changed his plans and returned to England. However, prior to his departure for the Netherlands the earl participated, for once, in an almost ordinary event of high society life, one which nevertheless left behind a striking and mysterious trace.

On June 11, 1600, the marriage of the son and heir of the Earl of Worcester and Lady Anne Russel, the queen's maid of honor, a cousin of Sir Robert Cecil, was celebrated in London. Many leading noblemen and their wives, as well as all the queen's maids of honor, attended the event; the queen had blessed the marriage. Rutland and the future Earl of Pembroke accompanied the bride to and from the church.

After some time (apparently not less than a year later), commissioned by the Earl of Worcester, who had received the post of Master of Horses to Her Majesty, left vacant after Essex, the artist Robert Peake set to work on a large painting (2.3 x 1.6 m.)[15] portraying the earl, his son, and the bride, as well as the participants in the wedding ceremony. But the central image in this large group is that of Queen Elizabeth, who looks much younger in the painting than she was at the time. The queen sits in a splendid palanquin ("canopy" — see Sonnet 125) carried by the royal palace servants, preceded by six Knights of the Order of the Garter stalking along in pairs. In the background there are royal guards and townspeople.

---

15. Some portraits on the canvas were obviously finished after King James Stuart had already acceded to the throne.

The picture was kept at Coleshill, Yorkshire, Lord Digby's estate, and was known to few people. It was only in the mid-18th century that art connoisseurs and collectors noticed the canvas. Really, the picture still produces an indelible impression. The artist managed not only to render the actual event that was taking place, but also to capture the atmosphere and spirit of the Elizabethan epoch. This picturesque, theatrical procession is one of the best and most forceful artistic monuments to the great empress of Britain and her time. The Digby family claimed that the picture portrayed the solemn procession on the occasion of the 1588 victory over the "Spanish Armada"; but when and how the canvas appeared in the house of Digby is still not known. For decades, British art experts puzzled over the mysterious canvas and proffered various hypotheses trying to fix the actual time of its creation and to identify the participants of the procession.

Extant letters from contemporaries and participants at the June 1600 nuptials have finally helped to elucidate the painting's subject. The central figures of the procession: the Earl of Worcester himself, the newly-weds, and then gradually all the lords — were identified and confirmed through comparison with other portraits, with the exception of one person — the fifth on the left — a young man with a small, perhaps fledgling beard, distinguished by his air of pensiveness and detachment. Several candidates were suggested, but the features in this portrait did not match up with their other known portraits.

Porohovchikov presumed that the thoughtful young man in Peake's picture is the Earl of Rutland, and he even reproduced this image on the frontispiece of his book in 1955. Because Rutland had indeed participated in the wedding ceremony, his name did figure in the debates about the canvas before Porohovchikov's hypothesis, but Rutland did not interest art scholars very much and besides, they had no other portrait of him from that timeframe, by which to judge. Since Porohovchikov failed to produce any additional evidence to support his point of view, it was neglected, and the pensive young lord remained a "mysterious Unknown" (to quote R. Strong[16]).

Now that we have determined that Isaac Oliver's noble youth sitting under Apollo's tree, against an Italianate backdrop, is the 20-year-old Rutland, we seem to have the proof needed to confirm Porohovchikov's surmise. In both cases, we see the face of the same person. In Peake's painting, he is four or five years older and has begun to sprout a beard, but the characteristic features of his face (particularly the nose, the shape of the eyes and lips), his melancholic and detached gaze, go beyond any chance similarity. This is the same person, and everyone to whom I have showed both images, in England and in Russia, tends to agree. It is also highly significant that, like Isaac Oliver, his friend the artist Robert Peake knew Roger Rutland well, and the steward's records testify that Peake was paid for the "portraits of my Lord and my Lady" (summer, 1599)! Precisely which portraits that refers to is difficult to say today, after the elapse of four centuries, with all their fires and wars; a portrait preserved at Belvoir

---

16. R. Strong is an eminent US expert on British portraiture of the 16th-17th centuries.

A procession with Queen Elizabeth on the occasion of a high society wedding. The fifth from the left is the Earl of Rutland. From the painting by R. Peake.

shows Rutland half-face, already with the beard and moustache, and dates to roughly 1610. Nevertheless, the enigma of the two most remarkable works of English portrait art appears to have been solved, and Rutland is the key to the solution.

One can imagine the atmosphere and feelings of Essex's entourage, his friends and relatives, as we feel it through the play "As You Like It." Registered in the same year, 1600, the comedy was first published only in the Great Folio of 1623, although it was presented to the new King James in 1603 at the Pembrokes' — at Wilton House, Wiltshire (which testifies to the importance the Pembrokes, who were close to Essex and the Rutlands, attached to the play). The subject is based mainly on "Rosalinde: Euphues Golden Legacie" (1590) by Thomas Lodge, but the names of the characters, apart from Rosalind's, were changed. In addition, important new characters appeared, including the melancholy Jaques and Touchstone, the clown. The main characters of the play are the sons of a certain Sir Rowland de Boys (de Bois, i.e. Rowland of the Forest). The de Boys family no doubt an allusion to the Rutlands, of Sherwood Forest, only the name of Oliver was given to the senior brother, whereas in the Manners family the name belonged to the younger one, the Catholic, who, as the junior son in a noble family, would have a limited inheritance and who schemed against Roger inheriting from his father the title, patrimonial castle and principal estates.

Lodge's work is a traditional pastoral novel lyrically presenting the delights of an idyllic life close to nature, far from the hubbub of the cities and the intrigues of royal palaces. Shakespeare seems to have been hinting at the actual situation of those days. The deposed Duke (the French king, in Lodge's romance) acquired the features of the Earl of Essex, debarred from the royal court and in disfavor — that is the accepted view among many Shakespeare scholars. However, few researchers have tried to identify the Duke's supporters who sympathized with him during his banishment, though the task is not complicated. Amiens and Jaques are clearly the loyal Earls of Southampton and Rutland, who stood by their friend through joys and sorrows all those years.

In Shakespeare's play, the character of Jaques is assigned a special role; he was not present in Lodge's work. Often serving as a mouthpiece for the author's ideas, he sadly and ironically contemplates the vanity and madness of the world. He has much in common with Berowne in "Love's Labour's Lost" and with Benedick from "Much Ado About Nothing." Hippolyite Taine wrote that melancholy Jaques was one of Shakespeare's dearest characters — "a transparent mask not hiding the outlines of the poet's face." This is Roger, Earl of Rutland, who persistently follows the Earl of Essex after he has returned from his travels and, in the words of Jaques, gained the "experience which wraps him in a most humorous sadness." Also, Jaques significantly adds: "I have gained this experience." Teasing, Rosalind advises him to go on wearing strange suits and criticizing everything in his own country, otherwise she will scarcely think he has really "swam in a gondola" — i.e. stayed in Venice. As we know, Rutland had visited Venice not long before. The playwright separates Jaques from the three sons of Rowland of the Forest (Rutland's three brothers), as well as from Rosalind —

the outcast Duke's daughter (the daughter-in-law of the Earl of Essex — Elizabeth Sidney), though introducing into the comedy Jaques and Rosalind's word play. (Similar contests take place between Benedick and Beatrice in "Much Ado About Nothing," and Biron and Rosalin in "Love's Labour's Lost"). Thus, Jaques is a gently ironical portrait of the young Roger Manners, Earl of Rutland. Nowadays readers of "As You Like It" would benefit if the publishers accompanied the play's reprinted texts with a picture of the young lord shown, like Jaques, "under an oak, whose boughs are mossed with age," pondering the transient vanity of the world. Perhaps, it would be useful for scholars and publishers of Shakespeare as well.

For all that, he was not quite an ordinary lord, this melancholy Jaques. Here is what he says to his patron, Duke Senior:

> *O that I were a fool!*
> *I am ambitious for a motley coat.*

Duke Senior
> *Thou shalt have one.*

Jaques
> *It is my only suit;*
> *Provided that you weed your better judgments*
> *Of all opinion that grows rank in them*
> *That I am wise. I must have liberty*
> *Withal, as large a charter as the wind,*
> *To blow on whom I please; for so fools have;*
> *And they that are most galled with my folly,*
> *They most must laugh...*

Jaques then asks leave to tell people what he really thinks of them:

> *Invest me in my motley; give me leave*
> *To speak my mind, and I will through and through*
> *Cleanse the foul body of the infected world,*
> *If they will patiently receive my medicine.*

But Duke Senior reasonably remarks that Jaques is unjust in criticizing the evil nature of people:

> *Fie on thee! I can tell what thou wouldst do...*
> *Most mischievous foul sin, in chiding sin:*
> *For thou thyself hast been a libertine,*
> *As sensual as the brutish sting itself;*
> *And all the embossed sores and headed evils,*

259

> *That thou with licence of free foot hast caught,*
> *Wouldst thou disgorge into the general world. (II. 7)*

These words seem to agree with Jaques' own confession that he has paid dearly for his experience, and seem to accord with Rutland's painful condition during and after his stay in Italy, and ultimately with his early death.

Jaques' response to Duke Senior merits a full citation:

> *Why, who cries out on pride,*
> *That can therein tax any private party?*
> *Doth it not flow as hugely as the sea,*
> *Till that the weary very means do ebb?*
> *What woman in the city do I name,*
> *When that I say the city-woman bears*
> *The cost of princes on unworthy shoulders?*
> *Who can come in and say that I mean her,*
> *When such a one as she such is her neighbour?*
> *Or what is he of basest function*
> *That says his bravery is not of my cost,*
> *Thinking that I mean him, but therein suits*
> *His folly to the mettle of my speech?*
> *There then; how then? what then? Let me see wherein*
> *My tongue hath wrong'd him: if it do him right,*
> *Then he hath wrong'd himself; if he be free,*
> *Why then my taxing like a wild-goose flies,*
> *Unclaim'd of any man...*

Here, Jaques is speaking about the social function of a writer and poet who condemns the unjust and those who indulge in vice; and he refers to himself!

And, finally, Jaques delivers the well-known monologue that exposes the essence of the Shakespearean vision of the world:

> *All the world's a stage,*
> *And all the men and women merely players:*
> *They have their exits and their entrances;*
> *And one man in his time plays many parts... (II. 7)* [17]

---

17. By the entrance to the Globe Theater, which opened shortly before this play appeared (and where the Earls of Rutland and Southampton were so frequently seen), was the image of Hercules holding the whole globe on his shoulders. The Latin inscription under the image conveys the same idea of the theatrical and ephemeral nature of human life and the world that is present in Jacque's monologue: "Totus mundus agit histrionem."

Perhaps, those who take the character of Jaques as a transparent mask on the face of the author are right; however, one cannot help feeling that the image of the strange young lord dreaming of being a court jester was envisaged by the compassionate eyes of a congenial soul, and shaped by the warm and tender hand of a woman. This is further supported by the epilogue delivered by Rosalind; is this the same woman evoked in Chester's poem in *Love's Martyr*, subtitled "Rosalins Complaint"?

In Lodge's romance, the legitimate king fights his usurping brother, and after the death of the latter he restores his rights. Shakespeare's play, of course, ends otherwise. The usurper musters an army to deal with Duke Senior and his supporters once and for all, but after meeting with an old hermit he is suddenly converted from his evil enterprise and "from the world," restoring his brother in all his rights and possessions. Thus — not very convincingly — the play presents the outcome of the "first Essex affair." The Earl did not win — after a long delay, his transgression was merely allowed to fade into the background. Still, his associates, including the author of "As You Like It," became more optimistic for the future. A new hope had appeared.

## CAMBRIDGE GAMES ON THE MUSES' HOME TURF

One by one, three other plays appeared at Cambridge University at roughly the same time as "As You Like It." The plays formed a trilogy which, as my latest studies show, is directly related to those unique personalities who preferred a fool's motley to any sumptuous attire.

In 1598, someone who was either a student at Cambridge or an alumnus maintaining close contact with the university wrote the burlesque play, "The Pilgrimage to Parnassus," which was staged that year by the students of St. John's College, Cambridge. It was followed by a sequel one year later — "The Return from Parnassus" — Part 1; and two years later, by Part 2. Of these three plays only the last was registered at the Stationer's Company; it was published in 1606. The first and second parts of the trilogy remained only in manuscript.

The plot of the "Parnassus" plays is not intricate. Some students set out to reach the seat of the Muses — Mount Parnassus. Along their way they traverse the lands of Rhetoric and Philosophy, and face the seductions of the voluptuary Amoretto, the votary of the wine cup Madido, and slothful Ingenioso, who has burnt his books and refused to trudge along to Parnassus. Nevertheless, the persistent pilgrims, Philomusus and Studiosus, overcome all the obstacles and temptations, and reach the cherished home of the Muses.

On the way back ("The Return from Parnassus"), new adventures await the travelers. They have to earn their way in life, and undergo all sorts of experiences, including fraud. They also try to make money at the theater, while the shrewd actors of Lord Chamberlain's Men, Burbadge and Kempe, are eager to make profit at their expense. We already know a little about this episode, particularly Kempe's remarks.

Both parts of "The Return from Parnassus" feature implicit and explicit allusions to the literary and theatrical life of those days; the play takes the form of a satirical review, and the author (or authors) are quite blunt in their comments. Special criticism falls on writers and playwrights. Ben Jonson is characterized as the "bold bastard, the wittiest brick-layer in England."[18] They say that Marston, who was then known only as a satirist, "lifts his leg and pisses at the whole world." Thomas Nashe (who had graduated from St. John College fifteen years before) is declared to be a literary hack. And, finally, the characters in the play, who treat all other writers without ceremony or respect, not only know perfectly well but greatly revere the works of Shakespeare.

In the first part of "The Return," a new and interesting character suddenly appears. Ingenioso warns all and sundry: they will see now a gull — a fool, a dupe, or a clown — and in fact, the new character is named Gullio. He is a great talker and pretends to be an aristocrat. He especially likes to enlarge upon his own business and interests. He brags about his rapier, whose origins give another clue to his identity: "This rapier I boughte when I sojorned in the Universitie of Padua. . . . By the heavens, it is a pure tolledo, and it was the death of a Pollonian, a German and a Duche men because they would not pledge the health of England . . . " Six months earlier, he dispatched a disrespectful Cambridge student to the next world. Prior to that, he had visited a Cosmopolis (apparently, Venice), and participated in naval expeditions to Spain and Portugal, as well as in the Irish campaign (i.e. under the Earl of Essex).

Listening to Gullio's stories, Ingenioso addresses caustic asides to the audience and questions Gullio about his love interest — one Lesbia. Gullio relates that he has written a sonnet commending Lesbia's squirrel and an epitaph upon her deceased little monkey. He wrote them while dressed in a luxurious jerkin, all trimmed in gold lace, apparel that cost him 200 pounds (a huge amount for that time). Ingenioso sneers — again, behind his companion's back — about the subtle wit one must have to poetize such trifles as squirrels and monkeys, suggesting that it means to "make something of nothing."

Gullio goes on about himself and his habits: "At the courte, I thinke I should growe lousie if I wore less than two suits of apparell a daye," and boots, he would change every two hours, leading Ingenioso to wonder whether this rich garb has been paid for as yet.

The conversation shifts to literary subjects. Ingenioso praises his counterpart's exquisite literary style, comparing it with Cicero's orations. Gullio responds that, to prove himself a complete gentleman, he always takes care to be the champion either in

---

18. In his youth, Ben Jonson had helped his step-father, a brick-layer.

poetry or in the tilting yard. And to support this statement, he quotes from Shakespeare's poem, "The Rape of Lucrece":

> *Gnats are unnoted everywhere they fly,*
> *But Eagles gazed upon with every eye.*

Gullio asserts that, in his day, there was a strong resemblance between himself and Philip Sidney, with the only difference being "that I had the better leg and more amiable face." But Gullio apparently means not only — and mostly not — the external, physical likeness: "His 'Arcadia' was prittie, so are my sonnets; he had bene at Paris, I at Padua; he fought, and so dare I; he dyed in the lowe cantries, and soe I think shall I; he loved a scholler, I montaine them — witness thy selfe . . . I also montaine other poetical spirites, that live upon my trenchers; in so muche that I cannot come to my Inn to Oxforde without a dozen congratulorie orations, made by genius and species and his ragged companions. I reward the poore ergos moste bontifillie and send them away."

So, Gullio not only presents himself as a poet, but also as a widely known Maecenas (not under this name, of course) — patron of scholars and writers. He continues: "I am very latelie registered in the roules of fame in an epigram made by a Cambridge man, one Weever-fellow, I warrant him els coulde he never have had such a quick sight into my vertues, howsoever I merit his praise. If I meet with him I will vouchsafe to give him condigne thanks." Aha! So Gullio (or, to be more precise, the one who hides behind this fool's mask) is a fellow student of the poet John Weever (1576-1632).

Ingenioso turns Gullio back to the subject of his love, and the latter bids him to depict his beautifull lady ("as sometime wooden statues represent the godess"), so that Gullio may rehearse amorous and courteous speeches afterwards to be addressed to her. This is followed by a dialogue which sheds important light on our topic:

Gullio
"*Pardon fair lady, though sick-thoughted Gullio makes a maine unto thee, and like a bold-faced suitor 'gins to woo thee.*"
Ingenioso (aside).
"*We shall have nothing but pure Shakespeare, and shreds of poetry that he hath gathered at the theatres.*"

Gullio is just opening his mouth to speak, but Ingenioso already knows that we shall hear "pure Shakespeare"? Though he does not miss the opportunity to give Gullio another jab, behind his back, it is clear that the Shakespearean "shreds of poetry" freely quoted by memory by the strange clown-aristocrat could not have been "gathered at the theatres." Ingenioso simply plays up to Gullio, meanwhile giving a wink to those few spectators (and readers) who know about whom and what he is speaking. The dialogue continues:

Gullio.

*"Pardon me my mistress, as I am a gentleman, the moone in comparison of thy bright hue a mere slut, Antony's Cleopatra a black-browed milkmaid, Helen a dowdy."*

Ingenioso.

*"Mark, Romeo and Juliet: o monstrous theft! I think he will run through a whole book of Samuel Daniel's."*

Gullio.

> *"Thrice fairer than myself, thus I began,*
> *The god's fair riches, sweet above compare,*
> *Stain to all nymphs, more lovely than a man,*
> *More white and red than doves and roses are."*

As Ingenioso has warned, Gullio speaks with the words of Shakespeare — this is the second stanza from "Venus and Adonis," scarcely modified. And Ingenioso reacts accordingly: "Sweet Mr. Shakespeare!" Just what does he mean? Is he expressing his pleasure at hearing the familiar Shakespeare lines, or is he addressing Gullio thus? Or maybe both? Further on, Gullio shows his erudition in English poetry, citing the verses of Spencer, Kyd, and Marlowe, and explaining to the rapt Ingenioso that when other cavaliers bestow jewelry on the ladies of their hearts, "I will bestow upon them the precious gravestones of my wit, a diamond of Invention, that shall be above all value and estime!"

Gullio is hurrying off to a dinner party with his friends — a countess and two lords. Therefore, he commissions Ingenioso to write some love verses for his lady.

Ingenioso.

*"My pen is your bounden vassal to commande; but what veine would it please you to have them in?"*

Gullio.

*"Not in one veine . . . make me them in two or three diverse veines, in Chaucer's, Gower's and Spencer's, and Mr. Shakespeare's. Marry, I think I shall entertaine these verses which run like this:*

> *"Even as the sun with purple-colour'd face*
> *Had ta'en his last leave on the weeping morn, etc."*

These lines begin the Shakespeare poem "Venus and Adonis," and the note "etc." in the play's text means that whoever is performing Gullio's role must recite the whole stanza, or maybe even more. But Gullio never damps his ardor: "O sweetest Mr. Shakespeare! I'll have his picture in my study at the courte." That must be another joke because, as we know, there is and has never been any authentic portrait of Shakespeare done in his lifetime. Where, then, is Gullio going to obtain Shakespeare's picture?

Ingenioso recites some lines from Chaucer's "Troilus and Criseyde" (with some of his own additions), but Gullio scolds both him and Chaucer, rejects Spencer, and insists on poetry in "Mr. Shakespeare's veine." Only when Ingenioso reads his verses imitating the Shakespearean does Gullio vouchsafe him any praise: "No more, I am one that can judge according to the proverbe 'lowem ex unquibus.'[19] Let this duncified world esteem of Spencer or Chaucer, I will worship sweet Mr. Shakespeare and to honor him will lay his 'Venus and Adonis' under my pillow" (Gullio has heard about "some King" who did so with Homer's books).

Gullio emits long tirades laced with references to Cicero and Ronsard, gives his translation of a little-known Italian proverb, and freely quotes Virgil's poems by heart, noting that such correct Latin as his can be heard only at Rheims or Padua: "It is my custom in my common talke to make use of my readings in the Greek, Latin, French, Italian and Spanish poets." Gullio also mentions his own poetry more than once, which appears to be widely famous across the whole country. But, "our base English wites have somewhat corrupted the generous spirit of my poetry."

Though Ingenioso often makes sarcastic asides about Gullio, he never ridicules his poetic activities. Moreover, he fulfills Gullio's instruction (for, rather than requesting, Gullio really orders Ingenioso) to draft for him some verses about his fair lady and the dialogue between the lady and Gullio. "When you have done," says Gullio, "I will correct these verses." Here is a very interesting form of creative collaboration: one makes literary drafts; the other corrects and polishes them. And to all appearances, Ingenioso is not alone in the ranks of literary apprentices, "'Genius-and-Species' and their ragged companions," who surround the eccentric Maecenas. The continuous eulogies to Shakespeare and recitations of his poems (which actually were not very widespread at the time) calls particular attention to the image of Gullio. In fact, such outspoken enthusiasm for and knowledge of Shakespearean texts is not expressed anywhere else in the writings of that period. Even Francis Meres — also a "university wit" — while expressing the highest regard for the works of Shakespeare, at about the same time, did so in a considerably more reserved manner.

Since most characters in the "Parnassus" plays obviously have real prototypes, 20th-century scholars have made several attempts to identify them; they were especially interested to know who hid behind the mask of Gullio. Notwithstanding Gullio's efforts to blend in, it is clear that he is no ordinary Cambridge student (or former student). He pretends to be a nobleman, his friends are earls and lords, he has recently been to other countries, including Italy, participated in the Essex campaigns, and is going to the Netherlands. He is from Cambridge, but he also maintains a study at Oxford and at the court. He patronizes poor students, writers and scholars. He has been educated at the University of Padua and while there he bought a precious sword made of Toledo steel, and we learn as well that an earl would like him to marry his daughter. And with all that, he turns out to be a widely known, even notorious, poet,

---

19. Gullio parodies the widely known Latin proverb, "Know a lion by his claws."

for whom the university writing fraternity makes poetical and dramatic drafts! His speeches are rich in erudition; he always turns everything to the "sweet Mr. Shakespeare," without whose picture and books under his pillow Gullio cannot really live, and while saying so, he seems to be softly laughing in some odd way.

Ingenioso introduced the eccentric young "lord" as a gull, and this is similar to, or perhaps the same as, the clown that Jaques (the melancholic person from the banished Duke's entourage in "As You Like It") wants to be:

> "O that I were a fool!
> I am ambitious for a motley coat."

Traditionally, a fool is a servant of the basest sort, an outcast, almost a human puppet, a toy and amusement for his lord and his guests. However, to perform the function, a man of motley despite being a social nonentity is allowed to do things that would not be permitted to anyone else: to laugh at everything and to tell the truth, even if it is unpleasant. And it is just that fool's privilege which Jaques craves. Gullio, the unique character in the "Parnassus" play, is the Jaques who has realized his dream and hides his face and true name under the motley's mask and fool's name.

Some scholars opine that the Cambridge wits used the guise of Gullio to portray the Earl of Southampton, who had graduated from St. John College a decade before, participated in the Essex campaigns, and patronized a number of writers (including Shakespeare, it is widely assumed). Elizabeth Vernon, whom he secretly married in 1598, could be his Lady Lesbia. In fact, Southampton and Gullio really do have some "points in common," but there are considerable disparities as well. These include the ten-year gap between the date of Southampton's graduation and the time (even approximately) when the action of the play takes place; the fact that Southampton had never been to Padua; and that by his nature and interests he was not much inclined to buffoonery. Even more weighty arguments against this hypothesis involve the name of poet John Weever, whom Gullio mentions as a fellow student who had registered his name in the rolls of fame. Weever studied at Queen's College in 1594-1598, and could never have been Southampton's mate either in the college or during his stay at Cambridge. Neither Professor J. B. Leishman,[20] who published and annotated "The Three Parnassus Plays" in 1949, nor other researchers have ever been able to name a likely fellow student of Weever who could have had something in common with Gullio.

However, an appropriate alumnus of the Queen's College does exist, one who matches all the parameters, and I am pleased to say that he is Roger Manners, the 5th Earl of Rutland.

He made his studies at Cambridge University from 1587 through 1595, and having been a student at the Queen's College for the first two years he continued to

---

20. *The three Parnassus Plays (1598-1601)*. Ed. by J.B. Leishman. L., 1949.

maintain close ties with the students there after he had moved to the other Cambridge college. Later on, after his graduation, he frequented Cambridge and spent the last months of his life there. Weever knew the Earl of Rutland, and he proved it by dedicating to him one of the first epigrams in his book *Epigrams in the oldest cut and newest Fashion.*[21] Only a few of the items there are addressed to nobles, among them Queen Elizabeth. Yet there are epigrams about Jonson and Marston!

John Weever's name may be found in almost all of Shakespeare's biographies. He was among the first to give high praise to the works of the Great Bard. Moreover, he thinks most highly of Shakespeare's poetic works "Venus and Adonis" and "The Rape of Lucrece," and of his dramas, "Romeo and Juliet" and "Richard III"; and he hints that there may be other works, too, with which he is not yet familiar:

> *"Honey-tongued Shakespeare, when I saw thine issue,*
> *I swore Apollo get them and none other..."*

Gullio says that in his epigram Weever has brought him fame. And as a matter of fact, amid the verses addressed to the university friends (some, under their student nicknames), the same book of epigrams features the "In obitum sepulcrum Gullionis"![22]

> *Here lies fat Gullio,*[23] *who caperd in a cord*
> *To highest heav'n for all his huge great weight*
> *His friends left at Tiburne*[24] *in the yere of our Lord*
> 1     5     9     and                         8
> *What part of his body French men did not eate,*
> *That part he gives freely to worms for their meat.*

This "epitaph" makes it clear that the person disguised under the Cambridge nickname of "Gullio" was well known to Weever, but such an impudent and mocking epitaph, in the Rabelaisian style appropriate to Falstaff, could hardly be called "fame," except in some ironic sense.

This Rabelaisian epitaph is an integral part of the play centered around the young lord, former Cambridge student, fellow of John Weever and congener of the melancholy Jaques. Gullio is his motley mask at which he, himself, laughs with Ingenioso. But what they both laugh at most are the uninitiated spectators and readers, who take this play in all good faith, though the authors and characters of the "Parnassus" plays tease them in almost every line.

---

21. Weever J. *Epigrams in the oldest cut and newest Fashion.* 1599. Reprint 1911 by R.B. McKerrow, p. 19.
22. "Epitaph for the late Gullio."
23. Ibid., p. 43.
24. Tyburn — an execution ground in London.

The noble young Cambridge graduate, a fellow of John Weever, was the Earl of Rutland who had recently come back from Padua, who had taken part in the Essex naval expeditions and the campaign in Ireland, who patronized Cambridge scholars and writers, and who that very summer of 1599 was courting the step-daughter of the Earl of Essex and soon married her. Everything Gullio tells us about himself precisely coincides with the known facts of Rutland's life at that period of time.

Rutland's, and nobody else's — that is beyond doubt, just like the fact that only he could have served as the prototype for melancholic Jaques, one of the two inseparable young lords who faithfully followed the banished Duke (Earl of Essex) into exile. It should also be noted that the languages which Gullio shows that he knows are the same ones mastered by Rutland; and the latter is also alluded to by the mention of his ailing feet and the Inn in Oxford (where at that time he was taking examinations in order to receive his second Masters degree). The clownish name of Gullio is a nickname for Shakspere, here playing the role of a human mask for the Earl of Rutland and caricaturing his patron. About this same time, the Stratfordian (under the similar name of Gullion) is also chosen as an object of satire by Joseph Hall, whose works seem to indicate that he was familiar with Shakespeare's. All of this supports the contention that some of Rutland's Cambridge fellows knew something about his games and human masks.

Gullio spouts unmetered dithyrambs eulogizing Shakespeare, whose name itself is repeated more than once; but, while he mentions that Weever has famed him in his epigram, Gullio for some reason avoids touching upon the fact that in another epigram, in the same book, Weever has famed — in the true sense of the word — Shakespeare!

Gullio or, to be exact, the one who hides behind the name, does have something to do with Shakespeare. Not for nothing does Ingenioso warn that when we are listening to Gullio, we hear "nothing but pure Shakespeare." When he promises to have a picture of Shakespeare in his study at the court, he must be jesting, and not only because there were no portraits of Shakespeare at the time. To see the main author of the Shakespearean poems and plays, all Rutland would have had to do would be to hang a mirror on the wall — or, place Isaac Oliver's miniature on his table.

Weever's "Epitaph for late Gullio" most likely alludes to the Shakespearean Falstaff, whom Prince Harry, having assumed the dignities of the crown, brought to justice together with his pals and merry friends. This also matches the rumor (heard from a contemporary of Shakespeare's) that Shakspere, in fact, went by the nickname "Sir John Falstaff." Falstaff is a hypostasis of Gullio.

For what, then, is Gullio grateful to Weever? For the fact that in his epigram-epitaph, having buried him alive, he sent him to the gallows and called him a syphilitic? No, he could not thank Weever for that. He means the other Weever epigram in the same book — the one which glorifies the works of William Shakespeare. Gullio never directly mentions that epigram, though he could not fail to note it since it is near enough to the humiliating "epitaph" addressed to him. However, that would be the epigram for which he thanks Weever — for the ultimate appraisal of

The poet John Weever, one of Rutland's Cambridge fellows, and one of the first to highly praise Shakespeare's poetry.

## The first weeke.

*Epig.13.* *In Rogerum Manners Rutlandiæ Comitem.*

It's not the sea which doth our land inclose,
That makes vs mightie to withstand our foes:
Nor farmes, nor mannours, but where manners be
There stands the cittie, from foes danger free,
If *Manners* then make vs our foes withstand,
MANNERS may wel be cald ROOT of the LAND.

*Epig.14.* *In Crassum.*

*Crassus* will say the dogge faunes with his taile,
To men of worth he writes for's best auaile:
*Crassus* thou lyest, dogs write not deedes of men,
Then thou the dog that snarlest at my pen.

*Mono-*

## The second weeke.

*Epig.21* *In obitum sepulcrum Gullionis.*

Here lies fat *Gullio*, who caperd in a cord
To hughest heau'n for all his huge great weight,
His friends left at *Tiburne* in the yere of our Lord
1    5    9   and   8
What part of his body French men did not eate,
That part he giues freely to worms for their meat

*Epig.22* *In Coam*

A nor Ω will *Coa* espie,
Till she ascend vp to the corner'd Π.

*Epig.*

## The fourth weeke.

*Epig 22. Ad Gulielmum Shakespear*

Honie-tong'd *Shakespeare* when I saw thine issue
I swore *Apollo* got them and none other,
Their rosie-tainted features cloth'd in tissue,
Some heauen born goddesse said to be their mo-
Rose-cheekt *Adonis* with his amber tresses, (ther
Faire fire-hot *Venus* charming him to loue her,
Chaste *Lucretia* virgine-like her dresses, (her:
Prowd lust-stung *Tarquine* seeking still to proue
*Romea Richard* more whose names I know not,
Their sugred tongues, and power attractiue beuty
Say they are Saints althogh that Sts they shew not
For thousands vowes to them subiectiue dutie:
They burn in loue thy childrē *Shakespear* het thē,
Go, wo thy Muse more Nymphish brood beget
(them.

*Romeo*

## The sixt weeke.

*Epig.11 Ad Io: Marston, & Ben: Iohnson.*

*Marston*, thy Muse enharbours *Horace* vaine,
Then some *Augustus* giue thee *Horace* merit,
And thine embuskin'd *Iohnson* doth retaine
So rich a stile, and wondrous gallant spirit,
That if to praise your Muses I desired, (mired
My Muse would muse. Such wittes must be ad-

*Epig.12 In tumulum Auari.*

Here lieth he who neuer aught
To man or woman gaue:
And now it grieues him that thou read'st
For nought this on his graue.

*Liue*

Pages from Weever's *Epigrams* (1599) with the names of Rutland, Gullio, Shakespeare, Marston, Jonson.

the works ascribed to "William Shakespeare" — there is nothing else to be thankful for. The "Parnassus" character of Gullio knows that the highest esteem, that fame, refers to the one who appears and will always appear under the various masks and nicknames of a fool.

Time and again, in the play, Gullio emphasizes "his own" poetic works, mentions his sonnets, and names classical writers and contemporary English poets. Other characters in the "Parnassus" plays refer to many poets and writers as well, and sometimes disparagingly. The same names occur in Weever's book of epigrams (which, incidentally, was not registered, and in spite of the date on the title page, 1598, there is evidence that it came out no earlier than 1599): the poet addresses Ben Jonson, Marston, Drayton, Samuel Daniel — those who just at that time were starting to form the Rutlands' poetic entourage. Besides the Earl of Rutland, the book of epigrams names Weever's professor at the Queen's College, William Covell — the same Covell who, as early as 1595, had listed Shakespeare among the poets and writers who graduated from the university. It would be no overstatement to say that the alumni and professors of the Queen's College at Cambridge were the first to note and greet the appearance of Shake-Speare's name in literature.

Gullio of course might also thank Weever for the epigram he directed to his fellow student, who shared the same year of birth, the Earl of Rutland. The verse is respectful and complimentary — just in the manner that a poor rhymer, a sizer[25] would have to use in addressing a young earl who happened to be with him at the same college. Here, Weever plays up the meaning of the earl's name, and calls him "root of Land." As to the epigram, which praises the works of Shakespeare, Gullio's words show that his college-mate had recommended Weever not to impose his raptures on him anymore. For the Earl of Rutland avoids curious, even if rapturous, eyes; he prefers to keep his literary and theater pursuits, his crafty acts, hidden; the world shall always see only his masks, his stage hypostases.

The poet John Weever, his book of epigrams, his relationship with the heroes of "Return from Parnassus" and in particular with Gullio, Shakspere, and Rutland, are important threads in the fabric of this story, and until now they have been unexplored and not properly understood. Meanwhile, their significance to the story of Shakespeare is hard to overestimate.

"The Return from Parnassus" contains yet another allusion to, scholars have assumed, Shakespeare. When Gullio leaves the scene after a good long talk, Ingenioso remarks after him (addressing the audience and readers): "Farewell base carle clothed in a satin suite!" J. Leishman and other researchers note that the phrase alludes to the widely known metaphor from "Henry VI," Part 3 — "a tiger's heart wrapt in a woman's hide," which was paraphrased by Robert Greene ("There is an upstart crow, beautified with our feathers, that with his Tygers heart wrapt in a Players hide") — which many

---

25. Sizer — a poor student who received an allowance toward college expenses and who worked for the college in return for this allowance.

scholars took as an attack on Shakespeare (i.e. Shakspere). However, these scholars (knowing nothing about Rutland) fail to understand the relationship between Gullio and Shakespeare, and so the question remains open for them. Only by understanding that Gullio is a friendly (though far from harmless) jest at both the Earl of Rutland and his human mask, Shakspere, can we elucidate the meaning of Ingenioso's remark, and put everything right.

It is often said that it may not be worth the effort to identify the real prototypes of dramatic characters, and anyway, the results are not always reliable. This sounds reasonable. But in the "Parnassus" plays, written for a very particular Cambridge audience, *almost all characters have real, specific prototypes,* whom the spectators recognized, just as they also understood the various hints abounding in the text (although, of course, some parts were more clear to one group or another, and much was largely obscure to the general public). It should also be borne in mind that Gullio appears only in the first part of "The Return from Parnassus" — which was never printed and in fact was not likely to be widely known.

Now, let us reread the scene when the students meet Burbadge and Kempe — the players from the Lord Chamberlain's Company, the cooperative enterprise where Shakspere was a shareholder. The actors are illiterate and greedy; they are eager to hire hungry students cheaply. Kempe makes fun of the students' deficiencies as actors — he once watched a comedy at Cambridge: ". . . they never speake in their walke, but at the end of the stage, . . . where a man can go no further." Burbadge hopes that a little teaching will mend these flaws, and besides, maybe the students will pen a play for the actors. But Kempe is portrayed as having his own goals: "Few of the University men playes well, they smell too much of that writer Ovid, and that writer Metamorphosis, and talke too much of Proserpina and Jupiter. Why here's our fellow[26] Shakespeare puts them all downe. . . and Ben Jonson too. O that Ben Jonson is a pestilent fellow, he brought up Horace giving the poets a pill,[27] but our fellow Shakespeare hath given him a purge that made him bewray his credit." The ignorance of the clown and dancer Kempe — he mistakes the title of the famous book from antiquity for its author — is shown in other ways as well. As to writings that "smell too much" of the Latin classics and old gods, Shakespeare's works mention Jupiter 30 times, Diana — 50, Apollo — 42, Venice — 17; and (as Kempe remembered) Proserpina — wife of Pluto, God of the underworld — 6 times. Therefore, the dancer Kempe had every reason to ascribe Shakespeare to the "University quills."

Of course, the "The Return from Parnassus" was written not by Burbadge and Kempe but by someone from that very circle of "university wits and quills" — the actors being quite unaware that somebody from Cambridge had put them into the play. The more so that not one of Parnassus plays was performed on a public stage; the

---

26. A choice ambiguity, as noted in Chapter 2.
27. To cure the incontinence of words.

William Kempe — the comic actor, dancer, clown

first two were never printed at all, and the last one was published only eight years later.

There are no documents to indicate that any one of the company's players regarded Shakspere during his lifetime as a writer or playwright. The first time a play was printed with the name of Shakespeare on the title pages was in 1598; and an author's name was never mentioned in the text of the actors' parts; in fact, it was probably of no interest to an ordinary player. Or to an audience, apparently. "Richard II" was repeatedly staged in London, but even some years later, when the Essex case was being investigated at the highest level, when the performance of that play was incriminating to the participants in the mutiny, no one even tried to find out who was the playwright.

As I have already mentioned, it is plausible to surmise that in some cases the plays might have come to the company through Shakspere, who perhaps had only to keep quiet about his principals and receive, from time to time, a purse of golden coins to invest according to his own prudent judgment. But this still does not mean that his fellows took him for a writer and dramatist. To some extent, the game that was going on over the similarity between the names of Shake-Speare and Shakspere might have been known to Richard Burbadge, who knew the earls of Rutland, Southampton and Pembroke and whom they trusted (not without reason — it was this same Burbadge who appeared with Shakspere at Belvoir after the death of the Rutlands, some days prior to Shakspere's eventual removal from London).

But judging by Gullio's revelations and Kempe's orations, the Cambridge authors of "The Return from Parnassus" did know about the mystery of the Shakespearean nickname and the role assigned to Shakspere from Stratford, in the game, and were happy to have a laugh over it. It seems they may still be laughing at the academic commentators of today.

19th- and 20th-century scholars have speculated as to the authors of the "Parnassus" plays (the three pieces were clearly written by different hands), but the problem still persists. The prologue to the first part of "The Return" skillfully alludes to the author's name, which, it says, resembles the name of the cheese produced at Cheshire (that is, it most likely sounds like Chester or Cheshire). Scholars have been unable to find any trace of a student with one of those names in the university lists in the mid-1590s. However, the author (or one of the authors) might have studied at Cambridge before that, and stayed in touch with the university (as was often done). Then we should recall the main author of Chester's collection, *Love's Martyr* — Robert Chester himself. He was educated at Cambridge (Trinity College) in the mid-1580s. His estate at Royston was located a few miles from Cambridge, and so it was easy and natural for him to stay in touch with the university public after his studies. In 1600, his name was listed among the students at the Middle Temple, closely related with Gray's Inn where Rutland did his studies; early in February 1602, Shakespeare's "Twelfth Night" was staged at Middle Temple. *Love's Martyr* testifies to the fact that Chester knew the secret of his noble young relative, the Earl of Rutland, and his wife, and could very likely be the author of at least one part of "The Return from Parnassus." However, for the time being, this is just a supposition which needs further study. Moreover, relatively recently F. Huntley and E. Honigmann[28] proposed John Weever as a potential author of the first Parnassus play ("Pilgrimage to Parnassus"). The name "Weever" coincides with the name of the biggest river in Cheshire, as the poet himself emphasized in one of his poems. There are other concurring facts and circumstances as well, which lend support to the hypothesis of his authorship.

However, Rutland's fellow-student John Weever is related to the Great Bard by another intriguing link. Scholars have long believed that the inscription on the Stratford wall monument was first noted by Dugdale in 1656; but it turns out that an extant manuscript of Weever's, dated three decades earlier, contains this inscription as well. Honigmann thinks Weever wrote down the inscription soon after the monument was erected. However, the text written in Weever's hand differs on two points from the text on the monument; for instance, it lacks the glaring orthographic error on the monument. Honnigmann presumes that Weever corrected the mason's mistake, which is quite possible. But that explanation does not hold water when we come to the other difference. Weever gives the date of Shakspere's death as April 24, 1616; the monument says April 23. It is unlikely that Weever could make such a mistake while transcribing the text from the monument. Weever did not copy the text; he was its author. It was the workman who, in the course of the transferring the text onto the stone, not only distorted it orthographically but changed the date of Shakspere's death (perhaps on the advice of the priest or someone else who knew the exact date). Thus, there is good reason to believe that besides being one of the first poets to hail Shakespeare, John Weever was also the first who paid homage to Shakspere, ten years after the death of the Earl of Rutland, identifying Shakspere with William Shake-Speare.

The Parnassus plays, Cambridge, the poet John Weever, his epigrams, his manuscripts — all these are highly promising areas for further study of the "Shakespeare authorship problem," the clues to its solution.

In his "Scourge of Villanie," anonymously published at about the same time (1598), John Marston addresses an unknown poet, absolutely unexpectedly and seemingly inexplicably:

> . . . *Far fly thy fame*
> *Most, most of me beloved, whose silent name*
> *One letter bounds. Thy true judical style*
> *I ever honour, and if my love beguile*
> *Not much my hopes, then thy unvalid worth*
> *Shall mount fair place when Apes are turned forth.*

---

28. Honigmann E.A.J. *John Weever.* Manchester University Press. 1987.

Thus Marston — one of Weever's addressees — prophecies the time when the "unknown" will achieve his honored place, and his screen, his "Apes," will be seen through. A silent name, that "one letter bounds," is Rutland's name — Roger.

## A FAVORITE ON THE SCAFFOLD. DOWNFALL.

The Earl of Essex and his supporters were wracking their brains for a way to win back the queen's favor and to oust the accursed Robert Cecil and Walter Raleigh; at secret meetings they sounded out the king of Scotland and the new Lord Deputy in Ireland, but their responses were not promising — neither James VI nor Lord Mountjoy showed himself eager to meddle in such a dangerous venture. Another hard blow was dealt to Essex's self-esteem and his financial state when Queen Elizabeth refused to renew his license on the duties from imported sweet wine. The monopoly she had granted to him ten years earlier was the major source of the earl's income, and without it he was on the brink of ruin. Essex became frantic, and feeling himself cornered he began to take the liberty of disrespectfully criticizing not only the queen's policy but her appearance as well — and there were, of course, people who were eager to bring these indiscrete utterances to the royal attention.

The government was warned about groups of suspicious persons loitering in London, and shocking rumors were set afloat in the city that Robert Cecil had allegedly promised the succession to the British crown to the Spanish Infanta, or that Raleigh intended to murder the people's favorite, the Earl of Essex. It was not difficult to trace the source of the rumors, and to find out what was discussed during Essex's and Southampton's secret meetings. It seems that Cecil decided to accelerate the course of events and to provoke Essex to action before he was ready; but it is possible that the following events took place spontaneously.

On Saturday, February 7, 1601, the queen's messenger came to Essex with an order to appear before the Privy Council. The plotters thought that this was a trap and decided to react immediately, though their actions look like a poorly conceived impromptu drama. Essex told the queen's messenger that he was ill, bedridden; and they planned a rebellion for the following day. The same Saturday night Sir Merrick, one of Essex's closest associates, went with some of his friends to the Globe Theater and urgently asked the actors to perform "Richard II" (as he explained later on, "to show the people that a monarch can also be deposed"). The actors refused to oblige: the play was too old and would not draw much contribution from the audience. Merrick offered forty shillings more than their ordinary pay, and the play was performed. It seems unlikely that the idea of generating popular support for the rebellion by reviving that play would have come from Sir Gilly Merrick, who had little in common with the Muses; it was more likely to have sprung from the earls of

Robert Cecil (first from the right)

Southampton and Rutland. However, the play, about events two centuries old, failed to stir up many Londoners.

Sunday, February 8, dawned, and about 300 of Essex's supporters, fervent and armed, gathered in the courtyard of his home. But the government had already taken the necessary precautions: the number of yeomen guarding the Royal Palace was doubled, and four dignitaries were sent to Essex House in order to receive explanations for the cause of this illegal assembly. The delegation was locked up in the house, and the mob then poured out into the street, loudly calling upon all and sundry to follow them. Their original plan was to go to the Palace, but Essex decided to head to the City, where he hoped the people would rally to him. Leading the way, side by side with Essex marched Southampton and Rutland, their swords unsheathed. However, the conspirators failed to receive any support in the City: even as they marched, preachers in all the churches were announcing the queen's injunction to the people: to arm themselves, and stay indoors awaiting further orders. The earl was declared a traitor. Some of his followers dispersed; others were blocked by the government army. An attempt to burst through the cordon failed, and some of the group were killed or wounded. The earl and his most loyal people barely managed to retreat to where they had started their chaotic procession a few hours before. They began preparing to mount a defense, but the government forces soon arrived with guns and encircled the house. Understanding that resistance was futile, the besieged conspirators were forced to surrender to the royal forces, with a knightly condition parleyed — free passage out of the house for the few ladies who happened to be there at the moment.

The trial was brief and severe, before a specially appointed jury of nine judges and 25 Peers of the Realm. Essex denied having any intention of harming Her Majesty herself, claiming that he only desired to remove her evil counselors. But the prosecutor — Francis Bacon — promptly proved that his actions were high treason. In the course of the proceedings, Essex behaved hysterically and tried to shift the blame onto others, including even his mother and sister. Rutland looked dismayed and excited. He ascribed his actions to loyalty, gratitude and family feelings toward Essex. To all appearances, the conspirators had not relied much on him, or they had consciously protected him from prosecution in case their enterprise failed — for they had not initiated him into their secret intentions, and Rutland sincerely believed that he was going to defend Essex against his enemies at Court. However, he told the judges everything he knew — and his unreserved testimony appears to have been very unfavorable for Essex and Southampton, which was not overlooked later on by their surviving adherents.

Five principal conspirators — Essex himself, Christopher Blount, Charles Danvers, Gilly Merrick and Henry Cuffe[29] — were convicted of high treason and were sentenced to death.

On February 25, 1601, aged 33, Robert Devereux, 2nd Earl of Essex, favorite and kinsman of the queen, mounted the scaffold, followed by three ministers. After the earl repented his sins, commending his soul into the hands of Lord, and pardoned the executioner who fell to his knees before him, Essex lay down on the scaffold, his head fitting to the block. Essex's last words, on the scaffold, were addressed to God: "When my life and body shall part, send thy blessed angels, which may receive my soule and convey it to the joys of heaven." Few people could hear these words. However, the author of "Hamlet" seems to echo them in Horatio's words of farewell to the prince of Denmark: "Good night, sweet Prince, and flights of angels sing thee to thy rest." The first axe stroke hit the head; the second hit the shoulder, and only with the third blow did the executioner cut off the earl's head, which fell onto the platform. The melodramatic revolt wrought its greatest carnage on its main hero.

Southampton was also condemned to death, but his sentence was commuted to life imprisonment, through the intervention of Sir Robert Cecil, petitioned by the earl's family.

After Essex's execution, the Earl of Rutland was shut up in the Tower. Both his younger brothers, Francis and George, who had also participated in the events of February, were imprisoned as well. Rutland's spirits were so low that the Privy Council specially ordered the superintendent of the Tower to keep watch over this prisoner and to assign a special man to look after him. Not so long ago, one could still read an Italian inscription on the wall of the cell where he was kept. Translated from Italian, it says: "O me — the most miserable of men!" According to the records of the Tower, no Italian was ever kept in that cell, and hence Rutland, who spoke fluent Italian, is most likely to have left the words.

Petitions by influential friends and family members, as well as the intercession of Robert Cecil himself (who, after Essex was executed, tried to win over the earl's former supporters, whom he deemed not very dangerous), contributed to softening Rutland's fate. Nevertheless, he was sentenced to pay an enormous fine of 30,000 pounds sterling, and was deported to the custody of his great-uncle at his estate at Uffington.

This was ruin. Financially destroyed, dishonored, morally crushed and humiliated, the Earl of Rutland spent over a year in the Tower and at Uffington. The appalling sight of the gory head of his friend, relative and patron, brutally hacked to death, haunted him. He was apparently also tormented by the thought of all the misery he had brought down upon his younger brothers and all his family, as well as by the effect his ingenuous statements at the trial had had on the fate of Essex and the other participants.

Finally, early in 1602, Robert Cecil managed to gain permission for the banished earl to move to Belvoir, and the fine was reduced by a third. The Rutlands were able to

---

29. Henry Cuffe — lecturer at the Queen's College, professor of Greek, secretary to the Earl of Essex. 1597 — Padua University. Author of the book, *The Difference of the Ages of Man's life*, written in 1600, published in 1607 with a foreword by R.M. (Roger Manners, who knew Cuffe well).

spend the next Christmas with their friends, the poet John Harington and William, Earl of Pembroke. But the situation was still desperate.

That very period, the years of Rutland's defeat, prison and exile, coincides with the dramatic shift in Shakespeare's creative activities, when the Bard turned from the light-hearted humor of his early comedies to the tragic perception of the world expressed in the great dramas written in the first decade of the early 17th century. The mood of the Uffington captive found reflection in the famous Sonnet 66:

> *Tired with all these, for restful death I cry,*
> *As, to behold desert a beggar born,*
> *And needy nothing trimm'd in jollity,*
> *And purest faith unhappily forsworn,*
> *And guilded honour shamefully misplaced,*
> *And maiden virtue rudely strumpeted,*
> *And right perfection wrongfully disgraced,*
> *And strength by limping sway disabled,*
> *And art made tongue-tied by authority,*
> *And folly doctor-like controlling skill,*
> *And simple truth miscall'd simplicity,*
> *And captive good attending captain ill:*
>
> *Tired with all these, from these would I be gone,*
> *Save that, to die, I leave my love alone.*

The tragedy "Timon of Athens," the work that was written several years later (although it may have been started earlier) and was never finished, brings to the forefront the despair and rage of the ruined Timon who generously spends all his fortune and then is spurned by his fair-weather friends and clients when he needs help. Only from the depth of his downfall is he finally able to see and comprehend the whole scope of human meanness, the sordid nature of those whom he earlier, light-mindedly, believed to be his friends; hence his disgust for people and his bitter misanthropy.

The tragic story of the Earl of Essex is echoed in "Julius Caesar" and "Coriolanus." The unusual play "Troilus and Cressida" came out in 1601-1602. Registered in early 1603, it was printed in a quarto edition only in 1609, and then with the title page asserting that the play was "acted by the servants of His Majesty" at the Globe Theater and was written by William Shakespeare. However, another quarto of the comedy has a different title page, with no mention of any stage production but bearing instead an anonymous preface from "A Never writer to an Ever reader." This very important epistle was written in extremely subtle euphuistic language; twice it is emphasized that the piece has *never* been staged, so that it has not been "clapper-clawed with the palms of the vulgar," or "sullied with the smoky breath of the multitude." Here, the sense of elitism and contempt for the ordinary audience goes beyond what would be expected even of the aristocrats; at the same time, the writer of the epistle praises the playwright, whose wit is so sharp that "all such dull and heavy-witted worldlings . . . coming . . . to his representations, have found that wit . . . they never found in themselves . . . feeling an edge of wit set upon them more than ever they dreamed they had brain to grind it on." The epistle's author regards "Troilus and Cressida" as the wittiest of Shakespeare's comedies. "And believe this, that when he is gone and his comedies out of sale, you will scramble for them and set up a new English Inquisition." The haughty contempt for the multitude, the artificially elegant and complicated speech of the preface, which would certainly be somewhat unclear to an ordinary reader, give me grounds to disagree with the view of some Western Shakespeare scholars that this preface was written at the publisher's request, to encourage people to buy the book. This is patently not the case, as further indicated by the author's reference to certain "Grand Possessors" of the plays, on whose will depended their appearance.

The comedy (which, by the way, was included among the tragedies in the First Folio of 1623) is a sharply satirical exposé of the classical Trojan War heroes, rash and obstinate, always ready to spill blood and kill each other. The women — Cressida and Helen — are disloyal, frivolous and false. Anikst has observed that "Troilus and Cressida" shares many of the ideas seen in "Hamlet": "This is a drama about broken ideals. It is apparent that the author is possessed with that mood which found expression in the words of Hamlet: 'Man delights not me: no, nor woman neither.'"[30] Bitterness, disappointment, contempt for the vanity and insignificance of human intentions bring "Troilus and Cressida" into the same realm as "Timon of Athens" and "Hamlet." It is also worth noting that most scholars of Shakespeare share the opinion that Thomas Dekker, John Marston and George Chapman evidently had a hand in some parts of "Troilus and Cressida."

Other plays classified as "dark" comedies — "All's Well That Ends Well" and "Measure for Measure" — also date to about the same period of time. Injustice, violence, lies, vice prevailing over virtue, innocent people tried and imprisoned — those are the themes at the heart of them.

## THE SHIP IS BOUND FOR ELSINORE: TWO "HAMLET" QUARTOS

On July 26, 1602, an entry was made in the Stationers' Register for "The Revenge of Hamlet Prince of Denmarke as it was latelie acted by the Lord Chamberleyne his servants." In 1603, the play was printed, and the title page announced: "The Tragicall Historie of Hamlet, Prince of Denmarke by William Shake-speare; As it hath beene

---

30. Anikst, A. A. *Shakespeare*, Moscow, 1964, p. 234 (in Russian).

diverse times acted by his Highnesse servants in the Cittie of London: as also in the two Universities of Cambridge and Oxford, and else-where."

In the meantime, Queen Elizabeth had died, on March 24, 1603, and King James had acceded to the throne with the assistance of Sir Robert Cecil and other courtiers. (How much it had cost the Earl of Essex, that he could not be patient for a couple of years!)

In "Hamlet," the great playwright appears before us, tragically reborn in the font of suffering. However, the obvious relationship between that radical shift and Essex's downfall has always been a difficult issue for biographers of the Stratfordian approach. For, what was the Earl of Essex to Shakspere, and what was the latter to Essex? Why should the death of a queen's favorite, so distant from him, wound him so painfully, and for life? The biographers have no choice but to note that Southampton, to whom two of Shakespeare's poems were dedicated, also suffered for his participation in the rebellion. This, they say, may also have affected the actor-playwright. But the facts show that after the destruction of Essex, Shakspere went on with his life as usual: in 1602, he purchased a big parcel of land in the vicinity of Stratford and bought a building as well. Neither would Essex's tragedy have strongly upset such non-Stratfordian "Shakespeare candidates" as Bacon or the Earl of Oxford, who took an active part in the trial and had a role in his conviction. But the tragic turning point in the Great Bard's mood, which took place after 1601, meshes perfectly with what we know of Rutland's biography.

As we have noted, the title page of the 1603 quarto edition called the company that performed "Hamlet" "His Highness' servants." The Register entry of 1602 called the actors who staged the play at the Globe Theater the "Lord Chamberlain's servants." One of the new king's first decrees regulated the patronage of actors' companies: henceforth, this was the privilege of the royal family. The Lord Admiral's Men were now called "Prince Henry's Servants," while the company playing at the Curtain Theater now bore the name of "Queen's Players." But the highest royal favor was won by the company that played at the Globe Theater, where William Shakspere was one of the principal shareholders and where the young earls of Southampton and Rutland had spent so much of their time during the year and a half prior to the tragic events of February 1601.

Within ten days of his arrival in London, the new sovereign ordered that the Keeper of the Privy Seal prepare a special Letters Patent for the company, now known as the King's Servants; the royal decree of May 17, 1603, even comprised the full text of the above patent — unprecedented in the history of England. It is no wonder that upon the receipt of such an injunction, the royal officers drew up the unique Letters Patent within record-breaking time, in just two days, and endorsed it by the royal seal, originally intended for the very important state deeds. The patent's text, coming from the king himself, was written in the style of Polonius in the scene introducing the actors who have just arrived at Elsinore, and bestowed on "these our servants Lawrence Fletcher, William Shakespeare, Richard Burbadge, Augustyne Phillipes,

King James I

John Heminges, Henry Condell, William Sly, Robert Armin, Richard Cowley, and the rest of their associates, freely to use and exercise the Arte and faculty of playinge Comedies, Tragedies, Histories, Enterludes, moralls, pastoralls, Stage plaies and suche others like as theie have alreadie studied or hereafter shall use or studie as well for the recreation of our lovinge Subjectes as for our Solace and plesure when we shall thincke good to see them duringe our pleasure . . ." It was also stated that when His Majesty's servants should show their art "within their now usual house called the Globe" or within any other city in the kingdom, then all justices, mayors, other officers and subjects of the King should "allow them such former courtesies as hath been given to men of their place and quality, and also what further favour you shal show to these our servants for your sake."[31]

Why would the king show such great interest in theatrical life in general, and in this troupe of players in particular, just a few days after his enthronement, when he had urgent state affairs to attend to? Someone in his close entourage must have had theatrical issues very close to his heart! Of course, these were the same noblemen, or some of them, who had tried to influence the course of history by staging the play "Richard II," and who before that had devoted so much time to the Globe Theater. They did not forget the actors under their patronage, even though any gathering of people including stage performances was banned in those days due to the plague — even the ceremonial procession in the streets of London to celebrate the coronation was delayed for almost a year. When the outbreak of the plague came to an end, "His Majesty's Men" were invited to the palace to perform for the royal audience at least twice a month, on average. Thus, from November 1604 to October 1605, the King's Men performed eleven plays before the king, including seven plays by Shakespeare, two by Ben Jonson, and one each by George Chapman and Thomas Heywood. The repertory speaks for itself. However, historians have looked in vain for other reasons for the king's kindness to the playwright whose plays he so enjoyed. A century later, it was rumored that a letter of commendation existed, written in the king's own hand to the Great Bard.

However, en route from Scotland to London, despite being in a hurry to get to the capital, the new king had made sure to stop at Belvoir. He was extremely kind to the Earl of Rutland, granting him the honorable post of Lord Lieutenant of Lincolnshire and making him Justice in Eyre of another sylvan Royal Park (in addition to Sherwood Forest). Rutland was fully restored in all his rights and relieved from paying the ruinous fine. His younger brothers and other people of his entourage were elevated to knighthood, including Henry Willoughby and Robert Chester from Royston. Southampton was released from the Tower and rehabilitated (although his friendship with Rutland was not restored). Instead, Walter Raleigh, who had witnessed Essex's execution on that fateful morning in February, 1601, fell prey to Robert Cecil's backstairs intrigue and was himself imprisoned in the Tower.

---

31. Quoted from: Schoenbaum S., op. cit., p. 321.

To the death of Elizabeth I, mourned by many poets of England, William Shakespeare did not respond at all. In the poem "England's Mourning Garments," Henry Chettle openly reproaches him for this silence, urging, "remember our Elizabeth" who, during her life, "opened her Royal ear to his lays." But the "silver-tongued" Shakespeare uttered not a word on the matter. The death of the queen meant the end of exile and ruin for the Earl of Rutland; and he was unlikely to forgive her the death of his idol.

> The mortal moon hath her eclipse endured
> And the sad augurs mock their own presage;
> Incertainties now crown themselves assured
> And peace proclaims olives of endless age.
> Now with the drops of this most balmy time
> My love looks fresh, and death to me subscribes... (Sonnet 107)

With the advent of King James, who always treated him well, a splendid career opened up before the Earl of Rutland, but still he preferred to stay away from court most of the time. Despite the cancellation of the fine, his financial position was strained, sometimes even desperate; this generous and kind man was apparently never good at the prudent management of money, as may be seen from his steward's housekeeping records.

Soon after ascending the English throne, the king entrusted the Earl of Rutland with an honorable task — to go to Denmark as the head of the official mission to congratulate the king's brother-in-law, the Danish King Christian,[32] on the occasion of his son's birth. On behalf of King James I, Rutland was to present to King Christian the decorations of the Order of the Garter. On June 28, 1603, the mission left England and after nine days at sea the delegation set foot on the soil of the Kingdom of Denmark.

The English king's envoy was received with great honor in the Danish king's residence of Elsinore. A retinue of Danish noblemen was appointed to look after the earl, and he was received in the king's private quarters at Kronborg Castle; the king conversed with him in Italian. There was no end to the festivities, feasts, libations and toasts. On July 10, the royal court held a banquet to celebrate the christening of the newborn prince; as was customary in the north, inconceivable quantities of alcohol were consumed.

The embassy included the royal herald William Segar; he kept a diary, which was later used by chronicler John Stow in the second edition of his "Annales," published in 1605. About the royal banquet Segar wrote, "... it would make a man sicke to heare of their drunken healths; use hath brought it into fashion, and fashion made it a habit, which ill beseemes our nation to imitate."[33]

---

32. Queen Anne, wife of James I, was the sister of King Christian IV.
33. See: *Hamlet.* Ed. by J.D. Wilson. Cambridge, 1997. Notes, p. 295-296.

Four days later, the Earl of Rutland went to Elsinore Castle to present King Christian with the decorations of the Garter, and at night the return banquet was hosted on board the British ship; tables were set on the upper deck. Each toast was accompanied by six, eight and ten cannon salutes; all in all, there were 160 rounds — one may calculate what volume of wine was drunk. Tired with "that Bacchanal way of spending time," to use Segar's words, on July 19 Rutland started on his journey back home, having perhaps reduced his planned stay in the over-hospitable Danish land.

On the high seas, the ship was caught in a terrible storm. For fourteen days the waves carried the ship along until finally the passengers and crew had already despaired; they were shipwrecked on the rocky beach of Yorkshire, near the cliff of Scarborough. Rutland's nautical experience was enriched with yet another tempest.

The next year, 1604, a new edition of "Hamlet" appeared. As the title page read, the play was "newly imprinted and enlarged to almost as much again as it was, according to the true and perfect Coppie." This edition is traditionally known by the name of Quarto 2 (as distinct from the 1603 edition, Quarto 1). The editions are quite different. While Quarto 1 had 2143 lines, Quarto 2 had 3719 lines, almost a 75% increase in size — but that was not the greatest change. The entire play was altered, and many characters received new names. Thus, the king's trusted minister Corambis became Polonius, known to us all; and the inseparable Rossencraft and Gilderstone were made more precisely into Rosencraus and Guyldenstern. The author's interpretation of many characters, including King Claudius, the queen, and Corambis-Polonius, also underwent changes. While the 1603 edition portrayed the latter as a harmless old man (though not devoid of weak points and demerits), the second quarto shows a cunning and unscrupulous but dull-witted old courtier who fully deserves the sarcastic treatment by Hamlet.

In the first Quarto, the queen stated quite plainly that she was not involved in the murder of her first husband, and when Hamlet told her of the crime, the queen readily committed to assisting him in wreaking revenge. In the second Quarto, her behavior is more ambiguous; she is now closer to Claudius and stays aloof from Hamlet, who is appalled by her incestuous marriage: "Frailty, thy name is woman!"

But most interestingly, Quarto 2 now truly recalls Denmark of the early 17th century, unlike the former edition's pseudo Denmark. It appears to show the author's knowledge of the Danish word "dansker" and of the tradition of burying kings in full warrior array, and particularly a knowledge of the pitiable passion of the Danish kings and noblemen for the "Bacchanal way of spending time." Hamlet explains to Horatio the meaning of the trumpet sounds and cannon volleys which accompany each bowl of wine drained by the king: "The King doth wake to-night and takes his rouse, keeps wassail, and the swaggering up-spring reels; and, as he drains his draughts of Rhenish down, the kettle-drum and trumpet thus bray out the triumph of his pledge . . . Yes, it is a custom: but to my mind, though I am native here and to the manner born, it is a custom more honour'd in the breach than the observance.[34] This heavy-headed revel east and west makes us traduced and tax'd of other nations: they clepe us drunkards, and with swinish phrase . . ." In the second Quarto, the description of the festivities at the king's court precisely matches the eye-witness accounts given by Segar,[35] who accompanied the Earl of Rutland. But Segar's notes were published in 1605, a year after this edition of "Hamlet"!

During Hamlet's meeting with his mother, Polonius, with her approval, hides behind the arras. Hamlet asks his mother to look at the pictures of his father and uncle: "This was your husband. Look you now, what follows: Here is your husband." Where are these portraits? What is Hamlet pointing at?

The large ballroom at Kronborg Castle,[36] where the Earl of Rutland was entertained by King Christian IV, is hung with tapestries displaying all the Danish kings in chronological order. In the 19th century, there were already some hundred pictures; in mid-century they were greatly damaged by fire, but some still survived.[37] It appears that the author of "Hamlet" knew about the portraits — that is, he knew about them immediately after Rutland's trip to Denmark and his visit to the royal castle. Segar's records devote a few lines to these tapestries, but as we have found out, his diary became known only after "Hamlet" was published.

19th-century Shakespeare critics assumed that Quarto 1 of "Hamlet" (found only in 1821) was a first edition of the great tragedy, later revised and enlarged by the author himself (as the title page of Quarto 2 indicates). In the 20th century, literary scholars commonly believed that the First Quarto was a "pirated" text, abridged and corrupted by whoever had transcribed it. However, the heroes' new names, the evolution of the images of the main characters and the appearance of specific Danish details testify against this opinion.

Generally speaking, the surmise about "pirating," of unauthorized copies of Shakespeare's plays, is just an attempt to explain a number of strange textual details and the circumstances under which these plays appeared. This hypothesis should not be used as a master key to unlock all the mysteries in Shakespearean textual study. The possibility exists that one or another edition was pirated — the First Folio's address to the reader also touches upon the notion of stolen or corrupt texts — but that does not mean that this is the answer to all riddles, and we can by no means exclude the possibility of author's revisions to an earlier version, as is apparently the case with "Hamlet." It should also be noted that all Shakespearean quartos indicate the strange nature of the relationship or, to be more precise, the lack of any relationship,

---

34. Curiously, in the First Folio of 1623, the next part of Hamlet's monologue with its sharp criticism of the drunken debauchery at the Danish royal court was excised. This was probably done because by then the English king was married to the sister of the Danish king, and could not be expected to tolerate such invectives.

35. This "coincidence" was however noted only two and half centuries later (1874) by Frederic James Furnivall.

36. This description of Kronberg's interior was kindly sent to me by A. Daniushevskaya.

37. See also: David Hohnem *Hamlet's Castle and Shakespeare's Elsinore.* Copenhagen: Christian Ejlers, 2000, p.36-40

between Shake-Speare and the publishers, in contrast to other poets and playwrights. Shakespeare took no interest in the publication of his works, and we have already discussed the far-fetched suppositions that the plays immediately went into the property of the actors' company.

Thus, everything is consistent in the revisions to "Hamlet." After Rutland's mission to Denmark, the text was revised, enlarged almost two-fold, and enhanced with specific details about Danish life. Various notions have been offered to explain how these details found their way into the work; some scholars even speculate that Shakespeare accompanied the Earl of Rutland during his visit to Denmark. I think that such a supposition is closer to the truth than others, though it would obviously be no use looking for the name of William Shakespeare in the list of Rutland's fellow travelers.

Only the biography of the Earl of Rutland makes it possible to understand how the author of "Hamlet" was able to learn so much about the customs and special details of life at the royal court of Denmark between the first and second editions of the play. While at Elsinore, the earl certainly met Rosencrantz and Guildenstern[38] again. Having analyzed these and other facts related to the two "Hamlet" Quartos and their texts, C. Demblon concluded that the play could only have been written by the Earl of Rutland. To put it more carefully, the play "Hamlet" could have been written either by Rutland himself or by someone very close to him, his spiritual and intellectual confidant.

## THE POETS OF BELVOIR VALE

Upon his return from Denmark, Roger Manners, Earl of Rutland, former student of Cambridge, Oxford and Padua, stayed at his Belvoir home, visiting court as infrequently as possible. He was often ill and only from time to time would "make those flights upon the banks of Thames" or visits to the universities, though he maintained steady contact with them.

In December, 1603, Rutland stayed at Wilton House — the Countess of Pembroke's estate, where the king came to watch "As You Like It"; this is the visit about which the Countess wrote to her son, asking him to bring the king, saying, "we have the man Shakespeare with us." Again, what a coincidence.

---

38. Few people know that the name Guildenstern is related not only to "Hamlet" but also to the history of Russia. In the autumn of 1602, Duke Johan of Schleswig-Holstein, brother of Danish King Christian IV, came to Moscow with a great retinue. Tsar Boris Godunov was planning to marry his daughter Ksenia to the duke. And now, among the duke's retinue we find the Danish nobles Aksel and Laksman Gieldenstern. However, soon after his arrival in Muscovy, Duke Johan fell ill and died, and his retinue returned to Denmark. In 1911, Aksel Guildenstern's extant notes about this mission were published in Russian by Yu. N. Sherbachiov.

In 1604, Rutland went to Oxford to participate in the formal ceremony conferring the Master of Arts degree upon the Prince of Wales, the young heir to the throne, in the king's presence. Many of the prince's tutors and teachers were close friends of the earl.

In addition to his illness and his financial worries, Rutland had difficulty with his Catholic brothers, especially the younger, Oliver, who was indirectly involved in the notorious Gunpowder Plot. The conspirators tunneled under the palace at Westminster and concealed in the basement of the building dozens of barrels of gunpowder. They planned to blow it up on November 5, 1605, when the king was to open the session of Parliament. Wishing to spare the lives of some of the lords, they warned them to keep away from Parliament that day — and that is how the plotters were caught. Curiously, among those whose lives the conspirators sought to spare was the Earl of Rutland; he was in no way connected with their designs.

At about this time, 1605-1606, Rutland was planning to leave England and travel for several years, but his poor health prevented it; this was the time when "King Lear" and "Macbeth" were created.

The nature of the relationship between the Earl of Rutland and his wife gradually ceased to be a secret, first among their friends and then generally. This, naturally, gave rise to rumors and idle gossip, which was unpleasant for the Lord of Belvoir and did nothing to encourage his cheery mood and sociability. Despite this and also the fact that Elizabeth often stayed away from Belvoir, the couple gathered around them an intimate circle of poets and playwrights including Ben Jonson, George Chapman, John Harington, Samuel Daniel, John Marston, Michael Drayton, Thomas Overbury, Thomas Campion, Francis Beaumont, John Fletcher, and women poets and patronesses like Elizabeth's aunt Mary Sidney Pembroke, her cousin Mary Roth, and her friends Lucy Harington, Countess of Bedford, and Anne Clifford, Countess of Dorset. And, of course, the Rutlands' constant and loyal friend — Mary's older son, William Herbert, Earl of Pembroke.

Ben Jonson used to visit the Rutlands, especially when they were staying in their London residence. To all appearances, his relations with the Earl of Rutland were not easy. On the one hand, he adored Philip Sidney's daughter, entertained her, and made every effort to be useful in her literary activities. On the other, Rutland did not trust him much, knowing his weakness for the gifts of Bacchus and his inability to hold his tongue after a good libation. This view is supported by an episode Jonson related to the poet Drummond, many years after the death of the Belvoir couple.

One day, Jonson was sitting at the table with the Countess of Rutland when her spouse came in. Later on, Elizabeth informed Jonson that he had rebuked her that she "kept table to poets" — or so the apparently offended Jonson put it afterwards. Having received Elizabeth's note, Jonson sent her a reply, which somehow fell into Rutland's hands. As far as can be seen, the episode had no consequences, but Ben Jonson did not forget it. Many scholars, noting Jonson's complicated and contradictory attitude to Shakespeare, have suggested that he was jealous of the other, far more talented, writer.

In many of his epigrams, addresses and other "verses on the occasion" abound in the names of everyone known to him, Jonson never overtly addressed the Earl of Rutland or mentioned his name. And when addressing Elizabeth Sidney Rutland in his poem, Jonson demonstratively interrupted himself in mid-phrase, rather than naming her spouse — and so the poem appeared in print — though that happened some years after Rutland's death. This silence was not due to Jonson's and other authors' reluctance to address the Earl of Rutland openly but because the name was taboo to them, at least from the early 1600s onward. And they maintained their silence, even after these amazing spouses both had quit this world.

Now that we know whom the authors of Chester's collection were mourning, we can also discern the always shadowy Rutlands and their poetic friends behind disguises in Jonson's pastoral play, "The Sad Shepherd, or a Tale of Robin-hood," a work which is commonly considered to be "obscure," being perhaps unfinished or incomplete, in the version that survived to 1640 when it was first published (i.e. after Jonson's death).

The play's action takes place at Sherwood Forest, the masters of which, Robin Hood and Maid Marian, invite to their feast a few guests whom Jonson calls the "shepherds [that is to say, poets] of Belvoir Vale." Readers of the play naturally associate the name Robin Hood with the image of the "kindly robber of Sherwood Forest" (the legendary folklore hero whose name is transcribed, traditionally but wrongly, in Russian as Robin "Good"). Studying Jonson's play, however, Robin's way of life, his occupation and his whole environment belie these customary associations.[39] Rather than a traditional brigand (the play does not, in fact, mention any of his "brigand's feats") the Jonson character is a noble lord surrounded by a large retinue including a chaplain, a bailiff, a steward, and special servants at his forest residence. His guests are refined poets and poetesses who live in a world of their own concerns and interests.

Ninety years ago, F. G. Fleay had already shown that the "The Sad Shepherd" was more than a purely pastoral work based on the motifs of the Robin Hood legend and characters who allegedly had no prototypes in the author's epoch. Basing his view on a score of conclusive proofs, Fleay identified the main heroes of the play with the Earl and Countess of Rutland. He noted " . . . the palpable identity of Robin and Maid Marian as possessors of Belvoir and Sherwood, with Roger, Earl of Rutland and Elizabeth, Countess of Rutland (for Belvoir was their seat and the Earl was Justice in Eyre of Sherwood Forest, its master)."[40] As for the name of "His Lady, the Mistris" —

---

39. In the play, Robin Hood is called "The chiefe Wood-man, Master of the Feast," and his name is hyphenated — Robin-hood. With the word "hood" thus emphasized, the name may be literally interpreted as "Masked Robin" or "Robin's Mask." In his play "Kings entertainment at Welbeck," Jonson provides an entire list of Robin's masks (hoods): red, green, blue, brown, orange, motley. There are different theories about the extent of Robin Hood's authenticity in history, and about the origin of his name. Here I focus on the name's meaning as emphasized by Ben Jonson.

Maid Marian, Jonson could not have meant it as a reference to the next Countess of Rutland (after 1612), the wife of Francis, who had a normal family and children.

By now, it is even more clear that the relationship of Jonson's Robin and Maid Marian,[41] masters of Belvoir and Sherwood Forest, mirrors the platonic relationship of the Turtle and Phoenix, the heroes of Robert Chester's poetic collection. And the guests of the forest masters treat them with timid adoration because they are the "wonder of the world, its renowned voice." Poet Clarion says: "Robin and his Marian, are the Summe and Talke/ Of all, that breath here in the Greene-wood Walke." And other poets add: "In Be'voir Vale! The Turtles of the Wood! The billing Paire!" Clarion also mentions their lofty deeds, their writings which can be compared with the best models of classical literature; and these words, which do not fit with the Robin Hood legends, resonate with the same sense of admiration that Jonson expressed in his epistles to Elizabeth Rutland and what he told Drummond in 1619 about her poetic talent.

Moreover, Jonson notified Drummond that he had written a "pastoral" entitled "May Lord" (this very strange title[42] may be interpreted either as the "Lord of May" or as the "Lord-Maid"), that in this pastoral he portrayed himself under the name Alkin, and depicted quite a group of persons including Elizabeth, Countess of Rutland, her cousins Lucy, Countess of Bedford, and Mary Wroth, her aunt Mary, Countess of Pembroke, and Thomas Overbury (all are poets), as well as the old Countess of Suffolk (in the image of the Witch) and her daughter Frances, who used to scheme against Elizabeth Rutland. This list is revealing in itself: the author explicitly confirms that his works (even the "pastorals") reflect actual contemporary events and had real prototypes well known to him, which means it should be possible for us to identify them.

No pastoral (play or poem) under the title of "May Lord" is known to us; perhaps Jonson renamed it at some point, and introduced some minor changes. In that case, "The Sad Shepherd" (which we may now interpret as "The Sad Poet") seems to fit the bill — and it is the only pastoral play by Ben Jonson that we know. And in this play we actually do come across the sage Alken, whose advice everybody respectfully seeks, as well as the witch of Papplewicke and her conniving daughter. Such characters are met

---

40. A significant topographical detail: Belvoir and the small valley bearing its name are located not on the territory that was then Sherwood Forest, but in Leicestershire, across the Trent River. And the only link between Sherwood and Belvoir are the Rutlands, owners of Belvoir and lords of Sherwood Forest. Therefore the mention of the "poets of Belvoir Vale" (where the ancient castle was the only hearth and home of culture) in the play, located at Sherwood Forest, can only relate to the Rutlands and their friends.

41. Maid Marian is now assumed to be the traditional character in some Robin Hood legends; but she first appeared at Robin's side not long before Jonson's "The Sad Shepherd" came out, in the play by Anthony Munday and Henry Chettle.

42. Some critics assume that Drummond made a mistake in recording the pastoral's name; however, the same name — May Lord — occurs in Jonson's play "Kings Entertainment at Welbeck," where the author praises Sherwood Forest. Thus, Drummond wrote the name correctly.

nowhere else in Jonson's works. In his 1905 debates with Fleay, the Shakespeare expert W. W. Greg admitted that "If it could be shown that, in drawing the characters of Robin and Marian, the author had any topical intention, we should have little difficulty in identifying them with the Rutlands; if, on the other hand, we knew that the Rutlands appeared in the play, we should at once say they could be none other than Robin and Marian. But we can be sure of neither."[43] It was difficult for Greg, known for his academic caution, to make a definite identification due to the lack of precise information at that time as to the date of Elizabeth Rutland's death — he personally accepted the wrong date of 1615, as stated in the Dictionary of National Biography. Thus, when he was working on Jonson's pastoral, he knew nothing about the Rutlands' almost simultaneous deaths, not to mention other facts relating to these mysterious figures, so close to Shakespeare and Jonson, that have come to light only in the course of more recent studies.

Today at last we have some additional facts to give us confidence in identifying Jonson's heroes. In combination with Drummond's notes, Jonson's epistles to Elizabeth Rutland, and particularly with Chester's collection, the contents of "The Sad Shepherd" testify that behind the masks of Robin and Maid Marian, like those of the Turtle and Phoenix, the author depicted the friends and patrons of the "poets of Belvoir Vale" — the real masters of Sherwood Forest, whose amazing alliance resulted in the summer of 1612 in their mystical and shocking union in death.

The poetic cycle "Underwoods," published in 1640, after Ben Jonson's death, comprises a poem named "A Celebration of Charis in Ten Lyric Pieces."[44] Jonson tells of an amazing woman whose beauty and wit refine and ennoble all she meets; he calls her his star, his goddess. "For this beauty yet doth hide, / something more than thou hast spied." Despite some promising hints, the prototype of this heroine was left unidentified by the pundits. But perhaps the task was absolutely hopeless? No! Analyzing the poem's sixth part, we hear the poet recall how he earned Charis' kiss "for what my Muse and I have done," and this occurred after a performance at the Royal Palace when

> . . . *the bride (allowed a maid)*
> *Look'd not half so fresh, and fair,*
> *With the advantage of her hair,*
> *And her jewels, to the view*
> *Of the assembly, as did you!*
> *Or, that did you sit, or walk,*
> *You were more the eye and talk*
> *Of the court, to-day, than all*
> *Else that glister'd in Whitehall . . .*

---

43. *Materialen zur Kunde des alteren Englishchen Dramas.* Louvain. 1905. Bd. 2. *Ben Jonson's Sad Shepherd.* Ed. by W.W.Greg. S. XIV - XVI.

44. See: Jonson B. Ed.by G.Parfitt. *The Complete Poems*, p. 126.

What festivity at the royal palace of Whitehall, related to Ben Jonson's activities and to a bride, eclipsed by Charis, could the author have in mind? Surely, this has to do with the performance of one of his play-masques[45] at Whitehall, and the reference to a bride makes it possible to definitely ascertain that Jonson is recalling none other than the splendid festivities at court on January 5, 1606. On this day all the nobility of England, with the royal family at the head, performed the masque-play "Hymenaei" specially written by Ben Jonson for the occasion of the marriage of young Robert, Earl of Essex (son of the mutineer executed in 1601, and the half-brother of Elizabeth Rutland), to the no less young Frances, daughter of the Earl of Suffolk. The costumes and scenic effects for the masque were developed by the famous architect Inigo Jones, and the music was composed by Alfonso Ferrabosco. This is the only wedding-masque by Jonson performed at Whitehall.

Immediately after the ceremonies, the 14-year-old bridegroom was sent to continue his education on the Continent, while young Frances was left home under the supervision of her mother, the Countess of Suffolk. The supervision turned out to be none too strict, and Frances failed to resist the temptations of the high and courtly life. Her admirers included the crown prince himself, but it was the king's favorite, the Scotsman Robert Carr, who became the object of her true passion. Upon his return to England several years later, the young Earl of Essex attempted to come into his conjugal rights, but Frances left him and threw in her lot with Carr forever. After a scandalous divorce suit (Frances and her supporters claimed that the Earl of Essex was impotent, and to "verify" this allegation a special commission of courtly ladies was established to examine Frances — whose face was covered by veil); the king, who was quite unable to stand up to any of his favorites' requests, sanctioned the annulment of this marriage that had been contracted under his own auspices. Frances was free to marry Carr.

Poet Thomas Overbury, an old friend of Carr, did not think much of the latter's desire to marry the divorcée, whom he saw as a shallow and dangerous person. All these events were directly related to Jonson's "Sad Shepherd," which included the poet Overbury, and the Countess of Suffolk and her daughter among the characters. Overbury's poem "A Wife," describing an ideal woman, is believed to have been written with the intention of steering his friend away from a marriage he thought was a poor risk; the model presented sounds like a poetic portrait of Elizabeth Rutland, of whom Overbury was enamoured — according to Ben Jonson. At Overbury's request, Jonson read (or gave) "A Wife" to Elizabeth, and said a few words in favor of the poem's author. Elizabeth kept in mind some lines from the poem. Thus, Carr's enterprising lady-friend had reason to view Overbury as her personal enemy; neither did she waste any affection on the sister-in-law whose virtues Overbury praised in

---

45. Play-masques were a sort of a ballet-pantomime; they were staged at court with the participation of the highest nobles of the kingdom.

contrast to her. Clearly, of this troubled trio (the Earl of Essex — Frances — Carr), Elizabeth Rutland sympathized with her brother; and realizing this, the Suffolks sought to weave some intrigue against the Rutlands and their entourage. In this context the characters of the old witch and her daughter plotting against Maid Marian become quite clear.

In 1613, after the Belvoir couple had died, Overbury, slandered by Carr, was sent to the Tower, and while imprisoned there he was poisoned to death with the direct involvement of Frances. It later came out that the poison had been administered to him with his meals, over a long period of time, after which stronger doses were injected — passed off as the medical treatment prescribed by his doctor. The poet died in terrible pain, and was buried, but the murderers were not able to keep their crime secret. More and more details of the murder were made public, and even the influence of the king's favorite was not enough to suppress the voices of the murdered poet's friends. In 1614, Carr and Frances were made the Earl and Countess of Somerset, but in 1616 they were found guilty of murder and spent the next six years in the same place where their victim had languished — at the Tower. Their untitled direct accomplices were hanged. Much in this dreadful story remains unclear, including the position of King James and his relationship with Carr, as well as the role of Thomas Campion — physician, prominent poet, composer and a close friend of the Rutlands.

Overbury's works were first published in 1614 and then went through several editions. In addition to "A Wife," the collection included his "Characters" and other works, plus many poems by the friends of the dead poet; they mourned his premature demise and demanded retribution. In nine years the book appeared in ten editions. And then, in 1622, the eleventh edition appeared, with Francis Beaumont's elegy on the death of the Countess of Rutland, which had been published nowhere before. The fact that the elegy appeared *on the tenth anniversary* of the Belvoir spouses' deaths, and in this book in particular, clearly confirms that the sensational Overbury case was a continuation of the tragic story of the leading lights of the "poets of Belvoir Vale."[46]

The festivities at Whitehall on January 5, 1606, lingered long in the memory of its participants, and not in memory alone. Some letters have survived, in which contemporaries described the event, and what is more important — the quarto book printed the same year by Valentine Simmes for publisher Thomas Thorpe, the same one who later, in 1609, would publish *Shake-Speares Sonnets*. This first edition of the play-masque "Hymenaei" provides very telling details (which Jonson omitted in later editions, after the bride's adultery was disclosed and after the scandalous divorce). The book also lists the names of the eight noble ladies, in the order they in which they

---

46. Ironically, the ill-fated poet Thomas Overbury was later related to Shakespeare's biography in another strange way. In the 18th century, a forger "converted" Overbury's (the so-called Janssen) portrait into a "portrait of Shakespeare" (with its elongated forehead, etc.), and such a depiction appeared in many editions of the Great Bard's works. In the 20th century the Folger Shakespeare Library in Washington, D.C. acquired the portrait. Several decades later, experts ascertained that it was a forgery.

stood on stage, in pairs, on both sides of the queen. One such pair was Elizabeth, Countess of Rutland, and her cousin and close friend Lucy, Countess of Bedford.

We know that in 1936 Newdigate, having found the manuscript copy of Ben Jonson's "Ode Enthusiastic," with an inscription "To Lucy, Countess of Bedford," assumed that she was the prototype of the Phoenix in Chester's collection. The same year he published the Shakespeare poem "The Phoenix and the Turtle" with a copy of the old, so-called Woburn portrait of Lucy Bedford, in the costume of the "Hymenaei" masque.

But besides the Woburn portrait there is also one known as the Welbeck,[47] portraying another of the ladies who participated in the play. That these ladies are represented in their "Hymenaei" costumes is proved by extant descriptions of the play's decorations and costumes. The Welbeck portrait pictures a lovely young woman with a slightly elongated face, auburn hair in small ringlets, and intent dark eyes. She stands against a stage backdrop — a flying cloud pierced with light emanating from the right upper corner. Her left arm rests on her thigh. The hair is pinned up with a precious adornment in the form of a small crown, from which a transparent veil falls. On the left side the hair is embellished with a white egret plume. The splendid apparel includes a white jacket ornamented with lace and golden embroidery, a strawberry-colored bodice, a short red upper skirt and long petticoat of bluish-green. Red stockings with golden clocks and blue shoes with red rosettes make the last touches to the attire. Her neck is adorned with a pearl necklace set with diamonds. Many details of the young lady's costume and footwear are decorated with precious stones and golden embroidery.

The Welbeck and Woburn ladies are dressed quite similarly, a circumstance which led to the Welbeck portrait being mistaken for a second portrait of Lucy Bedford.[48] But the faces of the young ladies are so dissimilar that one has to conclude that they are different women. Besides — the Welbeck lady is turned slightly to the right, and her egret plume is fixed on the left side of her hair, while the Woburn lady is looking somewhat to the left, and her plume is on the right. Clearly they stood on different sides of the queen, in accordance with Ben Jonson's scenario. Lucy Bedford, the Woburn portrait, stood to the right of the queen. We have other images of her which confirm the identification. The lady in the Welbeck portrait stood on the opposite side. C. H. Hereford and Evelyn and Percy Simpson, the most prominent authorities on Ben Jonson, came to the conclusion that the lady portrayed in the Welbeck canvas must be Elizabeth Rutland.[49] The scholars expressed their regret that there were no other paintings of the Countess of Rutland to compare to the

---

47. The portraits are called Woburn and Welbeck after the estates where they were kept in the 19th century

48. The portrait was also taken to be an image of Mary Fitton, mistress of the Earl of Pembroke, whom some Shakespeare scholars have believed to be the mysterious "Dark Lady" of the sonnets. Recently the portrait was even presented as such in an illustrated calendar. However, Mary Fitton did not take part in the performance of the "Hymenaei" masque.

Welbeck portrait; however, there is an obvious similarity between the face in this portrait and the image of Elizabeth's mother, Frances Walsingham, in the well-known portrait by William Segar[50] dating back to 1590,[51] when Frances was twenty years old, that is, the same age as her daughter at the time of this event in 1606. The face depicted in the Welbeck portrait is also quite similar to the face of Elizabeth Rutland's sculpture on the Bottesford tombstone.

The Welbeck portrait features another intriguing detail — the diamonds on Elizabeth Rutland look dark, almost black. Connoisseurs are at a loss to provide any definite opinion on the cause of such a strange phenomenon: either the lacquer or the pigment in this single instance happened to be low-grade and did not survive over time, or, perhaps at request of the clients, the artist intentionally painted this unique woman's diamonds in dark colors to hide their shine!

"A Celebration of Charis" and the play-masque "Hymenaei" are in many ways a continuation of the Jonson play that appeared as early as 1600, "Cynthia's Revels," full of allusions to Elizabeth Sidney, who had just become the Countess of Rutland. In his intriguing dedication, as also in some other instances of the play, Jonson plays up the semantic meaning of the Rutlands' surname — "Manners." The mention of Apollo, "who now guides Synthia," implicitly alludes to Elizabeth's recent marriage; she is also addressed in the author's inscription: "Thy servant, but not slave." A gift copy of the play has been found, with Jonson's dedicatory inscription to Lucy Bedford — "to Cynthia's fairest Nimph." Everyone knew that Elizabeth and Lucy were close friends. Another inscription from Jonson to Lucy, in the manuscript copy of the "Ode Enthusiastic" which was published later on, in Chester's *Love's Martyr*, when Jonson was out of England, testifies to the fact that the book was published with the Countess of Bedford's assistance.

Jonson's Charis, Elizabeth Rutland, was in the spotlight at the festivities at Whitehall on the occasion of her young brother's marriage. After the ascension of King James, Lucy Bedford was a permanent fixture at court entertainments, and her presence near the queen would not have surprised anyone. What actually made a stir was the appearance at the palace and the participation in the staged festivity of Philip Sidney's daughter, whose odd relations with her husband were apparently known to everybody by that time (and some people perhaps knew even more about the Belvoir couple). And therefore it was not surprising that all eyes were fastened on her, and the young wife-poet eclipsed all and sundry, including the bride.

Elizabeth's first and last participation in a royal pageant was clearly an exciting event that left a long-lasting impression on this book lover and forest recluse. The

---

49. See: *Jonson, B.* Ed. C.H. Hereford, P. and E. Simpson. Oxford, 1925-1952. Vol. 7, p. 208-209, XV - XIX; vol. 10, p. 465-468.

50. The painting, which is now in the US, has an interesting history. In the 19th century it was believed to be a portrait of Mary Stuart, and was even provided with an inscription to that effect.

51. See: Auerbach E. *Nicolas Hilliard.* L., 1961, p. 275. Pl 242 - portrait reproduction.

Rutlands' steward recorded considerable expenses — over 1000 pounds sterling — for the costumes and footwear for the masque and for the three-week stay at Whitehall (from December 16, 1605 to January 8, 1606[52]), which shows how long the rehearsals went on. Most likely, the portraits of Lucy Bedford and Elizabeth Rutland were painted just then, and one may imagine the anxiety and excitement experienced by the 20-year-old woman and her loyal poetic page Ben Jonson. He recollected these days with a sad smile many years later when Elizabeth Rutland, his Muse, his Charis, the incomparable Phoenix, was already long since gone to the Elysian Fields, and the festivities of 1606 were recalled only by a slender book — the first quarto of "Hymenaei," and by the echoes of the tragic events that came after.

In one of his elegies,[53] some allusions of which incline me to think that it was also addressed to Elizabeth Rutland, Jonson emphasizes that he is under a vow not to mention her name:

> *And such your servant is, who vows to keep*
> *The jewel of your name, as close, as sleep*
> *Can lock the sense up, or the heart a thought...*

And in the same elegy:

> *. . . sometime by stealth*
> *Under another name, I take your health...*


## THE COUNTESS OF PEMBROKE — MISTRESS OF POETIC ARCADIA IN FOGGY ALBION

In the earlier story about the Rutlands, Chester's book, and "The Sad Shepherd," we touched on Mary Sidney, who became Countess of Pembroke. This is a woman whose role in the history of English literature and in the creative formation of Shakespeare is becoming clearer only today.

We would know very little about this remarkable woman if it were not for the biographies of her brother, the most prominent poet of the English Renaissance, Philip Sidney. Studying his life and works, scholars inevitably come across Mary Sidney Pembroke. Paradoxically, it is only owing to her, to her talent, hard work and unselfish love, that future generations (including biographers) ever had a chance to read the works of Philip Sidney. As for her own immortality she, curiously enough, did not

---

52. All the dates in the book are given in accordance with the Gregorian calendar that was introduced in England only in the mid-18th century. Prior to that (including, thus, Shakespearean times) the New Year began on March 25.

53. In accordance with the numeration, adopted by Jonson scholars, it is elegy XL. See: Jonson, B. Ed.by G.Parfitt. *The Complete Poems*, p. 177-178.

Lucy Harington, Countess of Bedford, Elizabeth Sidney Rutland's closest friend, attired as a participant of the play-masque "Hymenai"

Elizabeth Sidney, Countess of Rutland, in a costume
for the play-masque "Hymenai"

worry at all; moreover, she rather seemed to take care that her name should always stay in the background. It was only in the early 20th century that researchers began to take notice of Mary Sidney Pembroke's contemporaries' opinions concerning her, her manuscripts and the lists of her works and letters — and gradually an amazing, multi-talented person came into view, together with her great contribution to the cultural treasury of not only Shakespearean England but of mankind as a whole.

An epitaph on the death of Mary Sidney was written by the poet William Browne of Tavistock, author of "Britannia's Pastorals":

> *Underneath this sable herse*
> *Lies the subject of all verse:*
> *Sidney's sister, Pembroke's mother.*
> *Death, ere thou hast slain another,*
> *Fair and learn'd, and good as she,*
> *Time shall throw a dart at thee.*[54]

Other contemporary writers and poets spoke of her in the same vein. For Edmund Spenser she was the "sister unto Astrophel, Urania, whose brave mind, as in a golden coffer, all heavenly gifts locked are." Samuel Daniel praised her for preserving English literature "from the hideous bestes — Oblivion and Barbarisme." Gabriel Harvey, in his pamphlet against Thomas Nashe, wrote that the Countess of Pembroke, if she only wished, could in a month demonstrate more works than Nashe wrote in his whole lifetime. Poet John Harington, in a private letter, wrote that: "In Poesie she is the mirror of our Age." Nathaniel Baxter called her poetic art god-like and likened it to Homer's. In "Wits Treasury," as we have already seen, Francis Meres said that she surpassed the poetess Sappho. Emilia Lanyer (we shall come across the name further on) mentions in her work the "many books she (the Countess of Pembroke) writes that are more rare." Walter Sweeper speaks of her home as a small university, while John Aubrey would write a century later that Wilton House, the home of Countess Pembroke, "was like a college . . ." These exalted praises (the list is far from complete) by no means rank as mere compliments — Mary Sidney is extolled not only as a patroness of the arts and literature, but above all as an author, an outstanding writer and poet.

This evidence, dispersed in various books by her contemporaries which were not reprinted and for the most part had fallen into oblivion, began to be conceived in the aggregate only in the past 100 years. The first work to concentrate on Mary Sidney came out in 1912 and was written by Francis Young. Further extensive studies on her appeared only in recent times (Ringler, Ratmell, Waller)[55]; manuscripts have been discovered with biblical psalms she translated, testifying to her years of work on them and serving as a good illustration of her creative capability.

---

54. *The Oxford Anthology of English Literature.* The Literature of Renaissance England. L., 1973, p. 597.

Mary Sidney, Countess of Pembroke

The poetess was born in 1561, to the family of Sir Henry Sidney, belonging to the so-called new nobility that replaced the ancient feudal families who had extirpated each other in the War of the Roses. Her mother came from the renowned Dudley family (the Earl of Leicester, favorite of Queen Elizabeth, was her mother's brother). Mary spent her childhood in Kent, at Penshurst, which Ben Jonson poetized later in the lyrical cycle "The Forest," where he also placed two poems from Chester's collection and his epistle to Elizabeth Rutland.

Contrary to her brothers, who were sent to school and to university, Mary was educated at home. The teaching found very fertile soil: the girl devoured every bit of knowledge, and demonstrated very early not only an interest in literature but an exceptional poetic gift, as well as an aptitude for music and foreign languages (French, Italian, Latin, Greek). At age fourteen, she accompanied her mother as a maid of honor and addressed Queen Elizabeth with her own poem, which George Gascoigne witnessed and noted in his own verse:

> . . . *young in years, yet olde in wit*
> *A gest dew to your race,*
> *If you hold on as you begine,*
> *Who ist youle not deface?*

As was customary at the time, she was married early, at the age of 15, to the rich and influential widower Henry Herbert, 2$^{nd}$ Earl of Pembroke, who is known in the history of the English theater as the patron of an actors company.[56] She moved to the Pembroke estate, Wilton House (Wiltshire, on the Avon River), which later on would gradually turn into the most significant literary center in England, and would deservedly be named as a "small university."

Upon his return from the Continent in 1577, her brother Philip Sidney stayed at Wilton House for long periods of time; there he created his "Arcadia" (later known as "The Countess of Pembroke's Arcadia"), "The Defense of Poesie" and other works. Her other brother, Robert, whose poems were found and published just recently, inscribed a manuscript book of his poems: "For my sister, the Countess of Pembroke." Here at Wilton, Philip Sidney reflected on the innovations needed to give an incentive to the development of English poetry, to raise it to the level of contemporary Italian and

---

55. See: Ringler W.A. (Jr.). *The Poems of Sir Ph. Sidney.* Oxford, 1962.

*The Psalms of Sir Philip Sidney and the Countess of Pembroke.* Ed.J.C.A.Ratmell. N.Y., 1963.

*Triumph of Death and other unpublished and uncollected poems by Mary Sidney, Countess of Pembroke.* Ed. G.F. Waller. Salzburg, 1977.

Waller G.F. *Mary Sidney, Countess of Pembroke: A critical study of her writing and literary milieu.* Salzburg, 1979.

56. This patronage was initiated when Mary became the mistress of the earl's home. Some scholars believe that Shakspere was among the players of the Earl of Pembroke, or had some relationship with the company in the early 1590s.

French poetry, to the level of Petrarch and Ronsard. He shared these plans and ideas with his sister, who became his student and confidante. Sidney used to note that, compared with Continental humanists, the English writers, and notably the poets, looked provincial. "Why England the Mother of excellent mindes should be growne so hard a stepmother to Poets?" he asked. About the lyrical poetry of his predecessors and some of his contemporaries, he remarked: "If I were a mistress, [they] would never persuade me they were in love."

Many poets and writers began coming to Wilton House for long stays. By the 1590s, hardly any prominent English poet or playwright failed to have some connection with the Wilton circle. The writers who stayed at Wilton composed and discussed their works; sometimes several persons wrote on a certain subject, and a kind of poetic contest ensued. Members of the circle corresponded with each other and extant letters give the impression of a formal, organized structure. Later on, some years after Philip Sidney's death, the poets of Belvoir Vale left the "university," but they never broke their ties with Wilton House.

Wilton-generated innovations enriched the English vocabulary, extended the imagery and expressiveness of the poetic language, eased earlier strict rules governing techniques of versification, and introduced Renaissance humanistic ideas into English literature. These innovations became widespread, and within a comparatively short time changed the face of the English literature in the late Elizabethan and early Jacobean periods.

The tragic death of Philip Sidney in 1586, at age 32, was a crucial event in the life of his sister (her father and mother died the same year). From this point on, the main aim of Mary's life was to preserve, edit and publish Philip Sidney's literary heritage, and to continue his cause — and this was truly a great deed of dedication and love. In his lifetime, Philip Sidney never published (and never prepared for print) his works, and at his death they mostly remained incomplete. Moreover, as he was dying, he asked her to destroy his manuscripts.

Mary did not quite find it within herself to do that; instead, she undertook to carry out the titanic work of saving her brother's literary heritage. She did an enormous job to edit and complete "Arcadia," and penned many poetic insets and some portion of the prosaic material. This book, whose role in the history of English literature is hard to exaggerate, was published in 1593 by the printer W. Ponsonby (the same who was sometimes referred to as the "court printer" of Mary Sidney). That same year the "Defense of Poesie" came out, and in 1598, a collection of Philip Sidney's works. The 1593 poetic collection "The Phoenix' Nest," containing the Wilton circle's elegies on the death of Philip Sidney, is also worth noting; many of the verses were addressed to the poet's disconsolate sister. In 1595, along with Spenser's "Astrophel," "The Doleful Lay of Clorinda," commonly believed to be written by Mary herself, was printed. Her efforts to preserve the works and perpetuate the memory of Philip Sidney took up at least twelve years of her life (of course, she had some assistance in this work, but she did the bulk of it). And in the many years that followed, she worked to complete the translation into English verse of the biblical psalms that he had begun.

Thus the works of Philip Sidney reached the reading public. Many of his contemporaries considered him a poetic demigod, and epithets such as "divine," "great" or "god-like" were often added to his name.

Mary Sidney's beautiful translations from French of Philippe de Mornay's "A Discourse of Life and Death" and Robert Garnier's tragedy "Marc Antonie" were printed in 1592, both accomplished at an artistic level unprecedented at that time. In 1593 she translated Petrarch's "Triumph of Death" from the Italian. (The manuscript of this translation has been found, and with it there is also a copy of the poet John Harington's letter to his sister Lucy, Countess of Bedford, where he offers to her attention some psalms rendered by Mary Sidney and refers to the owner of Wilton House as the "mirror of our Age in Poesie.") She translated other works by Petrarch as well, but these have not yet been found.

Through her translations, Mary Sidney revealed a new poetic facility in the English language, previously considered inadequate to render the deeply emotional, musical poems of the Italian poet. In doing so, she also brought into the poem her personal feelings, her love and devotion for her brother, the unceasing pain of irrevocable loss, the ache which nothing can alleviate, to which only poetry opens a gateway to the all-reconciling eternity.

Of special significance are her translations of the psalms, that were copied over by various people and came to light at various times. These manuscripts illustrate Mary Sidney Pembroke's ongoing devotion to poetic work, and the gradual and impressive growth of her mastery. Philip Sidney managed to translate 43 psalms; his sister translated the remaining 107, and also partially revised some of his translations. Seeking to achieve greater expressiveness, she experimented with poetic form, using distiches, tercets, quatrains (most often) and combined stanzas. The rhyming is highly varied and includes complicated and rare variants; the same rhyme scheme rarely repeats and both male and female rhymes are used. In metrics she preferred the iambic verse, but also often tried out other forms. There are alphabetic verses (the initial letter of successive lines occurring in alphabetical order), and extremely complex acrostics. The poet seems to have set her mind on demonstrating the untapped potentials of the English language and its prosody, and often achieved this aim with amazing virtuosity. Some of the translated psalms exist in four or five different manuscript versions, created at different periods in time; the consecutive variants demonstrate a persistent process of editing and revision, including radical changes. It is apparent that by the end of this lifelong work, which was unique (and not only in her era), she appears to be by far the more mature master, confident in herself and her art, a great poet preceding Donne and Milton.

She is also known to have published a well-known pastoral dialogue in the anthology "A Poetical Rhapsody" (1602), which, like the "England's Helicon" collection (1600) included works by members of the Wilton circle. Both editions, like the earlier collection "The Phoenix' Nest," demonstrate a high polygraphic level.

Mary Sidney's connections and influence in the world of publishing have not yet been studied completely, but it is obvious that through her "court printer" Ponsonby and later through his disciple Edward Blount she directed the work of publishing the "orphaned" works of Philip Sidney and other seminal works that left a clear trail in the history of English culture. And, unusual for an aristocrat, Mary Sidney Pembroke received some income from the publication of her and her brother's works (unlike Shakespeare!). Ben Jonson in his comedy "Epicene" alludes to this fact.

Like Ben Jonson and her son William, 3$^{rd}$ Earl of Pembroke, who presented Shakespeare's sonnets to Thorpe, Blount's friend and assistant, Mary Sidney Pembroke knew the true Shakespeare well. For the alliance of Rutland with her niece was contracted with her blessing and under her aegis, and she assisted them in their secret service to Apollo and the Muses, during their lifetime and beyond.

The circumstances under which the Great Folio appeared in 1623, in which 20 of 37 plays by Shakespeare first appeared in print, show that Mary Sidney Pembroke was directly involved in the creation of this phenomenon of world culture.

The date itself stirred no curiosity — no one ever even tried to explain why the book was published in just that year, until three centuries later, in 1925, when a persistent Englishman perusing the yellowed pages of printer John Bill's catalogue for the Frankfurt Book Fair found the following line in the list of books intended for print in 1622 and for sale at the autumn fair of that year: "The Plays written by Mr. William Shakespeare, all in one volume, printed by Isaac Jaggard, in folio." Thus, comparatively recently, it became known that the book was scheduled to appear in 1622 (and nobody ever noticed that this date coincides with the tenth anniversary of the Rutlands' death). To all appearances, the people preparing the edition were in a great hurry to meet the deadline. But in October of 1621, when the work was in full swing, printing was suddenly halted. Only after a very long interruption the book was published, late in 1623. Neither the adherents of the Stratfordian approach nor their rival Oxfordians have any reasonable explanation for that. The fact is that work stopped just a few days after Mary Sidney Pembroke's sudden death of smallpox at the end of September, 1621.

Her son William — Earl of Pembroke, Lord Chamberlain and King's confidant — stepped into the void and induced Ben Jonson to take part in the project by placing him in the position of Master of Revels, which allowed him to handle both new and old plays at his own discretion. Edward Blount obviously participated in the edition from the very beginning. These and other facts (including the dedication of the volume to her sons) prove that Mary Sidney Pembroke originally played the same role in the creation of the First Folio as she had done in the publication of Philip Sidney's literary heritage — the role of an initiator, editor and, partially, co-author. This is the only possible explanation for the modifications in this edition, so surprising to Shakespeare scholars, which shows significant abridgements and extensive author's additions as well. Mary Sidney's participation in the promotion of the books dear to her heart could never be reduced to simple proofreading of other authors' texts. She always appeared as a rightful co-author, a participant of the creative literary process. That she provided that contribution to Philip Sidney's literary oeuvre has been commonly acknowledged, and now the time has come to acknowledge her role in the formation of the Great Bard.

One of Ben Jonson's most "difficult" works, but at the same time most promising for researchers, is the play "The Magnetic Lady" (1632), which was timed for the 20th anniversary of the Rutlands' death. The author tells an allegorical tale of a Project Generall, the "Surveyor" of which dies before completing the project. The nature of this Great Project becomes clear from the remark of one of its executors, the assistants of the "Surveyor of the Projects Generall": "That is my industry. /As it might be your reading, studies and counsell."

On September 25, 1621, Mary died; she was buried in Salisbury Cathedral, but her grave was not graced with any monument. Three centuries later, in 1964, during a Shakespearean anniversary, her compatriots mounted a plaque on the cathedral wall with the epitaph written on her death by one of the youngest poets of the "Wilton university," William Browne from Tavistock — the initial lines in this, my story about the remarkable woman who was Mary Sidney, Countess of Pembroke.

The writer Gabriel Harvey and Mary Sidney's other contemporaries affirmed that she published comparatively few of her works under her own name but, if she wished, could have shown many of them. What would those have been? In the mid-17th century, Wilton House was severely damaged by fire. Apparently, that reduced to ashes almost all its former proprietress' papers, documents that could have shed light on her other works that appeared in various times under other's names or pennames. It is also known that her descendants, who were indifferent to the history of literature, lost a significant portion of her manuscripts. (One gentleman bought a handwritten text with the translations of some psalms along with some other "old papers" — to wrap up coffee; fortunately, his brother was smart enough to make a copy of the text, which survived).

Several authentic portraits of Mary Sidney exist. The most interesting and significant of them dates back to 1614, when she was already 53 years old. A woman with a beautiful, strikingly spiritual face is portrayed; her deep gaze reveals the intense work of a mind directed at us across the ages. In the upper right corner an intriguing inscription notes, "No Spring till now." That may be read in various ways, including a vow of silence.

Today, the words addressed to her memory by the poet Samuel Daniel, who knew her well, take on a new meaning. He predicted that the art of Mary Sidney would outlive the centuries and burnish her name for generations to come.

## THE TRANSFIGURATION OF CAPTAIN LANYER'S WIFE

In 1973, British historian and Shakespeare scholar A. L. Rowse declared that he had found the final clue to the mystery of Shakespeare's sonnets, and that the Dark Lady who gave the Great Bard such heartache was a certain Emilia Lanyer. Working at Bodleian Library and studying the casebook of the astrologer and healer Simon Forman (1552-1611), in the entry relating to his client Emilia Lanyer, Rowse read the illegible word "brave" as "brown," and this misreading became the chief argument for his identification, an error passed over with a touch of humor by today's scholars.

But Lesley Rowse made another and, in my opinion far more useful, contribution. In 1978, he reissued an extremely rare poetic book first printed in 1611 and written, as its title page says, by "Aemilia Lanyer, wife to Captain Alfonso Lanyer."[57] Rowse provided a foreword and, for publicity purposes, titled the reprint as "The Poems of Shakespeare's Dark Lady." In his foreword he repeated his allegations that Emilia Lanyer was the unknown lady of the sonnets.[58] Regardless of Rowse's surmise, the book itself shows its author to be a paradoxical person, a gifted poet, erudite and intellectual, whose ideas often were ahead of her time, a woman who deserved the high honor of being a literary coeval of Shakespeare!

As to the silence that greeted the appearance of Emilia Lanyer's volume (there were no comments, in 1611 or later on), Rowse could explain this only by small number of copies printed.

Notes in Simon Forman's diary (of 1597 and 1600) do not characterize his client Emilia Lanyer in any way that could lead one to anticipate that she had any literary inclination or aptitude. Emilia was born in 1569 to the family of a court musician, the Italian Bassano; she died in 1645. According to the diary, she caught the eye of old Lord Chamberlain Hunsdon, a patron of the actors' company, who made her his mistress; and she had a son by him. In 1593, "for cover," Forman writes, she was married off to Alphonso Lanyer, a minor courtier who for some reason was thought suitable for such a role. There is no evidence of her involvement in literature or poetry. Forman depicts his client as a person of quite dubious repute, who made a show of her former liaison with the aged Lord Chamberlain (who died in 1596) in front of this healer-astrologer, and who wondered aloud whether she herself might ever become a "real lady." Forman, who did not hesitate to serve as a panderer himself, characterizes her unambiguously as a "whore." Afterwards, she received a pension, but who granted that pension and what for, is unknown.

---

57. *The Poems of Shakespeare's Dark Lady "Salve Deux Rex Judaeorum"* by Emilia Lanier. Introd. A.L. Rowse. L., 1978.

58. Rowse identified the Fair-Haired Friend with the Earl of Southampton; and in his typical impulsive way he referred to all other hypotheses about the meaning and heroes of the sonnets as "absolute rubbish."

Thus, it comes as quite a surprise that in 1611 such a "lady of the demimonde," disreputable even in the eyes of Forman, suddenly came out with a serious poetic book wherein she appears to the reader as an apologist for religious piety and moral purity, and intolerant of sin in all its manifestations. One can only assume that in the course of a few years she underwent a momentous metamorphosis which, however, in no way affected her further life. Equally surprising, she suddenly turns out to be a master of the poetic word that is rich in meaning, thought and knowledge. Rowse justly regards the writer of the work as the best (along with Mary Sidney Pembroke) English female poet of the Shakespearean age.

Printed by Valentine Simmes for publisher Richard Bonian (names that are familiar in relation to the first editions of some of Shakespeare's plays), the book opens with the author's prefatory poems addressed to certain noblewomen, beginning with Queen Anne and her daughter, Princess Elizabeth; then, the king's relative, Arabella Stuart, who would later enter into a secret marriage without the king's permission, would be imprisoned in the Tower for that reason and there suffer a mental breakdown. These are followed by the poem "To all Vertuous Ladies in Generall," and then several pieces (also in verse) addressed to the countesses of Pembroke, Kent, Cumberland, Suffolk, Bedford, and Dorset — to each lady individually. These dedications are distinguished by the nuances of the author's attitude to each of them. These differences and shades are especially important when it comes to persons who are known in the history of literature, such as Anne Clifford, then the Countess of Dorset; "Bright Lucy," the Countess of Bedford; and of course Mary Sidney Pembroke. The latter was addressed by the longest poem (56 quatrains), entitled "The Author's Dream to Lady Mary, the Countess Dowager of Pembroke." Such familiarity between the commoner Emilia Lanyer and the highest ladies in the land, including Her Majesty and her daughter, is shocking. Judging by the text, she is obviously acquainted with them, and the poems convey her high respect but not servility. Thus, in her dedication to Arabella Stuart, a lady of the royal blood, the author regrets that while she has known her for a long time, she yet does not know her so well as she would desire![59]

After these dedications the book proceeds with the epistle "To the Virtuous Reader," cunningly ironical, and finally with a 57-page poem, the one that provided the title for the whole volume: "Salve Deus Rex Judaeorum." This is followed by a poem entitled "The Description of Cooke-ham," the contents of which seem to be unrelated to the preceding one. And, finally, the book is completed with a few lines on a separate page, addressed "To the Doubtful Reader," who receives the lucid "explanation" that the poem's (and the volume's) title was delivered to her in her sleep, many years before!

In the title poem, particularly in the section entitled "Eve's Apology in Defense of Women," the author develops a system of ideas arguing that the position of women in

---

59. An extant copy of the book was bound in parchment bearing the Coat of Arms of Crown Prince Henry. Apparently, this copy was presented to the prince, which in itself says a lot.

the society of those days was unjust. Such publicly stated views were radical, even unique, for those days; we may aptly call Emilia Lanyer a proto-feminist.

Unmasking the ancient and medieval prejudices about woman as a center of sinfulness (a vessel of sin), the author also treats correspondingly the scriptural plot describing the expulsion of the first man and woman from Paradise. She argues (not without irony) that it was Adam, not Eve, who was culpable in the Fall; and that men in general are more inclined to sin than women, to whom they cause so much suffering, and then blame them for everything. Eve, who yielded to temptation, is justified by her love for Adam, her woman's weakness; but the man is stronger — no one could force him to eat the forbidden fruit if he himself did not want to. And how unfair (and unworthy of the first man) to shift the burden of his responsibility onto the shoulders of the weak and loving woman. "Yet Men will boast of Knowledge, which he tooke / From Eve's fair hand, as from a learned Booke!"

The poet calls on women to win back their dignity, and on men to realize that women are right, and not to hamper their cause.

> Then let us have our Libertie againe,
> And challenge to your selves no Sov'raignitie;
> You came not in the world without our paine,
> Make that a barre against your crueltie;
> Your fault being greater, why should you disdaine
> Our being your equals, free from tyranny?

The author again and again emphasizes the purity, generosity, faithfulness and immaculate reputation of a woman. In her story about the great heroines of the Old and New Testaments, she omits the character of Mary Magdalene. Proceeding to the women of Greco-Roman antiquity, and devoting many lines to Cleopatra and her tragic love for Antony, she nonetheless makes clear her admiration for the modest and chaste Octavia. And this idea is present everywhere in her poem. Beauty must be united with virtue.

All this is a poor match with Simon Forman's introduction to Emilia Lanyer in his diary. Indeed, the sincerity and moral purity of the poetess are beyond doubt — her personality, her spiritual inner world and moral assessments are always in the foreground. But Forman knew Emilia well; she repeatedly asked his advice and let him into her intimate secrets.

The poems and dedication demonstrate that the author was extremely learned, in fact, amazingly learned for a woman of low birth, which is testified by a multitude of free references and allusions to scriptures and Greek-Roman mythology, literature and history.

"The Dream" addressed to Mary Sidney Pembroke indicates that both poet-wives share a common spiritual outlook, and that the poem's author is close to the Sidneys. She reveres Philip Sidney's sister for the feat of preserving his poetic masterpieces and

# SALVE DEVS

## REX IVDÆORVM.

### *Containing,*

1 The Pafsion of Chrift.
2 Eues Apologie in defence of Women.
3 The Teares of the Daughters of Ierufalem.
4 The Salutation and Sorrow of the Virgine Marie.

With diuers other things not vnfit to be read.

Written by Miftris *Æmilia Lanyer*, Wife to Captaine
*Alfonfo Lanyer*, Seruant to the
Kings Majeftie.

AT LONDON

Printed by *Valentine Simmes* for *Richard Bonian*, and are
to be fold at his Shop in Paules Churchyard, at the
Signe of the Floure de Luce and
Crowne. 1611.

Title page from the book *Salve Deus Rex Iudaeorum*

presenting them to the world. She pronounces the name of Philip Sidney with a pious adoration and her voice breaks, she is so shaken by his sad lot even after so many years. She also knows well that the Countess of Pembroke is a poet, writer and translator of psalms and other works (although, as already mentioned, Mary published almost none of her works under her own name).

> *For to this Lady now I will repaire,*
> *Presenting her the fruits of idle houres;*
> *Though many Books she writes that are more rare,*
> *Yet there is honey in the meanest flowers...*

The author repeats Shakespeare's conception of the theatrical, ephemeral nature of human life, the image of the world as a playhouse:

> *For well you knowe, this world is but a Stage*
> *Where all do play their parts, and must be gone;*
> *Here's no respect of persons, youth, nor age,*
> *Death seizeth all, he never spareth one...*

Emilia Lanyer's poetic language is strikingly picturesque and abounds in rich vocabulary, euphuisms, rare word combinations and subtle nuances of inflection bearing various significant overtones. Though this was her only book, there is nothing amateurish about it. Many of the stanzas may justly be regarded as among the highest attainments of 17th-century poetry in England.

But it is not only for its poetic merits and the apologetics on feminine equality that the book deserves close study. The question of the author's identity is also of paramount importance. On the title page of this, her only book, oddly named as it is and issued in a very limited edition (which would have been rather expensive), she represents herself unpretentiously as "Mistris Aemilia Lanyer, Wife to Captaine Alfonso Lanyer, Servant to the Kings Majestie." The name never appeared again in printed literature nor manuscripts of the era, although she lived on for many years. None of her contemporaries mentions that she had any ties with literature, and the archives yield only documents on her material lawsuits. Similarly, there is no trace of such an author in the literary milieu of Mary Sidney Pembroke (to whom she addresses herself in such a confiding manner), or of Lucy Bedford.

All the texts, especially the prefatory poems, show that the authoress is no stranger to high society; she is thoroughly familiar with the subtleties and conventions of upper crust life and shares the class attitudes and aristocratic prejudices of the time. It is plainly stated, more than once, that the book is of course meant only for the noble and honorable ladies of the kingdom; other women (unless they are biblical or mythological characters) are simply beyond her field of vision — this is not her world. As to the ladies of noble blood, she talks with them as equals; she tutors them on how to behave and how to dress. There is an immense gap between the shady "lady of the demimonde" portrayed by Forman and the high moral standards and outright rejection of vice expounded by the volume's author.

All these facts combined lead to the conclusion that the name of the "Wife to Captaine Alfonso Lanyer," appearing in literature but properly belonging to it neither prior to nor after the work in question, was a hoax and part of the intricately involved Game (though in anticipation of future doubts to this effect, the author or publisher, apparently teasing, ended the book with a special address "To the Doubtful Reader").

Clearly, we would stand little chance of success in our search for the true author of the book if it were not for a few telling circumstances. In the England of those days, there were few lady-poets. If one selects from this number only those who personally and intimately knew each of the nine above-mentioned highest-ranking noble ladies of the kingdom, and, moreover, takes into account the varying degrees of the author's closeness to each of them, which is obvious from the epistles, and analyzes the many specific allusions, by this means one may narrow in on the mysterious poetess who preferred to appear before those whom she addresses, those who are privy to the Game, in such a strange (for us) borrowed guise.

The poetic lines were written by a young woman — this can be felt by her emotions and sentiments — but not a young girl. The author is highly educated, knows much and has had time to think over many things. Of all those whom she addresses she is closest to Mary, Countess of Pembroke; she communicates with her not as a stranger but rather as a faithful daughter, and shows herself surprisingly well informed about the countess' unpublished literary works. And when it comes to Mary's brother, the hallowed Philip Sidney, the poetess can hardly control her voice — Sidney continues to live on in loving hearts, and death itself is powerless in the face of his glory, the rays of which illuminate the path for all who follow his way.

The special treatment of the Countess of Pembroke and her literary works, the daughter-like veneration of Philip Sidney's memory, the whole contents of the "Dream," and many other elements directly indicate the woman who was closest and dearest to Mary, her beloved niece and pupil Elizabeth, the only child of the great poet and warrior.

As we already know, in some of his works and in conversations with Drummond, Ben Jonson maintained — after Elizabeth Sidney Rutland was already departed — that she was not inferior to her great father in the art of poetry. Francis Beaumont also spoke of her poetic gift. But despite this high repute, not one line was printed and signed with her name, and neither has it been possible to identify her among the anonymous poets of those days. And only today, following the direction first indicated by the touching poetic address to Mary Sidney Pembroke and then by other obvious allusions, seeing through the odious disguise of the "wife to Captain Alfonso Lanyer," we may discern an amazing woman who always hid from curious eyes and, like her spouse, played hide-and-seek with the whole human race.

Rowse also remarked on the special note in the poet's voice when she recalls Philip Sidney, but he did not try to explain it. That these tearful lines were written by the poet's daughter, bred from the cradle to worship his memory, provides the explanation that puts everything in its place.

A very important allusion emerges in the poem addressed to Queen Anne, when the author says that her early years were blessed by the favor of the Great Elizabeth. The daughter of Philip Sidney was entitled to say so about herself, like no other English poetess: indeed, she received her name from her godmother, who made a special trip to attend her baptism. This allusion is expanded by another, even more significant point: the poetess follows the example of her late godmother, the Queen Virgin, and glorifies virginity. Such a notion has little in common with Lord Hunsdon's concubine and Captain Lanyer's wife, and sounds natural only from the lips of Elizabeth Rutland.

And if we look again at the names of the noble ladies whom the writer addresses as well-known acquaintances, something else becomes clear. I have already mentioned the Queen, her daughter, Arabella Stuart, and the Countess of Pembroke. The Countesses of Bedford and of Dorset (Anne Clifford) were Elizabeth Rutland's closest friends. Anne's mother, the Countess of Cumberland, was known for being deeply religious and having a strict sense of righteous conduct (a family portrait depicts her with a book of psalms in hands). As the poetess knows: in those instances where she quotes or indicates the Holy Scriptures, there are margin notes: "The Lady Margaret, Countess Dowager of Cumberland." It is hard to picture Emilia Lanyer anywhere near this strictly pious Puritan lady who, after the early death of her two sons, devoted all her time to raising her daughter, and to prayer. Elizabeth Rutland knew her well.

The other Countess, Catherine of Suffolk, was a lady renowned for her lack of scruples in achieving her goals; it was she whom Ben Jonson depicted as the old witch in "The Sad Shepherd." When her daughter Frances wed Elizabeth Rutland's half-brother, they became kin. The epistle from "Emilia Lanyer" to the Countess of Suffolk has an air of circumspection — hearsay about the liaison between Frances and Carr has apparently reached the Rutlands, but its possible consequences are yet obscure.

Thus, all the addressees of the author's prefatory poems are ladies who are very familiar to Elizabeth Rutland, and the epistles precisely confirm the peculiarities of her relationship with each one. As to the author's address to Elizabeth Rutland — of course, there is none.

The principal mood of the author is that of fatigue, sorrow and despair: " . . . I . . . live clos'd up in Sorrowes Cell . . . "

Such pessimism is often linked to a parting with the earthly world, with life. And just that frame of mind predominated over Elizabeth in 1607-1611, when she often stayed away from home, suffering from her status as a "dowager wife" and anxious for her fatally ill husband. It seems very likely that she had already made up her mind, with his consent, to follow her spouse upon his demise; this view is supported by the earl's will, in which she (a unique case!) is not mentioned at all. Francis Beaumont noted this mood in the last years of Elizabeth's life, in the elegy he wrote right after her death; the elegy also makes other allusions which prove that Beaumont knew the person disguised as "Emilia Lanyer" and the writings in her book of such limited distribution. Addressing the Countess of Pembroke, the poetess complains of the god of sleep, Morpheus, who takes away half of our life ("span of life"), which is so brief already. Mourning the loss of Elizabeth Sidney Rutland, Beaumont repeats this poetic metaphor and responds to it:

> *Why didst you die so soone? O, pardon me,*
> *I knew it was longest life to thee*
> *That ere with modesty was cald a span…*

A special role is played by the last poem, which appears after what would seem to be the end of an already finished book; and it, too, has a strange name: "The Description of Cooke-ham." The author of the poem, which greatly differs in its language, figurativeness and poetic form from the other texts in the book, describes a certain wonderful place, Cookham, left forever by its Mistress. From this place, from this height, a breathtaking view opens up:

> *A prospect fit to please the eyes of Kings,*
> *And thirteen shires appear all in your sight,*
> *Europe could not afford much more delight.*

The only English locality named Cookham is situated in Berkshire, a lowland from which one can see little enough of the shire it is in. Rowse fails to explain these lines and assumes that they testify to "a taste for great exaggeration." There is a place, though, from which, as they claimed back then, on a good day one could actually view the lands of thirteen (or twelve) surrounding counties — and that was Belvoir Castle. No other location in England matches the description, though there are hills far higher: Belvoir is uniquely situated among several small counties lying on a plain. It should be added that in the vale near Belvoir lie a number of settlements with names similar to "Cookham": Oakham, Langham, Edenham.

Western scholars, including Rowse, who studied the Emilia Lanyer book, assume that this final (one might say supplementary) poem describes that same Cookham in Berkshire. That is where the Cumberland estate was situated (which, by the way, was the object of a tenacious lawsuit among the heirs of the Earl of Cumberland who died in 1605). However, that place bore not the least resemblance to the heavenly nook depicted in the poem, never mind the fact that it was impossible to view thirteen shires from it. Moreover, the mistress of Cookham House, the Countess of Cumberland, was in her sixties (then regarded as a venerable age) in 1610, and did not quite qualify for the role of the incarnate Beauty recalled by the poem's author, kissing the bark of her beloved tree, which she had touched with her lips in the poet's presence.

The sun grows weak and his beams give no comfort, the tree branches droop, letting their tears fall in an agony of grief over the mistress forever gone. Flowers and birds, all the living beings in this most wonderful corner of the earth remember her, and grieve for her; and even the echo wants to reply to her last words; they all "did now for sorrow die." The hills, vales and woods, which were proud to have seen this *Phoenix*, are now disconsolate with grief. Her favorite tree, under which many a learned book was read, stands alone like an orphan. The mistress of the house "would often take the air" here with the Countess of Dorset,[60] "then a virgin fair." The author narrates how the beautiful lady gave the author a chaste yet loving kiss ("through" this favorite tree) before leaving. In his reminiscences about that day and her pure farewell kiss we hear the voice of a suffering and grieving friend:

> *This last farewell to Cooke-ham here I give,*
> *When I am dead thy name in this may live*
> *Wherein I have performed her noble hest,*
> *Whose virtues lodge in my unworthy breast,*
> *And ever shall, so long as life remains,*
> *Tying my heart to her by those rich chains …*

Many details indicate that this poetic epilogue depicts the Rutlands' castle of Belvoir and laments its late mistress, Elizabeth Sidney Rutland, who had penned the preceding addresses to the queen and the noblest ladies and who also authored the poem about Christ's Passions, which gave the name to the entire volume. The poem about "Cookham" was written in late 1609-early 1610; the most likely author was Francis Beaumont, who lived within a day's ride of Belvoir and undoubtedly (as his biographers maintain) visited it. He is also the author of a poetic epistle to the mistress of Belvoir Castle (dating to about the same period as "The Description of Cooke-ham"), as well as the striking elegy for her death. Both works have much in common with "The Description of Cooke-ham"; and they were published only after the death of Beaumont himself, in the postmortem collection of the works of Thomas Overbury, who was viciously murdered in the Tower. But in 1609-1610, Overbury was still free and, according to Ben Jonson, in love with Elizabeth Rutland. Therefore, his authorship of the poem about "Cooke-ham" cannot be ruled out entirely. The possibility also exists that Elizabeth Rutland herself wrote the poem about the true

---

60. Anne Clifford, daughter of the Countess of Cumberland, cousin of Lucy Bedford, friend of Elizabeth Rutland (five years her junior), became the wife of the Earl of Dorset in 1609. After his death, she married the younger son of Mary Sidney Pembroke, Philip, Earl of Montgomery. Thanks to her endeavors, the monuments to Spenser and Daniel and perhaps some others were erected.

Cookham House and its honorable and devout mistress, though the mention of the thirteen shires makes that seem unlikely. The research goes on, and any scholar may take part in it, considering that the authentic texts and papers are not as inaccessible today as once they were.

One of the problems hindering research into the circumstances under which the book was produced is the questionable dating. The entry in the Stationer's Register was made on October 2, 1610, and states the name of publisher R. Bonian and the title of the first poem — about the Passions of Christ. The record bears no author's name nor any mention of "The Description of Cooke-ham." The title page features the date 1611, and the table of contents omits "The Description of Cooke-ham." Here was the first reference to the author: "Written by Mistris Emilia Lanyer, Wife to Captaine Alfonso Lanyer Servant to the King's Majestie" — a rather extraordinary presentation. The author of the final poem and "all Creatures in this delightful Place" mourn the Phoenix who left them. Elizabeth Rutland departed this world in the summer of 1612, and was bewailed by Francis Beaumont in his stunning elegy. This originally led me to hypothesize that the poem about Cookham was written in the second half of 1612, and hence that the book as a whole could not have been printed earlier than this date.

But later on, after the first edition of *The Shakespeare Game* had already been published, I came across a fact which contradicted the hypothetical dating of "The Description of Cooke-ham" to 1612. One of extant copies of *Salve Deus Rex Judaeorum* bears an inscription noting that on November 8, 1610 it was presented by Alfonso Lanyer to T. Jones, Archbishop of Dublin. If that inscription is authentic, it testifies that the book was published not later than but somewhat prior to the date stated on the title page.

We do not know what, if anything, Captain Alfonso Lanyer knew about the true authorship of the book issued under his wife's name. Judging by what she told Forman, relations between the spouses were not particularly warm and confiding. However, it is a known fact today that Lanyer participated in the naval expedition to the Azores and in the Irish campaign with Rutland and Southampton, and was patronized by the latter. Mary Sidney Pembroke, Lucy Bedford, Anne Clifford-Dorset, as relatives and the closest friends of Elizabeth Sidney Rutland, must have known Emilia Lanyer. There is every indication, then, that there were some ties between the Lanyers and the Southampton-Rutland-Pembroke-Sidney circle, along with the "poets of Belvoir Vale." They rendered services to their patrons when needed, and fulfilled various errands, receiving certain benefits in exchange. Thus, in 1604-1605, those patrons obtained a good sinecure for Lanyer, who was granted a monopoly for weighing hay and thatch sold in London. It is worth recalling that William Shakspere also was involved in the hay and thatch business after he bought the right to collect the tithe on the value of these goods sold by the farmers in Stratford and its environs.

Of course, when Shakspere and Lanyer were required to keep mum about their high patrons' affairs or intentions, mum they were.

# Chapter 4. Thomas Coryate of Odcombe, the World's Greatest Legstretcher, Alias the Prince of Poets

*All the poets of England sing the praises to the Giant of Mind and his Crudities. — Across Europe at a gallop. — Cabbage as a dessert for the idiots readers. — To India, by foot, with His Majesty's Water Poet laughing all the way. — The Rabelaisian carnival.*

## All the Poets of England Sing the praises to the Giant of Mind and his Crudities

Studying the works of Ben Jonson, Michael Drayton, John Donne, John Davies and other poets of the Shakespearean age, I repeatedly came across the name of a certain Thomas Coryate, mainly through poems extolling his book, published in 1611, describing his travels all over Europe by foot. Commentators noted that the Coryate book received so many poetic panegyrics that some of them had to be placed in another edition.

The titles of his book and its sequel struck me as odd for travel works: *Coryats Crudities* and *Coryats Crambe*.[1] The panegyrics, too, are strange: a mixture of

---

1. In the originals, there were no apostrophes. In the context of the whole title, "crudities" may mean "absurdities," "immaturities," "undigested matter" or even "feces," because the Latin "cruditas" is translated as indigestion. *Crambe* in Greek and Latin means "cabbage." "Crambo" is also an old game in which one player sets a line, to which another is to come up with a rhyme, with no word from the first line repeated in the second. Then there is "Dumb Crambo," a similar game where the words are expressed in pantomime or dumb show.

extravagant eulogies, allusions laden with sometimes quite opaque meaning, and rudely grotesque jests. Meanwhile, since the purpose of publishing panegyrics to an author is, presumably, to praise him and to recommend his work to readers, it is hard to imagine that an author personally narrating his journey abroad would employ so much self-mockery, from the titles to auxiliary material like Jonson's "comments" on the drawings on the title-page of *Crudities*, which liberally ridicule the allegedly ill-fated traveler. However, for some reason Jonson referred to his couplets as a key to "unlock the mystery" of Coryate's book.

Referring to both author and book, John Donne uses such epithets as "greater than all," "not limited," "exceed the World," "Gyant wit" and even "Great Lunatique"! He notes the depth of Coryate's thought, his learning, and the precision of his descriptions, which he suggests may serve as models for any writer. Coryate's work is a masterpiece; it is destined to a great future — but in that future, he says, critics will not easily appreciate it because:

> As Sybil was, your booke is mysticall,
> For every peece is as much worth as all.

He does not seem to be kidding; even for such a philosophical poet as John Donne, there is something very significant about this book by an unknown writer and his seemingly ordinary journey to the continent. But what? Donne pointedly evades the question, using two Macaronic (made up of multilingual words) couplets.

Michael Drayton goes even further. On behalf of all poets, he addresses "dear Tom":

> You are our tutor who teaches us sing
> We are all thy Zanies,[2] thy true Apes.

All these hints, and the fact that an unprecedented number of prominent poets contributed to the book, inspired me to embark on a thorough study of everything related to Thomas Coryate and his works. However, very little had been published on the subject. In the course of almost four centuries, his Crudities were reprinted in England only twice, without commentary, while the first and only monograph about him[3] came out in 1962. No work on Coryate has ever been published in Russian.

The first background information on Coryate dates to the 17th century and Thomas Fuller's book about the sights ("worthies") of England (1662).[4] Fuller wrote that Coryate was a sort of buffoon and laughing-stock for Crown Prince Henry and his friends. He had an ugly head ("being like a sugar-loaf inverted, with the little end before . . . "), and "he carried folly (which the charitable called merriment) in his very

---

2. Servant of the proscenium, in the Italian comedy of masks.
3. Michael Strachan. *The Life and Adventures of Thomas Coryate.* L., 1962.
4. Fuller T. *Worthies of England – Somersetshire.* Ed. J. Freeman. L., 1952, p. 502.

Henry, Prince of Wales

face." Two hundred years later, in 1887, the *British Dictionary of National Biography* published a detailed article by A. Jessopp;[5] however, it included some inaccuracies and accepted at face value everything Coryate recounted on his own behalf, on an equal basis with historically-authenticated biographical information. Michael Strachan was not free of this flaw, either, though he had access to a far greater range of facts; he could not have failed to notice the highly dubious quality of many of Coryate's stories, the improbable nature of which was further emphasized by the entire chorus of poets who made so much fun of him in the pages of his own book.

Neither Jessopp nor Strachan could overcome the contradiction between their assertion of Coryate's humiliating position as a poor clownish imbecile, on the one hand, who was the butt of so many jokes among the courtiers and their literary friends, and, on the other hand, the extensive and profound learning which his book displays in many fields: politics, history, geography, architecture, classical philology (Latin, in particular), and his remarkable literary talent. And the jokes at his expense (as proved by some of the "panegyric verses") were far from innocent. When staging one of Jonson's play-masques at court, to the laughter of the spectators, he was pulled out of a trunk, wet to the skin and all shriveled up, soaked, apparently, with something more than water.

What do we know about him, for certain? Shakespeare's contemporary, Thomas Coryate (1577-1617) was born in the village of Odcombe, Somersetshire, into the family of a local rector who had once served as chaplain to the Earl of Pembroke. He studied at Oxford but left without a degree. How the poor undergraduate came to be in the entourage of the Crown Prince is not known for sure; his name does not appear on the royal household's extant payrolls (the prince's treasurer paid him 10 pounds only once).

Crown Prince Henry showed a keen interest in foreign countries and foreign policy. He had British ambassadors send him detailed reports on everything that was going on where they were posted; he also relished the stories and letters of his confidants from abroad. Many people were eager to foster his interest; they pinned their hopes for the future on him (in vain — he died prematurely in the autumn of 1612). In 1606-1609, some of his associates traveled to the Continent, including the young Earl of Essex and John Hurington, who regularly sent his patron detailed accounts about everything he saw,[6] and in 1608, the Earl of Rutland dispatched his servant, Nan Deleto, to France and Italy in order to obtain information.

At just that time, in May of 1608, Thomas Coryate tells us in his *Crudities* that he, too, overwhelmed with a passion for travel, crossed the Channel, and with empty pockets and no luggage went all across Europe to Venice (where he enjoyed a fairly long séjour), and then returned home, having surmounted such a "trifling" obstacle as

---

5. *Dictionary of National Biography*. L., 1887.
6. See: Stoye I. *English travellers abroad.* L. 1952.

the Swiss Alps. The whole journey, he claimed, took less than five months — by October 3, 1608, he was back in London.

And on November 26, 1610, two influential members of the Stationers' Company, Edward Blount and his partner William Barrett, officially registered the book entitled *Coryat's Crudities Hastily gobbled up in five Moneth travels...*[7] This was a very voluminous (950 pages) and very high quality publication: formatted in-quarto, the book is unusually free of errors and misprints, has exceptionally fine engravings, and used first quality paper with a large crown as a watermark. The book begins with a few couplets by Ben Jonson which, as mentioned above, he suggested should serve "to unlock the mystery" of the *Crudities* and which are "to be applied as mollifying Cataplasmes to the Tumors, Carnosities, or difficult Pimples, full of matter, appearing in the Author's Front, conflated of Striptike and Glutinous Vapors," arising out of the *Crudities*.

Then follows Coryate's message to the Prince of Wales, expounding at length on the motives that prompted him to make the trip and to relive it on paper. Modest of birth, Coryate either jokes familiarly with the heir to the throne or addresses him in an exaggeratedly courtly and stilted manner. Thirteen pages are devoted to a lengthy mock appeal to the reader, signed by the "Odcombian Legge-stretcher"[8]; then Jonson offers another work entitled "The Character of the famous Odcombian, done by a charitable friend." Since it concerns an author who was a complete unknown until then, the epithet "famous" can only be interpreted as comical. It appears that the native of Odcombe is possessed with an irresistible passion for travel (though he has yet to go anywhere). At the mere sight of a book cover mentioning "Frankfurt" or "Venice," he is "ready to break doublet, cracke elbowes, and overflowe the roome with his murmure." He is also keen on carousing, and, no less so, on Greek and Latin.

According to Jonson, Coryate is "a great and bold Carpenter of Words," or, as he would put it himself, a "Logodedale"[9] — that is, master of artful designs in words. In knowledge he surpasses an entire college, and at any party he is served as "the most exquisite dish." But above all, "in a word, he is so Substantiue an Author as will stand by himself without the need of his Booke to be joyned with him." What does that mean? The prosaic "Character" is concluded with the "Characterisme Acrostich," which maintains the same style and begins with the noteworthy words:

> *Trie and trust Roger, was the word, but now*
> *Honest Tom Tell-Troth puts downe Roger, How?*

---

7. *Coryates Crudities Hastily gobled up in five Moneth in France, Savoy, Italy, Rhetia commonly called the Grisons country, Helvetia alias Switzerland, some parts of high Germany and the Netherlands.* Newly digested in the hungry aire of Odcombe in the County of Somerset, and now dispersed to the nourishment of the travelling Members of this Kingdome. Printed by W.S. [William Stansby]. L., 1611.

8. Below the signature was the "tragic masque" — the same emblem found in "A Poetical Rhapsody," two Shakespeare plays of 1600, and in the new Grossart edition of *Love's Martyr* (on the half-title).

9. In Greek mythology, Daedalus was the builder of the Cretan labyrinth.

Title page of *Coryate's Crudities*

To the Righ Noble *Tom*, *Tell-Troth* of
his *trauailes*, the Coryate of Odcombe,
and his *Booke* now going to
*trauell.*

T rie and truſt *Roger*, was the word, but now
H oneſt *Tom Tell-Troth* puts downe *Roger*, *How?*
O f trauell he diſcourſeth ſo at large,
M arry he ſets it out at his owne charge;
A nd therein ( which is worth his valour too)
S hewes he dares more then *Paules Church-yard* durſt do.

C ome forth thou bonnie bouncing booke then, daughter
O f *Tom* of *Odcombe* that odde Iouiall Author,
R ather his ſonne I ſhould haue cal'd thee, why?
Y es thou wert borne out of his trauelling thigh
A s well as from his braines, and claimeſt thereby
T o be his *Bacchus* as his *Pallas* : bee
E uer his thighes *Male* then, and his braines *Shee*.

Ben. Jonſon.

A page from *Coryate's Crudities*. "Roger, was the word..."

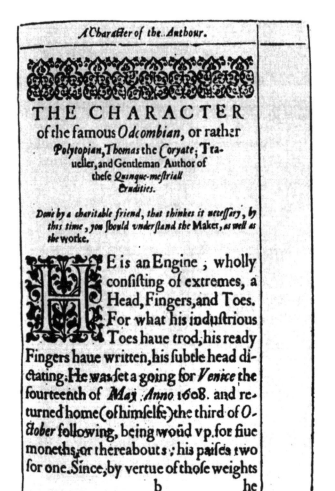

# THE CHARACTER

of the famous *Odcombian*, or rather
*Polytopian, Thomas* the *Coryate*, Tra-
ueller, and Gentleman Author of
thefe *Quinque-meſtriall*
*Crudities.*

*Done by a charitable friend, that thinkes it neceſſary, by
this time, you ſhould vnderſtand the Maker, as well as
the worke.*

HE is an Engine, wholly
confiſting of extremes, a
Head, Fingers, and Toes.
For what his induſtrious
Toes haue trod, his ready
Fingers haue written, his ſubtle head dictating. He was ſet a going for *Venice* the
fourteenth of *May Anno* 1608. and returned home (of himſelfe) the third of *O-
ctober* following, being woūd vp for fiue
moneths, or thereabouts; his paſſes two
for one. Since, by vertue of thoſe weights

b        he

A page from *Coryates Crudities.* "The Character of the
famous Odcombian, done by a charitable friend."

And thou O *Odcombe* laugh and tickle
To see thy *Pilchard* in his pickle,
Who late in Court, both wet and shrunck,
Lay close embrined in a trunck.

## François.

### *Asne-Bucephalæosis ou Recapitulation*
& Sommaire du gros fatras du Sieur
*Tho. Coriat.*

· Les poetes a leur Muses.

C'Est assez, belles Muses ;
Bouchez les escluses,
A l'Aganippée :
Où pour leur lippée.
Les Poetes grenouillens,
Et puis y gazouillent
D'une extreme rage
Leur doux chant ramage.
Eux faisans leur Feste
Au coq porte-creste :
Et lauants la teste
A la lour de beste :
Ont perdu toutes-fois

Et leur charbons & bois,
Leur peine excessiue,
Sauon & lessiue.
Leur rimes roulantes,
Et carmes coulantes,
De belle cadence
Comme sault en potence.
Sus doncq, belles Muses
Bouchez vos escluses,
Car Tom, le bon drole,
Ha ioué son role,
La farce est finie,
Tai toy, Poesie.

## Ital.

### Risposta delle Muse.

T Acete mattizche messer Thomasso,
D'vn Meuio è fatto vn Torquato Tasso ;

A page from *Coryate's Crudities*. Panegyrics to the author in various languages.

Il cui spirto gentil en vn batter d'occhio,
Trascorre dal capo, fin al ginocchio;
I piedi dan' salto, la tesla capriccii,
Quelli fan' il camino, questa s bisticci
  Pouero viandante chi preso me' lacci
D'amor, se ne tornò coperto di stracci.
Chi per no tener piu sale in Zucca
Che Canalio di Bergamo, ò bue di Lucca ;
Partissi sciocco, volgendosi pazzo,
Del mondo il scherzo, trastullo, e solazzo.

## Español.

### Concierto de los entrambos.

EA pues, acabense los chistes y pullas,
  Cantada la missa queden las casullas.
El Chronista Thomas pone fin al trauajo;
Despues de auerse mostrado badajo:
Y dicho donayres y mil disparates,
Que hazen ventaje de muchos quilates
A quantos han escrito. Quien vende tal mosto,
De poca cosecha haga su Agosto.
Y digan los niños ; Tata, madre, coco,
He aqui passa Tom tonto y loco.

### Explicit Glareanus Vadianus.

Additional panegyrics to the author of *Coryate's Crudities*, in various languages.

Jonson scholars have been unable to positively identify this mysterious Roger who was "put down" by Thomas Coryate. I recommend to their attention one Roger who was a good acquaintance of Ben Jonson, close to the Prince of Wales and his milieu, a strange man who was always hiding his face behind off-putting borrowed odious masks (starting with the clown Gullio and his Stratfordian prototype). That strange man was Roger Manners, the 5th Earl of Rutland.

The special foreword publicly states that the most prominent wits of the kingdom dedicated laudatory verses to the book. Each author's contribution is preceded by the announcement: "Incipit. . ." (i.e. "Begins so-and-so. . ."), and is followed by: "Explicit. . ." (i.e. "Finishes so-and-so. . .") — like a theatrical script. From the first author (using a Greek pen name which may be translated as "Friend of those who travel overseas"), the gentlemen are invited to laugh at this Thomas who is allegedly in possession of "wisdom's cell" and a key to unlock it, which, however, is not accessible to everyone.

> *Now Lordings mercy doe I aske,*
> *That since I under-went this taske*
> *His name I have concealed;*
> *He keepes the Magazine of wit,*
> *And beares the privy key to it,*
> *Which may not be reveal'd.*
> *Yet in despite of bread and ale,*
> *Unbuckled now shall be the male*
> *Betide what may betide;*
> *His name is Coryate I wish,*
> *But whether he be flesh or fish,*
> *I cannot yet decide.*

These "panegyrics" take up some 120 pages and are signed with the names of 56 authors who really include the "most prominent wits" and the greatest literary man in England at that time. This part of the book is stunning; Rabelais' famous stories would probably produce a similar impression if we came across them today and read them for the first time. There is nothing else like it in English literature — or elsewhere — before or since; this is not just a brilliant fireworks display of fantastic wit, but a carnival of laughter played out around the central buffoon — that of Thomas Coryate from Odcombe.

One third of the amazing list of authors who penned the "panegyrics" were connected with the royal court, another third with the London Inns of Court. Half of them are included in the *Dictionary of National Biography*. The most famous were Ben Jonson, Michael Drayton, John Donne, Henry Goodyere, Robert Cotton, Richard Martin, John Owen, Hugh Holland, Christopher Brooke, John Hoskins, Thomas Campion, John Davies of Hereford, John Hurington, Henry Peacham, and Inigo Jones

— shining stars of English poetry. Jonson and Holland actively participated, later, in Shakespeare's Great Folio; Richard Martin defended the legal interests of the actors' troupe named "The King's Men," and Christopher Brooke authored "The Ghost of Richard III," which alludes to Shakespeare. The "Northumberland Manuscript" (or part of it) was written by the hand of John Davies, who taught the crown prince calligraphy and who wrote the ambiguous rhyme, "To our English Terence, Mr. Will Shake-speare" (in 1610, not long before the Coryate book) — that striking address that claims that Shakespeare not only played kings' roles sometimes "in sport," but used to be a king's companion. Henry Peacham is known for his drawings (in the manuscript) depicting a scene from "Titus Andronicus" — *the only illustration* to a Shakespeare work made by one of his contemporaries.

All kinds of things pop up in those "panegyrics," which are sometimes untranslatable: there are poems in English and Latin, ancient Greek, French, Italian, Spanish, Flemish, and Welsh, as well as in fantastic "languages" — Macaronic, Utopian and Antipodal. There are acrostics and sonnets, poems set to music, and a syllabic verse in the shape of an egg. While seeming to "praise" Coryate, the writers roar with laughter at him, mocking him in puns and bending their words out of all proportion. Hugh Holland calls him "Topographicall and Typographicall Thomas" and draws a comparison between "Don Ulysses from Ithaca" and "Don Coryate from Odcombe," noting that "one Homer only sung Odysseus praise, but Coryates all the poets of our daies." Other authors also make a distinction between the two "travel writers," Homer and Coryate, and not in favor of the Greek. Christopher Brooke put it very simply:

> *Coryate hath writ a booke*
> *Bigger than Homer's, and (though writ in prose)*
> *As full of poetry, spite of Homers nose.*

Someone under the pen name of "Glarianus Vadianus" equates Coryate with Amadis of Gaul, the hero of a chivalric romance in prose, and even with the Maid of Orleans. There are verbose comparisons with Julius Caesar, Lycurgus, Solon, Pythagoras, Don Quixote, Pantagruel, Columbus, Magellan, Mercurius, Proteus, and others. Hugh Holland names him the Prince of Poets. John Hurington says:

> *Thou glorious Goose that kepst the Capitol,*
> *Afford one quill, that I may write one storie yet*
> *Of this my new-come Odcombe-friend Tom Coriet,*
> *Whose praise so worthy wits and pens inroll.*

The names of Coryate and of his native hamlet are mockingly played up in every possible way. Glarianus Vadianus displays his uncommon knowledge of languages and medicine in the poem entitled "A Sceleton or bare Anatomie of the Punctures and

Junctures of Mr. Thomas Coryate of Odcombe. . . ," which is surrounded in the margins with pseudo-academic comments and references to authoritative scholars.

> *O let the Hurlie-Burlie Fate*
> *Requite thy love with lasting hate;*
> *Long live, late come to thy enterring,*
> *Nor flesh, nor fish, nor good red herring.*
> *And thou O Odcombe laugh and tickle*
> *To see thy Pilchard in the pickle,*
> *Who late in Court, both wet and shrunck,*
> *Lay close embrined in a trunk.*

There is also "A Declaration of Nereus prophesies touching the fall of Glastenburie Abbey, and the rising of Odcombe, by two fishes. . . ," which specifies in a Rabelaisian style that the prophesy had been made in a tavern known for the fact that once upon a time a dog chasing a bear ran by, and they went so far north that both animals were frozen in the ice, and other such nonsense.

Another "compliment," by Jacobus Field, says:

> *Of all the Toms that ever yet were nam'd,*
> *Was never Tom like as Tom Coryate Fam'd . . .*
> . . . . . . . . . . . .
> *Tom foole may go to schoole, but nere be taught,*
> *Speake greeke with which our Tom his tongue is fraught,*
> *Tom-Asse may passe, but for all his long eares*
> *No such rich jewels as our Tom he weares.*

The collection concludes with some Macaronic verses by "Coryate himself," which show that he did not resent in the least all these put-downs from those whom he "invited so ingenuously to take part in the edition of his work." How can that be? Only an utter fool would not realize that he was being made a laughing-stock! Moreover, he willingly performed the final comical dance in that grotesque show. The author confirmed that he stood as the principal comical figure, as a clown who actively participated in the farce being played around him; the laughter is ambivalent, all-embracing. However, there are too many indications that it is not the author himself who is playing the role of a clown, here, but vice versa — the clown, the buffoon, is presented in the author's role.

The introductory "eulogies" are vitally important to any understanding of this extraordinary publication and its background; this unique collection remains the most striking phenomenon of Rabelaisian writing in the history of English literature, and it has not been properly understood and appreciated.

ACROSS EUROPE AT A GALLOP

Now let us focus on Coryate's travel notes themselves. First, as another introduction, the book features an address ascribed to German scholar Herman Kirchner — "On the benefit of travels," a long (40 pages) essay which manifestly but not grotesquely parodies the tiresome "works" of contemporary lovers of pseudo-scientific babble.

The description of Coryate's wanderings starts with a calculation of the mileage between the borough of Odcombe and the major European cities Coryate passes through:

Odcombe – London: 106 miles
London – Dover: 57
Dover – Calais: 27
Calais – Paris: 140, etc.

According to Coryate, using whatever means of transportation was available but most often shanks' mare, he covered a total distance of 1975 miles, traversing all of France and Italy up to Venice and then back to England, via the Swiss Alps, Upper and Lower Germany, and the Netherlands. The book provides the exact dates (and even hours) of his stay at every point, so that it is possible to calculate that he was actually in transit on no more than 80 days (the longest stop was in Venice; he also stopped in Paris, Padua and other cities). Thus, he bounced along through alien lands, taking difficult routes and visiting 45 cities, seeing their sights in detail, jotting down foreign-language inscriptions on monuments, and taking copious notes about everything he saw and heard, including geographic, historical and cultural facts — notes which subsequently made up such a large book, and at that he advanced at an average speed of 35-40 km per day, a pace that was, perhaps, inferior only to that of Pantagruel.

. His speed is clearly just one more farcical detail. Not for nothing did Coryate himself and his "eulogists" openly ask the ironic question: How did the Odcombian foot traveler contrive within such a short period of time to traverse so many countries and cities, to see and record so much, and all on an empty belly and empty pocket; and what should be done with those who would doubt his veracity?

How the trip was financed remains a puzzle. Overseas travel was costly; and Coryate repeatedly emphasizes his want of money. Also, as Jonson relayed in his "Charmes to unlocke the Mystery":

> *Old Hat here, torne Hose, with Shoes full of gravell,*
> *And louse-dropping Case, are the Armes of his travell.*

Then how did he live, how did he pay for his bed and board, at least? He didn't always sleep under haystacks — sometimes he put up at the most expensive and prestigious hotels. In Ly ons, he shared the "Three Kings," the best inn in the city, with such persons as the brother of the Duc de Guise and the French ambassador to Rome (it seems that Coryate missed the young Earl of Essex by one day, at "Three Kings"). And the Odcombian, penniless and worn out after a long journey, converses with these nobles in excellent Latin. In other places, he permits himself the most expensive pleasures, tasting choice dishes and wines. Such "discrepancies" permeate every stage of his journey — when he talks about himself, elements of falsehood, parody and buffoonery proliferate, making it clear that this aspect of his narration is purely literary and not to be trusted. It should be added that a permit was required to travel abroad in those days, specifying dates and other details. However, the usually garrulous Coryate says not a word about such things. Interestingly enough, Coryate's itinerary coincides (but in reverse) with that of Roger Manners, the Earl of Rutland, who had been to Padua twelve years before.

The quality and value of the factual content is high; the narratives about European countries are not over-burdened with elements of farce and buffoonery. The work actually conveys a tangible sense of life in Europe at the time. Each important city is granted its own section, where the author expounds its history and gives a general description with detailed accounts of folk traditions and customs, and expertly relates the most significant architectural constructions and renders the inscriptions and epitaphs on monuments and vaults. In some cases, he touches upon the subjects of public administration, intergovernmental relations, wars, diplomacy, and dynastic issues — all with competence.

Most interesting, as Strachan noted, is the fact that the author took such note of architectural monuments, many of which had never been described in any book before. He introduced the English to many of Palladio's works, such as the Basilica and Rotonda at Vicenza.

The panoramas of Lombardy, the Rhine, and Switzerland are magnificently portrayed. The Englishman is especially moved to admire the sun and colors of Italy, comparing the land with Paradise. One sixth of the book is dedicated to Venice, about which only two earlier books had been written in English (and the Coryate book conveys far more information and more striking impressions). The story about Venice is so colorful, comprehensive and accurate that Strachan believes it to be the most perfect ever written in any language.

Describing the Venetian way of life, Coryate covers gondolas and oysters, the monetary system and the status of women, foreigners and adherents of different faiths. At the theater, his attention is naturally drawn to the actresses — since, in England, all the roles were played by men. But on the whole, Coryate holds that Venetian theatrical art was inferior to that of Britain — which today sounds quite credible, coming from a contemporary of Shakespeare. Clearly following his own interests, the author describes the Venetian clowns, jugglers and all sorts of charlatans, and shares his impressions of the power and influence wielded by the courtesans. Penniless as he was, Coryate seems to have visited one of them, the wealthy (and very expensive!)

Margarita Emiliana, in her home. And a splendid engraving by William Hole portrays Coryate, suddenly appearing in exquisite dress and with stylish hair, and the Venetian priestess of love, rushing toward each other. Of course, the elegant garb of the Odcombian may be accredited to the imagination of the illustrator, though in this case (and other cases as well) it may not be that simple.

A long chapter is dedicated to Padua, its monuments, and the famous university. With special feeling, the traveler recollects what distinguishes Padua from other cities, describing the long roofed galleries running along the streets (like the arcade depicted in the portrait of the young lord, which I identified as the Earl of Rutland, who returned from Padua in 1597).

Wherever he stayed, Coryate associated with prominent scholars and connoisseurs of philology, rhetoric, and philosophy, with the renowned Swiss polyglot and orientalist Gaspar Waser, for example, and the theologians Bueler, Hospinian and others. He attended lectures on theology and ancient Greek literature, and compared them with those read at universities in England. At the end, the book even features Coryate's lengthy letters to those scholars and their no less wordy and vacuous replies. Generally, this "correspondence" in Latin and Greek has a playful and mocking tone, although it has been ascertained that the scholars did actually exchange letters with some Englishmen; Gaspar Waser, as we know, was in correspondence with the Earl of Rutland.

The book provides a detailed description of the widely known Frankfurt Book Fair, which Coryate visited in September of 1608. At that very time (naturally, just by coincidence) the fair was also attended by the young Earl of Essex, whom the Odcombian for some reason calls a cousin of the fourth degree. To declare himself a relative, even distant, of the nobleman who was raised with the Prince of Wales would be insolent for a man of humble origin. Unless the claim was made, say, by some relative of Elizabeth Sidney, Essex's half-sister — for instance, her husband, the Earl of Rutland — in which case, such a flippant definition of the degree and nature of their kinship would be quite appropriate.

Coryate passes along a great number of facts, dates, and names; his book amounts to an encyclopedia. In some cases, the author draws on existing works, be they in English, Latin or Italian (a language the Odcombian, by his own admission, had yet to learn).

The literary merits of the book are evident. It uses an impressive vocabulary, with words, expressions and entire pages in Latin and Greek. Coryate's "orations," parodying the hackneyed speeches of the university, manifest an excellent knowledge of classical rhetoric. The author clearly enjoys loading his language with euphuisms, hyperboles, rich and unusual metaphors. His narration is replete with new and audacious word-formations, including many derived from Latin and Greek roots (some of these have been carried over into modern English); the experiments show the hand of a skillful word master, a true Logodedale.

Right at the end, after the separate half-title, is a section of poetic opuses, mainly in Latin, which are credited to Thomas Coryate's late father, the Reverend George Coryate. They are addressed to various deceased but once powerful Elizabethan nobles — Lord Burghley, the Earls Robert Dudley of Leicester and William Herbert of Pembroke (grandfather of the 3$^{rd}$ Earl of Pembroke and the Earl of Montgomery, to whom Shakespeare's First Folio would be dedicated), and other aristocrats. There is also a verse addressed to Her Majesty Elizabeth herself — in which the humble pastor earnestly advises her to marry as soon as possible! These poetic compositions are scarcely veiled parodies and have nothing to do with the contents of the volume in general. The book is enhanced by an extensive alphabetical index, making this an early forebear of academic books today with their detailed reference sections.

And, finally, at the end, there are two pages containing errata, accompanied by the author's appeal to his readers. Misprints are very few (though Coryate claims that the actual number is much greater and invites the readers to join in searching for them). Among the errata noted by Coryate, the word "Manners" — with both small and capital letters — appears several times, appropriately and not. Thus, he recommends the reader to regard the word "Lordships" printed on page 297 as "Manners"! The word "Lordships" does not, in fact, appear on that page at all, but it would be extremely hard to imagine such a misprint. Of course, none of this would make any sense if we did not know that Manners was the patrimonial name of the Earl of Rutland. And the name Manners is played upon quite openly, here, just as it was played upon in Shakespeare's sonnets and some of Jonson's works, which we shall discuss later.

There is one more "coincidence." In the above epistle, Coryate flirts with the reader and begs to be excused for his "poor, superficial, smattering of Latin and Greek," although the book abounds in excellent Latin and Greek texts. This phrase later would be repeated word for word by Ben Jonson with respect to Shakespeare, although the latter's works likewise demonstrate more than competence in these languages. Obviously, it was not by accident that Jonson borrowed this phrase from Coryate's book, in the creation of which, like that of the Great Shakespeare Folio, he took a very active part.

The exact number of copies printed is not known. Very likely it was not large, maybe 100; 40 have survived. The most prominent publishers and printers were involved: Blount, Barret, Stansby, and the peerless artist and engraver William Hole. In polygraphic features — the quality of paper, composed set, printing, and unique engravings in particular — *Crudities* had few analogues in those days. Special gift copies were made for each member of the royal family. The crown prince's copy, stored now at the British Library, is velvet-bound, its edges and clasps gilded, the engravings thoroughly colored; and the colors and gilt have preserved their luster. This was clearly not a commercial endeavor. The numerous statements claiming that the beggarly Coryate published the book at his own expense are obviously more examples of pure buffoonery — it had to have been financed by those close to the Prince of

Wales, and papers left by Lionel Cranfield, one of the project's initiators, provide proof to this effect.

Soon, in *Crambe*, Coryate would relate a comic story about how he petitioned for approval to publish *Crudities*, and for greater "convincingness" his letter to the secretary of the Lord Treasurer was even pasted into the de luxe copy presented to Prince Henry — where it still can be seen. The letter is, of course, another parody; one would hardly have to humbly entreat such a minor official over a book that was created under the personal patronage of the Prince. The letter, including Coryate's signature, was written in the same copy-book penmanship as the captions under Hole's engravings; therefore, any suggestion that it was Coryate's true autograph (and the only one, at that) would not be credible.

Everything indicates the farcical nature of the publication, and this impression is only heightened by the striking events that took place after *Crudities* left the printing house.

### "Cabbage" As A Dessert For The Idiots Readers

The other book was published months later, also in London; it was far smaller (about 100 pages) but no less strange, and was hardly compatible with the author's solemn title: "Coryats Crambe or His Colwort Twise Sodden,[10] and now served in with other Macaronicke dishes, as the second course to his Crudities."[11] The title was artfully devised: "cabbage" was present both directly and indirectly, in Greek or Latin (Crambe), and the English (colewort), while "crambo," as mentioned above, is an old game that involves answering a riddle or deciphering a secret name.

*Crambe* contains another set of "eulogies" that allegedly had not fit into *Crudities*, the address to Prince Henry comically narrating the difficulties in obtaining approval to publish the previous book, and a series of orations which, Coryate said, he had delivered to His Majesty the King and to each member of the royal family individually. It also contains an abusive reply to the linen trader Starre, as part of a farcical lawsuit. Starre, Coryate claimed, had bet that Coryate would not return safely from his travels, but reneged on his wager. The merchant argued that it was simply impossible to visit and describe so many lands and cities within so short a time, and refused to pay. Basically made up of copious and comical curses, the "Petition to the Court" was signed by Coryate in Latin, English and Greek.

The reader is also offered a story about hostilities that broke out between the Odcombians and their neighbors, the community of Yeouvil (Coryate jokingly writes

---

10. "Crambe bis cocta" or "Crambe repetita" (Lat.) — "cabbage twice boiled," or "repeated" — a well-worn subject, stale news, etc.

11. *Coryats Crambe or His Colwort Twise Sodden, and now served in with other Macaronicke dishes, as the second course to his Crudities*. Printed by William Stansby. London, 1611.

this as Evil), the armed Odcombians allegedly being the first to launch the campaign, with the Yeouvilians advancing on Odcombe in response. In both cases the "hostilities" were successfully stopped only by means of lengthy speeches made by Coryate, sword in hand, accompanied by a martial band and volleys of musket fire (how did the martial band and muskets happen to appear in Odcombe?). Delivered in full accordance with the rules of declamatory art, quoting Homer, Xenophon and Livius, the orations of course are cited completely. This little spoof on the "war" between two tiny villages in Somersetshire takes up about a quarter of the book, and it would have fit quite nicely with the work relating the deeds of that other great traveler, Pantagruel.

Like the previous book, *Crambe* begins with a poem by Ben Jonson, in the same farcical style. Ben praises Coryate's "wise noddle" and his "untired feet," and as for those who do not believe that in the course of five months he was able to go around the world, and in the next five months to describe it all, he advises him to just piss on them! What else do suspicious readers want? — why, the book precisely indicates the day and hour when Coryate entered each city and when he left it! Besides, a "material proof" remains, a concrete bit of evidence: the sole pair of boots in which the Odcombian "limped" from Venice to England. The same footwear is mentioned by other smirking "eulogists," one of whom even pictured them wreathed with laurels. Coryate explains that upon his return he hung up his worn-out traveling shoes in a prominent place in the Odcombe parish church. Interestingly enough, a decade before, the comedian William Kempe had engaged to jig-dance all the way from London to Norwich, and afterwards he hung his shoes on the wall of the Norwich town hall. The parallel between Coryate and Kempe is also drawn in one of the "panegyrics."

Lawrence Whitaker's verse is set to music, the notes of which are printed alongside, and is entitled: "Course Musicke played upon the Odcombian Hoboy, to attend the second course of Coryat's Coleworts, and dittied to the most melodious Comicall ayre." Coryate is awarded with a new set of comic titles: Coryphaeus, Coryat the Great, etc., while Hugh Holland entitles his poem "To the Idiots Readers" Did he mean his contemporaries, only?

The five orations which Coryate claimed to have pronounced before the king and members of the august family are worthy of greater attention than has been given them heretofore. Whether at the court of the king of England and on the premises of the royal family as many as five special ceremonies were actually conducted one after another in April of 1611, just two or three days apart, and whether the poor Odcombian of humble station solemnly presented gift copies of *Crudities* first to the king,[12] then to the queen and finally to each of their three children, and whether at the same time he

---

12. Who actually acquainted the king with the *Crudities* and under what circumstances may be learned from Sir John Hurington's letter to the Earl of Pembroke (1611). Hurington relates how he presented the *Crudities* to the king, and how long the latter laughed at the panegyrics in honor of the "author." The letter, of which a copy is stored at the British Library, was shown to me by M. D. Litvinova.

The title page of *Coryat's Crambe*

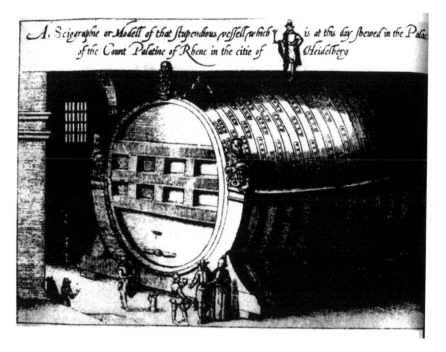

Coryate on the Heidelberg Barrel. Engraving by W. Hole.

really did deliver the speeches published in *Crambe*, is not known. But the fact that the story and the "orations" were permitted to be published proves once again that the edition was patronized at a very high level.

While they observe all the formalities of titling, the "orations" also feature a mocking, comical element, subtly calibrated to make the noble readers smile. Thus, the "naive" Coryate likens his address to King James, which took place on Tuesday, April 2, 1611, at 11 o'clock in the morning (what exactitude!), to the orations Demosthenes delivered to Philip of Macedon!

But it turns out that the great footman's solemn speechifying before the royal family was not limited to those five incidents. Seven pages of the book tell about the speech Coryate gave a month later, on May 12, to the young Duke of York (the future ill-fated King Charles I) on the occasion of his election and installation as a Knight of the Garter. This time, the commoner was a central figure at an important ceremony of state (attended only by the highest elite), recounting to the young duke in detail the history of the highest order of the realm, its status and the meaning of its emblem, and explaining to him the duties and responsibility that the Order's knighthood imposes on a newly inducted member. This "speech" displays a deep knowledge of the Order's history and heraldic details that were not widely known; it is an erudite and even unique piece on the subject.

The prince (still a boy) is addressed in a deferential and careful tone; slapstick is relatively rare here, but, for greater clarity Coryate divides his "report" into several parts, which he boldly likens in a Rabelaisian manner to a series of bottles, which he empties one after the other. The "oration" is in no way related to his travels; how he appeared in the august role of mentor to the highest pupil in the land remains obscure. There are no references to Coryate's speech in any official documents or in the correspondence of his contemporaries.

Finally, *Crambe* ends with a story wherein the author recounts that, after delivering his *Crudities* to the king, he put the rest of the presentation copies into a chest, loaded it on an ass's back, and set out to visit the other members of the royal family; and that he wrote on the trunk in big letters: "Asinus portans mysteria" — "An ass carries the mystery [or sacrament]."

And one more thing. At just about the same time a small book appeared in London, entitled *The Odcombian Banquet: Dished foorth by Thomas the Coriat, and Served in by a number of Noble Wits in prayse of his Crudities and Crambe too.*[13] The book comprised all the "panegyrics" from *Crudities* and an address to the reader, the author of which states in an ostensibly serious tone that he considered it sufficient to print only the complimentary verses, omitting Coryate's description of his travels altogether in order to spare the readers the extra expense, and because *Crudities* was excessive in size — its contents "could perfectly be stated on four pages"! It is strange that the anonymous

---

13. *The Odcombian Banquet: Dishes foorth by Thomas the Coriat, and Served in by a number of Noble Wits in prayse of his Crudities and Crambe too. Asinus portans mysteria.* Imprinted for Thomas Thorp. 1611.

## Incipit Hugo Hollandus.

### The same hand againe to the 'I-diots Readers.

Vpon fiue *principall Harangues* of the *Odcombian*
Orator, and. Priefo-Poët *Corÿate the Crude, Hugo-*
*nis Hollandi Carmen trimetrametrum kinnamis-*
*ticum fiue excommiafticum Odcomia-*
*fticum.*

IN fpeech there are eight parts (qyoth [a] hee).
But here in fiue nor one I fee:
So are they woue, and with that art.
(O monftrous skill!) part within parts.
  And yet his tongue that was the fhuttle,
In euery point is not fo fubtle,
But you may fee him here in groffe,
As well as Cheape or Charing Croffe.
  Now he that cannot here his found,
In ftudy, is or fleepe profound:
Our hath his eares pawn'd to the Pillery,
Or loft their vfe with great Artillery.
He iefts loud, and makes more noyfe
Then any of the *Roaring Boies.*
  Your tafte will tell you he is [b] frefh,
(Though he be neither fifh nor [c] flefh)
For here is not a dram of [d] falt
And yet no nofe can find a fault.
  Nay, euery Noddy-nofe may well
His fragrant flowers of Rhetoricke fmell:
Whereof who doth not like the fent,
Let him make triall by his [e] vent.

[a] In the Da-
tiue nor the
Genitiue cafe,
(that were
more then the
fufiæn cafe)
from which he
was miracu-
loufly and e-
raculoufly de-
liuered.

[a] The patron
of our lufticke
lineamentorit
*Willam Lily.*

[b] New out in
print.
[c] Which is but
part of the bo-
dy, and the
body part of
him.
[d] For Salt
ferues to keep
from tainting
and puttifac-
tion.
[e] The great
vent and fale
of his bookes.

As

Hugh Holland's address "To the Idiots Readers."

*Incipit Laurentius Whitaker.*

*(The ensuing verses of these three Authors were made since my booke of Crudities came forth.)*

**Course Musicke plaid vpon the Odcombian Hoboy**, to attend the second course of *Coryats* Coleworts, and *ditted to the most melodious Comicall ayre, borne and* brought vp in the Septentrionall suburbs, which the vulgar call, The Punks delight.

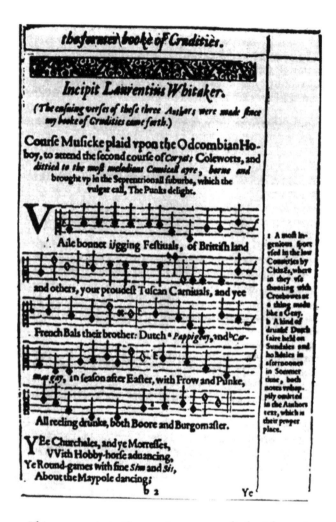

Aile bonnet iigging Festiuals, of British land

and others, your proudest Tuscan Carniuals, and yee

French Bals their brother: Dutch a *Pappigay*, and b Car-

mas gay, in season after Easter, with Frow and Punke,

All reeling drunke, both Boore and Burgomaster.

Yᴇᴇ Churchales, and ye Morresses,
  VVith Hobby-horse aduancing,
Ye Round-games with fine Shw and Sis,
  About the Maypole dancing;

b 2                 Ye

a A most Ingenious sport vsed in the low Countries by Clelses, where in they vse shooting with Crosbowes at a thing made like a Geny. b A kind of drunke Dutch faire held on Sundaies and holidaies in afternoones in Sommer time, both notes vnhappily omitted in the Authors text, which is their proper place.

 

    This panegyric to Coryate is even supplied with music, so that readers could sing it to the oboe.

writer should know about *Crambe*, which was just being printed; also that on the title page of *The Banquet*, Coryate's name is directly followed by the printed inscription: "Asinus portans mysteria."

In the final pages of *Crambe*, Coryate makes a fuss attacking an anonymous "hypercritic" who speaks scornfully about his work. But he appears to be hurt most of all by the fact that, expressly and with ill intent, the publishers of *The Banquet* placed the inscription on the title page next to his name and his books' titles, so that readers would regard Coryate himself as that same ass who bears the mystery on his back. Coryate glibly argues that it is not so, that he is not an ass; and he invents amusing curses especially for the occasion to insult the malevolent publishers of *The Banquet* in every way possible, until it becomes patently clear that he is indeed a buffoon, a straw man, a human mask hiding the true authors.

The farcical nature of the "polemics" becomes even more apparent when we learn that *The Banquet* was published by Thomas Thorpe (publisher of Shakespeare's sonnets, in 1609), a close and loyal friend of Edward Blount, who published *Crudities* and *Crambe*. To all appearances, they were in close collaboration[14]; the book was not registered, and few copies were printed. It was intended solely for the participants in the farce around Coryate, and served as its sequel. Serious-minded scholars who take at face value Coryate's tirades against the publishers of *The Banquet* are at a loss to explain any aspect of this story, and even their old fallback excuse of "piracy"[15] fails to clarify anything. But going ahead, I may now add that *Crambe* and *The Banquet* were the last books delivered to the fatally ill Earl of Rutland by his steward (who recorded the titles on one line, and this too indicates that both works were printed at the same time).

Related to the above, several handwritten copies of a poem have come down to us, in Latin (with, at the same time, a parallel translation into English), called "The Convivium Philosophicum" ("The Philosophical Feast"). The poem describes certain festivities "in the name of excellent food and good joke" that would take place at London's Mitre Tavern, most likely around the middle of 1611. In most copies, the author is listed under the pen name of "Rodolfus Calfaber." Each visitor is dubbed with a witty nickname (we now know who most of the guests were — and they are the same who participated in Coryate's books, the writers of the "panegyrics"). But, says the poem's author, the company will be incomplete without Thomas Coryate — in his absence, "the feast will want a tiller"! And when Coryate got enough drink in

---

14. Since *Crambe* criticizes the publishers of *The Banquet*, and *The Banquet*'s title page mentions *Crambe*, it is apparent that both books were being created at the same time. The word *banquet* in Jonson's lexicon means *dessert*.

15. The publication of illegally acquired or purloined texts was a routine practice in those days. However, some Western scholars are too quick to simplify any number of complex and seemingly inexplicable publishing events of the Shakespearean age (especially in relation to the Bard himself) by reducing them to instances of plain "piracy."

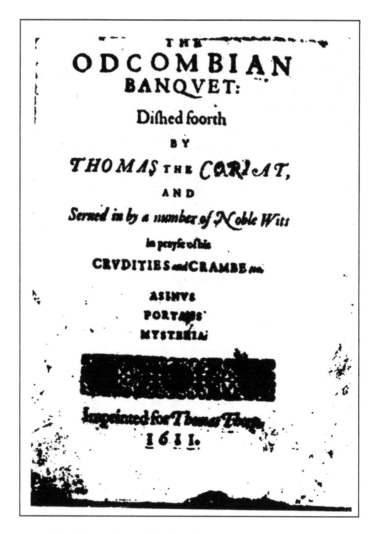

The title page from *The Odcombian Banquet*

him, what a good laugh you could have, what an earful of nonsense. Coryate is compared with the courtiers' anvil "to try their wits upon":

> For wittily on him, they say,
> As hammers on an anvil play,
> Each man his feast may breake
> When Coryate is fudled well
> His tongue begins to talke pelmel
> He shameth nought to speake.

The society meeting at the tavern is often referred to as the Mermaid Club, and playwright Francis Beaumont speaks of those meetings in his poetic "Letter to Ben Jonson":

> What things have we seen
> Done at the Mermaid! Heard words that have been
> So nimble, and so full of subtle flame,
> As if that every one from whence they came
> Had meant to put his whole wit in a gest,
> And had resolved to live a fool, the rest
> Of his dull life; then when there had been thrown
> Wit able enough to justify the Town
> For three days past, with that might warrant be
> For the whole City to talk foolishly
> Till that were cancell'd, and when that was gone
> We left an air behind us, which alone,
> Was able to make the two next companies
> Right witty: though but downright fools, more wise.[16]

This picture fully conforms with what the anonymous author of "Convivium Philosophicum" says, and with the breath-taking comic pirouettes in the "panegyrics" in *Crudities*, *Crambe* and *The Odcombian Banquet*. Here, we see the environment where these books were brewed — among the entourage of the Prince of Wales and the literary men around the Earls of Pembroke, Dorset, and Rutland — that very Roger who was "put down" by Thomas Coryate.

And thus, the fact that one of the five copies of "Convivium Philosophicum" was found at Belvoir Castle comes as no surprise.

---

16. See: Strachan M. *The Life and Adventures of Thomas Coryate*. L. 1962, p.145.

## To India, On Foot, with His Majesty's Water Poet Laughing All the Way

The next story of the extraordinary traveler and writer Thomas Coryate of Odcombe is told in his five "Letters from India," which came out in 1616-1618 in the form of printed pamphlets, as well as in a chapter of a book by geographer Samuel Purchas (1625)[17] and several pages in missionary Edward Terry's book about his stay in India. Once again, Coryate left no handwritten texts, not even a single reliable autograph.

In October 1612, one or two jovial gentlemen from the Mermaid Club, accompanied by Coryate, boarded a ship bound for the East. In the pages of *Crudities* and *Crambe*, the Odcombian had announced his intention to undertake another great tour.

As recounted in verses that appeared in London four years later, on the way to Constantinople a group of Englishmen went ashore in Troas and performed one more farcical play. Mistaking the ruins of an ancient construction for the remains of Homer's Troy, the Britons solemnly proclaimed the Odcombian "The First English Knight of Troy" (duly accompanied by such rites as genuflection, a tap on the shoulder with the flat side of a sword, etc.). Coryate climbed atop a rock and pronounced his regular "oration." And the anonymous author of the poem declares:

> *Coryate no more, but now a Knight of Troy,*
> *Odcombe no more, but henceforth England's Joy.*
> *Brave Brute of our best English wits commended;*
> *True Trojane from Aeneas race descended.*
> *Rise top of wit, the honour of our Nation,*
> *And to old Ilium makes a new Oration.*

While the Odcombian advanced to the East, acquiring new titles along the way, the foggy shores of Albion heard the voice of a new personage who carried on the grand-scale farce. A certain John Taylor, later widely known as His Majesty's Water Poet, published a pamphlet named *The Sculler's Travels...or Gallimawfry of Sonnets, Satyres. ..and a quarterne of new catched epigrams, catched the last fishing tide.*

As a matter of fact, this was a rather late debut; at 34, a man was no longer young by the criteria of those days. This is the first time Taylor's name appeared in the public press. He had taken part in Essex's naval campaigns, was wounded in the leg, and received a position as a kind of senior ferryman transporting passengers up and down

---

17. Purchas S. *Purchas his Pilgrimes: in five books*. Printed W. Stansby for H. Fetherstone. 1625. Materials about Coryate (scattered notes and also letters published earlier, recommended as "samples of Odcombian jokes") are placed in the 1st (book 4, ch. 17) and the 2nd (book 10, ch. 12) volumes of this gigantic — about 5000 pages in-folio — collection of stories and reports of voyages and war expeditions starting from biblical times.

the River Thames. As such, he claimed, he was also responsible for the collection of peculiar "duties": from every wine-transporting vessel, six gallons of his preferred drink, per boat. And thus, this sailor and oarsman, who had once flunked out of grammar school and who had never been actively involved in the world of letters, leapt to the literary fore in 1612 — and in the ensuing decades, his name turned up on an impressive number of short pamphlets in prose and verse (and in 1630, his collected works were published).

And it was with the same Coryate that Taylor began his literary career, choosing the Odcombian as the main object for his biting wit throughout the entire course of his first years as a writer:

> *What matters for the place I first came from*
> *I am no Duncecomb, Coxecomb, Odcomb Tom,*
> *Nor am I like a wool-pack, cramm'd with Greek,*
> *Venus in Venice minded to goe seeke;*
> *And at my backe returne to write a Volume,*
> *In memory of my wits Gargantua Colume.*
> *The choysest wits would never so adore me;*
> *Nor like so many Lackies run before me,*
> *But honest Tom, I envy not thy state,*
> *There's nothing in thee worthy of my hate;*
> *Yet I confesse thou hast an excellent wit:*
> *But that an idle Braine doth harbour it.*
> *Foole thou it at the Court, I on the Thames,*
> *So farewell Odcomb Tom, God blesse King James.*

In another pamphlet, Coryate is notified that the "game has begun" and it shall be aimed at him, though Taylor harbors no grudge against him: "for what an asse were I to hate just nothing?" This is followed by lengthy and amusing arguments with the "panegyrics" in the Coryate book. Taylor also recounts that Coryate, as he claims, complained to the king himself (!) of his gibes and offences; while to justify himself, the waterman allegedly petitioned the sovereign in verse, equating himself and Coryate with the two biblical harlots who had put their dispute to the judgment of King Solomon. King James, he said, replied that when the lords of his Privy Council were short of work, he would instruct them to define the difference between Thomas Coryate, the writer, and John Taylor, the waterman. This story is certainly a joke; besides, Coryate left England in 1612, the same year that the first Taylor pamphlet appeared.

Taylor's next two rollicking parodies in verse were published in 1613. The first was entitled, *Odcomb's Complaint, A Sad, Joyful, Lamentable, Delightful, Merry-go-sorry Elegie, or Funeral Poem upon the supposed Death of the famous Cosmographicall Surveior and Historiographicall Relator Mr. Thomas Coryate*. In his pamphlet, Taylor plays up in every possible way the news of the death at sea of the "Odcombian, Grecian, Latinian Great Tom-Asse," claiming that it is common knowledge in London. Taylor goes as far as to describe how Coryate drowned at sea, and says that the fish who ate his body became perfect Latin scholars and Hellenists. Coryate is "glorified" at the end of the poem with verses "In praise of Mr. Thomas, the Deceased, fashioned of divers Stuffs, As Mockado, Fustian, Stand-further-off, and Motly," with a lot of weird neologisms and puzzling puns, often on the verge of nonsense. Thus, the epitaph to the death of Coryate, "translated" by Taylor, as he affirms, from "the Bermudan and Utopian languages," recommends we pronounce the text with a grunting accent, similar to a boar's grunting:

> Hough gruntough wough Thomough
> Coriatough Odcough robungough
> Warawogh hogh Conitogh sogh wogh termonatogroph
> Callimough gogh whohth Ragamogh demagogh palemogh.

The other pamphlet followed three months later and in the same playful style has great fun with *The Eighth Wonder of the World, or Coriate's Escape from his supposed drowning*.

In 1616, the book entitled *Thomas Coriate, Traveller for the English Wits: Greeting. From the Court of the Great Mogul . . .* appeared in London (that is the date printed on the title page; but the book was never registered). It comprised four of "Coryate's letters" dating back to 1615, and verses making fun of Coryate, some of the rhymes being submitted as Coryate's own writings. Among other things, the book announces Coryate's appointment to the "rank" of Knight of Troy. Of special interest is the letter addressed "To the High Seneschall of the Right Worshipfull Fraternitie of Sirenaical Gentlemen that meet the first Fridaie of every month at the signe of the Mere-maid in Bred-streete in London . . ." This is the only contemporary reference to such a "fraternity." Whether Coryate confuses the siren with the mermaid by chance or as a joke is unknown. Also, who that "Seneschall" was is a question that remains to be investigated. The author signs the letter in dazzling terms: "The Hierosolymitan-Syrian-Mesopotamian-Armenian-Median-Parphian-Indian Leggestretcher of Odcombe in Somerset, Thomas Coryate."

In 1617, Taylor published a pamphlet in prose entitled *Three weekes, three daies and three hours observations from London to Hamburg* and parodying certain pages of *Crudities*. The book was dedicated "to the absent Odcombian Knight Errant Sir Thomas Coryat, Great Brittaines Error, and the World's Mirror . . . Cosmographical, Geographical describer, Geometrical measurer, Historiographical Caligraphical Relater and Writer . . . the Odcombian Deambulator, Parambulator, Ambler, Trotter, or untired Traveller . . . Knight of Troy, and one of the dearest darlings to the blind Goddess Fortune."

In 1618, his *Pennylesse Pilgrimage, the money-lesse Perambulation of John Taylor, alias the King's Majesties Water Poet, from London to Edinburgh*, was published. Taylor made a series

The title page of the book *Thomas Coriate, Traveller for the English Wits: Greeting. From the Court of the Great Mogul...*

of such journeys, and in his humorous accounts he openly parodies Coryate. To what extent Taylor's whimsical details should be trusted, one may judge from the way he describes his journey from London to Queensborough, Kent, in a brown paper boat with oars made of two "stock fish tied to sticks." Nevertheless, more than a few Western scholars have taken John Taylor's cock-and-bull stories seriously (and Coryate's, as well), and seem to take the inexhaustible Water Poet as a sort of Thor Heyerdahl of the Shakespearean era.

In the same year of 1618, Taylor (Coryate's persecutor, mocker, "enemy") published another (the fifth and last) Coryate letter from India, stylized as the revelations of a "simple pilgrim" and addressed to his mother, dated 1616. In addition, the volume features many of Taylor's verses, in which he continues to ridicule Coryate and "proves" that the letter was actually written by the Odcombian, and not composed by the Water Poet himself. However, when publishing his collected works 12 years later,[18] Taylor included the full text of that "letter from Coryate" — a very significant point.

The same 1618 volume contains an amusing oration by Coryate — an abracadabra that he allegedly pronounced before Emperor Jahangir, the Great Mogul, himself, and in Persian, at that! The book also features a "portrait" of Coryate, a full-page engraving: a man dressed quite fashionably, with a sword, but his high-crowned and befeathered hat is put just across his nose, hiding the forehead and eyes. The reader is allowed to examine only the lower part of the nose, the moustache and the beard of our great leg-stretcher, who stands with his arms crossed over his belly.[19] A masked face of the true author (or authors) is a key Rabelaisian feature of this farce that was played out not only on the pages of books but on the stage of life, as well.

For almost the whole year of 1613, Coryate and his traveling companion stayed in Constantinople, enjoying the hospitality of a certain Pindar, resident of the British Levantine Company (serving for all intents and purposes as the Ambassador of England), who was impressed by the letters of recommendation Coryate presented. The plan for further adventures apparently was unclear as yet. Rutland died in the summer of 1612, suddenly followed in November of the same year by the heir to the throne, for whom the Coryate books had been created. The Prince of Wales being the principal patron of the whole farce, the enterprise was halted in mid-air until other patrons stepped up, chiefly the Earl of Pembroke.

During the first half of 1614 Coryate, accompanied by another Englishman, meandered around the Middle East and visited the Holy Land. Finally, that September, he set out for India via Syria, Persia and what is now Afghanistan, and within nine

---

18. *All the works of John Taylor, the water poet*. L. 1630. It is dedicated to Marquis Hamilton and the two brothers, William, Earl of Pembroke, and Philip, Earl of Montgomery.

19. One may occasionally find this portrait in books on the art of the Elizabethan-Jacobean age in England and labelled as the "Portrait of a Melancholic"! What a twist of fate — melancholia would be the last feature one might ascribe to the Odcombian.

The portrait of Coryate with a hat covering the face.

The title page of *All the works of John Taylor, the Water Poet*

months reached his destination. In "his letters" he claims that the whole route from Jerusalem to India — 3,300 miles (5300 km) — across mountains, deserts and jungles — was covered exclusively on foot, making Coryate not just the first and only Englishman to accomplish such a feat but, it seems, the only such legstretcher in history. And it is just as well that "Coryate's letter from India" states: "I doubt whether you ever heard of the like in your life."

These "letters" published in London relate some colorful details about his fantastic travels and describe the Court and Empire of Great Mogul. Thomas Roe, admiral, traveler, diplomat and poet, a friend of Jonson, Donne, the Earl of Southampton and the Earl of Pembroke, wrote to Pembroke from India to let him know that the notes of a certain traveler, known to Pembroke, were ripe enough to make all the publishers in London happy to start printing them. This means that Pembroke who, among other things, was in charge of royal entertainment, was kept informed about Coryate's feats and the planned publication of a new book; the relationship between Coryate's farce, the patron of Shakespeare, and Ben Jonson is obvious. Closing his letter, Roe relates that the person (i.e. Coryate) was presently devoting himself to composing and rehearsing new orations, "mainly for our lady Hartford." In British society of the time, Countess Frances Hartford was known for her beauty and particular haughtiness, and it seems highly unlikely that this arrogant lady could have any interest in the humble Odcombian, impecunious as he was, and ugly to boot. Apparently this was a hint about preparations for another comic episode for the next book.

Somehow or other (perhaps, through the selfsame Roe and Pembroke), news of Coryate made its way to the king himself. Not long before his death, Coryate is known to have met a merchant who came from England, and was pleased at first with the latter's statement that the kind King James remembered his Odcombian; but he suffered an awful shock upon hearing just how the king had recalled his name: "Why, is that fool still alive?"

And he was not, in fact, alive much longer. He was ill and very weak, and over-consumption of the sack he was kindly treated to at the English factory only hastened his end. What a coincidence — as a matter of fact, the story that Ward heard and recorded several decades after the death of William Shakspere, at Stratford-on-Avon, was that he died of "fever" after a repast shared with friends who had come from London.

In December 1617, Chaplain Edward Terry,[20] with whom Coryate shared quarters during his last days, buried him somewhere in the area of Surat (the western coast of India). Concluding his story about the circumstances of Coryate's demise, Terry writes: "Sic exit Coryatus: Hence he went off the stage and so must all after him, how long soever their parts seem to be. . . " Terry also notes: "Yet if he had not fall'n into the smart hands of the wits of those times, he might have passed better." To what

---

20. Terry, E. *Voyage to East India*. L., 1655.

degree the chaplain of the East India Company was privy to the secrets of that kitchen where such eccentric dishes as *Coryate's Crudities*, *Coryate's Crambe* and *The Odcombian Banquet* had been prepared, several years before, cannot be traced.

At the end of 1618, a ship from India brought a letter from Thomas Roe, which conveyed, among other items, notification of the demise of Thomas Coryate. The news went almost unnoticed; and the only person to make a public comment was His Majesty's Water Poet — the Odcombian's ruthless ridiculer. The book describing Taylor's journey in a paper boat with two stock-fishes as oars includes heartfelt and "almost normal" verses bidding farewell to the main comic character of the strange play, a character who now quit the scene after eight long years of buffoonery:

> *O famous Coriat, hadst thou come againe*
> *Thou wouldst have told us newest direct & plaine...*
> *Of cranes, and pigmies, lizzards, buzzards, owles,*
> *Of swine with hornes, of thousand beasts and foules...*
> *But farewell Thomas, never to returne*
> *Rest thou in peace within thy forraigne Urne...*
> *But we must loose that which we cannot save.*
> *And freely leave theé whom we cannot have.*

## THE RABELAISIAN CARNIVAL

These words of the Water Poet were a contemporary's epilogue to the extraordinary life story and literary fame of Thomas Coryate of Odcombe. For some time, his name was still mentioned in works by others of his contemporaries. Four decades later, collecting information about Coryate for a book, Thomas Fuller was able to learn only that the man was a fool, a clown, amusing to the court and their literary friends and notable for the ugly shape of his head. Then came an almost complete silence. In England, torn apart by civil war and political factions, the eccentric traveler-legstretcher and his peculiar books seem to have fallen into complete oblivion; and later, the generation of the "Enlightenment" appears to have looked upon this stranger and his tales from the seemingly recent past with a bewildered consternation not unlike that of the Trojans crowding around the wooden horse left to them by the cunning Greeks, who had already sailed away.

*Coryate's Crudities* was reissued late in the 18th century, without any commentary. And not until another age elapsed were attempts made to define more precisely who was behind the pen names and to solve the riddles behind the laughter focused around the ridiculous Odcombian dressed in buffoon clothes with a head "like a sugar-loaf inverted."

The Coryate books and the whole paradoxical story around him are not widely known. In his study, Strachan praises the scientific and literary merits of *Crudities*, and regrets that Coryate found it necessary to envelope such valuable work in an inappropriate shell of foolishness. Strachan never focuses on the mocking, comical and sometimes purely fantastic character of the many details Coryate tells about himself, though these things often nonplus him. Neither he is able to account for the unparalleled collection of mocking "panegyrics," penned by the most brilliant English literary men, in what would appear to have started out as a purely geographic work. Indeed, what on earth was that long list of renowned authors laughing at, what made the Water Poet burst out laughing at the bare mention of the name of Thomas Coryate — what, after all, is the meaning of this decades-long circus around such an outstanding traveler and writer? Strachan fails to answer these questions because, like other British historians, he accepts the undisguised comedy, the impudent farce, at face value, and takes the meek clown and booze hound for a remarkable writer and a learned student of foreign lands. The farcical, carnival aspect, which is overwhelmingly important and determinant in the entire story of Thomas Coryate, the "Prince of Poets," is lost on them.

In his substantial study of the impact of Rabelais upon English literature (1967), Huntington Brown[21] noted the huge collection of panegyrics in *Coryat's Crudities* (he referred to it as an avalanche). The presence of Rabelaisian elements in the verses and in Coryate's book is beyond question; Rabelais is explicitly mentioned more than once, and the volume abounds in allusions and direct and indirect quotations from *Gargantua and Pantagruel*. However, Brown neglects other aspects of the farce around Coryate, the peculiarity of the whole business, and his close relationship with the Jacobean literary and theatrical world.

Many important aspects of the Coryate story have been neglected, including its documented relationship with the best-known (although always somewhere off stage) figure of the time. All these events take place near the Great Bard — literally! Thomas Coryate and William Shakespeare were not only contemporaries; they had the same publishers (Blount, Thorpe, Jaggard)[22], and the same patrons (the Rutlands and the Pembrokes); and the few poets who referred to the name of Shakespeare in their works are also among the ranks of Coryate's "panegyrists." And above all, both figures are closely associated with Ben Jonson, who publicly professed his personal acquaintance with both. In fact, addresses and verses by Jonson begin both *Crudities* and Shakespeare's posthumous Great Folio of 1623. Except for Ben Jonson, no

---

21. Brown H. *Rabelais in English Literature*. N.Y., 1967, p. 72-78.
22. About Blount, Thorpe, Barret, Jaggard, Fetherstone, Stansby and other publishers, booksellers and printers, one may consult the *Dictionary of Printers and Booksellers in England, Scotland and Ireland, and of Foreign Printers of English Books 1557-1640*. Ed. R. McKerrow. L., 1910.

Shakespeare contemporary directly pertaining to literature has anywhere near as many or as significant proven "points of contact" with the Great Bard as Coryate has; but the name of the eccentric Odcombian has only relatively recently begun to appear in some Shakespeare biographies. He is mentioned in discussions of Fuller's well-known (but far from reliable) description of verbal sparring between Shakespeare and Jonson, or in the context of more trustworthy facts about the wittiness and "practical jokes" of the gentlemen who met at the Mermaid Club and liked to call themselves the "British Wits."

Thus, British historians and literary scholars still regard Thomas Coryate as a sort of mysterious jovial sphinx. The longstanding mystique results in large measure from scholars' failure to appreciate the diversity of forms in which the comedic culture of the Middle Ages and Renaissance manifested itself. Among them, the most brilliant and well known (today), but not unique and unchallenged, is the masterpiece by François Rabelais. *Gargantua and Pantagruel* is a literary work, though its characters emerged from the depths of comedic folklore culture and do not fall into any academic canon whatsoever. As to the phenomenon known as Thomas Coryate, it is not only literary: much convincing evidence indicates that we are spectators of a farce, a grandiose decades-long carnival play, and the acts are constantly shifting from the printed page to the real-life stage, and vice versa. The farce is played out in such a daring manner and on such a breath-taking scale that its theatricality has never been adequately assessed in the context of the age in which it was generated — that of Shakespeare.

Like Rabelais' book, the Coryate farce may be compared figuratively with a chest whose clever decoration conceals its precious contents. However, the renowned French writer was not a clown or the butt of jokes: he was an author, and his readers laughed not at him but at the stories he related and the characters he invented; whereas Coryate himself stands as the central figure in the farce played around him, and he dances together with the wits who make fun of him. Moreover, he is no fantastic giant, but an ordinary man in flesh and blood, "inscribed" in Shakespearean England. He might be pushed wet and shriveled into a painted box or dragged across all of Europe and the deserts of Asia, ordained to the "rank" of a Knight of Troy, or trotted out before the king and the royal family. Books and letters could be published on his behalf, and he would always be at the center of the festival of laughter coming down to us from the pages of *Crudities*, *Crambe*, *The Odcombian Banquet*, the letters from India and the pamphlets of His Majesty's Water Poet.

It is a peculiar feature of the farce that, although the main book signed with Coryate's name has a grotesque title and is full of outlandish material, its backbone is of historical and literary value even now, a highly learned narrative about Europe as seen by a contemporary of Shakespeare and Jonson. And that mixture of genres — satire, burlesque, comedy — enveloping the serious texts, that constant invasion of literature into real life, the continuous presence of a buffoon disguised as the author, gives the whole enterprise the feel of a farcical play that was staged. But the secrets of this theater are all the more difficult to pierce, given the special (one might say, the English) way of laughing seriously when the limitations of reality are not discarded entirely but are used as stage props to obfuscate and confuse any readers outside the inner circle. In the Renaissance tradition, the fool often serves as a counterbalance to a man's claims for the power of his mind. The fool shares the stage with the hero; they are inseparable. We see, however, that this applies not only to fiction or theater personages. England has offered the world a formidable counterbalance to the great writer's, or writers', image.

The best way to make the farce look real to outsiders is, of course, the author's (authors') use of not only a pen name but a live and, furthermore, disagreeable mask, someone who presents no danger of divulging the secret; this also affords a fine opportunity to have a laugh at the readers' expense. In fact, no diaries, original letters or autographs from Coryate have survived, any more than they have from Shakespeare. As to the real authors and their assistants, some light is shed by the list of names under the "panegyrics," as well as by the postscript to Coryate's "letter from India" where he asks the "High Seneschall" to send his regards to the "true friends of literature." They include the poets John Donne, Richard Martin, Christopher Brooke, John Hoskins, Hugh Holland, Ben Jonson, of course, and the geographer Samuel Purchas. Some publishers are also mentioned — only five, but a very important five: in addition to Blount and Barret, who registered *Crudities* and *Crambe*, Matthew Lownes is mentioned — whose name is on the title page of the London edition of Robert Chester's *Love's Martyr*. We have already traced the Earl of Rutland's connection with the farcical play, and the evidence is quite abundant. It is clear that *Crudities* was based in part on his travel notes and impressions. Some of the "panegyric verses" also came from his pen. Perhaps it was he whom they addressed as "The High Seneschall of the Right Worshipfull Fraternitie of Sirenaical Gentlemen" or, as it is put in the same letter — as "Protoplast," i.e. "The First Man." The last books delivered to Roger Rutland before he died, to the "Roger put down by Thomas," were *Coryate's Crambe* and *The Odcombian Banquet*, and one of the five hand-written copies of *Convivium Philosophicum* is kept at Belvoir Castle. However, this "coincidence" among many others was never noted by scholars who held the keys to the farce but did not understand their meaning.

The Coryate play was never completed. The second book, which was intended to surpass the first — to describe the Orient as seen through the eyes of a pilgrim-buffoon, was never published; but Purchas' notes, Roe's diaries and Coryate's letters from India show the outlines and some details of the grand design. They lift the veil and expose the "technology" by which such a farce was created. The fact that the generations that followed were such appreciative spectators and readers, interpreting the Coryate farce as Coryate's True Story, may be regarded as the highest compliment to its creators. It is clear that many details of this story require further study. Highly promising archival materials remain to be tackled. However, the main point is now beyond doubt: this exceptional case vividly manifests the passion for the Game inherent in Shakespeare's generation, their effort to turn life's stage into theater, the craving for farce, practical jokes, and purification through laughter.

This is the realized dream of Jaques-the-Melancholic, and it is also a vital key to comprehending his other, more grandiose Game, the mystery of William Shake-speare. Perhaps that was what John Donne had in mind when he compared *Coryate's Crudities* (which he helped to create) with the Sibylline Oracles.

# INTERLUDE: EXCERPTS FROM THE BOOK "CORYATE'S CRUDITIES"

Some "Panegyric" Introductory Material
Honoring the Unordinary Legstetcher and Writer

**✳✳**

## The CHARACTER
of the famous ODCOMBIAN, or rather
POLYTOPIAN, Thomas the Coryate,
Traveller, and Gentleman. Author of
these Quinque-mestriall CRUDITIES.

Done by a charitable friend,[1] that thinkes it necessary, by
this time, you should understand the maker, as well as the worke.

He is an Engine, wholly consisting of extremes, a Head, Fingers, and Toes. For what his industrious Toes have trod, his ready Fingers have written, his subtle head dictating. He was set a going for Venice the fourteenth of May Anno 1608 and returned home (of himselfe) the third of October following, being wound up for five moneths or thereabouts; his paces two for one. Since, by vertue of those weights he hath bene conveniently able to visite Towne and Countrie, Fayres and Mercats, to all places, and all societies a Spectacle gratefull, above that of Niniueh, or the Citie of Norwich[2]; and he is now become the better Motion, by hauing this Booke his Interpreter: which yet hath exprest his purse more then him, as we the rest of his Commenders have don, so unmercifully charging the Presse with his prayse. But to

---

1. The "Character" and the acrostic that follows it seem to be more or less all of a piece, and therefore both are apparently by Ben Jonson. (– I.G.)

2. Norwich was razed to the ground by the Danes in the Middle Ages, just as the Assyrian capital Nineveh was destroyed by the Babylonians ages before. (– I.G.)

that Gale, he sets up all sayles. He will beare paper (which is cloth) enough. He hath ever since the first designe of printing hereof, bene a Delicijs to the Court; but served there in his owne cloathes, and at his owne costs; where he hath not bene costive of acquaintance to any, from the Palatine to the Plebeian, which popularity of his (it is thought by some of his Odcombians) may hurt him. But he free from all other Symptoms of aspiring, will easily outcry that; it being a motlie and no perfect ambition: the rather, because when he should have beene taken up for the place (though he hastily prevented it with a tender of himselfe) hee conditioned to have no office of charge, or neerenesse cast upon him, as the Remora of his future travaile; for to that he is irrecoverably addicted. The word Travaile affects him in a Waine-oxe, or Packe-horse. A Carrier will carry him from any company that hath not beene abroad, because he is a Species of a Traveller. But a Dutch-Post doth ravish him. The mere superscription of a letter from Zurich sets him up like a top: Basil or Heidelberg makes him spinne. And at seeing the word Frankford, or Venice, though but on the title of a Booke, he is readie to breake doublet, cracke elbowes, and ouerflowe the roome with his murmure. Hee is a mad Greeke, no less then a merry: and will buy his Egges, his Pudding, his Ginger-bread, yea cobble his Shoes in the Atticke dialect: and would make it a matter of Conscience to speake other, were he trusted alone in a roome with an Andiro of state. The greatest Politick that advances into Paules he will quit, to go talke with the Grecian that begs there; such is his humility; and doth grieve inwardly he was not borne that country man for that purpose.[3] You shall perceive a veine or thread of Greeke runne through his whole discourse, and another of Latine, but that is the courser.

He is a great and bold Carpenter of words, or (to expresse him in one like his owne) a Logodaedale; which voice when he heares, 'tis doubtfull whether he will more love at the first, or envy after, that it was not his owne. All his Phrase is the same which his manners and haviour, such as if they were studied to make Mourners merry; but the body of his discourse able to breake Impostumes, remove the stone, open the passage from the Bladder, and undoe the very knots of the Gout; to cure evewhere Phisyck hath turned her back, and Nature hung down her head for shame. Being not only the Antidote to resist sadness, but the Preservative to keepe you in mirth, a life and a day. A man might undo the Colledge that would practise with onely him. And there is no man but to enjoy his company, would neglect any thing but businesse. It is thought he lives more by letting[4] out of ayre, then drawing in, and feared, his belly will exhibit a Bill in chancery against his Mouth for talking away his meales. He is always Tongue-Major of the company, and if ever the perpetuall motion be to be hoped for, it is from thence. Hee will aske, How you doe? Where you have bene? How is it? If you have traveled? How you like his booke? With what newes? And be guilty of a thousand such curteous impertinences in an howre, rather than want the humanity of vexing you.

To conclude this ample Traveller in some bounds, you shall best know him by this: hee is frequent at all sorts of free tables, where though he might be as a Guest, hee will rather be served in as a Dish, and is loth to have any thing of himselfe kept cold against the next day. To give the Non ultra of him in a word, he is so Substantive an Author as will stand by himselfe without the neede of his Booke to bee joined with him.

Here endeth the Character attended with a Characteristic Acrostich.

---

3. Not to beg, but to talke Greeke the better with the naturall Grecians (*Jonson's note*).
4. I meane in the fore parts, not the hinder (*Jonson's note*).

## To the Right Noble Tom, Tell-Troth of his travailes, the Coryate of Odcombe, and his Booke now going to travell.

T rie and trust Roger, was the word, but now
H onest Tom Tell-Troth puts downe Roger, How?
O f travell he discourseth so at large,
M arry he sets out at his owne charge;
A nd therein (which is worth his valour too)
S hewes he dares more then Paules Church-yard durst do.

C ome forth thou bonnie bouncing booke then daughter
O f Tom of Odcombe that odde Joviall Author,
R ather his sonne I should have cal'd thee, why?
Y es thou wert borne out of his travelling thigh
A s well as from his braines, and claimest thereby
T o be his Bacchus as his Pallas: bee
E ver his thighs Male then, and his braines Shee.
                         Ben Jonson

**

## An Introduction to the ensuing verses

I[5] here present unto thee (gentle Reader) the encomiastick and panegyrick verses of some of the worthiest spirits of this Kingdome, composed by persons of eminent quality and marke, as well for dignity as excellencie of wit; such as haue vouchsafed to descend so low as to dignifie and illustrate my lucubrations without any demerit of theirs[6] (I do ingenuously confesse) with the singular fruits of their elegant inventions, which they have expressed in the best and most learned languages of the world, two only excepted, which are the Welch and Irish. But in that I exhibit unto thy view such a great multitude of Verses as no booke whatsoever printed in England these hundred yeares, had the like written in praise thereof; ascribe it not I intreate thee to any ambitious humour of me, as that I should crave to obtrude so many to the world in praise of my booke. For I can assure thee I solicited not halfe those worthy Wights for these verses that I now divulge; a great part of them being sent unto me voluntary from divers friends, from whom I expected such courtesie. At last when I saw the multitude of them

---

5. (Coryate.) Further in this chapter, notes are made by "Coryate himself" and his panegyrists; in the original, they are placed in the margins. (– I.G.)

6. Mistake me not Reader, I referre this word to the word Lucubrations.

to increase to so great a number, I resolved to put above a thousand of them into an Index Expurgatorius, and to detaine them from the presse. Whereupon the Princes Highnesse (who hath most graciously deigned to be the[7] Hyperaspist and Moecenas of my booke) understanding that I meant to suppresse so many gave me a strict and expresse commandment to print all those verses which I had read to his Highnesse. Since then that inevitable necessity hath beene imposed upon me, I have communicated that copious rhapsodie of poems to the world that my learned friends have bountifully bestowed upon me; wherein many of them are disposed to glance at me with their free and merry jests, for which I desire thee (courteous Reader) to suspend thy censure of me till thou hast read over my whole booke.

**\*\***

### Panegyricke verses upon the author and his booke

Incipit "Friend of the sojourner abroad":

Lordings, full well I hope you know
I never shot in Phoebus bow,
　　Or clim'd Parnassus hill:
Yet must I needes in dogrell rime
Crave your sweet patience for a time,
　　Full sore against my will.
I am not now to tell a tale
Of George a Greene, or Jacke a Vale,
　　Or yet of Chittiface:
But I must be the Chanti-cleere
Of one that is withouten peere
　　A horne replete with grace.
For he at Odcombe was y-bore,
Whereas the fates were heard to score
　　The fortunes of his birth:
Goe pretty dandy-prat to schoole
(Said they) thou shalt no little foole
　　Be counted for thy mirth.
The child in time was waxen great,
And all the Sophists he did great,
　　Their problems to confound;

---

7. You shall understand the meaning of this word in a marginal note upon the verses immediately ensuing.

Grammarians sore did stand in feare
The coinage of his words to heare,
  So uncouth was their sound.
For by a natural instinct,
 The Graces to his lips were linkt,
  (Forsooth his lips were faire.)
His mouth did open ere he spake,
And swifter farre then Ducke and Drake
  His words flew through the ayre.
The stony hearts that could not bide
A Church-Ale at Whitsontide,
  He suppled with his speech:
And like a Captaine bold and stout
He did advance his Eagles snowt,
  Faire thrive it I beseech.
Not Mahound, no nor Termagaunt
Could ever make halfe their avant
  Of deeds so sterne and fell,
As can this child Sir Thopas Squire,
Inspired with a sparke of fire
  Stolne out of wisdoms cell.
He hammers words upon his teeth
(Rime thereunto I can unneeth)
  Yet still I will proceede;
Like as a Beare doth licke her whelpe,
Their roughnesse so his tongue doth helpe,
  When polishing is neede.
Now Lordings mercy doe I aske,
That since I under-went this taske
  His name I have conceald;
He keeps the Magazine of wit,
And beares the privy key of it,
  Which may not be reveal'd.
Yet in despite of bread and ale,
Unbuckled now shall be the male,
  Betide what may betide:
His name is Coryate I wish,
But whether he be flesh or fish,
  I cannot yet decide.
For like the errant Knight Ulysses,

Through the Seas amongst the fishes
   He lanched forth his hulke:
The sides whereof were heard to groane
No lesse than twenty miles and one
   Under his grievous bulke.
Then either without scrippe or bagge
He usde his ten-toes for a nagge
   From Venice for to hie.
Thorough thicke, and thorough thinne
Untill he came unto his Inne,
   His winged heeles did flie.
He travaild North, he travaild South
   With [8]Hyperaspist in his mouth
   A word of his devising.
For nature  letters pattents gave
To him  the priviledge to have
   Of words naturalizing.
To trees and steeples as he went
He did his homage verament,
   And salu-ed them each one.
He registered their names always
Contrary if that any saies,
   The booke is to be showne.
A Cortizan then lycoras
More sweet in Venice towne there was,
   That wisht him for her owne:
But shee could never him hand fast;
For as a Gelding he was chast,
   Though Gelding he were none.
The Barcarvola appetite
His Gondola directed right
   Unto a female Elfe;
Yet would he not play Cupids Ape,
In Chaucers jest lest he should shape

---

8. A word that the author once used in an Oration to the Prince, metaphorically signifying (as being derived from these two Greeke wordes, that signifieth "above," and "a shield," that is, one that opposeth his shield in the defence of his friend against the blow of an enemie) a Patron, or Protector. Which word by a kind of conversion may be not improperly applied (as a certaine conceited gentleman lately said) to the author himselfe. Hyperaspist quasi hyperhorspist, that is, one upon whom never Asses pist, but Horses once pist on him, as when he lay upon straw at their heeles in Bergomo a Citie of Lombardie.

A Pigsnye like himselfe.
This wandring Squire  full oft I heard
The circle of his beard had squard,
  And  skowered every haire;
That sweeter then the Eglentine,
And then the purple Columbine
  He did appeare more faire.
He had a kind of simple blush
That kept him still from being flush,
  When ladies did him wooe:
Though they did smile, he seem'd to scowle,
As doth the faire broad-faced fowle,
  That sings To whit to whooe.
It was no crochet of his braine
That out his legs to so great paine
  In passing to and fro:
But sure it was the quintessence
Of study, that beyond all since
  Had made his wits to crow.
With Latin he doth rule the roast,
And spowteth Greeke in every coast,
  Ne'r may his well-spring fade:
He over-speakes the English tongue,
And picketh gold out of the dongue
  That ancient Poets made.
If any Zoilus will carpe,
Or take upon him for to harpe
  Upon his  learned strings:
On foote to Venice let him goe,
And then at his returning show
  What fruite from thence he brings.
For had our Coryate beene a Jade,
In halfe the journey that he made
  He had beene foundered cleane:
But now by foote, by cart, and saile,
Tom Coryate is come from Italie,
  From Italie I meane.
The squeazie humour of his braine
Before he parted from this maine,
  Near perished his skull:

Now since the Sunne beganne to sup,
And drinke those grosser vapours up,
  He is no more a Gull.
Oh let the fardels of his leaves
Be held more precious then the sheaves
  Pitched up in harvest time;
Ne ever any man alive
May see them saying from Queene-hive:
  Now Muse stay here thy rime.
      Explicit **"Friend of the sojourner abroad."**

**Incipit Joannes Harrington de Bathe (John Harington):**

Thou glorious Goose that kept'st the Capitoll,
  Afford one wuill, that I may write one storie yeat
Of this my new-come Odcombe-friend Tom Coryet,
  Whose praise so worthy wits and pens inroll
  As (with good cause) his custom is to glory it::
  So farre am I from judging his a sory wit,
Above earth, seas, ayre, fire,Ile it extol
  To Cinthias spheare, the next beneath the stares.
Where his vast wit, and courage so audatious
  Of equall worth in times of peace, and warres,
(As Rolands erst) encombring roomes capacious
  Lie stored some in hogsheads, some in jarres.
    This makes the learn'd of late in forren parts
    Find Phoebes face so full of wennes and warts.
      **Explicit Joannes Harrington de Bathe.**

**Incipit Henricus Goodier (Henry Goodyere):**

If in an evennesse all wisedome lie,
Tom thou art wise, thou dost all evenly.
Once thou didst wench, and thou wert carted once,
Once thou didst[9] steale, & once they beate thy bones.
Once didst thou beg, and if thou then didst get
Nothing by begging, thou art even yet.
What onely he saw he onely writes, if than
He onely reade it, hee's an even man.

---

9. Viz. Grapes.

Our spies write home no ill of him; he went,
He staid, he came an even[10] Innocent.
The jesuites could not shake him: for he would not
Take orders, but remaine an[11] Idiote.
If any thinke him dull or heavy, know
The Court and cities mirth cannot be so.
Who thinks him light, aske them who had the taske
To beare him in a trunke unto the maske,
He is so equall, that if he were laid
Into those scales whereby the proofe is made,
Whether the woman or the plume prevaile,
He and his booke would hardly turne the scale.

**Explicit Henricus Goodier.**

**Incipit Rowlandus Cotton (Rowland Cotton):**

Columbus, Magelan, and Drakes brave story
Are yet remembered unto their glory.
But thy high deeds with theirs when I compare,
I say thy travels have with theirs no share.
I wonder then this writhing age hath fail'd
To tell ere this how farre Tom Coryate sail'd
In five mon'ths time, and most or all on foote.
What man alive that ever else did do't?
It cannot be but that the world did looke
That you thy selfe hereof shouldst write a booke,
What good acceptance such a booke shall finde,
Thou need'st not doubt, there's no man so unkind
That will make scruple for to be thy halfe
Since thou the heifer art that beares the calfe.
Tis thy first borne Tom, I pray thee love it;
And whosoever shall thy issue covet,
I wish there may befall him this one curse,
To treade thy steps againe, and with thy purse.
Yet one thing Tom I do dislike is sooth,
Thou dost spare thy selfe to tell a truth.
What need'st thou in thy storie be so nice,

---

10. A harmlesse man.
11. A lay man, or private man, as being derived from the Greeke word, which signifieth a private man.

To tell thy child of all thy nits and lice?
Yet it becomes thee well, and much the rather,
The sonne, I thinke, will prove so like the father.
But pardon, Tom, if I no further tell
Those gifts which in thee do by nature dwell.
Who tells the Asse that he hath two long eares,
Or Chanti-cleare that he a coxcombe weares?
Why, all the world doth know as well as I
That never any did as much descrie,
So many nations, manners, and so soone,
Except alone the man that's in the moone.
Let other wits that with a nimbler wing,
Do cut the emptie ayre, thy prayses sing;
My Muse intreats thee to resume thy penne,
And to relate unto thy countrey-men
Whether thy father Joviall were or sad,
And what complexion thy faire mother had
When they were linked in wedlocks lovely band,
And whether of them had the upper hand:
How many mon'ths thy mother did intombe
Thy tender body in her fruitfull wombe:
What milder planet governed in the skie
In the horoscope of thy nativity,
Thy mothers midwife, and thy nurses name
The shire and houshold whence thy linage came.
Who trained up thy youth, and in what place,
Whether where Isis hides her dewie face,
Or where the silver streames of Chame do glide,
Shadowed with willowes upon either side;
That other men may learne to get a sonne
To see those countries which thy selfe hast done.
This calculation yet would breed a danger
And 'twere not fit to teach it every stranger;
Lest when the world thy learned booke should view,
A foole might get as wise a child as you.

**Explicit Rowlandus Cotton.**

**Incipit Joannes Donne (John Donne):**
Oh to what height will love of greatnesse drive
Thy leavened spirit, Sesqui-superlative?

Venice vast lake thou hadst seene, wouldst seeke than
Some vaster thing, and foundst a Cortezan.
 That inland Sea having discovered well,
A Cellar-gulfe, where one might saile to hell
From Heydelberg, thou longdst to see; And thou
This Booke, greater than all, producest now,
Infinite worke, which doth so farre extend,
That none can study it to any end.
Tis no one thing; it is no fruite, nor roote;
Nor poorely limited with head or foote.
If man be therefore man, because he can
Reason, and laugh, thy booke doth halfe make man.
One halfe being made, thy modesty was such,
That thou on th' other halfe wouldst never touch.
When wilt thou be at full, great Lunatique?
Not till thou exceed the world? Canst thou be like
A prosperous nose-borne wenne, which sometime growes
To be farre greater than the Mother-nose?
Go then; and as to thee, when thou didst goe,
Munster did Townes, and Sesner Authors show,
Mount now to Gallo-belgicus; Appeare
As deepe a States-man, as a Gazettier.
Homely and familiarly, when thou commest backe,
Talke of Will Conqueror, and Prester Jacke.
Goe bashfull man, lest here thou blush to looke
Upon the progresse of thy glorious booke.
To which both Indies sacrifices send;
The west sent gold, which thou didst freely spend,
(Meaning to see't no more) upon the presse.
The east sends hither her deliciousnesse;
And thy leav's must embrace what comes from thence,
The Myrre, the Pepper, and the Frankinsence.
This magnifies thy leav's; but if they stoope
To neighbour wares, when Merchants doe unhoope
Voluminous barrels; if thy leav's doe then
Convay these wares in parcels unto men,
If for vaste Tomes of Currans, and of Figs,
Of Medicinall, and Aromatique twigs'
Thy leav's better methode doe provide,
Divide to Pounds, and Ounces subdivide;

If they stoope lower yet, and vent our wares,
Home-manufactures, to thicke popular faires,
If omnipraegnant there, upon warm stals
They hatch all wares for which the buyer cals,
Then thus thy leav's we justly may commend,
That they all kinde of matter comprehend.
Thus thou, by mens which th' Ancients never tooke,
A Pandect makest, and Universall Booke.
The bravest heroes, for publique good
Scattred in divers lands, their limes and blood.
Worst malefactors, to whom men are prize,
Doe publique good, cut in Anatomies;
So will thy Booke is in peeces: For a lord

Which casts at Portescues, and all the board,

Provide whole Books; Each leafe enough will be
For friends to passe time, and keepe companie.
Can all carouse up thee? No: thou must fit
Measures; and fill out for the half-pinte wit.
Some shal wrap pils, and save a friends life so,
Some shal stop muskets, and so kill a foe.
Thou shalt not ease the Critiques of next age
So much, at once their hunger to asswage.
Nor shall wit-pyrats hope to finde thee lie
All in one bottome, in one Librarie.
Some leav's may paste strings there in other books,
And so one may, which on another looks,
Pilfer, alas, a little wit from you,
But hardly[12] much; and yet I thinke this true;
As Sybils was, your booke is misticall,
For every peece is as much worth as all.
Therefore mine impotency I confesse;
The healths which my braine beares, must be farre lesse;
Thy Gyant wit o'erthrowes me, I am gone;
And rather then reade all, I would reade none.

---

12. I meane from one page which shall paste strings in a booke.

**In eundem Macaronicon.**

Quot, dos haec, Linguists perfetti, Disticha fairont,
Tot cuerdos, States-men, hic liure fara tuus.
Es sat a My l'honneur ester hic inteso: Car I LEAVE
L'honra, de personne nester credito, tibi.

**Explicit Joannes Donne.**

**Incipit Richardus Martin (Richard Martin):**

To my friend that by lying at the signe of the Fox,
doth prove himselfe no Goose,
Thomas Coryate, the Traveller,
A Sonet.

O For a bonny blith and bounsing ballet
    To praise this Odcomb'd Chanti-cleere that hatched
    These Crudities which (with his shoes) he patched,
    All hitting right as it were with a mallet,
Before us here he sets both bag and wallet,
    Where met are many scraps (you see) unmatched:
    His feete, hands, head (daies and nights) walkt, wrote, watched:
    And hardly did he lie on any pallet.
Much oyle he sav'd both from his shoes and sallats,
    Which thriftily he ate while they were cobled;
    Then (for his fruite) these Cruduties he gobled,
    Which since he season'd hath for sundry palats.
To him therefore vaile travellers your bonnets,
Of him write Poets all your Songs and Sonnets.

**Explicit Richardus Martin.**

**Incipit Laurentius Whitakerus (Laurence Whitaker):**

To the most peerlesse Poetical Prose-writer, the most
Transcendent, Tramontane Traveller, and most single-soled,
single-souled, and single-shirted Observer, the Odcombian
Gallobelgicus.

Wonder of worlds, that with one fustian case,
One payre of shoes, hast done Odcombe the grace
To make her name knowen past the Alpine hils,
And home return'd hast worne out many quils
In writing faire thy large red-lin'd Rehearsall
Of what thou saw'st with sharpe eyes which did pearce all

Stone Tombes, great gates, and manners of the people,
Besides the height of many a Tower and Steeple,
Snailes, Butterflies, black sheep, black hogs, & Storks
And the neate use of eating meate with forkes:
And, that of stuffe thou might'st leave out no odd piece
To raise thy worke, th' hast writ o' th' Switzers Codpiece:
Thou saw'st the Venice Donna's & didst quarrel
With the Dutch Boore, thou saw'st the monstrous barrel:
But O thy temper! Seldome wast thou drunke,
Nor hadst but one night's solace with thy punke:
Nor in thy pilgrimage wert much a sinner,
But when thou didst stele bread to save a dinner.
Thou in all sorts of travel hadst thy part,
But most on foote, and sometimes in a cart.
Nor didst though scorne for all spruce Criticks mockings,
T' accept of gift a Prussian aged stockings.
Thow sawst the field of many a famous battell,
And home thou cam'st well furnisht with quicke cattell,
Yet must I say thy fortune therein was ill,
For thou wentst nak't to wash thy shirt at Basil;
And having seen Cloysters, and many a Monke,
Becam'st thy selfe a Recluse in a trunke.
But Il'e not write thy labours Inventory,
I'le say but this of thee, and of thy story,
   Thou well describ'st the marvels thou didst see,
   And this thy booke as well describeth thee.
      **Explicit Laurentius Whitakerus.**

**Incipit Hugo Holland (Hugh Holland):**

In persona & laudem authoris.
To Topographicall Typographicall Thomas.
I sing the man, I sing the wofull case,
The shirt, the shoes, the shanks that serv'd to trace
Seven Countries wide, the greater was the paine,
That two to one he ever came againe,
Yet two for one he came: O Muse, O Maid,
(If Maid or Muse) say what hath so beraid
This silly soule, and drove him to such labours,
As had his hide bene onely made for tabours?
Recount my Girle, what did he with the French,
Before he courted the Venetian wench?
How could he leave his well-boyl'd beere, & scape,
To drinke the raw bloud of the Germane grape?

372

Wherewith his waterie teeth being set on edge,
He nigh had lost of teeth his double hedge.
At home much did he suffer, much abroad,
And never once (poore Asse) did cast his load,
Yet further went then Scaracalasino,
And after litter'd lay at Bergomo.
This usage did he beare abroad uncivill,
At home too was he borne not farre from Evill.
In Odcombe parish yet famous with his cradle,
A chicke he hatcht was of an egge unaddle.
Whence a young Cockrel he was sent for knowledge
To Winchester, and planted in the Colledge:
Not there to prove a goose (for he is none)
But that he might with other Cocks come on.
Where loe a dwarfe in stature he so pliant,
Grew in the Greeke, that he became a Giant,
Pronouncing then Demosthenes each letter,
More plaine, and reading all then Homer better,
This Prince of Poets, that of Rhetoritians.
His Latin too deserves more praise then Priscians,
For Coryate lives, and Priscian is dead,
No marvaile; Coryate brake so oft his head.
Now when in Greeke and Latin he could gravell,
His schoole fellows, forsooth he needs will travel;
Not for bare language, but (his charges earning
On the by) on the maine, for reall learning.
Be Basil proofe and Zurich too, and Frankfort,
As thou in print maist see, if thou him thanke for't.
What would he with more tongues? He hath enough,
That which he hath is fine neat-leather tough:
And yet at Calais to confound the Masse
Some say he spake the tongue of Balaams Asse.
And others, that with Sampsons Asses jawbone.
He slew whole hoasts: so is he rough and rawbone.
T'were but a frump to name the Asses backe,
Each common traveller beares thereon his packe:
I therefore leave the Asse for feare he doubt,
Or others for him, that I should him flout.
But as the Serpent (not the goose) that hisses,
So is he wise, and equald with Ulysses;
Who townes of many men hath seene & manners:
The more was he beholding to the tanners.
If he had but one onely paire of shoes.
Then how much leather thinke ye could he loose?

He hath seene Paris garden and the Lions,
And Paris Garden of all France, and Lyons,
With all townes that lye twixt this and Venice,
Where (howbeit some say he played at tennis)
He more prevaild against the 'xcoriate Jewes,
Then Broughton could, or twenty more such Hughs,
And yet but for one pretty poore misprision,
He was high made one of the Circumcision.
But holla, that's a part that must be privy;
Now go we to the towne of learned Livy.
Where being before Licentiat, he Proceeded
To beg like a poore Paduan, when he needed.
Then through Vicenza and Brescia doth he goe
Among the Cogleons, those of Bergomo.
Who  made him lye in litter like a Villan:
Then views he, in his case of fustaine, Milan.
(Not Milan fustaine though) yet such a trophae
As might become a Soldan or a Sophe.
Which in his frontispice he doth extol
Like those of Marius in Romes Capitoll.
And well the case was lin'd with poudred Ermin.
Though others thinke it was some stranger vermin.
Now should I tell his travels with the Dutch,
But  that my Muse doth feare to drinke too much.
For if the water of poore Hippocrene
Doth make her drunke, what wil the wine of Rhene?
Both Heidelberg I passe, and the great hogshead,
Which he bestrid him selfe, like a great hogs-head.
Who list the paines or pleasure take  to looke,
Shall this and more finde printed in the booke.
Whose merits here I will no further raise:
That were my friend to sell and not to praise.
Perhaps I know some that have seene the Turke,
Yet would be whipt ere they wrote such a worke.
But what a volume here will rise anone,
When he hath seene both Turke and Prester John?
Enough; yet in his Crudities behoofe,
This will I say: It is a booke of proofe.
Wherein himselfe appears (I will be plaine)
No foole in print, nor yet a knave in graine.

# A Parallel betweene Don Ulysses of Ithaca and Don Coryate of Odcombe

### The preamble to the parallel

If moral Plutarch had done nothing else,
Yet would we praise him for his parallels;
Where he with every Greeke doth match a Roman.
I that would be his Ape, can fancie no man,
(Though learned Hackluyt hath set many forth)
Amongst our English, who for wit and worth
May be compared with the Ithacan,
Unlesse that Brute the brave Odcombian.
What do you tell me of your Drakes or Candishes;
We never were beholding to their standishes.
This man hath manners seene, and men outlandish;
And writ the same: so did not Drake nor Candish.
If Drake be famous because he did wander
About the seas, Tom may be well a Gander,
That ravisheth with his harmonious quill
More eares than any Swan on Parnasse hill.

### The parallel it selfe.

Ulysses was a merry Greeke they say,
So Tom is, and the Greeker of the tway.
Ulysses left at home an aged Syre,
And Tom an aged mother by the fyre.
Ulysses was an islander I trow,
How then? I pray you is not Coryate so?
Perhaps Ulysses did in wit excel,
Our Coryate though doth of more learning smell.
Ulysses had a ship of no great bulke.
And Coryate went to Calais in a hulke.
Ulysses in the Trojan horse was hid,
The Heidelbergian barrel Tom bestrid.
Good harnesse did Ulysses guarde and grace,
Where Coryate nought had but a fustian case.
Ulysses hardly from his Circe sluncke,
As hardly Tom from his Venetian Puncke.
By land Ulysses in a Chariot rode,
And Coryate in a Cart, the greater lode.
Ulysses with sterne Ajax had to doe,
With the Dutch Boore so had poore Coryate too.
At home left Ulix store of beasts and chattel,
And Coryate home came guarded with more cattell.
Ulysses us'd to drinke the Aethiop wine,
With whitson-ale his cap doth Coryate line.
Just twenty years Ulysses with his Greeks

Did wander: Coryate just as many weeks.
Ulysses all that while had but one carvel,
Tom but one paire of shoes, the greater marvell.
Minerva holpe Ulysses at a lift,
And Pacience Coryate, for there was no shift.
Ulysses heard no Syren sing: nor Coryate
The Jew, lest his praepuce might prove excoriate.
Ulysses had a wife to lust unprone,
But Coryate had a chaster, having none.
Ulysses seem'd a beggar all to torne,
So Coryate did; and was I dare be sworne.
Ulysses in his travel builded Flushing,
Where Coryate ending, or'e the Sea came brushing.
One Homer only sung Ulysses praise,
But Coryats all the Poets of our daies.

### The Epilogue of the Parallel.

Take reader with a laughing looke
This Odcombe new-come well-come booke.
Looke with the like thou take these parallels,
In sober sadnesse we shall marre all else.
For Coryate with us both will quarrel,
And teare himselfe out of his parell.
In each point they doe not jumpe,
I trust they doe yet in the lumpe.
Nor would I joyne them head and feete;
Lines parallel doe never meete.
Yet one day meete may thou and I,
And laugh with Coryate ere we die.

### Englyn un-odl inion.

Ynod y mourglod ae am arglwydh mawr,
Hwuad-mor cyfarwydh:
Dymma 'nawr Dwm un arwydh,
Ond thydan gwaithwdwn gwydh?

### Ad Janum Harringtonum Badensem, Equitem:
### Non Equitem Badensem, sed auratum.

These Latin verses following were written to be sent to the worthy and learned Knight above-named, by the Author of the former, for the obtaining of his encomiasticks upon my booke: but though they never came to that worthy Knights hands, I have thought good to insert them here, because it was the authors pleasure to have them printed with the rest of his Panegyricks.

O Bone, cui translatus olet miserabilis Ajax,
Qui sat es ingenio & carmine notus eques.
Inficiat furui vis ne fumosa Tobacci,
Neu piper attactu mordeat acre suo:
Ne scombros metuant (metuaunt quonque carmina scombros)
Thusue gravi piceum condat odore rogum.
His concede precor folliis, ferventer solentis
Sub Clypeo Ajacis posse latere tui.
    **Explicit Hugo Holland, Cambro-Britannus.**

**Incipit Christophorus Brooke Eboracensis (Christopher Brooke):**

As for these titles that follow, bestowed upon me by this worthy Gentleman, I would have thee know (reader) that as I acknowledge my selfe utterly unworthy of them, so I meant to have suppressed and concealed them, but that it is the Authors pleasure to prefixe them before his verses. Therefore for obeying of his will I have thought good, much against mine owne will, to expresse them in this place, even these.

To the no lesse learned, then wise and discreete
    Gentleman, Mr. THOMAS CORYATE,
In some few moneths travel borne & brought up to
    What you see viz.:
To be the delight of a world of noble wits,
To be a shame to all Authors, as the Gout and Quartan
    Feaver have bene to all Physitians.
This plaine song sendeth CHRISTOPHER BROOKE,
    His poore friends, to attend the
Descant of his famous booke, through all Hands,
    Tongues, Arts, Trades, Mysteries, and
    Occupations whatsoever.

The subtle Greeke Ulysses needs must travel,
Ten years, forsooth, over much sand and gravell,
And many Cities see, and manners know,
Before there could be writ a booke or two
Of his adventures: and he travel'd still
(Else there are lyars) sore against his will:
But this rare English-Latine-Grecian,
Of Orators and Authors the blacke Swan,
A voluntarie journey undertooke
Of scarce sixe moneths, and yet hath writ a booke
Bigger than Homers, and (though writ in prose)
As full of poetry, spite of Homers nose.
If he liv'd now that in Darius Casket
Plac'd the poore Iliad's, he had bought a Basket
Of richer stuffe to intombe thy volume large,

Which though (O noble Tom) at thine own charge
Art pleas'd to print. But thou needst not repent
Of this thy bitter cost; for thy brave Precedent
Great Caesar is, who penned his owne gestes
And (as some write) recited them at feastes,
And at's owne charge had printed them they say,
If printing had bene used at that day.
The Presse hath spent the three for one you got
At your returne: whats that? Poore thing God wot.
Manure this land still with such bookes my friend,
And you shall be paid for it in the end.
For I (me thinkes) see how men strive to carry
This Jovial Journall into each Library.
And we ere long shall well perceive your wit,
(Grave learned Bodley) by your placing it
Therefore lanch forth great booke like Ship of fame.
Th' Hopewell of Odcombe thou shalt have to name.
        **Explicit Christophorus Brooke Eboracensis.**

**Incipit Joannes Hoskins (John Hoskins):**

Cabalistical verses which by Transposition of Words,
Syllables, and letters, make excellent Sense, otherwise none.

    In laudem Authoris.
Even as the waves of brainlesse butter'd fish,
With bugle horne writ in the Hebrew tongue,
Fuming up flounders like a chafing-dish,
That looks asquint upon a Three-mans song:
Or as your equinoctial pasticrust
Projecting out a purple chariot wheele,
Doth squeeze the spheares, and intimate the dust,
The dust which force of argument doth feele:
Even so this Author, this[13] **Gymnosophist,**
Whom no delight of travels toyle dismaies,
Shall sympathize (thinke reader what thou list)
Crownd with a quinsill tipt with marble praise.

---

13. This word Gymnosophist is derived from two Greeke words, which signifie a naked sophister. And he therefore cals the Author so, because one day he went without a shirt at Basil, while it was washing.

ENCOMIOLOGICAL ANTISPASTICKS,
CONSISTING OF EPITRITS, THE FOURTH IN THE FIRST SYZUGIE,
WHICH THE VULGAR CALL PHALEUCIAC HENDECASYLLABLES; TRI-
MESTERS CATALECTIS WITH ANTISPASTIC ASCLEPIADS, TRIMETERES
ACATALECTICS CONSISTING OF TWO DACTYLICALL COMMAES OF
SOME LEARNED NAMED CHORIAMBICKS, BOTH TOGETHER DICOLI DIS-
TROPHI, RYTHMICALL AND HYPERYTHMICALL, AMPHIBOLOGICALL,
DEDICATED TO THE UNDECLINABLE MEMORY OF THE AUTARKESTI-
CALL CORYATE, THE ONLY TRUE TRAVELING PORCUPEN OF
ENGLAND.

Also there is this tune added to the verses, and pricked according to the forme of Musicke to be sung by those that are so disposed.

Dmired *Coryate*, who like a Porcupen, Doſt

ſhew prodigious things to thy countrimen.

Admired Coryate, who like a Porcupen,
Dost shew prodigious things to thy countrimen.
As that beast when he kils doth use his owne darts,
So doe thy prettie quils make holes in our hearts.
That beast lives of other company destitute,
So wentest thou alone every way absolute.
That beast creepeth afoote, nec absque pennis,
So didst thou trot a journey hence to Venice.
Live long foe to thy foe fierce as a Porcupen,
Live long friend to thy friend kinde as a Porcupen.
Henceforth adde to thy crest an armed Histrix,
Since thy carriage hath resembled his tricks.

No more but so, I heard the crie,
And like an old hound came I
To make it fuller, though I finde
My mouth decayes much in this kind.

379

The cry was this, they cri'de by millions,
Messengers, Curriers, and Postilians,
Now out alas we are undone
To heare of Coryates payre of sho'ne;
There is no newes we are more sorry at
Then this strange newes of [14]Rawbone Coryate
Who like a Unicorne went to Venice,
And drinking neither Sack nor Rhenish,
Home in one payre of shoes did trample,
A fearfull and a strange example.
But whats the newes of learned people
In Pauls Churchyard & neere Pauls steeple?
Hang up his shoes on top of Powles,
Tyed to his name in parchment rowles,
That may be read most legibly
In Tuttlefields and Finsbury.
Fame is but winde, thence winde may blow it
So farre that all the world may know it:
From Mexico and from Peru
To China and to Cambalu:
If the wind serve, it may have lucke
To passe by South to the bird Rucke.
Greater then the Stymphalides
That hid the Sunne from Hercules.
And if fames wings chance not to freeze,
It may passe North ninetie degrees,
Beyond Meta incognita,
Where though there be no hollyday,
No Christen people for to tell it,
Horrible Beares and Whales may smell it.
Thence may it on the Northern seas,
On foote walke to the Antipodes,
Whose feete against our feete do pace
To keepe the center in his place.
But when those fellows that do wonder
As we at them, how we go under
From clime to clime, and tongue to tongue,
Throughout their hemispheare along,

---

14. A great Gyant swift on foote, of whom mention is in Polychronicon.

Have tost these words as bals at tennis,
Tom Coryate went on foot from Venice.
This travelling fame, this walking sound
Must needs come home in coming round,
So that we shall cry out upon him,
His fame in travel hath outgone him.
When all have talked, and time hath tried him,
Yet Coryate will be semper idem.

**Explicit Joannes Hoskins.**

**Incipit Thomas Campianus (Thomas Campian):**

Medicinae Doctor.
In peragrantissimi, Itinerosissimi, Montiscandentissimique
Peditis, Thomae Coryati, viginti-hebdomadarium Diarium, sex pedibus
gradiens, partim vero claudicans, Encomiasticon.

Ad Venetos venit corio Coryatus ab uno
Vectus, & ut vectus, pene revectus eart.
Nave una Dracus sic totum circuit orbem,
At rediens retult te Coryate minus.
Illius undigenas tenet unica charta labores,
Tota tuos sed vix bibliotheca capit.

**Explicit Thomas Campianus.**

**Incipit Joannes Owen (John Owen):**

To the Reader, in Praise of this worthy Worke,
And the Author thereof.

The Fox is not so full of wiles
As this booke full of learned smiles:
Come seeke, and thou shalt finde in it
Th' Abridgment of Great-Britains wit.

**Explicit Joannes Owen.**

**Incipit Joannes Jackson (John Jackson):**

Can it
Be possible for
A natural man
To travel nimbler then
Tom Coryate can? No; though
You should tie to his horne-peec'd
Shoes, wings fether'd more then Mer-
Cury did use. Perchaunce hee borrowed
Fortunatus Hatte, for wings since Bladuds time
Were out of date. His purse he hath to print
What hee did write, else, who had read of thee, O
Wandering Wight? Who else had knowne what thou
Hast felt and seene, where and with whom; and how farre
Thou hast beene? Ere thou to Odcombe couldst thy Tro-
phyes bring? Thy hungry praises in his Egge I sing,
At thy request, else in another fashion I would
Have pointed at thy commendation: Thy other
Heliconian friends bring store of Salt, of
Pepper, and Vineger sowre, to furnish thy
Italian banquet forth, whereby is
Plainly shown thy wondrous worth.
Feast Coryate, feast the world
Still with thy travel, discharge
The Presse, and care
Not then who
Cavell.
**Explicit Joannes Jackson.**

**Incipit Michael Drayton:**

A brief prologue to the verses following.

Deare Tom, thy Booke was like to come to light,
Ere I could gaine but one halfe howre to write;
They go before whose wits are at their noones,
And I come after bringing Salt and Spoones.

Many there be that write before thy Booke,
For whom (except here) who would ever looke?

Thrice happy are all we that had the Grace
To have our names set in this living place.
Most worthy man, with thee it is even thus,
As men take Dottrels, so hast thou ta'n us.
Which as a man his arme or legge doth set,
So this fond Bird will likewise counterfeit:
Thou art the Fowler, and doest shew us shapes,
And we are all thy Zanies, thy true Apes.
I saw this age (from what it was at first)
Swolne, and so bigge that it was like to burst,
Growne so prodigious, so quite out of fashion,
That who will thrive, must hazard his damnation:
Sweating in panges, sent such a horrid mist.
As to dim Heaven: I looked for Antichrist
Or some new set of Divels to sway hell,
Worser than those that in the Chaos fell:
Wondring what fruit it to the world would bring,
At length it brought forth this: O most strange thing;
And with sore throwes, for that the greatest head
Ever is hard'st to be delivered.
By thee wise Coryate we are taught to know,
Great, with great men which is the way to grow.
For in a new straine thou com'st finely in,
Making thy selfe like those thou meant'st to winne:
Greatnesse to me seem'd ever full of feare,
Which thou found'st false at thy arriving there,
Of the Bermudos, the example such,
Where not a ship until this time durst touch;
Kep't as suppos'd by hells infernall dogs,
Our Fleet found there most honest courteous hogs.
Live virtuous Coryate, and for ever be
Lik'd of such wise men, as are most like thee.
         **Explicit Michael Drayton.**


**Incipit Joannes Davies Herefordiensis (John Davies):**

In the lowd, alowd, or well-deserved renowne of our Brit-
aine-Ulysses: his present worke, together with a description of
the particulars of the Vinet, Title-page, or Frontispice.

If Art, that oft the learn'd hath stammered,
In one[15] Yron head-piece (yet no hammer-head)
May (joyn'd with Nature) hit Fame on the [16]Cocks-combe;
Then tis that Head-peece that is crown'd, with [17]Odcombe
For, he hard Head (and hard, sith like a Whetstone
It gives wits edge, and drawes them too like Jetstone)
Is Caput mundi for a world of schoole-tricks,
H'hath seene much more then much, I assure yee,
And will see New Troy, Bethlem, and Old-Jurie:
Meane while (to give a Taste of his first travel,
With streames of Rhetoricke that get Golden-gravell)
He tells how he to Venice once did wander;
From whence he came[18] more witty then a Gander:
Whereby he makes relations of such wonders,
That Truth therein doth lighten, while Art thunders.
All Tongues fled to him that at Babell swerved,
Lest they for want of warme Mouthes might have sterved;
Where they doe revel in such Passing-measure,
(Especially the Greeke wherein's his pleasure)
That (Jovially) so Greeke, he takes the[19] guard of
That hee's the merriest Greeke that ere was heard of:
For, he as t'were his Mothers Twittle-twattle
(That's Mother-tongue) the Greeke can prittle-prattle.
Nay, of that Tongue he so hath got the Body,
That he sports with it at Russe, Gleeke, or[20] Noddy.
For his Invention, in his Bookes rare[21] Brass-face
Is seene the glory of it, that doth passe [22]Grace.
[.........................................]
Hold Muse, no more, unlesse thou wilt by martyr'd
Within his world of fame that ne're was quarterd:
For, if thou seek'st in numbers to containe it,
'Twil make thy browes sweate, and thy nose to raine it.
But though we cannot in this Frontispice
Number thy Stations, yet we may count thy lice,
Which (Tom) from one that (roaving) had no refuge,

---

15. Because like Yron it is strong to containe the resemblance of so many deere Observations.
16. A metaphore for the head.
17. Crownd together with Odcombe for producing him.
18. The word (more) for the reason of the excellency: and gander for the Rimes necessity.
19. He pleasantly preserves it in pristine purity.
20. Games at Cards, whereby is meant all manner of sports.
21. The Frontispiece graven in brasse.
22. Excels the grace of all other fore fronts or Title pages.

Drop downe, to make the Glories flood a Deluge.
Within which Flood my Muse (like a Diudapper,
In Fames wide mouth wagging my pen, her clapper)
Is so ore-whelm'd, that as shee strives for more breath,
The Flood ehgulphes her, and her wordes devoureth.
So fare well Tom (shee saies) great natures wonder,
I lye thy fame a thousand fathoms under:
For, it prevailes above the Alpes (high Mountaines!)
But when it ebbes, Ile spring in Castall Fountains.
All to bewet the earth with streames of praises
Running to none but thee in fluent Phrases;
Untill I make a second Inundation,
To wash thy purest fames [23]Coinquination:
And make it fit for finall [24]Conflagration,
So to prevent fell Envies indignation.
　　　Explicit Joannes Davis Herefordiensis.


Incipit Henricus Peacham (Henry Peacham):


To the famous Traveller ever to be esteemed the joy of his
Somersetshire, Thomas Coryate of Odcombe, professed enemy to
the Gentle-Craft or Mysterie of Shoo-makers.

Why doe the rude vulgar so hastily post in a madnesse
To gaze at trifles, and toyes not worthy the viewing?
And thinke them happy, when may be shew'd for a penny
The Fleete-steere Mandrakes, that heavenly Motion of Eltham
Westminster monuments, and Guild hall huge Corinaeus,
That horne of Windsor (of an Unicorne very likely)
The cave of Merlin, the skirts of old Tom a Lincolne.
King Johns sword at Linne, with the cup the Fraternity drinke in,
The Tombe of Beauchampe, and sword of Sir Guy a Warwicke:
The great long Dutchman, and roaring Marget a Barwicke,
The Mummied princes, and Caesars wine yet i'Dover
Saint James his Ginney Hens, the[25] Cassawarway moreover,
The Beaver I'the Parke (strange beast as er'e any man saw)

---

23. Alluding to that love which men bore to women in the old world, sith like love our Author beares to men; for whose love and commodity he hath put himselfe to this cost and pains.
24. Burning in flames of glory and wonder, as in the judgement-day.
25. An East Indian bird at Saint James in the keeping of Mr. Walker, that will carry no coales, but eate them as whot as you will.

Downe-shearing willowes with teeth as sharpe as a handsaw.
The Lance of John a gaunt, and Brandons still i'the tower;
The fall of Ninive, with Norwich built in an hower.
King Henries slip-shoes, the sword of valiant Edward.
The Coventry Boares-shield, and fire-workes seen but to bedward.
Drakes ship at Detford, King Richards bed-sted i'Leister,
The White hall whale bones, the silver Bason i'Chester;
The live-caught Dog-fish, the Wolfe and Harry the Lyon,
Hunks of the Beare-garden to be feared, if he be nigh on.
All these are nothing, were a thousand more to be scanned,
(Coryate) unto thy shoes so artificially tanned:
That through thicke and thinne, made thee so famous a Trotter,
And bore thee o're the Alps, where sidewaies, long, like an Otter
Thou climb'dst and clambred'st, there single solie recounting,
(Another Alcides) thy labours lustily mounting.
And as Alcides did scorne to weare any Linnen,
So Coryate shirtlesse did as well as if he had beene in
The bravest Lyons hide, with the taile downe fairly depending
But matchless Coryate, since now thy labour hath ending,
And since th'art well againe unto thy Country returned:
The very heeles by me shall be with laurel adorned.

### In the Utopian Tongue.

Ny thalonin ythsi Coryate lachmah babowans
O Asiam Europam Americ-werowans
Toph-himgi Savoya, Hessen, Rhetia, Ragonzie
France, Germanien dove Anda-louzie
Not A-rag-on o Coryate, o hone vilascar
Einen tronk Od-combe ny Venice Berga-mascar.
**Explicit Henricus Peacham.**


**Incipit Glareanus Vadianus:**

A skeleton of bare Anatomie of the Punctures and Junctures of Mr. Thomas Coaryate of Odcombe, in loose verse called
by the Italians, versi sciolti, because they go like Tom-boyes,
scalciati without hose of shoe, bootlesse: peruses this last Quarter of the Moone, and illustrated with the Commentaries of Mr.
Primrose Silkeworme, student in Gastroligia and Tuff-moccado.

Beauclerke[26] of [27]Odcombe, bellamy of fame,
Learnings quicke atome, wits glosse on Natures text,

Sembriefe of time the five finger of game,
Ambs-ace of blots, sweep-stake of what comes next.
March-pane of mirth, the [28]Genoua past of love,
The Graces [29]gallipot,[30] Musicks fiddle-sticke,
The spout[31] of sport, and follies turtle Dove,
Noddie turn'd up, all made, yet lose the tricke.
Thou Chesse-board pawne, who on one paire of shoes
Hast trode the foot-ball of this worlds center,
Discovering places[32] couch'd betweene the poles,
Where honest vertue never yet durst enter.
How should I sing thy worth in fitting layes,
With starveling verses of an hide bound Muse,
And crowne thy head with misletoe for bayes,
Unlesse thy[33] knapsacke did new thoughts infuse?
Such Gallo-Belgicke Mercuries are not chipt
From every billet, nor each axle-tree:
Nature her selfe in thee herselfe out-script
When she produced this vagrant Humble-Bee,
Whose buzze hath fild this worlds circled round,
Hing's on the Articke and Antarticke starre,
And whose great fame finds now no other bound
Then from the Magellan strait to Gibraltar.
Whose glorious deeds out-face and fiercely daunt
Guzman of Spaine, and Amadis of France,
Uterpendragon, Urson, and Termagant,
Great Don Quixote, and Joane of Orleance.
[...................................................]

26. A shrunke word of two into one, such as are, Hardyknowt, or Hogssnout, the name of pope Sergius. So Atome for Ah Tom.

27. The Arpinum of this second Cicero. A village before Ignoble: now by him raised to tenne rials of plate, and of which himselfe is the Chronological Mappe.

28. He meaneth a pantrie coffin made of paste, in which the white Blackmoore (as Gusman de Alparach calleth the Genouesi Moros blancos) stew certaine powerfull words called parole intoneate to charme Bridegroomes points nover L'esquilette.

29. It is a vessel into which womens teares blended with loves sighes are distilled through a serpentine or Crusible into a puer elexir, to cure Junoes kibe-heele.

30. The Augures lituus or bended staffe, wherein in the scale of Musicke men take the Altitude and elevation of a flat from the sharpe in Chromatique Symphonie.

31. The spout of sport, as a chimney is of smoake.

32. He meaneth the gallery of donna Amorosa the old Countess of Orgueil in Arabia deserta, which is a mere magazin of verdugals, whither those courteous dames called Cortesans (as M. Thomas himselfe hath elegantly unshaled the word unto us) that doe enter to barter or chaffer, elle perdent la vertu, mais la galle leur demeur.

33. He meaneth a soldiers or a travellers trusse, or fardle, or budget, which the old Romans called mulos Marianos.

Yet for all this, Tom, thou hadst proved soone
Abortive, and a foundling worth but little,
Had not thy sire, the man that's in the Moone,
Oft fed thee in thy youth with [34]Cuckow spittle.
Then treade the steps of th' Author of thy birth,
Who once every Moneth surround the earth.
            **Explicit Glareanus Vadianus.**

---

34. May it please thee reader to be advertised out of Germany, that this is nothing else but honie, called syderum saliva.

# Chapter 5. Death And Canonization Behind the Curtain

*The enchanted island of master magician Prospero and his bequest. — The faces of the dead were covered, and everybody was silent — Covert elegies. — And Manners brightly shines — When did the Shakespeare plays about the War of the Roses appear?*

## The Enchanted Island of Master Magician Prospero and His Bequest

In 1609, Rutland's health improved somewhat, while the favor of the king contributed to bettering his financial standing. He visited Cambridge, and took part in activities relating to the founding of a hospital and a hospice at Bottesford, not far from Belvoir Castle. Elizabeth had mostly been staying away from Belvoir in recent years, either at other Rutland family estates or at the home of her aunt.

On May 20, 1609, Thomas Thorpe, a friend and trusted associate of Edward Blount, registered at the Stationers' Company the book entitled *Shake-speares Sonnets*. At the time, Blount himself was busy publishing the voluminous *Coryate's Crudities*; later, the "Coryate" work would also involve Thorpe, who would release *The Odcombian Banquet*. On October 2, 1610, Richard Bonian registered the book entitled *Salve Deus Rex Judaeorum*, with no author's name. The volume would later appear with the name of "Emilia Lanier, wife of Captain Alfonso Lanier." Like Coryate's books, the license to publish this was issued by Doctor Mocket, chaplain of the Archbishop of Canterbury, an alumnus of Oxford. The latter's name had been among those to whom Coryate sent his burlesque greetings from India. In 1609, Henry Gosson published *Pericles*, which had been registered a year before by

The Earl of Rutland (circa 1610)

William Herbert, the 3d Earl of Pembroke

Blount; later Gosson would become the chief publisher of His Majesty's Water Poet pamphlets. Thus, all the above-listed books appeared in close interrelationship and were overseen by Edward Blount, with the Pembrokes standing behind.

Almost all Shakespeare scholars share the opinion that Shakespeare's sonnets were printed without any assistance from the author, perhaps even behind his back. However, opinions vary as to whom Thorpe addresses in his mysterious dedication. Thorpe's address makes it clear that this mysterious W. H., for one thing, appears in some of the sonnets and, for another, that this edition saw the light of the day owing to him alone, that is, "Mr. W. H." procured these sonnets for the printer without the author's consent. Most scholars, including such authorities as E. Chambers and John Dover Wilson, believed that the initials "W. H." masked William Herbert, the 3$^{rd}$ Earl of Pembroke. Having heard so much about the Rutlands, Pembrokes and Blount the publisher, we cannot but share the same view. The fact that the sonnets written by the Belvoir couple (mainly by Roger) showed up in the hands of their closest friends and relatives, the Pembrokes, seems quite natural; this was what Francis Meres implied, in his time. The liberty to hand over those lyrical and intimate verses to a publisher with no author's (authors') agreement could be taken only by such a person as the Earl of Pembroke.

In August 1610, the Pembrokes and Elizabeth came to Belvoir Castle. As discussed in earlier chapters, some visit to the ailing Rutland was mirrored at the beginning of Chester's poem, when Dame Nature (Mary Sidney Pembroke) and the Phoenix come to the Dove living atop a high hill, to give him a wonder-working balm they had received from Jupiter (King James), to salve his head and feet. Very likely, the "balm" is not a figment of Chester's poetic imagination, and the king ordered his physician to prepare some special arcanum[1] for the sufferer at Belvoir. But neither royal nor domestic medicines, nor even bloodletting — the favorite Aesculapian treatment of the age — was able to bring any noticeable relief.

The atmosphere at Belvoir, around the gradually fading Rutland and his poetic spouse, had an impact on the last Shakespeare play, "The Tempest." Although created in 1610-1611, the play would be placed first in the Great Folio, after the elapse of ten years, which testifies to the importance the editors attached to it.

Unlike other Shakespeare plays, no sources for the play have been definitively established. The plot is not very complicated. After a shipwreck, Prospero, the rightful Duke of Milan, whose throne has been usurped by his brother Antonio, finds himself and his infant daughter Miranda on a desert island which they share with another inhabitant — a subhuman creature named Caliban, son of the witch Sycorax. Prospero makes the creature his servant and, over the years, teaches him to speak.

Prospero masters the art of magic; he is capable of ruling over the spirits and natural calamities. In the course of their stay on the island, Miranda grows into a

---

1. In this context, it is worth noting that a legitimate sovereign in those days was commonly believed to be able to heal some human maladies by touching the patient with his hand.

young lady. Her father tells her the story of his brother's treason; the story provides much information about the interests and pastimes of the Duke of Milan who, in addition to being the very pinnacle among Italian princes in power and influence, also appears to be unrivaled in the liberal arts:

> *… … …those being all my study,*
> *The government I cast upon my brother*
> *And to my state grew stranger, being transported*
> *And rapt in secret studies.*

> *… I, thus neglecting worldly ends, all dedicated*
> *To closeness and the bettering of my mind*
> *With that which, but by being so retired,*
> *O'er-prized all popular rate, in my false brother*
> *Awaked an evil nature; and my trust,*
> *Like a good parent, did beget of him...*

> *... he needs will be*
> *Absolute Milan. Me, poor man, my library*
> *Was dukedom large enough: of temporal royalties*
> *He thinks me now incapable.*

Assured of the support of Alonso, the King of Naples, Antonio exiles Prospero and his daughter; they are put aboard the half-rotten ship, at the mercy of the sea. Out of compassion, noble Gonzalo provides them with clothes, victuals and fresh water; moreover, knowing how Prospero cares for his library, Gonzalo lets the exile take some of those volumes that he "prized above his dukedom." The twice repeated statement that Prospero values his books, his library, above all else, even the dukedom, should not be overlooked: it reflects the true interests of the true Shakespeare. Few researchers would challenge the fact that the author is often vividly felt through the words and philosophy of Prospero.[2] At the same time, Prospero speaks the language of a man used not only to meditation and reason, but also to command. Apart from his library and spiritual demands, Prospero's interests are the interests of a powerful seigneur who even in exile keeps to the habit of power forged since childhood.

On the deserted island, Prospero takes care of his daughter's education and upbringing:

> *… … … … … … … … … … … … … … …and here*
> *Have I, thy schoolmaster, made thee more profit*

---

2. At that, one cannot entirely equate Prospero with the writer of the play, as some scholars do. The matter is much more complex.

*Than other princesses can that have more time*
*For vainer hours and tutors not so careful. (I, 2).*

(This emphasis on the necessity of education contrasts with the priorities of William Shakspere of Stratford, whose wife and younger daughter were illiterate, while his older daughter could at best scarcely sign her name.)

Learning that there is a ship at sea with King Alonso and his courtiers aboard, including his brother Antonio, Prospero raises a terrible tempest, casting his enemies onto the shores of his island, where they are left to his mercy. Recovering from the shipwreck, the king's courtiers and hangers on are quick to show their wolf's teeth. Antonio incites Sebastian to kill the latter's brother, King Alonso, and to seize the throne. The Butler Stephano and clown Trinculo, both miserable drunkards, join Caliban in his plot to assassinate Prospero.

After he has disarmed his enemies, making them suffer and repent, Prospero suddenly gives up on revenge. He pardons the plotters, and helps the king's son Ferdinand and Miranda — who have fallen in love with each other. Then, Prospero sets free Ariel, the supernatural sprite who served him, and announces that he is no longer going to use magic:

... ... ... ... ... ... ...*I'll break my staff,*
*Bury it certain fathoms in the earth,*
*And deeper than did ever plummet sound*
*I'll drown my book. (V, 1)*

When Prospero, who has renounced his might, declaims his epilogue, we hear the voice of a tired, ill person. Though his throne is reclaimed in Milan, the conciliatory gaze of Prospero is fixed on his imminent demise: "Every third thought shall be my grave."

Almost all studies relating to "The Tempest" note the play's strong subjective basis. Prospero apparently is either the author or someone close to him, close to his thoughts and feelings. It has been widely assumed that this character, combining in one person wisdom, understanding of human frailty, and tolerance toward it, is a reflection of Shakespeare in his last years. Prospero bids farewell to life; his final words, as he leaves the scene, resonate with the unmistakable tone of a solemn last testament — a testament that many have tried to read and interpret. The Stratfordians find it particularly troublesome: in 1611, Shakspere was safe and sound, busy with his usual affairs. Only our knowledge of the last days of Roger and Elizabeth Rutland allows us to pierce the carapace of this play, and to properly read Prospero's Will, which differs so greatly from the famous Stratford testament that was drawn up five years later. On November 1, 1611, "The Tempest" was presented to the king at Whitehall Palace, and the sovereign — who possessed far richer information about Shakespeare than today's scholars, followed the performance with understanding and sympathy. Those who compiled and edited the First Folio were well aware of the play's significance — in addition to being placed first in volume, the play was printed with an exceptional degree of perfection, and the whole text is divided into acts and scenes and provided with a list of characters and their characteristics.

The play features some strongly realistic scenes which clearly indicate the sure hand of the author of "Hamlet" and "King Lear." This is especially true of the opening scene aboard the ship tossed about on a turbulent sea, amidst a merciless tempest: a tremendously impressive and convincing episode. The atmosphere on this foundering ship, the crew's desperate attempts to fight the elements — the whole scene is conjured up by a few remarks and commands that show that whoever wrote these lines had firsthand experience in seafaring and bad weather at sea.

Searching for the sources of the plot, scholars have puzzled over the location of the island where the play takes place. Given that King Alonso's ship sails from Tunis to Naples, the island should be somewhere in the Mediterranean. However, the sprite Ariel mentions the "dew of the Bermoothes." Are we to understand (as some biographers assume) that the author actually believed that the Bermuda Islands were situated in the Mediterranean? As in certain other Shakespearean plays, the geographic names here are of course imaginary or stylized, not real.

Long ago, Shakespeareans noted that many of his plays are permeated almost obsessively with the theme of hostility between brothers, with the junior usually plotting against the senior, the rightful head of the family. That sort of rivalry is inherent in "As You Like It," "Much Ado About Nothing," "Hamlet," "King Lear," "Macbeth," and finally in "The Tempest." Some advocates of the Rutlandian thesis have tended to interpret the twice-repeated theme of brother-against-brother (Antonio versus Prospero, and Sebastian versus Alonzo) as proof of dire schemes woven by Rutland's brother, Francis. The latter, they said, was in a hurry to eliminate the Earl, who was sick and deep in his books and queer affairs, and besides had no direct heir. The above Rutlandians fancied that the deceased Rutland had written "The Tempest" in order to act upon his brother and his accomplices, to reproach them and to make them abandon their treacherous designs. Scholars have even assumed that despite such exhortations his criminal brother carried off his plot and killed Rutland and his wife.

Today, after decades of research and the analysis of innumerable documents, it is safe to say that assertions and assumptions about the violent death of the Belvoir couple are off the mark, and the Chester book confirms that. However, the character of the wise magician, the Duke of Milan, preparing for the end and bidding farewell to his books and works, does bear a strong resemblance to the master of Belvoir Castle, who was fading away just when this last Shakespeare play was being created. I will avoid discussing in detail the possibility of reliably identifying a real-life Miranda. The unique relationship between Roger and Elizabeth Rutland, resembling as it did the alliance of a young lady with her older brother or a loving and wise father-tutor; the similarity of Miranda to Maid Marian in Ben Jonson's "Sad Shepherd"; and a number of allusions in Francis Beaumont's and John Fletcher's plays, as well as in Chester's collection, trace obvious parallels between Miranda and the soon to be "Love's Martyr" — Elizabeth Sidney Rutland.

Rutland's condition, his strength waning (the Turtle looked "as if his name [were] writ in Death's pale book"), must have been noted and discussed by his closest associates, his brothers in particular. Those whispers, and maybe even practical steps that would be taken in anticipation of an imminent outcome, would not go unnoticed by the ailing and apparently very suspicious person. His relations with his two Catholic brothers had never been very warm, while his attitude to the youngest, Oliver, who had close ties with the Jesuits, was definitely hostile (as manifested earlier in "As You Like It"). Although no trace of any malicious intent has been documented on the part of Francis, who was next to inherit the title, Rutland seemed to doubt his loyalty. Besides, he could not help thinking about his spouse, a fragile being who after his departure would be left alone in that world of base passions, greed and prevailing evil.[3] Her false status in the eyes of society apparently troubled the women with whom she was intimate — Mary Sidney Pembroke, Lucy Bedford and Mary Roth. What was more, she herself now saw the future in a gloomier light. The chivalrous admiration of such brilliant personages as Thomas Overbury or Francis Beaumont could of course take the edge off the generally dull prospects; however, deep in her heart she had already decided to take her life after Rutland, though both he and her friends participating in the creation of "The Tempest" tried to convince "Miranda" that a chance to find another love and simple human happiness should not be deemed impossible, even if it were delayed.

Meanwhile, the Pembrokes' efforts to change the situation, "to bring Turtle to the Phoenix' bed," were at that time also shared by Ben Jonson, who wrote two play-masques dedicated to reconciliation and the revival of love after a discord: "Love Freed from Ignorance and Folly" and "Love Restored."

"The Tempest" includes other allusions to Belvoir Castle and its proprietors. Thus, finding that the sage Prospero possesses a superhuman power, Sebastian exclaims: "Now I will believe that there are unicorns,"[4] and that in "Arabia there is one tree, the phoenix' throne, one phoenix at this hour reigning there." Antonio and Gonzalo agree with him: yes, they have really seen these miracles on the "island," yes, the unusual manners of the islanders have amazed them (III, 3). Unusual Manners? In another instance (II, 1), Gonzalo is delighted with the lush and lusty look of the "island's" grass, while Antonio suddenly adds that "the ground indeed is tawny." [5]

---

3. Let us recall the last line of Sonnet 66.

4. There are two unicorns in the Rutland coat-of-arms.

5. In Rutland County, one often comes across soil that is reddish because it contains ferrous ores. There are various opinions about the origin of the name of the county. It may indeed have come from the Old English and French *rutilant* (red), which stems from Latin. Antonio certainly plays up this etymology. Earlier, I noted that Roger Manners' fellow student poet Weever played with the name of the county and Roger's title as "Root of Land."

John Fletcher

The weird, unparalleled figure of Caliban has been food for much speculation.[6] Some scholars would regard him as typifying the future "cad to come"; others politicize the scene, calling him a native enslaved by colonizers and rising against his oppressors. But apparently no one noticed the parallels between the images of that son of the "damn'd witch Sycorax" and the rude and uncouth cattleman Lorell, son of the Papplewick witch in Ben Jonson's "Sad Shepherd." Like Sycorax, Jonson's witch confines her victims within a gnarled and cloven pine tree and keeps at her service an efficient sprite (here, named Pack; Ariel, in "The Tempest"). Jonson told Drummond that the witch in his pastoral was the Countess of Suffolk. It should be added that, after the scandalous marriage of her daughter to the young Earl of Essex, Elizabeth Rutland's half-brother, aware of the latter's relationship with her husband and anticipating his imminent demise, the above-mentioned lady was open about her plan to bring together Elizabeth and her younger son; in the same way the witch of Papplewick tries to throw together her son Lorell and Maid Marian, while Caliban once attempted to rape Miranda. The correspondences are striking. There might be another prototype, too, of the ungrateful barbarian — someone from among those whom Rutland, like Prospero, "taught to speak"; in any case, the figure of Caliban is not a fiction but a biting and contemptuous lampoon of a real and abhorrent person who happened to appear in Belvoir Vale and harbored a grudge against his masters.

"The Tempest" is not the Duke of Milan's first Shakespearean appearance: we find the bearer of this title among the dramatis personae of "The Two Gentlemen of Verona," as well as in the Beaumont and Fletcher play "The Woman Hater" (1607). "The Triumph of Love," generally attributed to Beaumont alone, introduces the Duke of Milan Rinaldo and his "hidden" Duchess Cornelia; the Massinger play of 1620 was entitled "The Duke of Milan"; and Milan was also the setting for Jonson's play "The Case is Altered." Such a bias toward Milan and its rulers is interesting both as a simple fact and due to the similarity of the situations and allusions in the above plays. It is also noteworthy that "The Triumph of Honour," which is believed to have been penned by Beaumont as well and was part of the same cycle of four plays as "The Triumph of Love," introduced the character of the Duke of Athens, bearing the name of Sophocles, and his wife Dorygen was called an "example of chastity." What ties all these works to "The Tempest" is not just literary fashion, but a shared cast of characters, the poetic Belvoir couple and their tragic story.

As has been acknowledged in many Shakespeare studies, it was John Fletcher who finished the Bard's last play, "Henry VIII," in 1613. This fact defies Stratfordian biographers: William Shakspere is known to have lived three long years after that. Advocates of Oxfordian, Derbian, and other non-Stratfordian theories and hypotheses also fail to provide any satisfactory explanation. The Rutlandian school stands apart — when the Rutlands passed away, who but Fletcher could finish writing the play

---

6. Mills A.D. *The Popular Dictionary of English Place-Names.* Oxford, 1996.

they left behind, who but the faithful "poet of Belvoir vale," Rutland's friend and a companion of Francis Beaumont.

## THE FACES OF THE DEAD WERE COVERED AND EVERYBODY WAS SILENT

Rutland's illness progressively worsened; in the spring of 1612, he was taken to Cambridge to Doctor William Butler, then widely renowned. At times, Rutland could not even speak, having been stricken by paralysis (as a certain John Torys wrote from Cambridge in a letter which has survived to our day).

On May 8, 1612, at Cambridge, in the presence of his beloved brother George, the Master of Belvoir Castle and the "chief man of Sherwood Forest" signed a will declaring: "I, Roger, Earl of Rutland . . . being sick of body, but of good and perfect memory thanks be given to Almighty God do make and ordain this my last Will and Testament. . . ." He made his brother Francis, who was next in line after him, his principal heir. The legacy provided adequately for other members of the family, and specially provided for the education of his under-aged nephews. The servants were not forgotten — Francis was instructed to reward each of them to the extent of their worth and time of service; and a large sum was earmarked for the construction of a hospital and hospice at Bottesford, as well as for both of the colleges where Rutland had made his studies — the Queen's College and Corpus Christi. Only to Elizabeth, Countess of Rutland, his legitimate spouse, the testator bequeathed absolutely nothing; he did not mention her at all.

That the Will of a distinguished lord should omit any reference to his wife is obviously extraordinary. Indeed, the wife was often designated executrice of the estate, and the Rutlands' parents were no exceptions. Philip Sidney and John Manners had both appointed their widows to administer their affairs and property in accordance with their last wills and testaments. The complete absence of Elizabeth Rutland in her husband's will contravenes not only with her legal rights but the traditions of both families. During his life, in spite of sometimes rather stringent means, the husband had never denied Elizabeth payment of her personal expenses (her dress and jewelry for the "Hymenaei" masque alone cost over one thousand pounds). When she resided in London or at any other Rutland estate, the steward duly fulfilled the instructions of the Earl and sent her ample sums of money. How could he leave her out of his will?

Claude Sykes, who thoroughly studied all the documents relating to the Earl of Rutland, failed to focus on Philip Sidney's daughter, whose role was not quite clear to him. He explained the absence of her name in the will by suggesting that, "For Rutland she was already dead,"[7] using the term metaphorically. Nevertheless, having studied

---

7. Sykes C.W. *Op. cit.* p. 194.

Robert Chester's volume and knowing about the events of the summer of 1612, after Rutland's death, we can now repeat the words in their strict sense.

Indeed, according to Chester, it is hardly by chance that the Phoenix departs her terrestrial life right after the Turtle: they have arranged in advance to quit this world together. Thus, Rutland had no reason to bequeath anything to his wife, knowing that she would follow him. Like him, she already needed nothing in this world.

Roger Manners, Earl of Rutland, died at Cambridge on June 26, 1612. Though his body was embalmed (the steward recorded the payment to the embalmer), it was not delivered to the earl's family estate, only some 60 miles away, until July 20. Traditionally, prior to a funeral, the coffin would be exhibited at the home of the deceased to allow relatives and household members to bid him farewell. This time, custom was not observed; and historian Irwin Eller could provide no reasonable explanation for that in his recent study of Belvoir Castle.[8] The closed coffin was immediately transferred to the church in nearby Bottesford, and committed to the earth at the Rutland patrimonial vault, next to the graves of the late earl's father and mother. Moreover, from the moment the procession arrived from Cambridge, no one was allowed to see the decedent's face! And as if this were not mysterious enough, two days later the last offices were duly solemnized at the castle and the church, without the deceased. The parson was apparently unsure how to handle this, since he felt compelled to make a special record in the parochial register.

Why was the burial so rushed; why was no one allowed to see the late earl's face? Those who organized the funeral — Roger's brothers Francis and George — might have had a very powerful reason for acting this way, but what reason could there be? Of course, we may suppose that the face of the deceased had been disfigured in his death agony; or that he had been murdered (if we overlook such facts as, firstly, the "apoplectic stroke" he was stricken with shortly before death; secondly, the presence of his devoted brother George at his bedside till the dismal end; and, thirdly, Chester's Phoenix commenting on the smile fixed upon the face of the dead Turtle). But the embalmers of those days were, as now, capable of making presentable any body entrusted to them even under worse circumstances. No, the reason was evidently different. Especially since the papers from Belvoir indicate a new and no less interesting fact: the Countess of Rutland was not present at her own husband's funeral, although, as the Robert Chester poem tells us, she was at his deathbed during his last days and hours:

> *Look what a mirthful countenance he doth beare,*
> *Spreading his wings abroad, and joes withal…*

The Turtle dies in front of the Phoenix — Elizabeth was a witness to the epilogue of Rutland's dramatic life.

---

8. Eller L., *The History of Belvoir Castle*. L., 1866.

Elizabeth's absence from her husband's funeral cannot be explained by the platonic nature of their relationship. In the eyes of the whole world, she was his rightful spouse, the Countess of Rutland, and had hosted guests as the mistress of Belvoir Castle not long before. But now, during the queer funeral rites for a person who was already interred, she was far away. Preparations were under way for the next act of the tragedy, as was learned from a letter, found relatively recently, from a very well-informed witness of the events. Here is what John Chamberlain, a London rumor-monger, wrote to Sir Dudley Carleton on August 11, 1612: "The widow Countess of Rutland died about ten days ago, and is privately buried in Paul's, by her father, Sir Philip Sidney. Sir Walter Raleigh is slandered to have given her certain pills that dispatched her."[9]

Thus, Elizabeth died in London on August 1, ten days after the bizarre obsequies of the Earl of Rutland at Bottesford. Gossip attributing her death to poison obtained from Walter Raleigh confirms that she departed of her own free will. It should be borne in mind, however, that it was out of the question to speak openly about a suicide — the church condemned self-murderers, and even prohibited burying them within a church cemetery (recall how poor Ophelia was buried!). It is not clear how Elizabeth Rutland could have received poisonous pills from Walter Raleigh who had already been imprisoned in the Tower of London for eight years, sentenced to death. It is true that his confinement was not too severe: he continued his botanical experiments at the tiny little prison garden, wrote a book, and in addition to his wife and son, was visited by other guests including Queen Anne herself in the company of Crown Prince Henry, who held the notorious seafarer in high regard. Under such circumstances, Elizabeth might have had no difficulties in obtaining "pills" from Raleigh, who could have had them prepared "just in case" by his stepbrother Adrian Gilbert, who was staying at the home of Mary, Countess of Pembroke, and used to concoct all sorts of medicines.

Unlike her husband, Elizabeth Rutland was buried right after her death, but also in secret, at night, at the country's principal cathedral. Her remains were deposited in the grave of her father, the first poetical Phoenix of England. Such quick and secret burial bespeaks preparation beforehand and proves that everything was done in accordance with ante-mortem orders from Elizabeth herself. It may be appropriate to cite here some lines from a poem which Elizabeth Rutland could not have failed to know. The verse completes the collected works of poet Nicolas Breton (1592): "The Countess of Pembroke's Love":

> *Oh, let my soule beseech her sacred rest*
> *But in the ashes of the Phoenix Nest.*

This expression, "The Phoenix Nest," became the title of a 1593 poetic collection incorporating elegies on the death of Philip Sidney

---

9. Sykes C.W. Op. cit. p. 202.

Tomb for Roger and Elizabeth Rutland in St. Mary the Virgin Church in Bottesford (one cannot see, here, the cherubs on the rear columns)

Wall monument to Shakespeare (Shakspere) in the Holy
Trinity Church in Stratford (full view). The top part (coat of
arms, skull) resembles that of the Rutlands' tomb.

Philip Sidney's funeral was celebrated with great pomp, on a national scale, in February 1587, and with many a poetic repercussion, but no memorial was erected over his grave; only a plaque inscribed with a few lines was attached to a column standing next to his final resting place. The poet's sister and friends seemed to assume that, being alive in his works, he needed no other monument. Nothing was changed at the church and the site around the poet's grave after his daughter was secretly interred. Half a century later, however, the Great London Fire turned the old wooden Cathedral of St. Paul to ashes, also destroying the archives with the record that must have existed to document the burial of Sidney's daughter in "England's Phoenixes Nest." Thus, for several centuries, the date and circumstances of her demise puzzled historians and literary critics who came across her name while studying the works of Ben Jonson and Francis Beaumont.[10]

That John Chamberlain was correct in his letter about the death of Elizabeth Rutland is supported by the fact that her burial was never recorded in the register of the parochial church of Bottesford, which serves as the family shrine of the Manners, earls of Rutland. Nevertheless, the sculpture at her husband's vault portrays not him alone, but her as well. They are shown reclining, side be side, upon the deathbed, their palms folded in prayer, as if they were both buried here. There is some evidence that her image was added somewhat later. However, all the records of burials at the vault in the late 16th-17th centuries, as well as the parish register with these records, have been fully preserved, which precludes there being any mistake; the remains of Elizabeth Sidney Rutland never reposed beneath the sculptural monument bearing her image.

The questions still confound most researchers. Why was Rutland's corpse interred so promptly upon delivery from Cambridge, two days prior to the official funeral rites? Why was no one permitted to see his face?

Despite the conjectures that such details are wont to inspire, the notion that Rutland could have suffered a violent death is groundless and in conflict with many facts, even more so in connection with Elizabeth. Any such violent deed could not have gone unnoticed. Her many relatives and friends were at the pinnacle of society, and were received by the king himself. They would not allow any suspicious action to go unexamined, and a murder, whatever forces involved, could not have been covered up; the case of Sir Thomas Overbury shows that the king himself was unable to prevent the exposure and trial of the participants in a murder.

Facts that have newly been established, documented materials, and finally the unveiled mystery of Chester's book enable us to reconstruct the course of events that took place in the autumn of 1612 at Cambridge, Belvoir and London.

---

10. After the Great Fire of 1666 and the erection of the new cathedral, its basement (crypt) with tombs was inaccessible to visitors. In the 19th century, the crypt was cleared, the seeping water was dried up and it was opened to visitors. I went there and happened to see, on an inner wall of the crypt, the new memorial plaque with the name of Philip Sidney. In today's Britain, few persons are aware that the ashes of his one and only daughter repose there as well.

The closed coffin, delivered from Cambridge directly to the church of Bottesford a month after the death of the Earl of Rutland, held the body of another person. Thus it was immediately interred; nobody was able to see the deceased face; and the funeral ceremonies were conducted only two days later. The widow was not present at the burial because at that very moment she and a few of her most loyal friends were taking the embalmed body of Rutland to London. It took several days more to carry out the final preparations — many details had to be envisaged to hide the mystery of "Shakespeare" behind an impenetrable curtain forever. And finally — poison, death, the secret nighttime burial of the married couple at St. Paul's Cathedral, in "the Phoenixes nest" — beside Philip Sidney. Those few who knew everything were bound by an oath of secrecy, while others had to content themselves with guesswork and snippets of gossip (as is manifest from the letter of the generally well-informed John Chamberlain). Then came the desired oblivion.

By now, the story of the Belvoir couple might only seem improbable to those who prefer to overlook the wide array of above-adduced facts, who fail to recognize in them the hand of the greatest master of mystique — the Belvoir Turtle, who played his role consistently in both his mortal and eternal lives.

Several weeks later, Belvoir Castle hosted His Majesty the King and the Crown Prince. They stayed for three days. Whether they were privy to the secret of the Belvoir couple's interment is unknown, but there can be no doubt that the king had been initiated into the secret of Shakespeare long ago.

After yet another seven months, the new master of Belvoir sent for Shakspere and Burbadge. To all appearances, Shakspere was ordered out of London after he had been paid by the steward, Thomas Screven, for the well-known "My Lord's impreso."[11] Shakspere rushed to wind up his business in the capital, cast off his troupe of actors, and went back to Stratford for good. The "Grand Possessors" would need him again only ten years later, when they deemed it necessary to erect a small monument close by his grave at the local church in Stratford.

Thus, in the summer of 1612 Roger Manners, Earl of Rutland, and his wife Elizabeth ceased to exist on earth; their departure coincides with the end of Shakespeare's creative activities — a fact for which neither the adherents of the Stratfordian theory nor those who favor other non-Stratfordian hypotheses can account. This goes hand in hand with one other vital fact: when an outstanding couple who had been very close to the most famous poets and writers of the epoch left the stage, almost simultaneously, all these people were absolutely silent. Not a single elegy was written (despite tradition) on the death of Rutland, either by his numerous Cambridge friends, whom he had patronized and helped in so may ways, nor by the

---

11. Thomas Screven served as the steward of the Rutland family under both Roger and his successor Francis; thus he could use "My Lord" referring to either the former or the latter. If he meant the recently deceased Roger, then the word "impreso" may be interpreted as a conventional expression meaning a mask.

The cherub sculptures on the Rutland (left) and Shakspere (right) tombs are identical in conception.

"poets of Belvoir vale," or the minstrels around the Prince of Wales, who had participated in the creation of *Coryate's Crudities*. Nobody said a word.[12] Even more amazing is the fact that no one reacted to the death, following so closely on her husband's, of the sole daughter of Philip Sidney, revered by all the literary men of England and moreover, according to Ben Jonson, a remarkable poet herself. Jonson, who knew and adored her, also kept silent, though he was used to respond with heartfelt elegies on the demise of almost everyone he knew (and even some he did not know). In the summer of 1612, Jonson was away from England; when he came back later in the year, the news of Elizabeth's death must have shocked him, but nevertheless he showed no reaction openly. In his *Works*, 1616, he included two poetic addresses to the Countess of Rutland which had been written during her lifetime and were known to their common friends (Lucy Bedford, for instance), but he never uttered a syllable about her recent death. If one did not know the reason, this would look like an appalling, shocking silence!

Other people who knew her well also behaved as if they had lost their tongues: Samuel Daniel, John Donne, John Marston, George Chapman, Michael Drayton, Mary Roth, Lucy Bedford, even Mary, Countess of Pembroke, who had fostered her. But the mysterious demise of Philip Sidney's daughter could not have left them unmoved (and what John Chamberlain was able to sniff out was, of course, no secret to her closest friends and relatives). Like the death of the great poet and playwright William Shakespeare, historians have found the departure of the Belvoir couple to be ringed with a wall of strange and impenetrable silence, a silence that could not have been caused by lack of knowledge, let alone indifference. The only possible explanation is that they were forbidden to write about the double death.

While those in the know clearly had been bound to secrecy, young Francis Beaumont was apparently not a part of it. A year before the demise of Elizabeth Rutland he wrote a poem, which he entitled "a strange letter," wherein he expressed his deep admiration of this remarkable woman.

> I never yet did a living woman praise
> In prose or verse.

He rejects the well-worn manner of burdening women with flattery, because he understands whom he addresses now.

> I can, by that dim fading light,
> Perceive of what or unto whom I write.
> … … … … … … … … … … … … … … … … …
> I lose my ink, my paper and my time

---

12. By comparison, when his friend the 3rd Earl of Southampton died in 1624, many poets of England openly lamented his death.

> *And nothing add to your o'erflowing store*
> *And tell you nought, but what you knew before.*

And here is Beaumont's conclusion:

> *But if your thoughts, which I must respect*
> *Above your glorious titles, shall accept*
> *These harsh disordered lines, I shall ere long*
> *Dress up your virtues new, in a new song;*
> *Yet far from all base praise and flattery,*
> *Although I know what'er my verses be,*
> *They will like the most servile flattery shew,*
> *If I write truth, and make the subject you.*[13]

Alas, Beaumont was afforded just such an opportunity all too soon. The elegy he wrote three days after the death of Elizabeth Rutland is permeated with deep grief:

> *I may forget to drinke, to eat, to sleepe,*
> *Remembring thee, but when I doe, to weepe...*

He mourns for her whose life began with the loss of her great father; he expresses sorrow that the source of woman's happiness, marriage, was, "to believe rumours," just a fiction because

> *Blessing of women — marriage was to thee*
> *Nought but a sacrament of Miserie;*
> *For whom thou hadst, if we may trust to fame,*
> *Could nothing change about thee, but thy name.*
> *A name which who (that were againe to doo't)*
> *Would change without a thousand joyes to boot*
> *In all things else, thou rather leadst a life*
> *Like a betrothed virgin than a Wife.*

Deploring the loss of Elizabeth Rutland (judging by the text, Beaumont did not know or preferred not to touch upon the cause of her death), he expresses his faith in the immortal value of poetic ideals. Unable to go on, he has to fall silent.

> *I will not hurt the peace which she should have*
> *By looking longer in her quiet grave.*

---

13. Gayley Ch. M. *Beaumont, the Dramatist.* NY. 1912. p. 150-151, 155-158.

Francis Beaumont

Beaumont's biographers note that this elegy rises above all his other poetic works for its intensity of feeling, the weight of the ideas expressed and the tragic tonality. In his conversation with Drummond in 1619, Ben Jonson mentioned the elegy in admiring terms. When Beaumont himself died, in 1616, John Earle spoke highly of the latter's elegy for the death of Elizabeth Rutland, and called it:

> A Monument that will then lasting be
> When all her marble is more dust than she.[14]

And in the epitaph for Francis Beaumont himself, his brother John mentioned the above elegy in terms that intimate that it was the untimely demise of Philip Sidney's daughter that gave the young poet such a great shock that he was unable to recover. Despite the esteem accorded this elegy, it was published only six years after the death of Francis Beaumont. As to the others, they still maintained their silence.

## COVERT ELEGIES

Thus, the fact that Ben Jonson, who knew her so well, did not say a word about the death of Elizabeth Rutland in his *Works*, published just a few years later, in 1616, and did not mention it later on either, testifies beyond a doubt that the topic was banned. Yet, Ben Jonson could get around the strictest prohibitions like nobody else, without formally violating them (that is, he did not name names, but he penned verses "with double    meaning" intended for the initiated few). In this difficult art, Jonson attained great mastery, surpassing in it nearly all[15] his contemporaries. Careful analysis of those works and the circumstances under which they appeared provides us with additional telling allusions.

The portion of his *Works* entitled "Forest" consists of fifteen verses, most of which are directly addressed to members of the Sidney family and their circle. There are, as we know, also two poems (numbers X and XI) from Chester's collection about the Turtle and the Phoenix. The verse under number IV, named "To the World," has a subtitle: "A Farewell for a Gentlewoman, virtuous and noble." It is a dramatic monologue, a bitter farewell to an imperfect world full of vanity and falsehood, which the eminent lady quits, judging by her speech, voluntarily.

> *I know thou whole art but a shop*
> *Of toys, and trifles, traps, and snares,*

---

14. Gayley Ch. *Op. cit.*, p. 156.

15. The reader understands why the word "nearly" is necessary, for one of Jonson's contemporaries was William Shakespeare.

> *To take the weak, or make them stop:*
> *Yet art thou falser than thy wares.*

Fate gives her an opportunity to start a new life, but she rejects it. Her voice is tinged with a weary and bitter resolution. Having realized the fleeting essence of the world of vanity, and on the verge of a tragic choice, she does not wish to start over; she does not want to be "a bird who

> *. . . having 'scaped, shall I return,*
> *And thrust my neck into the noose,*
> *From whence, so lately, I did burn,*
> *With all my powers, myself to loose?*
> *What bird, or beast, is known so dull,*
> *That fled his cage, or broke his chain,*
> *And tasting air, and freedom, will*
> *Render his head in there again?*

No, she rejects such an opportunity: "My part is ended on thy stage."

Jonson's commentators have not yet been able to identify this lady who so dramatically bids farewell to the world, to its stage. But is it really so hard to recognize her among the heroes and characters of the little "Forest," of all of Jonson's poetic collections the most closely tied to the Sidneys? Who else among Jonson's acquaintances, belonging to the Sidney family, left this world under similar circumstances several years before the book was issued, that is, before 1616? Only the lady whose death, as has become evident, could not be mentioned openly. The answer is unequivocal: It was she, Elizabeth Rutland, the young lady-poet, who had a chance to start a new life after the demise of her husband. It was she who rejected the chance, having no desire "to come back to the cage," who refused "to play her part on the stage of the world." She took her own life several days after Rutland's funeral at Bottesford; and she had taken care that her own burial would be secret. "A Farewell for a Gentlewoman, virtuous and noble" is the parting monologue of the Chester Phoenix and a place for it certainly could have been found in that collection if Jonson had been in England when Chester and Blount started to compile the secret book dedicated to the Rutlands' memory.

Another poem, "Eupheme,"[16] written at about the same time as "To the World," was first published only in 1640, after Jonson's death, in the poetic cycle *Underwoods*. It consists of ten parts, all the titles of which had been announced previously, but then it turned out that the texts of four of them (just those which, judging by the titles, speak about the heroine's occupation with poetry and about her spouse) were lost! About half of the remaining parts contain awkward additions, evidently made later.

---

16. Eupheme is a new word created by Jonson from the Greek Euphemia — "glory," "veneration."

Sometimes, in prose, they lead the reader astray; there are even some unfinished sentences. These apparent, nearly flagrant additions are addressed to Jonson's patron during the last years of his life, Sir Kenelm Digby, and his young wife, Venetia, who died in 1633. In parts that remained unchanged and unabridged, the poet speaks about the lady who had been his Muse, his inspirer,

> *I call you muse; now make it true:*
> *Henceforth my every line be you...*

He bids her farewell; his grief is boundless, and he reproaches those who could not stop her, who could not talk her out of taking that irrevocable step. There are lines that speak directly about Elizabeth Sidney's poem about Christ's Passions:

> *... She saw him on the cross*
> *Suffering and dying to redeem our loss!*
> *She saw him rise, triumphing over death*
> *To justify, and quicken us in breath!*

Jonson dedicates as much as 25 lines to her poem — not his usual practice.

Like many other verses in the *Underwoods* cycle, Jonson's poem was created when Digby's wife was still a child, and it is implausible that she could have inspired every line there written. In the extant part of the poem, there are many lines that have nothing to do with Venetia Digby. Besides, Jonson lived for four years after her death and he had enough time and creativity to compose and complete a memorial poem (or elegy) dedicated to the late wife of his patron. Still, he preferred to make explicit additions to several parts of the poem about Elizabeth Rutland and her husband that had long been kept in his desk. He could not publish it as it was, so he simply removed those portions where he could not avoid mentioning her and could not disguise her by additions and deletions. Thus, he managed to preserve about half of the basic text, and Jonson scholars have yet to evaluate it properly.

The third and fourth parts of "Eupheme," which have none of these additions and deletions, are of enormous interest. Here, the poet explains to the artist what the portrait, the image of his fair Muse, should look like. Even if the artist could render her outer traits (though he must never reveal her identity), one could never depict on canvas her high and clear mind, her speech (by which one should understand, poetry) like music and full of meaning; only a poet could show all that. Jonson presents the same thought, expressed in nearly the same words, in his address to the reader concerning the "portrait" of Shakespeare made by Droeshout for the Great Folio!

Certainly, it is odd that "Eupheme" was published with half of the parts "lost," with additions and deletions made exactly at the places where the poet's contemporaries, even those who were not very well aware of the topic, still could have recognized Philip Sidney's daughter. But the oddest thing is that the third and fourth parts were included in the first collection of Shakespeare's poetic works, published the same year, 1640, and were placed right after the elegies dedicated to the Great Bard! What has this poem by Jonson, or at least those two parts, to do with Shakespeare, and why did the editor John Benson find it appropriate to include them in the book? None of the Western Shakespeare or Jonson scholars has ever tried to explain that. I shall add that those two parts of "Eupheme," in the Shakespeare book of poetry, are followed by a poetic letter from Beaumont to Jonson: the very verse in which he recollects the merry meetings at the Mermaid Club among gentlemen who liked to call themselves the "British Wits."

After 1612, a number of works appeared with clear hints at a heavy loss suffered by English literature. William Browne from Tavistock, in the second book of "Britannia Pastorals" (written in 1614-1615 and dedicated to the Earl of Pembroke) enumerates the greatest poets of England, "whose equals Earth cannot produce again"— Philip Sidney, George Chapman, Michael Drayton, Ben Jonson, Samuel Daniel, Christopher Brooke, John Davies of Hereford, George Wither. Then he speaks about two other poets:

> *Two of the quaintest swans that yet have beene*
> *Failed their attendance on the Ocean's queene*
> *Remond and Doridon, whose haplesse fates*
> *Late severed them from their more happy mates.*

The list of "most skilful poets" lacks the name of Shakespeare; whom did William Browne mourn under the names of Remond and Doridon, "two most perfect poets" who had died not so long before? We can narrow in on those "recently deceased" poets by reading Browne's first book of "Pastorals," issued in 1613 but written several years before, where we see that at that time both Remond and Doridon were still alive. They were inseparable; their songs were echoed by forest birds. Doridon vowed fidelity to Remond. Every attempt by scholars of English literature to find out who were the persons under these name-masks has been futile up till now. Browne's "Pastorals" give us two recently deceased poets and other allusions to the Belvoir couple as well, bringing these "Pastorals" closer to Jonson's *Sad Shepherd* and Chester's *Love's Martyr*. The same may be said of Christopher Brooke's "The Ghost of Richard III," John Fletcher's "Upon an Honest Man's Fortune" and the final pieces of his tetralogy *Four plays in One* ("Triumph of Death" and "Triumph of Time"), and Robert Herrick's "To the Apparition of his Mistresse calling him to the Elizium."

In 1615 John Stephens (of Lincoln's Inn) came out with a book, *Essays and Characters*. In one of the profiles, under the title "A Worthy Poet," a portrait is presented which, in the opinion of John Dover Wilson, refers to the Great Bard (as he appears to us in the pages of his works). Stephens writes:

A worthy poet is a purest essence of a worthy man: he is confident of nature in nothing but the form and an ingenious fitness to conceive the matter . . . His works do every way pronounce both nourishment, delight and admiration to the reader's soul: which makes him neither rough, effeminate, not windy: for by a sweet contemperature of tune and ditty he entices others to goodness, and shows himself perfect in the lesson . . . He hath more debtors in knowledge among the present writers than creditors among the ancient poets. He is possessed with an innocent liberty, which excludes him from the slavish labour and means of setting a gloss upon frail commodities... Neither does he passionately affect high patronage, nor any, further than he may give freely, and so receive back honest thanks. The dangerous name and the contempt of poets, sprung from their multitude of corruptions, prove no disadvantage or terror to him: for such be his antidotes that he can walk untouched, even through the worst infection . . . He only among men is nearest infinite: for in the scenical composites, of a tragedy or comedy, he shows the best resemblance of his high Creator: turning his quick passions, and witty humours to replenish and overcome into matter and form as infinite as God's pleasure to diversify mankind . . . Silver only and sound metal comprehend his nature: rubbing, motion, and customary usage, make the brightness of both more eminent. No marvel though he be immortal, seeing he converts poison into nourishment, even the worst objects and societies to a worthy use. When he is lastly silent (for he cannot die) he finds a monument prepared at others' cost and remembrance, whilst his former actions be a living epitaph.

Citing these lines, Wilson noted: "Had the writer Shakespeare in mind?"[17] E. Fripp was even more definite, and Anikst is inclined to agree with them: "There was no other writer who corresponded so perfectly to this profile, and I am ready to join the opinion of those scholars. But the book was published in 1615, when William Shakespeare [i.e. Shakspere — I.G.] was still alive and well. Can it be that this description, especially its final part ('monument,' 'epitaph') refers to a living man?"[18] But is it not clear that the author is speaking about a writer who was not alive in 1615?

In the first decade after the Belvoir couple's death, their names were not the only ones shrouded in silence; the name of Shakespeare, too, could hardly be heard. His works were seldom published, despite the fact that editors had the right to do so, as confirmed by records in the Stationers' Register; and Shakespeare's books were selling well. More than a half of the plays that comprise what is now Shakespeare's canon had not yet been published, and nobody knows where they were at the time. It looks as though "the Grand Possessors of Plays," among whom were Mary Sidney Pembroke and her son, the powerful Lord Chamberlain, the Earl of Pembroke, thought that the time for the presentation of the "complete Shakespeare," as well as for the erection of a

---

17. Cit. by Wilson, John Dover. *Life in Shakespeare's England.* — Harmondsworth: Penguin books, 1951. — pp. 188-190.

18. E. I. Fripp also noted that.

monument in Stratford that would serve as a basis for the future cult, had not yet come.

That is why, in 1619, when Thomas Pavier and William Jaggard wanted to publish a score of Shakespeare plays and those that were considered his (probably they wanted to issue even more), in one volume, they were stopped and had to sell separately what had already been printed, falsely back-dating the title pages. Since Pavier and Jaggard had legal rights for about half of those plays, Stratfordians are in a bind. What coherent explanation can be given for those false dates? The only convincing answer, based on facts, is now evident: the Earl of Pembroke gave a spoken order to the Stationers Company to prevent the appearance of any books with the name of Shakespeare on them. Until further notice.

## AND SHINES

At last, the "Grand Possessors" decided that the time had come to present the Great Bard William Shakespeare to the world. The summer of 1622 was the 10th anniversary of the death of the Belvoir couple. This was the year in which the full collection of Shakespeare's works was intended to appear (as we now know from the catalogue of the Frankfurt Book Fair) and the monument was placed in the Stratford church. This small wall memorial was made in 1622 by the Janssens, the stonecutters who created the monument to Rutland. The Janssens, fulfilling the wishes of their high patrons, saw to it that the external aspects of these two tombs were similar.[19] But the "Grand Possessors" did not manage to issue the large volume on schedule. The work began in April 1621, under the auspices of Mary, Countess of Pembroke, but was suspended after her sudden death in September. As we know, Blount managed to publish the book only in the autumn of 1623.

But the year of 1622 was not uneventful: after having lain in hiding, nobody knows where, the never before published "Othello" appeared, along with reprints of "Richard III" and "Henry IV." Also in consecutive edition of Overbury's book, Beaumont's elegy on the death of Elizabeth Rutland at last was printed. This was also the year that the now well-known poem by William Basse was written (it was published 18 years later in an edition of "Shakespeare's poems"). Basse pays great tribute to Shakespeare, who, he says, merited being buried in Westminster Abbey next to Chaucer, Spenser and Beaumont. Let us note that Beaumont, who died the same year as Shakspere but seems to have been treated rather better, was indeed buried with the appropriate veneration and was mourned by numerous friends.

---

19. We have already spoken of the surmise that the author of the inscription on the Stratford memorial was Rutland's fellow student poet John Weever.

Ben Jonson

After the death of Mary, Countess of Pembroke, her son, Lord Chamberlain, showed great benevolence to Ben Jonson. The latter was made the Master of Revels, which included responsibility for the censoring of plays. Jonson's predecessor, Sir George Buck, was pronounced mad; probably the poor man lost his way in the intricate phantasmagoria of the "Grand Possessors." In order to prevent anyone from unraveling that riddle, the old registration books were burned. So were Ben Jonson's study and library, so that he would not be tempted to publish the contents. Jonson recollected with melancholy the lost manuscripts and registers, and also the fire of 1613 that burned down the *Globe* theater, in the poem "Execration upon Vulcan." Thus the "Grand Possessors" once again proved their foresight and a determination that stopped at nothing. By the way, Jonson, who contributed extremely important work to the creation of the First Folio (he wrote two addresses on behalf of the actors: to Pembroke and Montgomery, and to the readers; he also wrote two major introductory poems) was consoled by the fact that his remuneration was doubled. Expenses for the creation of the Great Folio have been estimated at 6000 pounds sterling; sales brought in only some 1500 pounds. At the time, only the "Grand Possessors," the Pembrokes and the Dorsets above all, could have covered the great deficit. As we know, besides Jonson, memorial verses in the Great Folio were contributed by Leonard Diggs, who mentioned the Stratford monument that would be dissolved by time, an anonymous I. M., and our acquaintance Hugh Holland, the one who supplied the address to the "idiots readers" in *Coryate's Crambe.*

1632 was the 20th anniversary of the Rutlands' death. It comes as no surprise that the second edition of the Shakespeare folio, now customarily called "The Second Folio," was issued the same year. The major figure behind that publication was Robert Allot, to whom Blount had shortly before assigned the right to publish a number of books, including sixteen Shakespeare plays. The Second Folio is largely a reprint of the First, only with some misprints and grammatical errors were corrected. The work was not laborious, and the volume appeared on time.

The Second Folio contained the same Droeshout engraving allegedly depicting Shakespeare — with a face-mask, inverted tunic and other strange details — that so puzzles Shakespeareans. Also reprinted from the First Folio was Jonson's controversial address to the reader, advising us not to look at the "portrait," and his poem "To the Memory of My Beloved, the Author Mr. William Shakespeare: And What he hath Left Us." We have already examined that remarkable poem, a chef d'oeuvre worthy of the genius to whom it was dedicated. Now, let us focus on those lines which we did not touch upon before.

Jonson exclaims (as if contradicting William Basse):

> … … … … … … … *Soul of the age!*
> *The applause, delight, the wonder of our stage!*
> *My Shakespeare, rise; I will not lodge thee by*
> *Chaucer, or Spencer, or bid Beaumont lie*

*A little further, to make thee a room:*
*Thou art a monument, without a tomb,*
*And art alive still, while thy book doth live,*
*And we have wits to read, and praise to give.*
*That I not mix thee so, my brain excuses;*
*I mean with great, but disproportioned muses:*
*For, if I thought my judgment were of years,*
*I should commit thee surely with thy peers,*
*And tell, how thou didst our Lyly outshine,*
*Or sporting Kyd, or Marlowe's mighty line.*
*And though thou hadst small Latin, and less Greek,*
*From thence to honour thee, I would not seek*
*For names; but call forth thundering Aeschylus,*
*Euripides, and Sophocles to us,*
*Pacuvius, Accius, him of Cordova dead,*
*To life again, to hear thy buskin tread,*
*And shake a stage: or, when thy socks were on,*
*Leave thee alone, for the comparison*
*Of all that insolent Greece, or haughty Rome*
*Sent forth, or since did from their ashes come.*

The comment about Shakespeare's "small knowledge" of Latin and Greek cannot be taken seriously. Nowadays, Shakespeare scholars know full well that the Great Bard's works attest to the contrary — he demonstrates almost perfect knowledge and fluent use of Latin and Greek sources.[20] Certainly, Jonson considered himself the greatest expert in Latin and Greek of all the writers and poets in England (and so he forthrightly declared to Drummond in 1619); he did not think much of the others' capabilities in that area. Besides, the creators of the Great Folio were consciously, if cautiously, working to craft the image of the Shake-speare to a legend that would acquire a more definite shape over time.

Jonson calls Shakespeare "sweet swan of Avon." We all know that Stratford is situated on the River Avon; but there are six rivers bearing that name in England, and one of them is close to where the Rutlands lived.[21] Then Jonson reminds us of Shakespeare's "flights" to the banks of the Thames, those "flights" that Queen Elizabeth and King James so enjoyed. Nobody has ever shown that either of those monarchs was acquainted with the Stratfordian; but they knew Rutland well, and

20. Let us recollect that Thomas Coryate spoke about his "poor command of Latin and Greek" in the same tongue-in-cheek tone, while the books bearing his name are full of passages demonstrating a thorough knowledge of those languages. Jonson seems to be "quoting " Coryate!

21. On the banks of the other Avon lived Mary (Sidney) Pembroke; and opposite her estate was a village named Stratford! A portrait etching from 1618 shows her in a dress with a lace collar decorated with images of swans.

James especially saw him during the "woods earl's" infrequent flights to the capital (and probably Mary Pemboke, as well.)

Jonson goes on:

> *Triumph, my Britain, thou hast one to show,*
> *To whom all scenes of Europe homage owe.*
> *He was not of an age, but for all time!*
> *And all the muses still were in their prime,*
> *When like Apollo he came forth to warm*
> *Our ears, or like a Mercury to charm!*
> *Nature herself was proud of his designs,*
> *And joyed to wear the dressing of his lines!*
> *Which were so richly spun, and woven so fit,*
> *As, since, she will vouchsafe no other wit.*
> *The merry Greek, tart Aristophanes,*
> *Neat Terence, witty Plautus, now not please;*
> *But antiquated, and deserted lie*
> *As they were not of nature's family.*
> *Yet must I not give nature all: thy art,*
> *My gentle Shakespeare, must enjoy a part.*
> *For though the poet's matter, nature be,*
> *His art doth give the fashion. And, that he,*
> *Who casts to write a living line, must sweat,*
> *(Such as thine are) and strike the second heat*
> *Upon the muses' anvil: turn the same,*
> *(And himself with it) that he thinks to frame;*
> *Or for the laurel, he may gain a scorn,*
> *For a good poet's made, as well as born.*

Then come some lines that sound queer enough in English, and are always rendered into Russian approximately at best, so that the intricate word play for which Ben Jonson is famous goes unseen and unheard. Here, Jonson plays with Manners, Rutland's family name, which of course may be understood as "customs," "mores," "habits," "ways," etc. The word "manners" occurs in Shakespeare's sonnets three times (39, 85, 111) and each time the sonnet's meaning becomes clear if the word is treated as a *proper* noun. For instance, the first line in Sonnet 85:

My tongue-tied Muse in m a n n e r s holds her still . . .

It may mean literally: "My Muse, tongue-tied, keeps quiet." Why is "in manners" added here? The line makes sense if the word "manners" is understood as a proper name, though it is not written with a capital letter: "My Muse remains silent in me,

Roger Manners." In Sonnet 111, Shakespeare rebukes the goddess Fortune that made him dependent on public subsidies. In the fourth line, the word "manners" appears, with the verb in singular, which means that here again, Manners is a proper name. Rutland's adherents attribute the sonnet to 1604-1605, when Rutland, in a very tight financial situation, had to beg the government for subsidies ("alms").

Word play with the name Manners is also present in both Weever's epigram and the Coryate book; it is positively striking when it appears out of nowhere at the end of *Coryate's Crudities.*

Away back in 1598, John Marston, in his anonymously published book *Scourge of Villanie,* unexpectedly addresses an obscure poet:

> … … … … … … … … ….*Far fly thy fame*
> *Most, most of me beloved, whose silent name*
> *One letter bounds. Thy true judicial style*
> *I ever honour, and if my love beguile*
> *Not much my hopes, then thy unvalued worth*
> *Shall mount fair place when Apes are turned forth.*

What "silent name" begins and ends with one and the same letter but Roger?

Thus, Marston foresees the time when this unknown will achieve his place of honor, and his masks, his "apes" (remember Jonson's "Poet-Ape"?) will be removed and he will be recognized.

Jonson joined the game in the epigrams published in his *Works* in 1616. In the 9th Epigram, he asks those whose names may be met in his book not to look for his degrees of rank and title; "it is against the manners of an epigram." This may be taken as an assurance that Jonson would adhere to the form and traditional character of the poetic genre of an epigram (though it is not clear why such an assurance is necessary); but the expression "against the manners" may be understood as a sly hint that the epigram is intended against the Manners. The more so that in the following, 10th Epigram (and Jonson meticulously arranged the verses himself), he addresses a lord who called him a poet in jest, and says:

> *Thou call'st me poet, as a term of shame,*
> *But I have my revenge made, in thy name.*

Here we should also recollect the episode Jonson related to Drummond: that Rutland once rebuked his wife for receiving this poet at her table. Epigrams 9-10 testify once again that Jonson did not forget that, although, it seems, he did not make too much of it, either.

Epigram 77 is dedicated "To One that Desired Me Not to Name Him."

> *Be safe, nor fear thyself so good a fame,*
> *That, any way, my book should speak thy name:*
> *For, if thou shame, ranked with my friends, to go*
> *I'm more ashamed to have thee thought my foe.*

Epigram 49 is addressed to a playwright:

> *Playwright me reads, and still my verses damns,*
> *He says, I want the tongue of epigrams;*
> *I have no salt: no bawdry he doth mean.*
> *For witty, in his language, is obscene.*
> *Playwright, I loathe to have thy manners known*
> *In my chaste book: profess them in thine own.*[22]

Here again is a tantalizing play on words. The key phrase, "I loathe to have thy manners known" could be construed as, "I have no desire to unmask you, Manners."

Now let us come back to Jonson's poem on Shakespeare, in the Great Folio, where Jonson surpassed himself in wordplay. After the line "For a good poet's made, as well as born," we find the family name of Rutland in a context that not only confirms its presence in the Great Folio, but also discovers the character of the presence:

> *And such wert thou. Look how the father's face*
> *Lives in his issue, even so, the race*
> *Of Shakespeare's mind, and manners brightly shines*
> *In his well-turned, and true-filed lines:*[23]
> *In each of which, he seems to shake a lance,*
> *As brandished at the eyes of ignorance.*

The verb "shines" is singular, and "manners" becomes the subject of the verb: before it there is a comma, disjoining this part of the composite sentence from the previous one, and changing the sense of the sentence significantly. The word "turned" has many meanings, including "changed," "reversed" etc.

All these (and other) devious and elegant tricks are for the benefit of those few who knew the role played by Roger Manners, the Earl of Rutland, in creating the works and the very image of the Shake-speare; to them, these lines say: as the father's face shows in his posterity, so does Shakespeare's mind, and Manners brightly shines

---

22. An anonymous verse from the early 17th century questions Jonson's talents as an epigram writer. There are grounds to think that the verse was either written or inspired by Rutland, whose attitude towards the latter — who could hardly keep his mouth shut — was rather conflicted. Most Shakespeare scholars think that Ben Jonson's attitude towards Shakespeare was similarly complicated.

23. Emphasis mine — I.G.

in his excellent lines; in each one he is shaking his lance, brandishing it in the face of ignorance. The last two lines bring to mind Shakespeare's Sonnet 76: "That every word doth almost tell my name."[24] In both cases, the author hidden under a mask laughs before the blind eyes of Ignorance and Misunderstanding. Besides, Jonson here directly evokes the name of the real Shake-speare. "Manners" was not the only family name Ben Jonson experimented with,[25] but it is perhaps the one he used most significantly — although the significance is so commonly overlooked.[26]

Just as one can discern the traits of the parent in his creation, so Manners shines in Shakespeare's lines. Jonson's most famous poem, always present either in full or in part in every Shakespeare biography along with his address to the reader about the notorious "figure" on the Droeshout engraving, is one of the momentous keys to deciphering the "Shakespeare mystery." Jonson, who could not openly say everything, left hints along the way to the truth and urged would-be readers: "Look at the book, not the portrait." He repeated this warning in another address to the reader, in the two lines opening his own collection of epigrams:

> *Pray thee, take care, that tak'st my book in hand,*
> *To read it well: that is, to understand.*

Like the needle of a compass always pointing North, Jonson's gaze in many of his works is directed toward Sherwood Forest and its extraordinary masters, hidden from the eyes of misunderstanding by the veil of a legend in whose creation Jonson was destined to play a considerable part.

The scenarios of his play-masques and entertainment are an inadequately researched aspect of Jonson's work; many of them contain hints at the Belvoir couple and their secret, which became the mystery of the century, of the whole new era. In the foreword to the masque "Hymenaei," Jonson said outright that his masques are not meant simply to entertain the nobles but are "a mirror of life" and contain important secrets understood only by the chosen. But it is quite a challenge to discern in that mirror the traits and traces of actual situations and prototypes of the allegoric characters, and an insurmountable challenge if the daring sleuth has no reliable key.

---

24. Sonnet 76.

25. Jonson several times played with the meaning of his contemporaries' proper names (for example Vere, Radcliffe et al).

26. One cannot say that no Shakespeare or Jonson scholar has ever noticed this hardly accidental comma. Any attentive reader of the English original would stumble upon it: Jonson inserted it here, disconnecting a composite sentence in such a way that "manners" can be the only subject to referenced by the predicate "shines". Stumped by that anomaly, some scholars treat the famous poem without much ado. Placing Jonson's eulogy in their over-erudite reissues of Shakespeare's works, they just delete (without any comment!) the "bad" comma that is so much in the way. And so Jonson was "corrected" in the last complete Oxford collection of Shakespeare works, edited by leading English Shakespeareans, Stanley Wells and Gary Taylor. *William Shakespeare. The Complete Works.* General editors Stanley Wells and Gary Taylor. Clarendon Press. Oxford, 1994, p. XLVI.

And then there are the peculiarities of the genre; for a masque was a sort of a ballet pantomime, the performers of which were eminent persons and members of the royal family — King James was fond of those exuberant spectacles.

The plot of a masque is not always clear cut; not all the lines are developed during a performance; and the text may abound in hints and double entendres that would be understood only by a few. Hints at real situations, which are incorporated in the masque, are allegorical and often fantastically distorted; all this takes place against a background of decorative and purely entertaining material. English researcher D. B. Randell notes that the mind-boggling obstacles encountered while trying to penetrate the secrets, dead ends and traps of Jonson's masques are such "that a scholar, who desires a reputation for sanity hardly ventures to touch the subject."[27] That fear of falling into a trap has kept most explorers of literature out of this part of the academic jungle, so that attempts to untangle the secrets of the masques have been very rare. A certain parallel can be found with the problem of Shakespeare authorship and identity, a problem that many academicians who cherish "the purity of their reputation" try to avoid. The similarity in how these problems are treated does not seem to be accidental.

The masque "The Gypsies Metamorphosed" was a great favorite with King James; it was performed in his presence three times during 1621 (on August 3 in Burley-on-Hill, August 5 at Belvoir and early in September at Westminster). The masque, whose "gypsy" characters represent certain unnamed members of the upper aristocracy, contains tantalizing hints at some extraordinary secret known only by a few. One of the characters asks another: "What must a man do, to enter your company?" — that is, to become a "gypsy." The response is that "such a man must be privy to mistery, which is worthy of the history. There is much to be done, before you can be a sonne, or brother of the Moone." "'Tis not so soone acquired as desired." In the epilogue, the author himself (Jonson) says that though these "gypsies" and the secrecy around them may appear strange to uninitiated spectators, the topic is not for outsiders to pry into, that is why "the good Ben . . . forgot to explain all that."

There are many allusions to Belvoir and its former owners, among them "the absent Maid Marian" and the "wit cracking cheater, the first lord of the Gypsies." It turns out that the latter was fond of visiting the famous cave, "Devil's Arse," situated not far from Rutland County, and even invited the very Devil to call upon him there. Ben Jonson went to see the cave himself and mentions it in several other masques in connection with Robin Hood and Sherwood Forest (as we know, in the "Sad Shepherd," under the name of Robin Hood, the head man of Sherwood forest, Jonson presented Rutland, who was Justice in Eire of Sherwood Forest).

All that, and the three consecutive presentations of the masque before the king, coinciding in time with a weird and mysterious voyage to Belvoir (the Venetian ambassador reported to the Doge that the cavalcade proceeded in complete silence), may lead us to conclude that the secret of the "Gypsies" was connected with the

27. Randell, D.B. *Jonson's gypsies unmasked.* Durham, 1975, p.13.

mystery of Belvoir, and the masque was written on the occasion of the upcoming tenth anniversary of the couple's death.

D. B. Randell notes with wonder that in the same year (June 27, 1621), poet George Wither was jailed because, in his poem "Wither's Motto *Nec habeo, nec careo, nec curo,*" he tried to touch on the same topic to which the Jonson masque about "gypsies" was dedicated. In December of the previous year, the Lord Chancellor Francis Bacon had written and the king had signed a special "Proclamation against Excess of Lavish and Licentious Speech of matters of State." In July of 1621, one more strict royal proclamation was issued, threatening transgressors and chatterboxes with death. Soon after this, Jonson excoriated George Wither, in the figure of the impudent satyr Chronomastix, in the masque "Time Vindicated to Himself and to his Honours," which was presented at court during Christmas of 1622 and published in quarto in 1623. Here, we meet Fame, sent by Time. Chronomastix, pursuing Time, is about to flagellate it; but having stared in the face of Fame, stops and in amazement and drops his whip:

> … … … *My Mistris! Fame!*
> *The lady whom I honour and adore!*
> *What lacke had I not to see her before!*
> *O, pardon me …*

He promises that, for the future, to "serve Fame / Is all my end and yeat my selfe a name," but Fame sends him away with disdain: "Away, I know thee not, wretched imposter . . . / goe revel with thine Ignorant admirers, / Let worthy name alone . . . " Further on, the masque glorifies the protected Time and Love, whose faces, however, are always shadowed. Their unseen presence creates harmony and adorns the world.

It is common knowledge that Jonson's attacks were aimed at Wither, but his unmerciful frenzy strikes some as disproportionate, considering that the poet had already suffered enough from the authorities. Jonson also lashed out at the publisher and others involved in the publication of Wither's book. Scholars have not been able to establish a reason for Wither's official persecution and Jonson's severe attacks. Later on, when the episode was long past, Wither complained that he was prevented from naming and glorifying "these rising stars," that his "brave attempt" was a failure.

Whom did Wither have in mind, that he recognized as "rising stars" and wished "to bring to shining"? He had dared to approach the banned topic that could be broached only by such trusted authors as Ben Jonson, the royal pensioner. Let us note that the whole story took place just at the time when work was in full swing on the Great Folio, approaching the anniversary of the Rutlands' death. The character of the accusations lodged against Chronomastix (that is, against Wither and his editor) in the context of Jonson's masque, and with "Gypsies Metamorphosed," indicates that Wither had nearly revealed the secret that he had learned by chance and that was sealed under the highest patronage. The story allows for a better understanding of that strange and complete silence on the part of English writers and poets who published not a single line, openly, commemorating the demise of the Shake-speare (whoever he had been and whenever he had died — in 1612 or in 1616). Only after the appearance in 1623 of the Great Folio, sponsored by the Pembrokes, which determined the contours of the future cult, was the unwritten ban taken off the name of Shakespeare — though still no definite biographical data appeared about him. Interestingly, poet and playwright Thomas Heywood had started a reference work in 1614 entitled *Biographies of all English poets*, where a chapter about Shakespeare could not be omitted; but as one might by now expect, the composition disappeared without any trace.

Some special significance seems to lurk in Jonson's play "Magnetic Lady," for he gave it a subtitle, "Humours Reconciled." In the introductory part, Boy, the "poetry shop" assistant, explains that after "Every man in his Humor" and "Every man out of his Humors" and other plays, the author is now finishing with a work conceived long ago about a lady who reconciles all the humors. Though the name of the lady is "Loadstone" and means "magnet," the title of the play (he explains) derives from the Latin "magna" — great, magnificent. Such an explanation indicates that the play deals with things that are far from ordinary; and while Lady Lodestone really is a magnet attracting and uniting people around her, the author, through his character, interprets the title as "The Great Lady."

The heroes of the play are taking part in a mysterious enterprise, which Sir Moath Interest characterizes by saying: "That is my industry/ As it might be your reading, studies and counsel." Obviously, the project has to do with some form of publication. Then the attention of the dramatis personae is concentrated on the Great Lady's niece, who turns out to be pregnant; everyone anticipates the appearance of a midwife who is called to help the child into this world and "to deliver everybody from suffering." Then everyone scrutinizes the "babe." "Your name's not in it," says the mathematician Compass to the lawyer Practice, who answers: "It has the seale, which is the maine. And registered . . . I am much bound into you. You have all the law and parts of Sir Squire Practice." Then he breaks the news: "Mr. Thin-wit — Surveyor of the Project generall . . . is dead this morning." The heroes go away with the "babe" and the cradle in a carriage to implement their "project."

Back in the "poetic bookshop," the witty Boy discusses with the clients a risky question: whom is the author presenting under one or another mask? He evades the question and explains that some people's specific traits are certainly given in the allegorical figures, but the heroes of the play are not their exact replicas. The "lock" sealing the play is not to be opened so simply; there is definitely a secret here, one that cannot be revealed. One of the women states this quite definitely: "Be friends and keepe these women-matters, smock-secrets to ourselves, in our owne verge. We shall marre all, if once we open the mysteries of the Tyring-house, and tell what's done within. No Theatres are more cheated with appearances, or these shop-lights, then the Ages, and folke in them . . . " The last sentence is indeed fraught with meaning!

The presentation and publishing of the play in 1632 ran into serious difficulties, resulting in accusations against the censor, author, and actors, and two petitions to high authorities protesting their innocence have been found.

All these quirks and obfuscations point to the same conclusion: the project in which the characters are engaged, the babe, the weighty words about theater and publishers' secrets, about the ages and people that should not know these secrets, testify that Jonson was consciously and deliberately, albeit in an extremely confused form, speaking about the publication of the First Shakespeare Folio a decade before, about the godmother and major figure of the "project," the Great Magnetic Lady, Mary (Sidney) Pembroke, and her faithful assistants.

Only when we know the facts pertaining to the "poets of Belvoir vale" can we see the common thread that ties together the multiple significant hints scattered in Ben Jonson's poems, plays and masques. He confirms several times (in 1623 and after) that he knew Shakespeare, so he knew who he was; the Rutlands and the Pembrokes are the only "pretenders" with whom Jonson was on close terms, and this makes the reading of each of his testimonies invaluable. The strands of the momentous mystification which is the glory of the epoch are deviously woven into many of his works. He never could say it all openly, but he took pains to help posterity unravel the Game some time in the future; he left his clues more than once. Here I have touched upon only a few such hints.

The 20th century saw a revival of interest in the works of John Donne (1572-1631), one of the major poets of Shakespearean England. They have now been studied, analyzed, translated[28] and classified.[29] Still, very few scholars ever wondered that Donne, who was closely acquainted with nearly all the writers and poets of England in those years, never mentioned the name of the greatest of his contemporaries, William Shakespeare, and never commented on or reacted in any way to his death — though the elegy by William Basse written in 1622 first appeared in the posthumous publication of John Donne's works (evidently, it was found among his papers after his death). Donne could not help but have known Rutland, with whom he had taken part in Essex's Azores expedition, and then they met at the house of Egerton, when Essex was there under arrest. In 1607-1610 Donne helped Rutland's capellan Thomas Morton during his polemics in the press, with Rome; it was Morton who at the time advised Donne to enter the church, and Donne later followed this counsel. Donne also took part in the "panegyric following" of Coryate's books. He knew well the "Bright Lucy," the Countess of Bedford, closest friend of Elizabeth Sidney Rutland, and often visited her at her house. Several of his poetic works are addressed to the Countess of Bedford. Donne surely was well acquainted with the daughter of Philip Sidney, and he had to

---

28. Among Russian translations of Donne, the most widely known are by Joseph Brodsky; among literary studies the books by A. N. Gorbounov and S. A. Makourenkova stand out.

29. Gorbunov, A. N. *John Donne and English poetry of the 16th-17th Centuries* (in Russian). M., 1993. Makourenkova, S. A. *John Donne: poetry and rhetoric* (in Russian). M., 1994.

John Donne

John Donne's tomb — the only statue in St. Paul's Cathedral surviving the Great Fire of 1666.

have been impressed by her tragic and sacrificial demise. In 1621, he became dean of St. Paul's Cathedral, where she was buried, and he certainly knew that. And yet he never openly mentioned her name, or Rutland's.[30]

Still, the Belvoir couple, especially Elizabeth, is often present in Donne's poetic heritage. Of course, owing to the peculiarities of life (and probably his fidelity to the vow to silence), his perception and images are more "metaphysical" than his friend Ben Jonson's, who, it seems, was almost physically tortured by the requirement to keep quiet. In the poem "Funerall," Donne asks those who would prepare his body for burial:

> *Whoever comes to shroud me, do not harm*
> *Nor question much*
> *The subtle wreath of hair about mine arm ...*

(He also speaks about "a bracelet of bright haire about the bone" in the poem "Relique.") The talisman, token of a secret, should not be touched for it represents another poet's soul, a remembrance of her, when she was taken to heaven. She left the talisman in order to inspire and uplift the mind of the poet:

> *These haires which upward grew, and strength and art*
> *Have from a better braine,*
> *Can better do it; Except she meant that I*
> *By this should know my pain,*
> *As prisoners then [as in Shawcross] are manacled, when they are condemned to die*
> *What ere she meant by it, bury it with me,*
> *For since I am*
> *Loves martyr, it might breed idolatrie,*
> *If into others hands these Reliques came...*

In this mysterious verse infused with perennial pain (the same pain one feels when reading Beaumont's elegy on Elizabeth Rutland's death), John Donne, calling *himself* "Love's martyr," repeats the title of Chester's collection.

Donne's works include a poetic letter written jointly with the poet Henry Goodyere to an anonymous poetic couple; half of the verse is Donne's, the other half, Goodyere's (intermittently). The poets send the letter to the addressees as a pledge of

---

30. The tombstone of John Donne, who was also buried in St. Paul's Cathedral, has had a wonderful, even mystical fate. The monument is a bit peculiar. According to his Last Will, Donne is presented in a mortal shroud standing on a low, thin urn as if guarding the ashes contained there. During the Great Fire of 1666, all the monuments in St. Paul's cathedral were reduced to charred ruins. The only monument found intact among the awful debris was the statue of John Donne upon a fragile urn. Nowadays, centuries later, the statue of poet-priest stands in its place in the dormitory of the cathedral, still guarding the eternal peace of the souls who trusted him with their presence.

fidelity; they submit completely. The unknown couple is likened to the Sun that warms everyone; in them both dwell all the Muses. Donne and his friend are eager to meet them.

> *Heere in our Nightingales, we here you singe*
> *Who soe doe make the whole yeare through a springe,*
> *And save us from the feare of Autumns stinge.*
> ... ... ... ... ... ... ... ... ... ... ... ... ... ...
> *. . . should wee more bleed out our thoughts in Inke*
> *Noe paper (though it would bee glad to drinke*
> *Those drops) could comprehend what wee doe thinke.*
> *For t'were in us ambition to write*
> *Soe, that because wee two, you two unite,*
> *Our letter should as you bee infinite.*

To whom, in 1608-1610, could such a letter be sent, full of boundless veneration? Donne's biographers are at a loss, for as a rule they are not well informed about the "poets of Belvoir vale."

Scholars who have studied the Shakespeare poem about the Turtle and the Phoenix and the Chester book note the obvious recycling of some of their images and expressions in Goodyere's poem in the book *The Mirror of Magestie* (1618) and in a mysterious poem (how often one has to use the word!) "The Canonization," by Donne. This borrowing has inspired the notion that the anonymous verses in Chester's collection were written by Goodyere and Donne ("Ignoto" and the "Chorus of Poets"). That possibility cannot be excluded, but considerable investigation would be required to verify it. Still, "The Canonization" could have become a part of Chester's *Love's Martyr*.

"The Canonization" begins with the lyric hero's address to some friend:

> *For Godsake hold your tongue, and let me love,*
> *Or chide my palsie, or my gout,*
> *My five gray haires, or ruin'd fortune flout...*

He goes on:

> *Alas, alas, who's injur'd by my love?*
> *What merchants ships have my sighs drown'd?*
> *Who saies my teares have overflow'd his ground?*

Weakness, early aging, gout, paralysis (contraction of the brain vessels) are diseases Rutland suffered from; he was plagued too by debts and muddled business affairs. And this unusual, venerating love ("not passion, but peace and quiet") associated with tears, torrents of them — that was the relationship of the Belvoir pair, their platonic love, so torturing for both of them, making them both one single spiritual entity.

> *Call us what you will, wee'are made such by love*
> *Call her one, me another flye,*
> *We'are Tapers too, and at our owne cost die,*
> *And wee in us finde the Eagle and the dove.*
> *The Phoenix riddle hath more wit*
> *By us, we two being one, are it.*
> *So, to one neutrall thing both sexes fit.*
> *Wee dye and rise the same, and prove*
> *Mysterious by this love.*

Now, we hear the voice of the heroes of the Chester book, the voice of the Turtle and the Phoenix:

> *Wee can dye by it, if not live by love,*
> *And if unfit for tombes and hearse*
> *Our legend bee, it will be fit for verse;*
> *And if no peece of Chronicle wee prove,*
> *We'll build in sonnets pretty roomes;*
> *As well a well wrought urne becomes*
> *The greatest ashes, as halfe-acre tombes,*
> *And by these hymnes, all shall approve*
> *Us Canoniz'd for Love.*

And the last lines are:

> *And thus invoke us: You whom reverend love*
> *Made one another hermitage;*
> *You, to whom love was peace, that now is rage,*
> *Who did the whole worlds soule extract, and drove*
> *Into the glasses of your eyes*
> *So made such mirrors, and such spies,*
> *That they did all to you epitomize,*
> *Countries, Townes, Courts: Beg from above*
> *A patterne of your love!*

It is quite clear that we are being shown a spiritual union, joint poetic (sonnets, hymns) creativity. The heroes perceive the world so that afterwards, with the might of their artistic imagination, they can revive it in their art, in their poetry, which is timeless. Like Chester's Turtle and Phoenix, Donne's heroes are secretly serving Apollo, and staying out of the limelight. If literary scholars of ages past did not dissemble their confusion, contemporary Western specialists on Donne have not infrequently allowed those stunning lines to drive them to try to insert into "The Canonization" some metaphysics of sexual emotion, ignoring the purely spiritual nature of the love that connected the heroes and was inseparable from their service to the highest art. The same holds with the Chester book, where modern adepts of the C. Brown hypothesis tend to see the poem-requiem as a wedding hymn. More soundly, we can focus on what "The Canonization" tells us about the amount of wit that was put into the Phoenix riddle.

So the heroes of "The Canonization" are the heroes of the Chester collection, the Turtle and Phoenix, that unique poetic couple that quit this world in complete silence, having left behind the incomparable Perfection, their great creations, their only monument. "And Manners brightly shines\ In his well-turned and true-filed lines:\ In each of which, he seems to shake a lance, \ As brandished at the eyes of ignorance."

"The Canonization" is one of Donne's hard-to-date works; a recent opinion suggests that it belongs to the late first-early second decades of the 17th century. The timing coincides. The poem was first printed posthumously in the 1633 edition, wherein some extraneous creations appeared among authentic Donne works, having probably been found among his papers (as was the case with the William Basse poem). If Rutland wrote "The Canonization," his capellan Thomas Morton could have brought the poem to Donne, as he was close to both. When the Belvoir couple died, Donne, like Jonson, was abroad; he did not arrive home until a month after the tragic event. But whether John Donne wrote this stunning revelation, or these are *ante mortem* lines by the Turtle in person, its connection with the poems of Chester's collection is beyond dispute (to a certain extent all researchers agree with that).[31] And the mystery of the queer poetic works is opened with one key: Belvoir.

The 1630s saw the demise of Jonson, Donne, Drayton, Pembroke, and many other people of the Shakespeare generation who were personally acquainted with the Shake-speare. Southampton, Buckingham, the Countess of Bedford, and King James had passed away still earlier. Hard times were ahead; in 1640, the Long Parliament was convened and soon its war with the king broke out, ending in a Puritan victory. The Puritans prohibited theatrical entertainment; the muses were at bay. The next, third edition of the Shakespeare Folio only came out after the Restoration, in 1663, when few of Shakespeare's contemporaries were still alive. The Shake-speare's creations, "his orphans," went into the custody of new generations who readily accepted the sacred legend about him. The Belvoir couple had achieved that long-sought oblivion — and for several centuries, nobody gave them a thought.

---

31. One cannot exclude the possibility that "The Canonization" (if it was written by Donne) was intended for the Chester collection, but for some reason was not included.

## WHEN DID THE SHAKESPEARE PLAYS ABOUT THE WAR OF THE ROSES APPEAR?

The idea that Shakespeare was a mask hiding Roger Manners, 5th Earl of Rutland, was first submitted early in the 20th century by K. Bleibtreu and S. Demblon, and then was further developed and supplemented by P. Porohovchikov and K. Sykes. They concentrated mostly on Rutland (though Porohovchikov thought that the first Shakespeare poems were written by Bacon); they greatly underestimated the roles of Elizabeth (Sidney) Rutland and Mary (Sidney) Pembroke. Still, the extremely vigorous activity of the "Shakespeare-Oxford" school, both in Britain and the US, left the figure of Rutland in the shadows, despite the high authenticity of facts testifying to his connection with the Shakespearean oeuvre.

My investigation of the Chester collection, Coryate's books, Emilia Lanier's poem (first via microfilm, then the originals), and the "Parnassus" plays has shown that only by factoring in the Belvoir couple can we make sense of numerous historical and literary facts that previously defied explanation, and in the final analysis, get to the bottom of the brilliant Shakespeare game.

Now, before we come to the conclusion of our story, let me give a short summary of major facts and arguments confirming the Rutlands' presence behind the Shakespeare mask. We have already documented that, following in Shakespeare's wake, one stumbles across Rutland time and again, either alone or with his wife or others from his circle. Those encounters are so numerous and interconnected that it cannot be a matter of chance. The Rutlands and Shakespeare cannot be separated.

\* \* \*

The first Shakespeare poems contain the author's dedications to the Earl of Southampton, whose friendship with Rutland at the time is plentifully documented; and later on it was noticed (and again, remarked upon in writing) that the two young earls were spending all their days and nights at the theater. John Florio, who taught them both Italian, is represented in the play "Love's Labour's Lost" as the teacher Holofernes. Another character in the play, Don Adriano de Armado, is a mock portrait of Antonio Perez, who was well known to Rutland.

The first to acknowledge and accord high regard to Shakespeare's playwriting were Rutland's Cambridge University fellows Weever, Barnfield, Covell, and later Meres.

A number of Shakespeare's plays take place in just those cities of northern Italy that Rutland visited and adored — and not in Rome, which he missed, by the way. He studied at Padua University; according to Demblon, the Danes Rozencrantz and Guildenstern also studied there. Tranio in the "Taming of the Shrew" enumerates subjects taught in Padua, and the city is also mentioned in other plays.

The Rutlands' monument, crowned with an image of wings in flight — a symbol of Spirit overcoming Death, symbol of the Phoenix arising from the ashes.

The difference between the two principal versions of "Hamlet" that have come down to our day trouble scholars. But now we can see that true-to-life details of the Danish royal court and even of the private royal residence were injected into "Hamlet" only after (right after!) Rutland's visit to Elsinore.

In the student play "The Return from Parnassus," the character Gullio — an early buffoonish mask of Rutland and a caricature of Shakspere as well — turns out to be an author of sonnets and assumes the praises that (Rutland's fellow poet) Weever applies to Shakespeare.

Rutland was a close friend and relative of Essex, whom Shakespeare treats with great sympathy in "Henry V." Rutland even went to war at Essex's side, and stood up with him in his failed mutiny. The tragic breakthrough in Shakespeare's creativity coincides with this fiasco and its calamitous (for Essex, and for Rutland too) results.

The daughter of the great poet Philip Sidney, Elizabeth became Rutland's wife; she was also a talented poet who always hid her authorship. Rutland was close friends, all his life, with her cousin the Earl of Pembroke and his mother Mary , the Countess of Pembroke. The Earl of Pembroke is believed to be the person who gave Shakespeare's sonnets to the publisher; and the posthumous Great Folio was dedicated to him. Mary was the sponsor, partial co-author and editor of this edition.

Rutland was one of the initiators and authors of the great literary farce around the court jester Thomas Coryate, who was credited with several books and was proclaimed the greatest traveler and writer in the world.

In Shakespeare's sonnets and in Ben Jonson's poem dedicated to Shakespeare's memory, in the Great Folio, Rutland's family name Manners is the object of repeated wordplay. Jonson was very familiar with the Rutlands; he visited their home; he called them and their entourage the "poets of Belvoir vale." Several poetic works by Jonson are addressed to Elizabeth (Sidney) Rutland — both openly and covertly.

The demise of the two Rutlands in the summer of 1612 coincides with the cessation of Shakespeare's creative output. "Henry VIII," which appeared later, was finished by Fletcher.

The deaths and funerals of the Rutlands were shrouded with mystery. Their friends could mourn them only secretly, under allegorical names, in the poetic collection entitled *Love's Martyr*, which was published as a very limited edition, without registration, and with false dates. It also includes the poetic work ("cantoes") of "The Turtle" (Rutland), that are so similar to the Shakespearean poems and sonnets.

The first complete collection of Shakespeare's plays, published as the First Folio, was slated for the summer of 1622, that is, for the tenth anniversary of the Rutlands' death. The Second Folio was issued in 1632, marking the twentieth anniversary. Of all the serious pretenders to the role of Shakespeare, Rutland is the only one whom Shakspere knew personally and whose house he visited.

In the Rutland family crypt in Bottesford, on their grave, a tombstone made by the Janssen brothers was erected in 1617-1620. Soon thereafter, the same sculptors also made a wall monument for the Stratford church, near Shakspere's grave, which in many outward details is similar to the Rutlands' monument.

Several months after the Rutlands' demise, Shakspere received a sum of money from their steward and left London forever. The Rutlands are the only contemporaries who are known for sure to have paid Shakspere for anything.

Rutland was one of the best-educated people of his time. He knew the foreign languages which can be traced in Shakespeare's works. He complies in every regard with the characteristics of Shakespeare-the-author as deduced and formulated by Looney. That is particularly true of such traits as his ambiguous feelings for women, a tendency to generosity and magnanimity, tolerance for Catholicism, eccentricity, and a passion for mystery and secrecy.

Nearly all the books used by Shakespeare as sources were part of the Belvoir library (many of them are still there). There is also a manuscript version of the song from "The Twelfth Night," written, as Porohovchikov established, in Rutland's hand. This is the only authentic manuscript of a Shakespearean text.

\* \* \*

Even this incomplete list of details reviewed in the preceding chapters is impressive. None of Shakespeare's contemporaries, no other "claimant" for the "throne of the Great Bard" (including William Shakspere) can match anything like this collection of authentic facts about his connection with the Shake-speare, with his works. All this, despite the fact that everything pertaining to Rutland's literary activity, as is evident from many episodes, was shrouded with secrecy, and the manuscripts — after being copied — were annihilated. The existence of a version of the song from "Twelfth Night," written in Rutland's hand, is an extremely important piece of evidence and finding it was a rare piece of luck. And lastly, adequately read, Chester's collection and "Coryate's" books are certainly   literary facts of major distinction.

In England and the US, Rutland and his wife are very little known. That is not because the facts on which the Rutlandian hypothesis is based are inauthentic or dubious. The facts are verified and documented, but even most Shakespeareans are not familiar with their totality; coming across isolated details, scholars cannot perceive their full significance, their connection with "the Shakespearean mystery." And then, this hypothesis was generated by French, Belgian and German researchers (Demblon and Bleibtreu are still not translated into English). But the main problem is inertia, and the tendency to prefer the habitual approach to Shakespeare. Even among those who reject the traditional Stratfordian view, the Oxfordian and Marlowean hypothesis prevails. And one certainly should not forget the extremely complex character of the centuries-long arguments.

Similar situations are known in the history of other branches of knowledge — the way to the truth is not simple and straightforward, but a ceaseless accumulation and perception of authentic facts makes the final selection of ideas and hypotheses inevitable.

The facts that form the basis of the Rutlandian hypothesis have never been refuted by anybody, in the East or West; they are objective and well-documented. Critics can only differ over details of the interpretation, over how to fill in some of the gaps, and over the extent and nature of the Rutlands' and other Belvoir poets' participation in the creation of specific works.

Let us consider now the arguments of some of those who criticize the Rutlandian hypothesis: A. A. Smirnov (1932), F. Wordsworth and R. Churchill (1958). In his introduction to M. Zhizhmor's play discussed earlier, Smirnov writes about Rutland: "In the Italian university where Rutland studied, there were also two Danish students, Rozencrantz and Guildenstern . . . The most that we can assume is that Rutland was Shakespeare's informant . . . Young aristocrats' ("gilded youth") contacts with actors were usual at the time." About Rutland's possible participation in the creation of Shakespeare's plays: "Certainly 'prodigious children' existed in every age, but one can hardly imagine a 14-year-old boy creating plays not only of great artistic value, but also fit for presentation on the stage. Nothing in Rutland's biography indicates that he possessed any literary talent or a prominent mind in general." Smirnov was not, evidently, aware of John Florio's allusion to Rutland's literary abilities in his dedication of the Italian-English dictionary, or Jonson's epistle to Elizabeth Rutland in which he said that her consort had fallen in love with the art of poesy, and many other items that reflect on this question.

F. Wordsworth tackles the Baconian, Derbian and Oxfordian hypotheses in detail in his book[32]; he writes very little about Rutland. He seems to find the argument of Rutland's youth incontestable.

R. C. Churchill[33] tries to cast doubt on some of the facts. Thus, in reference to Shakspere's receiving payment at Belvoir for the "impreso," he repeats the opinion voiced early in the 20th century that it was just a namesake, for it was not plausible that a renowned playwright would deal with such a commission as making an impression or a shield for participants in a tournament. But Shakspere was not alone in this; he was accompanied by Richard Burbage, and most scholars (including Chambers and Schoenbaum) long ago conceded that the Belvoir steward's records relate to Shakespeare (i.e. Shakspere). Indeed, doubts that a famous poet and playwright could be invited from London to perform such a modest task (for a modest sum, by the way), support the view that William Shakspere was neither a poet or a playwright.

Churchill mentions Rozencrantz and Guildenstern from Padua University, but offers no comment on the fact; he does not even notice Shakespeare's special affinity for Padua and its university. As to the appearance of new and accurate details about

---

32. Wordsworth F.W. *The Poacher from Stratford.* Los Angeles, 1958.
33. Churchill R.C. *Shakespeare and his betters.* L., 1958.

the Danish court in the second quarto of "Hamlet," Churchill notes that some of the Earl of Leicester's actors visited Denmark in 1585 or 1586. Churchill even tries to reconstruct a possible conversation between Shakespeare and a member of the troupe; he notes with sympathy that poor Shakespeare must have been tired of hearing the endless talk about their visit to Denmark. Even if one overlooks the fact that the tour took place some fifteen years before "Hamlet," then a fundamental question remains: why did the Danish details appear only in the Second Quarto, i.e. in 1604, that is, right after Rutland's mission to Denmark? Churchill also mentions Rutland's young age, asserting that he could not have written all three parts of "Henry VI," "A Comedy of Errors," "Richard III," and "Titus Andronicus" at the age of 15 to 18 years.

Anikst, in his article "Who Wrote Shakespeare's Plays?"[34] (1962), generally repeats the same line as Churchill. "All the arguments in favor of Rutland's authorship fall apart like a house of cards when the reader learns the earl's date of birth. He came into this world on October 5, 1576. The first plays by Shakespeare, as has been established, was first staged in 1590. Then it would follow that Rutland began writing at the age of 13-14 years . . . "

This is the principle argument for all critics of the Rutlandian hypothesis, and it is based on a serious misconception. It is high time that this "decisive argument" was put to the test.

When they refer to Shakespeare plays that were staged as early as 1590, Demblon and Porohovchikov's opponents first and foremost have in mind "Henry VI." Somehow, they fail to mention the fact that it is not known exactly what play was performed at that time; they also gloss over a number of problems pertaining to the trilogy about the War of the Roses — problems that are quite important.

In 1594, "The First part of the Contention betwixt the two famous Houses of Yorke and Lancaster . . . " was published, without any author's name. It covers the second part of the story in what the Shakespeare canon knows as "Henry VI." Published in 1595, "The True Tragedie of Richarde Duke of Yorke, and the death of good King Henrie the sixt . . . as it was sandry times acted by the Right Honourable the Earle of Pembroke his servants," corresponds to the third part of "Henry VI" in the Shakespeare canon. Most Shakespeare scholars, starting from Malone and going through the end of the 19th century, asserted that Shakespeare did not write these plays; they considered the most probable authors to be Marlowe, Green, Peele or Kyd. The text of both plays differs greatly from the text of the second and third parts of "Henry VI" that appeared for the first time in the Great Folio, that is, only in 1623. The text in the Folio is one and a half times larger, and while the older plays served as a basis, they are hardly identical. Out of 2000 lines in the old play, only 500 in the second part are untouched; the rest are either omitted or changed; and 1700 entirely new lines have appeared. Similar drastic rewriting occurred with "The True Tragedy," which became the third part of "Henry VI." Actually, new plays were created whose artistic

---

34. *Questions in Literature*, 1962, No. 4.

value is much higher. As to the first part of the trilogy, it first appeared in the Great Folio and has no known theatrical predecessors. These and other facts were long considered proof enough that the two earlier plays did not belong to the Great Bard; they were written before his time!

Still, late in the 19<sup>th</sup> century, another point of view cropped up, claiming that the earlier plays were not sources used by Shakespeare but were inaccurate (pirated) copies of Shakespeare's plays. That hypothesis was supported and further developed by P. Alexander (1924) and his followers, but there is no basis whatsoever for considering it a complete solution to the problem. Shakespeare's authorship of the two earlier plays about the War of the Roses was never proven; it is only a supposition. How could one think it proven when, besides textological analysis, we have authoritative testimony provided by Francis Meres and William Shakespeare himself!?

In 1598, Francis Meres in his *Wits Treasure* enumerated all the plays written to date by Shakespeare, *but he did not mention "Henry VI."* Scholars agree that Meres was remarkably familiar with Shakespeare's works. Out of twelve Shakespeare plays named by Meres, only six had been published by then, and four were issued anonymously. A Cambridge graduate, Meres was also familiar with Shakespeare's sonnets, which were published only a decade later. Meres' list is a universally recognized basis for dating early Shakespeare plays, and Meres did not merely omit some part of "Henry VI" — *he did not mention the trilogy at all*. It is hard to conceive how such an impressive piece of evidence could be ignored, but this is exactly that happens in modern Shakespeare studies — the absence of "Henry VI" in Meres' list is ignored. The lame excuse is usually given that by 1598 those chronicles were no longer being performed. But if these two early plays also belong to Shakespeare (as most modern Shakespeareans now believe) and were published only three to four years before Meres' book, how could he "forget" them? No; *Meres knew that these chronicles were not Shakespeare's*, and any other treatment of this evidence is wishful thinking.

Shakespeare himself corroborates this view: in 1593, referring to the poem "Venus and Adonis," he calls it "the first heir of my invention." But many Shakespeareans take even this evidence with a grain of salt: Shakespeare allegedly had in mind only the noble occupation of poetry and did not count plays written for public theater, which were "considered at the time works of low genre" (yet Meres did not consider them such?). Here again we have a casuistic treatment of the evidence; those who so greatly believe in the early dating of Shakespeare's first works are ready to ignore important facts that stand in their way.

Thus, there is no serious factual basis for dating the beginning of Shakespeare's activity to earlier than 1592-1593 — only speculation. Once that becomes clear, the arguments in favor of Rutland's authorship do not "fall apart like a house of cards" when we learn the earl's date of birth. In 1592-1593, Rutland was 16-17 years old and had studied at Cambridge University for six or seven years. He was a young but intellectually quite mature person. In any case, there is no doubt whatsoever that he could have written "Venus and Adonis" by then, never mind such a weak play as "Titus Andronicus" (1593-1594). Other plays usually attributed to the year 1593 include only "Richard III" and "The Comedy of Errors." The text of the first, however, was published in 1597 (when Rutland was 21 years old), and the second was published only in 1623.

So the major argument against Rutland's authorship — his age — is not valid. Neither are the complaints that Shakespeare's plays contain geographical errors regarding northern Italy and Bohemia — in fact, it is the critics of the Rutlandian hypothesis who show their poor knowledge of those details in different historical periods.

The problem is, there has been no scrupulous, objective and solid analysis of the Rutland hypothesis in modern Western Shakespeare studies. The Rutlands and their weird relations are nervously avoided by scholars ignorant of the corpus of historic and literary facts connected with them. Even the works of Demblon, Porohovchikov, and Sykes failed to reflect the fundamental point that the publication of the First Folio was timed to coincide with the tenth anniversary of the Rutlands' death and the second came out on the twentieth. The roles of Elizabeth Sidney and the remarkable Mary, Countess of Pembroke have not been understood, let alone the self-evident fact that Demblon et al. were not familiar with the results of today's research.

Still, though numerous facts point again and again to Roger and Elizabeth Rutland (though not only to them), hiding behind the mask/pen name of William Shakespeare, we may as well answer the questions usually put to non-Stratfordians:

- Why should the authentic author (authors) so diligently hide their names for so long?
- Why, besides the pen name, did they create a living mask, a stalking horse, William Shakspere from Stratford?
- How did they manage to keep this mystification a secret?

At various times, non-Stratfordians have given various answers to the first question. In the case of Francis Bacon, they suggested that such a link could have hindered his career. Others have claimed that the authentic author (Rutland, for instance) belonged to the political opposition and needed a pen name to cover up some conspiracy. We often hear the opinion that for a person of high social station, a titled lord, it would have been unseemly to admit to such lowly activity. One cannot fully agree with this argument. Such an occupation was, indeed, not particularly esteemed in an eminent lord, but neither was it considered inappropriate (the more so given that the pen name of Shakespeare first appeared in connection with refined poems).

Let us recollect once again that many aristocratic figures were partial to literature, and even King James was not averse to publishing his poetry and prose under his own name; in 1598, Meres mentions Lord Buckhurst (the Earl of Dorset), and the Earl of Oxford among the best authors; play-masques were written even by the First Minister Robert Cecil and Francis Bacon (who became Lord Chancellor in 1618).

There is no basis for asserting that it would be impossible or inadmissible for an aristocrat to acknowledge his involvement in literature or playwriting.

However, when a writer is reluctant to publish under his own name for personal reasons, that is a different matter. Many writers have chosen that route, and a list of pen names would fill several volumes.

In certain periods, it was even the fashion to write under a pen name. Out of twenty poets who contributed to the poetic collection *The Phoenix Nest* (1593), not one put down his proper name; some gave initials, and some of the contributors have never been identified to this day.

In his dictionary *A World of Words*, John Florio mentions "a sonnet by one of my friends" who prefers to be an authentic poet rather than to bear the name; he almost surely means Rutland. "Shakespeare" knew the value of his own talent but he was wary of literary vanity. In general, a predilection to secrecy and mystification was one of his most prominent traits; he even took special care that his own funeral would be cloaked in a veil of secrecy.

In Jonson's play "Epicoene" (1609), there is a curious conversation among three young cavaliers: Dauphine, Clerimont and Daw. The latter is partial to poetic activity, himself, but treats poets with disdain:

> Dauphine. "Why, how can you justify your own being a poet, that so slight all the old poets?"
> Daw. "Why, every man, that writes in verse, is not a poet; you have of the wits that write verses, and yet are no poets: they are poets, that live by it, the poor fellows that live by it."
> Dauphine. "Why, would not you live by your verses, Sir John?"
> Clerimont. "No 'twere pity he should. A Knight live by his verses. He did not make them to that end, I hope."
> Dauphine. "And yet the noble Sidney lives by his, and the noble family is not ashamed of it."

Here, Jonson was probably again recollecting Rutland's rebuke to his wife for receiving Ben the poet at her table. Also of interest is the insinuation that the Sidneys had some income out of publishing. But most important is that we see Jonson trying to understand the reason for keeping the authorship secret, a secret to which he was witness and which was hidden first of all in the identity of Rutland himself.

And how can we answer that question? For those who perceived the world as a great stage, a pen name was not enough. That is why a living mask was being sought, and the most odious personalities were preferred — people who had nothing to do with writing. For Rutland's incarnation of Jaques the Melancholic, he needed not only a mask but the mask of a jester, an outrageous one. And an illiterate or semi-literate person (or a half-wit and drunkard, like Coryate) was preferable, because he would never have any documents that could later spoil the Game.

Who was the first to notice the shrewd Stratfordian in the acting cast, or even earlier in his native town, we may never know, but it seems that some insight may be gleaned from the episode in "The Taming of the Shrew," when the Lord picks up the tinker Sly. Certainly, the funny resemblance of Shakspere's name to Rutland's supposed student nickname, the Shake-speare, was significant. During his lifetime, Shakspere's role in this play was not difficult at all; no one among his friends and fellow townsmen took him for a writer and a poet, and otherwise he had only to keep his mouth shut. It is possible that sometimes the actors obtained plays through him. He may have performed some other errands on behalf of Rutland and he may have been paid handsomely for that. His fellow actors certainly knew that he had eminent patrons, and that was enough for them. The most knowledgeable was Richard Burbage, of course, but he was a reliable man. It is owing to Shakspere's patrons that the troupe became the "Servants of His Majesty" and made a good income. Nothing definite is known about the troupe's possible participation in the publication of Shakespeare's plays (much less the poems and sonnets) except for the ornamental appearance of the names of the actors Heming and Condel under an address composed by Ben Jonson to Pembroke and the readers of the First Folio.

Elizabeth (Sidney) Rutland joined the Game in the middle of the first decade of the 17th century; her hand is noted in some sonnets, and in the last plays, "Cymbeline," "The Winter's Tale," and "Pericles." Modern Shakespeare biographers, dividing the Bard's works into three (some of them four) periods, note that after the great tragedies Shakespeare suddenly started writing romantic plays and fairytales with happy endings. The reader already knows that Jonson and Beaumont had a high regard for the literary talent of Philip Sidney's daughter — and that not a single line signed by her was published.

"As You Like it" was penned by Mary (Sidney) Pembroke; she also undertook the major final literary editing of many texts included in the First Folio. Specifying each participant's contribution to the works will be an enormous research project in itself, a task that will be complicated by the fact that in some cases the plays borrowed liberally from earlier works.

The fact that the secret of the pen name/mask was maintained does not in itself present anything extraordinary. Many pen names of that era have never been decoded, though Shakespeare's case, of course, is the most prominent one. The circle of initiates was evidently small: the Pembrokes, the Southamptons, the Dorsets, Lucy Bedford, several poets including a few of Rutland's fellow Cambridge students, and Jonson, Donne, Drayton, Marston, Chapman. Jonson's words and much other evidence suggest that the secret was known to Queen Elizabeth and, after her, to King James. To the latter, with his love of literature and theater, and of mystery as well, such a game steeped in mystique must have been most sympathetic. His multiple visits to the Rutlands' castle, the arrival of the king and prince of Wales at Belvoir right after the death of its owners, and the fact that the king who valued Shakespeare's works nearly

The title page of *The Works of King James*

as highly as the Bible paid no heed at all to the man from Stratford — all this is evidence that the king was in on the game, and that in itself says much.

Jonson's early epistle to Elizabeth Rutland supports a surmise that those initiated "outsiders" may have been sworn to secrecy; one could pay dearly for a misstep. Let us recollect the vow upon his sword that the Danish prince requires from his friends:

> *... That you. At such times seeing me, never shall,*
> *With arms encumbere'd thus, or this head-shake,*
> *Or by pronouncing of some doubtful phrase,*
> *As 'well, well, we know', or 'we could, an if we would'*
> *Or 'If we list to speak', or 'There be, an if they might,'*
> *Or such ambiguous giving out, to note*
> *That you know aught of me: — this not to do,*
> *So grace and mercy at your most need help you,*
> *Swear." (I, 5).*

Certainly, the specific forms provided for keeping the secret may have been different, but there is no doubt that Rutland and his friends took pains to guard him from curiosity, idle or otherwise. After all, they managed to keep secret even the burial place of Philip Sidney's daughter!

As to the Stratfordian, his activity as a shareholder of the acting troupe in London, as a purchaser of the church tithe and usurer in Stratford, took place in an environment where books were not read and nobody cared who had written what. In Stratford, during his lifetime and many years after his death, nobody ever took him for a writer. The mask only took its final shape around the tenth anniversary of the Rutlands' death, when it was bolstered by the collection of works prefaced with a queer "portrait," and by a wall monument in the Stratford church. The luxurious book, the "portrait" ("My Lord's 'impreso'") and the church monument (though the images do not resemble each other at all) were destined to appear before posterity as an authentic image of "The Titan in a vacuum." The great legend about the genius bard from Stratford was gathering strength for its journey across the centuries and continents.

The devious mystification was carried off meticulously, with a fine understanding of human psychology and of how mankind's perception of the past is created. But the legend so crafted had its Achilles' heel; its creators probably could not fully compensate for the fact that William Shakspere from Stratford was not a puppet, but a live and enterprising person. Though he did not leave behind any traces in letters or documents (written by himself), the evidence of his real existence still survived in the church, town and court archives. At least, these tracks remained in obscurity for a long time, so the legend was strengthened in the minds of new generations; the Stratfordian cult was generated and took root.

Then arose questions that were hard to answer convincingly (such is, unfortunately, the fate of many cults). Inquiring minds started to search for the Titan's links with his time. At first, such links were just conjecture or were invented on the basis of what was written in the First Folio and on the Stratfordian's tombstone. But later on (alas, alas!), the real, authentic traces of William Shakspere began to come to light. Those traces revealed a stunning abyss separating the literary creations and their alleged creator, revolting to some of those researchers who found them. And so, time started "to dissolve the Stratford monument."

But the cult, long ago separated from the era that gave it birth, was now functioning of its own accord and acquired new, not only decorative but also academic accessories of many pages, and became practically an official symbol of the cultural and spiritual values of mankind. What a bizarre abode of great souls!

# CHAPTER 6. FOR WHOM THE BELL TOLLED

*Coming back to Chester — Hunting unicorns in the heart of Washington and London.*
*Robert Chester defies American and English scholars — The bell tolled for Shakespeare*

## COMING BACK TO CHESTER

Let us come back to Chester's book *Love's Martyr*, where we started our narration. Now that we are better acquainted with the history of the Shakespeare authorship controversy and the polemical passions that swirl about it, with the tragic story of the couple from Belvoir and their close ties with Ben Jonson and other members of a narrow poetic circle, the reader can more readily evaluate the significance of *Love's Martyr*.

An analysis of literary and historic facts has shown that dates on the title pages of the book's various editions are pure mystification; the book appeared much later than 1601. The reference to death, and the name of John Salusbury (who died in summer of 1612), enables us to specify the genuine date of the book's publication more precisely, and through that to identify the prototypes of the Turtle and the Phoenix, the extraordinary Rutlands, who left this world at the same time Salusbury did. Many a coincidence testifies to the fact that Chester's heroes are the Rutlands. We have the innocent, purely spiritual nature of the marriage of the lords of Belvoir, their secret service to the Muses, the circumstances of their death, the extremely mystifying burial and many other events detailed in the previous chapters. Even the ills that plagued Chester's Turtle are the same that Rutland suffered from; the unique topographical features of Belvoir are also easily identified. Ben Jonson (who visited the Rutlands' house more than once and deeply venerated Philip Sidney's daughter) and other authors of the Chester collection were among the "poets of Belvoir Vale."

An impressive list of incontestable coincidences points time and again to the Belvoir couple. Even a small portion of them should persuade us to drop obsolete hypotheses based on poor information. *Love's Martyr*, allegorically hinting at the truth about the love and cruel fate of the "Phoenix and the Turtle," was finished in the immediate aftermath of a tragic event — the death of the Rutlands. The book was printed in a very limited edition; it was never sold freely; and those copies became the property exclusively of the initiated. We already know that for years after the Rutlands' demise it was prohibited to mention their names publicly. Only many decades later, when the times had changed, the strange book with conflicting title pages became a curiosity for book lovers. Then it caught the attention of Shakespeareans, because the Great Bard's name was printed there, and Alexander Grossart (probably incited by R. W. Emerson) published the full text with his commentary. A long and involved process of scholarly research was set in motion and, while it is not completely over, yet, the main riddle of the Chester collection, the mystery of its unique heroes, at last has been solved.

## Hunting Unicorns in the Heart of Washington and London:

### Robert Chester Defies American and English Scholars

I first published the results of my research on Chester's book and the poem about the Turtle and the Phoenix in a Russian academic journal, *Shakespeare Readings of 1984*. My first major task was to publicize the revised printing date and the identity of the prototypes of the collection's heroes, and to touch off a scholarly discussion on those points. I thought it inexpedient to discuss the broader perspectives those new facts opened up for the greater controversy over Shakespeare's authorship. After many years of ideological pressure, the non-Stratfordian line of thinking was viewed with considerable reserve in Russian academic circles, and any attempt to say too much at once might have delayed or even prevented publication of the article. Besides, one could also easily predict the reaction of British and American Shakespeareans: any "heretical," non-Stratfordian work is usually discarded at first sight, even if it contains solutions to specific problems. It was important not to discourage those scholars who had at their disposal all the material and the original sources, but rather to induce them to study Chester's book, to review old hypotheses that had been discarded and to verify new facts and arguments. Some form of academic cooperation would only emerge if the painful question (for most of them) of the Great Bard's identity were not immediately broached. Therefore I did not go beyond a few vague hints in this delicate vein, in my first article, and focused mostly on the date of issue and the identification of the prototypes, points that are important enough in themselves. I had to take a similar course while preparing an article on Thomas Coryate for publication, not to mention other books connected with his name, in *Shakespeare Readings of 1985*.

However, those literary scholars, historians, and philologists who had long evinced a keen interest in the Shakespeare authorship controversy picked up on those hints and understood the impact that a new reading of Chester's collection and of "Coryate's" works might have on the centuries-long argument about the Great Bard; I am deeply grateful to them for their help during further my stages of study, especially while researching the watermarks.

Proof that had been obtained analytically had to be substantiated empirically. Evidence that my dating is correct was obtained by Marina Litvinova in Washington, DC, in 1988, and by Igor Kravchenko in London in 1989. They discovered identical, heretofore unknown, watermarks in two copies of Chester's book. A short notice about this discovery appeared in academic publications both in English and in Russian.

After a time, the Folger Shakespeare Library, with the help of the Soros Foundation, provided me with an opportunity to go on with my research for several months using the richest library collection. The job was immense: to verify whether the watermarks appeared in other books and documents of the time, to check the original books published by Blount, Lownes, Field, and Allde, to look through a number of works by Shakespeare, Jonson, and Chapman, to analyze material discovered by the historical commission in Belvoir late in the 19th century, and to look for additional evidence of games played out around Thomas Coryate.

The Folger Library is situated in the heart of Washington, DC, next to the Library of Congress, not far from Capitol Hill. It was built in 1932 and endowed with funds provided by the oil magnate Henry Clay Folger and his wife Emily, for the preservation of a collection of books and manuscripts of the Shakespearean era. Henry Folger got the idea to create such a library while he was a college student listening to R. W. Emerson's lectures on Shakespeare. This was the same Emerson who was amazed by traditional biographies of Shakespeare, for he could not reconcile them with the creative power of the author; he was one of the first people in the 19th century to sense that the poem about the Turtle and the Phoenix was linked to the death of some mysterious but quite real couple, engaged in poetry. He called on scholars to reveal the mystery of the poem and the whole of the Chester collection.

The Folger Library contains the largest collection of Shakespearean materials in the world, including first editions. It has practically all the reference books imaginable, in many languages, literature on all types of arts, originals and copies of painting,[1]

---

1. Many Shakespeare portraits acquired at different times for large sums of money decorate the walls of the Library. Among them are renowned examples such as the Ashburn and Janssen pictures that turned out to be fakes. The rest may be called, at best, inauthentic.

sketches and etchings, and old maps. In a word, it is a researcher's paradise. As a rule, no more then a few dozen people are studying in its reading rooms.

At last, I could hold in my hands that small volume, the Chester collection, that I had been studying from so far away via microfilm and Grossart's reprint. The Folger copy has its own story: it crossed the ocean in the 20th century, after having changed hands several times in Britain. Who was its first owner is unknown. I looked at the pages, held them up to the light, and saw the contours of the long-sought watermarks, among them the unusual unicorn with crooked hind legs. Laetitia Yeandle, curator of Early Books and Manuscripts, and Elizabeth Welsh, supervisor of the Reading Room, were keenly interested in my research and lent me all possible help. We sent facsimile copies of the watermarks to the Huntington Library (California)[2] and to the National Library of Wales (where the fourth copy recently "showed up," minus the first and last pages). Soon we got our answers: the watermarks in those copies are the same.

In his response from California, the advisor of the Huntington Library asked Laetitia Yeandle to send his congratulations to the sponsors of the research for such a successful and compelling result. A note from a bibliographer, Dr. Noel Kinnamon, was attached to the reply, saying, "The watermarks on the last pages are particularly interesting, perhaps suggesting something about the make-up and printing of the volume." Unfortunately, what he meant I could not discover, for I had no way to get in touch with him; one can only hope that either he or some other American specialist will keep on studying the Huntington copy.

In the meantime, in Washington I began to study the watermarks used in the Shakespeare age. Naturally, I started with the paper on which Richard Field and Edward Allde printed their books, and the printers who catered for Blount and Lownes. I checked the watermarks and other technical details: the fonts, decorative elements, publishing dates, registration, and in varying degrees the books' contents. Most of these books are not fiction, but theological, medical, philosophical, or moral in nature, pamphlets on important events, etc. It was not easy to navigate through this sea of ancient folios and brochures without missing something important. But I was lucky — just before my arrival, the third volume of the bibliographical catalogue was issued (the result of many years' work by several American bibliographers), in which all the publications of the era were linked by editor and printer.[3] That sped my work along nicely. As a result, I could ascertain that the paper on which the Chester book was printed is unique. Not one other British book (at least, among those that are kept in the Folger Library) has been printed on paper with such watermarks. There are six watermarks in the Chester collection altogether; one was found in a manuscript copy

---

2. The library was founded in the town of San Marino by the railroad tycoon Henry E. Huntington, a worthy rival of Folger.

3. *A Short Titles Catalogue of books, printed in England, Scotland and Ireland, and of English books, printed around 1475-1640. Vol. 3. A printers and publishers index.* By Katharine F.Pantzer. L., The Bibliographical Society, 1991.

of an old letter, but that mark is not unique — it is listed in a special reference book. But the strange unicorn was never found anywhere else.

It seems that the client (most probably Edward Blount) brought to Field's or Allde's printing shop a stack of paper received from the sponsors of the publication (Lucy Bedford or Mary Sidney Pembroke, for instance), including the paper with the strange unicorn watermark (there is another kind of unicorn in the Rutland coat of arms, and noble families sometimes ordered special paper). In every other instance, the printer made at least several books on the same paper; so this is another piece of evidence that Chester's book was not ordinary in any sense, for editor or printer, and they took exceptional measures in order to conceal the circumstance and date of its appearance.

In a month's time I made a momentous discovery. Among the books printed by Field and Allde in 1612-1613, I found copies of the above-mentioned clandestine pro-catholic composition by Roger Widrington (Thomas Preston). Different copies carry different title pages, with imaginative names of printers and fantastical places of issue ("Cosmopolis," "Albinopolis"). This typographic game has already been solved (The Pollard and Redgrave Short Title Catalogue unequivocally qualifies Preston's works published by Field and Allde as mystification[4]). But only now it became known that at the same time (1612-1613) both printers were engaged in another, even more important mystification, the Chester book (where many elements of composition coincide with those used for "Widrington").

Something new, strange, and probably quite promising came as a surprise. When Grossart reprinted the Chester book for the first time in 1878, he tried to reproduce with every method available at the time all the technical elements of the original, including the decorations. The reproduction was not a facsimile as we understand it now. The original pages, including the title page, were not photocopied; the illustrations, emblems, ornaments were redrawn by a copyist; similar fonts were selected for the text and captions. Some inaccuracies still appear, but with such a manual approach to the copying, there could not be great deviations. Studying the Folger and London microfilm copies and the Grossart edition, in Moscow, I was struck by the second title pages introducing the poems by Marston, Chapman, Shakespeare, and Jonson. Under the title, where the printers usually place their emblems, the Folger and London copies actually carry the emblem of Field's printing house. The Grossart edition, however, has a tragic mask, with rings, and under it the Field motto — "Anchora Spei." The mask does not resemble any of the known Field versions; it has nothing to do with it at all; but it can be found in several editions of important poetic works and also on the title pages of two Shakespeare plays issued in 1600 by other printers.[5] H. E. Rollins noted the strange mask, but it was not clear to

---

4. *Ibid.*, vol. 1-2. First compiled by Pollard A.W. and Redgrave G.R., 1976, 1986, NN 25596, 25597, 25602.

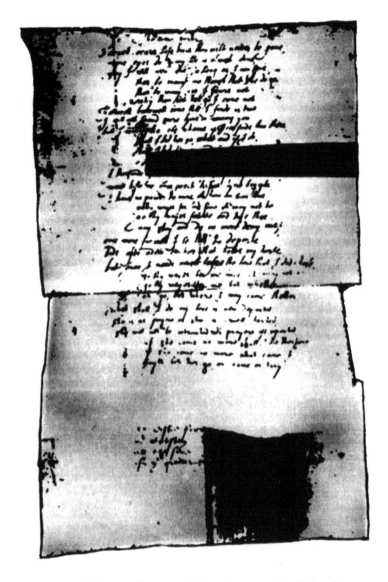

Text of the song from "Twelfth Night," in Rutland's handwriting

him whether it was a purely decorative element or the sign of an author belonging to a certain society or circle.

Because the second titles of the Folger and London copies feature Field's emblem, very large and clear, which does not resemble the mask at all, I first came to suppose that Grossart had made a replica of the half-title on the third copy (now known as the Huntington copy, but in the 19th century all the copies were still in Great Britain). However, I did not have a microfilm copy from the Huntington Library. Later on, in Washington, I received photocopies from California and saw that the Huntington copy bears the same Field emblem as both the others, and not the mask. Where did Grossart get the image of the tragic mask; how did it appear in his edition? I showed the strange second title in the Folger Library to Professor Peter Blayney, a prominent book specialist and bibliographer; he suggested that it was just carelessness on the part of the copyist who worked for Grossart. That is hard to agree with: the emblems are totally different, and a heer carelessness is highly improbable. Was it some kind of bad joke? Whose, and what for? In such a serious edition? How could the diligent and meticulous Grossart overlook such a thing, for it is a glaring discrepancy! If we exclude the possibility of a temporary mental derangement, we can only conclude that Grossart had at hand one more copy of Chester's book that we know nothing about nowadays. There is no evidence to support such a conclusion, and the tragic mask in Grossart's edition remains unexplained. Nobody studying the Grossart edition of *Love's Martyr* has ever concentrated on the strange reproduction of the second title.

Then I got my hands on the records of the Royal Historical Manuscripts Commission that studied manuscripts and other rarities from Belvoir Castle at the end of the 19th century. There, I saw the note about a verse (ten lines), the second part of which is used in Shakespeare's "Twelfth Night." Piotr Porohovchikov asserted that these lines were written by Rutland; no handwriting examination has been made till now. No other manuscript with such a direct bearing on Shakespeare texts has ever been found! This is inconceivable, when so many theories swirl around nearly every line of Shakespeare. If only one sentence written in Shakspere's hand could be found, what a commotion it would produce.

The list of Belvior manuscripts contains the very rare anonymous satirical poem, "Convivium Philisophicum," about a feast in a London tavern where all the prominent English poets are invited. Among them, the most welcome was Thomas Coryate from Odcombe.

---

5. In R. B. McKerrow's reference book, such a mask with initials of A.H. is found under number 379 as an emblem of printer A. Heart, dated to 1613. However, the same mask (without any additions) is also printed on the title pages of "Poetic Rhapsody" (1602, 1611). H.E. Rollins pointed out several cases of the mask in editions from 1582, 1583, and 1585, and also at the end of "Juvenalies" by John Donne (1633). One may also add to that Shakespeare's "Much Ado about Nothing" and "Henry IV" – the second part (1600), a collection of epigrams by G. Owen (1612), who was close to Rutland, "Coryates Crudities" and titles in the 2nd (posthumous) volume of Ben Jonson. Quite a mysterious mask!

*If Coryate be not invited*
*The feast will want a tiller...*

The man the "British Wits" pronounced the greatest writer and traveler is still listed as such on the pages of eminent American and British reference books.

The household notes of the Rutlands' steward (and distant relative) Thomas Screven are another source by which to trace the interests of the Belvoir couple. They contain many entries about the purchase of books, among them many that would serve as sources for Shakespeare's plays. Sometimes whole boxes of books were delivered. The last entry of this kind included books from the Coryate series: *Crambe* and *Banquet*. This is the steward's last entry during the life of Roger Manners, the 5$^{th}$ Earl of Rutland; he may just have had a chance to look through the "Coryate" pages, with a smile. The next entry came on July 19; two surgeons were paid for the last medical treatment of "my Lord" and for embalming the body of the deceased — 70 pounds. Then the large sum of 145 pounds was paid to the Garter King-of-Arms and his men for participation in the ceremony of Rutland's burial on July 22 (two days after his interment!). Seven months later, on March 31, 1613, the famous entry was made that incited scholars' interest in Rutland: Shakspere and Burbadge are paid for "my Lord's impreso."

And at last I was able to see the edition that had caught my interest long ago but that had been so far out of reach: the very rare book by John Davies of Hereford, *The Muses Sacrifice*.[6] I have already spoken about Davies' ambiguous poetical address to "our English Terence, Mr. William Shakespeare." There is no doubt that Davies,[7] a poet among the brilliant suite of the Prince of Wales, the Pembrokes, Rutlands,[8] etc., a very active member of the Coryate farce, was party to the mystery of the Great Bard: he hinted at that many times. The book, in its small format (octavo), was printed by Thomas Shodham for George Norton. Like the Chester collection, the book was not registered with the Stationers' Company; the title page bears no date of printing, but the last page has the date 1612. I called it "the title page," but if that is what it is, it is very strange; I have never come across another one like it. It bears an engraving two centimeters wider than the format of the book, and so its edge is folded according to the book's width. It seems likely that the engraving was printed separately and was not intended for this edition. It contains no name of author, printer, or editor, no place of printing — in a word, it lacks all the usual printing data. Only at the top, outside the

---

6. Davies J. *The Muses Sacrifice*. L., 1612.

7. See: *The Complete Works of John Davies of Hereford*. Collected and edited with memorial introduction, notes and illustrations by A.B.Grossart. Reed. AMS Press, N.Y., 1967.

8. In the book by John Davies of Hereford, *Microcosmos* (1603), dedicated to the King and Queen during their first year of incumbency, there are some sonnet-addresses to the Rutlands, Pembrokes, and Derby. Of special interest is the sonnet addressed to the Earl and Countess of Rutland (Roger and Elizabeth). They are called "Right right Honorable," the poet's veneration of them is immeasurable, and he finishes the sonnet with a plea to count him as one of their "own."

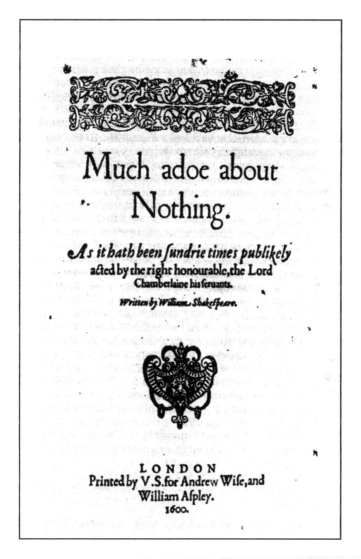

Much adoe about
Nothing.

*As it hath been sundrie times publikely
acted by the right honourable, the Lord
Chamberlaine his seruants.*

*Written by William Shakespeare.*

**LONDON**
Printed by V.S.for Andrew Wise,and
William Aspley.
1600.

Title page from "Much Ado about Nothing" by Shakespeare,
1600. In place of the printer's emblem is a tragic mask with rings.

The enigmatic mask also appears in *Coryates Crudities*, under the signature of the Odcombian Leggestertcher and his Address to the reader.

# HEREAFTER
## FOLLOVV DIVERSE
Poeticall Essaies on the former Subiect;viz: the *Turtle* and *Phœnix*.

*Done by the best and chiefest of our*
moderne writers, with their names subscribed to their particular workes:
*neuer before extant.*

And (now first) consecrated by them all generally,
*to the loue and merite of the true-noble Knight,*
Sir Iohn Salisburie.

*Dignum laude virum Musa vetat mori.*

MDCI.

The half-title of Chester's collection as it is presented in all
the three extant copies.

# HEREAFTER
## FOLLOVV DIVERSE
Poeticall Eſſaies on the former Subiect; viz: the *Turtle* and *Phœnix*.

*Done by the beſt and chiefeſt of our*
moderne writers, with their names ſub-
ſcribed to their particular workes :
*neuer before extant.*

And (now firſt) conſecrated by them all generally,
*to the loue and merite of the true-noble Knight,*
Sir Iohn Salisburie.

*Dignum laude virum Muſa vetat mori.*

*Anchora Spei.*

## MDCI.

The half-title of Chester's collection in Grossart's reissue
of 1878. How is it that the tragic mask, familiar to us, appears
here?

458

frame of the engraving (also wider than the format of the book) is the title: "The Muses Sacrifice"; and at the very bottom on the left side, a note, "for G. Norton" and the signature "W. Hole." William Hole was a famous artist who, as mentioned, also illustrated *Coryats Crudities*.

The picture presents a scene on Parnassus. At the altar of the god Apollo, patron of arts, the hearts of the couple that had served him are burned in the sacrificial fire. Apollo and an angel of Pure Love, who is treading on Cupid, the god of carnal love, keep the fire going. The allegory is quite transparent: the traditional bow and arrows of the prostrated Cupid are scattered nearby, for they are of no use here. Around them kneel all the nine Muses who, in mourning, stretch their arms to the sacrificial flames. Above the angel's head flies a (turtle-) dove. The right top corner contains several lines:

> We sacrifice this Hart
> In flames of love and arte.
> While drops of beauty grace
> Make both to burne apace.

Only eight copies of the book survive, two without the title page with the engraving. The Huntington copy contains the poetic lines in the top right corner *in toto*; in the Folger copy, the right side of the inscription is blank (either cut out of the engraving plate or covered by a piece of paper during printing). The intention is evident — a lay reader has no idea what event is represented in the picture. Still, the event is shown in minute detail and reflects the mourning described in the Chester book. Here is the (Turtle-) Dove, the spiritual nature of the couple's relationship, their selfless service to Apollo, Parnassus, and the year 1612. The engraving is an authentic illustration to *Love's Martyr* and probably was originally meant for it. It is odd that nobody among those who studied the Chester book or Shakespearean poetry ever thought of putting the Hole engraving into one of the many reprints of the Shakespeare poem about the Turtle and the Phoenix or in John Donne's *The Canonization*. It would be right at home.

The contents of the Davies' book are revealing. First of all, it begins with a poetic dedication to three eminent ladies, the closest friends of Elizabeth Sidney Rutland: Mary Sidney Pembroke, Lucy Bedford and Elizabeth Cary. Most of the book is dedicated to religious and philosophical ruminations on life and death, on sin and retribution for it, expressed in poetic form. These reflections are preceded by "A Funeral Elegie on the death of the most vertuous, and no less lovely, Mrs. Elizabeth Dutton," Lord Ellesmere's granddaughter. We learn that young Elizabeth was engaged at the age of eleven to John Datton, who was 15 at the time. Two years later he died, leaving Elizabeth "a virgin widow," and three years later, in October of 1611, she died also. This sad story is put down in dry prose, but in the elegy itself Davies speaks of the high veneration that he feels toward his heroine:

"The Muses Sacrifice." Hole's engraving of 1612. Scene on Parnassus: surrounded by all the nine Muses, Apollo and the Angel of Pure Love (treading upon Cupid) keep the fire going, in which burn the hearts of the chaste couple who had secretly served poesy.

*My Muse shall labour on this ground of Fame*
*To rise a Pile of Rime, whereon thy name*
*Shall ever shine, through Wits Celestial Flashes*
*Until another Phoenix of the Ashes*
*Produced be …*

Whom is the poet talking about? Could the Phoenix, whose "name shall ever shine, through wits celestial flashes," "ground of Fame" be the girl, nearly a child, who passed away before she really began to live? The text of the elegy does not contain any mention or allusion to the Hole illustration, but one may suppose that those few English researches who studied the John Davies book did not dwell on the engraving,[9] taking it only as an illustration to a simple and sad story of a very young couple. But what had these children to do with the service to art, to poetry; why Parnassus, Apollo, the Muses? No, Hole's picture has nothing to do with the untimely death of those children, who could not have possibly left behind anything of value. Their names only figure in the Davies book as the name of John Salusbury figures in the Chester collection, or the name of Venetia Digby in Ben Jonson's "Eupheme" — they are only substitutes for a true story about love, poetic service and cruel fate, the Turtle and the Phoenix, that is, Roger and Elizabeth Rutland.

Laetitia Yeandle, having diligently examined the engraving, agreed that it offers convincing insight into the Shakespeare poem about the Turtle and the Phoenix; she wondered at my being so lucky to find it. However, I came upon it not by luck but by correctly dating and identifying the characters of the Chester book. The circle of the Sidneys, Rutlands and Pembrokes, their poetic milieu, the almost simultaneous demise of the Belvoir couple in the summer of 1612 — here is the period and here are the signs indicating where to look for convincing evidence. Findings are not accidental! Such an event as the mysterious death (for many people, a mysterious disappearance) of Philip Sidney's only daughter *had to* provoke some response, albeit camouflaged and intended for a only few initiated persons. Such traces and responses, as the reader can see, turn out to be plentiful and there is every reason to expect further new and wonderful findings.

Laetitia Yeandle is a highly skilled specialist in ancient manuscripts and printed matter, whose goodwill and helpful attitude is immeasurably useful to those who study in the Library. Aside from her, in my contacts with American Shakespeareans I limited myself to discussing only the actual problems of my research: dating, identification of prototypes, and the meaning of certain allusions. I tried not to touch

---

9. The copy of the Davies book in the British Library in London has no title page. Hole's engraving was kept separately in the British Museum (at that time, in the same building); however, in April of 1995, I was unable to examine it, for the room where it was located had been flooded just several days before, and was closed to visitors for a long time. Only this part of the building was affected!

461

on the contentious problem of the Great Bard's identity, "the Shakespeare question"; and neither did I hear other Shakespeare scholars discussing the issue among themselves. The cult of Shakespeare established in Britain and the US long ago is closely linked to Stratfordian reliquae and university professors adhere strictly to this tradition (I have never met any exceptions in academic journals). The cult naturally includes not only the works of the Great Bard but also his biographical canon that was refined long before the advent of modern historical methods based on critical verification of sources and extraction of authentic facts out of legends and hearsay. Discussions with non-Stratfordians (in America, they are mostly Oxfordians) never take place in academic journals, but mostly in the general media and sometimes even in the courtroom. This, along with the weakness of the Oxfordian thesis, reveals the low academic level at which the debate is usually conducted. It would not be an exaggeration to assert that, for university professors, there are no problems connected with the personality of Shakespeare.

The extremely narrow specialization of studies inclines academic Shakespeareans to dig into specific issues, leaving aside broader problems and specific problems that their "neighbors" are dealing with. More often than not, they have only a very vague notion what their colleagues are up to. Jonson students are not always well-versed in Shakespeare biographies; Shakespeare students do not always have a profound understanding of Jonson's poetry, although they and "Conversations with William Drummond" are the very important key to Shakespeare. Some areas of inquiry have not been touched upon for decades; the Chester book is a vivid example. Even in those cases when Western Shakespeareans come across important facts unknown heretofore, they deem it necessary to cram them into the Procrustean bed of tradition in assessing the Great Bard. That prevents them from grasping the significance of their findings in a broad sense. The Stratfordian legend, a Rabelaisian mask placed over a whole era, peculiarly distorts our view of cultural life in Britain during the reigns of Elizabeth and James. "Official" Shakespeare scholarship declines to peep behind that mask. One can hardly imagine that Ptolemy's theories could hold sway in astronomy today, but Shakespeare studies are not natural science; and in the humanities, where relations between accurate facts and cherished tradition are much more delicate, this brilliant game created four centuries ago is still able to go on.

In the basement of the Folger Library, where the open stacks are located, there are several shelves of works on this authorship question. They are seldom visited. There are thick volumes by Baconians who bent their minds over ciphers in which they think the great philosopher left secret messages about his authorship; almost nobody reads these books nowadays, though not everything in them is nonsense. There are volumes promoting Derby, Marlowe, Rutland, Oxford and others, and volumes promoting group authorship theories. Demblon's books are here, never translated into English in the 80 years since they first appeared. This cellar shows how difficult it is to find authentic truth, when it is so cunningly hidden. One of my new American acquaintances, seeing me there, said in jest that this section should be closed off with iron bars. Apparently, he wanted to protect a foreigner from the bad influence of these "fakes." Then I thought of Kozma Proutkov's[10] bad luck! Had he been born like Thomas Coryate in another time, in another place, the name of this "great writer" would have adorned the pages of eminent English biographical dictionaries and encyclopedia right up until our day.

A short article about my work on *Love's Martyr* was published in the American journal *Shakespeare Newsletter*, in 1989. But only specialists at the Folger Library knew that Russian researchers had found the unique watermarks in Washington and London. I therefore showed the translation of my article from *Shakespeare Readings 1984* (with additional material on watermarks) to my colleagues working in the Library — Professors Winfried Schleiner, Kennet Gross, Patricia Steinlein, and Park Honan. The new dating of the Shakespeare poem and identification of the Turtle and the Phoenix prototypes seemed to them convincing enough (certainly, as I mentioned, the question of Shakespeare's identity is not directly broached in the article). The most encouraging response came from Professor Park Honan, who wrote on April 22, 1992:

> This is the only entirely convincing article on the poem that I have read, and it seems to me, your identification of Roger Manners, Earl of Rutland and his wife Elizabeth née Sidney is very, very well-established. (Your writing is so lucid, logical and well conducted that it was impossible to stop reading!) Now, I wonder what could be said in the way of an aesthetic appreciation of the poem? Why does it seem to have some universal applications? Why does it please us? But even for these questions, you have done brilliantly the most difficult thing and given us invaluably the groundwork. You are at once patient, charitable, but properly dismissive about the earlier "identifications."[11]

Because the article was published in a Russian academic journal, my American friends urged me to offer it to an American journal so that American and English scholars might become acquainted with the new hypothesis and take part in discussions. I followed the advice and forwarded the translation of the article to *The Shakespeare Quarterly*.

In the meantime, some Washington journalists got wind of the investigation. A mysterious 400-year-old unicorn found in the heart of Washington (and London) by people who had come for just that purpose from Moscow?! I had several conversations with Linda Feldman of the *Christian Science Monitor*. Professor Donald Foster from

---

10. The fictional hero and pseudo-author of several books of poems and aphorisms invented by a group of Russian writers in the second half of the 19th century.

11. Analyzing and shooting holes in my predecessors' hypotheses in relation to the Chester book, I bore in mind that they were only the first attempts to understand the mysterious events, attempts that did help clarify certain aspects despite the false starting points (such as giving credence to intentionally mystifying dates). To the question of why the poem makes such a strong impression, the real answer is that its true profundity is only clear once we know the whole truth about the great tragedy of the Belvoir couple, that was hidden for centuries behind the Stratfordian mask.

Vassar College soon explained to her that Shakespeare's poem-requiem and the whole of the Chester collection are dedicated to Sir John Salusbury's wedding and his daughter's coming of age; Foster did not see any reason to doubt that. I had to tell Feldman that the professor (with whom I am not acquainted) had merely passed on one more old and implausible story. At the moment, I did not think much of it, and the newspaper article soon was published.[12]

Professor Peter Blayney became another opponent. He asked outright why I doubted the date printed on the title page. It became apparent that Blayney, a bibliographer and book expert, considers only the appearance, that is, the physical, printing evidence; the facts "hidden in the texts" are of minor interest to him. And furthermore, in this case he was willing to pass over those facts that are inconvenient for the established tradition (for instance, the fact that Field and Allde participated in another mystification in 1612-1613). Incidentally, Blayney did not see the translation of my article; he only learned that it gave an untraditional interpretation of the dating of *Love's Martyr*. Later on, when I became acquainted with his excellent book in London bookshops,[13] I came to a better understanding of his motives. He had not made a special study of the Chester book but mentioned it in his work (just on the basis of the entry in *A Short Titles Catalogue*) as the only example to substantiate the surmise that Lownes (who had settled in 1610 in the bookshop "Bishop's Head") sold off the books left by his predecessor Blount. A new dating may have required Blayney to abandon that example and reconsider Lownes and Blount's relationship — to consider that there was more to it than the mere purchase of a bookshop. There are no, and have never been, documents spelling out the conditions of this transfer of ownership, never mind any "remainders" of the Chester book.

Unfortunately, there was no other chance to reach wider circles of American (and English) scholars, then. *The Shakespeare Quarterly* would not print my article, for their reviewer, like D. Foster, was an adherent of the C. Brown hypothesis. From the text of the review kindly given to me by the editors, it was evident that the anonymous reviewer considers the Brown version the only possible solution to the puzzle that the Shakespeare poem and the Chester book represent. He found no insurmountable inconsistency in the mournful tone and the idea of a wedding and coming of age.

But the abundant errors in the review show, among other things, that the author himself had not read *Love's Martyr*, and all his knowledge of it came from reference books. He did not even know the name of the London copy of the Chester book, and he was not aware that both its main heroes die! He takes John Salusbury for one of the poets who authored the collection.

---

12. Professor Foster became famous in 1995, when he declared to the whole world that the anonymous "Funeral Elegie," dated by 1612 and signed "W.S.," was Shakespeare's. For seven years, he persistently defended his opinion, and many trees were sacrificed to produce the paper filled with articles on this "discovery," until, at last, Foster himself acknowledged it was totally unfounded (*see* W.S. Niederkorn, "A Scholar Recants on His 'Shakespeare' Discovery," in *The New York Times*, June 20, 2002).

13. Blayney P.W.M. *The bookshops in Paul's Churchyard*. L., The Bibliographical Society, 1990.

The review contains some controversial assertions that it would be useful to discuss. For instance the reviewer, like some other Western scholars, thinks that it was meaningless that a work might be issued without being duly registered in the Stationers' Register in Shakespearean times. I would not dwell here on the details of rule and custom prevailing in the Stationers Company, but would advise such scholars to consult the "Records of the Court of the Stationers Company" and the relevant entries in the Register.[14] It was published long ago and can be found on the shelves of the Folger Library and the British Library. All those willing to study historical facts, and not to rely only on fashionable theories, will find entries detailing fines and other penalties for Company members who evaded registration. For instance, in September of 1613, our old acquaintance Edward Allde was fined for just such a peccadillo (this episode coincides in with the printing of the Chester book). In the article I emphasized that the lack of registration for Chester's book is not direct evidence of false dating, but it does exclude the possibility of confirming the printer's dating and gives us good reason to doubt it, especially considering the professional status of Blount and Lownes and their usual practice. The reviewer tries to distort the significance of this incontestable argument, trying to present the question as if the dating problems come up *only* because of the lack of registration. He himself considers that inconsequential, for he relies on the notorious "average of 30 per cent," and he does not know that Blount and Lownes do not conform to that statistic.

The intriguing substitution of the title page in the London copy, in which the old title and the name of the author disappeared and a new title with a strange "misprint," a different date and the emblem of another printer were inserted, the reviewer naturally "explains" on supposedly "commercial" grounds. Perhaps Matthew Lownes sought to offload the remainders he had received from Blount. My article thoroughly addressed such conjecture, but the reviewer ignored that.

He did not waste a word on the extremely important internal evidence contained in the text of the Chester book, although a great part of the article he reviewed was dedicated to it. He simply dismissed such unique facts as the similarity of the Turtle and the Phoenix's history with the strange marriage of the Rutlands and their strange demise that coincided with the death of John Salusbury, the peculiarities of Ben Jonson's contribution in view of his special attitude towards the Rutlands, etc. It is hard to imagine how a scholar could pass over such striking and incontrovertible facts, recently brought to light. After all, it is no surprise, then, that the reviewer had nothing to say about the Russian researchers' discovery of watermarks heretofore unknown in Washington and London.

I do not dwell on this episode in order to complain about the practice of anonymous reviews in American academic journals. It may have its positives traits. But under such circumstances a reviewer, sticking to preconceived and false views, may

---

14. *Records of the Court of the Stationers Company 1602-1640.* L., The Bibliographical Society, 1957, p.138; *A Transcript of the Registers of the Company of Stationers of London 1554-1640.* Ed. by Edw. Arber. L., 1875.

block his fellow scholars' access to new ideas. Some scholars (if they do have a chance to become familiar with research that was produced in a foreign language) may find it very useful and relevant, as Professor Park Honan found in the case of my new dating and identification of the Turtle and the Phoenix prototypes. Directed filtering is actually censoring of academic information, including international information, and is inconsistent with what one expects in the US. This trend is characteristic of contemporary academic Shakespeare studies, however, and it does not facilitate progress in this branch of science.

The episode with the anonymous reviewer is important in another respect as well. It testifies to the lack of serious academic debate over new hypotheses. Opponents of my hypothesis have not found mistakes or inconsistencies in the main thrusts of my article. The heroes of the Shakespeare poem and the Chester collection are identified. It will only be a matter of time and academic objectivity for the truth that has been revealed to become evident to everybody.

My article about the Turtle and the Phoenix was published in English after all in 1998, in a collection issued by Delaware University.[15] In the foreword, the compiler Prof. Joseph Price finds my arguments for dating the Chester collection to 1612 and the identification of its heroes with the Rutland couple convincing. I hope that this publication will enhance the opportunities for American and English scholars to participate in further research in a promising direction. Further investigation is needed on books published by Field, Allde and Jaggard, on paper with the same watermarks as in Chester's book, with the same decorations, insets and other polygraphical details. The printer could not possibly have used the font only once and then discarded it. The same holds true for the paper. That means that someplace in London, Washington or California, in an academic library, in some special storage place, a coveted book (maybe more than one) that is capable of confirming this important and difficult problem is still waiting for us — just as an unseen unicorn waited for so long.

I have invited my English and American colleagues to an academic discussion about Chester's book.[16] Now, I repeat the invitation (one may even consider it a challenge). And it is not even necessary to tackle "the Shakespeare question" right off the bat, if it scares off so many scholars, for the problem of dating and identification of prototypes deserves (and requires) a deep and objective discussion, the time for which now has come. I am fully aware of the difficulty of enticing my Western colleagues into a full-fledged discussion when the topic touches upon this delicate "question."

Backstage at the theater of English and American literary scholarship, the Greatest of Writers and Travelers, Prince of Poets, the indefatigable Leggestretcher

15. Gililov I. "For whom the bell tolled." In: *Russian essays on Shakespeare and his contemporaries*. Newark: University of Delaware press; London: Associated Universities Presses. 1998.

16. See: Gililov I., "Shakespeare studies: Cooperation and polemics." In: *Science in Russia*, 1994, N 3, p.82.

from Odcombe Thomas Coryate, is also waiting his turn, supported by His Majesty's grinning Water Poet, John Taylor. They too have something to say to posterity.

## The Bell Tolled For Shakespeare

Having identified the prototypes of the Turtle and the Phoenix, we can make the next and final step in appreciating the meaning and import of the Chester book as a golden key to the "Shakespeare mystery," for the secret of the Great Bard is first and foremost the secret of the extraordinary Rutlands.

On June 26, 1612 in the city of Cambridge, after much suffering, "the dark dimme Taper" died; the heart of "the Knight of Honor and Magnanimity" stopped beating, the soldier, traveler, poet and dramatic writer, "elixir of all joes," an extraordinary person who combined the highest wisdom and multifarious knowledge with eccentric pranks, the scholar from Padua, the university fellow of Rosencrantz and Guildernstern, the first of the "poets of Belvoir Vale," who preferred "to be a poet rather than to bear that name," the "pure Dove" of the Chester book. Now we know more about that tragic life — for really it was high tragedy — carefully hidden from curious eyes behind a jester's mask, shrouded by mystery.

Several days after his mysterious burial, his poetic lady took her own life, "his pure Maid Marian," the daughter of Phoenix, and Phoenix herself, object of Beaumont's and Overbury's veneration, "the noblest Charis," designated "Nature's fairest creature" by Ben Jonson, and only a "visible image of Turtle's wife." Before that, she did everything to "spare the Turtle's blood," so that "from their ashes a new Phoenix should rise," their creative heritage left for the edification and wonder of this world. She tells how her friend took his last trial:

> *Look what a mirthful countenance he doth beare,*
> *Spreading his wings abroad, and joes withal …*

The Phoenix sees how the mind of her friend, even on his deathbed, keeps a sly smile and acquires mighty wings, departing to "teach this spoiled world" to listen to the voice of Truth and to see Beauty.

> *I come sweet Turtle, and with my bright wings*
> *I will embrace thy burnt bones as they lie,*
> *I hope of these another Creature springs,*
> *That shall possesse both our authority:*
> *I stay to long, o take me to your glory.*

Someone unknown (an Ignoto) also writes about the expected appearance of a new Phoenix, whom he imagines to be a "rare live urne."

"We'll build in sonnets pretty rooms." They did not wish for any other monument. And John Marston, time and again, as if he was afraid that we would mistake his meaning, describes the Perfection left behind by the couple, their works of genius that appeared before the "poets of Belvoir Vale" after the Turtle and the Phoenix left this world. Let us recollect that during their lifetime more than half of the Shakespeare works were still unknown; they were polished and printed only by the tenth anniversary of the Rutlands' death. But not every morsel of this heritage was published. As testimony to that, we have the so-called apocryphal plays that the publishers of the Third Folio later on tried to introduce into the Shakespeare canon; and there is more.

Testifying to the same effect are the poetic works placed by Chester after his poem and especially designated by him as the ones "written by the Paphian Dove to the beauteous Phoenix." I noted in the first chapter that in the 20th century some scholars did concentrate on this collection of brilliant acrostics, in which the firm hand of a master surpassing in his poetic art all the other authors presented in the Chester collection — the best English poets of the time. Most of all, the researchers were impressed by the wonderful similarity and many coincidences in topics, images, and poetic language of these "Turtle-Dove's cantoes" with the poetic lines of Shakespeare, first and foremost with his sonnets. In Elizabethan poetry there are no other "coincidences" like these. No wonder the Shakespeare poetry expert G. W. Knight, meticulously examining endless "Shakespeare locations" in the "Turtle-Dove cantoes" exclaimed: "This is pure Shakespeare!"[17]

Who else at the time could write with such authentic Shakespearean might, with such poetic mastery; who could see and feel in such a Shakespearian way the same collisions of life (extraordinary as they were) and express his vision and his thoughts with such Shakespearian vocabulary and images except the Great Bard himself, whose hand we know not only by his early poems on classic topics but also by his sonnets and the "Passionate Pilgrim"? That is why Knight, after much deliberation, came to a tentative conclusion that Shakespeare, after placing his poem "The Phoenix and the Turtle" in the collection, went on to take part in other portions of the Chester work as well, which is most evident in the "Turtle-Dove's Cantoes." As far as I know, nobody has offered any other explanation for the phenomenon. Only now can we say, much more coherently: the wonderful acrostics of the Belvoir Turtle really are Shakespeare poetry, because under the mask of "William Shake-speare" the Turtle and the Phoenix were hiding, first of all. Humanity thus acquires a superlative collection of Shakespeare poetry bearing the clear and incontestable seal of Shakespeare's genius

---

17. I have already noted that the "Turtle-Dove's Cantoes" are in many respects more Shakespeare-like poetic material than the poem "The Phoenix and the Turtle," though the latter appears above the name of Shakespeare.

that extends and develops the motifs and images of the Shakespeare sonnets ("The Cantoes," according to many indications, were written later than many of the sonnets). "The Turtle-Dove Cantoes" are a key to the sonnets that many generations of Shakespeare researchers have toiled away at; they are the key to Shakespeare's heart. Thirty-four pages of Shakespeare's poems, unknown before — and what poems! And that is only part of the wonderful Shakespeare heritage that fell into the lap of the friends of the Turtle and the Phoenix as their parting gift.

Now we know that English writers and poets did not sit silently by when the Great Bard died. They paid tribute to those who were Shakespeare; and they did so in a book, deviously disguised with a mask worthy of the masters of creative secrecy, Roger and Elizabeth Rutland. Thus did the Chorus of Poets, the best in England, bid the couple farewell, in lines "shadowing the Truth and varied from Multitude."

But if the Chester collection is a mournful response to that tragic death, a secret farewell to "William Shake-speare," then one can rightly ask: what is the wonderful poem known by the name given to it in the 19th century, "The Phoenix and the Turtle," and in our time customarily considered a Shakespeare work (though, as we know, in the past, well-substantiated doubts were expressed on this account)? For in the Chester book Shakespeare's name appears under the poem. How can we explain the fact that it mourns the death of those who worked under the same name?

Let us, however, recollect the way the poem is placed in the Chester collection. Its first part is printed on two pages without a title (the only such item in the whole book) and without signature. The second part, "Threnos," a requiem on the deceased Turtle and the Phoenix, occupies a separate page and has a separate title. The top and the bottom of the "Threnos" is framed with borders, and under the last line is printed the name "William Shake-speare" (with a hyphen to emphasize its literal sense). The absence of the title before the first part is not due to a lack of space — one or two lines could have been put on the following page. The compositor did it on purpose, and the reason for that is clear to us now. The absence of a title before the address to the participants in the funeral ceremony and the special arrangement of the "Threnos" serve a function; the poem(s) are made to stand out in the collection dedicated to the Turtle and the Phoenix. It is no accident that the mourning poem got into the Chester book, despite the comments from Shakespeare researchers who have not had time to read the book.

Shahany, Garnett and others who thought that the poem is not Shakespeare's (and it really does not look like any of his poetic works or poetical texts in plays) were inclined to think that it was written by John Fletcher. The "Threnos" in its poetic form and language is extremely similar to several lines written by Fletcher in 1616 and 1621. This similarity is not accidental: Fletcher helped create, and finished, Shakespeare's "Henry VIII," "Two Noble Kinsmen"[18] and probably some other plays. One of the

---

18. The play is among the so-called apocryphal Shakespeare works.

"poets of Belvoir Vale," he is the most probable author of the poem "The Phoenix and the Turtle."

Placed on a separate page, framed by a border the way obituaries are today, the "Threnos" really is a found obituary, a requiem for Shakespeare. The last lines rhyme with the name of Shakespeare; the name becomes part of the poetic text and merges with the last sentence:

> *To this urne let those repaire*
> *That are either true or faire*
> *For these dead Birds, sigh a prayer.*
> *William Shake-speare.*

Thus, the name William Shakespeare here is not a signature — it is a grieving sigh, a moan from a person who came to pray to the urn filled with the ashes of the Turtle and the Phoenix. If one uses present day punctuation and places a semicolon at the end of the last line, then one finally discovers the real meaning of the line, of the requiem, and, at last, of the whole Chester book:

> *For these dead Birds, sigh a prayer: William Shakespeare.*[19]

The Chester collection *Love's Martyr*, for so long so inaccessible and mysterious, and the moving requiem in it, is the heart-rending farewell song sung by the poets of Belvoir Vale over the fresh grave of the real Great Bard — Roger and Elizabeth Rutland. All-wise Providence took care that the requiem for the Great Bard would take a worthy place among his works of art. As befits a requiem, "The Phoenix and the Turtle" is now usually found crowning the collected works of William Shakespeare.

---

19. There may be other explanations for the name of Shakespeare under the "Threnos." Beside the Rutlands, there were other people who lent a hand to the "Shakespeare" enterprise (for instance, Fletcher or Mary Sidney Pembroke, or even Bacon), who could sign with this name, thus symbolizing continuation of the game after the death of its creators and principal actors.

Certain uncompromising proponents of the Stratford story may start from the fact that Shakspere, who visited Belvoir in the spring of 1613, was certainly acquainted with its recently deceased lord (citing the appearance in "Hamlet" of realistic details from Denmark, and Rutland's friendship with Southampton, and other convincing evidence), and assert that Shakspere took part in compiling the book dedicated to the memory of the earl and his spouse. Such an explanation would easily match the Stratfordian biography of the Great Bard and would not necessarily require its professional "defenders" to confront the new dating and identification of the heroes of the "Phoenix and the Turtle," although the aspects of our investigation connected with the "Shakespeare authorship question" would not be acceptable to this category of Shakespeare scholars.

## AFTER WORD

I thought it would be appropriate to end the book with a mention of Vladimir Nabokov's penetrating poem, written in 1924 in Russian (here translated by A. Vagapov), simply entitled: *Shakespeare*.

One of the greatest writers and poets of the 20th century, a great thinker and versatile in literature, Nabokov did not as far as I know delve into Shakespeare studies. But he perceived the image of the real Shakespeare (which is very close to Rutland's portrait!), probed his high thought and understood his pain, his revulsion to vanity.

> *Disdaining stage alarms and agitation*
> *You put aside without hesitation*
> *The leaves of laurel woven in a wreath.*
> *You hid your monstrous genius for ever*
> *By putting on a mask, however,*
> *You left us what you had beneath.*

Nabokov surely did not know much about Elizabeth Rutland, Mary Pembroke, the game around Thomas Coryate and many others that were discovered later. Behind the mask and name of Shakespeare he could discern only one person. His understanding of the nature of the real author's relations with his "living mask" is not quite accurate. Shakspere did not sign any plays, poems or sonnets; he could not have done it, for pay or for any other reason. But those are only details; Nabokov's work in this case is not an academic article, but a poetic work of art. The last line is striking. Certainly, Nabokov did not study the Chester collection, and did not know how, with a smile, the Turtle departed. But he visualized the scene; he even saw the smile on the lips of the dying man!

> *But when you duly felt that God was going*
> *To turn you out of life, you thought*
> *Of secret manuscripts and copies, knowing*
> *That all the common talk would not*
> *Depreciate your eminence and greatness,*
> *And you would go through centuries, in hiding,*
> *Like immortality itself remaining faceless...*
> *And you set out for the journey, smiling.*

Through the centuries, through seas of words, one poet discovers another. . .

2135687